Shinto in History

Curzon Studies in Asian Religion

Series Editor: Sue Hamilton, King's College, London

Editorial Advisory Board:

Nick Allen, University of Oxford
Catherine Despeux, INALCO, Paris
Chris Minkowski, Cornell University
Fabio Rambelli, Williams College, Massachusetts
Andrew Rippin, University of Calgary

Curzon Press publishes a Series specifically devoted to Asian Religion, considered from a variety of perspectives: those of theology, philosophy, anthropology, sociology, history, politics and literature. The primary objects of study will be all the religious traditions of the Indian sub-continent, Tibet, China, Japan, South-East Asia, Central Asia, and the Near and Middle East.

The methodology used in the works published in the Series is either comparative or one focused on (a feature of) a specific tradition. The level of readership ranges from undergraduates to specialist scholars. The type of book varies from the introductory textbook to the scholarly monograph.

Tradition and Liberation
The Hindu Tradition in the Indian Women's Movement
Catherine A. Robinson

Shinto in History
Ways of the Kami
John Breen and Mark Teeuwen

Beyond Personal Identity
Dōgen, Nishida, and a Phenomenology of No-Self
Gereon Kopf

*Proposal or scripts for the Series will be welcomed by the Series Editor
or by Jonathan Price, Chief Editor, Curzon Press.*

Shinto in History

Ways of the Kami

Edited by
John Breen and Mark Teeuwen

CURZON

First Published in 2000
by Curzon Press
15 The Quadrant, Richmond
Surrey, TW9 1BP
http://www.curzonpress.co.uk

Editorial Matter © 2000 John Breen and Mark Teeuwen

Typeset in Horley Old Style by LaserScript Ltd, Mitcham, Surrey
Printed and bound in Great Britain by
Biddles Ltd, Guildford and King's Lynn

British Library Cataloguing in Publication Data
A catalogue record of this book is available from the British Library

ISBN 0–7007–1170–8 (Hbk)
ISBN 0–7007–1172–4 (Pbk)

CONTENTS

PREFACE

All essays by Japanese authors in this volume have been translated by the editors. Japanese and Chinese personal names are given in the traditional order, with the family name first. Japanese common usage is followed in choosing the name by which the person in question is best known.

Chinese names and terms are given in the *pinyin* transcription, followed, if relevant, by the Japanese reading. For Japanese names and terms, the Hepburn transcription is used. Characters are given in the text only when this is deemed necessary for the argument, or when characters are so obscure as to be difficult to find in reference works and dictionaries.

Dates prior to 1873 are given according to the traditional lunar calendar. They have not been changed to corresponding solar dates. Therefore, 'the second month of 1297' does not correspond to February 1297 in the solar calendar. For the sake of brevity, dates have sometimes been given in numbers, e.g., 'Keichō 3/8/18.' This stands for 'the 3rd year of Keichō (1598), 8th month, 18th day.'

Finally, a note on periodisation. A number of conventional period names are used in the text, sometimes without dates. These periods with their dates are as follows:

Nara period:	710–794
Heian period:	794–1185
Kamakura period:	1185–1333
Nanbokuchō period:	1336–1392
Muromachi period:	1392–1568
Momoyama period:	1568–1600
Edo period:	1600–1867
Meiji period:	1868–1912
Taishō period:	1912–1926
Shōwa period:	1926–1989

ACKNOWLEDGEMENTS

The editors are grateful to the publishers Iwanami Shoten, Taimeidō and *Shintō Shūkyō* for permission to carry translations of articles by the Japanese contributors. Isomae's article first appeared in *Shisō* (Iwanami Shoten); it subsequently appeared in abbreviated form in a recent edition of Acta Asiatica. Sakamoto's essay is a chapter from his *Kokka Shintō keisei katei no kenkyū* Iwanami Shoten, 1996. Nitta's contribution is a chapter from *Kindai seikyō kankei no kenkyū*, Taimeidō, 1997 and Sonoda's article apeared in *Shintō Shūkyō*.

We also wish to thank David McCarthy of LaserScript for the typesetting and our editor at Curzon, Jonathan Price, who was patient, helpful and a pleasure to work with.

CONTRIBUTORS

Tim Barrett
Professor of East Asian History, SOAS, University of London
Select publications
Singular listlessness: a short history of Chinese books and British scholars, Wellsweep, 1988.
Li ao: Buddhist, Taoist or neo-Confucian, OUP, 1992.
Taoism under the T'ang, Wellsweep, 1996.

Brian Bocking
Professor, Department of the Study of Religions, SOAS, University of London
Select publications
Nagarjuna in China: A translation of the Middle Treatise, Edwin Mellen Press, 1995.
A popular dictionary of Shinto, Curzon Press, 1996.

W. J. Boot
Professor of Japanese, Leiden University
Select publications
The adaption and adaption of Neo-Confucianism in Japan: the role of Fujiwara Seika and Hayashi Razan, Leiden PhD dissertation, 1982.
'The religious background to the deification of Tokugawa Ieyasu,' in Adriana Boscaro et al. eds., *Rethinking Japan, vol. 2: social sciences, ideology and thought*, Global Books, 1991.

John Breen
Senior Lecturer in Japanese, SOAS, University of London
Select publications
Japan and Christianity (edited with Mark Williams), Macmillan, 1996.
'Accommodating the alien – Ōkuni Takamasa and the Religion of the Lord of Heaven' in Peter Kornicki et al. eds., *Religion in Japan – arrows to heaven and earth*, CUP, 1996.
'The imperial oath of April 1868: ritual, power and politics in restoration Japan', *Monumenta Nipponica*, 51, 4 (1996).

Allan Grapard
ISF Professor of Shinto Studies, University of California, Santa Barbara
Select publications

The protocol of the gods: A study of the Kasuga cult in Japanese history, University of California Press, 1992.
'Religious practices in the Heian period' in *The Cambridge History of Japan, vol. 3*, CUP, 1998.

Nitta Hitoshi
Assistant Professor, Kōgakkan Daigaku, Ise
Select publications

'Meiji kenpō seiteiki no seikyōkankei: Inoue Kowashi no kōsō to naimushō no seisaku o chūshin ni' in Inoue Nobutaka and Sakamoto Koremaru eds., *Nihongata seikyō kankei no tanjō*, Daiichi Shobō, 1987.
Kindai seikyō kankei no kisoteki kenkyū, Taimeidō, 1997.

Isomae Jun'ichi
Associate Professor, Nihon Joshi Daigaku
Select publications

Dogū to kamen: Jōmon bunka no shūkyō kōzō ('*Clay figurines and masks: the structure of religion in the Jomon period*'), Kōsō Shobō, 1994
Kiki shinwa no metahisutorii ('The metahistory of *Kojiki* and *Nihon shoki* mythology'), Yoshikawa Kōbunkan, 1998.

Kamata Tōji
Professor of Religions, Musashigaoka Women's College and Kokusai Nihon
Select publications

Ikai no fuonoroji – junsui kokugaku risei hihan josetsu, Kawade Shuppan, 1990.
Shūkyō to reisei, Kadokawa Shoten, 1995.
Sei naru basho no kioku, Kōdansha, 1996.

Nicola Liscutin
Research Fellow, Deutsches Institut für Japanstudien, Tokyo
Select publications

'Daijōsai – the great festival of tasting the new fruits: some aspects of its history and meaning', in *Transactions of the Asiatic Society of Japan*, 4th series, vol.5, 1990.
Kamo no Chōmei: Aufzeichnungen aus meiner Hütte, Japanische Bibliotek, Insel Verlag, 1997.

Nelly Naumann
Formerly Professor of Japanese, Albert-Ludwigs-Universität in Freiburg im Breisgau

Select publications

Die einheimische Religion Japans vols. 1 and 2, Brill, 1988 and 1994.
Die Mythen des alten Japan, Beck, 1996.

Sakamoto Koremaru
Professor, Kokugakuin Daigaku, Tokyo
Select publications

Nihongata seikyō kankei no tanjō (edited with Inoue Nobutake), Daiichi Shobō, 1987.
Meiji ishin to kokugakusha, Taimeidō, 1993.
Kokka Shintō keiseikatei no kenkyū, Iwanami Shoten, 1994.

Bernhard Scheid
Researcher, Institute for the Research of Intellectual History and Culture of Asia, Austrian Academy of Sciences, Vienna
Select publications

Im Innersten meines Herzens empfinde ich tiefe Scham: das Alter im Schrifttum des japanischen Mittelalters, Austrian Academy of Sciences, 1996.

Sonoda Minoru
Professor of Anthropology, Kyoto University and Chief Priest of Chichibu Shrine in Saitama.
Select publications

Matsuri no genshōgaku, Kōbundō, 1990.
Shintō: Nihon minzoku shūkyō, Kōbundō, 1994.
Shintō no sekai, Kōbundō, 1997.

Mark Teeuwen
Lecturer in Japanese, University of Oslo
Select publications

Watarai Shinto: An intellectual history of the Outer Shrine in Ise, Leiden, 1996.
Nakatomi Harae Kunge: Purification and enlightenment in late-Heian Japan (with Hendrik van der Veere), München, iudicium verlag 1998.

Anne Walthall
Professor of History, University of California, Irvine
Select publications

Social protest, popular culture in 18th century Japan, University of Arizona Press, 1986.
Peasant uprisings in Japan: a critical anthology of peasant histories, Chicago University Press, 1991.
The weak body of a useless woman: Matsuo Taseko and the Meiji restoration, Chicago University, 1998.

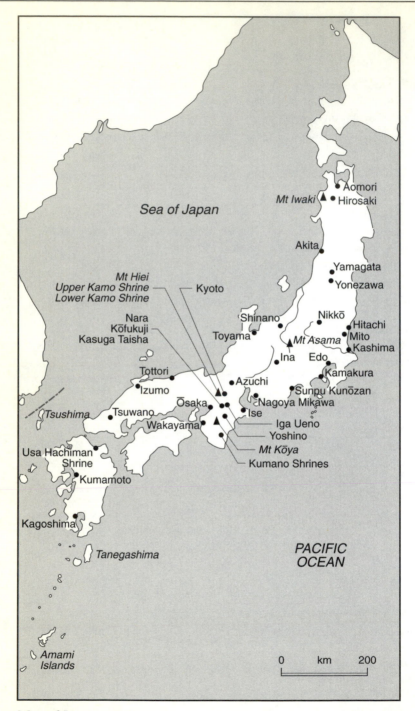

Map of Japan

CHAPTER ONE

Introduction: Shinto past and present

John Breen and Mark Teeuwen

The Shinto present

The place of Shinto in the religious scene of contemporary Japan as a vibrant, independent and coherent religion would seem self-evident. Shrines, the concrete symbols of Shinto, dot the landscape of urban and rural Japan.[1] Shinto shrines, with their distinctive *torii* gates and *shimenawa* ropes can be discreet, nestled in wooded precincts, or tucked away behind rows of shops; they can also be more imposing, defining the landscape in which they are set. The ancient shrines at Ise and Izumo and more modern creations like the Meiji and Yasukuni shrines in Tokyo are examples of the latter type. The material symbols which such shrines have in common, and which distinguish them from other religious structures, like those of Buddhism, say, attest to a shared heritage. Shrine priests across Japan are distinguished from Buddhist monks, other religious figures and the laity, by black *eboshi* hats, garments of white silk, and the *shaku*, a wooden implement priests carry on ceremonial occasions. It is evident, then, to even the most casual observer that Japan's 100,000 or so shrines, and their attendant priests, do indeed belong to one and the same tradition. The organisational structure one would expect of an independent and coherent religion is apparent, too. Some 75% of the nation's shrines and priests belong to *Jinja Honchō*, a charitable organisation based in Tokyo. The majority of the remainder of shrines are dedicated to the rice deity, Inari, and are affiliated to the Fushimi Inari shrine in Kyoto. There are also two institutions that train men and women from all over Japan for the shrine priesthood: Kokugakuin University in Tokyo and Kōgakkan University in Ise.

Again, there is manifest the uniformity of practice to be expected of a coherent and distinct religious tradition: from participants' washing of hands and rinsing of mouths on passing under the *torii*, through the casting of coins and ringing of the deity-summoning bell (*suzu*), to the clapping of hands and bowing of heads as greeting to the kami deities. Events in the annual and life cycles provide the main structures for such shrine practice. Shrines have their own special 'feast days' to mark founding and other unique events, but there is, for the rest, a striking synchronicity amongst shrines throughout Japan: New

1

Year, the Dolls' festival in March (*hinamatsuri*), children's day in May (*tango no sekku*), the *tanabata* and *bon* festivals in July and the autumn harvest festival, all of which draw many contemporary Japanese to shrines. Likewise, the birth of a child, special (November) ceremonies in a child's third, fifth and seventh years, coming-of-age ceremonies (on 15 January), and weddings, too, provide opportunities for shrines, their priests and parishioners all over Japan to engage in the practice of what we now know as 'Shinto.'

To the extent that such practice is sustained by any sort of 'theology' at all, and not simply by a need to confirm and strengthen family, communal or even national ties, it is apparently a straightforward and simple one: the kami, whatever their identity and provenance, will, when addressed with correct etiquette, appropriate prayers and adequate offerings, deign to confer blessings on the supplicant. Invariably the blessings sought and won are of a this-worldly variety: success in exams, recovery from sickness, longevity, the flourishing of a business, a happy marriage or an easy birth are typical examples.

Yet another dimension of Shinto is suggested by the typical location of shrines in the heart of the natural environment, at the feet, or on the summits of mountains, backed up against wooded copses, in the vicinity of waterfalls. Shrine practice invests in mountains, trees, rocks and other natural phenomena a sacred quality and identifies them as the dwelling places of kami deities. These facts point up a defining relationship between Shinto and nature, which is everywhere underscored and articulated in the available literature on Shinto in Western languages. The same literature points to still another dimension of Shinto thought and ritual, much less evident to the casual observer: the centrality of the imperial institution. We are told that imperial myths, such as those articulated in the eighth century *Kojiki* and *Nihon shoki*, rites, such as the *Daijōsai* enthronement, and imperial deities, foremost among whom is Amaterasu, the Sun Goddess, and imperial shrines, like that of Amaterasu in Ise, constitute Shinto's most holy texts and practices, its central deities and most sacred places. A cursory exploration of imperial ritual in contemporary Japan – the enthronement rituals for the present emperor, Akihito, say – is sufficient to confirm that it does indeed share key symbols with local shrine cults. From the involvement of ritualists clad in *eboshi* and white silk garb, to the emperor's veneration of Amaterasu both in the palace and subsequently, too, at Ise, the symbolic commonality is evident.

It is here, in the literature on the centrality of the imperial institution in Shinto, that we stumble upon a suggestive anomaly. For, despite the evident, and significant, commonality on the symbolic level, there is no evidence at all that such shrine practices and kami beliefs as are common among the Japanese today are dominated by, or even consciously related to, imperial themes. Still less are local practices and beliefs sustained by belief in, or even intimate acquaintance with, imperial practices and beliefs. The slippage here is that between a self-consciously 'Shinto' establishment and the national, not to say nationalistic, agenda professed by the majority of its members on the one

2

hand,[2] and local shrines and the practices and beliefs of ordinary Japanese who venerate there, on the other.

There is further, striking evidence of a dislocation between image and reality, between what are central and local agendas. The Shinto establishment lays claim to some 110 million Shinto practitioners, a figure which corresponds to some ninety percent of the population of Japan. This statistic is reproduced annually in government surveys on religious affiliation. Yet all the indications are that 'Shinto' – as opposed to, say, *jinja* or kami – has no meaning at all for the vast majority of Japanese, regardless of generation. Japanese attend shrines and beseech kami at festivals and on other occasions, too, but they have no awareness that their practice constitutes something called 'Shinto,' or that they themselves are 'Shintoist.' They certainly do not, themselves, profess affiliation to the Shinto religion. The striking statistic, it turns out, is obtained by the government's Office for Cultural Affairs (*Bunkachō*) asking shrine priests to submit parishioner numbers; these figures themselves are obtained from local government population registers.

These slippages suggest that there is an obvious case for deploying the term 'Shinto' with very considerable caution in discussions of contemporary Japanese religiosity. We argue that it is vital to distinguish between shrine cults – the reality of those multifarious activities and beliefs that are manifest in shrines both local and central – and 'Shinto' – the ideological agenda of the establishment, rooted especially though certainly not uniquely, in reverence for, or at least identification with, the imperial institution. There is, of course, no denying the continuities across shrines, from the smallest rural shrine to that of the imperial ancestress in Ise, in terms of symbols, practices and, indeed, beliefs – at least at a basic level. And yet it remains that these continuities fail conspicuously to converge with the establishment's articulation of Shinto. We clearly overlook this slippage, these tensions and contradictions, at our peril. 'Shinto' is not, then, in any obvious sense, what contemporary Japanese 'do at shrines,' nor what they think before the kami, since it is not what they themselves understand that they do and think; Shinto is, rather, what the contemporary establishment and its spokesmen would have them think and do.

The main focus of our concern in this book is Shinto in history, not in the present, but any historical exploration might usefully begin with an awareness that the contemporary dislocation between centre and periphery, image and reality, is not a new phenomenon; it is a contemporary manifestation of an age-old dimension to the problem of Shinto present *and* past.

The Shinto past

Until the relatively recent publication of a series of seminal articles by the historian Kuroda Toshio, the Shinto establishment's construction of the Shinto past went unchallenged by specialists writing in Japanese, English and other

Western languages. To this day, that construction remains largely unquestioned in non-specialist literature. There is some value, therefore, in a brief rehearsal of both the establishment position and Kuroda's incisive critique of it.

In a nutshell, 'establishment' spokesmen, like Hirai Naofusa, have disseminated the view in English as well as Japanese that Shinto is the indigenous religion of Japan, and has continued in an unsevered line from prehistorical times to the present; that Shinto is unique in, say, its attachment to nature, and, as such, constitutes the basis of Japanese culture. Hirai and others argue further that Shinto constitutes, and has always done so, the ultimate expression of Japan's unique polity, centred on the imperial institution. Critical to the persuasiveness of the arguments of Hirai and others like Joseph Kitagawa who follow him very closely, are the structural subdivisions of Shinto: 'shrine Shinto,' 'folk Shinto' and 'sect Shinto.'[3] Shrine Shinto has existed, according to Hirai, 'from the beginning of Japanese history' and has its most lofty expression in the religious devotions of the imperial family to Amaterasu;[4] by folk Shinto, or 'popular Shinto,' 'the substructure of Shinto faith,' Hirai seems to refer to all other practices before the kami that do not take place at 'established' shrines. Sect Shinto, finally, comprises the thirteen new 'Shinto-type' religious sects that sprang up in the social tumult of the nineteenth century. In this seamless multi-layered vision offered by the establishment, there is no room for dynamism, contradictions or tensions. The emphasis is on continuity and changelessness, rather than change.

Kuroda's main counter to this view, as articulated in English in a seminal article entitled 'Shinto in the history of Japanese religion,' is that 'Shinto' as the distinct, autonomous and independent religion we know today is an invention of nineteenth century Japanese ideologues.[5] Before the Meiji policy that authorised the 'separation' of Shinto and Buddhism, Japanese religious culture had been to all intents and purposes defined by Buddhism.[6] Shrines and shrine-based practice were nothing more than Buddhism's 'secular face';[7] kami, for their part, were understood to be 'manifestations of the Buddha.'[8]

The path to the revolutionary change in early Meiji was paved, of course, with the writings of various intellectuals in the preceding Edo (1600–1867) period, men like Motoori Norinaga (1730–1801) who conceived of kami and shrines as constituting a tradition quite distinct from, and unquestionably superior to, Buddhism. It was Motoori and others like him who 'firmly fixed' the definition of Shinto as the indigenous religion of Japan.[9] These men owed an intellectual debt, in their turn, to the writings of men like Yoshida Kanetomo (1435–1511), but Shinto theorists of the medieval period *prior* to Yoshida, such as the Watarai school at the Outer Shrine of Ise, were all 'adherents of the orthodox [Buddhist] teachings.' None of these men questioned for a moment that Buddhism constituted the 'over-arching principle.'[10] It is nonsensical, Kuroda asserts, to talk of Shinto as though it existed as an independent religion at this or, indeed, at any earlier age in Japanese history.

4

Contrary to the claims of some, then, the state formalisation of kami rituals and the state ranking of shrines during the Heian period (794–1185) did not mark Shinto's emergence as an 'independent' indigenous religion; indeed, these developments coincided precisely with new theological formulations that sought to explain kami in Buddhist terms, defining the kami as 'transformations of the Buddhas manifested in Japan to save all sentient beings.'[11] Kuroda's critique of the religious situation in pre-Heian Japan is more provocative still. 'Shinto' in its earliest usage in, say, the *Nihon shoki*, was, he insists, a referent not for some indigenous creed at all but, rather, for Taoism. The characters read as 'Shinto' in Japanese were used in eighth century China to mean Taoism, and it would have been natural for Japanese to use the same term in the same way. 'Teachings, rituals and even the concepts of imperial authority' – everything from the veneration of swords and mirrors to religious titles and the physical structure of the most sacred shrine of Ise – all spring from Taoism; so, too, were local beliefs defined by Taoist influence.[12] Taoism totally pervaded early Japan's religious milieu, obliterating what indigenous practices may have existed prior to that foreign creed's advent. 'Shinto,' in its earliest known usage, was then nothing but a Chinese cultural import.[13]

The new enthusiasm for the study of Shinto in academic circles outside Japan is due, in no small degree, to Kuroda's ground-breaking contribution.[14] For all its incisiveness, however, Kuroda's approach is itself not problem-free. It leaves us with a portrayal of Japanese religious history potentially as devoid of dynamism as that of Hirai and the Shinto establishment. Hirai posits Shinto as the seamless cultural-religious historical backdrop against which all religious phenomena including Buddhism are subtly transformed even as they were effortlessly accommodated. Kuroda, in his turn, accords to Buddhism a function not altogether dissimilar: Buddhism is the over-arching, defining influence within which all other religious phenomena were transformed in time, even 'to the point of obliteration.'[15] Kuroda disassembles the construct of a continuous Shinto tradition, stating that it is 'no more than a ghost image produced by a word linking together unrelated phenomena,'[16] but in the process he comes very close to writing out of Japanese history not only 'Shinto,' but shrines, their priests, kami and distinctive religious practices as well. *Pace* Kuroda, it is vital that we remember that many shrines, priestly lineages, kami beliefs and rites do display a remarkable degree of continuity over very long periods of time. There is similarly a striking degree of continuity over time in the imperial institution: its symbols, myths, and some of its rites. It is incumbent on us to explore these continuities and their inter-relationship further.

With regard to the former, the symbols of *torii* and *shimenawa* are of verifiably ancient pedigree; so, again, is local shrine practice and belief unquestionably ancient, at least in such basic terms as the supplicant's recognition of the need for purification before supplication, say, or the summoning of kami by hand-clapping, and the propitiation of the kami, whatever their provenance, for benefits of a this-worldly nature. The identification, evidenced by shrine location, between beliefs, practices and the natural environment is also verifiably ancient. To insist on the existence of continuity in local symbolism, practice and belief is not, of course, to deny the possibility of more or less profound influences from, say, Buddhism, Taoism or other imported practices at various historical stages; it is not, in other words, to deny the reality of change that lies at the heart of any tradition.

With regard to the imperial institution, we need to note that it was in the late seventh to early eighth century that the *Nihon shoki* and the *Kojiki* texts were written, the Ise shrines were commandeered by the ruling elite as the ancestral shrine of the imperial family, and the annual *Niinamesai* ritual (as well as its grander version, the once-in-a-reign *Daijōsai*) was reformulated and staged as a celebration of the emperor's privileged relationship with the Sun Goddess, Amaterasu.[17] While it is true that there were historical breaks in the performance of, say, the *Daijōsai*, it remains that the symbols of the imperial institution, whatever their ultimate provenance, have their roots firmly embedded in ancient Japan. Again, it is important to bear in mind that from Japan's ancient period this imperial symbolism, however indebted to Taoist ideas, was never superseded; it was never overtly challenged or discredited by any group of intellectuals, nor was it at any time replaced.[18] This applies to all intellectuals, but most obviously to those various self-consciously 'Shinto' groups of men that formed at different stages of Japanese history: the men who ran the *Jingikan* or 'Department for the Affairs of the Deities' in the classical period, for example; the Watarai priests at Ise in the medieval period, or the Yoshida and Shirakawa priests and the nativist exponents of the pre-modern period.

None of these groups 'overcame' imperial symbolism, or denied its validity, but it remains incumbent upon us to consider critically the place of imperial symbolism in their thinking and writing. The nature of the metaphysical, or more practical, negotiations these thinkers conducted, willingly or otherwise, with regard to the imperial institution and its symbolism is one of several areas demanding our concern. Another is the relationship between the imperial centre and the aforementioned groups of intellectuals on the one hand, and rural, local shrine cults on the other, especially at the times when those intellectuals were most active: what influence, if any, might each have exerted on local shrine cults, their beliefs and practices? Such an investigation might enable us to talk with Sonoda Minoru of the 'Shintoisation' of shrines in ancient Japan; that is, the 'subverting' of specific local shrines, and their subjection to the influence of the central imperial cult. It might, again, prove more accurate to speak of a succession of attempts at 'Shintoisation' in the classical, medieval, early modern and modern periods, since in each of them the national or universal agendas that constituted 'Shinto' adopted different guises. Shinto as articulated by the Watarai priests was different from that articulated by Yoshida Kanetomo, which in turn differed from that of, say, Edo nativists.

Kuroda's critique discourages explorations of this sort, largely because of his insistence that Buddhism explains all. It is conceivable that in his enthusiasm to challenge the Shinto establishment view, he overlooks other dimensions to the dynamism of Japanese religious culture. One concerns the fraught question of the transformation of Buddhism in Japan. If we can divest ourselves of the idea that all shrine practice and all patterns of belief in kami necessarily constitute 'Shinto,' it becomes easier, perhaps, to ask whether indigenous practice, influenced to a greater or lesser extent by Buddhism, Taoism and Asiatic patterns of folk religious practice, did not in some profound way leave its mark, in its turn, on the various forms of Buddhist practice adopted in Japan. Was it not owing to more or less indigenous habits of faith disclosed in shrine practice that Japanese Buddhism adopted the unique forms that it did? Arnason points out that 'the distinction between the inhabited lowlands and the mountainous regions seems to have been particularly important for the development of religious symbolism and the acculturation of Buddhist ideas,'[19] and indeed, mountain cults of at least partly indigenous origin have shaped much of Japanese Buddhism. Also, from its very inception Japanese Buddhism related to the kami in a very active way, incorporating them into Buddhist ritual and practice. There has been a tendency among specialists of Japanese Buddhism to marginalise kami-related aspects of Japanese Buddhism and exclude them from the 'real' Buddhist tradition. However, the influence of kami ritual and mythology especially on the esoteric Buddhist sects (Tendai and Shingon) was profound, and continued over centuries. The comments of Kushida Ryōkō in his classic *Shingon Mikkyō seiritsu katei no kenkyū* are worth heeding: 'Monks of the medieval period no longer regarded the kami classics as *geten*, works from outside the Buddhist tradition. Not only were they Buddhist works (*naiten*), [to these monks,] the kami classics were the very essence of the Buddhist teaching.'[20] The mere fact that to this day most temples have a small shrine within their grounds demonstrates that kami-cults have penetrated deeply into Buddhist practice; and the abundance of Buddhist theological texts, many of them still practically unexplored, dealing with subjects such as kami purification or the religious meaning of the three Imperial Regalia, demonstrates that topics that most would classify as 'Shinto' also held the intense interest of Buddhist monks and their patrons over many centuries.

Not only, then, can Buddhist ideas and ritual forms be seen to have influenced shrine practice and Shinto thought throughout the medieval period; but Buddhist thought and practice, too, were transformed under the influence of kami cults. If we accept Kuroda's argument in its most extreme form, and adopt his stance that there was no distinct 'Shinto' tradition of thought during the pre-modern period, we render ourselves unable either to explain the process of amalgamation that dominated pre-modern Japanese religion, or to see the Shinto tradition that rose to prominence in the Edo and modern periods in its proper historical context.

If one provisional conclusion can be drawn from the above, it is that the paths of the kami through Japanese history have been manifold. Kami have formed the focus for a great variety of local cults, many of which persisted largely unchanged through many centuries. They have played a central role in imperial ritual, and continue to do so to this day; they have penetrated deeply into the ritual and theology of Japanese Buddhism; and finally, they have inspired a range of theological constructs, which are generally brought together under the term 'Shinto.' The ideological agenda of the modern Shinto establishment, that we define as 'rooted . . . in reverence for, or at least identification with, the imperial institution,' is but one in a long succession of such theologies. Already in the fifteenth century, Yoshida Kanetomo identified three different categories of 'Shinto,' each with a radically different agenda. This 'establishment view,' which, as demonstrated by the essays of Isomae Jun'ichi, Nitta Hitoshi, and others in this volume, was itself the product of very specific historical circumstances, imposes on all kami cults an hierarchical blueprint which categorises all kami-related phenomena (in order of diminishing importance) as constituting, leading to, or branching off from a single 'Way of the Kami.' It is as an alternative to this view that we propose a multiplicity of 'Ways of the Kami,' each grown out of different historical and social circumstances, and each with its own ritual and theological agenda. Such an approach promises not only to open our eyes to aspects of kami cults and Shinto traditions that have previously been ignored, but also to throw new light on the rituals, beliefs and ideas of such cults and traditions that have been studied only through the lens of the above-mentioned notion that they, ultimately, formed part of a single 'Way of the Kami.'

It is only recently (and largely under the influence of Kuroda's work), that scholars have begun to look beyond the 'establishment view' of Shinto and the kami. For the most part, moreover, their studies are confined to specialist journals, and have yet to leave their imprint on the general understanding, inside Japan and out, of Japanese religions. The aim of this volume is to bring together in an accessible fashion a number of essays on Shinto and the kami that explore some of the issues raised above. The essays included in this book deal with kami and Shinto-related subjects ranging from the beginning of the historical period (the seventh century), until, roughly, 1945. Regrettably, lack of space precludes us from doing justice to two important themes: the growth and development of so-called 'sect Shinto' in pre-war Japan; and the complex dynamics of Shinto issues in the post-war period. We hope that there will be an opportunity to address these themes in separate volumes.

The classical period is covered by four essays. Tim Barrett discusses the profound formative influence of Taoism on Shinto in early Japan. Barrett provides abundant historical examples of the relationship between Shinto and Taoism during this early period, and gives special attention to the adoption in Japan of the imperial title of tennō (Ch. tianhuang), its background, and its religious and political implications. Sonoda Minoru focuses on the relationship between shrine cults and nature mentioned above as one of the enduring traits of kami cults. His essay explores the ritual means by which early Japanese transformed their natural surroundings into a cultural landscape, infused with religious and historical meaning. Referring to early mythological materials as well as early poetry, Sonoda uncovers the deep symbolic meaning of woods and forests in shrine worship. Nelly Naumann discusses the establishment and the functions of the *Jingikan* or 'Department for the Affairs of the Deities,' which was set up in the seventh century as part of contemporary attempts to reorganise Japanese government along the lines of the Tang Chinese bureaucratic state. Naumann provides a detailed overview of the state cult of which this office was in charge, and of the Chinese and indigenous sources from which it derived.

Allan Grapard closes this section with a discussion of the central role of both shrine and temple ritual in the Japanese state of the Heian period. He addresses this issue from various angles, offering analyses of the institutional framework within which rituals were performed, the political dimensions of this body of rituals, and their economic significance. Grapard opens up a tantalising perspective on these matters by calling upon us to reconsider ritual in terms of 'production, ingestion, and digestion.'

Topics from the medieval period are discussed in two essays by Mark Teeuwen and Bernhard Scheid. Teeuwen explores the functions that kami, and especially Amaterasu, performed in esoteric Buddhist thought and ritual, which, as pointed out by Kuroda, formed the dominant religious paradigm of the age. Discussing esoteric Buddhist forms of kami purification, shrine worship, and kami court ritual, Teeuwen describes the emergence of a Buddhist kami discourse that was instrumental in the subsequent development of Shinto into an independent religion. Bernhard Scheid's essay provides an analysis of Yoshida Shinto's central doctrinal text, the fifteenth-century *Yuiitsu Shintō myōbō yōshū*. He demonstrates in detail how esoteric, exoteric, and ritual elements are revealed in this text, and discusses how the dichotomy of open versus secret defines its structure. Scheid's analysis not only sheds new light on Yoshida Shinto thought and ritual, but also offers an example of how texts of this *kenmitsu* type (which constitute the majority of Japanese medieval religious literature) can be fruitfully read.

The section on the Edo period is opened by Wim Boot. Boot offers a detailed study, on the basis of primary sources, of the deification of Tokugawa Ieyasu as Tōshōgū Daigongen in the early seventeenth century. Comparing this event with the earlier deifications of Toyotomi Hideyoshi and of Fujiwara no Kamatari (quoted as precedents in the polemics that accompanied Ieyasu's deification), Boot sheds new light on its religious significance, and argues against the interpretation that this deification was a politically inspired exercise of bakufu propaganda. Brian Bocking focuses on *sanja takusen*, a distinctive type of hanging scroll inscribed with oracles of the Ise, Kasuga and Usa Hachiman shrines. Bocking uses this scroll, produced through some six centuries, as a window through which to view the dynamic development of Japanese religions over this long period of time. Bocking's choice of focus eloquently reveals the limitations inherent in the conventional method of tracing 'Buddhist' and 'Shinto' history as two separate fields of study.

9

The transition from Edo Japan to Meiji Japan is the underlying theme of the essays by Nicola Liscutin, Anne Walthall and John Breen. Liscutin studies the diverse religious phenomena that gave meaning to the sacred mountain of Iwaki in Tsugaru. She analyses the Iwaki 'cults' in terms of the mountain's sacred topography, and explores the religious dynamics sustained by the Iwaki shrine-temple complex in the pre-modern period. Her particular concern is to demonstrate how this dynamism expired and how the religious complexity of the site unravelled under the edicts of the early Meiji state.

Anne Walthall explores the Shinto thought of Hirata Atsutane from a new perspective. She asks how Hirata's ideas were transmitted to and enacted by his 'posthumous disciples' in the Ina valley. The religious and political fervour of these Hirata followers, of different social classes, found concrete expression in the creation of a shrine to Hirata. Walthall exposes the cultural and intellectual milieu of this little studied rural community and locates it in the context of late Tokugawa history. Finally, John Breen takes a new look at the 'separation policies' of the Restoration government. His focus falls less on the edicts and their consequences than on the people who formulated them, the ideologues, and the bureaucrats whose support was essential to their implementation. He questions the received wisdom of the Shinto perpetrator – Buddhist victim framework, and finds evidence of a more complex history in the unpublished writings of ideologues and bureaucrats as well as in the experiences of a provincial shrine priest.

Nitta Hitoshi, in the first of four essays to deal with late nineteenth and early twentieth century Shinto, explores the dynamics of the process that resulted in Shinto being defined as 'non-religious.' Nitta finds the key dynamic to lie not so much in the duplicity of Meiji bureaucrats seeking to circumvent the Meiji constitution's provisions for religious freedom; still less, at least in early Meiji, did it lie in the Shintoists themselves. Nitta proposes rather that we locate the origins of that idea in the logic of Shinshū Buddhists. In short, Buddhists' role in the creation of what we now know as 'state Shinto' was critical. Sakamoto Koremaru analyses this 'state Shinto' construct from an institutional perspective. The creation of the *Jinjakyoku* in 1900 was a landmark development as, for the first time since the very early Meiji years, shrines and priests were brought under the wing of a dedicated government office. The promise of an improvement in fortunes was hardly realised, however. The government gave little commitment to shrines and their priests despite vigorous campaigning by shrine clergy through the first two decades of the twentieth century. We overlook at our peril, Sakamoto argues, the ideological and emotional distance between the bureaucrats and the Shintoists who staffed such institutions as the *Jingiin*.

Kamata Tōji divides his attention between two men of unrivalled stature in the Shinto world: the twentieth century ethnologist Orikuchi Shinobu and the nineteenth century thinker Hirata Atsutane. Kamata adopts what might be called a psycho-historical approach to expose the obsession of both men with the Other Realm. Where some have suggested the influences of Christianity or

10

Pure Land Buddhism, Kamata uncovers a dimension of an entirely different order. Was it not, he asks, because of their physical disfigurement and the accompanying psychological torment that both Hirata and Orikuchi suffered that explains their turning from this world and seeking solace in the Other? The 'disfigurement' of Kamata's title might be seen as referring both to the physiognomy of the men he studies, and to the effect of that physiognomy on their brands of Japanese nativism. Isomae Jun'ichi, finally, highlights the thought of Tanaka Yoshitō (1872–1946) who, as the founding father of modern Shinto studies, was a little known yet central figure in the history of Shinto's modern development. Tanaka was driven by a desire to construe for Shinto a metaphysics that would enable it to stand shoulder to shoulder with Western religion and philosophy. He became one of the leading theoreticians of state Shinto. Isomae's essay sheds light not only on the formation of state Shinto thought but also on its sources, its institutional foundations and the limits to its influence.

Notes

1 Here we adhere to the somewhat arbitrary convention of referring to 'Shinto' institutions as 'shrines' and those of Buddhism as 'temples'.
2 For an analysis of *Jinja Honchō*'s position on these matters, see Teeuwen 1996b.
3 Hirai Naofusa, 'Shinto', *Encyclopaedia Britannica*, 276. For Joseph Kitagawa, see his *Religion in Japanese history* (1966) and *On understanding Japanese religion* (1987).
4 Ibid.
5 Kuroda Toshio 1981: 3.
6 Kuroda Toshio 1981: 11.
7 Kuroda Toshio 1981: 15.
8 Kuroda Toshio 1981: 12.
9 Kuroda Toshio 1981: 19.
10 Kuroda Toshio 1981: 18.
11 Kuroda Toshio 1981: 8. Most influential of the scholars who argue thus about Heian religion is Takatori Masao 1977.
12 Kuroda Toshio 1981: 9. This interpretation of the term Shinto in ancient Japan was first proposed by Tsuda Sōkichi, e.g. in his *Nihon no Shintō* (1949). For a further discussion, see T.H. Barrett's essay in this volume.
13 Hori Ichirō anticipated Kuroda's identification of early Japanese religious practice with that in China in his classic *Folk religion in Japan: continuity and change* (1968). Japanese practice was striking, he argued, for the similarities it bore to early religions on the Asiatic continent, and was doubtless indebted thereto. Hori was, for this reason among others, also reluctant to apply the term 'Shinto' to early Japanese religion. He chose, albeit with a disconcerting lack of consistency, to talk of 'proto-Shinto' or simply 'folk religion' – hence the title of his still valuable and provocative book.
14 Among recent studies of special interest are several by Allan Grapard and Neil McMullin. See especially Grapard 1988 and McMullin 1987.
15 Kuroda Toshio 1981: 20.
16 Kuroda Toshio 1981: 20
17 See on this, Matsumae Takeshi, 'Early kami worship', in *The Cambridge history of Japan*, vol. 1. Matsumae would have us locate the origins of 'Shinto' in pre-historic Japan.

18 Eisenstadt speaks eloquently of the inability of other intellectual traditions to overcome the imperial ideology. (Idem, *Japanese civilisation: a comparative view*, see especially Chapter 10: 'Some aspects of the transformation of Confucianism and Buddhism in Japan', 219–62.)

19 Arnason 1997: 126.

20 Kushida Ryōkō 1964: 275.

CHAPTER TWO

Shinto and Taoism in early Japan

Tim Barrett

The study of Shinto with regard to its relationship with the Chinese religion of Taoism (or Daoism, as it is now sometimes termed, in deference to the official romanisation of Chinese used in China and in this study) is, as most scholars would agree, whatever their personal opinions on that relationship, an underresearched area, and so it would as yet be foolish in the extreme to try to venture any generalisations on the topic in all its complexity. The following remarks focus therefore on the early period of this relationship as posited by Kuroda Toshio, since this has the greatest direct bearing on our understanding of the nature of Shinto itself. But it is worth pointing out that the most perceptive and balanced survey of the whole topic, compiled by the late Anna Seidel shortly before her untimely death, does emphasise that Taoist influence on indigenous Japanese religion, especially as transmitted through the medium of Buddhism, stretched from early times through to the Kamakura period and beyond.[1] As a consequence, the reader must bear in mind that the tentative suggestions made in this chapter refer primarily to the Nara period and the century or so leading up to it, and may have little validity before or after. Even so, the state of research on Chinese and Japanese religion during that time does now allow us to start to clarify a number of formerly obscure points, and gives us the hope that continued joint research in this area may offer new understandings of Japan's religious development.

But if we start from Kuroda's attempt – already discussed in the Introduction – at rethinking the meaning of Shinto, our first admission should be that the meaning of Taoism too has been something that has likewise generated considerable debate amongst students of Chinese religion in times past, and that the understanding of the term now most commonly accepted in academic circles is somewhat at variance with that which is nowadays becoming increasingly familiar in the English-speaking world in general.[2] For the simultaneous progress made both by translators of ancient texts like the *Daode jing* and by teachers of techniques loosely associated with the martial arts and with Chinese medical practice has concentrated popular attention on phenomena that either antedate or postdate the main canonical forms of the Taoist religion, leaving an excluded middle largely as yet known only to academics.

True, medicine and the martial arts share some common elements with Taoism amidst the closely-tangled strands of Chinese cultural history, but they – and their influence in Japan – are both probably best considered separately. The *Daode jing*, the *Zhuangzi*, and one or two other texts from ancient China share a bibliographical label and indeed a form of genetic relationship with Taoism, but one of the convictions of contemporary scholars most baffling to the ordinary reader is that none of the men and (for all we know) women who composed these texts would have considered themselves as 'Taoists', so for all their undoubted appeal to a Japanese readership, too, throughout Japanese literary history, the influence of their ideas as such also falls outside the scope of these remarks.

But what such texts provided, quite apart from glimpses of a continuously developing Chinese religious environment more rigorously excluded from Confucian literature, was a non-Confucian image of sagehood which served as a rallying-point for distinct, well-organised religious movements at a subsequent stage of Chinese history.[3] For after four centuries of unity, the collapse of China's imperial system in the second century of the Common Era had profound consequences in the religious sphere, since during that long span of relative stability the unseen world of the spirits had come to be thought of as highly organised, a bureaucracy as systematic as that of the emperor. When the emperor's officials could no longer control events the population seems to have turned, amidst natural disasters and epidemics, to the priests of this unseen bureaucracy, who were propagating cults like that headed by the Celestial Master Zhang, leader of an alternative empire legitimated not by Confucius, but by a commission passed on by the divinised Laozi, supposed author of the *Daode jing*. The introduction of the 'imperial metaphor' into Chinese religion gave it notions of structure, hierarchy, and membership of a bureaucracy which have endured to this day, even though the immediate reaction of the warlords who dismembered China into 'Three Kingdoms' was to obliterate by violence or at best incorporate into their own regimes organisations which they saw as rivals for power.

The power of organised religion, however, could not be suppressed for long, especially after the spread in China of Buddhism, a well-developed world religion based on a scriptural heritage emanating from an enlightened founder with a message addressed to all mankind, or rather to all 'sentient beings', to adopt the Buddhist perspective. The influence of Buddhism was perhaps marginal in the first organised Chinese religious movements, but in time it offered an increasingly clear model for Chinese emulation, providing for example a scriptural format for fresh revelations from purely Chinese deities in the late fourth century, who proclaimed to a dispossessed aristocracy in South China messages reaffirming their cultural values and threatening apocalypse to the displaced regime of Northern origins which had come to occupy their territory.

To my mind a crucial point was then reached during the late fourth and early fifth centuries which saw the formation of organised religions in China in the guises in which they dominate our sources for the rest of the imperial age. For it seems to me that a further period of instability and religious rebellion led governments in both North and South China to the conclusion that cooperation with established religions was a better policy than either attempts at complete suppression or a *laissez-faire* attitude to the religious environment. As a result we see the emergence under state guidance of well-defined and well-regulated forms of both Buddhism and Taoism. Though it is quite clear that the former faith had entered China not simply as the belief of a distinct clergy but also as a congeries of religious practices followed by the populace without much reference to that clergy, the Buddhist scriptures (and canon law) were now taken as the norms against which the state would judge its performance, and new offices were instituted to provide a hierarchy of monk-officials to enforce those norms, something which the religion had hitherto entirely lacked in China.[4]

Taoism, by contrast, was much more of a novelty, at least as regards its name, which is now used to describe organised Chinese religion for the first time. But just as the very different doctrines to be found in the vast mass of Buddhist scriptures could be seen as constituting one religion by appealing to the notion of a hierarchy of different levels of truth, so the various currents of Chinese religious thought already given some coherence by the notion of a bureaucratic hierarchy of gods could be brought together into one overarching religion, whose various texts were now to be organised in a single canon. At the same time it would be naive to assume that beyond the purview of the state either Taoism or Buddhism meant anything very much: where there was no state-recognised clergy tied to scriptural norms, ordinary people continued to construe the religious meaning of the Buddha, Laozi, or any other figure very much as they pleased, though since almost all our sources stem from educated persons close to the centres of power, the common practices and beliefs of ordinary people are precisely those which are most obscure to us.[5]

Yet before we turn to Shinto and Japan, a further development, perhaps already implicit at this point but only entirely clear by the mid-fifth century, needs to be taken into account. That is that beyond a mere rapprochement with religion the new situation also allowed for an advance towards the purposeful ideological use of religion to meet state needs, though where two religions now coexisted, a choice had to be made in the interests of ideological unity. First to make this choice in the mid-fifth centry were the Northern Wei, who opted for Taoism and persecuted Buddhism; in the early sixth century, the Liang dynasty in South China seems to have restricted Taoism in favour of Buddhism; and in the late sixth century the Northern Zhou turned once more to Taoism and persecuted Buddhism a second time. This last episode has been studied in some detail by scholars specialising in both religions, and we should note that surviving materials on Northern Zhou Taoism show that its victory was not an unambiguous one: forms of Taoism that appeared troublesome to the state are ignored in its ideological synthesis, which gives not unnaturally a special place to the emperor himself.[6] Now that we have introduced the term

15

Taoism as the self-designation of the state-recognised form of the religion, we may perhaps designate this variety of the religion positively manipulated by the state as State Taoism, by analogy with the State Shinto of recent memory.

The foregoing sketch of Taoism has of necessity been highly selective; it has also been in some ways partisan. Not all scholars in the West would subscribe to my own analysis, but for present purposes it may serve to carry the argument forward, since in deferring the use of the term Taoism until the early fifth century it coincides with the interpretation of the development of the religion espoused by a good number of Japanese scholars. And argument there has certainly been in Japan concerning the relevance of Taoism to Japan's own religious traditions, with the most recent wave of it sparked off by the publication of the very remarks of Anna Seidel already referred to above. From the eirenical mode of survey scholarship we must pass in short order to polemics, and in particular to the views of Fukui Fumimasa.

Fukui Fumimasa is the son of one of Japan's pioneering scholars in Taoist Studies, a seminal figure equally at home in the study of Buddhism, both Chinese and Japanese, and since he has inherited his father's breadth of erudition, his opinion, it must be said, carries great weight, even if in polemical contexts it is only evidence rather than erudition *per se* which can clinch matters.[7] In reviewing Anna Seidel's survey of Taoism he found occasion to criticise several points which need not detain us, and which in any case provoked responses from her friends. On her account of Taoism and Japan, he does complain that her views derive not from original research but from the opinions of other Japanese scholars, and in particular he thinks it 'unfair' (using the English term) that she should cite the controversial research of Fukunaga Mitsuji without mentioning his own criticisms of Fukunaga's work.[8]

We need not detain ourselves with Fukunaga's work, either, since it has already been surveyed in English in a loyal but admirably objective survey of the controversy between Japanese scholars over Taoism and Japan published by Fukunaga's leading Western student, Livia Kohn.[9] Of particular value for our immediate purposes is the condensation by Fukui of his own position into four key arguments, presented in English translation. Rather than run the risk of misrepresenting his views through paraphrase, I will cite the four numbered points verbatim, but will follow each with comments of my own. Though naturally I cannot claim like erudition to him, especially with regard to Japanese sources, I have carried out my own study of the Taoism of the seventh and eighth centuries, in particular of what I have dubbed 'State Taoism', in the light of which I feel that some reconsideration of the arguments so far advanced is possible.[10]

'(1) It is a matter of common knowledge in Japanese history that the Japanese government officially rejected the introduction of Taoism to Japan. Clear evidence of this appears in the *Tō daiwajō tōseiden* (Account of the expedition to the east by the Great Master [Jianzhen] of the Tang) by the eighth-century Japanese scholar-official Ōmi no Mifune. Yet advocates of the above theory are either ignorant of this historical fact or else for some reason disregard it in their arguments.'

In the source named, which relates the adventures of a Buddhist ordination master who is invited to Japan but finds his plans constantly thwarted by bureaucratic opposition or by shipwreck, we find that finally in 754 some Japanese envoys in China who happen to be devout Buddhists themselves approach him with the following message: 'We, your disciples, have long known that you tried five times to cross the sea to Japan, wishing to propagate the Teachings. So now that we meet you face to face we pay obeisance and are overjoyed. We have already recorded your honourable name and that of five of your disciples in the study of *vinaya* [Buddhist Canon Law] and have memorialised the Chinese emperor that you should spread the Buddhist Precepts in Japan, but the emperor required that you should go taking Taoist priests with you. The ruler of Japan formerly did not revere the dharma of the Taoist priests. So we memorialised that Chun Taoyuan and four others should be detained and kept to study the dharma of the Taoists, and therefore we memorialised that your name for its part should be dropped. We ask that you yourself should come up with an expedient. We have four ships ready with official goods for our country. They are fully prepared to depart, and so there will be no problem in your leaving'.[11]

Now the sentence concerning 'the ruler of Japan' in context need not be a statement of official policy. It might represent the Chinese emperor's reason for sending Taoist priests; it might represent the envoys' personal, Buddhist reasons for not going through with the plan proposed by the Chinese emperor – their desire to keep the Taoists out of Japan. The whole paragraph is simply explaining why their own plans to arrange an official trip for the master to Japan were thwarted, and why they are asking him to 'use his initiative' and come with them anyhow. The key sentence might in isolation be interpreted to mean that Japanese official policy prevented them from taking Taoists to Japan, but there is absolutely no supporting evidence for this.

There is, indeed, firm evidence to the contrary: as long ago as 1981 the Chinese scholar Bian Xiaoxuan pointed out that a second independent eyewitness account of this conversation survives, and this reads as follows: 'We your disciples have long known that you wish to go to Japan to spread the Precepts, and now that we meet you face to face, we pay obeisance and are overjoyed. We have now memorialised the emperor listing your name, saying that taking you to Japan is no trouble. It is simply that the emperor reveres the Taoist priests, and wishes to dispatch them to the Eastern Land to spread their dharma. However we disciples do not revere their *dharma*, so as an expedient we memorialised that the plan be stopped, yet we renew our encouragement and invitation to you.'[12] This account, then, supports the second option, that the refusal to take Jianzhen as part of a deal spreading Taoism in Japan was a private decision by the envoys.

Furthermore, diplomatic records on the Chinese side show that the Japanese ruler as recently as 735 had specifically asked official envoys to request from the emperor not only the *Daode jing* but images of Taoist gods.[13] The 'ruler of Japan' had changed by 754, but not the emperor of China, who perhaps felt that he was simply fulfilling the earlier Japanese request. It is also worth bearing in mind that both events in any case cannot be read simply as records of religious preferences since they formed part of the currency of interstate diplomacy: the Chinese emperor in question had created the most fully wrought version of State Taoism ever to appear in Chinese history, a State Taoism very much centred on his own person, and the conduct of the Japanese may be read simply as designed to appeal to his prejudices (in the first instance) without directly involving themselves in his ideological schemes (in the second).[14] Since countries such as Tibet are on record in the eighth century as asking China for Buddhist teachers even when we know that the religion was already present there, we cannot even deduce for certain that there was no Taoism in Japan at this time; at best we can conclude that if it was present, it cannot have been well established.[15]

'(2) Ever since ancient times Taoism has never existed in Japan as a religion or religious group, and Buddhism has exerted far greater influence on Japanese society. This is a fact that cannot be ignored. But the reasoning of the advocates of the above theory starts from the premise that there were contacts between Taoism and ancient Japan, and they pay no attention to the relationship between officially sanctioned Buddhism and unsanctioned Taoism or to the difference in the relative importance of the two.'

The 'above theory' here is that of Taoist influence on Japan. Fukui's counter-argument concerning the preponderant influence of Buddhism I would not seek to deny, though his remarks do invite one or two qualifications. First, though officially recognised Chinese Buddhism was also officially recognised in Japan, influences on that country did not arrive solely through official channels, and Japan was open to influence from the relatively unknown Buddhism of the 'ordinary Chinese' to which I have drawn attention above. Whether this rather flexible form of religious practice should be called Buddhism is an interesting point: from a late twentieth century position, we might well take it as our normative model of what Buddhism 'really' was, rather than privilege the official, canonically-determined form of Buddhism sanctioned by East Asian rulers. But, to concentrate on the issue in hand, we should further note that the inexistence of Taoism as a religion or religious group in early Japan represents an argumentum ex silentio susceptible of disproof, though not disproved; the description of Taoism as 'unsanctioned', furthermore, rests on a hypothesis which we have already shown to be unsafe in our comments on argument (1) above.

'(3) Taoism is an amalgamation of various ancient folk beliefs and other religious elements that evolved into a 'religion' in northern China in the fifth century A.D. Therefore the origins of some of the individual constituent elements of Taoism may be traced back to ancient China, and it is also possible to discover similar phenomena in ancient Japan. However, even though these may be regarded as forming a part of "Chinese religion", they cannot be subsumed under the name of "Taoism", which was established only in the fifth century, for this would result in a historical perspective that runs counter to the flow of history. When discussing Taoism as a religion, one should restrict oneself to the fifth century and later, when Taoism had been established as a national religion and the term "Taoism" (*daojiao*) had assumed the same meaning that it has today, otherwise terminological confusion will ensue.'

Again, it will be seen that my own understanding of Taoism accords very much with that put forward here by Fukui, with the possible exception that I do not see the situation having quite reached stability by the fifth century. Also we should perhaps beware not simply of the points made by Fukui, but also of the 'unfairness' of denying the name 'Taoist' to elements of earlier religion taken up by later Taoists and reaffirmed by them. My own account, which here accords with that of other Western scholars, sees earlier elements reaffirmed by later Taoists as integral to their religion, not borrowings which may be methodologically detached at will.[16] If it could be shown (and I would hasten to reassure Fukui that on his understanding of Taoism I do not think this is the case) that such elements reached Japan in a Taoist context (i.e. through identifiably Taoist scriptures, preaching or rituals), then their presence in Japan would constitute Taoist influence.

'(4) This point is related to (3). There are instances in which mere folk beliefs of Chinese provenance among the religious beliefs of ancient Japan are referred to as "Taoism". When discussing the possible existence of Taoism in ancient Japan, one must first demonstrate that religious phenomena such as a religious group professing "Taoism," groups of adherents, scriptures containing the names of Taoist deities and Taoist rituals actually existed in ancient Japan, for if the evidence cannot be discovered, then the use of the term "Taoism" only leads to confusion. However, positive evidence of such phenomena has been found in neither ancient literary sources nor archaeological remains.'

This conclusion certainly requires qualification, if only because scriptures containing the names of Taoist divinities are most certainly listed in one ancient literary source from Japan. This is the *Nihonkoku genzaisho mokuroku* of Fujiwara no Sukeyo, who died in 898. As a traditional East Asian bibliographical label, 'Taoist' does not accord with the definition espoused both by Fukui and myself, so most of the titles listed in Fujiwara's catalogue of books present in Japan in his day under this heading do not concern us. But two titles listed, the *Benji jing* and the *Lingbao jing*, are quite irrefutably scriptures of the Taoist religion.[17] How and when they arrived in Japan we cannot tell, nor whether anyone there read them, and since they seem to have been in a fragmentary condition perhaps their presence counts for very little. But it counts, and cannot be ignored.

It is necessary, however, to go somewhat further. The working definition of Taoism arrived at by Fukui emerges over the course of his four arguments as one based very much on a certain model of what Taoism was, a religion comparable to Buddhism. I would not deny the importance of that model in the fashioning of Taoism – indeed, I would see it as crucial. But Taoism was not simply – especially in the seventh and eighth centuries of the Common Era – a religion like Buddhism. It had inherited from the second century close connections with Chinese conceptions of empire, and it had therefore the potential to be transformed into an ideology, State Taoism as I have termed it, propagated through the organs of the state as much as of the Taoist religious community.

Now during the seventh and eighth century Japan adopted a large number of Chinese political institutions. This was done without the presence in Japan of any Chinese bureaucrats – save the occasional hapless envoy – and indeed very largely without the training of Japanese personnel in China for subsequent bureaucratic employment in their home country. The key to this great transfer of culture was not propagation by adherents to Chinese political norms, but through the medium of texts, which allowed for an understanding at a dispassionate distance of how Chinese bureaucracy worked, and how it might be adapted independently to the Japanese situation.[18] What if the Japanese encountered Taoism not simply as a religion, but as part of the Chinese polity?

Such a view would have been unthinkable until quite recently, since it has been taken as axiomatic that Chinese political institutions were an exclusively Confucian preserve. That axiom is now untenable, as far as the historical epoch in question is concerned, as my remarks on the emperor's plan of 754 have already indicated.[19] But the high point of Taoist integration into political life achieved in 754 was the result of a gradual process, and if we are to trace the Taoism that might have been known to the Japanese through political texts, we must trace developments before that point with all due caution, mindful of the ideological tendency of the Tang imperial regime to rewrite history as it went along, updating the past to accord with the present.

My account of the development of Taoism above ended in the late sixth century with the imperial Taoism of the Northern Zhou and its great persecution of Buddhism. The premature death of the Northern Zhou ruler allowed his dynasty to be replaced by one founded by a former subordinate of his under the dynastic title of the Sui. The Sui regime pursued a cautious ideological policy, leaning heavily towards Buddhism without penalising non-Buddhists, especially after it had achieved the political reunification of the whole of China using the war machine bequeathed by the Northern Zhou and had therefore to bend its efforts to a cultural reconciliation and reunification of North and South. It is noteworthy that the Sui were the first Chinese dynasty with which the newly emergent centralising Japanese state came into contact, so the practice of using Buddhism as an officially sanctioned religion would have been demonstrated to the Japanese as a political reality.[20]

When the second ruler of the Sui overreached himself in the process of empire building, attempting to incorporate the kingdoms of the Korean peninsula into his state and to link North and South China logistically through the creation by forced labour of a lengthy canal system, China fell apart into civil war. Amongst the many contenders, a general from the same northeastern military background as the Northern Chou and Sui founders named Li Yuan proved the eventual winner and founder of the much more stable Tang dynasty. Yet it would be wrong to suppose that Li Yuan rose to power on the strength of a fully fledged alternative to the Sui ideology: Stephen Bokenkamp has recently studied in some depth the prophetic verses used by the nascent Tang forces to justify their cause, and while they appeal to popular forms of messianic expectation reflected in some Taoist texts, they are not narrowly Taoist in any sense that would satisfy Fukui, but include symbolism equally redolent of popular Buddhist messianism – a rather potent form of religiosity deemed heterodox by our orthodox Buddhist sources.[21] The text that preserves this material, a diary of events by a Tang supporter named Wen Daya, has practically nothing to say concerning Taoism as such, though it does record Li Yuan's cautious acceptance of declarations of support relayed to him from the god of Mount Huotai.[22] It may be that 'in Taoist literature the gods of Mount Huotai were identified as Taoist deities', but once again we should beware: Taoism liked to coopt such powers into their own system, yet this did not mean that they became exclusively Taoist.[23]

Even so, one of the most striking features of Wen's work is the way in which it preserves an account of the founding of the Tang which for dynastic reasons (the usurpation of Li Yuan's son, Li Shimin, who thereafter tried to minimise his father's contribution) might well have been suppressed. Denis Twitchett has noted that Wen's diary was eventually listed by Fujiwara no Sukeyo, and it may be that from the start it was for propaganda reasons so widely distributed that it proved to be out of the question to try to suppress it.[24]

Now if this stirring tale of the seizure of empire did actually reach Japan quite rapidly (perhaps via the embassies of the mid-seventh century), this might possibly explain the appearance in the *Nihongi* description of the seizure of the throne by Tenmu in 672 of messages of support from similar gods – once past the opening chapters, theophanies are actually rather rare in this account of early Japanese history, and although these passages may have been invented *ex nihilo*, we know that the authors of the *Nihongi* frequently turned Chinese texts to good account.[25]

But if this suspicion is worth raising even in the case of the first steps towards religious legitimation taken by the Tang, for reasons that will eventually become apparent, their subsequent course bears even closer reflection. If we stick closely to contemporary documentation, ignoring later historiography, the first move came in 620, when Li Yuan visited a famous Taoist institution associated in particular with Yin Xi, the border guardian to whom Laozi is said to have handed the *Daode jing* before disappearing from China for good.[26] Though this institution was (and is) generally known as the Louguan ('Towering Monastery'), he renamed it the Zongsheng-guan, 'Monastery of the Sage's Lineage' because, as an inscription erected in 626 makes clear, Li Yuan asserted that he himself was descended from the sage Laozi, who from early times had been claimed as a bearer of the Li surname.[27]

Given that Laozi in a Taoist context was not only a sage but a divine eternal being of cosmic significance – in short, a god – this amounted to an unambiguous affirmation of his divine descent.[28]

Naturally, Buddhist apologists, on the qui vive after more than a half century of particularly intense ideological competition, were not prepared to accept these dynastic pretensions, which soon enough emerged as favouring patronage of the Taoists over their own religion. Their champion during this era was the fearless and very erudite Falin (572–640).[29] His line of defence on the matter of Taoist gods and their descendants may be traced back to the Liang dynasty of the early sixth century, an era (as we have noted in passing) of strong Buddhist influence from the Emperor on down, which seems to have been particularly concerned to draw up an inventory of its dual cultural heritage, Buddhist and Chinese, defining through classic works of reference what from each stream of culture was considered worth preserving, especially in the latter case. It has been shown that Falin accordingly quotes an encyclopedia (the bulk of which is now lost) to stress that he has no quarrel with the 'normative' view of China's origins enshrined there, that at the dawn of time this world was the domain of a numinous figure known as the *tianhuang* or 'Heavenly August One'.[30] Indeed, this primal ruler – for whom there were loose analogies in Buddhism – is mentioned by him in his writings with considerable frequency.[31] But any other higher gods as described by the Taoists he denounces as mere sectarian inventions, introduced to compete with Buddhism. As for Laozi, he was simpy a man, albeit a wise one.[32]

On this point, he was immovable, and when brought up before the emperor himself (by this time, the usurping son, Li Shimin) on the grounds of slandering the imperial family, he even pressed his case further, denying that the Li rulers had any legitimate claim to descent from Laozi in any case. The infuriated monarch was only narrowly dissuaded from executing him forthwith, and he was lucky to be sent into an exile from which he never returned. His biography, giving details of these dramatic events, was promptly banned as soon as it appeared as well, though as one monkish bibliographer of the next century notes (no doubt with secret satisfaction) 'People keep making copies, generation after generation'.[33]

But although the inscription of 626 (which was penned by a very famous literary figure) and the polemical writings of Falin were doubtless widely circulated and may have arrived therefore in Japan, they were essentially private documents which would not necessarily have attracted the attention of the 'modernising' rulers of the Japanese seventh century. Chinese state publications incorporating the new imperial notions of divine descent were, however, soon to be produced.

Earliest of these, it would seem, was a text, now lost, giving a revised history of his father's reign compiled by the historians of Li Shimin in 643.[34] We cannot be absolutely certain that this ever reached Japan, but similar or identical material certainly did.[35] And a twelfth-century epigrapher's comment on an eighth-century inscription is quite clear as to a vital part of the contents of this text, which are repeated in a slightly different form in the inscription itself. Laozi is said to have appeared in 620 and announced: 'Tell the Tang Son of Heaven for me "I, Lord Lao, am your ancestor"'.[36] Lord Lao, it should be noted, was specifically the term for the divinised Laozi used in the contemporary Taoist religion.

To my mind, however, it was Li Zhi, son of Li Shimin, who took the boldest steps to identify the cause of his dynasty with that of Taoism.[37] The most dramatic ideological move of all came in 674, when he abandoned the time-honoured Chinese term for emperor, and declared that his title was now *tianhuang*. As we have seen, Buddhist polemicists had already gone on record as seeing the term as a legitimate one in Chinese culture, so they were in no position to protest, but it must be noted that even so the title resonated with specifically Taoist meanings too, and so represented a very clever ideological compromise.[38]

It hardly seems possible that such a radical innovation went unnoticed in Japan, and there is certainly evidence in Fujiwara no Sukeyo's bibliography that a work by Li Zhi's chief historian of the cult of the divine ancestor, a Taoist priest named Yin Wencao (622–688), did arrive there at some point.[39] True, official contacts between China and Japan seem to have lapsed between 669 and 702, but even this may be due to deficiencies in our sources: one recently published early edition of a collection of Tang materials refers to an embassy in 670 hitherto unknown to historians.[40] Absence of official contacts in any case would not have cut off completely the supply of Tang documents to Japan.

But the crucial question is whether the rulers of the Japanese state had somehow anticipated the Chinese in adopting the term at an earlier date themselves. For *tianhuang* is no more and no less than the best-known Japanese term for emperor, *tennō*, in its Chinese reading. Whether the Japanese usage is actually earlier or not, we need to see it against a Japanese awareness of its signification in the Chinese texts available at the time of its adoption. And in the latter case, it is quite clear that it represents a term which, if not 'Taoist' in the narrow sense, even so had strong Taoist overtones, and was at the very least strongly connected with a conception of rule by monarchs of divine descent which had been deliberately built up in China over the course of half a century.

As it happens, the recent work of Joan Piggott on the emergence of the Japanese monarchy shows decisively that the majority of Japanese experts on Japanese history are now very much in favour of a date later than 674 for the first use of the term in Japan, and the evidence would indeed seem to point to as late as after 690.[41] This position has only been arrived at after extensive debate: one study which reached this conclusion as early as 1983 already lists thirty-one different opinions on the topic.[42] By the following year, however, evidence not only for the later date but for Chinese influence had been put on record.[43] In the light of this, it is interesting to find at least one Japanese scholar still preferring to think that the term was used at an earlier point, even if not in a systematic way. That scholar, apparently the only one to have communicated his researches in a European language, is Fukui Fumimasa.

In an erudite but usefully concise review of the major developments in scholarship with regard to the introduction of the term *tennō*, Fukui endorses fully the scholarship used by Piggott in so far as concerns the official adoption of the term, but points out that this can still be reconciled with earlier theories suggesting that it was first borrowed from China at the end of the sixth century.[44] The problem here is once again with the evidence: the only source appearing to date any instance of the term so early, though accepted by the first generation of critical scholars, has long been abandoned as a reliable witness on the basis of later research, which research Fukui himself notes without fully indicating its significance.[45]

The source in question is an inscription on a Buddhist statue dated apparently to 607, which has excited almost as much scholarship itself as the larger question of imperial terminology upon which it bears: some dozen contributions already by 1974, according to one useful survey of that date.[46] No one finds the apparent date now tenable, though most assign the statue and inscription to somewhat later stages of the seventh century; a similar inscription on another statue elsewhere bearing the title *tennō* is at least dated to 666.[47]

Now while I am not aware of any direct evidence rendering the inscription of 666 problematic, I have come across some apparent evidence suggesting that the 607 inscription may have been tampered with very much later, in medieval times, to bring its terminology into line with what had at that point become standard; such a possibility of course might in any case apply to the 666 inscription also. The evidence is by no means ideal; it occurs in a source which is certainly not free from simple copyist's errors itself. But it does give a plausible reading for the 607 inscription which raises the possibility that it (and also earlier written sources) originally contained another term in place of that which now reads *tennō*.

The readings in question may be found in a commentary of 1547 by the monk Shōyo, the *Shōyoshō*, on earlier literature concerning Shōtoku Taishi, the famous royal prince responsible for his influential support of the Buddhist religion in Japan.[48] He is in part referring not simply to the inscription but to an earlier reference to it by another commentator, Jungen, in 1239 or thereabouts: I cannot trace the reference in this commentary as it now stands, but Jungen does at one point exhibit the same usage.[49] This (though in his own comments Shōyo reverts to the normal term) gives the reading *ten'ō*, Chinese *tianwang*, 'Heavenly King' where the text now reads *tennō*.

Given the similarity in pronunciation, and the occasional carelessness of medieval writers, it might not do to make too much of this, especially since earlier quotations of the inscription, including one in a manuscript dating back long before Shōyo's time, consistently give the current reading.[50] Yet there is firm evidence that at the start of the seventh century the Japanese relayed to China the information that their monarch was called by them *ame no kimi*, 'Lord of Heaven', a title for which *tianwang* would surely be an appropriate equivalent. In fact the modern Chinese pronunciation of the reported title would be *abei jimi*, but despite past attempts at interpreting the first two syllables as meaning 'great' (which would provide yet another term, 'Great King', known to have been used in early Japan), a gloss preserved in a collection of Chinese documents to the effect that the meaning was 'Heaven's child' (perhaps a Chinese misunderstanding of a Japanese gloss as 'Son of Heaven', the Chinese synonym for 'emperor'?) effectively rules out that possibility.[51]

That 'Heavenly King', *tianwang*, would have been an attractive title in early seventh century Japan is suggested by its previous popularity in North China. In China's distant past it had been a term implying paramountcy rather than centralised rule, and in the late fourth and early fifth centuries it was revived by various non-Chinese rulers – perhaps to convey the same overtones, but also perhaps (as I have suggested elsewhere) in order to incorporate not only familiar Buddhist images of martial power (it equates with the Buddhist Sanskrit term devarāja) but Inner Asia notions of legitimation by sky gods as well.[52] In any case, even if the evidence for the adoption of the term is not overwhelming, it is certainly much better than for the adoption of the term *tianhuang* prior to its choice by the Chinese for ideological reasons as an imperial title.

It may even be that when that time did come in Japan also, the ideological reasons were understood, and that the choice was deliberate. Li Zhi, who coined the title in China as part of what can only have been a deliberate ideology designed to raise his rather humble standing in terms of contemporary aristocratic genealogy to an unquestionable semi-divine status (hence his father's sensitivity to Falin's frankness), was succeeded by his wife, the Empress Wu, who was genealogically not in a position to benefit from this glorification of the Li clan. As scholars have shown, she had associated herself very closely with his rule, accepting a change of title to *tianhou*, 'Heavenly Empress', at the same time as her husband changed his own self-designation to *tianhuang*, so his death left her in the awkward position of trying to rule through her sons as a 'Holy Mother'. When the Li clan resisted her dominance, she was obliged after some hesitation eventually to come up with a completely different Buddhist form of legitimation from 690 onwards, and abandon the notion of rule by divine descent so carefully nourished by her husband and his predecessors.[53] At that very point the Japanese throne fell to an empress also. But, crucially, in the close-knit royal genealogy of Japan, this empress, Jitō, was herself an emperor's daughter as well as an emperor's widow.[54] If in Japan it was she who first took over the term *tianhuang*, then the message in the contemporary East Asian world could only have been that she wished to stress her legitimation by continuity of descent, and that whatever the pace of change in Japan at that time, no switch to Buddhist forms of legitimation was contemplated.

Such an interpretation can only remain hypothetical in the absence of any supporting materials, but in order to explore the continued divergence between Chinese and Japanese terminology following the time of Li Zhi there is certainly an interesting body of evidence which so far appears to have been entirely overlooked. Japanese scholars such as Fukui tend to stress that the term *tianhuang* was only in use in China for a very short time, during the latter years of Li Zhi's life, and so naturally seek for internal causes in Japan for the adoption and retention of the term. Unfortunately, they are mistaken. While it is true that the Empress Wu came up with a sequence of alternative titles for herself, and also true that after her removal her sons and successors did not themselves turn back to make use of the term *tianhuang*, which tended to be used only in conjunction with her title in a way that summoned up memories they preferred to forget, that is only part of the story.

For the term remained in use, long after Li Zhi himself had ascended to be with his divine ancestor, in order to signify not that late emperor, Li Zhi, specifically, but *any* emperor in the Li imperial line, at least in the vocabulary of ordinary Chinese. The first to notice the evidence for this were traditional Chinese epigraphers, who point out that in dedications of Buddhist statues, which always ask for the resultant benefits to accrue to family ancestors and more occasionally to China's rulers as well, the *tianhuang* and his empress attracted dedications not simply after Li Zhi's death (as in an example dating to 687) but even in 692, after his empress had changed her own title and selected (as we have noted) an entirely different ideology making the term meaningless.[55] An even clearer case of popular inertia in dropping the terminology introduced by Li Zhi has been detected on a Buddhist manuscript by Tonami Mamoru, who finds *tianhuang* being used unthinkingly to mean emperor in a dedicatory colophon even after the death of the Empress Wu and the return to the pre-Li Zhi official terminology for emperors, as late as 709.[56] In fact, the compendium of inscriptions on early Chinese images published as long ago as 1915 by Ōmura Seigai shows that this example too is by no means out of the ordinary: dedications to the *tianhuang*, meaning simply the current emperor, may be found not only in 706, but as much as half a century after the death of the official bearer of the title, in 733.[57]

Why would the Japanese wish to retain a word for emperor which was still current in China, but only as a rustic solecism amongst country folk, who maintained a certain affection for the uneventful rule of the Empress, whilst better educated people saw it as an anachronism from a time when life at court had been for those at the top of society too eventful by far? The answer surely must lie in the difficulties the Japanese faced in conducting diplomatic relations with China whilst sustaining their own ambitions to imperial status.[58] Any coincidence of overtly imperial terminology was bound to provoke a furious response on the part of the Chinese, but *tennō*, though it undoubtedly meant 'emperor', from the late seventh century onward probably only elicited a wry smile from Chinese bureaucrats amused by what they would have considered quaintly inappropriate Japanese attempts at mimicking their terminology. Pragmatically, the divergence suited both parties.

Our quest for Taoist influence has come a long way, and ended up rather far from the hypotheses of Kuroda Toshio with which we started. As a case study, however, the history of the term *tennō* does illustrate some of the problems involved in talking of Taoist influence. Its Chinese form, *tianhuang*, was undoubtedly chosen as part of an ideological attempt to bend Taoism to the service of the dynasty, yet for political reasons the choice could not be an openly sectarian one. Its further adoption in Japan could have been due to analogous considerations, but its persistence was probably due to non-religious diplomatic factors. If we speak, as both Kuroda and Anna Seidel do, of a 'pervasive' Taoist influence on Japan, then that word's overtones of 'low-profile', 'insidious', might suit the case, but if the meaning of 'omnipresent' is to the fore, as it usually is, then despite the heavy influence of continental (that is, not only Chinese but also Korean, to say nothing of Indian and Inner Asian) religion on Japan, I would side with Livia Kohn in questioning its appropriateness.[59]

Even so, the role of State Taoism in influencing the articulation (presumably – though this needs to be established – not the origin) of Japanese ideas of sovereignty based on divine descent – something normally considered part of the sphere of State Shinto – evidently does need to be carefully investigated. When, for example, Li Zhi said of his son 'His divine mirror shines afar', what would a contemporary Chinese bureaucrat have thought of such rhetoric?[60] Would it have seemed Taoist?[61] And with what degree of literalness would a contemporary Japanese bureaucrat have interpreted the phrase, had he read it? Can any verbatim Japanese borrowings of such rhetoric be identified? To what extent might both Tang and Japanese representations of divine descent have been affected by earlier examples – for instance by the non-Chinese Northern Wei, who claimed descent from the Yellow Emperor and also included a goddess in their genealogy?[62] Even more appositely, one notes that the Northern Zhou, predecessors of the Sui, claimed descent from a Chinese divinity (Shen Nong), bore a clan name (Yuwen) translated as 'Heavenly Lord', and initially ruled from 557 to 559 under the title 'Heavenly King' also.[63] So when we come to the seventh century, how explicit at the formative stage were any claims to current divinity hidden in the broader ideological agenda?[64]

My own remarks have subjected the comments of Fukui Fumimasa on Japan and Taoism to as stringent a critique as possible, because ultimately his central contention has to be accepted: that no one has as yet subjected both Chinese and Japanese materials to the necessary close analysis over an extended body of documentation. The aim of the foregoing reconsideration, therefore, has been simply to introduce something of the issues at stake and the materials and methods which might be used to replace mere controversialism and resolve those issues in future on the basis of the existing evidence. While Fukui is right to assert that such an undertaking demands greater erudition than most of us possess – hence my initial reference to the probable appearance of joint research in future – I hope that enough will have been said to show that the effort should prove worth while for anyone bold enough to take up the challenge.

Notes

1 Kuroda Toshio 1981:1–21; Seidel 1989–90: 223–347 (see for Japan 299–304).

2 Scholars in the field of Chinese religion now have a number of studies in English which may be used to trace the course of their debates over the scope of the term Taoism. See e.g. Kirkland 1992: 77, n.4 and the text of the article itself; Katz 1995: 37, n.78 (and generally 32–38 and notes) for just some of the recent scholarship written in the shadow of this issue, to say nothing of discussions in other languages. The debate will doubtless continue: on the issue of membership of a (or the) medieval Taoist tradition, see Barrett 1999.

3 The account of Taoism given here represents, of course, a personal interpretation geared towards the main topic under discussion, i.e. influence on Shinto. For a standard account, cf. Robinet 1997.

4 For one aspect of the introduction of this Buddhist state hierarchy, see Barrett 1996b: 1–7.

5 The implications of this for the study of Buddhism in China have been most cogently made by Zürcher 1982: 161–176.

6 I have in mind here Lagerwey 1981 which reviews our main source on the Taoism of this dynasty.

7 For the position of Fukui senior in Taoist Studies, see the Introduction to Maspero 1981: xv. The most convenient source for the views of Fukui Fumimasa in English is Fukui 1995: 1–18; n.7 on p. 9 of this article lists earlier polemics for and against in Japanese, one or two of which will be mentioned below.

8 Fukui 1993: 63–67.

9 Kohn 1995: 389–412. Pp. 401–405 in particular are devoted to the 'Iconoclastic Position' of Fukunaga cum suis.

10 Fukui's summary (I have retained his Wade-Giles transcriptions in quoting him) is at Fukui 1995: 6; the study of State Taoism (not a term I used at the time that it was put together, in the early 1980s) is Barrett 1996a, which represents a first draft towards a chapter for the *Cambridge History of China*.

11 Mabito 1979: 83. This Chinese variorum edition represents the most convenient and carefully edited text to date; since Western language translations are too old or too unreliable, I have also checked this against the Japanese translation of Ishida 1970: 331.

12 Bian 1980: 36 citing a text, *Ganjin wajō san iji*, by his Japanese disciple's disciple, Hōan, reproduced as an appendix in Wang's edition, p. 116, from *Dainihon Bukkyō zensho*.

13 *Song-ben Cefu yuangui* 1989: 999. 11a–b. This partial but early edition of a standard collection of Tang documents compiled in 1013 was not available at the time that I undertook my earlier study; although it unfortunately lacks the main section on Taoism, it is clearly superior in its text to the Ming edition used by scholars before its publication.

14 Apart from my own survey, already mentioned, it is now possible to point to Benn 1987: 127–145, which is based on a detailed doctoral dissertation.

15 For a Tibetan request for Buddhist teachers, see Wang 1991: 2055, another compilation of documents, which records under the year 781 (when Tibet was certainly already familiar with Buddhism) a Tibetan diplomatic request for good Buddhist teachers to be sent to them; despite rather fraught relations with the Tibetans, such a scheme was put in place.

16 Thus Robinet 1997: 2–3: 'Its history shows us how ceaselessly it has proceeded by "recursive loops", taking up its past like a bundle under its arm in order to travel farther towards new horizons and, as it goes, gleaning all sorts of treasures along the way.'

17 See Fujiwara no Sukeyo 1976, reprint of 1936: 12; cf. Noguchi et al 1994: 549–550, 612, respectively, for information on these titles. For Fujiwara's catalogue, see Wang 1991: 47–52 which makes the point that losses through fire shortly before it was compiled suggest that it only gives a partial guide to literature available at an earlier date.

18 This point is particularly stressed by the most recent Western study of Japan's contacts with China at this point, von Verschuer 1985: 216–222, 230.

19 The recognition of non-Confucian elements in the historical conception of emperorship in China is now apparent also in such works as Ching 1997, which devotes its sixth chapter largely to this topic, although it would be possible to take this approach much further now, especially with China's so-called 'alien' dynasties. To cite just one other example, Siklós 1996: 14, demonstrates that the Manchu Emperor was *inter alia* considered – at least by his Mongol subjects – an embodiment of the terrifying Tantric deity Vajrabhairava. Emperorship in China was much of the time every bit as religious a role as it was in Japan.

20 See Wright 1957: 71–104.

21 Bokenkamp 1994: 59–88.

22 Wen 1983: 23.

23 The quotation is from Wechsler 1985: 69, following the verdict of Miyakawa Hisayuki. Note, however Barrett 1996a: 54–55, for an example of a Taoist takeover, and compare Faure 1993: 158, which cites sources suggesting that one of the mountain gods concerned, in Buddhist eyes, had already been converted to their religion.

24 Twitchett 1992: 41, n.14; Fujiwara's catalogue is not actually named, but that is the source of the reference to Japan. The construction put upon the information given here is, however, my own.

25 Sakamoto et al 1965: 404–5; Aston 1956: 317–18.

26 This figure, and the history of the legend associated with him, are the topic of a detailed study by Kohn 1997: 83–139.

27 This episode is the topic of a detailed and careful study by Otagi 1993: 275–322. A typeset edition of the original inscription may be found in the standard collection for Taoist epigraphy, Chen 1988: 46–48. The Yin family asserted that they had been maternal relatives of Laozi, too, a claim which Kohn (see p. 118 of the article cited in the preceding note) is disposed to view as a Tang innovation, though I myself believe that such a move would have been very dangerous at the time, given the sensitivity of the Tang rulers to competition over genealogical status which comes out in the case of Falin, mentioned below, and also in Twitchett 1973: 62. In fact the earliest source for the story, a lost text known as the *Xuanzhong ji*, is already quoted in the early sixth century *Shuijing zhu*.

28 The notion that Laozi was not merely a philosopher but a divine figure who incarnated himself repeatedly in human history goes back to the second century CE, as was established by Anna Seidel in one of her earliest publications (listed on p. 336 of her 'Chronicle') and subsequently elaborated in a series of later articles. By 620 it was a prime tenet of Taoist belief, widely accepted beyond narrowly Taoist circles – hence the widespread messianism to which we have already alluded.

29 For a synopsis of the full range of polemics at this time, with further references, see Kohn 1995: 180–186.

30 See Katsumura 1978: 674.

31 A cursory scan through his writings in volume 52 of the Taishō Canon (herinafter T.) edition reveals not only the reference used by Katsumura (preceding note) on p. 490b, but also on pp. 475a, 488c, 500a (which deals with the astral overtones of the term), 511c (associating the term with the emperor himself), 524a (citing the Confucian *Li Ji* as a proof text to demonstrate that there were no higher gods), at the very least.

32 Falin's strategy in trying to deny Taoism any cultural space at all forms the starting point for a very interesting essay on the conception of a 'teaching' or 'religion' at this time by Kobayashi Masayoshi, now included in Kobayashi 1990: 511–538.

33 For an excellent study of Falin's career, see Tonami 1993: 243–274; the final quotation is from T.55.746b.

34 This work, the *Gaozong shilu*, is described by Twitchett 1992: 123–125, who suggests that Li Shimin did not induce these men to falsify events, but certainly managed to influence them.

35 Twitchett 1992: 213, n.10.

36 This is cited in the edition of the inscription in Chen 1988: 114, from the *Jinshi lu* of Zhao Mingcheng (1081–1129), cf. the inscription text on p. 112.

37 See Barrett 1996a: 29–45.

38 See in particular pp. 36–37 of the account cited in the preceding note.

39 Yin and his works are treated at Kohn 1997: 114–1188 and Barrett 1996a: 33–34. Ohase's edition of the *Nihonkoku genzai sho mokuroku* lists Yin's work on p. 12, and also on p. 11, another text linking the Li family with the Yellow Emperor, apparently the same as that quoted by Kohn on p. 119 of her article from a late T'ang source.

40 *Song-ben Cefu yuangui*, 970.10b – this edition has already been cited, n.13 above.

41 Piggott 1997: 144, and 361–2, nn.57–60.

42 See Mori 1983: 27, n.1

43 See Kawakita 1984: 207–230. Evidence suggesting that even the earliest signs of a trend towards divinisation of the Japanese emperor may be placed well into the second half of the seventh century continues to accumulate: cf. Toyama 1998, a reference I owe to Professor Richard Bowring.

44 Fukui 1996: 403–410: see especially the conclusion on the final page.

45 On p. 408, n.10 of the article cited in the preceding note, which concerns the research of Fukuyama Toshio: this has a direct bearing on the evidence he has already cited on p. 405 from the research of Tsuda Sōkichi (1873–1961).

46 Horii 1974: 242–260. Horii lists nine predecessors in his first note, besides the redoubled efforts of Fukuyama, to whom Fukui refers.

47 This latter inscription is covered in Fukui's account of Fukuyama's research, and also by Horii.

48 The reference occurs in the second part of this work, p. 470a in the edition of Takakusu and Mochizuki 1942. Both the text of this volume and its pagination (I have cited the continuous, Roman numeral pagination, with a and b for upper and lower frames of text) are identical throughout with the equivalent volume of materials in the *Dai Nihon Bukkyō zensho* series, but with the addition of useful bio-bibliographical notes as an appendix.

49 Jungen's work, itself a distillation of earlier commentary, has survived – though perhaps not intact – and is included in the same collection under the title *Kenshin Tokugō guketsu shō*. On p. 120b, he refers to the Emperor Bidatsu by the same anomalous term quoted from him and from the inscription in 1547.

50 See the *Kamitsumiya Shōtoku hōō teisetsu*: 44b in the collection, and note the remarks of Piggott 1997: 295–6, on the value of this source. Cf. also pp. 100b, 288a, for other quotations from the inscription, and p. 15b for a textual note suggesting that *tennō* was in medieval Buddhist circles unfamiliar enough for a careless copyist to corrupt it into a more familiar term.

51 For earlier confusion in Western scholarship over this term in the *Sui shu*, compare Steininger 1956: 184 following Florenz; von Verschuer 1985: 8, evidently following Wada Sei and Ishihara Michihiro; cf. too the first page of Fukui 1996. There is still room for doubt over how *kimi* may have been written in Japan, but for *ame* now see Du You 1988: 4995.

52 See Barrett 1996b: 6, n.33.
53 See the summary in Barrett 1996a: 40–43, for the changes forced upon the empress, which are generally read in the light of hindsight as the outcome of a long-term quest for power in her own right, but are equally well accounted for through sheer immediate expediency.
54 Piggott 1997: 68, provides a useful chart illustrating the interrelationships of this period.
55 See Lu 1985: 210a, 211a.
56 See Tonami 1982: 607–8.
57 Ōmura 1915: 573, 581, referring to rubbings in the possession of the scholars Luo Zhenyu and Naitō Konan; for some earlier examples in 674, 678, 681 and 692 (as above), see pp. 499, 553, 555 and 505 respectively. Of course most later inscriptions show a due change in terminology; not everyone was 'behind the times'.
58 These difficulties are noted by von Verschuer at the start of von Verschuer 1985: xv; she considers the question of royal titles on pp. 7–8, though without reference to Li Zhi's title, in the course of a very useful chapter comparing Japanese goals and practices with those of other 'tributary states' during this period.
59 Kohn 1995: 407.
60 The quotation is taken from a document preserved in Song 1959: 93.
61 The mirror as a symbol suggesting Taoist influence on Japan was the topic of one of Fukunaga's pioneering explorations, listed as Fukunaga 1973 in Kohn 1995: 408
62 Wei 1974: 1–3. In the collection *Shōtoku Taishi goden sōsho* used above, this Wei descent from the Yellow Emperor is cited in the early fourteenth century on p. 253a from a Chinese chronology, probably (as with the quotation of a Taoist religious text on p. 301b) known only through an encyclopedia. Medieval knowledge of Taoist literature is, of course, a separate topic: it is touched upon in my note, Barrett 1994: 71–77. Fujiwara 1976: 8, suggests that another history of the Northern Wei was present in Heian Japan, but does not list Wei Shou's compilation, which was subject to strong criticism not long after its compilation in 554: see Ware 1932: 33–45. This, unfortunately, has little bearing on when the legends recorded by Wei Shou were first transmitted through some textual or oral medium to Japan.
63 *Zhou shu* 1: 1; 3: 46; 4: 58. This particular source was compiled by Linghu Defen between 623 and 636: see McMullen 1988: 165–166; not only is it listed as existing in Heian Japan, according to Fujiwara 1976: 8, but even a manuscript fragment at least as old as the Heian period was discovered during this century at a shrine: cf. Yoshikawa 1968: 539–549. Once again (cf. preceding note) this has no real bearing on when the information cited from this source could have reached Japan.
64 Benn 1987: 137–139, shows that the emperor of China in the mid-eighth century expected his image to be worshipped and also claimed to be in some sense immortal – something of a departure from the Chinese norm, though Ōmura 1915: 440 notes from a ninth century source images of the Empress Wu, presumably for worship, made in 702. Whether this stage had already been reached by the late seventh century deserves careful consideration. Some Taoist texts from before the Tang certainly contain the notion of kingship by divine descent, with reference to the Han dynasty: cf. Bokenkamp 1997: 214. Yet it is likely that the information cited in the two preceding notes reached Japan more rapidly than any overtly Taoist works. Also, if I say nothing here about Korean kingship, this is largely because of difficulties in reconstructing the way it was viewed at the time of greatest Korean influence on Japan, rather than because I discount its significance.

CHAPTER THREE

Shinto and the natural environment

Sonoda Minoru

Socio-ecosystem civilisations and *fūdo* cults

C.W. Nicholl (b. 1940) is a Welsh naturalist who lives on the Kurohime mountain plateau in Nagano Prefecture. In an essay, entitled 'Sacred groves' and published in *Jinja Shinpō* in 1991, he wrote:

> I saw a cave surrounded by tall trees. There was no sound but the cries of birds and monkeys, and the rushing of a pretty waterfall – a beautiful place indeed. A short, dark-skinned hunter, wearing no more than a straw apron, and holding a bow and some poisoned arrows in his hand, picked a flower and put it into his hair. Someone asked: 'How do you know there are deities in this place? Can you see them?' I thought it a silly question, but the hunter replied with a smile: 'The deities are invisible, but I know they are here even though I can't see them.'

In his essay Nicholl stresses the importance of shrine groves, and it is to illustrate this point that he introduces this episode from his travels in Africa: his meeting with a pygmy hunter in the Congo, who offered to show the tourists a place his people revered as sacred. Nicholl, sharing the feelings of the hunter, concludes: 'Whatever the country and whatever the religion, I am not so immature as to doubt the presence of the invisible in sacred places and sacred forests.'

The pygmy people Nicholl refers to are the Mbuti, who live as hunter-gatherers in the Ituri rainforest. Roaming through the vast virgin forests of the Congo in small kin groups, their lives are completely attuned to the ecosystem of the forest. Their primitive religion of spirit worship, too, can be described as an 'ecological religion,' in which the ecology of the forest is identical to their religious world. If we take a broader perspective, it is clear that the religions of those few among the so-called native peoples that remain in primitive civilisations around the world can likewise be described as cosmologies developed by people whose lives are entwined with the ecology of the area. These religions, too, are 'nature religions' and can be described as 'ecological religions.'

All ancient civilisations originated in production economies such as agriculture and cattle breeding. In their initial stages, one part of society singled out one element from the natural ecology and 'civilised' daily life by improving upon that element and managing it. In these ancient civilisations, man formed societies that were independent from the natural ecology, and by cutting down forests, cultivating the land, and growing crops and pastures set out to change the natural conditions according to his needs. Of course, at this stage man lacked the modern techniques to control nature, and these civilisations were restricted by the natural climate and ecology of the region. If we are to label civilisations of this type with a view to their relation to the natural environment, we may say that they had moved from the phase of 'ecosystem civilisations' to a new phase of 'socio-ecosystem civilisations.' The religions of these ancient civilisations can likewise be described as belonging to a type of 'socio-ecological religions,' which developed from the 'ecological religions' mentioned above.[1]

The reason why I use the term 'fūdo cults' (fūdo saishi) in this context, is that this term most accurately describes the character of Japanese kami and their cults, rooted as these are in a religio-cultural cosmology that corresponds to the socio-ecosystem stage.[2] In an agricultural civilisation, the natural environment ceases to be purely 'natural.' Transformed by influences from human society, the environment becomes a 'cultured nature,' infused with the spiritual culture of its inhabitants. It is to avoid this self-contradictory term that I will here adopt the concept of fūdo as developed by Watsuji Tetsurō, as a tool to point up the inherent relation between environment and religion.[3] According to Watsuji, the given natural environment or 'climatic fūdo' becomes at some stage of its transformation by humans internalised as an 'historic fūdo,' determined by the culture of the inhabitants who build their society in that environment. Fūdo, then, denotes not only the external, natural climatic and geographic features of a region, but also refers to an internalised nature, infused with a cosmological and spiritual Lebenswelt construed by the people living in the region. Further, phenomenological theories about society point out that although nature is transformed into fūdo as the members of a society develop their surroundings into a lived-in environment through their livelihoods as farmers, herds and so on, that is not all: at the same time, they develop a shared appreciation of the natural landscape and build a symbolical world inspired by that landscape.[4] Indeed, the word 'cult' itself is related to words such as 'culture' and 'cultivation,' which all derive from a root that combines meanings ranging from 'tilling the soil,' through 'dressing oneself' and 'conducting oneself,' to 'doing worship.' Thus by cultivating nature and transforming it into a lived-in fūdo, societies at the same time construe a religious cosmos in which they can feel spiritually at ease.[5]

In the religious culture of ancient civilisations which relied on agriculture, myths explaining how the natural environment could be improved upon and how more crops could be grown occupied a central position. A famous myth, for example, tells how a human being killed 'Terra Mater' and obtained various kinds of crops from her dead body. This interpretation of the annual cycle of seasons as the death and rebirth of the land recounted the origins of agriculture, and developed into myths and rites of sacrifice and praying for abundant crops. In Japanese mythology, too, variations on this myth can be found.

The Chapter of the Age of the Gods in *Kojiki* (712) tells how Susanowo, after being expelled from the Plain of High Heaven, asked Ōge-tsu-hime for food. When Ōge-tsu-hime prepared and served him a meal from materials that she procured from her nose, mouth, and anus, Susanowo was so enraged by the impurity of the meal that he killed her. Then, *Kojiki* tells us, silk worms were produced from her head, rice seeds from her eyes, millet from her ears, small beans from her nose, wheat from her genitalia, and large beans from her anus. One version recorded in *Nihon shoki* (720) recounts a similar myth, in which the deity Tsukiyomi killed the deity Ukemochi, from whose body the five kinds of grain were produced. While the details of these two variants differ, both tell of the killing of a female earth deity, whose dead body produced precious crops.

This is a story type common in South-Asian mythologies, belonging to the 'Hainuwele'-type myths that occur in Melanesia and Indonesia; it also shares many traits with stories linked to grain cultivation and slash-and-burn agriculture – the culture of the evergreen broad-leaf forests that cover southern China and South-East Asia.[6] But however that may be, it will be clear that it was the development of agriculture that allowed mankind to render its societies autonomous from the natural environment and that produced new environments that I termed 'socio-ecosystems'; and that, moreover, it was agriculture that made it possible for the shared, subjective culture here termed '*fūdo* cults' to develop. In other words, the myths which recount how crops were obtained through the sacrifice of an 'earth mother' deity or a food deity symbolise the transformation of the natural environment into *fūdo* – a transformation that was central to the development of ancient culture. This is why 'cults' – etymologically related both to 'cultivation' and 'culture' – were the religious form most appropriate to the formation of *fūdo*.

Here I would like to introduce a story told by an old man from the Namekata district, and recorded in *Hitachi-kuni fudoki* (eighth century). According to this story, the local lord Matachi of the Yahazu clan wished to reclaim a marshy valley to the west of his mansion, but found that work was hindered by snakes locally known as 'Yato (or Yatsu) no kami.' Matachi donned his armour and chased the snakes away to the back of the valley. Planting a stick in the ditch that marked the foot of the mountains, he said to the snakes: 'The area above this stick will henceforth be the land of the gods; the area below will be fields of human beings. From now on, I will myself become a priest and worship the gods, so I pray you not to bear a grudge against me.' At this place he founded a shrine and worshipped the gods, and this shrine is the present Yato Jinja in Shinden, Tamatsukuri-machi. The old man concludes that, thanks to this Matachi, the reed plains of the past were replaced by paddy fields, and he tells us that the descendants of Matachi continued to revere Yato no Kami to his day.

This story may serve as an example of how the people of antiquity, as they reclaimed paddy fields along water systems, regarded animals living in the wild as kami endowed with spirits and worshipped them. The same *fudoki* includes another tale, told by an old man from the Naka district, according to which a maiden from the village of Ubaraki was visited every night by a man of unknown name and appearance, conceived, and gave birth to a snake. The snake spoke to its mother by night but not by day, and was raised by her as the child of a kami. Similar, well-known tales can also be found in *Nihon shoki* and *Kojiki* (in their respective chapters on Emperor Sujin). The first tells how Ōmononushi, the kami of Mt. Miwa, made nightly visits to the maiden Yamato-totohimomoso-hime and was at long last found to be a snake; the latter relates that a female medium by the name of Ikutamayori-hime was visited by the kami of Mt. Miwa and gave birth to his son Ōtataneko, who again, the text hints, had the body of a snake. Also in later, medieval story collections and foundation legends we can find similar tales. An example is a long tale from the tenth chapter of Agui's *Shintōshū* (1352–61?), entitled 'The foundation legend of Suwa.' When the beloved wife of Kōga Saburō, the third son of the *jitō* of the Kōga district in Yamato Province, was abducted by a troll-like being called a *tengu*, he searched for her at sixty-eight sacred mountains throughout the country, all called 'Ontake,' without finding her. He then entered a cave at Mt. Tateshina in Shinano Province, where he found seventy-three more caves and seventy-two subterranean lands. Having travelled through all these lands, he finally succeeded in returning to the surface at the top of Mt. Asama in Shinano. However, when he emerged from the Netherworld Saburō appeared as a kami in the form of a large snake.

Similar foundation legends of ancient shrines, featuring local kami in the form of snakes that are deities of both water and thunder, are common throughout Japan, and illustrate the transformation of untamed nature into *fūdo*. When Kōga Saburō emerged from his travels in the Netherworld, he had become the kami Suwa Daimyōjin. The fact that he appeared as a kami in the form of a snake corresponds with the beliefs in snakes and dragons that surround the Suwa shrine to this day.[7]

Fūdo cults in small basins

Japan is a mountainous archipelago with a warm and wet monsoon climate, divided by numerous small streams and rivers that run from small basins in the interior to delta plains of various sizes on the coast. Most of these plains are relatively small and surrounded by mountains, opening up only on one side to the ocean; therefore one could say that these, too, are in fact 'basins' of a kind. Yoneyama Toshinao has pointed out that the Japanese islands can thus be said to consist of more than one hundred 'basins,' and that these formed their own small 'basin universes' from prehistory and antiquity down to the Edo period.[8] Of course, each of these basins has its own climatic and geographical peculiarities and its own history, but nevertheless, the environmental conditions they offer are similar in many respects. The 'far mountains' that rise in the distance form the source of water; the lower and closer 'village mountains' are cut by numerous valley streams that form diluvial plateaus and feed the lowlying marshland at the centre of the basin; and these streams then converge into the main river which runs into a lower-lying basin or a coastal plain. The broad-leaf forests that covered the far mountains were inhabited by bears, wild boars, deer, wolves, snakes and other wild animals. Although these mountains were used for hunting and gathering, they remained the almost exclusive domain of small numbers of mountain dwellers, and to the villagers from the basin below represented a mysterious and sacred realm. In the lower hills, settlements developed in places that were blessed with a reasonable amount of sunshine and a good water supply. Mixed grains and vegetables were grown on small burnt fields, and the 'village mountains' were used as sources of firewood and charcoal. In the basin itself, moreover, the marshes were turned into paddy fields through a slow and steady improvement of water supply and irrigation. Here, intensive rice cultivation was conducted by close-knit communities consisting of kin groups (ie) and villages (mura) tied together by bonds of blood and locality. This occupational structure continued to exist in the various basins at least until the early years of the Shōwa period (1926–89).

The 'small universes' constituted by these basins found expression in the form of *fūdo* cults, and it was through their early development of such cults, from the Kofun period (c. 250–552) onwards, that the Yamato clan, who dominated the largest developed basin of the period around Nara, laid the foundations for the ancient state of Japan.

The *fūdo* cults of the Nara basin were developed between the fourth century, under the so-called Miwa court of Emperor Sujin, and the later seventh century, during the reigns of Emperors Tenmu and Jitō. These cults were included in the 'Festivals of the Four Seasons' (*shijisai*) executed by the *Jingikan* as state rituals under the *ritsuryō* system: the festivals of Toshigoi in the second month, of Ōimi in Hirose and the Wind Gods in Tatsuta in the fourth and seventh months, and of Tsukinami in the sixth and twelfth months.[9] In the prayers (*norito*) read at these festivals, which are recorded mainly in book 8 of the *Engi shiki* (927), the local kami of the Nara region were invoked and invited to take part in the Toshigoi and Tsukinami festivals: the six kami that protected the six imperial estates (*miagata*) of Takechi, Katsuragi, Tōchi, Shiki, Yamanobe, and Sou, all in and around the Nara basin; a further fourteen kami of forests and water (*yamaguchi no kami*) residing in the foothills at Asuka, Iware, Osaka, Hatsuse, Unebi, and Miminashi, as well as Yoshino, Kose, Kamo, Taima, Ōsaka, Ikoma, Tsuge, and Yagyū; and finally the kami of the four watersheds or water sources (*mikumari no kami*) in the 'far mountains' around the basin: Yoshino, Uda, Tsuge, and Katsuragi. Further, at the biannual Ōimi festival in Hirose priests prayed for a good water supply during the

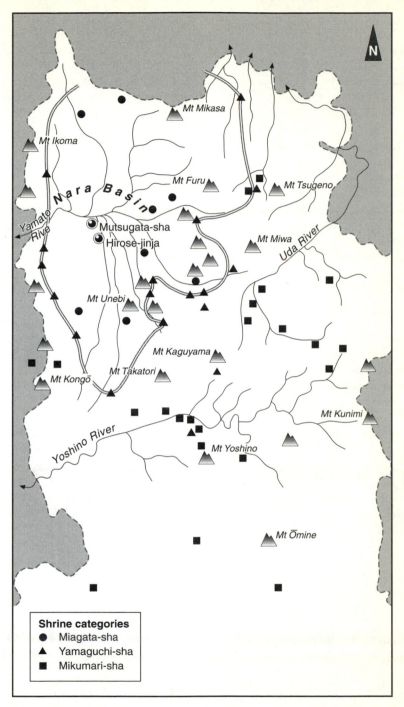

A cosmo-topographical system of the shrine cults in and around the Nara Basin

coming agricultural season at the shrine of Wakauka no Me, a female food deity in charge of the foodstuffs used by the emperor, again also inviting the kami of the six imperial estates and the fourteen foothills mentioned above. The Hirose shrine was located in the centre of the Nara basin, at a large shoal (*hiro-se*) where streams from the four directions flow into the main Yamato River.

If we look at the locations of the shrines of the various kami invoked at these rituals, we find that the six shrines of the kami of the imperial estates were set in the agricultural area at the centre of the basin; the fourteen shrines of the kami of forests and water were scattered over the foothills at points where small streams run into the basin plain; and the four shrines of the watersheds lay in the 'far mountains' that did indeed form the basin's watersheds. As the ancient Yamato state took form, moving north from the Itabuki and Kiyomihara palaces at Asuka, through Fujiwara-kyō, to Heijō-kyō (Nara), these three kinds of kami, distributed along the Yamato river system from the watersheds in the mountains down to the centre of the basin, constituted a three-dimensional sacred world that permeated the *fūdo* cult of the ancient state.[10] Higuchi Tadahiko, who is a specialist in landscape engineering, has categorised Japan's landscapes into 'basin landscapes,' 'valley landscapes,' 'foothill landscapes,' and 'plain landscapes' and defines the Nara basin in particular as an example of the (quintessentially Japanese) 'Akitsushima Yamato'-type.[11] Higuchi draws attention to the fact that it was in this setting that foreign culture was adopted, accommodated, and nurtured; and it is indeed worth pointing out that while the Yamato state originated through its contacts with the continent, it did so while including the region's *fūdo* cult in its state ritual.

However, as the Yamato state took on ever larger dimensions in the seventh and eighth centuries and palaces and large temple complexes were erected throughout the Nara basin, the upper reaches of the Yamato and Yodo Rivers became deforested. As a result, floods and droughts became more frequent and the loss of top soil in these areas became severe. *Shoku Nihongi*, for example, records in an entry dated Hōji 6 (762)/4/17 that a ship with envoys to Tang China was grounded on a sand bank in Naniwazu Harbour (in Osaka Bay).[12] This must have been the result of the loss of large amounts of soil into the Yamato and Yodo rivers. The imperial court reacted at a relatively early stage by taking measures against over-exploitation of the natural ecosystem and by protecting forests and improving rivers. An example of this can be found in book 19 ('Prohibitions') of *Ruijū sandai kyaku*, where we find the following comment accompanying an order to local officials (*daijōkanpu*) regarding a 'prohibition against cutting mountain forests bordering on streams' (dated Kōnin 12 (821)/4/21):

Your tasks are not limited to the damming of ponds. The infiltration of water depends on the combination of water and trees. Therefore you must make sure that trees grow abundantly along the banks. The sources of great rivers are in dense woods, while the headlands of small streams are bare. Thus we know that the volume of a river depends on the mountains [it derives from]. When clouds empty their rain on a [wooded] mountain, the river [emerging from it] will supply nine village units (*ri*) with water; when a mountain is bare and shaven of its trees, its valley streams will dry up.

The text continues first by quoting an earlier order from 806, reminding officials that even at that date over-exploitation of river basins was forbidden in the interest of irrigation. Then it goes on to state that while there are at present restrictions on the use of the 'far mountains' that feed the large rivers, there are no such restrictions relating to the 'village mountains' that are the source of smaller streams. This has caused the peasants to deforest these mountains, leading to damage to crops because of frequent droughts. Therefore, the text concludes, the felling of trees along streams, springs, and ponds that irrigate paddy fields will henceforth be forbidden both on private and public lands.

Prohibitions against the felling of trees like the above show that the imperial estates in the Home Provinces (known as *miagata*) as well as other agricultural estates developed in other provinces (known simply as *agata*) were areas of advanced agriculture, reclaimed along water systems and at the centres of the country's basins, and that the 'village mountains' and 'far mountains' surrounding these basins were set aside for the maintenance of water resources. Moreover, the more remote mountain areas were also subject to religious taboos, and thus remained untouched virgin forests; the foothills, however, were sources of building materials, firewood and charcoal, and were easily over-exploited. In the Home Provinces, especially, great quantities of timber were used for the construction of large palaces and temples, leaving lower-lying areas and foothills within easy reach of the building sites bare. In other provinces, too, the construction of governmental compounds (*kokuga*) and *kokubunji* temples required large amounts of timber.

There was, however, one category of natural forests that survived even in the plains and the foothills, protected by strict traditional taboos. These were the so-called *kamu-tsu-mori* or *kamu-tsu-yashiro*, groves where the kami resided, and the sacred mountains known as *kamunabi-* or *mimuro-yama*. An example can be found in book 1 of *Ruijū sandai kyaku*, which starts with 'shrine matters.' Beginning with an edict of Emperor Shōmu from 725, stating that purity is an absolute priority in revering the 'kami and buddhas' and must be maintained at 'all shrines in all provinces,' this book lists many *Daijōkan* orders pertaining to the repair and maintenance of shrine precincts.[13] Particularly eye-catching among these are an order from Shōwa 8 (841)/3/1 'prohibiting hunting and the felling of trees in the kami-mountains of the Kasuga shrine,' and orders for the protection of the precincts and kami-mountains of the Upper and Lower Kamo shrines in Yamashiro Province and of the sacred lands of the Amashi shrine on the upper reaches of the Nibu River in Yamato Province. Since access to the forests and mountains where the kami were worshipped had been prohibited long before these orders were issued, it is only natural that there would have been taboos on hunting and the felling of trees in these areas. Even some two centuries earlier, Emperor Kōtoku (r. 645–54) had been criticised for 'lacking respect for the kami' when he used wood from the precincts of the Ikukunitama shrine in Naniwa (modern Osaka), probably for the construction of a palace or temple.[14]

Above, we considered the *fūdo* cult of ancient Yamato in some detail; but in other advanced areas in Japan the same pattern repeated itself. In the low-lying areas with their paddy fields, one found the wooded precincts of 'field shrines' (*ta no miya*), 'village shrines' (*sato no miya*), or 'shrines of the kami of the *agata*' (*agata ni masu kami no yashiro*); in the foothills, there were the 'wooded hills' (*moriyama*) of 'mountain shrines' (*yama no miya*) or 'shrines of the kami of the mountain gates' (*yamaguchi ni masu kami no yashiro*); and the remoter mountains were the sacred domain of 'outlying shrines' (*oku no miya*) of 'kami of the watersheds' (*mikumari no kami*).[15]

Shrine groves and 'hometown cults'

The myths in Japan's classics include tales about kami that reflect the archipelago's wooded landscape. In the Chapter of the Age of the Gods in *Nihon shoki*, there is the tale of Susanowo who after his expulsion from the Plain of High Heaven descended towards the Korean state of Silla together with his son Itakeru. From there Susanowo sailed to Izumo where he reached the head-waters of the river Hi. Here he defeated a large serpent in whose tail he found the famous Herb-Quelling Sword, which he presented to Amaterasu. Later, we hear that Itakeru had brought a large quantity of tree seeds from the High Plain of Heaven. He sowed none of these seeds in Korea, saving them all until he arrived in Japan, where he spread them from Kyushu over all the land, covering the mountains in green. This version in *Nihon shoki* states that it is due to this act that Itakeru is praised for his merits, and that Itakeru is a 'great kami who resides in Kii Province.' In another version, following after this, Susanowo says: 'Korea is rich in gold and silver, and the land over which our descendants shall rule will need good treasure ships.' Accordingly he pulled out the hairs of his beard and scattered them over the land, where each hair immediately changed into a cedar tree (*sugi*). In the same way, the hairs from Susanowo's chest were turned into cypress trees (*hi-no-ki*), the hairs from his buttocks into black pines (*maki-no-ki*), and the hairs from his eyebrows into camphor trees (*kusu-no-ki*). This work done, Susanowo announced: 'Use cedar and camphor wood when building ships; use cypress wood when building splendid halls and palaces; use black pine wood for coffins when burying the dead. Tree seeds useful for all these various purposes have been sown and have sprouted in the land.' Then, three of Susanowo's children, named Itakeru, Ōya-tsu-hime, and Tsuma-tsu-hime, sowed tree seeds in all corners of the land, until they finally reached Kii

Province. Finally, this version draws to a close by stating that Susanowo left from Mt. Kumanari to the Netherworld.[16]

Thus Susanowo, as a typical culture hero, created trees from his own bodily hair and left instructions on their various uses. Moreover, making his children sow seeds he changed the Japanese islands into an archipelago of green mountains. The fact that this unique myth was born and handed down in ancient Japan shows that the inhabitants of these islands had a devout interest in the preservation and cultivation of forests from a very early age indeed.

Antiquity gave way to the middle ages and the early modern period, and the *ritsuryō* system with its court culture was replaced by successive *bushi* shogunates, bringing far-reaching changes to society. However, throughout these changes both the successive central authorities and local rulers, whether they were *shugo*, *jitō* or *daimyō*, continued to treat shrines and their lands with respect at least during times of peace, protecting their property and donating new estates, repairing shrine buildings, and urging priests to carry out their rituals in a strict manner. The *Goseibai-* or *Jōei shikimoku* (1232), for example, a 51-article law code issued by the Kamakura shogunate, began with an article concerning 'maintaining shrines and concentrating on ritual,' and explained to bakufu magistrates both the reasons why this was important, and the concrete duties this entailed for them.[17] This notion in medieval *bushi* law influenced the later Tokugawa shogunate as well as individual *daimyō*. During the Tokugawa period, special officials protected and oversaw temples and shrines (*jisha bugyō* – another institution dating from the Kamakura period), and, partly in the interest of suppressing Christianity and winning the hearts of the people, all domains vied with each other in constructing new temples and shrines and in making donations to existing ones.

The Meiji government, however, destroyed much of the traditional shrine cults in its attempt to strengthen state control over the traditional religions. In Meiji 1 (1868), the new government moved to make Shinto a state religion by restoring the 'unity of rites and government' and 'separating Shinto and Buddhism.' In the first and fourth months of Meiji 4 (1871), the *Daijōkan* issued regulations that confiscated shrine and temple lands (*shajiryō agechirei*) and abolished the traditional system of hereditary succession of priests (*seshū shinshoku haishirei*). Because of these regulations, many ancient shrines lost the sacred mountains and lands that had formed the basis of their *fūdo* cult, and as hereditary priests were forced to find other employment ritual traditions were broken. Moreover, the Meiji government made a limited number of 'government shrines' (*kansha* or *kankokuheisha*) into state institutions, and separated them from the large majority of smaller regional and prefectural shrines that were distinguished from the above as 'popular shrines' (*minsha*). As a result, the religious character of both categories of shrines was lost. As the *kansha* were turned into little more than venues for the execution of state rituals, many of the *minsha* were destroyed due to the policies of 'one *ujiko*, one shrine' in Meiji 29 (1896) and of 'shrine rationalisation' of Meiji 40 (1907).

41

The latter endeavoured to reduce the number of shrines to one per village by means of forced shrine mergers. Needless to say, these policies destroyed many of the local *fūdo* cults that had continued since antiquity, as well as the 'hometown cults' that had defined village communities since the middle ages.[18]

The term 'hometown cults' (*kakyō saishi*) is a methodological concept that I employ to grasp *ujigami* cults in local communities and their mythological cosmologies in their totality, as symbolic structures relating to the *fūdo* of the region. Until the onset of the modern period Japanese villages and towns were local communities not only in the modern sociological sense, but also in a spiritual sense: communities of ancestors and descendants worshipping kami and buddhas. The inhabitants shared livelihoods in the primary sector, such as agriculture, forestry and fishing, and while being internally divided into different social classes, these communities also constituted communal 'sacred worlds' which guaranteed the spiritual security of their members. Since this fact has been dwelt upon by many scholars not much will need to be said about it here; but if we accept that this shared love for one's hometown and this communal subjectivity were important features of traditional communities, we might from the standpoint of the sociology of religion describe such communities as 'hometown societies.' Moreover, because this concept of 'hometown societies' stresses the shared cultural subjectivity of the inhabitants, it helps us to understand the relative imperviousness to change displayed by village societies in the face of social and economic changes both within and around these societies. An important factor contributing to the durability of village life has been its 'hometown cults,' which defined the sacred order of the village in the two dimensions of space and time.[19]

The characters now normally read *jinja* 神社 ('shrine') were in ancient sources mostly read *kamu-tsu-yashiro* (e.g., in *Engi shiki*) or *mori* (both 'kami grove'). Both readings can be found in the *Man'yōshū* (eighth century). *Yashiro* occurs, for example, in the following two poems exchanged between an unnamed woman and Saeki no Akamaro (in which Akamaro's wife is likened to a fearsome kami):

woman:
Chihayaburu / kami no yashiro (神の社) shi / nakariseba / Kasuga no nohe ni / awa makamashi wo
Thousand-rock-smashing, a fierce deity abides in the godly shrine:
But for her I'd be well pleased to sow our millet in Kasuga fields. (3:404)

Akamaro:
Kasugano ni / awa makeriseba / shishimachi ni / tsugite ikamashi / yashiro (社) shi urameshi
Had we sown millet in the fields of Kasuga,
I'd go every night to stalk deer amid the grain –
Oh, how I hate that shrine! (3:405)[20]

One of many examples of the reading *mori* is the following sequence from a longer *chōka*:

> . . . / *Yamashina no* / *Iwata no mori* (社) *no* / *sumekami ni* / *nusa torimukete* / *ware wa koe-yuku* / *Ausakayama wo*
> Offering a branch to the Great Deity of the Iwata grove in Yamashina, I cross Mount Ausaka. (13:3236)

Yashiro had the meaning of a sacred place where a kami must be worshipped, and usually referred to a space surrounded with a *shimenawa* rope where no-one was allowed to enter. It was exactly because 'Kasuga fields' was a *yashiro* that no millet could be sown there. Reading the characters 神社, 社, and 杜 *mori* ('grove'), moreover, was a Japanese innovation with no basis in Chinese practice. This reading reflects the fact that Japanese shrines were originally sacred groves or forests inhabited by kami.

The most ancient form of shrines was in most cases a grove or a wooded hill (*moriyama*), used for the performance of rituals at the foot of the mountains. At Ōmiwa shrine in the Nara basin, there is no kami-hall; instead, this shrine retains the ancient ritual form in which the mountain rising behind the shrine is itself regarded as the kami's place of residence. The nearby Isonokami and Kasuga shrines also have their 'kami-mountains' in Mts. Furu and Mikasa. The Upper and Lower Kamo shrines in Kyoto, moreover, have kami-mountains in Kōyama and Mikageyama. It is at the foot of these mountains (or, rather, hills) that the kami of these shrines manifest themselves during the so-called *miare* and *mikage* rituals, which form the secret centrepiece of the famous Aoi festival.

'Kami-mountains,' which occur in ancient texts as *kamunabi(yama)*, appear throughout the country in place names such as Kōyama or Miyama (神山), Miyayama (宮山), Mitake, Ontake or Utaki (御嶽), Ōyama or Daisen (大山), Moriyama or Muriyama (森山), and so forth. There are also local sacred sites which seem to bear no relation to forests or mountains, such as the Obotsuyama in the Amami islands, Garōyama on Tanegashima, Moidon in Kagoshima Prefecture, Kōjin no Mori in Nishi-Iwami, or Tentōzan on Tsushima; but even these refer to hills or mountains that dominate the view from the village or to low, wooded hills of a pleasing shape. Most of these hills and mountains are vital sources of water or eye-catching landmarks. In villages on the shores of lakes or on the sea coast, small reefs and islands in the offing (which were also rich fishing grounds) were often regarded as 'kami-islands' (*tategami* or *kamishima*), and in a similar way capes and coastal mountains which served as landmarks for navigation were often the object of religious practices.

Recently, modern linguistics has developed the striking hypothesis that the word kami is related to *kuma* ('corner, nook') and *kumu* ('to hide'), and originally referred to the spiritual quality of the mountains and valleys that were the sources of water.[21] The ancient word *matsuri* denoted rituals of 'waiting' (*matsu*) for the appearance (*miare*) of a kami that was usually hidden. These words convey some idea of the way in which the people who settled in

Japan's mountainous islands and tilled their soil came to revere the spiritual quality hiding in the woods and mountains as kami, and thus transformed the landscape into a living cosmos.

Underlying the 'hometown communities' of Japanese villages and towns is a ritual structure of 'mountain shrine – village shrine – field shrine' (or *oku no miya* 'outlying shrine' – *jinja* 'shrine' – *karimiya* 'temporary shrine'), focusing on the village shrine where the *ujigami* resides.[22] The village shrine was originally a sacred grove (*yashiro*) where the kami from the mountain shrine would be invited to stay during his visit to the village; but later, shrine buildings were erected in such groves and they developed into village shrines where the *ujigami* resided permanently. This did not mean that the kami ceased to embody the 'remote,' 'liminal' sacred space of the forests on the borders of village life. To the contrary, in traditional Japanese dwellings and villages an 'outlying' room or sacred grove set apart from the quarters of everyday life formed a 'remote' and 'liminal' space at the symbolic centre of these dwellings and villages.[23] The field shrines or temporary shrines (often called *kamiyado*, *tongū*, or *otabisho*) outside the village served as temporary abodes for the kami during festivals only, when the kami where worshipped among the fields on which the villagers' livelihood depended.

Communities characteristic of Japan did not centre on an open square, but formed around a crossroads.[24] *Ujigami* rituals led the kami along the roads from the mountain shrine to the village shrine and from the village shrine to the field shrine in a procession, thus transforming the entire village community into a sacred, liberated space. During this period of festivities (*hare*), the village is turned into a market place and the community is re-invigorated. As the whole village shares in the excitement of the festival, the 'hometown community' that is at other times of the year maintained by the quiet and transparent cosmology of the shrine grove is restored.[25]

Conclusion

After the impoverishment of shrine life caused by the state cult imposed on shrines by pre-war governments, village life was further transformed by the rapid industrialisation and urbanisation of the post-war period. In towns and villages alike, modern local societies have severely damaged the environment for the cause of economic development. This has undermined traditional 'hometown cults,' and has taken 'hometown communities' to the brink of collapse. The period of rapid economic growth from the 1960s to the 1980s has done particularly severe damage to the country's natural environment through overdevelopment and frequent pollution. The price of consumerism and material wealth has been paid in the form of the disintegration of 'hometown communities' and spiritual confusion, and in the 1990s this has undoubtedly been one of the reasons for the frequent occurrence throughout Japanese society of events that border on the pathological.

However, it is also a fact that for these very reasons local groups throughout Japan are making persistent efforts to construct, restore or maintain old and new 'hometown communities.' At this very time, when the preservation of the environment on a global scale has become an urgent, international concern, the *fūdo* and hometown cults described in this essay have again become a focus of interest. The shrine groves that more than eighty thousand shrines in Japan have preserved from the countless pressures of centuries, and the religious symbolism of shrine fields and kami mountains are being rediscovered and revalued as expressions of Japan's ancient animistic view of life. This suggests new possibilities for shrine life in the future. The recent grand rebuilding of the Ise shrines – which are representative of all shrines in the country – in 1993, after a ritual process that took eight years to complete, is in fact a *fūdo* cult on a grand scale. The large quantity of cypress wood used for this rebuilding was all raised as 'sacred trees' (*goshinboku*) in mountain forests. Without the ancient forest culture that has made this possible, it will soon become impossible to hand down this grand vicennial ritual, with its history of some twelve centuries, to our descendants.

Notes

1 The concept of 'socio-ecosystems' is my own, developed in the context of my research into *fūdo* cults. In recent years, however, I have found that Hagino Kazuhiko of Ehime University, who is a specialist in forest ecology and forestry, employs exactly the same term when discussing the relation between civilised society and the natural environment. This convinced me that this concept is viable across disciplines. For a detailed discussion of this concept, see Sonoda et al. 1985: 1–12, and Hagino Kazuhiko 1994: 6–16.
2 See chapter 5 and appendices 1 and 2 in my *Matsuri no genshōgaku*, 1990.
3 Watsuji Tetsurō 1935, especially chapter 1, 'Fūdo no kisoron', 7–23.
4 See Sonoda et al. 1985 vol. 2, chapter 4, 'Yamato ni mieru fūdo no shūkyōteki kōsei', 239–58.
5 Cf. Kimura Bin 1981: 306–8.
6 Ōhayashi Tarō 1973, chapters 1 and 2, 1–103.
7 ST vol. *Shintōshū*, 277–317.
8 Yoneyama Toshinao 1989: 185–202.
9 See Nelly Naumann's essay in this volume for further details.
10 See Sonoda et al. 1985 vol. 2: 254–6, and Sonoda 1990: 256–68.
11 Higuchi Tadanao 1975: 84–162, and 1981, chapter 2, 47–177.
12 *Kokushi taikei*, vol. *Shoku Nihongi* II, 287.
13 *Kokushi taikei*, vol. *Ruijū sandai kyaku* I, 6–31, and II, 606–7.
14 *Kokushi taikei*, vol. *Nihon shoki* II, 215.
15 See also my publications on the relation between forests and *fūdo* cults in other regions: on the Takayama/Furukawa basin in Gifu Prefecture in Sonoda 1990: 268–315; on the Suwa basin in Nagano Prefecture in Sonoda 1989: pp. 44–87; and further the Chichibu basin in Saitama Prefecture, the Ichinomiya basin in Hyōgo Prefecture, and the Tōno basin in Iwate Prefecture.
16 Itakeru also appears in *Kojiki*, in the tale of Ōkuninushi's escape from the Netherworld. Here, Itakeru is called 'Ōya-biko no Kami of the land of Ki [=Kii].'

The 'land of Ki', of course, bears this name because of the abundance of its trees (*ki*), and this deity is the kami of the Itakiso shrine (mentioned in *Engi shiki* as a major shrine with a principal kami) in Itakiso in the present city of Wakayama. The female kami Ōya-tsu-hime and Tsuma-tsu-hime are also revered at shrines in the city of Wakayama: Ōya-tsu-hime shrine in Udamori and Tsuma-tsu-hime shrine in Hirao (both major shrines with principal kami).

17 *Gunsho ruijū* vol. 22, 1.
18 Sakamoto Koremaru 1994: 305–36; Morioka Kiyomi 1987; and Sakurai Haruo 1992.
19 See Sonoda 1989.
20 Translations from Edwin A. Cranston 1993, vol. 1, 498–9.
21 Sakakura Atsuyoshi 1982: 89–107; also Sonoda 1989: 63–9.
22 See Kageyama Haruki 1971.
23 Maki Fumihiko 1978.
24 Kamiyo Yūichirō 1977.
25 Sonoda 1989: 73–8; Ueda Atsushi 1984; Okatani Kōji 1987.

CHAPTER FOUR

The state cult of the Nara and early Heian periods

Nelly Naumann

Legislation and the Chinese model

The seventh century in Japan is marked by successive attempts to reform the entire political structure of the country, taking the Chinese Empire and its institutions as a model. At the beginning of the eighth century, as a result of this process of adoption and adaptation, the Japanese state emerges as a well-organised bureaucratic entity, governed by newly promulgated laws.

This process of adaptation met with many difficulties, as recurrent attempts at legislation during this time show. The *Ōmi-ryō* and the *Kiyomihara-ryō*, codes promulgated during the reigns of Emperors Tenchi (r. 668–71) and Tenmu (r. 673–86) respectively, are both lost. They were superseded by the Taihō-code, drafted in 701 and promulgated the following year. This code too is not extant, but it can to a certain degree be reconstructed from citations in the *Shoku Nihongi* and *Ryō no shūge*. It is generally supposed that the first extant body of laws, the Yōrō-code of 718, is in part at least a revised version of the Taihō-code. In this code the *Jingikan* or 'Department [for the Affairs] of Deities' takes the place of honour at the head of all other organs of administration. Fascicle 6 of the Yōrō-code contains the *Jingi-ryō*, the laws regulating the duties of this department; they comprise what we term 'State Cult.'[1] Particular points are explained in two commentaries, an official one, the *Ryō no gige* of 834, and a 'scholarly' one, the *Ryō no shūge* of 880.

The *Jingikan* was the counterpart of the Chinese *Libu* or 'Ministry of Rites,' the most important political institution in China. Its four sections dealt with the rites proper, with the state cult, with sacrifices and offerings, and with the reception of foreign guests. No comparable institution formerly existed in Japan, yet quite a number of entries in the *Nihon shoki* give evidence that during the reign of Tenmu the government for the first time started activities which later on would form the nucleus of a state cult proper. To understand the mechanisms which led to the formation of this entirely new concept of a Japanese state cult it will be useful to take a look at analogous proceedings in China. When in 221 B.C. the Chinese Empire had been united under Qin Shi Huangdi, one of the most important efforts consisted in the unification of

47

religious rites. Orders were given that whatever could be ascertained regarding sacrifices for Heaven and Earth, for holy mountains and waters, and for ancestor spirits and deities should be collected and set down in the right order.[2] Likewise, the Han Emperor Wudi too, well aware of his position as the highest and unique ruler of the world in a religious sense, ordered learned men to lay down the fundamentals of a state cult by reverting to the rites of the Zhou. This state cult was praised as a revival, a restoration of the old, while in reality it was a new creation out of existing sacral concepts, religious rites and practices, and relics of old cults which in the course of some decades had crystallised into fixed rituals.[3]

The key figure in a similar development in Japan was Emperor Tenmu. While he was still following the Chinese model in several ways, his own experience of a war of succession – if not Chinese history – told him of the dangers threatening a dynasty the legitimacy of which depended on the Chinese idea of a 'Mandate of Heaven' which in turn could be bestowed on any usurper. Thus he fell back upon the myth of a divine command to rule the land given to the ancestor of his dynasty at the very beginning of history, and valid until the end of history. The *Kojiki* was drawn up by Tenmu first of all to insist upon this legitimation and to document the unbroken line of his dynasty once it had received the heavenly command. On the other hand, his thorough indebtedness to Chinese ideas concerning the character and status of a ruler can easily be perceived in the first sentences of the *Kojiki*. They suggest that the emperor is equated with Ame no Minakanushi, 'Lord of the August Center of Heaven,' personified by, and residing in, the pole star. In China, during the Han period, the pole star appears as a symbol or embodiment of *taiyi*, the 'Great One(ness).' *Taiyi* stands for *dao*, another name for the primeval, undefinable entity in which everything originates; at the same time, deified, it stands also for Tiandi or Tianhuang Dadi, the 'Celestial Emperor,' the Supreme God, whose abode is the pole star. Thus it is no mere accident that during Tenmu's time the Chinese compound *tianhuang* 'Celestial Emperor,' now pronounced as Sinico-Japanese *tennō*, became one of the official appellations of the emperor, and that the different buildings of the imperial court were given the names of the corresponding celestial palaces. Last but not least, it was only from Emperor Tenmu on that the emperor was deemed to be kami, a living god. All in all, mythic tradition, Taoist thought and political speculation appear skillfully blended.[4]

The *Jingikan* and its administrative duties

The *Jingikan* and its predecessor

The *Jingikan*, the 'Department [for the Affairs] of Deities,' is mentioned for the first time during the reign of Empress Jitō (645–702, r. 686–97),[5] but it had a predecessor, the *Jinkan* or *Kami no tsukasa*, 'Office [for the Affairs] of

Deities,' which appears to be a new institution inaugurated during the reign of Emperor Tenmu as a counterpart of the Chinese *Libu* mentioned above. This office appears exclusively in connection with the festival of the 'Great Tasting' or 'Tasting of the New [Food].'[6]

The few entries in the *Nihon shoki* mentioning the *Jingikan* do not tell us much. For further information we have to turn to the Yōrō-code. There we find that, despite the exalted position of the *Jingikan* at the head of all other organs of administration, the rank of its chief, the *jingihaku*,[7] is of a relatively low order within the hierarchy of state officials (Junior 4th Rank, Lower Grade). From this we may recognise the true value of this exalted position – it was only nominal.

According to fascicle 2, § 1 of the Yōrō-code, the staff of the *Jingikan* consists of a head of the department, two assistant heads, two secretaries, two clerks (each both 'senior' and 'junior' respectively), 30 deity households (kanbe), 20 diviners, 30 attendants, and two servants. The same paragraph lists the tasks for these officials. The duties of the head of the department consist in 'the supervision of the festivals for the deities, of the registers of the *hafuribe* and the *kanbe*, the 'Great Tasting,' the 'Pacification of the Spirit' (*chinkon*), the Sacred Maidens, divination, and all decisions of the department. The other officials have to act in accordance with this. The assistant heads have the same duties. The secretaries are bound to keep everything in the right order; they supervise the correspondence, care for delays and mistakes, and are informed about the vigils. The clerks accept what comes to hand and draw up excerpts; they compare and control the correspondence, point to delays and mistakes, and recite the official letters.'[8] Thus the 'Department [for the Affairs] of Deities' appears for the most part as a board of management.

Nakatomi and Inbe

The *Nihon shoki* records that Empress Kōgyoku appointed Nakatomi no Kamako head of the *Kami no tsukasa* on New Year's Day of her third year (644/2/13); he, however, declined.[9] No such office existed at the time, thus this anachronistic notice has no other purport except to stress the claim of the Nakatomi clan to this office. Actually, not only members of the Nakatomi clan were appointed; for example, for twenty-five years, beginning in 741, members of the Kose, Ishikawa, and Fun'ya held the position. Very often the senior assistant head too was a Nakatomi while the junior assistant head and other minor officials were members of the Inbe clan.

Both clans, Nakatomi and Inbe, were originally religious functionaries, the Nakatomi evidently serving as diviners, the Inbe preparing and taking care of the offerings. It would lead us too far to follow up the history of these two competing clans, and it will suffice here to point out that, except for a short period after Tenmu's war of succession, when the Inbe gained the upper hand, the Nakatomi held the higher position. It is Nakatomi no Ōshima who in his capacity as *jingihaku*, head of the *Jingikan*, recites the *ama-tsu-kami no yogoto*, the 'Congratulatory Words of the Heavenly Deities,' during the official enthronement ceremony of Empress Jitō on New Year's Day of the fourth year of her reign (690/2/14) while Inbe no Shikobuchi offered her the regalia, sword and mirror.[10]

The short description of the enthronement ceremony of Empress Jitō, evidently designed by Tenmu and here enacted for the first time, shows how mythic tradition was skillfully exploited; in particular, the correspondence with the scene in front of the Heavenly Rock-Cave as described in the *Kojiki*, when Ame no Koyane, ancestor of the Nakatomi, recited his 'mighty prayer' (*futonoritogoto*) to lure the sun-goddess out, and Futodama, ancestor of the Inbe, offered her a *sakaki*-branch adorned with mirror, jewels and 'soft offerings' (*nikite*), cannot be overlooked.[11] At the same time the mythic scene serves as a precedent for the prerogatives of both families.

The subordinate officials of the Jingikan

When Inbe no Hironari presented his *Kogoshūi* to the throne in 808 it was not only to deplore the favours meanwhile shown to the Nakatomi and the disregard of his own clan; he points to other grievances as well. In his opinion, families that originally took part in the preparation of the 'Great Offerings,' the Sarume, the mirror-makers, jewel-makers, shield-makers, weavers, etc., had been forgotten.[12] But even the commentaries to the Yōrō-code seem to be uncertain about what had happened to those families. It is only the later regulations which inform us about the tasks the *kanbe* of the *Jingikan* had to perform, under the control of Nakatomi and Inbe, from preparing the necessary utensils for the festivals to enacting songs and dances.

No details are given regarding the diviners (*urabe*). It is quite certain, however, that scapulimancy had been abandoned in favour of the Chinese practice of tortoise shell divination. The best diviners in the service of the *Jingikan* came from Tsushima, Iki, and Izu; two of them had to attend to the persons of the Emperor and the crown-prince. Otherwise divination was necessary for many occasions, especially in connection with the 'Great Tasting' and other festivals.

Persons controlled by the Jingikan

The *Jingikan* was in charge of the household-registers of two groups of people, the *hafuribe* (priests of low rank) and the *kanbe* ('deity households'). These were households assigned to shrines; taxes and corvee of these serfs were controlled by the provincial authorities who also arranged for their allotment to the shrines to which they belonged. In 692 two 'deity districts' of Ise are mentioned; later reports show that in 723 there were altogether eight deity districts, all very probably cultivated by *kanbe*. The Izumo, Munakata, Kashima, Katori, and Awa shrines owned one district each; in Kii two shrines shared one deity district. There is a constant tendency to expand these possessions; toward the end of the twelfth century the Ise shrines alone owned eight deity districts.

The same tendency is apparent in regard to the deity households which provided the income of the shrines. It appears that at the beginning of the ninth century there were 5,884 deity households belonging to 170 'eminent shrines,' most prominent among them the shrine of Yahata (Hachiman) in Usa (1,660 households) and the Ise shrines (1,230 households). These are, however, small numbers in comparison with those providing for the great Buddhist temples (e.g., the Tōdaiji with 5,000 households) or even of high officials (e.g., 2,000 households for a *daijin* 'great minister'). There must have been many shrines with very small incomes or even no income at all. This is another grievance of Inbe no Hironari, who also complains that although during the Tenpyō era (729–49) registers of deities had been prepared, only shrines connected with the Nakatomi, big and small, had been included, while even important shrines belonging to other clans had been omitted. Thus the full income provided by the government went into the pockets of the Nakatomi, including the government offerings granted on certain festivals.[13]

No such register of deities is extant. Sporadic notices point to a gradual realisation of a register of 'official' shrines. For the beginning of the tenth century the *Engi shiki* ('Procedures of the Engi era', see below) lists '3,132 Heavenly and Earthly Deities [within] 2,861 shrines, in which 271 deities are worshiped jointly.' Of these, 492 are major, 2,640 are minor deities, a distinction which refers to the donor (government/provincial) of the offerings at certain festivals and the way they are presented ('on tables,' 'below the tables').[14]

The other group of people to be registered by the *Jingikan* were the *hafuribe*. They formed part of the priesthood serving in permanent positions at the officially registered shrines. These *hafuri* usually came from old, local *hafuri*-families.[15] If there were no such families to be found, someone from a *kanbe*-family had to be appointed and, if no *kanbe* were available, some other person was chosen, as the *Ryō no gige* (1, KT 29) explains – which again demonstrates that there were shrines without any official income apart from the offerings. It also suggests that the duties of the priest at such a shrine were rather insignificant. In contrast to this, a priesthood came into existence at the more important official shrines where the positions of *kannushi* 'deity-master' or *jingūji* 'shrine-functionary' were, like all other functionaries, subject to rotation in office, initially after four years, then later after six years. As with landed property and income, the number of officials shows a constant tendency to increase.

Finally, there were the *mikannagi* 'Sacred Maidens.' These were girls serving at official shrines as well as at the palace and the *Jingikan* itself. They had various duties to perform, but their original function of serving as mediums through whom the deities revealed their will was rapidly lost.

The State Cult proper: the festivals

The Jingiryō

As mentioned above one of the duties of the head of the *Jingikan* consisted in the supervision of the festivals for the deities; among these are expressly identified the 'Great Tasting' and the 'Pacification of the Spirit.' Both these ceremonies centred on the emperor. The relevance and extent of this task are set down in fasc. 6 of the Yōrō-code, the *Jingiryō* ('Laws [regarding the cult] of Deities').'[16] § 1 of this fascicle recapitulates: 'At all times, the *Jingikan* makes offerings to the Heavenly and Earthly Deities according to the usual rules.' §§ 2–9 enumerate the festivals due within the course of the year: 'Festival Praying for the Harvest' (*kinensai* or *toshigoi no matsuri*) in the Second Month; 'Festival for the Pacification of the Flowers' (*chinkasai* or *hanashizume no matsuri*) in the Third Month; 'Festival of Deity Raiment' (*kanmiso-matsuri*), 'Felicity-Herb-Festival' (*saigusa no matsuri*), 'Great-Taboo-Festival' (*ōimi no matsuri*), 'Wind-God-Festival' (*kazekami no matsuri*) in the Fourth Month; 'Festival in the Course of the Months' (*tsukinami no matsuri*), 'Festival of the Banquet of the Roads' (*michiae no matsuri*), 'Festival of the Pacification of the Fire' (*chinkasai* or *hoshizume no matsuri*) in the Sixth Month. In the Seventh Month the Great-Taboo-Festival and the Wind-God-Festival are repeated, in the Ninth Month the Festival of Deity Raiment, this time connected with the 'Festival of the Divine Tasting' (*kanname-sai* or *-matsuri*). In the Eleventh Month follow the 'Festival of the Joint Tasting' (*ainame no matsuri*) on the upper Day of the Hare, the 'Festival of the Great Tasting' (*daijōsai* or *ōname no matsuri*, also *ōnie no matsuri*) on the lower Day of the Hare, and the 'Festival of the Pacification of the Spirit' (*chinkonsai* or *tamashizume no matsuri*) on the Day of the Tiger. In the Twelfth Month the festivals of the Sixth Month are repeated.

Two paragraphs are devoted to the 'Great Purification' (*ōharae*) which requires assistance from outside the *Jingikan*: 'At all times, for the Great Purification on the last day of the Sixth and Twelfth Month the Nakatomi offer the purification-hemp. The Chroniclers (*funhitobe*) of the East (Yamato) and the West (Kawachi) offer the purification-sword and read the purification words. When this is finished, the Hundred (all) Officials, men and women, assemble at the place of purification. The Nakatomi recites the purification words. The diviners perform the purification' (§ 18). 'The taxes due for the Great Purification are 1 sword, 1 hide, 1 hoe and miscellaneous things per district. Each household gives 1 bunch of hemp. The local governors (*kuni no miyatsuko*) give 1 horse' (§ 19).

Several paragraphs deal with details regarding the accession to the throne. For this occasion offerings for all deities, partial abstinence during one month, severe abstinence during three days, and preparation of the offerings within three months are prescribed (§ 10). On the day of accession the Nakatomi recites the congratulatory words and the Inbe presents the regalia as already described in the case of Empress Jitō (§ 13; see above). § 14 states that the Great Tasting must be performed by the provincial governors for one year and for one sovereign, otherwise by the *Jingikan*.

The abstinence prescribed in § 10 needs further comment given in § 11. During partial abstinence all offices work as usual, but it is forbidden to visit people in mourning or the sick or to eat meat. There should be no death sentences and no condemnation of criminals, no music or any occupation with anything defiled. During severe abstinence only the presentation of offerings is allowed. Before and after severe abstinence partial abstinence has to be kept. The duration of abstinence depends on the rank of the festival, as set forth in § 12: one month for Great Festivals, three days for Medium Festivals, and one day for Minor Festivals. The proper offices are responsible for the timely announcement of abstinence (§ 15).

General regulations concerning the offerings are listed in § 16. It is the duty of the highest functionary of the pertaining office to control the liquids, food, and fruits to be offered. They must be absolutely pure and accurately measured. The rank of the messengers due to bring the offerings to the respective shrines is cared for in § 17. If offerings have to be sent apart from the usual festivals the messenger must be someone 'of the Fifth Grade or above.' The last paragraph (§ 20) deals with taxes and corvee of the deity-households as already mentioned above. Within these laws there are again many regulations which point to a Chinese model, as e.g. the division of the festivals into 'Great,' 'Medium' and 'Minor Festivals,' while the regulations concerning abstinence are a direct copy of the Chinese model.[17]

From the Jingiryō to the Engi shiki

The instructions given by the *Jingiryō* appear to have been very scanty, so that specific regulations (*shiki*) for carrying out the prescribed tasks were drawn up during the Kōnin (810–24) and Jōgan eras (859–74). Evidently both supplementations (of which nearly nothing remains) proved insufficient, so at the command of Emperor Daigo a third compilation was completed during the Engi era (901–23) and presented to the throne on January 21, 928 (Enchō 5/12/26).

Here, within the first ten fascicles of the *Engi shiki* everything concerning the duties of the *Jingikan* appears established in minute detail.[18] At the same time it becomes apparent that during the roughly 200 years since the Yōrō-code was drawn up those tasks had considerably increased. There were new institutions under the administration of the *Jingikan* such as a 'Bureau of the Consecrated Imperial Princess in Ise' (fasc. 5) and likewise an 'Office of the Princess Consecrated to the Kamo Shrines' (fasc. 6). The shrines and buildings belonging to the Ise shrines as well as their festivals are treated in a separate fascicle (4). There are newly inaugurated festivals, while the old ones had become more and more elaborated, involving an increasing number of staff members (fasc. 1 and 2 deal with the 'Festivals of the Four Seasons,' fasc. 3 with 'Extraordinary Festivals'). Fasc. 7 is given over entirely to the 'Great Tasting of the Enthronement.' For the first time the *norito* or 'Rituals' recited during the festivals are recorded (fasc. 8) and there is, also for the first time, a register of deities receiving official offerings (fasc. 9 and 10).

If we consider the modest attempts at a revival of the Ise-cult and the creation of a sequence of festivals within the four seasons during the reign of Tenmu, as well as the measured approach of the *Jingiryō* based on Tenmu's arrangements, then the regulations of the *Engi shiki* appear as the end of a development characterised by unchecked growth in every respect: the number of shrines receiving official offerings at certain occasions, the number of such occasions, the scope of the festivals and the staff. However, there is reason to doubt whether the regulations laid down in the *Engi shiki* and promulgated in 967 were ever fully implemented.

The festivals: warding off evil

No contemporary source exists that gives evidence for the religious ideas underlying the state cult; these ideas must be deduced from the cult ceremonies which for their part constituted the state cult proper. The festivals listed in §§ 2–9 are all identified as acts of offering by the use of the Chinese word *ji* 'sacrifice.' The Japanese word *matsuri*, used to translate this word, signified essentially the same concept during the eighth century. This shows that the presentation of offerings was the most important part of the entire ceremony. The festivals, thirteen in all, six of which were repeated in the second half of the year, can be arranged into three groups: petition offerings, thanksgiving offerings, and offerings for warding off evil.

Five festivals belong to this last category; two of them are repeated. With the 'Pacification of the Flowers' one appealed to the Great God of Miwa, well-known as the great helper in the case of epidemics. The 'Felicity-Herb-Festival' was addressed to a side-shrine of this same god. The festival took its name from the herb (*saigusa* or *yamayuri* 'Lilium auratum') with which the wine-jars were decorated; it became obsolete early so that little is known about it.[19] It seems possible that both festivals resume an older local tradition. The 'Festival of the Banquet of the Roads' was conducted 'at the four corners of the capital' by the diviners and was meant to bar the entrance of evil spirits into the capital. It was also the diviners of the *Jingikan* who for the 'Pacification of the Fire' made fire by using a fire-drill and deposited offerings outside the four corners of the Palace to ward off all danger of fire. These last two cases point to a mixture of Chinese ideas with old magical practices.

In a broader sense the 'Pacification of the Spirit' may also be counted in the same category. A ceremony of 'inviting the soul' (Chin. *zhaohun*) was enacted for Emperor Tenmu for the first time in 685.[20] A late reading tradition interprets this as *mitama-furi*, 'stirring up the vital power.' It was performed on the 24th day of the Eleventh Month, a day near the winter solstice when the sun reaches its lowest point and will, from this day on, regain its full strength, with the intention of strengthening or restoring the vital power (*tama*) of the emperor in analogy to the sun. Thus the ceremony reenacts the mythic scene in which the sun-goddess is lured out from the Heavenly Rock-Cave, the emperor being equated with the goddess. But the day chosen was also the Middle Day of the Tiger. Fixing this festival on the Middle Day of the Tiger rather than on the day of the solstice proper points to Chinese ideas: the most acute danger for the life of the emperor (likened to that of the sun) arises from the combination of winter-solstice/Day of the Tiger because the tiger is the devourer of light and life.[21] The ceremony was later elaborated to comprise further elements of the 'pacification,' i.e. the 'arresting' of the soul. The commentary of the *Ryō no gige*,[22] which speaks of 'inviting the free-rambling yang and arresting it in the body,' again shows the presence of Chinese ideas. Thus the ceremony combines magical devices of 'arousing' with those of 'arresting': garments are shaken and knots are tied in a cord which then is enclosed in a box while a Sacred Maiden (a descendant of the Sarume) standing on top of an overturned tub taps it with a spear counting from one to ten, imitating the dance of the goddess Ame no Uzume in front of the Heavenly Rock-Cave. Later this ceremony was also enacted on behalf of the empress and the crown-prince.

Not until the *Engi shiki* does it become clear that the offerings on the 'Festival of the Pacification of the Spirit' are presented to the 'Eight Deities of the *Jingikan*' and the god Ōnaobi. This god as well as some of the 'Eight Deities' clearly owe their existence to speculative thinking of the late seventh or early eighth century. When Izanagi cleanses himself after his visit to the world of the dead Ōmagatsui, a god who causes '(moral) crookedness and defilement,' first emerges, then Naobi, the god who does the mending, the annihilation of the actions of the former, comes forth – thus the *Kojiki*. As a set the 'Eight Deities' appear for the first time in the *Kogoshūi*.[23] Conspicuous are the two deities heading the group: Takami-musubi and Kami-musubi. In the *Kojiki* they form, together with Ame no Minakanushi, a triad at the beginning of all creation, corresponding with the two creative forces, yin and yang, emerging out of the primeval dao.[24] Kotoshironushi and Mike-tsu-kami are known from mythology. The goddess Ōmiya no me seems connected with the Inbe; together with Takami-musubi she receives special offerings. The three remaining and hitherto unknown deities point to a connection with the Mononobe clan. They derive the first part of their names, which hint at the restoring of life, directly or indirectly from those of certain gems from among the ten 'Heavenly wondrous treasures' given to Emperor Jinmu by Umashimaji no Mikoto, ancestor of the Mononobe, on the Day of the Tiger in the Eleventh Month in his first year 'to pacify his spirit' (*Sendai kuji hongi* fasc.7: 202). The second part of their names is *musubi* ('effecting force of creation'), thus linking them at the same time with Takami-musubi and Kami-musubi. In explaining the procedures of the *chinkonsai* the *Jōgan gishiki* (fasc. 5, KS 139) has the

'Divine Treasures' being brought in by the *kanbe* and put in the place of honour. This can only refer to the treasures of the Mononobe supposed to have been given to Jinmu; they are not mentioned in the *Engi shiki*.

This important ceremony was performed in the Palace on the day before the 'Great Tasting,' that festival which after the accession to the throne and as part of the relevant ceremonies was celebrated in an outstanding and most solemn fashion.

The festivals: petition offerings

Like the festivals discussed above the 'Great-Taboo-Festival' of Hirose and the 'Wind-God-Festival' of Tatsuta are all 'Minor Festivals'. Ōimi 'Great Taboo' is another name for the food-goddess venerated in the Hirose shrine. The rituals for both festivals pray for 'sweet water' and for 'keeping back bad winds and wild waters' in order to assure a good harvest.[25] Both shrines are mentioned for the first time during the reign of Emperor Tenmu; from then on offerings were presented twice every year.

Entries in the *Shoku Nihongi* for 702 and 706 suggest that the *toshigoi no matsuri* 'Festival Praying for the Harvest' and also the *tsukinami no matsuri* 'Festival in the Course of the Months' (both are festivals of the middle category) are already riveted in the Taihō-code.[26] There are strong indications that the *toshigoi* may even go back to Tenmu. The *Engi shiki* delineates in every detail the procedure of the *toshigoi* which takes place on the fourth day of the Second Month. Fifteen days in advance the preparation of the offerings begins; the responsible persons are named, and species and exact amount of the offerings are minutely described.[27] They are controlled by persons from the Inbe clan. At dawn on the day of severe abstinence (after three days of partial abstinence) the offerings are set on top of offering tables or on mats spread in front of these within the court of the *Jingikan*. Then in set order all the civil officials of the capital march in through the different gates and take their respective seats. The Nakatomi now recites the ritual, and after that the Inbe are called to distribute the offerings to the representatives of the shrines. When all is carried out the participants retire. For the *tsukinami* the procedure is the same, and the provincial offerings are distributed in the same way and at the same time at the provincial headquarters. The designation *tsukinami* seems to point to an originally monthly performance, but there is no evidence for this supposition.

The rituals for the two festivals are also the same, apart from a short passage which is lacking in the ritual for the *tsukinami*. The poetic diction of the ritual cannot distract from the fact that the central declaration of the prayer can be reduced to a simple *do ut des*, and the promise of more offerings if the deities will grant what they are being asked to provide. The petitions are limited to freedom from evils, good harvests, and the well-being of the emperor; the prayers are directed to the Heavenly and Earthly Deities in general, the imperial ancestor deities (whoever is meant by this), the deities of the harvest, the deities which are venerated by the diverse Sacred Maidens (*mikannagi*) of the *Jingikan* (i.e. the Eight Deities of the *Jingikan*, the deities caring especially for the Palace and the Palace-gates and the deities caring for the country in general), Amaterasu, and finally to the deities of the six *miagata* or imperial domains in Yamato and the deities protecting the entrances up into the mountains and the tributary streams in the same province.[28] The geographical details indicate that the prayer was composed between 672 and 710, a period during which the festival itself was created. The supposition that the festival has its roots in folk customs and is 'extremely old' cannot be maintained.[29]

The *toshigoi no matsuri* may be taken as a model. It opens the cycle of the yearly festivals of government offerings; the petitions brought forward are comprehensive. All officials are duty bound to attend and all officially registered shrines receive their share of government offerings. Here then the State, represented, indeed personified, by its hierarchically arrayed officials, faces a likewise hierarchically arranged community of deities in order to express the requests of the state and to offer something in advance. If the requests are granted, more will follow. It is easy to recognise here the analogy to the Chinese state cult in which, as Eichhorn explains, human relations with supernatural forces were strictly regulated in each and every detail, and their management restricted to the heads of government, resulting in a system in which all religious measures, as well as all political ones, were precisely calculated before the fact and then executed according to prescribed norms.[30]

In establishing the state cult, however, as in other respects as well, not a copy of the Chinese model but rather an adaptation to Japanese conditions was intended. Thus, as Ellwood has already pointed out,[31] the *toshigoi* had been created in imitation of the corresponding Chinese festival, and even identically named. Methods resembling the practice of presenting offerings to a multitude of deities, at the same time expressing their difference in rank by gifts differing in species and amount as well as by the way of presenting them ('on tables,' 'below the tables') are also encountered in China. That on the occasion of a festival of this kind it was possible to represent the state itself by its assembled officials must have appealed to the Japanese authorities; but other important Chinese ceremonies – the ploughing by the emperor, the tending of silkworms by the empress on New Year – even though tried once in 758,[32] did not gain a footing.

In 914 Miyoshi Kiyoyuki presented a memorial to the throne in which he speaks to the meaning of the *toshigoi* and the *tsukinami*, at the same time confronting the ideal with the reality – a reality which shows the thoroughly 'practical and economic' utilisation of offerings; he complains that no representative ever actually carried the offerings intact to his shrine but that instead everyone consumed them beforehand. It is vain to look for any kind of personal religious feeling here. This is indeed excluded from the beginning – it is not the individual human being and his relations with the supernatural forces that are in demand; it is the state, and only the state, personified and represented by its officials, that enters into relations with the host of deities. And it is in their capacity as representatives of the state that those officials fail in the eyes of Kiyoyuki.

The Festival of Deity Raiment

This festival forms a category in itself; there is no petition and no thanksgiving. Instead it serves to provide raiment for the sun-goddess in Ise who appears anthropomorphised throughout. Thus the (*Kōtaijingū*) *Gishikichō* of 804 mentions as equipment for her shrine mosquito-nets and coverlets, jackets, skirts, girdles and scarves, socks and boots, combs and dressing-cases.[33] With this in mind it seems quite natural to imitate the court-society in following the Chinese model of dress-changing at the seasonal turning-points of the year, that is, in the Fourth and, one month earlier than the court, in the Ninth Month. The *Kogoshūi*, however, tries to connect the festival with a mythic precedent.[34] The precise description of the festival beginning with the (*Kōtaijingū*) *Gishikichō* makes it a model case showing continual enlargement in every respect.[35]

The festivals: thanksgiving offerings

There remain three festivals of thanksgiving offerings: the Divine Tasting, the Joint Tasting, and the Great Tasting. The designation of the last one is inconsistent; it took some time until 'Tasting of the New' was used for the annual festival and 'Great Tasting' for the enlarged ceremony performed only once after the accession to the throne. All these festivals are described by the Chinese word *chang* 'to taste, to prove,' designating at the same time the imperial autumnal offering of first fruits when the 'Son of Heaven' tastes the new cereals after having offered part of them to his ancestors. Millet, sesame, and rice were the fruits he offered and tasted in turn during the three harvest-months.[36] The feudal lords too had to perform the *chang* in the same way.[37] This is the alleged ideal, but it is precisely this Chinese ideal which we may not overlook as a factor in the process of creating the Japanese state cult. In a historic context the 'Tasting of the New' is mentioned for the first time in 642. Empress Kōgyoku celebrated it in her First Year 11/16, and on the same day 'the Prince Imperial and the Oho-omi each personally tasted the new rice' – 'probably . . . in their own houses,' as Aston comments.[38] It was a private ceremony as prescribed by the Chinese model.

This is not to deny that there also existed a Japanese tradition of 'tasting the new [food]'. Old Japanese *niFinaFë*[39] and *niFunami* (*Man'yōshū* poem 3460, Azuma dialect) testify to the word, and a legend in the *Hitachi fudoki*[40] shows that it meant a nocturnal rite performed within the family, with the doors barred against anyone from outside. The *Kojiki* poem (its geographical location points to Tenmu) speaks of the 'house' of tasting the new and thus leads to the myth of the sun-goddess and the palace where she wanted to celebrate it. This mythic precedent is supplemented by a pseudo-historical one, with Kamu Atakashitsu-hime, wife of the Heavenly Grandchild, performing the rite,[41] but no true creation-legend is ever given. It might very well be that the mythic and pseudohistorical scenes are later accretions seeking to prove the high antiquity of the rite that by now formed the most conspicuous part of the state cult.

The 'Divine Tasting' was one of the important festivals at the Ise shrines; official offerings were brought to the shrine by a special messenger. It seems to have been celebrated for the first time in 721, and a detailed description is already given in the (*Kōtaijingū*) *Gishikichō* of 804.

The 'Joint Tasting' followed the same intention: offerings were sent to several shrines within the nearby provinces, the number of which increased rapidly, from eight shrines named in the *Ryō no gige* to 71 deities in 41 shrines in the *Engi shiki*. The offerings given for the occasion were of various kinds: raiment of diverse kind, salt and sea-food, dried meat, receptacles and vessels, and rice in sheaves for the preparation of sake.

The Great Tasting

To sketch the festival of the Great Tasting in all its details as regulated in the *Engi shiki* would take us too far. As a consequence of its political significance it grew into a whole complex of rites, while the Tasting of the New is hardly discernible from the *jinkonjiki* 'Divine Present Partaking of Food,' a rite performed following the *tsukinami*. This rite is mentioned for the first time in 790; later (840) *jinkonjiki* is even used to designate the Tasting of the New.

The preparatory rites for the Great Tasting begin in the spring following the accession to the throne and culminate in the offering of the first fruits of the sacred crop to the emperor. From here on he plays the role of the sun-goddess, tasting the new food, as well as that of the Chinese emperor presenting the *chang*, the autumnal offering of first fruits to his ancestors. On the day of the festival proper within the courtyard of the *Jingikan* offerings are presented to the same deities as on the *tsukinami*; the secret rite performed by the emperor in person takes place during the night. Within each of two specially erected buildings a room is prepared containing a couch for the deity and two sitting mats, one for the emperor, the other for the deity. Two food-mats are spread out, and the emperor himself fills the dishes for the deity. Boiled rice, several side dishes, and white and dark rice wine are offered and evidently partaken by the emperor. Thus a third element enters the rite: a joint meal, i.e., communion with the deity. It is generally believed that the deity thus entertained is the sun-goddess, but there is no certainty on this point; it might also be Takami-musubi.

The strong political significance of the rite may not be overlooked. In the Festival of the Pacification of the Spirit the emperor is already likened to the sun-goddess; this time, by tasting the new food according to mythic precedent, he appears as her representative. Again, in their joint meal, he receives the blessing of the attending deity by re-enacting the mythic scene of the investiture of the Heavenly Grandchild. This finds expression in the couch: it is a replica of the True Seat of Takami-musubi, decked with the coverlet which Takami-musubi cast over his August Grandchild whom he sent down from Heaven to rule Japan. Thus the emperor, descendant of the sun-goddess as well as of Takami-musubi, succeeds rightfully to the throne, himself now elevated to the state of *aki-tsu-mikami*, 'God Present.'

The Great Purification

As the *Jingiryō* shows, the Great Purification consists of two clearly distinguishable parts, one to be performed by the Chroniclers of the East and the West, one by the Nakatomi serving in the *Jingikan*. The purification words read by the former, in the *Engi shiki* designated as 'charms' or 'spells,' are in Chinese; they are addressed to the full host of Taoist deities, from Huangtian shangdi, the Supreme Ruler of Heaven, down to the Five Rulers of the Five Directions and the Four Climates of the Four Seasons. 'Fortune effigies' are presented to them, praying to ward off calamities; a golden sword is presented, praying for the prolongation of the imperial reign. 'We pronounce the spell: To the East as far as the Fusang [-tree, where the sun rises], to the West as far as Yuyuan [where the sun sets], to the South as far as the Flaming Brightness, to the North as far as the Weak Waters, over a thousand cities, a hundred countries, may [the emperor] prudently reign ten thousand years! Ten thousand years, ten thousand years!'[42]

The independence of this magic-imbued portion of the rite as well as its essential difference from the ceremony conducted by the *Jingikan* is clearly shown by the fact that in 702, after the death of ex-Empress Jitō, this part took place but not the Great Purification proper. The *Jōgan gishiki* (5, KS 145f.) gives precise instructions for the drawing-up of the officials on the platforms and booths erected in front of the Suzaku-gate where the ceremony of the purification takes place and where the *Jingikan* beforehand has arranged the offerings. When the complicated ceremony of reporting and taking seats is finished the great minister gives orders to perform the purification, and at last 'the *Jingikan* distributes the cut hemp, and the Nakatomi comes forth and reads the *norito* summoning everyone to listen. When this is done the hemp is taken up. Then those of the fifth rank and above perform the purification and leave, scattering the cut hemp.'

If the primary intention of the Chinese rite was to ward off calamities and invite an everlasting reign for the emperor, the norito of the Great Purification shows at once that it serves a different purpose: all the *tsumi* perpetrated consciously or unconsciously by the court and the officials shall be removed by it. The *tsumi* are enumerated; they consist in the 'heavenly' *tsumi*: breaking down paddy dikes, filling in ditches, etc., up to flaying alive or backward and scattering excrement, namely all the misdeeds perpetrated by the god Susanowo in heaven, and in the 'earthly' *tsumi*, namely cutting living skin, cutting dead skin, leucodermia, excrescences, the *tsumi* of intercourse with one's mother, one's daughter, a woman and then her daughter by previous marriage or vice versa, the *tsumi* of copulation with an animal, calamity of creeping worms, of gods on high, of birds on high, the *tsumi* of causing death to livestock and other evil magic. 'May all these *tsumi* depart!' And in truly beautiful poetic language all the *tsumi* are declared certain to be driven away so that none remain; they are carried away by the responsible deities in streams and rivers to the nether regions and in the end they are dissipated. From now on no *tsumi* remain.

The *norito* as well as the ceremony lead to a series of questions. What is meant by *tsumi*? How is the term *harae* 'purification' to be understood? As a special ceremony the *ōharae* was inaugurated by Emperor Tenmu; but what was its purpose as part of the state cult? To understand the development and the meaning of the ceremony it is necessary to go back to the reforms of the Taika era when for the first time the Chinese law system was introduced. Before this *tsumi* designated 'misdeeds, offences,' and these called for *harae* 'compensation, payment.' According to a kind of prescriptive right the wronged person himself asked for the compensation. Now, as practice of the 'unenlightened vulgar' this was strictly forbidden,[43] but the change-over to the new law must have been difficult. On the other hand, *harae* means also 'exorcism,' as of evil demons, and according to the *norito*, this newly created *harae* causes the dispersion and annihilation of the *tsumi*. But when the *Jingi-ryō* asks for special taxes from the districts and local governors while the *Engi shiki* mentions *mi-agamono* 'recompensation gifts,' the old idea of compensation still seems somehow present even though there is no claimant. At the same time the hemp as well as the effigies mentioned in the 'spell' of the Chroniclers and those serving as *mi-agamono* according to the *Engi shiki* suggest the idea of a transfer of the *tsumi* onto them.[44] Here the idea of *misogi* 'ablution' comes in, a method to cleanse *kegare* 'cultic defilement.' Thus it becomes evident that the character of *harae* has been changed; it has taken over traits of *misogi* as well.

The list of 'heavenly' and 'earthly' *tsumi* as enumerated in the *norito* shows that this term too has changed its meaning. The Great Purification under the legendary Empress Jingū mentioned in the *Kojiki*[45] is clearly anachronistic but if only because of that fact, it shows all the more what Tenmu had in mind when he inaugurated the ceremony. Quite contrary to the *norito* (which seems to be composed only during the eighth century) there appear, apart from the misdeeds of Susanowo, only the *tsumi* of intercourse of parents with children and copulation with animals. The enlarged list of *tsumi* in the *norito* certainly applies a new meaning to the term, but it is difficult to find a common denominator.

As far as the list enumerates offences against property, body and life, infringement of conventions (thus intercourse between brother and sister seems exempted), and practices of black magic, *tsumi* can be understood as misdeeds or offences as before. But what about the 'calamities,' skin diseases, and cutting living or dead skin? The last could be seen as defilement, but an intrusion of the Buddhist belief that killing and eating meat is a 'sin' is also possible. The calamities as well as the skin diseases can be understood as the effect, the visible sign of a divine curse, usually the response to the breaking of a taboo. That all these different kinds of *tsumi* can simply be wiped away just as defilement is cleansed by ablution shows clearly enough how the meaning of the word *tsumi* has changed. Still, there are of course the criminal laws regulating the punishment of any offence whatsoever. This change of meaning has caused many translators to use the term 'sin' as an equivalent for *tsumi* which, however, does not fit. 'Sin' refers to something personal or individual, while the state cult ceremony of the Great Purification is addressing the collective, not the individual. How little the ceremony impressed those individuals personally is demonstrated by the lack of attendance of the officials obliged to be present – in 979 for instance not even a single one of the high officials appeared.[46]

Norito and Yogoto

By means of the festivals and through the body of its assembled officials the state itself appeals to the deities for the welfare of the state and its people. This finds expression not only in the offerings but also in the official prayers or 'rituals,' the *norito*. As the first attempts to create a 'state cult' occur during the reign of Emperor Tenmu, so the oldest *norito* bear traits which suggest their formation during the same time or shortly thereafter, as already pointed out above. They are newly created texts composed especially for the newly created festivals and written in a language which in its wealth of poetical representation resembles the poetry of Kakinomoto Hitomaro (around 700), while its bureaucratic-stereotyped flourishes remind us of the diction of eighth century imperial decrees (*senmyō*). The *norito* for the *toshigoi* and the *ōharae* display many original and beautiful traits; the *norito* for the *toshigoi* in particular provides a pattern for all later *norito*. Thus, apart from short sections alluding to the festival for which they are intended, most *norito* can hardly claim originality since previously fixed figurative passages are handled like set pieces, inserted and grouped as required in order to produce new rituals. This holds especially true in the case of festivals inaugurated after the *Jingiryō* was promulgated.

Rather than glorifying and eulogising the deities invoked, the *norito* eulogise and glorify the offerings that are either dedicated on the spot or are promised to be given to the deities in future; and the requests that are given weight by the offerings are clearly stated. Only two of the surviving rituals do not fit this scheme, the 'Congratulatory Words (*yogoto*) of the Heavenly Deities' recited by a Nakatomi during the enthronement ceremony, and the 'Divine Congratulatory Words of the Local Chieftain of Izumo' delivered on the occasion of his succession. Both, the Nakatomi and the Izumo Chieftain, speak on behalf of their deities, and the deities themselves congratulate and bless the sovereign. The 'Divine Congratulatory Words of the Local Chieftain of Izumo', first mentioned in 716, is one of the oldest rituals, and one of the most beautiful. The Nakatomi ritual, although attested since Empress Jitō, is only known in a text of 1142. In both cases the blessing is intended for the emperor as *aki-tsu-mikami* 'God Present', which points to their composition not before Tenmu.

As a direct and intimate meeting and communion between emperor and deity during the rite, the Great Tasting stands out against all other state cult festivals where generally 'the state' represented by the officials confronts the deities. In the same way these *yogoto* as blessings of the emperor by the deities stand out against the rest of the rituals in which the state as such appeals to the deities. But it is not the emperor as a human being who is addressed; the blessing is intended for the sovereign, the '*ōyamatoneko sumeramikoto* who as God Present rules the Great Land of the Eight Islands.' Here too, the political dimension may not be overlooked.

The emperor, a 'God Present'

The title of the emperor mentioned above and used as a general opening formula in the senmyo texts is but one of several variants prescribed by the Yōrō-code for written documents. Very probably already devised in the Taihō-code, in the *Nihon shoki* they are also used as anachronisms in the decrees of Emperor Kōtoku. Three of them contain the term *aki-tsu-mikami*, 'God Present.'

The divinity of the emperor, claimed for the first time by Tenmu, rests on two conditions: the divine descent and the 'Heavenly Sun-Succession.' As only a member of the imperial family, descending from the sun-goddess, could succeed on the throne, it is after all the office which conveys the divinity. This principle only slowly takes definite shape. Toward the end of the seventh century the stereotype *ōkimi wa kami ni shi maseba* 'because the Great Prince is a god' found in poems of the *Man'yōshū* is also used for imperial princes (the sons of Tenmu). In spite of the claim for divinity maintained by the titles of the emperor, during the Nara period and even later this did not lead to further consequences. emperors and empresses during this time were extremely involved with Buddhism, notably Emperor Shōmu (r. 724–49) and his daughter, Empress Kōken (r. 749–58, and again 764–70 as Empress Shōtoku);[47] others, like Emperor Kanmu (r. 781–806), sympathised with Chinese ideas. It is only later that the possibilities inherent in the idea of the divinity of the emperor were realised, speculatively developed and exploited.

It is in connection with this complex of ideas in their original form that the cult of the sun-goddess in Ise as ancestress of the imperial clan was re-animated by Emperor Tenmu.

State cult, deities, and religious belief

As stated above (section 2.4) only a limited number of deities received official offerings and were invoked in the *norito*. Apart from the deities of the imperial family, these were in most cases deities worshipped as *ujigami* 'clan-gods' by powerful clans, and by shrines of local importance. The sun-goddess worshipped in Ise as the ancestress of the imperial family can be seen as the model for the cult of *ujigami* coming into vogue during the eighth century. Just as only members of the imperial clan were allowed to worship at Ise, so also *ujigami* were worshipped exclusively by a certain clan. They were not necessarily ancestor gods, and there is no genuine connection here with an ancestor-cult. Thus even the presentation of offerings for the imperial tombs (*nozaki*) at the end of the year appear as official, not as private acts.[48] The great bulk, namely 2,207, of 'minor' deities receiving only provincial offerings, remain nameless; only the name of the shrine is given. For this reason it is difficult if not impossible to form an opinion about their character. What can be said with certainty is that all these shrines and deities were of limited, local importance only.

The picture that emerges here is that of a great number of small, unconnected cultic or religious entities. Personal religious attachment to certain deities is more or less predetermined by local or family ties, if such attachment is not already directed toward Buddhism. By the great number of deities and shrines to which official offerings are presented the state cult tends to evoke the picture of a homogeneous religion, but although there are single cults of local gods or clan-deities in abundance there is no coherent 'religion' binding them together, no clear ideas forming a religious system apart from the belief in this or that god of limited power who might help on this or that occasion if properly propitiated, or who would otherwise send his curses.

But this lack of a coherent religion is not the only reason why – as some readers may have noticed – the term 'Shinto' is avoided throughout this paper. When the word appears for the first time in the *Nihon shoki* it is used in conformity with the ideas promulgated by Emperor Tenmu and it designates, in the given context, 'the way [of the emperor] as a god.'[49] It is not used in the sense of an 'indigenous religion' in contrast to Buddhism – and in particular, it is not used in the anachronistic sense of the later propagandistic contexts that strive to present 'Shinto' as a religion going back to the age of the gods.).[50] 'Shinto' as a word designating a coherent religious system was introduced for the first time by Yoshida Kanetomo (1435–1511).[51] Neither the state cult nor individual belief in one or the other indigenous god falls into this category.

Conclusion

By means of the state cult of ancient Japan the state becomes the mediator between the deities and the people. Following its own hierarchic organisation the state designs a universe of gods organised by ranks bestowed upon them according to a scheme that thus exactly reproduces its own hierarchic organisation. In due time and in accordance with their ranks they receive the official offerings, which on their part presupposes the obligation to fulfill the expectations set upon them. After the accession to the throne the emperor communicates with his ancestor deities. Now himself 'God Present' he is confirmed in his office – an act repeated every year, thus renewing the relationship.

The scheme of a state cult developed around the turn of the seventh and eighth century; it was only gradually worked out in detail, and up to a certain degree the system remained open. When, with the *Engi shiki*, every single detail was fixed and the state cult reached its splendid culmination point (on paper at least), the germs of decay were already present. The divinity of the emperor, derived from his office, becomes the more conscious the more he is deprived of real power, and the more his role is restricted by the court ceremonies. This development goes together with the decay of the state based on the law-codes of the Nara period. At the same time this caused not only the decay of the ceremonial observances regulated by these laws but also of the official cult system as a whole.

Notes

1 For another and more detailed treatment of this general question the reader is invited to consult Naumann 1988: 141–86.
2 Cf. Eichhorn 1973: 95.
3 Cf. Müller 1980: 200, 267.
4 For details see Naumann 1996; see also Tim Barrett's essay in this volume.
5 In 689, Jitō 3/8/2 (*Nihon shoki* = NKBT 68: 498–9; cf. Aston 1956: II, 394).
6 Tenmu 2/12/5; 5/9/21; 6/11/27 (NKBT 68: 414–5; 426–7; 430–1. Cf. Aston 1956: II, 324, 333, 338).
7 Several entries mentioning a *jingihaku* before the time of Jitō (Keitai 1/2/10, Kinmei 16/2, and Kōgyoku 3/1/1) are clearly anachronistic. See also below.
8 Cf. Aida 1964: 92.
9 NKBT 68: 253; cf. Aston 1956: II, 184.
10 NKBT 68: 500/501; cf. Aston 1956: II, 395.
11 *Kojiki* = NKBT 1: 80/81–82/83; cf. Philippi 1969: 83.
12 *Shinchū Kogaku-sōsho* 1: 554; cf. Florenz 1919: 450ff.
13 *Kogoshūi, Shinchū Kogaku-sōsho* 1: 553; Florenz 1919: 446.
14 *Engi shiki* 153; cf. Bock 1972: 113.
15 The original function of the *hafuri* as well as the etymology of this important early term are discussed in Miller-Naumann 1991.
16 Cf. Aida 1964: 335–66
17 Cf. Eichhorn 1973: 213ff.; Eichhorn 1976: 166ff.

18 Translation: Bock 1970, 1972.
19 See Antoni 1988: 116ff.
20 NKBT 68: 473; cf. Aston 1956: II, 373.
21 Cf. Naumann 1997.
22 1, KT 29.
23 *Shinchū Kogaku-sōsho* 1: 551; Florenz 1919: 433ff.
24 See above and Naumann 1996.
25 Cf. Bock 1972: 72–5.
26 *Ōmitegura* 'great offerings' to be distributed to the local governors of all provinces are mentioned for 702 (Taihō 2/2/13; *Shoku Nihongi* 2, KT 14; cf. Snellen 1934: 199). For 706 (Keiun 3/2/26) nineteen shrines are mentioned as being 'included among those where annual prayers (*kinen*) were said and *mitegura* offered' (*Shoku Nihongi* 3, KT 26; Snellen 1934: 230).
27 *Engi shiki* 1, *Shinchū Kogaku-sōsho* 3: 1–3; cf. Bock 1970: 59–65.
28 *Engi shiki* 8, *Shinchū Kogaku-sōsho* 3: 135–137; Bock 1972: 66–70.
29 Cf. Naumann 1988: 158.
30 'Alles in allem aber waren die Beziehungen der Menschheit zu den außermenschlichen Mächten klar geordnet und ihre Handhabung auf die Spitze der Regierung beschränkt, wo jeder religiöse Schritt so wie jeder politische genau vorgeplant und in festgelegten Formen vollzogen wurde' (Eichhorn 1973: 139ff.).
31 Ellwood 1971: 18.
32 This was done only in a simulative fashion; the plough and 'silkworm-broom' used on this occasion are still preserved among the treasures of the Shōsōin. Both are unsuitable for any real work. See also *Man'yōshū* poem 4493 (NKBT 7: 470–1).
33 *Gunsho ruijū* 1: 6; cf. Naumann 1983: 33.
34 *Shinchū Kogaku-sōsho* 1: 546; cf. Naumann 1983: 26ff.
35 *Gunsho ruijū* 1: 32, 37ff.; for details see Naumann 1983: 20–34.
36 Cf. Couvreur 1950: I, 376, 381, 389.
37 Ibid. 289.
38 NKBT 68: 243; Aston 1956: II, 177 n. 1.
39 *Kojiki*, NKBT 1: 320–1.
40 NKBT 2: 38–41.
41 *Nihon shoki* 2, NKBT 67: 156–7.
42 *Norito*, NKBT 1: 426/427–428/429. Bock 1972: 84, n.376 speaks of a 'precedent in ancient China' pointing to the chapter *chunguan* in the *Zhouli*: 'The female shamans have charge of the yearly seasonal driving out and ceremonial bathing' (cf. *Zhouli* ch. 26: 949) and again: 'female priests have charge of the seasonal prayers and sacrifices to ward off calamity' (this probably refers to *Zhouli* ch. 8: 286ff., *tianguan*). This seems rather far-fetched.
43 Cf. Aston 1956: II, 220ff.
44 Effigies were rubbed in order to transmit defilement to them from the person rubbing. More than 1,000 wooden effigies used for this purpose and thrown into the river during the Nara Period have been found while doing river-conservancy work at Sunairi site, Izushi-machi, Hyōgo Prefecture. Around the beginning of the Heian Period tightly spread branches along the river-bank were used as a 'purification-bridge'; however, the number of effigies found within this later layer is much smaller, thus 'allowing us to trace the changes in the purification ceremony' (*Kodaishi hakkutsu '88-'90*: 233).
45 NKBT 1: 228–9.
46 *Shōyūki*, cf. NRD 3: 197b s.v. *ōharai*.
47 Performances of Buddhist ceremonies like the *Ninnōe*, the principal aim of which was 'to give peace and prosperity to the Empire' (de Visser 1935: I, 182), were ordered by the emperors or empresses beginning in the seventh century, while other

Buddhist ceremonies such as the *Gosaie*, celebrated in the Imperial Palace, became the rule only during the ninth century. In all these cases Buddhist monks and priests were ordered to pray on behalf of the state and the Emperor in their capacity as members of a religious body. This was in sharp contrast to the practice of the state cult; in these Buddhist ceremonies it was not the state as such that was acting by way of the officials who were its representatives.

48 For details see Naumann 1988: 183–5.
49 NKBT 68: 154–5; for details see Naumann 1970 passim; Naumann 1988: 137ff.
50 See also Naumann 1988: IXff.
51 For details see Naumann 1994: 60–2.

CHAPTER FIVE

The economics of ritual power

Allan G. Grapard

Toward a ritualised state

The matter at hand begins with the coup d'état of 645, followed by the Taika Reform engineered by Imperial Prince Naka no Ōe (Emperor Tenchi after 668) and his advisor Nakatomi Kamatari (614–69). With respect to the issue of shrines and temples and their relation to political authority, the Taika Reform represented a major change: the government's Chinese-inspired technology of power, combined with both a thoroughly revamped set of institutions specialising in ritual and with Buddhist institutions, radically transformed Japanese concepts of ownership and techniques of fiscal management. Imperial territoriality was being formed, and I will follow Maurice Godelier in defining territory as 'the portion of nature and space that a society revendicates as that space where its members will permanently find the conditions of, and the material means for, their existence.'[1] Territory was also the object of representation, a representation that is clearly stated in the first official records of the imperial state, and which proposed that the universe was in part a 'visible' realm consisting of the material world, and, in another part, an 'invisible' realm consisting of 'forces' that suffused that material world. These latter forces were considered the most important and, thus, became the object of what today we would call 'symbolic behaviour,' namely, ritual.

One of the more significant developments of the one hundred and fifty years before the beginning of the Heian period (794–1185) was the creation of capital cities designed on a Chinese model.[2] This development was significant for four major reasons. First, it suggests that the state was conceived of in a radically different way than it had been prior to the Taika Reform. Second, it marks the formation of a centre vis-à-vis a periphery, and a new type of relationship between the imperial lineage and its surrounding houses and clans. Third, in the realm of ritual and liturgical organisation this signalled the fact that centralised ritual practices would play a strategic role in the formulation of the imperial state. And fourth, it meant that the economy changed. We have to linger here for a few moments and imagine some effects of the appearance of large, Chinese-style cities such as Naniwa, Fujiwara-kyō, Heijō-kyō (later named Nara), the short-lived Nagaoka-kyō, Heian-kyō (later named Kyoto), and others. First, an immense architectural effort symbolised by large palaces and monumental Buddhist temples displaying power and wealth of theretofore unimaginable scope.[3] Second, the creation of markets to sustain a growing urban population, but also the impoverishment of the lower segments of society who came to live on the margins of the cities. And last but not least, transformed social relations, increased interactions with Korea and China, and a new polity.

The Taika reformers conceived of the structure of their polity in terms of a separation of (and, at the same time, of an interdependence between) cultic and policy-making duties, the former being concerned with the invisible realm, and the latter, with the visible realm. Cultic duties were determined by the 'Office of the [rites dedicated to] the kami of Heaven and Earth', also referred to in English sources as the Bureau of Worship (*Jingi-kan*), while policy-making functions were to be discharged by the Bureau of State Affairs (*Dajō-kan*). The *Jingi-kan* determined ritual practice pertaining to the conduct of political affairs and of social matters within the court, and also functioned as an apparatus of control of the main sacerdotal houses of the time.[4] Of great importance is the fact that the *Jingi-kan* was thought to be above the purely policy-making organs of government; this does not mean that ritual matters took precedence over policy-making, but implies that ritual matters were central to the definition of the imperial state and of its social construct, and to the legitimation process of some decisions made by the government. If one looks at the rank of members of both sets of offices, however, it soon becomes evident that reality was at a variance with the official line: all members of the *Jingi-kan* had much lower ranks than those of the *Dajō-kan* (to put it in a nutshell: the Fujiwara 'political' house was always above the Nakatomi 'sacerdotal' house from which it had originated in 669 C.E.). This is not to say that ritual was unimportant: the social construct, the imperial state, and the policies made by that government were not only legitimised, but coloured by, and grounded in, ritual considerations. The rituals dedicated to the kami of Heaven and Earth served to reinforce the power structure which lay claim to the territory, especially since the kami of Heaven were related to the socio-cosmic construct of the imperial state and to its main houses, while the kami of Earth were related to other matters: as a general rule, few of the latter were the ancestral kami of the main aristocratic houses. In other words, the world of shrines dedicated to those kami portrayed in the imperial mythology (recorded in Kojiki, 712 and Nihon shoki, 720) as having an important role was intensely sociopolitical. The dominantly protocolar character of ritual in shrines seems to have been established, in part, in order to control rivalries, to manage jealousies, and to pacify people who had been hurt by the vast redistribution of power and the above-mentioned changes which followed the Taika coup d'état.

Here it is necessary to point out that Kamatari was a member of the Nakatomi sacerdotal lineage, which specialised in scapulimancy and had fairly close ties to the rulers by virtue of its techniques of prediction and purification rituals. A few years after the surname Fujiwara had been granted to Kamatari's descendants, it was stipulated that Nakatomi house members should retain their own surname and occupation, and the politically created Fujiwara house went on to specialise in governmental matters. Interestingly, the Fujiwara house remained concerned with ritual matters throughout its existence, and this has consequences for establishing a proper perspective on ritual and economy, ritual and kinship, and ritual and politics. Indeed, one might say that the Fujiwara house was a central force behind the formulation of the imperial state and of ritual; this view is supported by the following.

Fujiwara Fuhito (659–720), the elder of Nakatomi Kamatari's two sons,[5] ordered in 718 an amended version of the *Taihō ritsuryō* codes enacted in 702; known as *Yōrō ritsuryō*, these codes were enacted in 757. The sixth part (*hen*) of the codes contained the *Jingi-ryō*, 'Codes for [rites dedicated to] the kami of Heaven and Earth,' and consisted of twenty articles (*jō*) dealing with rites of a public character performed by members of the *Jingi-kan*. There were then nineteen such rites to be performed in the course of the year, and they took place at Ise and the ancient shrines of Ōmiwa, Hosoi, Izakawa, Hirose, and Tatsuta, all located in the Yamato region. These rites were 'official' or 'public' in the sense that they involved the participation of an imperial emissary, usually of the Nakatomi sacerdotal house, and were performed by sacerdotal officiants of the leading houses at the time: the Nakatomi, Inbe, Ō, and Urabe houses. Members of the bureaucracy of civil officials belonging to both the *Jingi-kan* and *Dajō-kan* were expected to participate (and received emoluments for their attendance) in the seven top national festivals: Toshigoi, Tsukinami, Kanname, Niiname, Kamo (all Middle Festivals); and Ōmi and Kaze-no-kami (Small Festivals) – while the officials of the *Jingi-kan* in charge of ritual conduct (*saikan*) were celebrating eleven lesser festivals in the presence of an Imperial Messenger.

About one hundred years later, Emperor Seiwa (a grandson of Fujiwara Yoshifusa, 804–72) was placed on the throne in 859 (Jōgan 1), and he ordered the compilation of new codes and regulations, some of which concerned the conduct of rituals in shrines sponsored by the court. Known as *Jōgan kyaku-shiki*, these codes were enacted in 869 and 871. They indicate an even greater formalisation of ritual procedures, and evidence a growing emphasis on hierarchy. More importantly, however, they reveal that the imperial state became responsible for rituals dedicated to kami that were enshrined in formerly private shrines; that is, there was an accelerating trend toward what Okada Shōji has called *kōsaika*, 'transformation [of private rituals] into state-sponsored rituals.'[6] Such ritual festivities came to be known as 'official rites' (*kansai*); among those, three rose to great prominence over time and were called 'ritual festivities requested by imperial order' (*chokusai*): Kasuga, Kamo, and Iwashimizu.[7]

Yet another hundred years later, in 967, the *Engi-shiki*, 'Procedures of the Engi Era,' were enacted almost forty years after their completion by Fujiwara Tokihira (871–909) and Fujiwara Tadahira (880–949) on order of Emperor

Daigo (whose mother was a Fujiwara). The *Engi-shiki* gives directions for 132 full-fledged *matsuri*, 410 Extraordinary Rites, and special directives for the Ise Shrine, the Consecrated Imperial Princess residing at Ise, the Princess Consecrated to the Kamo Shrine, and the imperial enthronement ritual named *Senso daijōsai* – all in all potentially as many as five hundred rites performed over the course of one year and all supervised by the *Jingi-kan* and paid for by 'the government.' At a minimum, about two hundred rituals had to be performed every year in shrines the *Jingi-kan* was said to supervise.[8]

It is clear that many if not most of the laws and regulations mentioned in the last forty books of the *Engi-shiki* were applied for only a short time, and that the majority died a slow death leading to the demise of the System of Codes in the mid to late Heian period. Some historians have characterised the *Engi-shiki* as a model for an unrealised utopia, while others have upheld it as a model of the ideal functioning of the ritualised state.[9] Others, however, point out that the regulations on ritual expenditure were so demanding that the system of imperial offerings soon collapsed in the context of famines or requests for weapons, and that this collapse forced the imperial state to limit its sponsorship to what later came to be called the Twenty-Two Shrines system, to which I will return below.[10] Morita Tei reveals that as early as 914, sacerdotal officiants of the *Jingi-kan* appropriated offered silk and weapons, drank all the rice wine, and sold the horses on the market as soon as they were taken out the imperial palace.[11] One reason advanced for this state of affairs is that the rituals had, in the minds of some, lost effectiveness because they had not originated in an urban environment and because of the growing power of Buddhism, which promised salvation and relief to people who could not be helped otherwise. Morita agrees with Kumagai that it was this situation that led the imperial state to focus on the Twenty-Two Shrines. While there is some truth to this statement, it does not explain why the Procedures of the Engi Era were subsequently enacted in 967, and concerned many more shrines.

Be that as it may, if one adds to the number of rituals prescribed by the Procedures of the Engi Era the number of rites performed for the state in Buddhist temples and sponsored by the government, we have thousands of ritual occasions. And if one adds to those the plethora of rites performed by individuals and groups not sponsored by the state, one conclusion becomes inescapable: Japan existed predominantly in a ritual mode. This apparently key feature of Japanese culture has been given scant attention by academics in the past, and this lack of attention may prevent an adequate understanding and characterisation of what that culture was. Some might wish to argue that ritual functions and policy-making functions were merged earlier on in Japanese culture; it is becoming clear, however, that these two functions, dependent on each other as they were conceived, merged further rather than separated in the course of the Heian period. As suggested earlier on in this discussion, a very large number of ritual functions originally ruled to be private matters became state matters. I have underlined this point in my study of Kasuga, but the matter needs further elaboration on the social conditions of the phenomenon.[12]

Furthermore, if one follows Sakurai Yoshirō's views, the state in the medieval period itself should be described as a ritual state (*girei kokka*).[13] There is therefore a need to suggest that other approaches to the study of ritual might be envisioned. Little has been done on the topic of the economic issues related to ritual performed in Japanese history, both as a matter of how much it cost, and as a purely theoretical issue. The following discussion does not claim to be exhaustive and will merely suggest possible avenues for future research. It will focus on the framework within which ritual was performed in Heian Japan: the institutional framework (government offices, shrines, temples); the political framework (ideology of the protection of the imperial state by associated shrines and temples); and the economic framework (regulations of offerings, lands, and theoretical issues). Statements concerning the social framework will be dispersed throughout the discussion.

The institutional framework

The 'Bureau of Yin and Yang' (Onmyō-ryō)

The Bureau of Yin and Yang was created under the Yōrō System of Codes in 718 by Fujiwara Fuhito and others.[14] Although it was conceived on the model of its counterpart established by the Tang dynasty, it was different in scope and partly different in structure. The Bureau was governed by a director under whom four administrators oversaw the activities of specialists in four major fields. The director himself was responsible for astronomy and the calendar, while he also observed and interpreted climatic phenomena. In the advent of any abnormalities (*i*) in the natural cycles, he reported secretly to the emperor. Under the four administrative aides to the director were six Masters of Yin and Yang (*onmyōji*) who specialised in divination (*uranai*) and in geomancy (*fūsui* – Ch. *fengshui*). The four major fields of investigation were, in descending order of importance: Yin and Yang, Calendar, Astronomy, and Time. Each of these fields was under the supervision of a scholar (*hakase*), who taught his skills to ten students in each of the first three fields, while two scholars taught twenty students in the field of time measurement. These two scholars were helped by twenty-three assistants. Murayama Shūichi notes that by the year 720 the Bureau of Yin and Yang employed a total of eighty-nine officers instructed by four scholars who were all either of Chinese or Korean origin, and who were all in their fifties. By comparison, the same bureau in China employed a grand total of 1,413 people whose functions were roughly divided between astronomy and the calendar on the one hand, and divination on the other. The pre-eminence of these fields was reversed in Japan. A final distinction between the Chinese and Japanese systems must be added: in Japan plastromancy was not assigned to the Bureau of Yin and Yang, but to the *Jingi-kan*, where it was performed by the Nakatomi and Urabe sacerdotal lineages.

Upon the occurrence of a baleful sign (*yō*), the masters of Yin and Yang decreed a number of taboos, restrictions, and restraints. Baleful signs came to be seen in each and every aspect of life; for instance, after a fire destroyed a large part of Kyoto, wearing red clothes was forbidden. From 960 onwards, the masters of Yin and Yang began to perform rites to placate calamitous forces; these were known as *kasai matsuri*, 'calamity rites,' and were related to the fire that had engulfed the imperial palace that year for the first time since the creation of the capital. This fire caused great anxiety among the aristocracy, and the government ordered that offerings be made immediately to Ise and other shrines, and that the fire be reported to the mausolea of Emperors Tenchi, Kanmu, and Daigo. The following year (961), the first *kasai matsuri* was held within the compounds of the imperial palace. Documents left by the Abe sacerdotal house indicate that the pillars of various buildings of the imperial palace were decorated with swords on which inscriptions were engraved. These inscriptions show that Taoism was an aspect of the protection of imperial buildings in Heian Japan. The Bureau continued to exist during the early Heian period, but did not develop because of the combined influences of Esoteric Buddhism, and of the 'Way of Lodgings and Planetoids' (*sukuyōdō*) and mountain asceticism (*shugendō*), in which various strains of Yin and Yang practices and notions (*onmyōdō*) evolved. For these and other reasons that are yet to be determined, the early Heian government did not support the activities of the Bureau of Yin and Yang; it was disbanded in 820. Instead, the government relied on both Shingon and Tendai esotericism to perform a number of rites which in earlier years would have been the domain of the *Onmyō-ryō*.

The ritual world of shrines

A salient feature of the world of shrines during the Heian period was the reformulation and codification of ritual practices under the aegis of the government and the dominant sacerdotal lineages. The Procedures of the Jōgan Era and the Procedures of the Engi Era unified these practices. These documents indicate that the 'worship of the kami of Heaven and Earth' was redefined during the Heian period according to specific notions held by the government. It must be noted that most shrines that came to be supported by the imperial state in Heian had been either maintained or built privately by the major social lineages and houses (*uji*), even though some (if not most) were subtle indicators of those lineages' claim to a privileged relationship to the imperial lineage and thereby to the imperial state. What changed during the Heian period was that the government, even while recognising the private character of those shrines, began to acknowledge them as its own symbols, and therefore made offerings of food and various products and in some cases set up government representatives to oversee the architectural development of shrines with funds provided by the state.

But before we discuss these shrines, it is best to address briefly the existence of Buddhist temples erected near the grounds of shrines, the *jingūji*. The *jingūji* were institutions symbolising early trends of non-exclusive attitudes toward autochthonous and imported creeds and practices, while they were at the same time institutions expressing the power of houses concerned with controlling cultic matters, such as the Fujiwara house. The Buddhist clergy administering those shrine-temples performed Buddhist rites in front of the kami, chanting Buddhist scriptures with the avowed goal of releasing the kami from their unenlightened state of being and guiding them toward the Buddhist goal of awakening. This was probably one of the strategies used by Buddhism to gain converts in remote areas, but it was also a strategy aimed at installing representatives of the government in distant places of cult. Indeed, government provisions concerning the number of monks that could be ordained by temples under government supervision stipulated that a certain number would specialise in shrines; they were called *shinbun dosha*, 'monks ordained for the worship of the kami.' The Heian period saw the creation of temples on the grounds of shrines on a massive scale, but the term *jingūji* tended to be abandoned. This suggests that the function of temples vis-à-vis shrines evolved toward increasing control (if not domination), as is shown by the system of imperium-sponsored shrines and temples called traditionally, though incorrectly, the 'Twenty-Two Shrines' (*nijūnisha*).

The Twenty-Two Shrines system[15]

The term *nijūnisha* indicates twenty-two shrines which became the object of imperial support during the first part of the Heian period, and thus became major symbols of the cultic system of the imperial state. By the middle of the ninth century, this system showed a trend toward the unification of ritual modes and the stabilisation of a government ideology concerning relations between shrines and temples. At the time of ritual performance, which followed the seasonal cycle overlaid with calendrical principles originating in India and China, the emperor or some of his representatives would participate in rites according to strict standards laid down by the government, make offerings the value of which was set forth in decrees, and provide economic support for the sites of cult. The appearance of that system heralded a significant step in the evolution of cultic and policy-making institutions and practices, as well as a major increase in state control. This evolution led to the systematic institutionalisation of the dominant Heian government ideology, namely, the 'protection of the imperial state (by shrine-temple multiplexes)' (*chingo kokka*), and the mutual support between the imperial state and the combined exoteric-esoteric system (*kenmitsu taisei*) of temples and shrines.

The shrines under consideration were located, for the most part, in the Kinai area (the five provinces immediately surrounding the capital), and most were included in the list of major shrines established by the *Engi-shiki* for the reason that they were related to the central lineages supporting the imperial house, or to other lineages of historical importance.[16] Those shrines included in the list of twenty-two but not in the *Engi-shiki* are sites of cult which gained popular significance thereafter, or which were created at the time to accommodate the court. The origins of the majority of these shrines go back to antiquity, when they already represented specific connections between cultic and sociopolitical concerns. It is those concerns that came to be expressed and reinforced by the creation of the system and its accompanying representation.

The process of quasi-unification of these shrines may have begun at the onset of the Heian period for, when the list appears for the first time in documents in 966, sixteen shrines were included that had long been the object of imperial offerings. These were separated into an Upper Group of seven shrines, a Middle Group of seven, and a Lower Group of two to which were added three shrines in 991, one in 994, and three in 1039. The list is as follows:

Upper Group
Ise, Iwashimizu, Kamo, Matsuno'o, Hirano, Inari, Kasuga

Middle Group
Ōharano, Ōmiwa, Isonokami, Yamato, Hirose, Tatsuta, Sumiyoshi

Lower Group
Hie, Umenomiya, Yoshida, Hirota, Gion, Kitano, Nibunokawakami, Kibune

The organisation of the twenty-two shrines into three groups exhibits two rationales: one geopolitical, and one political. In the first case, five of the first seven shrines are located in the province of Yamashiro, where the capital Heian-kyō is located; the two other shrines are Ise (in Ise Province) and Kasuga (in Yamato Province), dedicated respectively to the ancestral and tutelary kami of the imperial lineage and of the Fujiwara house. The second seven shrines are located in the Yamato region, with the exception of the Ōharano and Sumiyoshi Shrines; the Ōharano Shrine (in Yamashiro Province) is the Kasuga Shrine that had been duplicated in the Nagaoka capital, while the Sumiyoshi Shrine (in Settsu Province) was directly related to imperial mythology and imperial enthronement ceremonies, particularly during the Heian period. The last group of eight shrines is located in the Kinai provinces and specialised in placating droughts or various noxious forces that made themselves evident during the period. In other words, the first group is close to the capital, the second group represents the past history of the lineages in Yamato, and the third group represents a larger concern with the periphery.

In the case of political rationale, it must be pointed out that the Fujiwara house made sure that its major shrines would be represented in the three classes of shrines: Kasuga in the first, Ōharano in the second, and Yoshida (the Kasuga Shrine of Kyoto), in the third. This indicates that the Fujiwara house emphasised its presence at the three levels of organisation. Equally important is the often ignored fact that these Twenty-Two Shrines were associated with

Buddhist temples located on or near their precincts. By the middle of the Heian period the Twenty-Two 'Shrines' had become major shrine-temple multiplexes (*jisha*), consisting of complex combinations and interactions between autochthonous (or foreign) kami and imported buddhas and bodhisattvas, between sacerdotal lineages in the shrines and Buddhist lineages in the temples, between administrative and economic structures of the two types of institutions, and between modes of cult, all under the aegis of the state. Many of the shrines and temples had been created by the Fujiwara house, or were restored by members of this house during the Heian period. This indicates that the Fujiwara house consolidated its grip over the country in part through the formation and administration of shrine-temple multiplexes to which the imperial house made offerings, and from which it requested the performance of sumptuous rites for the protection of the realm under its governance. At the time of the Jōwa Incident of 842, in which the Fujiwara house began to assert its centrality in decisions concerning the choice of emperors, the government requested the performance of rituals by one hundred Buddhist monks within the imperial palace, and asked them to read the Sutra of the Buddha of Medicine, to perform rites dedicated to that Buddha, and further requested readings of the *Daihannya-kyō* within the imperial palace. The Jōwa Incident was the first in a series of coups engineered over a period of one hundred years by the Fujiwara house to ensure that emperors would be chosen exclusively from among children born of a union between a reigning emperor and a woman of Fujiwara birth. This enabled the Fujiwara ministers to govern in the name of their grandchildren and thus control the imperial lineage. Cultic activity was an essential feature of their claim to legitimacy in that context, and this point is symbolised by the Fujiwara creation of the Iwashimizu multiplex founded to protect Emperor Seiwa, who ascended the throne in 859.

The soon dominant modality of relationship between cultic and policy issues, which took the name of mutual support between these institutions and the imperial state (*ōbō buppō*), was thus institutionalised in a system (*taisei*) of non-Buddhist shrines and Buddhist temples of exoteric (*ken*) and esoteric (*mitsu*) Buddhism (that is, *kenmitsu taisei*).[17]

The political framework

The *Nihon shoki* could not have put it more succinctly:

> 'Let the public matters which thou hast charge of be conducted by my grandchild, and do thou rule divine affairs. . . . Let the August Grandchild direct the public affairs of which I have the charge. I will retire and direct secret matters.'[18]

These lines have been interpreted to mean that the realm of the visible (public affairs), together with the realm of the invisible (ritual matters) formed the basic structure of the polity and governed the relations that obtained between political and sacerdotal functions. The realm of the invisible, which preceded in cosmogony the appearance of visible forms, was thought superior, and that is the reason why the *Jingi-kan* was set above the *Dajō-kan*. As we have seen, however, reality was the reverse in terms of actual behaviour and ranks, thus leading to fundamental ambiguities and tensions between these two basic social functions, and between those and the economic function. Claims to legitimacy to govern the realm of public matters needed grounding in the realm of the invisible, but precisely because of its fundamental opacity, the latter could only be hinted at through exceedingly visual means: ritual within a specific space and time, and economic exchange (food offerings, gifts, phonetic formulas). There is no ritual without these prerequisites. The *Kojiki* and *Nihon shoki*, therefore, indicate the structure of the imperial state and its main functions, and thus pay a great amount of attention to social matters, which they surrounded with much ritual display.

With regard to the new conception of the state, the compilation of the *Kojiki* and *Nihon shoki* fixed the myths and symbols which became central to the definition and the legitimation of the state. With regard to the new relationship between centre and periphery, the creation of [Buddhist] temples and the erection of [Shinto] shrines in the capital as well as in the provinces show a new type of institutional organisation and cultic emphasis. Their establishment reveals the delineation of geopolitical spheres of influence and an attempt to unify ritual and liturgical notions and practices. The appearance of those texts and institutions expresses forcefully that the cults dedicated to the kami of Heaven and Earth were being unified at the level of the imperial state. The need for such unification might be explained according to the following three hypotheses. First, in maintaining a single realm of symbols, ritual, and protocol, the state was hoping to institutionalise its control over houses and lineages surrounding the imperial family. Second, the control over shrines was accompanied by an equal increase of control over Buddhist temples. And third, there arose a need to ground the definition and legitimacy of the centralised state in a symbolic and ritual realm pertaining to both shrines and temples.

The Buddhist realm

Many of the most important temples of the Nara period (710–94) were dedicated to the welfare of the spirits of departed leaders of the main lineages, while a number of shrines were dedicated to the ancestral and tutelary kami of the very same lineages. Concerned perhaps that the private character of these institutions might lead to an excessive fragmentation of society, the government transformed many such temples into imperium-sponsored operations, and, as we have seen, gave a new and unified structure to the cults in the main shrines to ensure that they were directed toward the imperial state rather than toward private interest. Ritual and liturgical practices of the

Heian period are thus marked by the creation or enlargement of shrines and temples supported by the government, by the codification of rituals performed therein, by the emergence of new schools of Buddhism, by the appearance of a pre-eminence of practice over theory, and by the associations of kami to buddhas and bodhisattvas worshipped in adjacent Buddhist temples. The gradual association of some temples to shrines seems to have been related to the formulation of the protection of the imperial state (*chingo kokka*), and to the creation of the ideology of mutual support between the imperial state and Buddhism (*ōbō buppō*). These features will be analysed below via a discussion of the ideology of protection of the imperial state through ritual.

Chingo kokka theories and practices

In its narrow meaning the term *kokka* refers to the imperial lineage and supporting houses (*ka*) which govern the realm of the country (*koku*); in its larger meaning, however, it denotes the imperial state at large, with an emphasis on its geopolitical domain or territory. As such, the phrase *chingo kokka* refers to a government ideology legitimated by rituals performed by both sacerdotal lineages in specific shrines and Buddhist lineages in specific temples, in the name of the imperial lineage and its satellite households, particularly the Fujiwara. The term is of Sino-Japanese origin, but the concept of protection of a state was also present in Buddhism in India. It was developed to a great extent in China (one of the scriptures on which Buddhism relied for those rituals, the *Ninnō-kyō*, is actually an apocryph conceived in China),[19] and from there made its way into Japanese theory and practice.

Starting in the late tenth century, shrine-temple multiplexes came to be governed by aristocracy-born ecclesiasts (the so-called *monzeki* temples governed by *kishu*, 'noble seeds,' from main lineages, and by *ryōke*, 'members of good households' of lesser aristocratic birth).[20] This means that these multiplexes represented house-oriented private interests, even when their public rhetoric was geared to the state. This was one way in which the principle of a tight relation between political authority and kinship ties resisted the trend toward state control mentioned by Okada Shōji. A second reason why this trend stalled is connected with the decline of the System of Codes during the second half of the Heian period: shrine-temple multiplexes garnered vast land estates free from taxation, and thus developed into major economic and ideological units which, by the end of the Heian period, came into conflict with the imperial state, with warrior houses, and with each other. Indeed, during the period a few emperors attempted to curb the growing political, economic, and military power of these sites of cult, but the private interests of specific sites of cult overrode any other interest. As a result, violent conflict erupted even between multiplexes which should have been unified at least at the doctrinal level, and was also directed against decisions of the state the multiplexes wished to protest against.[21] It took centuries for the warrior governments of later ages to control the military and economic power of these institutions.

Buddhist rituals

Saichō (767–822) and Kūkai (774–835) introduced to Japan new rituals for the protection of the imperial state. During his stay in China Saichō had learned a number of rites to this effect, but the full-fledged development and performance of rituals by the Tendai lineage did not occur until Saichō's disciples Ennin (794–864) and Enchin (814–91) returned from China with the latest developments in the field, and thoroughly transformed Tendai into an esoteric ritual tradition geared to the protection of the imperial state.[22]

When Kūkai returned from China in 806, his expertise was immediately sought by the government. He set to the task of reproducing mandalas and altars for protective rituals and performed initiatory unctions (kanjō), allowing monks and aristocrats alike to be participants in the esoteric doctrine and the rituals connected to it. The government requested in 816 that he build an Initiation Hall within the compounds of the Tōdaiji in Nara for the protection of the imperial state. In 834, one year before his death, Kūkai saw to it that a special building designed for the performance of those rites was built within the imperial palace. That is the Shingon-in, in which Shingon's major rite for the protection for the imperial house, the goshichinichi no mishihō, was performed during the second week of the first month. The first ritual Kūkai performed for the protection of the imperial state was in 810, the year after the rebellion of Fujiwara Kusuko (fl. 810) which signalled the decline of the Shiki branch and the surge to power of the Northern branch of the Fujiwara house. Kūkai obviously sided with the Northern branch, since it is reported that he performed in 814 the rituals for the opening of the Nan'en-dō at the Kōfukuji in Nara, which remained for centuries one of the salient symbols of the dominance of the Northern branch of the Fujiwara house. In a document asking for permission to perform this ritual, Kūkai stated that past rituals for the protection of the imperial state had emphasised the chanting of scriptures; but he stressed that rituals would be far more effective if they were based on esoteric doctrine and on the adequate formulation of potent formulas and charms (darani). The scriptures used for those rituals were already used during the Nara period: they were the Konkōmyō-kyō,[23] the Daihannya-kyō,[24] and the Kongōhannya-kyō,[25] on which Kūkai wrote several interpretive documents (kaidai).[26] In the time of Kūkai, aristocrats requested the performance of those rituals for themselves or members of their family. Several such requests are mentioned in Kūkai's works, accompanied by the petitions he wrote for those rites.[27] Another trend, known as 'day chanting of scriptures, and evening rites of penitence,' surfaces as early as 833 in court orders to perform such rites against epidemics, and in 834 against threats to crops. In both cases the court ordered that various temples dedicate three days to readings of the

Kongōhannya-kyō, and three evenings to rites of penitence. The rites of penitence in question were those associated with the scriptures dedicated to the Buddha of Medicine, and were known as *Yakushi keka*. By the second half of the ninth century, however, the evening sessions tended to be devoted to the recitation of charms and spells dedicated to the Buddha of Medicine or to the Bodhisattva of Compassion, and were followed by the recitation of mantras known as *kōmyō shingon* and *Shaka butsugen shingon*.

Beyond those rites, Esoteric Buddhism initiated the performance of specific rites dedicated to individual members of the pantheon. Among these were two major rites for the protection of the imperial state, performed in competition by Shingon and Tendai. The major Shingon rite was *Daigen(sui)-hō* 大元(帥)法, and the main Tendai ritual performed over the centuries for the protection of the imperial state was *Shijōkō-hō* 熾盛光法. In 850 the Shingon monk Jōkyō (fl. 866) requested that the rite be performed by fifteen monks, as in the case of the other main Shingon ritual performed in the Shingon-in, the *goshichinichi no mishiho* created by Kūkai in 834. The Daigensui ritual was performed in the imperial palace every year, with even more regularity than the *mishiho*, but it was abandoned in early Meiji.[28] Various Shingon lineages also specialised in the performance of rainmaking rituals. Rituals performed to cause rain to fall were important matters of state directly related to the emperor, and were requested from both shrines and temples. The *Engi-shiki*, for instance, mentions the existence of as many as forty-nine shrines specialising in such rituals in the Kinai area alone. On the Buddhist side, Shingon specialised in the performance of such rituals, but there are few records showing that Tendai monks performed them. Two major types of 'Buddhist' rain rituals existed during the Heian period: the *Kujaku-hō* ('ritual of the Peacock'),[29] which became the speciality of the Hirosawa branch of Shingon, and the *Shōukyō-hō* 請雨経法 (based on the scripture of the same name),[30] in which the Ono branch of Shingon specialised.

On the Tendai side, Ennin went to China in 838, stayed for nine years, and brought back a number of rituals, the most important of which was the *Shijōkō-hō*, which became the central Tendai rite for the protection of the imperial state. The word Shijōkō, which means 'radiance of a vivid fire,' is the name of one of several personified emanations springing from the cranial protuberance of the Buddha.[31] Ennin's first performance of the ritual took place either in 849 or 850 on Mt. Hiei. Its principal object was the annihilation of natural catastrophes, but it came to be associated with the emperor in a direct way, and was requested by the government whenever military danger faced the court. From that point on the court looked to the shrine-temple multiplexes it sponsored for Tendai or Shingon Esoteric Buddhist rituals; by the tenth century it was also asking for help from thaumaturgists who had trained in mountain areas in order to gain supernatural forces and who were reputed for the efficacy of their rites and incantations. One began to see an increasing number of mountain ascetics (*yamabushi*) at court.

The privatisation of ritual activity

The position of the emperor declined while the power of the Fujiwara house grew. By the tenth century, as government came under the control of Fujiwara regents, rituals that had been performed in the name of the emperor came to be requested by aristocrats for their own welfare. After the exile of Sugawara Michizane in 901 the government forbad the performance of such rituals for private purposes, but the practice resurfaced with increased vigour, perhaps in connection with the disintegration of the social system based on the Codes and the emergence of private concerns and individual competition within given houses. The most widely performed rituals at an individual level for the aristocrats were the *Fugen enmyō-hō*, a ritual for enhanced longevity dedicated to the bodhisattva Samantabhadra,[32] and the *Fudō-hō* ('ritual of Acala'), performed in a wide variety of contexts.[33] The Fudō-hō was even more widely appropriated by the nobility since it required less lengthy preparations. It seems that Fujiwara Tokihira was the first to request its performance to cure a personal disease, and then to ensure the safe birth of one of his children in 903. Yet another rite of importance throughout the Heian period at state and personal level was the *Daiitoku-hō*, dedicated to Yamāntaka.[34]

The economic framework

Even a cursory reading of the *Engi-shiki* impresses upon the reader the fundamental features of ritual in shrines during the Heian period: the performance of codified behaviour focusing on a specific relationship to a divine entity by a strictly defined social body, within the confines of particular spatial arrangements and at strictly defined times of the year, month, and day. This relationship was expressed by purification and by various offerings, among which the offering and sharing of food took precedence. A second striking characteristic concerns the strict regulation of expenditures by the government at the time of ritual observances. This suggests that private houses were probably competing in prestige through outlays of wealth, ranging from amounts of rice offerings to ceremonial clothing and horses. There are grounds for thinking that private gifts sometimes reached astronomical figures. This competition was brought under control by the stipulations of the *Engi-shiki*, but it returned to the fore when the government began to commend land to centres of cult as a reward for success in rituals. Furthermore, since many of these landholdings were partly free from taxation, a number of people began to commend parts of their land to centres of cult 'for spiritual protection' – that is, in order to avoid taxation. Land was commended to specific shrines and/or temples, not to 'Shinto' or to 'Buddhism.' Hence, ritual came to be ever more connected to economics: the maintenance of the realm of the invisible required much visible, material stuff, and just as much work.

The amounts of offerings stipulated by the regulations contained in the *Engi-shiki* stagger the imagination. They were products from the land and the sea, foodstuffs, cloth, paper, metals, and various other man-made objects such as bows, arrows, spears, swords, quivers, and so forth. They involved several networks of producers located in various provinces, from which certain products were required as both direct and extraordinary tax payments.

In order to form an idea of the scope of economic outlay required by rituals performed in the name of the imperial state, it will suffice to take the example of the first *matsuri* listed in the *Engi-shiki*, Toshigoi, which was held annually on the fourth day of the second month and was one among the Festivals of the Four seasons originally based on the *Jingi-ryō* of the eighth century. The Toshigoi *matsuri* was dedicated to the 3,132 kami listed in the *Engi-shiki* and was performed in the *Jingi-kan* in the presence of a host of officials, as well as in the provinces under supervision of the governors. Of these 3,132 kami, 492 were ranked as major kami (304 worshipped by the central government with offerings on top of offering-tables, and 188 by provincial governments), while 2,640 were minor kami (433 worshipped by the central government with presentations on mats on the ground, and 2,207 worshipped by the provincial governments). The *Jingi-kan* alone thus made offerings to 737 kami, of which 30 were enshrined in the Imperial Palace, 3 within the capital, 53 in Yamashiro, 128 in Yamato, 23 in Kawachi, 1 in Izumi, 26 in Settsu, 14 in Ise, 1 in Izu, 1 in Musashi, 1 in Awa, 1 in Shimōsa, 1 in Hitachi, 5 in Ōmi, 1 in Wakasa, 1 in Tango, 3 in Harima, 1 in Aki, 8 in Kii, and 2 in Awa.

The breakdown of offerings is as follows. Each of 198 shrines was offered:

Five *shaku* of pongee, 1 *shaku* each of 5 five colours of thin pongee, 1 *shaku* of coloured hemp-cloth, 2 *ryō* of bark-cloth, 5 *ryō* of hemp, 1 *jō* and 4 *shaku* of tax cloth, a sword case of pongee (3 *sun* of pongee), a sword case of common cloth (3 *sun* of cloth), 1 *yokura-oki* offering table, 1 *yakura-oki* offering table, 1 shield, 1 spearhead, 1 bow, 1 quiver, a pair of deer antlers, one mattock, 4 *shō* of sake, 5 *ryō* of abalone, 5 *ryō* of bonito, 2 *shō* of dried meat, 6 *ryō* of wakame seaweed, 6 *ryō* of *arame* and other assorted seaweeds, 1 *shō* of salt, 1 wine-jar of sake, 5 *shaku* of leaf-matting for wrapping.

There were also 106 presentations of the following items:

Five *shaku* of pongee, 1 *shaku* each of five colours of thin pongee, 2 *ryō* of bark-cloth, 5 *ryō* of hemp, 1 sword case of coloured hemp cloth, 1 sword case of pongee (3 *sun* of pongee), 1 sword case of ordinary cloth (3 *sun* of cloth), 1 *yokura-oki*, 1 *yakura-oki*, 1 shield, 1 spearhead, 5 *shaku* of leaf-matting for wrapping.

Furthermore, each of 375 shrines received:

3 *shaku* of pongee, 2 *ryō* of bark-cloth, 5 *ryō* of hemp, 1 *yokura-oki*, 1 *yakura-oki*, 1 shield, 1 spearhead, 1 *jō* and 4 *shaku* of tax-cloth, 3 *shaku* of leaf-matting for wrapping.

Also, for 65 of the presentations 1 mattock and 1 quiver were offered; for 28 presentations, 1 additional mattock was offered; for 3 presentations, 1 quiver was offered, and for 58 presentations, 3 *shaku* of pongee, 2 *ryō* of bark-cloth, 5 *ryō* of hemp, 1 yokura-oki, 1 *yakura-oki*, 1 shield, 1 spearhead, and 3 *shaku* of leaf-matting for wrapping were offered. These preparations and offerings were to be reported to the *Jingi-kan*.

The total is thus as follows:

Pongee	1,810.96 yards [both plain and dyed]
Hemp-cloth	95.21 yards [both plain and dyed]
Bark-cloth	14, 998.83 yards [yū]
Hemp	75, 510.32 yards
Tax-cloth	3,321.87 yards [primarily of hemp, by simple collection]
Common cloth	39.45 yards
Yokura-oki	737 stands [offering tables, 1 shaku 2 sun high, made of 4 pieces of wood]
Yakura-oki	737 stands [offering tables, 2 shaku 4 sun high, made of 8 pieces of wood]
Shields	737 items
Spearheads	737 items
Bows	198 items
Quivers	266 items
Deer antlers	198 pairs
Mattocks	291 items
Sake	316.8 gallons
Sake jars	198
Abalone	81.675 lbs.
Bonito	81.675 lbs.
Dried meat	158.4 gallons [from deer or other animals]
Wakame seaweed	98.01 lbs.
Arame seaweed	98.01 lbs. [and other assorted seaweeds]
Salt	79.2 gallons
Leaf-matting	1,168 yards [for wrapping].

In addition, 24 horses were offered, one each at the Ise and Watarai Shrines, one at Mitoshi Shrine, two at the Hall of Eight Deities (*Hasshinden*) of the *Jingi-kan*, and one each at the following water shrines: Amakashi, Asuka, Iware, Osaka, Hase, Yoshino, Kose, Kamo, Taima, Ōsaka, Ikoma, Tsuke, Yagyū (all of the *yama-no-kuchi* type), and to Yoshino, Uda, Katsuragi, and Tsuge (Chikkei), these last four being of the *mikumari* type.[35]

That is not all. In the case of the Provincial Governments, ritual presentations were made to 2,395 kami, broken down as follows: 188 major kami (33 in the Tōkaidō Region, 38 in Tōsandō, 13 in Hokurikudō, 36 in San'indō, 12 in San'yōdō, 19 in Nankaidō, and 38 in Saikaidō) received a combined total of 2,824 yards of silk thread and 2,824 yards of floss silk. The remaining 2,207 minor kami (680 enshrined in the Tōkaidō, 340 in Tōsandō, 338 in Hokurikudō, 523 in San'indō, 124 in San'yōdō, 134 in Nankaidō, and 69 in Saikaidō) received a combined total of 22,100 yards of silk thread and 22,100 yards of silk floss, for a grand total of about 50,000 yards of silk thread and floss. In addition, twice a year in relation to this Toshigoi *matsuri*, the thunder kami of Sōnami in Yamato received the following: 42 yards of pongee, 2 skeins of silk thread, 26 oz. of floss silk, 2.5 yards each of five colours of thin pongee, 1.65 yards of coloured hemp-cloth, c. 30 yards of tribute cloth, c. 30 yards of tax cloth, 2.64 lbs. each of bark cloth and hemp, 4 mattocks, 2.5 bushels of rice, 8 gals. of glutinous rice, 4 gals. each of soybeans and red beans, 8 gals. of sake, 40 bundles of rice-in-ear, 5 lbs. each of abalone, bonito and assorted dried meat, 5 salmon, 8 gals. assorted sushi, 5 lbs. of *wakame*, 5 lbs. assorted seaweeds, 5 lbs. of salt, money for purchase of fruit (amount according to season), 2 white-wood boxes, 4 cypress-wood boxes, 1 high table, 2 earthenware jugs, 4 cooking-pots, 20 uncovered dishes, 4 gourds, 1 bale of oak wood, 4 straw-mats, 6 food-mats, one palanquin (foregoing required for the *matsuri*); 30 yards of tax cloth, 2.5 lbs. each of bark-cloth and hemp, 4 mattocks, 4 gals. of dried meat, 15 lbs. of *wakame*, 15 lbs. assorted seaweeds, 1.6 gals, of salt, 2 earthenware bottles, 5 saucers, 2 seat-mats, 1 palanquin (foregoing required for the purification).

For the ritual, a tunic of the colour assigned to the rank of the Nakatomi sacerdotal officiant charged with making the offerings, as well as 18 yards of dark-blue pongee and 17 yards of green silk for the lining were to be prepared. Furthermore, the sacerdotal officiants participating in all rites mentioned above were provided with clothing and ceremonial robes, hats, shoes, and daily allotments in the form of rice, sake, sushi, abalone, squid, bonito, salt, and seaweed, in amounts varying with their ranks.

It is not possible to have an exact sense of the overall tally of emoluments, allotments, and offerings, or of the number of officials, officiants, potters, weavers, farmers, fishermen, hunters, and other artisans who were involved in this one specific *matsuri*, but it should be clear by now that the enterprise was of a very large scale and involved a considerable geographical area and a vast number of man-hours, all geared to final ritual performances that may have lasted just a few hours. The avowed purpose of it all? The Toshigoi *matsuri* was held to avoid natural calamities and to call in a year of abundant crops. All the kami invoked in these rites performed all over the country were, indeed, related to the food production process: rice production, water amount and quality, thunder kami related to rain, noxious influences and disease-causing agents.

The economy of expiation and purification

The *Engi-shiki* regulated and re-formulated rituals of exclusion and purification with a long and interesting history. Two are of some significance for a consideration of economic principles: the ōharae ('great purification') rites and the *michi-ae* ('crossroads') rites and formulas. Perhaps the most famous case in Japanese mythology is that of Susanowo no Mikoto, brother of the ancestral deity of the imperial line, who was expelled from Takama-ga-hara for having broken a number of taboos. Susanowo's beard, hair, and nails were cut (or pulled), he was required to provide one thousand tables loaded with gifts, and he was then expelled, with those as symbols of expiation (*harae-tsu-mono*). Now, *Nihon shoki* states that in the fifth month of 667, expiatory offerings consisted of horses, cloth, swords, deer hide, mattocks, short swords, sickles, arrows, rice ears, and hemp. However, in an edict of the seventh month of the same year, the expiatory offering is stipulated to be 'one slave,' onto which the transgressions of the populace were attached; the slave was then expelled, and put to death.[36] The expulsion of slaves (or quasi-outcasts) is also attested in 809, in a case in which a slave was exiled to Tsushima Islands in the place of somebody else accused of a transgression.[37] While *Engi-shiki* does mention the offering of slaves in other instances, the text stipulates that in the case of the Ritual of Great Purification to be held on the last day of the sixth and the twelfth months 'gilt and silvered effigies' were to be prepared. It is thought that these effigies came to replace the slaves; the puppet-like entities were then subjected to projection of all transgressions, and taken by members of the Urabe sacerdotal lineage to rivers into which they were cast.

This ritual brings to mind the Greek ritual involving the pharmakoi. In this respect Jacques Derrida wrote:

The character of the pharmakos has been compared to a scapegoat. The evil and the outside, the expulsion of evil, its exclusion out of the body (and out) of the city – these are the two major senses of the character and of the ritual.

Harpocration, commenting on the word pharmakos, describes them thus: 'At Athens they led out two men to be purifications for the city; it was at the Thargelia, one was for the men and the other for the women.' In general, the pharmakoi were put to death. But that, it seems, was not the essential end of the operation. Death occurred most often as a secondary effect of an energetic fustigation. Aimed first at the genital organs. Once the pharmakoi were cut off from the space of the city, the blows were designed to chase away or draw out the evil from their bodies. . . . 'Finally, they burnt [them] with fire with the wood of wild trees and scattered the ashes into the sea and to the winds, for a purification.' . . .

The ceremony of the pharmakos is thus played out on the boundary line between inside and outside, which it has as its function ceaselessly to trace and retrace. . . . These expulsions took place at critical moments (drought, plague, famine). Decision was then repeated. But the mastery of the critical instance requires that surprise be prepared for: by rules, by law, by the regularity of repetition, by fixing the date.[38]

The critical issue with respect of the relation between these matters and economics is the need for expiatory offerings or gifts. This problem concerning a sort of restitution is too considerable to be treated in this paper, and I will simply refer the reader to Derrida's notes on the Indo-European words surrounding 'gift' (present, poison, marriage) in connection to his analysis of the pharmakos. A further point of comparison between Derrida's analysis and the rituals of expiation, expulsion, and purification in classical Japan is the fact that Susanowo became the central figure of the Gion cult, dedicated to placating the entities responsible for epidemics. This cult, best known today for what is actually a 'cleaned-up' and miniaturised version of the Gion Festival, was a major phenomenon of the Heian period and was sponsored by the imperial state. Furthermore, it is clear that there is a certain kind of link between expiation and propitiation, of the same kind as between insider and outsider, purity and pollution, and so forth: these oppositions tirelessly retrace boundaries invisible to the naked eye, and the rituals tirelessly intimate a correlation (an equivalence?) between transgression and value. In other words, value is set by law, which itself depends on transgression and a certain type of rationality that determines equivalencies and subsequent modalities of exchanges. And I suspect that such is the rationality that is embedded in the institutions of the government and ritual, and that this rationality determined the equivalence between the price of a slave and that of gold and silver effigies, and of wooden effigies that were fabricated by the Imperial Bureau of Carpentry according to precise regulations set forth in chapter 34 of the *Engi-shiki*. A small price to pay for a magical pharmacy.

Sinologists will no doubt recognise here continental elements; attention has been drawn in the past to the Buddhist and Taoist components of these rituals, and to Korean components. One of these elements that needs underlining is that the formulas of purification set forth in the *Jingi-ryō* were to be uttered or chanted in Chinese; another is that the gold and silver effigies were called *rokujin* 禄人 (as I believe they were called in China), and that they were first presented to the emperor, together with gilt swords, while chanting formulas wishing for a prosperous and longlasting reign. Practices based on Yin and Yang notions infiltrated the ritual world of shrines as well, but particularly so in the evolution of practices of purification. The Nakatomi, Urabe, Abe, and Kamo sacerdotal houses were responsible for these rituals, intended to protect the body, the imperial city, and the country against epidemics. An excellent example is provided by the *michi-ae* rites, of which we have some record in the *Engi-shiki*.[39] These rites were performed at crossroads and at the various entrances to the capital at the time of epidemics, but in particular also at the time of the approach of foreign missions. These *michi-ae* rites consisted in offering food and in formulating incantations, probably of Chinese origin.

A notable characteristic of ritual in Heian was the emphasis on hierarchy and code, and on the observance of protocol. This emphasis can be understood from two related perspectives: a sociological concern and a concern with purity and pollution. In the case of the neighbouring temples, although Buddhism was not geared toward the exclusion of any member of the social body (with the significant exception of the almost systematic exclusion of women), in fact the higher echelons of the priestly hierarchy came to be reserved for leading ecclesiasts born from those noble lineages which had dedicated or created the temples in the first place. Thus, principles of exclusion tended to remain important aspects of the social construct of the time.

Temples and shrines as economic power-blocks

A dominant feature of economics with regard to ritual activity during the Heian period must have been the appearance of land estates (*shōen*). According to the letter of the System of the Codes, the emperor was the only person to claim ownership of the land, and the capital cities acted as immense 'black holes' that engulfed the products of the nation. The roads were constantly carrying taxes, produce, and various products that filled the storehouses and granaries of the court, as well as the major markets. This type of relation between the centre and the periphery could not last long, and very soon after the beginning of the Heian period aristocrats, shrines, and temples began to receive control over pieces of land, either already cultivated, or for development. In the case of shrines and temples, which played a major role in the development of arable land, the estates were partly tax-free. Soon, these institutions began to behave as though they were the owners, and created their own economic systems: production systems, distribution systems, and storage as well as retail systems. As a consequence, the economy of the state was de-centralised, one might say, and the unified economic arrangement laid out in System of the Codes simply fell apart and was replaced by various local networks related to the *shōen*. It seems that a majority of the estates that were commended by the emperor or aristocrats to shrines specialised in the production of food, and that estates commended to temples generally specialised in other products. If one looks at the original production sites of the huge amounts of food products required for rituals sponsored by the imperial state, it is clear that they were often related to shrines, while the estates of temples provided both natural and man-made materials, and quickly managed to control guilds of producers and artisans in a way that most shrines did not. Furthermore, I am not aware of a single shrine's involvement in loans during the Heian period, but many temples did have offices of change and loans at high interest.

In the slowly evolving system of combined shrines and temples, the temples had the upper hand in almost all respects, from basic economic resources to the appointment and control of sacerdotal officiants. By the late Heian period the shrine-temples complexes were the largest land-owners in the country and represented a formidable economic and political power, which they protected through the creation of local guards and armed militias, even against the central government. Indeed, not only were their estates free of most taxation, they actually were granted (or sometimes took) the right to deny entry to their estates to the representatives of the government (*funyū-ken*), and they charged a fee to whomever had to pass through their domains. The *Heihanki* thus complained in 1158: 'The Province of Yamato has become the possession of the Kasuga Shrine and the Kōfukuji: not one single square foot of public fields is left in the Province.' Another good example is provided by the sacred perimeter (*kekkai*) of Mount Hiko in Kyushu: granted by Emperor Go-Shirakawa in 1181, it was 7 ri (c. 17 miles) on each side, was entirely tax-free, legally free from any official ingerence, and even served as an asylum for people sought by the state; it ultimately evolved into a thoroughly independent entity. Yet another example will make enough of a point: Mount Hiei was one of the most powerful shrine-temple complexes during the Heian period, and its military might sent shudders down the spine of aristocrats; its complex of shrines and temples (as noted above, the shrines were sponsored by the imperial state as one of its twenty-two sites of cult) covered the mountain and its foot, and its roads and paths were probably constantly busy with bulls, horses and men carrying to the temples the wealth issued from the many estates the complex owned in various parts of the country. A city eventually arose at its eastern foot (Sakamoto) and became quite wealthy.[40]

Now, what kind of ideology would make this possible? A short detour through hell might provide the beginning of an answer. Inoue Mitsusada quotes *Konjaku monogatari* (early twelfth century) and other documents to show how the fear of hell was widespread in the popular world of the late Heian period.[41] However, this fear to fall into hell did not arise spontaneously among the populace, but was spread by *hijiri* (itinerant ascetics) and temple shōen-holders. These taught that hunting and fishing were activities causing one to fall into hell, and that one should instead devote oneself to the practice of good (*jiriki sazen*). Thus, as Fabio Rambelli would say, hell was an ideological instrument for social control: it was used to force people to work within the shōen and not outside in competing productive activities, and thus ensured that they would 'give' their labour to capitals or temples.[42]

Taira Masayuki makes a similar point when he writes that precepts against the taking of life (*sesshō*) determined fall into hell, and hindered productive activities.[43] Not only hunting or fishing, but also tilling the soil (killing of insects), cutting trees to make firewood, growing silkworms, or engaging in the activities of a samurai led to such a destiny. The precepts were thus interpreted to be closely related to the social organisation and economic relationships within the shōen: the fish caught was offered to the deities (or at least brought to temples or shrines), and fishing was thus transformed into a salvational activity; in the same way, activities deemed 'dangerous' to personal salvation, if performed for a temple (or with the sponsorship of a temple), acquired a highly meritorious value because they involved the protection of Buddhism and therefore the state – the *kenmitsu* regime. Still according to Taira, the ideology of *kenmitsu* institutions concerning land determined the transformation of taxes and corvées due to the landholders into religious offerings, and the acquisition of those taxes by the temples was related to the promise of divine protection. For example, in a strategy to organise hunters or fishermen under its control, the Suwa Shrine was among the first to assert that killing sentient beings could produce karmic merits: if they were offered to a kami identified as a suijaku or emanation of a Buddhist divinity, fish were said to produce a bond (*kechien*) with the *honji* or Buddhist 'original source' of that kami. That is, independent activity of fishermen or hunters led to the karmic retribution of hell, while the same activity, if controlled by a religious institution, produced karmic benefits because it helped to lead ignorant beings to salvation. The same ideology was used in order to justify war. Such an ideology functioned perfectly in relating the peoples' hopes for salvation to the management of the shōen.

A second, important material consequence of the *honji suijaku* ideology and praxis was the fact that any action against the land-owners acquired religious 'value' and became an 'evil karmic act' (*akugō*); those who did not comply with the shōen economic, political, and social order were considered 'enemies (*onteki*) of the buddhas and the kami,' and accordingly would suffer divine punishment (*butsubachi* or *shinbatsu*) for two generations. In particular, the enemies of the buddhas and the kami were explicitly identified as lepers or medicants (*kojiki*), of whom it was said that they would fall into hell in their next life. *Shōen* monks performed rituals of witchcraft and black magic (*juso*) against subversives (those who did not comply with the economic orders of the religious institutions). In the Kongōbuji (the main temple of Shingon Esoteric Buddhism at Kōyasan), for example, the names of those who had not yet paid their taxes or who resisted the temple's authority were written down and a divine punishment was invoked upon them during the 'ceremony of the four seasons' (*shiki kitō*). The Kōfukuji invoked such punishment upon the enemies of the temple even if they were members of the Fujiwara house, whom it could strike from the house's register. Those rituals for divine punishment were not deemed to be against Buddhist ethics, because they were considered to be aimed at destroying the afflictions (*bonnō*) of the temple's enemies and thus lead them to salvation. Needless to say, the more the landholders spoke about the salvation of the masses, the more they increased their own wealth and power. In other words, the landholders were identified with the buddhas and kami that were the objects of cult, while the common folks and servants were identified with the dominated ones in need of salvation.[44]

In conclusion: theoretical issues

It is worth noting in this respect that Catherine Bell's *Ritual Theory, Ritual Practice*, says little about the relationship between ritual and economics. So far as I can tell, the only mention of the issue in her otherwise sustained and high-quality critique is her footnote to the effect that Bourdieu has something interesting to say about the 'gift'.[45] I would like to hear her opinion concerning the relationship between the 'mis-recognition' of which ritualists are said to be guilty with regard to their own activities, and what I think might be a 'mis-recognition' of economic facts which manifests itself as an emphasis on epistemological issues to the detriment of actual practice. As Bell rightly points out, past theoreticians of ritual have been victims of their own culturally-determined epistemological categories (if not biases); and I wonder whether our lack of attention to economic factors in ritual might be such a case. No ritualist I can think of among the Baruya of Papua New Guinea, the Brahmins of Kerala, the Taoist masters of Taiwan, the Shinto officiants of Japan, the monks of Bali, or the Catholic priests of France performs for free, or for matters that are not explicitly related to human exchanges or to any exchange *tout court*. And I wonder whether they do so, not just for money or any other form of payment, but *because* ritual is fundamentally inseparable from what Georges Bataille calls 'the accursed share' (*la part maudite*).[46] In all the manifestations of ritual I have briefly examined above, ritual's relation to the state was connected to consumption; this feature is apparent in all the texts and examples, but also in the phenomenon of the ritual festivity aptly analysed by Bataille.[47] I would submit that economic factors are a central part of all rituals, and that one might engage in studies of the economy of gesture (from obeisance to dance and agonistic contests), of the economy of preparation of materials, of the economy of exchange (of material stuff against hopes for, say, good crops, but also of social exchange), of the economy of speech, of the economy of time and space, of the economy of signification and memory, of the economy of calculations that sustain oracular practice and divinatory acts, of the economy of food, and last but not least, of a general economy of power.

Whether one looks at the *Engi-shiki* or at the *Gyōrinshō* (1154), which is perhaps its closest Buddhist equivalent, the first thing that jumps to the eye is the universal presence of lists. Jonathan Z. Smith has argued that 'lists' were intrinsically related to the establishment of the canon, and thereby to the formation of law. He writes:

> The Iatmul enumeration is a simple catalog which organises a heterogeneous group of materials around the single principle: the first performance of a cultural activity is to be celebrated. However, the schema according to which the various items are listed and grouped is more complex. It does not testify merely to the centrality of the notion of 'first time,' but represents a map of a particular culture's selection, out of the multitude of elements which make up their common life, of *those which are capable of bearing obsession*, those which are understood as significant. Properly interpreted, it is a diagram of the characteristic *preoccupations (as well as the occupations)* of the Iatmul. . . . I would note that the catalog is organised around the rubric: relations with strangers.[48]

In this regard, then, ritual might be said to represent a society's 'nervous system,' not only in the derived sense of obsession observed by Freud in both neurosis and religion ('little preoccupations, performances, restrictions and arrangements in certain activities of everyday life . . . elaborated by petty modifications . . . and little details'), but also in the sense recently given by Michael Taussig.[49] Ritual might also represent what I wish to describe as a society's digestive system, run by a very large appetite, conspicuous consumption, exuberant excess, and surplus throwaway. When asking what circulates in the fluidity of goods that form part of the economy of shrine ritual, one is struck by the awesome presence of food. Food recipes and ritual definitions share a number of fundamental features, and I wish to elaborate briefly on the issue. In his chapter on 'Sacred Persistence,' Smith writes:

> Almost the first thing observed by any traveler, be he professional or amateur, is the wide diversity between peoples as to food, both with respect to things they will eat and things they will not eat. . . . Granted that food is best understood as a cultural rather than a natural category, the dynamics of its limitation and variation are more complex than a simple relativism might suggest. A given foodstuff represents a radical, almost arbitrary, selection of the incredible number of potential sources of nutriment that are at hand. But, once the selection is made, the most extraordinary attention is given to the variety of its preparation. That is to say, *if food is a phenomenon characterized by limitation, cuisine is a phenomenon characterized by variegation*. . . . As one thinks of the possibilities for applying this general model of cultural activity to religious phenomena, one finds himself both assisted and left unsatisfied by the studies of historians of religion. . . . The historian of religion has been less convincing in explicating the second moment in our model: that of ingenuity, of cuisine. In part this is because historians of religion have traditionally resisted the anthropological as the cost of preserving the theological, preserving what they believe (I think wrongly) to be the 'irreducible, *sui generis*' nature of religious phenomena. . . . Thus ingenuity is often displaced as mere routinization or swallowed up by postulating some ontic primordium which manifests itself in a variety of forms, apparently independent of human agency. *Both degrade the anthropological dimension in a way I find inexcusable, the former by robbing it of its significance, the latter by denying its existence.*[50]

And so, keeping our eyes on the anthropological, we might begin asking questions concerning restraints and taboos against certain foodstuffs that are so prevalent in the rituals of shrines and temples, and cast an eye in the direction of the stupendous food offerings that mark the beginning of ritual, and the extraordinary banquets that close it. Recipes and modes of offering (styles determined by rank: either on top of offering tables or upon mats on ground) seem to be the result of lists that are memorised and recorded, whose elements are subjected to analysis in terms of patterns and then used in a proscriptive manner. Recipes and rituals are indeed rule-governed activities, but they both involve spending and, if I may be pardoned the pun, provisions. In the realm of temples, food was also extremely important, not only in terms of the restrictions placed on types of food, but also in symbolic terms, since it was believed that the Buddha had bequeathed part of his body as food for future generations, in a general equation of the kind: relics = rice grains. This goes a long way to explain why rice production was such an important matter for both shrines and temples. Production, ingestion, and digestion thus appear to me to be root metaphors of some interest; indeed, they occur clearly in Japanese myths, as in the following example:

Tsuki-yomi no Mikoto, on receiving this command, descended and went to the place where Uke-mochi no Kami was. Thereupon Uke-mochi no Kami turned her head towards the land, and forthwith from her mouth there came boiled rice: she faced the sea, and again there came from her mouth things broad of fin and things narrow of fin. She faced the mountains and again there came from her mouth things rough of hair and things soft of hair. These things were all prepared and set out on one hundred tables for [the visitor's] entertainment. Then Tsuki-yomi no mikoto became flushed with anger, and said: 'Filthy! Nasty! That thou shouldst dare to feed me with things disgorged from thy mouth.' So he drew his sword and slew her. . . . At this time Uke-mochi was truly dead already. But on the crown of her head there had been produced the ox and the horse; on the top of her forehead there had been produced millet; over her eyebrows there had been produced the silkworm; within her eyes there had been produced panic; in her belly there had been produced rice; in her genitals there had been produced wheat, large beans, and small beans. . . . Ama-terasu no Oho-kami was rejoiced and said: 'These are the things which the race of visible men will eat and live.' . . . She forthwith sowed for the first time the rice in the narrow fields and in the long fields of Heaven. That autumn, drooping ears bent down, eight span long, and were exceedingly pleasant to look on. Moreover she took the silkworms in her mouth, and succeeded in reeling thread from them.[51]

This myth speaks for itself. It is small wonder that the enthronement of the emperor is predominantly a matter of cultivation and sharing the first fruit. For it is all, after all, a matter of *production*, either of food, or of the actualisation of wishes, or of the imagination of society.

Notes

This is the revised version of a paper first presented in Paris under the auspices of the Committee for Scholarly Cooperation in East Asian Studies between Europe and North-America, June 1996, and presented as amended at Stanford University, Evans Wentz Symposium in Buddhist Studies, May 1998. I wish to thank here the organisers of these meetings. A shortened version in French was published in *Cipango* 6 (Autumn 1997): 111–50, under the title 'Aspects Économiques du Rituel.'

1 Godelier 1984: 114.
2 See Wheatley and See 1978.
3 Few Buddhologists have commented on the fact that Buddhism was, perhaps predominantly, an immense architectural phenomenon: from Ajanta to Sigiriya and Borobudur, from Dunhuang to Changan and to the Tōdaiji of Nara, Buddhism has radically transformed and often actually constructed the landscapes it settled in. Why Buddhologists would have preferred to emphasise documents over monuments is a matter of some importance. The political, institutional, and

economic history of Buddhism might serve, however, as another and perhaps more realistic framework within which to assess the history of Buddhist ideas.

4 On the *Jingi-kan*, see also Nelly Naumann's essay in this volume.

5 The other son became a Buddhist monk who went to China and, upon his return, initiated a cult dedicated to his father at Tōnomine; he was subsequently poisoned. See Grapard 1984: 240–65.

6 Okada Shōji 1986: 2–101.

7 These ritual festivities still include an imperial envoy at the present.

8 It should be noted that some, but not all, of these rituals were part of the cycle of annual observances (*nenjū gyōji*) the aristocracy engaged in during the Heian period and after.

9 Felicia Bock, for example (whose immense labour should be underscored), states that 'regulations for worship of the deities – that is, the first ten books on the *Jingi-kan* – had a greater vitality and something close to immortality.' Bock 1970, Vol. 1: 58.

10 See Kumagai Takanori 1984: 353–71.

11 Morita Tei 1991: 20. This is based on Miyoshi Kiyoyuki's 'Memorial on Twelve Opinions' of 914, parts of which are elegantly translated in Bock, 1970, Vol. 1: 13–4.

12 Grapard 1992.

13 Sakurai Yoshirō 1993.

14 The following discussion is based in part on Murayama Shūichi 1981, and *Onmyōdō sōsho* vol. 1. The reader may also refer to Saitō Tsutomu 1947, and Bock 1985.

15 For a larger discussion of the system, see Grapard 1987: 246–69.

16 See Bock 1970 and 1972.

17 These issues have been studied in detail in Kuroda Toshio 1980 and 1983.

18 Aston, trans., *Nihongi* (1972): 80.

19 *Ninnō-kyō*, properly, *Ninnō haramitsu-kyō*, in T 8, no. 245 (in Kumārajīva's translation), and no. 246 (in Amoghavajra's translation).

20 Not surprisingly, the first *monzeki* was the Ichijō-in (created between 978 and 983) of the Kōfukuji, whose abbot was Jōshō, grandson of Fujiwara Moroyasu, then Minister of the Left.

21 See Gaston Renondeau 1965, and also Kuroda Toshio 1980.

22 The best treatment of the variegated aspects of Tendai esoteric practices and ideas is in Misaki Ryōshū 1988, 1992, 1993 and 1994.

23 *Konkōmyō-kyō*, T 16, no. 663.

24 *Daihannya-kyō* (properly, *Maka hannya haramitsu-kyō*), T 8, no. 223.

25 *Kongōhannya-kyō* (properly, *Kongō hannya haramitsu-kyō*), T 8, no. 235.

26 See for instance his *Ninnō-kyō kaidai* in *Kōbō Daishi zenshū*, vol. 1, 329, and his *Kongō hannya-kyō kaidai*, ibid., 489.

27 See examples of these petitions in Watanabe Shōkō and Miyazaka Yūshō, eds., 1965: *Shōryōshū*, *kan* 4, no. 20, for a petition for a ritual for the imperium, and for rituals for aristocrats see *kan* 6, no. 46, no. 50, no. 52, no. 55, and others.

28 The ritual was subsequently reinstated with the provision that it be performed only once during the reign of an emperor. It was last performed, officially, in 1928; however, extraordinary performances took place during the Second World War.

29 The peacock ritual is in the *Dai kujaku myōō gazō danjō giki*, T 19, no. 983 [a].

30 *Shōu-kyō* (properly, *Daiunrin shōu-kyō*), T 19, no. 989. The ritual is *Daiun-gyō kiu dampō*, T 19, no. 990. Such rites were already performed during the Nara period, but in the Heian period eminent thaumaturgists were called upon. A famous case is that of the Ono lineage thaumaturgist Ninkai (born 951), who came to be known as *ame sōjō*, literally, the 'Monacal Rector of Rain.' He performed the ritual successfully nine times between 1028 and 1044.

31 The Japanese generic term used to refer to those emanations is *Butchō* (Skt. *Buddhosnīsa* or *Usnīsarāja*). The *Shijōkō* emanation under discussion here is the object of the *Shijōkō daiitoku shōsai kichijō darani-kyō*, T 19, no. 963; and of the *Daiitoku kinrin butchō shijōkō nyorai shōjō issai sainan darani-kyō*, more commonly called *Shōjōsainan-gyō*, T 19, no. 964. The oldest extant ritual text, *Shijōkō dōjō nenjū-gi*, T 46, no. 1951, was compiled by Fabao Tashi (946–1032).

32 This ritual was based on the *Kongō jūmyō darani-kyō*, T 20, no. 1134 [b], and is described in the *Kongō jūmyō darani-kyōhō*, T 20, no. 1134 [a].

33 There were several forms of Fudō rituals, variously emphasised in Shingon and Tendai lineages. The main texts on the topic are contained in T 21.

34 Daiitoku-hō. There are several texts describing varied rites dedicated to Daiitoku; of central importance are those contained in T 21, no. 1214 and no. 1216. See Robert Duquenne 1983: 652–70.

35 On these shrines, see also Sonoda Minoru's essay in this volume.

36 Mitsubashi Takeshi 1984: 311.

37 *Ibid.*

38 Jacques Derrida 1972. English translation by Barbara Johnson (1981): 130–3.

39 See Bock 1970:86, and 1972:90–2.

40 The *monzenmachi* of Sakamoto, regarded today as one of the best preserved cities of the genre, does not allow insight into its Heian-period size; what we see today was built after Mount Hiei was reduced to ashes by Nobunaga, and is therefore considerably smaller

41 Inoue Mitsusada 1956: 138ff; see also Inoue 1971.

42 Personal communication. Rambelli is working on an extensive treatment of hell as a social phenomenon within the kenmitsu system.

43 Taira Masayuki 1992: 247–9.

44 I am indebted to Fabio Rambelli for the above three paragraphs.

45 Catherine Bell 1992.

46 See Georges Bataille, trans. Robert Hurley, *The Accursed Share* (1991). See also Pierre Clastres, trans. Robert Hurley, *Society Against the State* (1982).

47 Bataille 1973: 73.

48 Jonathan Z. Smith 1982: 46 (emphasis mine).

49 Michael Taussig 1992. I wish to add here Taussig's quotation of Philip Abrams to suggest that discussions of ritual and state that do not involve critical theorising concerning the notion of state as an imaginary institution might miss something interesting: 'The state is not the reality which stands behind the mask of political practice. It is itself the mask which prevents our seeing political practice as it is [and] it starts its life as an implicit construct; it is then reified—as the *res publica*, the public reification, no less – and acquires an overt symbolic identity progressively divorced from practice as an illusory account of practice.' (113).

50 Jonathan Z. Smith 1982: 39–42. (Emphasis on the last line is mine).

51 Aston, trans., *Nihongi* (1972): 32–3.

CHAPTER SIX

The kami in esoteric Buddhist thought and practice

Mark Teeuwen

The amalgamation of kami cults and Buddhism began almost as soon as Buddhism arrived in Japan. It is usually described as a process in three stages. First, the eighth century saw the appearance of 'shrine-temples' (*jingūji*), founded by itinerant mountain ascetics at the request of provincial lords and village heads, whose local kami asked to be saved from their kami state by means of Buddhist ritual. The idea behind these shrine-temples was that kami could be rendered both more beneficent and more powerful when served a menu of Buddhist services. The building of temples at shrines resulted in integrated temple-shrine complexes that became hot-houses of the amalgamation process.[1] Towards the end of the same century, a parallel process inaugurated a second stage with the identification of the kami Hachiman as a protector-deity of the Buddhist Law, and, somewhat later, even as a bodhisattva. This was followed by the adoption of tutelary kami (*chinju*) by temples all over the country. Now, shrines were built at temples, taking the institutional amalgamation of kami cults and Buddhism an important step further. The third stage of the process began in the ninth century, which saw the origin of the notion that some kami are skilful means, emanations of buddhas, bodhisattvas or devas who 'soften their light and mingle with the dust' (*wakō dōjin*) in order to lead us to the Buddhist Way. Between the ninth and eleventh centuries, an increasing number of kami were 'promoted,' in Buddhist terms, from potentially dangerous spirits whose character should be improved through contact with the Buddhist Law, to local emanations of buddhas and bodhisattvas, embodying their wisdom or compassion.[2] By worshipping such kami, it was now possible to unleash the magical powers (*riyaku*) of Buddhist divinities ranging from Śākyamuni to Fudō Myōō, or to escape to the Pure Lands of Amida, Kannon or Yakushi.[3]

However, this was not yet the end of the career of kami within Buddhist thought and practice. The twelfth and thirteenth centuries saw yet another shift in the Buddhist perception of kami. During this period, selected kami were promoted from 'secondary' emanations (*suijaku*) of 'primary' Buddhist divinities (*honji*), to embodiments of Dainichi's universal enlightenment. It is this last development that will be explored in this article. These kami, which were all related to Amaterasu in some way or other, became *honzon* (the focal divinities of rituals) of some of the most elaborate esoteric rituals of the country, and penetrated to the core of Buddhist doctrinal studies. This new view of kami that I shall analyse here had a profound influence not only on esoteric Buddhism, but also on the subsequent development of Shinto thought and practice. As will be argued below, it was this new brand of Buddhist kami thought that lay at the basis of the first schools of 'Shinto thought' (such as Watarai or Ise Shinto, Sannō Shinto, Miwa Shinto, Goryū Shinto, and Urabe or Yoshida Shinto). In this essay, I hope to make clear that it was this kami thought and practice, pioneered among monks of the esoteric Buddhist sects, that opened the way for kami cults to develop into something that may be meaningfully referred to as 'Shinto': a religious tradition that consciously and explicitly defined itself as non-Buddhist and self-contained.

Kami as paragons of inherent enlightenment

The shift in the role of kami within esoteric Buddhist discourse from secondary emanations to embodiments of universal enlightenment can be exemplified by looking at Tendai writings on the Hie shrines, the tutelary shrines of the Tendai headquarters on Mount Hiei. In *Yōtenki*, a source from the early thirteenth century, the main kami of the Hie shrine of Ōmiya is depicted as an emanation of Śākyamuni. Since Japan is a tiny country, this text argues, full of 'people with little talent or goodness,' and where the Buddha's teachings are of no avail, Śākyamuni appeared at the foot of Mount Hiei 'as a kami, in order to warn against impurity and admonish the faithless, to punish laxness and encourage serious practice (*shōjin*), to reward the faithful and punish those without faith, and to fulfil wishes for this life and the next.'[4] While this text praises worship of the kami as 'a worldly method (*sehō*) identical to the Buddhist method (*buppō*),'[5] it is nevertheless clear that kami ritual is here recommended only because adverse circumstances in *mappō* Japan have made the Buddhist methods infeasible. About a century later, however, *Keiran jūyōshū* (c. 1318–19) paints a radically different picture of the kami of Hie. In this work of encyclopedic proportions, by the Tendai scholar-monk Kōshū (1276–1350), the kami of Hie are no longer secondary emanations of Śākyamuni; they have become embodiments of Dainichi (Skt. Mahāvairocana), the 'World-Buddha' of universal enlightenment, of which Śākyamuni himself was but a temporary manifestation: 'The kami (*shinmei*) are Dainichi; Śākyamuni is a buddha emanating from [the kami/Dainichi]. Our country is the Original Land of Dainichi, and India is the Land of Śākyamuni's manifestation.'[6] Here, 'the kami' are declared to be the supreme divinities of the esoteric teaching, while Śākyamuni was 'merely' a teacher of exoteric (and less profound) doctrines: 'Because the exoteric lineages are based on the Buddha, they regard Śākyamuni as their lord and teacher, who acquired Buddhahood in eight steps (*hassō sabutsu*).[7] [Esoteric] Shingon, however, teaches that the uncreated, original state (*musa honnu no tai*) of all sentient beings, just as they are, is the Dharma body. Therefore we revere the kami of the Ancestral Shrine and the Shrine of Grains (*sōbyō shashoku* – i.e., the seven Hie shrines, or the Inner and Outer Shrines of Ise), and through [these kami] the original state [of inherent enlightenment] of the sentient beings themselves.'[8]

This interpretation of the kami of Hie was based on ideas about inherent enlightenment (*hongaku*), which state that all sentient beings, or indeed all phenomena, whether sentient or not, exist only in the meditation of Dainichi and are therefore enlightened as they are: the 'uncreated, original state of all sentient beings as they are is the Dharma body (the embodiment of Dainichi's universal enlightenment).'[9] Teachings based on this notion taught that one could realise one's inherent enlightenment in this life and in this body by attaining union (*kaji*) with Dainichi or one of his countless emanations. In this state of union with Dainichi, one would become aware of the ultimate unity of self and Dainichi, of one's innate passions (including one's desire, anger, or ignorance) and enlightenment, and of birth-and-death and nirvana. Inherent enlightenment was moreover contrasted with 'acquired enlightenment' (*shigaku*), a term here used to refer to all 'exoteric' methods of attaining enlightenment, as exemplified by Śākyamuni's 'acquiring of Buddhahood in eight steps.' Such methods were considered inferior to the esoteric method of Dainichi.

In *Keiran jūyōshū*, the kami are no longer a last resort to which the Buddha has no choice but to turn in *mappō* Japan. The kami of Hie have become the very entity of universal enlightenment, paragons of an 'uncreated,' natural enlightenment that is superior to the 'acquired' enlightenment of exoteric Buddhism. In the process, moreover, Japan has changed from a 'tiny land even among tiny lands' (*shōkoku ni arite mo shōkoku*), far removed from the centre of Buddhism, to the 'Original Land of Dainichi' (*Dainichi-hongoku*) – an example of the ubiquitous use of paronomasia in esoteric discourse, inspired by *Dai-nippon-goku*, 'Great Japan.' *Keiran jūyōshū* elaborates on this idea by stating that the nine sections of the capital correspond to the nine assemblies of the Kongōkai mandala (representing Dainichi's wisdom), the five provinces of the central region around the capital to the Taizōkai mandala (representing Dainichi's compassion), and the seven circuits (*dō*) of Japan to the Soshitsuji mandala (representing the ultimate oneness of Dainichi's wisdom and compassion). In this way, the whole of Japan becomes a representation of Dainichi's Dharma realm.[10]

A similar view of kami is expressed in a large body of literature, produced during the Kamakura and Muromachi periods, that taught esoteric Buddhist doctrine through the medium of kami myth. In *Keiran jūyōshū*, which is but one example of such literature, Kōshū interprets the myth of Amaterasu's retreat into the Rock-Cave of Heaven as a Japanese, encoded version of the universal esoteric Buddhist myth of the Iron Tower. The latter explains how Nāgārjuna (c. 2nd century CE) received the sutras of esoteric Buddhism from

Kongōsatta (Skt. Vajrasattva) after he succeeded in entering an iron stupa in South India. The tower then functions as a metaphor for the universal enlightenment of Dainichi inherent in all sentient beings:[11]

> Question: What of the association of the kami (*shinmei*) with the Iron Tower?
>
> Answer: When Amaterasu became angry because of Susanowo's acts of evil and retired into the Heavenly Rock-Cave, the world was plunged into darkness. Then, the eight myriad kami gathered in front of the cave and danced. Ame no Koyane and Tajikarawo stood to the left and right of the Rock-Cave, and the eight myriad kami lit a fire and performed a *kagura* dance. Amaterasu responded to the *kagura* of the kami, and some of her divine light illuminated the faces of the eight myriad kami; and the kami said: *Ara omo-shiro ya* – 'How wonderful,' or, 'How white our faces'; this is the origin of the word *omoshiro*. Then Ame no Koyane and Tajikarawo pulled open [the gates of] the Rock-Cave; for these two deities are kami of great power. This is a paraphrase of the account in the *Nihongi* (720).
>
> When we relate this to the [Buddhist] teaching (*hō wo motte kore wo awasureba*), [we see that] Amaterasu is the Dharma body of one's own nature, or the King of Dharma nature. Susanowo is ignorance, or Devadatta.[12] The Iron Tower is the stupa of the Dharma realm. Retiring into the Rock-Cave and closing it means that ignorance follows Dharma nature; opening the Tower means that Dharma nature follows ignorance. The two kami of great power are the two methods of concentration and wisdom (*jō-e*) – think of the sutra that reads: 'The power of concentration and wisdom is magnificent; with it the sentient beings can be saved.' Lighting a fire is the teaching of the various skilful means. The eight myriad kami are the eight myriad Buddhist scriptures. Ultimately, the retreat into the Rock-Cave stands for the ignorance of the sentient beings; the opening of the Rock-Cave stands for the opening of the gates of the Dharma realm.[13]

Here, the myth of Amaterasu's retreat into, and reappearance from the Rock-Cave of Heaven has become a metaphor for the realisation of one's inherent enlightenment, made possible by the helpful means laid down in the 'eight myriad' Buddhist scriptures. Similar esoteric explanations of kami myth were recorded in prodigious quantities at both shrines and temples throughout Japan between the late thirteenth and fifteenth centuries. Their influence spread to the interpretation of literary texts such as *Kokin wakashū* and *Ise monogatari*, as well as to collections of warrior tales, legends, and Noh pieces. The body of this literature is so large that it has recently come to be studied as a genre in its own right: the 'medieval *Nihongi*' (*chūsei Nihongi*).[14]

As noted briefly above, these new interpretations of kami all hinged on new theories about Amaterasu and the Ise shrines. Typically, the section on Sannō (i.e., the kami of Hie) in *Keiran jūyōshū* sets out by arguing that 'Amaterasu and Sannō Gongen are identical.'[15] The shrines and shrine-temple complexes at which kami interpretations of this type were developed and from which they spread – the Hie shrines, Miwa, Kumano, Yoshida, and Ise itself – all identified their kami as spirits of Amaterasu. At Miwa, for example, *Miwa Daimyōjin engi* (late thirteenth century) states that during a seven-day retreat at Ise, a 'voice from the void' revealed to the famous monk Eizon (1201–90) of Saidaiji that Dainichi had left 'traces' (*suijaku*) both in heaven (as 'Amaterasu') and on two places on earth: first as Ōmiwa Daimyōjin at Miwa, and later as Kōdaijin ('the Imperial Great Deity') at Ise.[16]

The esoteric kami discourse outlined above was built on three pillars: the association of Amaterasu with Dainichi (supplemented by the association of various kami with Amaterasu); the notion that Japan was the 'Original Land of Dainichi'; and *hongaku* thought. Individually, these 'pillars' can be traced back centuries before they were combined into a more systematic body of kami thought and practice. The association of Amaterasu with Dainichi may go back as far as Gyōgi (668–749). The earliest reference to the theory that Japan is 'the Original Land of Dainichi' is in Seizon's *Shingon fuhō san'yōshō* (1060).[17] *Hongaku* thought, finally, is thought to have developed fully in the course of the late Heian and early Kamakura periods (the twelfth century). These building blocks were put together and combined into a more coherent kami discourse by monks of the esoteric sects in the course of the thirteenth century.

There was, however, more than a 'discourse' alone. A fact that is often overlooked is that these esoteric kami ideas were grounded in ritual practice. It is in this ritual practice that the rationale behind the interpretation of kami as paragons of inherent enlightenment becomes clear. In this article, I shall briefly explore three instances of esoteric Buddhist kami discourse and their ritual backgrounds. All three focus on Ise and its main kami, Amaterasu, but represent different stages in the development of esoteric Buddhist Shinto. After these three brief excursions, it will be possible to draw some conclusions about the social and theological dynamics that informed the penetration of the kami into the heart of esoteric Buddhism, and the influence this had on the formation of shrine-based Shinto schools.

Esoteric purification: *Nakatomi harae kunge*

With the exception of a small number of extremely short texts, *Nakatomi harae kunge* is widely regarded as the first text of 'Ryōbu Shinto' – a term referring to theories and practices handed down in various lineages, based on the association of the Inner and Outer Shrines of Ise with the Taizōkai and Kongōkai mandalas.[18] The origin of this text is much debated, but the most convincing research to date links the text with Sengūin, a shrine-temple located on an estate of the Ise shrines some twenty-five miles south-west of Ise, and to Sengūin's head temple, Onjōji at the foot of Mt. Hiei. It is dated variably to the mid- or late twelfth century.[19] As indicated by its title ('Reading and explanation of the Nakatomi formula'), this text provides an esoteric interpretation of the Nakatomi formula, a purification formula used in purification rituals for private patrons by 'Yin Yang masters' (*onmyōji*) and shrine priests alike. This formula was a slightly adapted version of the Formula of Great Purification (*Ōharae no kotoba*), recited by a Nakatomi priest at the biannual court ceremony of Great Purification. Recitation of this formula had become part of standard *onmyōji* practice by the tenth century, and soon penetrated into certain esoteric Buddhist rituals as well.[20]

Nakatomi harae kunge, then, is an esoteric treatise, written by a monk of one of the esoteric sects, on a rite that was usually associated with *onmyōji* and shrine priests, but that had come to form part of integrated rituals that combined elements from different traditions.[21] Naturally, the unknown scholar-monk who was the author of the text drew on explanations of the Nakatomi formula by its current performers – in this case, ritualists linked to Ise, perhaps even Ise priests, who in the course of the twelfth century began travelling the country to establish ties with local land-owners and rising *bushi* leaders, urging them to donate lands to the Ise shrines, and offering to perform rituals of private purification for the attainment of a wide variety of aims, such as victory in battle or recovery from illness. *Nakatomi harae kunge* gives clear clues to the way in which these ritualists explained and presented the formula to their patrons.

The Nakatomi formula starts out with a mythological account of the founding of the imperial lineage; it then lists the sins 'perpetrated by the people,' and prescribes purification rites such as the cutting of pieces of wood and sedge reeds, and the chanting of 'heavenly ritual words.' The formula closes with a description of the removal of all impurity from the Japanese islands by kami of the river rapids, the sea currents, and the wind, to the Netherworld, where all impurity is finally 'lost.' *Nakatomi harae kunge*, now, identified these kami as emanations of Enma-ō (King Yama, the King of Hell) and his retinue, and at the same time stated that these kami are identical to the kami that dwell in the main auxiliary shrines (*betsugū*) of the Ise shrines.[22] The kami of the river rapids (Seori-tsu-hime), for example, is associated both with Enma-ō, and with the 'turbulent spirit' (*aramitama*) of Amaterasu that resides in the Aramatsuri shrine, an auxiliary shrine of the Inner Shrine in Ise.

It would seem that lingering in the background here is a ritual focusing on Enma-ō. The most obvious candidate is *Enmaten-ku*, a ritual performed by monks of various esoteric lineages to heal illness, prolong life, or secure the safe delivery of a child. This ritual implored the 'divine magistrates' (*myōkan*) of the realm of the dead, who were thought to control the fate of all human beings both before and after death, to grant the ritual's patron a longer and more successful life. Together with similar rites, such as the esoteric Buddhist *Myōdō-ku* and *Hokuto-hō* and the *onmyōji* ritual *Taizanpukun-sai*, *Enmaten-ku* was one of the most popular and common rites ordered by court nobles during the Insei period (1087–1192).[23] The 'magistrates' invoked in *Enmaten-ku* included both Buddhist figures (such as Enma-ō), and deities of Daoist origin (such as Enma-ō's 'chief officer' Taizanpukun, and fate-ordaining stars such as *shimei* and *shiroku*); exactly the same list recurs in *Nakatomi harae kunge*. The image conjured up by this web of identifications is one of travelling Ise ritualists who offered to chant the Nakatomi formula as a close equivalent from their own kami tradition to the Buddhist ritual of *Enmaten-ku*, that was more familiar to their patrons.

The scholar-monk who wrote *Nakatomi harae kunge*, however, used this understanding of the Nakatomi formula only as a starting point for his own doctrinal interpretation of the practice. While the ritual practice on which this text is based focused on Enma-ō, the doctrinal explanation of the formula focuses on Dainichi. The chanting of the Nakatomi formula is explained as a practice similar to the chanting of *darani* or esoteric spells: as a way to attain union (*kaji*), and thus realise one's 'bond with Dainichi' (*hongan*) – a synonym for one's inherent enlightenment. This, the text argues, is because the kami are 'spirits' (*tamashii*) of the various buddhas, who constitute their essence (*shō*). It is through the kami that Dainichi activates the Nakatomi formula with his 'permeating power' (*jinzū*). The formula is in fact an aspect of this permeating power, made out of the compassion of the various buddhas emanating from Dainichi. If used properly, it is a 'teaching of meditation' (*yuga no kyōhō*) which will bring the practitioner good results on various levels according to his capacity.[24]

Nakatomi harae kunge also reinterprets the kami myths that feature in the formula in a way that reminds one of the passage in *Keiran jūyōshū* quoted above. When the descent of the Imperial ancestor Ninigi to Japan is recounted in the formula, for example, *Nakatomi harae kunge* explains this as a mythological account of Dainichi's application of skilful means. Similarly, Amaterasu's act of sending Ninigi to Japan to make it into a 'peaceful land,' as described in the formula, is explained as a reference to Dainichi's act of 'sending Śākyamuni's teaching and disciples in all directions.'[25] These interpretations lead up to the concluding statement of this section of the text, where it is argued that Ninigi's land is 'the Original Land of Dainichi,' a 'Buddha land' where all sentient beings 'receive the majestic and divine power of the buddhas' and 'dwell together in bliss with the various buddhas.'[26]

The most striking feature of the text, however, is the author's treatment of the concept of impurity that lies at the heart of the Nakatomi formula. In a revealing passage, the author points out that the duality of pure versus impure is not 'real,' but is a projection of our own conditioned minds. For the esoteric practitioner, then, purification is not so much a method of removing external impurity, as a meditation practice tailored to deliver his mind from its conditioned state. If carried out correctly, to perform purification is therefore 'the same as to return to the wondrous state of the syllable *a*, in which everything is unborn (*aji honpushō*),' and it will lead the practitioner to 'instantaneous enlightenment.'[27]

In this early text of esoteric kami discourse, then, we already see many of the features that were to characterise texts of this genre in the ensuing decades. A doctrinal exposition focusing on Amaterasu and Dainichi is superimposed on the ritual association of Amaterasu with Enma-ō. Moreover, kami myths

101

are furnished with a new interpretation, as metaphors for esoteric Buddhist teachings. Finally, the aim of kami ritual (here kami purification) is redefined as reaching enlightenment in this body, through union with Dainichi.

Esoteric shrine worship: *Ise kanjō*

In the course of the second half of the thirteenth century, esoteric kami ideas and practices began to be handed down in the form of 'initiations' (*kanjō*). *Kanjō* came in many different forms, ranging from very elaborate (such as the *denbō kanjō* that raises the initiate to the status of *ajari* or master), to very simple (such as *kechien* or 'bond-establishing' initiations for laymen, in which the initiate simply establishes a bond with a divinity by throwing a sprig of anise onto a mandala spread out in front of him; or advanced initiations between masters, which are not accompanied by any form of ritual).[28] It would seem natural to assume that kami initiations, which went under a great variety of names including *Shintō kanjō*, *shinmei kanjō*, *jingi kanjō*, *Ise kanjō*, *Nihongi kanjō*, *Reiki kanjō*, and others, began as simple affairs. What is certain, is that they developed into a very elaborate and highly ritualised system in the course of the medieval period.[29]

What was central to all kami initiations was the instruction of the practitioner in a secret technique enabling him to attain union (*kaji*) with a specific kami, or the kami in general, and thus generate both this-worldly and other-worldly results. The initiating master taught his disciple (or fellow-master) a mudra and a mantra, or a sequence of mudras and mantras, as well as an accompanying visualisation. An early example of such a technique, which I shall discuss here in some detail, is the *Ise kanjō*, which can be traced back at least to 1289, and probably to 1262.[30] The contents of this initiation have been preserved on slips of paper called *kirikami*, often extremely brief and concise initiation documents handed down from the initiating master to his initiate as a memory aid and as proof of the fact that the initiation has taken place. These documents outline the (often spurious) origin and transmission lineage of the secret knowledge, describe the mudras, mantras and visualisations that form its essence, and explain the rationale behind the technique in an 'oral tradition' (*kuden* – i.e., instructions written down only in secret initiation documents).

The practice revealed in *kirikami* for the *Ise kanjō* consisted of five steps.[31] First, arriving at the *torii* or shrine gate, one was to form the mudra of the 'closed stupa' (*heitō-in*) and vocalise the syllable *a*. This mudra and mantra both represent the Taizōkai, or Dainichi's compassion. Then, arriving in front of the main hall in which the kami is enshrined, one formed the mudra of the 'outer five-pronged vajra' (*gegoko-in*) and vocalised the syllable *ban*, both representing the Kongōkai, or Dainichi's wisdom. Thirdly, one visualised the kami body while forming the mudra of the 'eight-petalled lotus' (*hachiyō-in*) and vocalising the syllable *un*, both of which represent the mind of enlightenment (*bodaishin*). In meditation, the eight-petalled lotus formed by the hands is visualised as

'closed stupa' mudra (*heitō-in*)

'outer five-pronged vajra' mudra (*gegoko-in*)

'eight-petalled lotus' mudra (*hachiyō-in*)

corresponding to both the shrine hall and, at the same time, the organ of the human heart – both of which, by no coincidence, are bright red.[32] The syllable *un* is visualised as resting between one's hands, and is seen at the same time as the kami body within the shrine hall, and as the mind of enlightenment within the organ of one's own heart. The fourth and fifth steps consist of chanting (three times each) a *ge* or Buddhist *gāthā* verse, and a *waka* or Japanese poem, each expressing the notion that the kami, as an embodiment of one's own inherent enlightenment, dwells within one's heart/mind (*kokoro*). This *ge* and *waka* read:

南無本覚法身本有如来自性心壇内護摩道場
namu hongaku hosshin honnu nyorai jishō shindan-nai goma dōjō
I place my trust in the *goma* hall that is within the altar of my own heart and my own nature, where dwells the original Tathāgata of the Dharma body of inherent enlightenment.

ちはやぶる我が心よりするわざを いづれの神かよそに見るべき
chihayaburu / waga kokoro yori / suru waza wo / izure no kami ka / yoso ni mirubeki
The acts of my own mind, born from the womb – what kami could one find anywhere else?[33]

The *kirikami* of this initiation further reveal that the syllable *un*, that is at the heart of the ritual, represents not only the mind of enlightenment, but is also the seed syllable (*shuji*) of Aizen Myōō or King Rāga. This figure (which is also bright red) represents human lust and desire, and personifies the insight that one's innate desires are no other than inherent enlightenment itself.[34] As such, Aizen Myōō is a potent *honzon* in practices that stress physical, 'uncreated' enlightenment.

The practice revealed in *Ise kanjō* thus teaches the practitioner that the kami dwells in his own heart/mind. The initiate is taught to visualise the kami as the syllable *un*, representing both the mind of enlightenment and his innate desire, in the guise of Aizen Myōō. The insight to be gained from this is that enlightenment and desire are identical. Up to this point, there is little that sets the teachings of this initiation apart from mainstream esoteric practice; but this is not all. The *kirikami* go on to teach that the kami of the Inner and Outer Shrine of Ise appear in our world as a golden and a white snake, and in attached *kuden* point out that Aizen Myōō's *siddham* seed syllable *un*, too, has the form of a snake.[35] It would seem that it was this teaching, the revelation that both the kami of Ise and Aizen Myōō are snakes, that constituted the centre piece of the *Ise kanjō*.

Keiran jūyōshū throws more light on the significance of the image of the snake in this context. This text argues that the kami (*shinmei*), when they 'soften their light and mingle with the dust,' always take on the body of a snake, and explains that this represents the 'three poisons' of greed, anger and ignorance.[36] These 'three poisons' also occur in an *Ise kanjō kirikami*, which defines greed as Aizen Myōō, anger as Fudō Myōō, and ignorance as Amida, and points out that the seed syllables of these divinities (*un*, *kan*, and *kiriku*, Skt. *hūṃ*, *hāṃ*, and *hrīḥ*) are all variations on the same 'snake-formed' syllable *ka* (Skt. *ha*).[37] The conclusion to be drawn from all this is that the kami, as snakes, physically represent the highest form of inherent enlightenment: the 'three poisons' themselves. Relating this point to an anecdote from the Lotus sutra, *Keiran jūyōshū* reminds the reader that at Vulture Peak, there was among Śākyamuni's audience an 'eight year-old dragon girl' who 'to the Buddha appeared as a snake of 16 *jō* (c. 48 m).' The text concludes: 'Therefore the appearance of the uncreated, original state (*musa honnu*) of all sentient beings is as a snake. This uncreated state, without change, opened up as the original Dharma body, and thus [the dragon-girl] attained enlightenment.'[38]

The association of kami with Buddhist divinities such as Aizen Myōō, Fudō Myōō and Amida *as snakes* throws a revealing light on the development of kami as outlined above: from deluded and violent beings wishing to be saved, first into secondary 'traces' (*suijaku*) of Buddhist divinities, and finally into embodiments of inherent enlightenment. The appearance of new ways to relate kami to Buddhist thought and ritual did not cause earlier notions to be abandoned; rather, older notions were built upon and infused with new meaning. The kami were such compelling candidates as paragons of inherent enlightenment precisely because of the fact that they were regarded as beings of desire, violence and delusion. The *Ise kanjō* and *Keiran jūyōshū* show that the kami were elevated to the highest position on the Buddhist ladder of sacredness not because they were now perceived as enlightened beings, but rather because the greed, anger and ignorance ascribed to them since ancient times had come to be regarded as the highest form of enlightenment. It was not the character of the kami that had changed, but the esoteric Buddhist evaluation of that character.

Finally, it should be noticed that in this ritual practice, Dainichi has had to make place for more dramatic characters, and appears at most as a distant unifying principle on a doctrinal level.

The kami and esoteric court ritual: *sokui kanjō*

As a last example of esoteric Buddhist kami thought and practice, I shall briefly touch upon an esoteric image of Amaterasu that is at the heart of the most secret initiation of all: the imperial enthronement initiation (*sokui kanjō*).[39] In this initiation the imperial regent (*kanpaku*) revealed to the new emperor a secret mudra and mantra (or a series of such mudras and mantras) to be performed by him on his way to the enthronement platform on the day of his accession to the throne. Documentary proof that this ritual was actually practised as part of enthronement ceremonies exists for Emperor Fushimi (in 1288);[40] it became standard practice from Emperor Go-Komatsu (1382) onwards. However, the *sokui kanjō* also had a life of its own, apart from imperial practice, within Tendai and Shingon esoteric lineages. Here it developed a large range of ritual forms and corresponding 'oral traditions' that were handed down as the 'ultimate secrets' of those lineages. While these traditions tell us little about actual imperial practice, they reveal a great deal about esoteric Buddhist views on the emperor, the imperial regalia, and Amaterasu.

While different lineages preserve a great variety of ritual manuals for the *sokui kanjō*, ranging from quite simple to very elaborate, the focus of all variants is on the 'mudra of rule over the four seas' (*shikai ryōshō-in*) as the secret mudra, and the mantra of Dakini (Skt. Ḍākinī) as the secret mantra to be performed by the emperor on the day of his enthronement. While this choice of mudra needs little explanation, the fact that Dakini should be invoked as the *honzon* of this important ritual is striking. According to Shingon lore, *dakini* are flesh-eating demons who have the ability to foresee the death of human beings six months in advance, and who then proceed to eat out their victims' hearts, without killing them. It is said that Dainichi 'tamed' these demons, and taught them to instruct their victims in the 'method of Shingon' during the last six months of their lives. In return, Dainichi allowed the *dakini* to devour their victims' bodies after death. The *dakini* were included in the outer enclosure of the Taizōkai mandala, and were believed to grant unlimited powers to those who successfully invoked them.[41] Moreover, *dakini* were in Japan associated

'mudra of 'rule over the four seas' (shikai ryōshō-in)
note: a number of alternative traditions can be found in *Mikkyō daijiten*

with foxes (and, of course, with the kami of foxes, Inari), perhaps because they were traditionally accompanied by jackals (*yakan*). The standard Japanese image of Dakini shows an attractive-looking young woman, seated on a white fox, and holding a wish-fulfilling gem (*nyoi hōju*) in her hand – the latter symbolising the unlimited powers that can be acquired by those who have mastered the ritual of *Dakiniten-hō*.

Again, *Keiran jūyōshū* supplies us with some revealing hints about the *honzon* of this ritual:

Question: What was the appearance of Amaterasu when she was hiding in the Rock-Cave of Heaven?
Answer: Since Amaterasu is the sun deity, she had the appearance of the sun-disc. Another tradition says: When Amaterasu retired into the Rock-Cave of Heaven after her descent from Heaven (*sic*), she took on the appearance of a dragon-fox (*shinko* or *tatsugitsune*).[42] Uniquely among all animals, the dragon-fox is a kami that emits light from its body; this is the reason why she took on this appearance.
Question: Why does the dragon-fox emit light?
Answer: The dragon-fox is an expedient body of Nyoirin Kannon. It takes the wish-fulfilling gem as its body, and is therefore called King Cintāmaṇi.[43] . . . Further, one tradition says that one becomes a king by revering the dragon-fox because the dragon-fox is an expedient body of Amaterasu.[44]

Here, we learn that the *honzon* of the esoteric enthronement ritual is in fact a 'dragon-fox,' who is an 'expedient body' (*kegen*, *ōgen*) of the wish-fulfilling gem (which is in turn identified as an expedient of Nyoirin Kannon, the 'Kannon of the wish-fulfilling *cakra*'), as well as of the imperial ancestor Amaterasu. Thus we arrive at a complicated web of identifications: Dakini = dragon-fox = wish-fulfilling gem = Amaterasu. It was this combined deity that was at the centre of the *sokui kanjō* – which was alternatively known as *shinko-hō*, 'the ritual of the dragon-fox.'

A striking aspect of the Dakini mantra in this imperial ritual is its sexual connotation. *Kirikami* of the *sokui kanjō* reveal that this mantra represented the unity of Dainichi, expressed by the union of the Kongōkai and Taizōkai mandalas (*ryōbu funi*).[45] These mandalas depicted Dainichi not only in his aspects of wisdom and compassion, but also in his male and female aspects. The Dakini mantra, then, was explained to express the sexual union of the emperor (embodying the male, Kongōkai aspect of Dainichi) and the empress (embodying the female, Taizōkai aspect of Dainichi).[46] It should perhaps be stressed here that such a 'left-handed' interpretation of the union of Kongōkai and Taizōkai was not limited to the heterodox Tachikawa sect; it was very much part of mainstream esoteric thought in both Tendai and Shingon lineages.[47] It should not come as a surprise, then, to find that by 1288, when the *sokui kanjō* was first practised, this esoteric view on imperial sexuality already had a long tradition. It can be traced back at least to the Tendai abbot Jien (1155–1225).

Jien had a dream about the three regalia and their esoteric significance shortly after Emperor Antoku drowned at Dan no Ura in 1185, taking one of the regalia, the sword, with him to the bottom of the sea. Jien's dream must be seen in the context of the imperial rituals that formed part of his duties as the highest Tendai prelate. As *Tendai zasu* ('abbot'), Jien was in nightly attendance at the imperial palace, where together with his Shingon counterpart, the abbot of Tōji (*Tōji chōja*), he performed *yorui kaji*, a ritual for the health and safety of the emperor, in a room known as the *futama* ('the second room'), where a Kannon image was enshrined. This *futama* shared one thin wall with the *yoru no otodo*, the room where the emperor and empress slept in the presence of the imperial sword and jewel, which were laid out on a table placed between the imperial pillow and the *futama* wall.[48] Jien's dream (which Jien recorded in *Jichin oshō musōki*, 'Record of Abbot Jichin's [=Jien's] Dream Vision') was quite obviously inspired by this ritual context. Jien dreamt that the sword and jewel were transformed into the emperor and empress themselves, who embraced and thus formed the 'sword-and-sheath' mudra (*tōshō-in*) of Fudō Myōō. Born from their union was the third of the three regalia, the mirror preserved elsewhere in the imperial palace (in the *naishidokoro*), which represented the new emperor, Amaterasu, or Dainichi.[49]

It is not entirely clear whether Jien's dream record had a direct influence on the development of the *sokui kanjō*, or merely expresses ideas similar to that *kanjō*. It is striking, however, that in his record Jien referred to a remark in a report on the enthronement of Emperor Go-Sanjō in 1068 (*Go-Sanjō-in onsokuiki*), by the court scholar Ōe no Masafusa (1041–1111). In this report, Masafusa mentioned that on the enthronement platform the emperor was not carrying a *shaku*, and that it 'seemed as though he was forming with his hands the 'wisdom-fist' mudra (*chiken-in*) of Dainichi.'[50] Kamikawa Michio suggests that Jien may well have intended the 'sword-and-sheath' and 'wisdom-fist' mudras to replace the sword lost by Emperor Antoku. In relation to the *sokui kanjō*, it is worthy of note that the wisdom-fist mudra features prominently in many of the more elaborate *sokui kanjō* manuals. In these manuals, the wisdom-fist mudra accompanies the Dakini mantra, and is then followed by the 'mudra of rule over the four seas.'[51] The wisdom-fist mudra, finally, is very suggestive in a sexual sense: it is formed by folding the fingers of the right hand around the upright index finger of the left hand – an obvious symbol of

'wisdom-fist' mudra (*chiken-in*)

penetration, and thus a perfect companion to the Dakini mantra expressing the union of emperor and empress (or Kongōkai and Taizōkai).[52]

Also in relation with the *sokui kanjō*, it is worth noting that the most important rituals performed in the *futama* by the abbot of Tōji (the highest Shingon prelate) focused on the wish-fulfilling gem, which is such a central element of the *honzon* of this initiation. In the *goshichinichi no mishihō* ('seven-day practice'), for example, which was an annual ritual performed at the palace by the abbot of Tōji, the abbot aimed to invigorate the powers of the emperor (and thus of the nation) by activating the wish-fulfilling gem in meditation. There were various theories about the whereabouts of this gem, or even of the number of such gems, which were in fact small silver bottles containing grain-sized relics (*shari*) of the Buddha. The gem referred to in the 'seven-day practice' was said to have been given to Kūkai (774–835) by his Chinese teacher Huiguo (746–805), and according to an apocryphal testament of Kūkai (*Nijūgokajō goyuigō*, eleventh century) it had been buried in the mountains near the temple complex of Murōzan to guarantee the 'safety of the nation.' In relation to this practice, the Kannon image in the *futama* was sometimes identified as Nyoirin Kannon. Moreover, if the 'seven-day practice' was successful, it was said that the number of relics preserved in two silver bottles at Tōji (which were somehow 'one' with the gem at Murōzan) would increase in number. The newly created relics were counted each month, and distributed between the emperor and the retired emperor, who passed some of them on to their retainers.[53]

The above may suffice to show that the *sokui kanjō* formed part of an intricate system of esoteric imperial rituals. Nodal points in this system were the sexual union of the male and female aspects of Dainichi, and the wish-fulfilling gem. The first can be seen as an esoteric Buddhist equivalent to the kami rituals performed at the imperial court, which were primarily concerned with the fertility of land and people. While stressing this same theme of imperial fertility, the unity of Kongōkai and Taizōkai also represented the most profound truth of esoteric Buddhism: it was by gaining insight into this unity that one could attain instantaneous enlightenment. The second, the wish-fulfilling gem, was central to the relation between the Shingon sect and the imperial court. This gem was regarded as a Buddhist relic of extraordinary powers, dedicated by Kūkai to the protection of the Japanese state; in practice, it functioned as the chosen *honzon* for rituals performed to ensure the health, longevity, physical vigour and spiritual power of the emperor, or the safe birth of the crown prince – in other words, it was an imperial treasure that ensured the physical safety of the emperor and the continuation of the imperial line.[54] The spiritual power of the emperor was 'boosted' by the ritual activation of this gem, and subsequently demonstrated to retainers by means of the distribution of newly created 'sub-gems.' In this manner, the wish-fulfilling gem displayed both the power of the emperor (ruling or retired) over his retainers, and that of its caretakers, the Shingon sect, over the emperor. As such, it was a potent symbol of the interdependence of imperial rule and the Buddhist Law (ōbō buppō), and the closest Buddhist equivalent to the kami treasures in which imperial sovereignty was thought to be vested: the three imperial regalia.

In the sokui kanjō, these two focal points of esoteric imperial ritual were particularised in Dakini, who holds the wish-fulfilling gem in her hand, and is seated on a dragon-fox whose body, too, is a wish-fulfilling gem. In this image of Dakini, the gem, and the dragon-fox, all the elements of esoteric imperial ritual are combined into a single, powerful figure. It is probably no coincidence that this figure, otherwise known as Inari, was also the tutelary deity of the Shingon head temple Tōji. In the sokui kanjō, however, no reference is made to this; instead, it is explained that the dragon-fox/wish-fulfilling gem is an 'expedient body of Amaterasu,' the ancestor and protector of the imperial lineage. Tōji kuden elaborated on this point by claiming that the sokui kanjō was first taught by Amaterasu (= Dakini = dragon-fox) herself, to Nakatomi no Kamatari (614–69), the ancestor of the Fujiwara and therefore of the imperial regents who initiated the new emperor in this kanjō.[55]

Discussion

In Nakatomi harae kunge, Amaterasu (or her turbulent spirit, to be precise) appeared as a kami who transports our defilement to the Netherworld; in the Ise kanjō, as a snake embodying the 'three poisons' of greed, anger, and ignorance; and in the sokui kanjō, as a 'dragon-fox' and a demon. In the first, moreover, Amaterasu was associated with Enma-ō, the 'King of Hell'; in the second, with Aizen Myōō, the 'King of Desire'; and in the third, with the flesh-eating Dakini – all Buddhist divinities with outspokenly demonic features. Clearly these associations are fundamentally different from other current honji suijaku theories, which explained that Amaterasu's 'Original Source' was the 'World-Buddha' Dainichi, the benevolent Kannon, or the ruler of the world of man, Bontennō.[56]

One scholar describes the association of Amaterasu with 'extreme impurity' in Nakatomi harae kunge as a 'dangerous tale,' and argues that the notion that 'pure and impure are not two' adduced elsewhere in the text was inspired by the 'shock' this tale gave its author.[57] We have seen, however, that this was but a first step in a development that took Amaterasu into ever more 'shocking' terrain. The snake at the centre of the *Ise kanjō* was a very common figure in Buddhist legends of the Heian period, where the snake appeared as 'the evil inside us all,' symbolising in particular our 'detachment to things of this world' and our 'sexual appetites.'[58] In these legends, stories about the defeat of snakes by monks and the subsequent salvation of their victims abound; but in the *Ise kanjō* this same snake has become the *honzon* of an esoteric ritual, embodying the highest truth of Buddhism. The fox whose guise Amaterasu takes in the *sokui kanjō* was in many ways a similar figure to the snake, and the two have even been described as regional variations on a single theme: while the fox is the chosen witch animal in most regions of Japan, the snake replaces him in some.[59] Since 'dragon' and 'snake' are not seldom used interchangeably, the 'dragon-fox' may even represent a composite figure in which the two have been amalgamated. In legends and folktales, the fox tends to appear as a *femme fatale* and a trickster, seducing and mocking the virtuous, and not seldom inflicting serious harm and damage. Like the snake, then, he (or she) was hardly an obvious candidate to serve as Amaterasu's ultimate expedient, especially in this highest imperial initiation.

The snake and the fox of the *Ise* and *sokui kanjō* both fall into the category of kami variously referred to as *jitsurui*, 'the real kind,' or simply *jitsu*, 'real [kami].' This category was contrasted to *gonge*, *suijaku*, or simply *gon*, 'emanations' – kami who are expedient 'traces' of buddhas or bodhisattvas, and who have appeared among us in order to guide us to salvation. Unlike these 'emanations,' kami of the 'real kind' had no Buddhist credentials. *Shoshin honkaishū* (1324) describes them as 'human beings or animals who are revered as kami in order to pacify them and stop them from laying curses (*tatari*) and harassing [people].'[60] There was nothing 'expedient' about these 'real' kami; they were simply vicious, dangerous, and a general nuisance.

It was in these 'real' kami that esoteric monks took an interest in the course of the Kamakura period. To these kami, they applied the same paradoxical logic that informed the prominent positions in esoteric thought and ritual of demonic Buddhist divinities such as Aizen Myōō (lust), Fudō Myōō (anger), or Dakini (impurity). Aizen Myōō, for example, personifies the violent passions that are innate in all sentient beings, and symbolises the insight that these passions are identical, just as they are, to the pure mind of enlightenment. Aizen Myōō, then, is seen as identical to Kongōsatta (inherent enlightenment) and, ultimately, Dainichi (universal enlightenment). In Aizen rituals, which were among the most secret of the esoteric tradition, the power of these violent passions became an enlightened force that none can resist.[61] It was the technique of tackling (seemingly) unenlightened forces, realising their source in Dainichi's universal enlightenment, and then focusing them in a secret ritual that was at the core of esoteric practice in Japan – or, indeed, of 'Tantrism' in general.[62] Applying this ritual rationale to the kami, it becomes clear that the '(seemingly) unenlightened' kami would be the most ritually powerful. Also, it follows quite logically that these kami should be identified as the very stuff of inherent and, indeed, universal enlightenment.

Clearly there is an essential difference between *esoteric* associations between 'real' kami and Buddhist figures like Aizen Myōō, Fudō Myōō, or Dakini – and, by extrapolation, Kongōsatta and Dainichi – and *exoteric* associations of the *honji suijaku* kind. This does not mean, however, that esoteric lineages rejected the latter. Rather, esoteric monks devised complicated networks of associations by combining the two. Amaterasu did not cease to be associated with Dainichi or Kannon; rather, these associations were given new ritual power by particularising these overarching figures in the form of very 'real' and concrete beings. Amaterasu was Dainichi not just in theory, but in the powerful, familiar guise of witch animals, *via* demonic figures such as Dakini and Aizen Myōō. Similarly, Amaterasu was Kannon in the particularised guise of Nyoirin Kannon, appearing as a frighteningly 'real' fox. An example of the practices this inspired is the performance by Eizon of Aizen rituals of exorcism (*jōbuku*) for protection against the Mongols, in front of an altar (*zushi*) that contained mirrors carrying spirits of the kami of the Inner and Outer Shrine of Ise. Eizon had received these mirrors 'from Amaterasu herself' in 1280, on one of his pilgrimages to these shrines.[63]

Moreover, knowledge of these 'particularisations' and the practices based on them was shrouded in secrecy and further empowered by the mysterious solemnity of initiations. Full and partial initiations moved freely across sectarian lines. They were exchanged between monks of various esoteric lineages as well as shrine priests, and inspired new insights, ideas and ritual practices in those who received them. *Bikisho*, a text from 1324, is a good example of the flow of esoteric kami knowledge. *Bikisho* contains secret Shingon theories about the *sokui kanjō*, the central pillars of the Ise shrines, and some esoteric drawings relating to the Ise shrines, discovered at the imperial palace. Kadoya Atsushi has unravelled the web of initiations that led to the compilation of this text, which was written by a certain Chien who is otherwise unknown. Chien got his information at Sekidera, a clan temple of Outer Shrine priests in Ise, from a monk called Chibu Risshi, in return for an initiation from one of the Shingon Hirosawa lineages. In return, Chibu Risshi passed on the secret knowledge outlined in *Bikisho*, which he in turn had received from Dōjun (fl. 1321), the abbot of the prominent Shingon temple Daigoji, and from Watarai Tsuneyoshi (1263–1339), a leading Outer Shrine priest.[64] A few years later, we find further revelations relating to these same secrets in *Tenshō Daijin kuketsu* (1327), a text by Kakujō (c. 1273–1363), who belonged to Eizon's lineage.[65]

All this suggests that 'secret' information travelled widely and rapidly among lineages, temples, and shrines, where such knowledge was flaunted, hinted at, and exchanged by religious specialists of wideranging provenance. These then went on to select and combine, rearrange and expand, and, most importantly, to write things down and systemise them in new ritual forms. It was this activity, at places like Sekidera, that informed the dynamism behind the baffling array of associations, initiations, and practices produced by esoteric Buddhist Shinto.

At Ise, places where secret knowledge could be developed and exchanged were perhaps particularly numerous and prominent. In 1275, for example, Tsūkai (1234–1305) of Daigoji had founded two 'chapels for Buddhist services to the kami' (*hōrakusha*) within the precincts of the two Ise shrines, to pray for divine assistance in defeating the Mongols. These chapels belonged to the nearby temple of Daijingū Hōrakuji, an old clan temple of the Nakatomi where Tsūkai was the abbot, and which he brought under Daigoji control. Five years later, in 1280, Eizon founded a temple named Kōshōji not far from the Inner Shrine, which remained under the control of Saidaiji. At these places, monks and priests met, mixed, and exchanged information, and they became centres of theological expertise. It was at temples like these that works such as *Reikiki*, a true encyclopedia of Buddhist kami theories, were compiled;[66] these works then formed the basis for the multi-layered initiations that would dominate the further development of esoteric Shinto lineages.

Shrine priests joined in this exciting theological activity. At Kōshōji, for example, monks from the same Arakida clan that staffed the Inner Shrine (Dōjō, Shun'yu) copied and preserved Shinto texts, and developed and passed on secret knowledge about the kami.[67] Esoteric Buddhist theories dominated the writings of medieval shrine priests. This was true for obviously Buddhist schools such as Miwa, Sannō or Goryū Shinto; but also for Watarai or Ise Shinto, which, misleadingly, has been described as an attempt to 'emancipate Shinto from the Buddhist-dominated Shinto-Buddhist amalgamation.'[68] A single glance at Watarai Ieyuki's (1256–1351?) digest of Watarai Shintō, *Ruiju jingi hongen* (1320), which was to prove the most influential and lasting work of this tradition, is enough to reveal that he relied heavily on *Reikiki*, and most so in the most secret and crucial part of this work, on the mirrors of the Ise shrines.

Historically speaking, the most important aspect of the esoteric Buddhist kami discourse outlined here was perhaps that it was *via* this discourse that shrine practice embarked on the long road that would eventually result in the emergence of a non-Buddhist, self-sufficient religion named Shinto. As argued above, this discourse contrasted the Buddha to the kami by stating that while the former represents the (inferior) 'acquired enlightenment' of exoteric Buddhism, the latter embody the (superior) 'inherent enlightenment' of esoteric Buddhism. Here, for the first time, kami are given precedence over the Buddha. At Ise, Tsuneyoshi translated this into the theory that monks were 'of no use' at Ise, because as representatives of acquired enlightenment, their presence could only defile the Ise shrines, which are the domain of Dainichi's undiluted universal enlightenment.[69] Around the same time, this discourse gave rise to the theory of 'inverted *honji suijaku*,' according to which the kami are the source of the buddhas, rather than the reverse.[70] Here, the kami are for the first time presented as religious forces in their own right, rather than as secondary 'traces' of Buddhist divinities. This represented a first tentative step towards the non-Buddhist Shinto of later ages. This step became possible only because monks of the esoteric sects had invested kami of the 'real kind' with sublime powers of their own, and it would prove to be a seminal event in the development of Shinto into the independent religion that it is today.

Notes

My special gratitude is due to Murei Hitoshi of Kōgakkan Daigaku in Ise who most generously shared his knowledge of these matters with me during a brief stay in Ise in December–January 1997–8. My thanks go also to the Japan Foundation Endowment Committee, who made the stay possible. The illustrations are from Inatani 1993.

1 See Grapard 1988.
2 On these developments, see e.g. Yoshie Akio 1996 and Susan Tyler 1989. A useful summary of the development of Japanese research into these matters can be found in Itō Satoshi 1998.
3 The three shrines of Kumano, for example, the destination of grand court pilgrimages during the twelfth century, were identified as emanations of Amida (Hongū), Senju Kannon (Nachi), and Yakushi (Hayatama), and as entrance gates to their respective paradises of *gokuraku jōdo*, *fudaraku jōdo*, and *jōruri jōdo*.
4 ST vol. Hie: 81; quoted in Sueki Fumihiko 1993: 354.
5 ST vol. Hie: 78; Sueki 1993: 356.
6 ST vol. *Tendai Shinto ge*: 410; Sueki 1993: 365.
7 The eight steps here referred to are descent from heaven, conception, birth, becoming a monk, conquering demons, reaching enlightenment, turning the wheel of the Law, and extinction.
8 ST vol. *Tendai Shinto ge*: 410; Sueki 1993: 365. ST vol. *Tendai Shinto ge*: 405 explains why the Hie shrines carry the titles of *sōbyō* and *shashoku*.
9 On *hongaku* ideas and their position within medieval Buddhist thought, see *JJRS* 22-1/2, Spring 1995, with articles by Sueki Fumihiko, Jacqueline Stone, Paul Groner, and Ruben Habito on this subject. See also Ruben Habito 1996.
10 ST vol. *Tendai Shinto ge*: 410–1.
11 On this legend, see Yamasaki 1988: 87–9.
12 Śākyamuni's erring cousin, who, among other things, plotted to kill him.
13 ST vol. *Tendai Shinto ge*: 412–3.
14 For this term, see Itō Masayoshi 1972.
15 ST vol. *Tendai Shinto ge*: 405.
16 Murayama Shūichi 1974: 326. It is of course no coincidence that Ōmiwa Daimyōjin is given precedence over Ise in this Miwa text.
17 On the association of Amaterasu with Dainichi by Gyōgi, see Kushida Ryōkō 1964 (1973): 233–9, and Nishida Nagao 1978–9: vol. 4, 10 ff. For *Shingon fuhō san'yōshō*, see Kushida 1964 (1973): 277.
18 For a lucid discussion of this confusing term, see Kadoya Atsushi 1995: 61–6. This volume also includes a useful bibliography of medieval Shinto.
19 For more detail, see Teeuwen and Van der Veere 1998. An extract from this monograph has appeared in Tanabe, ed., 1999.
20 See Watabe Mayumi 1991: 49–95. A translation of the *Ōharae no kotoba* can be found in Philippi 1959.
21 The text is thought to have been inspired by *rokuji karinpō*, a large-scale ritual of exorcism performed by monks of the highest rank for members of the Imperial House and the Kamakura shogunate. The earliest description of this ritual can be found in *Gyōrinshō* (compiled in 1154). *Rokuji karinpō* can be translated as 'river-

bank ritual of the seed-syllables of the six Kannon,' and was a combination of the Buddhist ritual of *rokujikyō-hō* or *rokuji-hō* ('ritual of the six-syllable sutra') with the *onmyōji* ritual of *karin-harae* ('river-bank purification'). See Murayama Shūichi 1976: 38–9 and Kushida 1964 (1973): 258.

22 ST vol. Nakatomi harae chūshaku: 11–2.
23 On these rituals, see Hayami Tasuku 1975: 234–61.
24 ST vol. Nakatomi harae chūshaku: 3–4.
25 *Ibid.*, 3; see Teeuwen and Van der Veere 1998: 66–7.
26 ST vol. Nakatomi harae chūshaku: 5.
27 *Ibid.*
28 See Yamasaki 1988: 175–7. *Kanjō* translates Skt. *abhiṣeka.*
29 For an example of a highly developed system of successive kami initiations, see Hatta Yukio 1991: 70–107, describing *Miwa kanjō* in detail.
30 For the date 1289, see Kushida Ryōkō 1979: 513; for 1262, see Itō Satoshi 1997: 64.
31 See Itō Satoshi 1997: 64–5, and Yamamoto Hiroko 1990: 144–6.
32 Since the Ise shrines themselves are notoriously not red but left unpainted, this throws up the question whether the ritual described in this initiation was in fact performed at Ise. First of all, it should be noted that Ise mandara from the medieval period routinely depict the Ise shrines as red, and while these mandara are more schematic than accurate, the possibility that the Ise shrines were in fact painted red during the medieval period cannot be ruled out. While it is therefore quite possible that this ritual was performed as part of Ise pilgrimages, it would nevertheless seem likely that it was more commonly performed at temple *chinju* shrines, or perhaps even as a purely mental exercise, simply because Ise pilgrimages must have been relatively rare occasions.
33 In other words: the kami is nothing else than the activity of one's own mind, which is inherently enlightened. For *chihayaburu* in the meaning 'born from the womb' (an interpretation based on reading the compound as *chiha-yaburu*, 'tearing a thousand petals,' and common in Ise-related initiations), see Susan Blakeley Klein 1997: 456, and 1998: 29–33.
34 For a detailed treatment of Aizen Myōō, see Goepper 1993.
35 Yamamoto 1990: 145; Itō Satoshi 1997: 66–70. Itō discusses the relation of *Ise kanjō* with the Tachikawa ritual of *Denbu Aizen-hō*, which was practised in both Tendai and Shingon lineages since 1210 at the latest. Its *honzon-zu* (a scroll used as a focus for a ritual) shows Aizen Myōō as a snake, carrying a wish-fulfilling gem on its head, and seated on an eight-petalled lotus. Itō cites examples of use of this *zu* in *Ise kanjō* initiations.
36 ST vol. Tendai Shinto ge: 415.
37 Itō Satoshi 1997: 66. Fudō Myōō is Skt. Acalanātha, Amida is Amitāyus or Amitābha.
38 ST vol. Tendai Shinto ge: 415. This is a reference to the Devadatta chapter of the Lotus sutra, which recounts how this dragon girl attained instantaneous enlightenment after presenting the Buddha with a 'precious jewel'; see Burton Watson 1993: 187–9.
39 For detailed descriptions of this *kanjō*, its practice, and its backgrounds, see Kamikawa Toshio 1989: 106–39, Abe Yasurō 1989: 113–69, and Yamamoto 1990.
40 Fushimi noted in his diary (*Fushimi Tennō nikki*) that he was instructed by the *kanpaku* (Nijō Morotada) in 'secret mudras, etcetera, for the enthronement' on Shōō 1 (1288)/3/13, and that he 'formed mudras and chanted mantras' while proceeding to the enthronement hall on 3/15. No further details are known. Kamikawa 1989: 112.
41 *Mikkyō daijiten*, 1552–3. Interestingly, Dakini also features prominently in the retinue of Enma-ō, and in that capacity developed into a popular object of worship among the Heian nobility.

42 *Shin* or *tatsu*, which usually denotes a calendary *eto* sign, combines the notions of 'dragon' and 'dawn; sun, moon and stars; celestial lights,' and is therefore more expressive in this context than my translation suggests.

43 Cintāmani is Sanskrit for 'wish-fulfilling gem.'

44 ST vol. Tendai Shinto ge: 424.

45 Kawakami Toshio (1989: 119), for example, quotes one tradition of this mantra as follows: 'Initiate [the emperor] in the wisdom-fist mudra (*chiken-in*) . . . and in [the following] two mantras: the mantra of Dainichi of the Kongōkai, *dakini bazaradado ban*, and the mantra of Dainichi of the Taizōkai, *dakini a-bi-ra-un-ken.*' As explicitly stated here, these mantras denote the two mandalas; the wisdom-fist mudra (which will be discussed further below) denotes their unity.

46 Abe Yasurō 1989: 141. This explanation was especially current at Daigoji Sanbōin (one of the three most prominent Shingon temples).

47 On the Tachikawa sect, see Sanford 1991.

48 This sword was actually said to be a copy of the original sword, found in the tail of a dragon by Susanowo, which was preserved at the Atsuta shrine. For the reading *yorui*, I relied on Abe Yasurō (1989), 123; this compound is more commonly read *yoi*.

49 Abe Yasurō 1989: 139. My account of Jien's dream is slightly simplified. The mirror in the *naishidokoro* was thought to be a copy of the mirror handed to Ninigi by Amaterasu, and preserved at the Inner Shrine in Ise.

50 Quoted in Kamikawa 1989: 110. Kamikawa rejects the possibility that this remark could imply that the *sokui kanjō* was performed already at this early date, which is a full two centuries before the first recorded performance, and more than a century before Jien's dream record (116). A *shaku* is a flat wooden baton that formed part of formal attire, perhaps best described as a 'hand-held tie.'

51 *Ibid.*, 119. See also note 44, above.

52 On this mudra's sexual connotations, see Saunders 1960 (1985): 102–7.

53 Abe Yasurō 1989: 124–7.

54 *Ibid.*, 127–33.

55 See Abe Yasurō 1980. According to this *engi*, handed down in many versions, Amaterasu/Dakini appeared as a dragon-fox to kidnap a young boy. She taught this boy a 'secret technique' (*hihō*) and gave him a 'wisteria sickle' (*fuji-maki no kama*), telling him that these would preserve the imperial lineage. With this sickle, the boy (later to become known as Fujiwara no *Kama*tari) beheaded the rebel Soga no Iruka and thus saved the throne; as a reward, he was raised to the position of minister, in which he initiated the emperor in Amaterasu's 'secret technique.' For obvious reasons, this *engi* is also current in texts related to the Fujiwara shrines of Kasuga and Kashima. The Tendai *engi* of the *sokui kanjō*, however, is completely different; here, the practice is traced back to an initiation received by King Mu, the fifth king of Zhou, from Śākyamuni himself. See Abe Yasurō 1984.

56 See Kubota Osamu 1973: 299 ff., Agatsuma Matashirō 1982, and Itō Satoshi 1996: 251 ff. Bontennō (Skt. Brahmarāja) rules over the Realm of Desire (*yokukai*), which includes our human world, from his abode in the highest heaven (*shozenten*) of the superior Realm of Pure Form (*shikikai*), and features in many texts as the Buddhist 'Source' of Amaterasu, who dwells on the Plain of High Heaven.

57 Sakurai Yoshirō 1993: 262–70.

58 Kelsey 1981: 110.

59 This was first pointed out by Yanagita Kunio; see Carmen Blacker 1975 (1986): 51.

60 The *locus classicus* of this distinction is article 5 of Jōkei's *Kōfukuji sōjō* (1205). See Hirazawa Takuya 1997: 77. In *Shintōshū* (late fourteenth century), the kami (*shintō*) of the *jitsu* category are simply typified as 'all snakes and demons' (Hirazawa, 79).

61 On Aizen rituals, see Goepper 1993 chapter 12 and Yamamoto Hiroko 1997.

62 Fabio Rambelli (1994: 376) characterises Tantrism as 'a complex magico-ritual apparatus that systematically reverses the renouncement ideals proper to religious institutions, especially Buddhism, although it does not necessarily conceive of itself as an opposition ideology.' The 'magico-ritual' reversal of destructive passions (here embodied by the kami) into forces of universal enlightenment in twelfth and thirteenth century Japan is perfectly compatible with this Tantric paradigm. Also, strikingly, this reversal was not part of an 'opposition ideology' but was at the core of Shingon and Tendai imperial and state ritual.

63 See Kondō Yoshihiro 1959; also Kushida 1964 (1973): 310.

64 Kadoya Atsushi 1993.

65 Itō Satoshi 1995.

66 Hiraizumi Takafusa (1995: 244–7), for example, argues that Tsūkai's Daijingū Hōrakuji would be the most probable location for the compilation of this text.

67 Itō Satoshi 1993.

68 Joseph M. Kitagawa 1987: 159.

69 In *Daijingū ryōgū no onkoto* (1335); see Teeuwen 1996: 106–7. This theory appears earlier in *Keiran jūyōshū*, ST vol. Tendai Shinto ge: 412.

70 Sugahara Shinkai (1992: 175) argues convincingly that 'the idea of inverted *honji suijaku* first arose in the age of Jihen (dates unknown; most active in the 1330s), and Jihen was the first to systematise it as a Shinto theory.' Jihen was a Tendai monk close to Tsuneyoshi.

CHAPTER SEVEN

Reading the *Yuiitsu Shintō myōbō yōshū*: A modern exegesis of an esoteric Shinto text

Bernhard Scheid

Introduction

In the later Muromachi period (1336–1568), a sacerdotal shrine lineage called the Yoshida-Urabe began to expound what they called Yuiitsu (the One-and-Only) Shinto. Right from the beginning the Yoshida enjoyed reasonable success in establishing this teaching as a kind of Shinto orthodoxy. The implications of their success are still widely open to research, yet no specialist would deny that Yoshida or Urabe Shinto, as it is called today, was one of the most influential brands of Shinto in the Late Medieval and Early Modern periods. Also, there is no disagreement about the fact that Yoshida Shinto was profoundly determined by its founder, Yoshida Kanetomo (1435–1511), who drafted numerous prayers, instructions, manuals for religious ceremonies, and, last but not least, his main doctrinal text, the *Yuiitsu Shintō myōbō yōshū* or Essentials of Names and Laws of the One-and-Only Way of the Kami (hereafter *Myōbō yōshū*).[1] Nevertheless, as Allan Grapard has written: 'In spite of the centrality of [Kanetomo] in the Japanese medieval world and in the history of the Japanese tradition in general, there are no studies of him and his thought in English.'[2] In addition to an introductory article that deals primarily with the significance of Yoshida Shinto in general, Grapard himself improved on this situation by translating the *Myōbō yōshū* into English.[3] Since then, Yoshida Shinto has also been given attention in a study of Watarai Shinto by Mark Teeuwen.[4] Teeuwen discusses it as the main proponent of Shinto in the late Medieval period to develop and distribute the ideas of the early Watarai priests of Ise. We should add that the *Myōbō yōshū* was translated into German as early as 1940 by Ishibashi and Dumoulin, and that the influence of the *Myōbō yōshū* on Neo-Confucian thinkers like Hayashi Razan has been discussed in a German study of Tokugawa intellectual history by Klaus Kracht.[5] However, none of these studies has gone so far as to analyse the contents of the *Myōbō yōshū* systematically. Japanese specialists have also failed to rise to the challenge.

The most obvious reason for this lack of research seems to lie in the nature of the text itself. The *Myōbō yōshū* presents itself as an 'esoteric' transmission, which is to say that its doctrines are more or less by definition secret, obscure, and not immediately intelligible. Ever since the Edo period, scholars and theologians alike have become increasingly critical towards theological discourse of this kind. Yoshida Shinto, as expounded in the *Myōbō yōshū*, has often been regarded as a confusing, eclectic hotchpotch of heterogeneous doctrines, based on arbitrary identifications of numeric isomorphisms, and so is discarded as nothing more than a pale imitation of esoteric Buddhism, larded with some Taoist ornamentations.[6] Even Allan Grapard portrays Kanetomo as living in a 'never-ending prison of resemblance,' and regards Yoshida Shinto more or less as a dead end in Japanese intellectual history.[7]

In contrast to this evaluation, I would like to point out that this esoteric discourse was by no means peculiar to the *Myōbō yōshū* or the texts of Yoshida Shinto. There is, in fact, a dense network of texts, ranging from the Kamakura through to the Edo period, authored by Buddhist monks, Shinto priests and even Neo-Confucian scholars, which I would subsume under the label 'esoteric Shinto.'[8] These texts are 'esoteric' in the sense that they rely on traditions that, allegedly, have been transmitted in secret in the past and are to be kept secret in the future, too. Many not only deal with the kami, but also show a strong orientation towards Chinese cosmology which they superimpose on the national mythology of world creation. On the other hand, they frequently refer to all kinds of ritual practices such as mantras, mudras, and *kaji* that derive from esoteric Buddhism. Esoteric Shinto discourse is thus clearly eclectic, but that should not imply that it is unsystematic. It certainly built on 'invented traditions,' but that does not mean it allowed for unlimited, arbitrary invention. The various texts may centre their speculations on different shrine traditions, but in the final analysis they are all part of a combined effort to overcome the notorious lack of a systematic, comprehensive indigenous theology. Certain nationalistic overtones are also therefore characteristic of esoteric Shinto discourse.

In this essay, I read the *Myōbō yōshū* as an example of precisely this esoteric Shinto tradition. I deal with the specific significance attributed to secrecy, the adoption of the fundamental cosmic principles of Taoism, and the efforts to create a ritual system that could compare with Buddhism. I do not go too much into the details of the relations between Yoshida Shinto, Watarai Shinto, Ryōbu Shinto, and other specific Shinto lineages, but the reader should bear in mind that the *Myōbō yōshū* is presented here as just one paradigmatic text among many others that can facilitate an understanding of the modes and tenets of Shinto discourse in medieval Japan. I concentrate, moreover, on the expositions of Yuiitsu teaching proper, which form the central, yet most impenetrable part of the *Myōbō yōshū*. In addition to these doctrinal expositions, the text deals mainly with the different kinds of Shinto and the relationship between Shinto and Buddhism in general. These passages are comparatively easy to understand and well known. They include Kanetomo's famous classification of three kinds of Shinto: Honjaku-engi Shinto, based on the *honji suijaku* theory; Ryōbu-shūgō Shinto, based on the amalgamation of

Dainichi and Amaterasu; and Genpon-sōgen Shinto, Kanetomo's own teaching which, he claims, 'has existed since the foundation of the Japanese nation.'[9] The last is singled out by Kanetomo as the most basic, original teaching of the kami, and contrasted with the other two, which are both said to be influenced by Buddhism to some degree. The relation between Buddhism and Shinto is further discussed in the so-called 'tree theory' which identifies Shinto as the basis (= roots and trunk) of Confucianism (= twigs and leaves) and Buddhism (= flowers and fruit). Consequently, Kanetomo adheres to the inverted version of the *honji suijaku* theory, which identifies the kami as the origin (*honji*) of the buddhas (*suijaku*). These arguments are not strictly anti-Buddhist, nor do they question the coexistence of kami and buddhas which was commonplace at that time. Rather, they aim for a value shift within this syncretistic world view: a reversal of the master/disciple relationship between Buddha and kami teaching.

In spite of the fact that most of the *Myōbō yōshū*'s arguments concerning the relationship between kami and buddhas had already been formulated in earlier texts, the *Myōbō yōshū* is commonly credited for its novel usage of the term 'Shinto' in the meaning of a non-Buddhist, independent religious tradition (similar to its present-day meaning). However, as we will see in detail below, in the central, doctrinal part of the text the term 'Shinto' is to be understood as the deeds or activities of the kami, much in the same sense as in older texts. This is only one example to suggest that the specific doctrinal expositions of the *Myōbō yōshū* somehow stand apart from the rest of the text. We may perhaps call them the 'esoteric part' of the text. This esoteric part may be particularly responsible for the bad image of the *Myōbō yōshū*. However, as I endeavour to show below, difficulties in understanding this part of the text might be equally due to our implicit expectations of any form of literature: that a given text will want to be readily understood, just by reading. We thus tend to interpret the *Myōbō yōshū* as an exoteric text, and disregard the fact that a teaching which calls itself 'secret' or 'esoteric' would constitute a contradiction in terms if it were capable of understanding without tutorial guidance. This should not exclude the possibility that the text actually contains some message. In order to decode this message, however, we should be prepared for some obstacles. We must not expect it to be spelled out, for example, that there is a correspondence between microcosm and macrocosm, and that, therefore, the laws which govern and structure the universe simultaneously govern and structure the human body. Such general remarks do not befit an esoteric teaching. Equally, there is no attempt to translate a highly specialised terminology into common language, nor to define terms, except for a definition consisting of further new terms. Any object may be referred to by more than one term and any term may refer to more than one object. In particular, every object is liable to be identified with the class of objects it belongs to. Thus, the level of abstraction is always ambiguous. Many statements are connected by a causal conjunction (*yue ni, sunawachi*), but to grasp this causality requires very careful reading and specialist knowledge. The *Myōbō yōshū* may have been intended as an introduction to Yoshida Shinto, but its didacticism seems to be built on the principle that, for the new apprentice, most arguments should become understandable only in retrospect. The aim is not to convince by immediate meaningfulness; rather, the text sets out to conceal matters in such a way that they become meaningful only step by step.

Chinese cosmology

The often confusing question/answer sequences of what I shall call the esoteric or doctrinal part of the *Myōbō yōshū* lose much of their arbitrariness when one realises that there is a correspondence between the organisation of the arguments and the orderly principle these arguments refer to. This principle is derived from Taoism and is mentioned in a passage from the *Daode jing* quoted at the end of the *Myōbō yōshū*:

> The Dao gives birth to the One. The One produces the Two; the Two produces the Three; the Three produces the ten thousand phenomena.[10]

Translated into modern language, we may infer from this statement that there is a monistic principle which first develops into a dualistic principle, and then into a triadic principle to create all phenomena of the universe. Instead of 'produce' or 'develop,' the verb 'split' would be equally correct. There are several terms in Taoism which refer to the monistic principle: the term Dao itself, the 'Great One' (*taiyi*), the 'Great Ultimate' (*taiji*), the 'Original Qi' (*yuanqi*), or 'Primordial Chaos' (*huntun*). They all refer to a basic form of existence, which is common to every aspect of the world. The monistic principle is at the same time the modifying power and the modified substance that lead to the diversification of existence into the phenomena of the visible world. Also, it is the form of existence to which every single entity eventually returns, and forms the utopian topos of the Taoist sage's quest for a life in harmony.[11]

The first step of this diversification is the partition of the One into Two, that is, the dualistic principle of Yin and Yang. Yang ascends and becomes Heaven, Yin settles and becomes Earth. To provide for a dynamic creative process, however, a sphere which allows both to mingle is necessary. This sphere is identified as Man, resulting in the triadic principle of Heaven, Earth, and Man, also called the 'three powers' (*sancai*, J. *sansai*), or 'three foundations' (*sanyuan*, J. *sangen*). Richard Wilhelm compares this conception to Hegel's dialectic principle of thesis, antithesis and synthesis.[12] According to Isabelle Robinet, Heaven and Earth are related to Man as father and mother, for they create him, nourish him, carry him and give him shelter. At the same time, Man acts as a 'hybrid in-between,' both separating and uniting Heaven and Earth.[13] Whatever interpretation we choose, we should keep in mind that in this triadic principle, Heaven, Earth, and Man also serve as the headers of a classificatory system, and are thus put formally at the same logical level, in contrast to Western thinking which would tend to place one of them either above or below the other two.

From Kanetomo's writings we can infer that this concept must have had a great impact on his thinking.[14] However, there is no systematic explanation of it in the *Myōbō yōshū*, except for the short quotation from the *Daode jing* cited above. Moreover, in referring to the respective monistic, dualistic and triadic principles, Kanetomo often uses terms different from the Taoist sources which are either his own inventions or taken from previous esoteric Shinto texts.

Let me briefly mention some additional Taoist concepts that will prove useful in understanding the *Myōbō yōshū*. As we have seen, the 'three foundations' structure the universe vertically: Heaven – which is Yang – at the top, Earth (Yin) at the bottom, and Man (the result of both) in the middle. There is, however, also a horizontal structure, which divides space into five categories – the cardinal directions and the middle. This corresponds to a temporal division – the four seasons and the 'axis of time.' These categories do not imply a static structure, but form a system of cyclic changes. Known as the 'five phases,' often symbolised by certain natural elements (water, fire, wood, metal, and earth), they represent the laws according to which things change until they return to the point of repetition where the cycle starts afresh.[15]

In his classical work on Chinese thought, Marcel Granet has shown how these basic categories of space and time relate to, or rather transform into, all the other numerical sets which came to be regarded as meaningful representations of the cosmic order. The number five corresponds to the four directions (N, S, E, W) plus the middle. If one adds the directions NW, NE, SW, and SE, one gets the number nine. Nine can be graphically represented in the form of a square consisting of nine divisions:

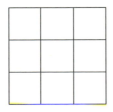

This square is regarded as the ground plan of the Earth. Further, it serves as a basic diagram in the cosmogonic speculations of *Yijing*-divination. It would lead us too far to repeat Granet's demonstrations how the numbers 8, 10, 12, 15 and many more can also be related to this basic square. Suffice it to say that not only the numerical categories, but also the way of thinking described by Granet are fundamental to understanding the epistemological setting of the esoteric discourse in the *Myōbō yōshū*.

The monistic principle

Let us now take a look at the basic, ultimate entity in the *Myōbō yōshū* which becomes the central issue right at the beginning of Kanetomo's doctrinal expositions. Referring to his term 'Genpon-sōgen Shinto,' Kanetomo explains genpon and sogen as synonyms of the One. *Genpon* 元本, which might be translated as 'original beginning,' is said to predate Yin and Yang and the first moment of diversification 一念.[16] The explanation of the term *sōgen* is similar, but somewhat more specific:

Q7:[17] What is *sōgen*?
A7: *Sō* 宗 ('ancestor') reveals the original kami (*genshin* 元神), predating the diversification of the One Qi 一気未分. Thus, all phenomena return to that one and true origin. This is called *sō*. *Gen* 源; ('source') reveals the transformation of the kami, as they soften their glare and merge with the dust.[18] Thus, it unfolds the basis of benefit for all sentient beings. This is called *gen*. Hence the verse:
  Sō is the return of all phenomena to the One.
  Gen is the unfolding of all bonds between living beings.[19]

In this explanation we find two aspects of the One which are also present in Taoism: the One as the basic entity from which everything evolves; and as the entity to which everything returns.[20] In a later passage the very term *shintō* is interpreted as a synonym of the same monistic principle:

A36: *Shin* (as in Shinto) is the spirit-ancestor (*Reisō* 霊宗) of all the ten thousand things in Heaven and Earth. Therefore, it is said that *shin* existed before Yin and Yang 陰陽不測.[21] *Tō* 道 is the origin of all activities. Therefore, it is said that the Way is not the ordinary way.[22] Thus, there is nothing [. . .] that is not Shinto. Hence the verse:
  Shin is the mind (*shin/kokoro*) of all beings.[23]
  Tō is the source of all activities.[24]

Here another double aspect of the ultimate principle that we already mentioned in connection with Taoism appears. The original One – to call it by the most neutral term – can be understood both as something substantial from which everything is made, and as something functional which stimulates all development. It is at the same time the 'clay' from which the cosmos is formed, and the 'hands' which form it.[25] Thus, both the pantheistic world view of kami worship, and the tendency towards monotheism which Ōkuwa Hiroshi finds in the *Myōbō yōshū* are equally compatible with this monistic conception.[26]

There is a wide range of additional names and terms that refer to this same principle. Among them, there are more abstract terms such as '(God of the) Great Origin' (Taigen or Taigenshin), 'spirit' (*rei*), or 'mind' (*shin/kokoro*), but also – more personalised – the 'Divine ancestor of the Heavenly Deities,' Ame-no-kami-no-mioya, or – as in Watarai Shinto – the first mythological deity,

122

Kuni no Tokotachi or Ame no Minakanushi. On the other hand, we must not overlook the fact that words like 'mind,' 'spirit,' 'divine,' and even 'Shinto' may also take on a much narrower and more specific meaning. While Kanetomo – as already mentioned – is frequently regarded as the first to use 'Shinto' in the sense of a 'religious teaching,' he also uses the term 'the Eighteen Shinto' to refer to a specific esoteric ceremony. Shinto in this case is thus a kind of ritual. Again, at one point, Kanetomo prefers to write *shintō* with characters meaning 'the true way' 真道 arguing that *shin/kami* is 'the general denomination of all spiritual beings (*reisei* 霊性) good and bad, false and true'.[27] Moreover, the characters *shin/kami* and *rei* 'spirit' are often used simply as adjectives to convey a mysterious, sacred quality. The fact that, for Kanetomo, a word seems to be the more attractive the more meanings it contains, certainly contributes to our difficulties in accessing the *Myōbō yōshū*.

The dualistic principle

The space reserved for the introduction of the monistic principle in the *Myōbō yōshū* is admittedly not very large. I am quite certain that Kanetomo had in mind (among others) the sequence '1, 2, 3, [all]' when he started his doctrinal explanations with a reference to the 'original beginning'; yet other references to the monistic principle are also to be found in later passages. Thus, concerning '1', my claim that this sequence forms the organising principle of the *Myōbō yōshū* may be open to debate. The 'dualistic section' which follows the brief monistic one, however, is easier to identify. This part of the text refers to a number of dualistic conceptions, and also arranges the question-answer pattern accordingly.

The dualistic section begins with A8, where we learn that Yuiitsu Shinto is composed of exoteric (*ken*) and esoteric (*mitsu*), or plainly open (*kenro* 顕露) and mysteriously secret (*on'yū* 隠幽), teachings. Even Kanetomo could not ignore the fact that this corresponds to the coexistence of exoteric and esoteric doctrines in Japanese medieval Buddhism which Kuroda Toshio called the *kenmitsu* system.[28] In a later passage in the *Myōbō yōshū*, however, he argues that the two-fold structure of his religious system was of pre-Buddhist origin.[29]

The organisation of this structure forms the main issue of the following question-answer sequels. These never forget to add a secret, esoteric aspect after each explanation of the corresponding exoteric one. Proceeding in this way, the text runs through a list of topics: canonical scriptures, the proper time and space for rituals, ritual sites, and prayers. As long as Kanetomo deals with the 'open' aspect, the student of Shinto meets with more or less familiar issues; the 'secret' aspects, on the other hand, always remain ill-defined and mysterious. In the following, I discuss the two conceptions 'purity' and 'treasure,' both of which contain an open and a secret part. These examples illustrate how Kanetomo skilfully used the dichotomy of secret versus open to synthesise traditional 'Shinto' and 'non-Shinto' elements into a religious system of his own.

Purity: ritual time, ritual space

Let me mention only briefly the distinction between open and secret canonical scriptures mentioned at the beginning of the dualistic section.[30] According to the text, the open teaching is contained in the three classics *Kojiki, Nihon shoki,* and *Sendai kuji hongi,* and the secret teaching in three secret classics with the ornate names *Tengen jinben jinmyōkyō, Jigen jinzū jinmyōkyō,* and *Jingen jinriki jinmyōkyō* for the secret teaching.[31]

Next, Kanetomo arranges the open and the secret parts of his religious system under the headers 'outer purity' (*geshōjō*) and 'inner purity' (*naishōjō*). These are originally Buddhist concepts that were also adopted by earlier esoteric Shinto thinkers, most notably the Watarai of Ise. They defined outer purity as ritual purification of the body by external means such as, for example, taking a bath, and inner purity as the purification of the heart or mind. Kanetomo appears to be influenced by these definitions, but uses these terms in an even broader sense. In the context of the *Myōbō yōshū,* 'purity' (*shōjō*) assumes the meaning of ritual in general. 'Inner purity' thus refers to the system of 'esoteric,' 'outer purity' to the system of 'exoteric' rituals. The first items classified under the headers of outer and inner purity in the *Myōbō yōshū* are the two stages of ritual time in traditional Shinto rites, *chisai* and *sansai* (severe and light observance of taboos, also pronounced *ma-imi* and *ara-imi*). These formed the basis of the twofold conception of purity already in Watarai Shinto.[32]

Kanetomo, however, does not stop at this. Next, he declares that inner purity is also the place of ritual performance (*dōjō*), or altar (*dan*) reserved for the central, esoteric ceremonies, while outer purity is the space used for the peripheral, ordinary rites. These two realms of ritual space are consequently called inner and outer space (*naijō, gejō*). Further, he refers to the inner space by the name of *saijō* (place of worship). This term can be applied to all places of kami worship, but seems to refer specifically to the *Daijōsai* (the 'Great Rice Offering Ritual'), which is a part of the imperial enthronement ceremony. During the *Daijōsai* the emperor himself is subjected to the taboos of *sansai* and *chisai*. He is the main ritualist who serves food directly to his divine ancestor, Amaterasu, in temporary shrines called Yukiden and Sukiden, built especially for this occasion. This term *saijō* was adopted by Kanetomo for his own, newly built sanctuary, called Taigenkyū Saijōsho ('Shrine of the Great Origin – Place of Worship'). Thus, when Kanetomo uses the term *saijō,* he refers primarily to his own ceremonial centre, but at the same time implies some connection with one of the most sacred national ceremonies, performed only once in each imperial reign.

The intimate connection of the term *saijō* (and, possibly, also *chisai* and *sansai*) with the *Daijōsai* ceremony is further borne out by the fact that the following questions and answers in the *Myōbō yōshū* (Q17–A20) all concern details of precisely that ceremony, relating in particular to the two temporary shrines, Yukiden and Sukiden. Kanetomo equates the names Yuki and Suki (which refer to the provinces from which the rice used in the ceremony has been taken) to the deities of Heaven and Earth, to Yin and Yang, to the Inner and Outer Shrines of Ise, and to the Taizō- and Kongōkai mandalas of Dainichi Nyorai. Also, he adds two names of his own, Bansō-dan (or 'altar of the All-*Ancestor*') and Shogen-dan (or 'altar of the All-*Source*'), that refer back to his initial explanation of *sōgen*. These altars are said to be used exclusively for esoteric rites, and are reserved for the worship of the Heavenly (Bansō) and Earthly (Shogen) deities, respectively. The Yuki and Suki shrines, on the other hand, are used for exoteric as well as for esoteric rites (which suggests that Kanetomo regarded the *Daijōsai* as a ceremony containing both esoteric and exoteric elements).

In the passages relating to 'purity,' we encounter a significant effort to establish analogies between Kanetomo's 'exo-esoteric' structure and the traditional system of court ritual laid down in the Taihō codex. To this end, Kanetomo concentrates on the *Daijōsai*, which is indeed one of the most secret ceremonies of the Japanese court. Even in the *Gyodaishishō* of Ichijō Kaneyoshi (1402–81), one of the few historical sources which refer to it, it is said that apart from the regent (*kanpaku*) and the personal diviner of the emperor (*miyaji*), nobody knows any details.[33] Now, Kaneyoshi himself held the post of *kanpaku*, while *miyaji* was a function traditionally performed by the Urabe.[34] Thus, if we trust Kaneyoshi's report, Kanetomo must indeed have had a privileged knowledge of this ceremony. Even if the details of Kanetomo's esoteric ceremonies in the Taigenkyū Saijōsho were, as we may assume, quite different, they were related by their names to this most sacred imperial offering ritual.

In the passages dealing with the *Daijōsai*, we find a direct reference to the concept of Yin and Yang, which we would have expected earlier if the model '1, 2, 3, all' (in which '2' clearly represents Yin and Yang) had been strictly adhered to. However, the importance of this concept is not immediately self-evident in the case of the *Myōbō yōshū*. In the passage in question, Yin and Yang could be called the most elementary dualism in a series of correspondences starting with Heaven and Earth, Inner and Outer Shrine of Ise, the twofold mandalas of Dainichi, and so forth, but contrary to what one might expect, this series is kept separate from the series open-secret, inner-outer, peripheral-central, and so on. This is not to say that the concept of Yin and Yang was not important to Kanetomo's teaching. On the contrary, as we will see below, Yin and Yang were regarded as corresponding to the most basic modes of religious worship, approach (to a deity) and retreat. Moreover, ritual texts of Yoshida Shinto reveal that Yin and Yang determined virtually all ritual movements. It is indeed strange, therefore, that this importance is hardly reflected in the *Myōbō yōshū*, especially in the section on dualistic patterns. One possible reason for this could be that Yin and Yang are implicitly subsumed under the categories open-secret; but in the discussion of Yuki and Suki it becomes apparent that Yin and Yang, Heaven and Earth and so on, are to be found in the open and in the secret realms. Thus, the two respective lines that divide the dualistic realms of 'Yin-Yang' and 'secret-open' do not overlap. Rather, we may imagine them as two crossing axes. Both Yin and Yang are present in secret and open, and vice versa: secret and open rituals worship Heaven and Earth (Yang and Yin), and neither Yin nor Yang is exclusively related to esotericism or exotericism.[35] Also, they do not constitute a secret or open section within the secret. There is no ontological reduction of the Yin-Yang opposition to the opposition of open versus secret.[36]

In principle, it should not have been too difficult to relate open and secret to the concepts of Yin and Yang, as such correspondences already existed in the Taoist tradition. However, for Kanetomo this might have posed a problem. As we have already seen in the above examples, he used the secret-open (or esoteric-exoteric) opposition systematically to add new ideas to the codified courtly Shinto tradition. Moreover, there is a clear bias toward the secret, which is the distinctive part of Yoshida Shinto, and is often referred to by names such as Yuiitsu's 'fundament' (honbun) or 'name and law' (myōbō). If Yin and Yang were to be applied to the kenmitsu pattern, however, this would certainly imply that secrecy was Yin, which traditionally does not only represent the female, but also the dark, hidden, and earthly, while openness would be Yang and would thus represent the male, bright, and celestial. Thus, even if Yin and Yang are said to complement each other, and not to compete with each other, the bias conventionally tilts toward Yang. Applied to Shinto, this might lead to the conclusion that 'open' ceremonies would address the deities of Heaven, and 'secret' ones the deities of the Earth. In short, if Kanetomo had applied the pattern of Yin and Yang to his system in a straightforward manner, he would have had difficulties in maintaining the implicit priority of the secret over the open, and of specific Yuiitsu elements over traditional Shinto.

Treasures

An explanation of the term 'treasure' forms part of an extensive exposition of the various terms that make up the formula Mujō reihō shintō kaji. This formula may be translated as 'Kaji of the Unsurpassable Spirit-Treasure Kami-Way,' but no translation can do justice to the multifarious meanings Kanetomo ascribes to it. It actually featured in ritual prayers of Yoshida Shinto, and thus reminds us of the Amidist nenbutsu or the Namu myōhō rengekyō of the Nichiren sect. It is an emblematic formula representing the practitioner's adherence to a certain religious teaching, and it implies the spiritual benefit to be gained from this teaching. Kanetomo develops large parts of his explanation of Yuiitsu Shinto in the form of an interpretation of this formula. Kaji is, of course, a term from esoteric Buddhism, and is difficult to translate. Originally referring to the attainment of mystical union with a buddha, it also came to signify the power associated with this mystical state, and finally with the magical spell used to attain this power. What is more, the utterance of the word *kaji* itself is said to lead to *kaji*-power. To recite the phrase *Mujō reihō shintō kaji* serves, therefore, as a mystical or magical means to attain what is implied in the phrase, probably a mystical union with the way of the kami. I return to this question below.

'Treasure' (*hō*) in this formula denotes two different sets of treasures, the Ten Treasures and the Three Treasures. Both refer to specific objects mentioned in the National Histories. The Three Treasures are the well-known three Imperial Regalia, mirror, *magatama*-jewels and sword, which are, ideally at least, in the possession of the emperor. The Ten Treasures consist of similar objects, but occur only in the *Sendai kuji hongi*, and are therefore less well-known. Kanetomo maintains that they are now stored in the 'Inner Place,' which is to say in his own sanctuary, the *Saijōsho* mentioned above. This implies that they are a) in the possession of the Yoshida, and b) part of the secret realm of Yuiitsu Shinto. The Ten Treasures in the *Sendai kuji hongi* are actually magical objects with various supernatural powers. Kanetomo describes them in the following way:

A28:
'Treasure' denotes the ten divine treasures handed down to us by the kami. They are spiritual treasures related to the true practice of mysterious exercises (*myōgyō*). Hence the verse:
> The ten divine treasures are the ten good deeds in the ten worlds;
> the ten minds and the ten stages.[37]
> Each of them is perfection (*enman* 円満), each is completion (*jōju* 成就),
> and divine response as we desire (*nyoi kannō*).[38]

The first part of this verse refers to the ten Buddhist virtues and the ten steps to spiritual perfection. The second part mentions three qualities which exhibit the supernatural character of the Ten Treasures: they bring about perfection (*enman*), completion (*jōju*) of ourselves or our wishes, and, finally, they produce every divine response we might desire (*nyoi kannō*).

As in the examples above, Kanetomo is free to interpret the Ten Treasures in whatever way he wishes, because they are part of his secret realm and thus by definition accessible only to the Yoshida. Therefore, one might expect the Ten Treasures to be considered superior to the Three Treasures, just as the secret classics of Yuiitsu Shinto are superior to the commonly known National Histories, which belong to the open tradition. In this case, however, Kanetomo seems to hesitate to conceive of something more profound and dignified than the three Imperial Regalia. He describes the relationship between the two sets of treasures in the following way:

Q33: Do the Ten Treasures and the Three Treasures relate to each other as relative and absolute (*gon-jitsu*), or as superior and inferior?

127

A33: They relate to each other as relative and absolute, but not as superior and inferior. The Ten Treasures are spiritual treasures which pervade all ten worlds. They are provisional [emanations] that reveal the absolute [form] (gon ni shite jitsu o arawasu). The Three Treasures [on the other hand] are: First, the spirit (rei) of the ten kinds of perfection; this is the Yata mirror. Second, the treasure (hō) of the ten kinds of divine response; this is the curved Yasaka-jewels. Third, the kaji of the ten kinds of completion; this is the Grass-cutting sword. They are absolute, and yet provide [the basis] for the provisional [emanations] (jitsu ni shite gon o sonau). This is the reason why they relate to each other as relative and absolute, but not as superior and inferior. In the last instance, the spiritual power (reitoku) of the Ten Treasures and the Three Treasures is the divine treasure of government (tōgyo) . . . This is what is meant by the term 'Unsurpassable Spirit-Treasure' (mujō reihō).[39]

This paragraph presents us with a number of problems, but first of all it should be noted that Kanetomo deals primarily with the relationship between the metaphysical concepts behind his two sets of treasures, rather than with the treasures as physical objects. Now, what is the meaning of the distinction of gon and jitsu? Rendered sometimes as 'provisional' and 'real,' or as 'relative' and 'absolute,' these expressions constitute a concept which was used to explain the varieties and contradictions within the various kinds of 'truth' found in the Buddhist canon, some being of absolute, some of only relative significance. In the honji suijaku theory this conception was also applied to the relationship of kami and Buddha, the former being explained as 'provisional' emanations of the latter. Kanetomo's specific attribution of gon and jitsu, however, is somewhat surprising. According to orthodox Buddhist argumentation, one would expect the open, visible aspects of reality to be provisional or of relative existence. They are usually considered to be the outer appearance of an absolute, yet hardly conceivable reality which is hidden beyond the relative. In the case of the treasures, however, Kanetomo reverses the order. The Ten Treasures (stored in the 'Inner Place' and thus part of the hidden), are gon, provisional or relative, while the Three Treasures (which we would expect to be part of the 'open') are jitsu, fundamental or absolute. Even if Kanetomo denies any hierarchical implication in this context, it seems due to the exalted status of the Regalia that he diverted from his established pattern, by which he attributed a more profound and fundamental significance to the secrets belonging specifically to his own tradition.

Now, what is this 'real' or 'absolute' metaphysical conception symbolised by the Three Treasures? If we may be permitted to regard the expressions 'spirit,' 'treasure,' and 'kaji' in the above definition simply as rhetorical ornaments, we may say that the Three Treasures are defined as 'perfection,' 'completion,' and 'divine response.' In Kanetomo's teachings, these terms form a triad which is encountered quite frequently. I have not yet been able to determine the exact meanings of each term, but together they seem to refer to a stage of perfect happiness and omnipotence.[40] The Ten Treasures, on the other hand, denote aspects of, or steps towards this stage of happiness and omnipotence. In the *Myōbō yōshū*, we do not find a more specific characterisation than 'the ten good deeds in the ten worlds' and 'the ten minds and the ten stages.' It seems, however, that these ten aspects or steps constitute something like a *conditio sine qua non* necessary to achieve the perfect stage of the Three Treasures.

The whole passage might be considered of secondary importance, if it were not for the fact that, besides a purely metaphysical interpretation, there is a striking political connotation as well. As already mentioned, he who possesses the Three Treasures can be nobody else but the emperor, and he who (allegedly) possesses the Ten Treasures must be the head-priest of the Yoshida house, who is in charge of the 'Inner Place.' Neither their identity, nor their relationship is mentioned with a single word in the text, yet we may assume that the relationship between the respective treasures also has some bearing on the relationship between their owners. We may try to drive our interpretation even a little further: if the Three Treasures are effective only in combination with the Ten Treasures (as implied in the *Myōbō yōshū*), the emperor is in need of the Yoshida head-priest to prepare him for the proper execution of his imperial role.

This interpretation would perhaps appear rather far-fetched, were it not for a short remark at the end of this explanation of the term 'treasure': 'In the last instance, the spiritual power (*reitoku*) of the Ten Treasures and the Three Treasures is the divine treasure of government (*tōgyo*).' In spite of the Buddhist overtones of his terms, which would suggest a rather metaphysical, other-worldly concern, this remark reveals that Kanetomo also had quite concrete, this-worldly aims in mind. In the light of the term *tōgyo*, we can regard the above-mentioned state of happiness and omnipotence as the ideal condition of secular government. In short, Kanetomo seems to be aiming at something similar to the *ōbō–buppō* ideal, which implied a perfect government by a combination of secular (lit. 'kingly') and Buddhist law. Replacing Buddhism, Kanetomo's ideal might be termed *ōbō–Yoshida-hō*. Certainly, this idea was not merely wishful thinking. In fact, Kanetomo initiated Emperor Go-Tsuchimikado (1442–1500, r. 1465–1500) in a set of rituals in 1480, a few years before the most plausible date for the first draft of the *Myōbō yōshū*.[41] Reading the above explanation of the two kinds of treasures, we should therefore take into account that Kanetomo actually did establish himself as a religious instructor of the emperor.

We can infer from this example that Kanetomo's attempt to explain the universe from a kami-centred point of view led him – like Jien (1155–1225) and Kitabatake Chikafusa (1293–1354) before him – to the issue of imperial rule, both on the level of discourse and in reality. In contrast to these political thinkers, however, Kanetomo chose an indirect method to combine belief in the kami with the question of political legitimation. He did not raise the question of imperial government or of his own priestly functions directly, but preferred to interlard his religious system with symbolic references to the ceremonial structure around the emperor, such as the Imperial Regalia or the *Daijōsai*. While linking his religious system with this structure, these references also imply some manipulations of the structure as a whole. The traditional ceremonies become merely the 'open part' of a system that also contains a 'secret part,' accessible only to the Yoshida and their disciples.

The triadic pattern

Beginning with an esoteric explanation of the term 'Shinto,' Kanetomo eventually turns to a triadic pattern, which becomes, at the same time, the object of his explanations and the principle which determines the question-answer sequels. Here, each topic is considered from three different angles, and each new term is given a threefold interpretation. The pattern is somewhat obscured, however, when Kanetomo at one critical point goes into great detail, as if he had forgotten about the third part of his answer. It takes careful reading to discover the point where the third explanation of the issue in question is finally taken up again.

Yet, understanding the arrangement of this section is not enough to understand its actual purpose. Since the language here becomes increasingly ambiguous and metaphysical, we may try to identify a comprehensive, philosophical exposition of Shinto in this triadic section. However, Kanetomo's philosophical world view is never fully expounded; the explanation always seems to stop short, hiding one's view of the whole. On the other hand, it is apparent that this part of the text leads us deeper into the ritual system of Yoshida Shinto. It mentions the most important liturgical implements, and gives meaning to certain methods of prayer and ceremonial behaviour. These implements and ceremonies, however, are part of the 'secret realm' of Yoshida Shinto and must therefore not be described too plainly, in order to keep them secret. The reader is often left uncertain whether the text refers to a specific item or to a general category. The obvious intention is to hide the level of abstractness of a remark, and thus make it contain as many meanings as possible. In this way, Kanetomo anchors various polymorphous items in a system of polymorphous symbolic relations. The metaphysical theories behind this system of relations might be called Taoist, or Buddhist, or Shinto. In any event, such theories are not the primary focus. If they surface in the course of Kanetomo's esoteric explanations, this seems to be merely as a side effect of his attempt to create a system both flexible and meaningful, that integrates the heterogeneous parts constituting Yoshida Shinto.

The ritual items that are prominent in the remaining 'esoteric' part of the *Myōbō yōshū* are referred to by the names 'Altar of the Nine Parts,' 'the Eighteen Shinto,' and 'the Etiquette of Advance and Retreat.' The fact that we have little notion of the actual appearance of these items is one of the major reasons for the cryptic nature of the *Myōbō yōshū*. Even though I can not claim a thorough understanding, I endeavour below to demonstrate that we can gauge the actual implications of these terms only by keeping a balance between theoretical and practical interpretations.

The 'triadic section' begins with a reference to the *sandai* 三大 or three forms of 'thusness' (*shinnyo*, Skt. *tathatā*, the inherent, 'real' aspect of all phenomena) in Buddhism (Q37).[42] In the *Myōbō yōshū*, the *sandai* appear as aspects of 'Shinto' and thus represent three forms or aspects of 'kami activities.' However, since this triad is neither explained nor mentioned again in the *Myōbō yōshū*, it seems safe to say that it serves mainly to introduce the Taoist categories of Heaven, Earth, and Man, the 'three foundations' (*sangen*), which become the basic headers to which all subsequent triads are related in some way. Kanetomo's arguments are structured as follows. Each of the three foundations has a specific power or property: 'divine transformation' (*jinben* 神変), 'divine permeation' (*jinzū* 神通), and 'divine force' (*jinriki* 神力). Together, these are subsumed under the term *sanmyō* 三妙 ('the three mysterious [properties]'). Further, each of these properties can be applied by the individual believer or priest by way of a ritual practice. This practice is called *sangyō* 三行 ('the three exercises'). The above-mentioned *sandai* function as a kind of super-triadism, uniting *sangen*, *sanmyō*, and *sangyō* under one header. However, as I shall try to show in detail below, these three conceptions are actually related to each other in a vertical relationship.[43] This relationship is also the basic arrangement of Kanetomo's arguments in this section. It is obscured, however, by the fact that Kanetomo first deals at length with *sangen* (the three foundations, Heaven, Earth and Man) and *sanmyō* (in particular A38–A45), and returns to *sangyō* only much later (A53–A63).

The Altar of Nine Parts and the Eighteen Shinto

The passages on *sangen* and *sanmyō* combine these two triads to arrive at a number of multipliers of three. These multipliers are related to several items in this context, but the most prominent seems to be what is called the 'Mysterious Altar of Nine Parts' (*kyūbu no myōdan*, A42–A45). These nine parts are derived from the *sangen* and the *sanmyō* in the following way: Heaven, Earth, and Man each possess a privileged property. Heaven possesses 'divine transformation,' Earth 'divine permeation,' and Man 'divine force.' However, each of the *sangen* may also take command of the other two properties. (As in the case of perfection, completion, and divine response mentioned above, it is not easy to define and translate these properties, or grasp what unites and what separates them.) Heaven's main property is 'divine transformation,' and it is exemplified by the sun, the moon and the stars. Temperature, time, and weather conditions, on the other hand, are attributed to its minor properties (A43). Earth's main property is 'divine permeation,' and this is exemplified by the tides of the ocean and by the fact that Qi is everywhere.[44] Other properties are the different forms of landscapes and the growing and flowering of plants. Man's main property is 'divine force' and is exemplified by ritual gestures:

bowing, offering, and forming mudras with one's hands. Man's minor properties are to chant prayers and to meditate (A44). These last attributions are particularly interesting, as they contain a concrete message: man's way to express his fundamental nature is through religious behaviour, in particular through physical ritual acts. Vocal and mental acts are less important. I return to this below.

Thus, the attribution of the three mysterious properties to the three foundations results in nine categories. These categories comprise a number of phenomena which may perhaps be described as 'expressions of the three foundations by way of the three properties'. Now, what is the purpose of these categories? What do they actually stand for? Are they intended as an explanation of such phenomena as time, weather, tides, and ritual behaviour? Perhaps. But their main significance in this context appears to be related to the 'Altar of Nine Parts.' If we imagine this altar as something the intended reader of the *Myōbō yōshū* was, or could become familiar with, the fog begins to clear: the purpose is to make this object meaningful. Its constituting parts, beyond their actual function or significance, now also contain a symbolic meaning. It is enough that this symbolic meaning hints at a cosmic order. To expound this order in detail is entrusted to the classics of Chinese and Indian philosophy, which are – as Kanetomo tells us – nothing but the twigs and blossoms of Shinto itself.

This interpretation would become much more plausible if the 'Altar of Nine Parts' were to be encountered outside the *Myōbō yōshū* too. However, I must confess to having found no evidence that there ever existed an object known by this name. My belief, therefore, is that it may refer to a basic structure found in several, or perhaps all altars of Yuiitsu ritual. This would explain why it is not mentioned in the manuals of Yoshida Shinto that I have had access to. What I did find were several descriptions and graphical representations of Yoshida altars, which differ somewhat according to the ritual performed. Basically, the 'altar' is a low table of square or octagonal shape,[45] either of which could be easily divided into eight surrounding, and one central, part. In the middle of this table there is typically a plate with a bowl in the middle, surrounded by eight similar objects. Moreover, the octagonal ground plan of Kanetomo's hall of worship, the Taigenkyū, also conforms to this nine-fold pattern. The nine parts of this pattern can, of course, be symbolically related to the nine divisions of the Earth mentioned above, which also occur in the *Myōbō yōshū*, or to the representation of Dainichi surrounded by eight Buddhas in the Kongōkai mandala. In any event, there is ample evidence that Yoshida ritual and architecture made use of the number nine in various ways. The Altar of Nine Parts may thus be understood as a kind of mandala, as a diagram of the symbolism inherent in all these nine-fold ritual objects of Yoshida Shinto.

The next major issue to be discussed in the *Myōbō yōshū* is called the 'Eighteen Shinto,' and the explanation here is still more obscure. According to the *Myōbō yōshū*, the Eighteen Shinto are composed of the five phases found in Heaven, Earth, and Man (fifteen in all), plus three 'Shintos' labelled the

'Shinto of perfect fundamental Qi' (Heaven), the 'Shinto of correspondence with the One Spirit' (Earth), and the 'Shinto of completion of life/destiny' (Man) (A48–A51). In this case, however, it is not difficult to find a corresponding 'symbol' in ritual practice. It is called *Sangen jūhachi shintō gyōji* ('Ceremony of the Eighteen Shinto [contained in] the Three Foundations'), and is one of the three most important esoteric ceremonies of Yoshida Shinto (the so-called *sandan gyōji* 三壇行事). Among these it had the lowest degree of secrecy, and was thus the first to be encountered by a new apprentice.[46] In contrast to the explanation in the *Myōbō yōshū*, the number 18 may actually have been derived from a purification ritual of the six senses (*rokkon shōjō*) which is performed three times. Such an explanation can be found in some minor texts by Kanetomo himself.[47] Moreover, a *rokkon shōjō* ritual is actually part of the Eighteen Shinto ceremony. The term *rokkon shōjō* can be encountered in the Lotus sutra and applies to various Buddhist rites.[48] Rituals consisting of eighteen steps seem to have existed also in esoteric Buddhism.

Concerning the question as to whether it is absolutely necessary to know about the Altar of Nine Parts or the Eighteen Shinto (Q52), Kanetomo asserts at the end of this passage that even the prayers of those who know nothing about them will be accepted by the kami, since every single reverence in front of the kami is endowed (*sonau*) with these altars and 'Shintos.'

Kaji

The next topic is Kanetomo's unique interpretation of *kaji*. The difficulties inherent in this word have alrady been mentioned. Needless to say, Kanetomo does not derive his usage of the term *kaji* from Buddhism.[49] Instead, he traces it back to the names of the shrines of Kashima and Ka[ji]tori (which are both somehow related to the Yoshida shrine). In this connection he calls *kaji* the secret art to govern the 'yonder' (*kashiko*) from here. *Kaji* is therefore a means for taking control of the spiritual world.

This aspect is further emphasised when Kanetomo equates this magical *kaji* with the homophone Japanese word for 'rudder' (*kaji* 舵). When the rudder was invented by Empress Jingū, the auspicious name *kaji* (written with the Buddhist characters) was chosen for this magnificent tool by which ships can be directed at will. Apart from its practical use, the rudder is thus a representation of *kaji* as applied in ritual: seizing the rudder is a visible expression of divine force; to move it expresses divine permeation; to direct the boat where one wishes expresses divine transformation.

Thus, a synthesis of Kanetomo's statements leds us to surmise that *kaji* refers to a process which starts with a specific rite (a 'tool,' for instance, a formula), the proper performance of that rite (similar to the handling of the rudder), the gaining of 'mystical properties' (which corresponds to the *kaji* union with a Buddhist divinity in esoteric Buddhism), and the usage of these

133

properties for the specific purposes addressed in the ritual (the fulfilment of prayers by 'governing the yonder'). Sometimes the magical powers involved in this process are rendered specifically as '*kaji*-power,' while the term *kaji* itself seems mostly confined to the uttering of *kaji*, that is, a *kaji*-formula. In general, however, we have to take into account that the term *kaji* may equally denote both the whole of this process, and every individual step of it. Again, we are confronted with the eternal problem of ambiguity concerning the level of specificity of a given term.

The same process referred to by the term *kaji* seems also to be associated with the term 'the three exercises' (*sangyō*). *Sangyō* and *kaji* appear therefore more or less synonymous. This, at least, is implied in the subsequent passages of the *Myōbō yōshū* where we find the following verse:

> A54: The exercise of the property of Heaven is the *kaji* of divine transformation.
> The exercise of the property of Earth is the *kaji* of divine permeation.
> The exercise of the property of Man is the *kaji* of divine force.
> Applying these one realises the prayers of oneself and of others.[50]

Let us recall, at this point, that Kanetomo began his exposition of the various triadisms by explaining the meanings of the term 'Shinto' in *Mujō reihō shintō kaji*. Kanetomo's interpretations in the preceding passages can be summarised as follows: *shintō* first refers to the *sangen*, that is the three fundamental categories which developed from the original One; it can further refer to their 'mysterious properties' (*sanmyō*), that is, to all sorts of supernatural or divine powers. And, finally, it can refer to the 'three exercises,' that is, exercises or ritual acts that use *kaji*-power to apply the mysterious properties to a certain religious purpose. Thus, even if the *Myōbō yōshū* still does not tell us exactly what these 'three exercises' are, we now know that they are more or less identical with *kaji*, and that *kaji* seems to be the privileged way to gain control over super-natural powers. To perform the three exercises and thus gain *kaji*-power is obviously connected with the recitation of a certain *kaji*-formula, but may imply some additional ritual acts such as mudras and other gestures, as well as implements that accompany the recitation. In any event, it seems that we have arrived at some kind of understanding of the vertical relationship between *sangen*, *sanmyō* and *sangyō* and their relation to *kaji* in Yoshida Shinto.

The five phases

At this point, however, quite out of the blue, the *Myōbō yōshū* addresses the meaning of the term *sangyō* again, and explains it in a completely different way, that seems to render invalid our translation as 'three exercises':

> Q56: What leads to the appellation *sangyō*?

A56: It is the five phases (*gogyō*) of Heaven, the five phases of Earth, the five phases of Man. Hence the verse:

San is derived from the three foundations (*sangen*),
gyō is the name of the five phases (*gogyō*).[51]

The subsequent questions and answers deal at length with all sorts of correspondences between the *gogyō* and other sets of five found in the realms of Heaven, Earth, and Man. For each of the three foundations, there is a separate set of *gogyō*. Moreover, each of these three sets of *gogyō* is connected with a set of five Shinto deities which Kanetomo selects quite arbitrarily from *Nihon shoki* and *Sendai kuji hongi*.[52]

The obvious objective of this new definition of *sangyō* is to include the teaching of the five phases into the cosmology of the *Myōbō yōshū*. This objective is in itself not at all unnatural. As mentioned above, in Taoism the *gogyō* are intimately associated with the *sangen*, as they represent (at least according to Robinet) the horizontal structure of the universe, while the *sangen* represent the vertical structure. The problem is that Kanetomo includes the concept of the five phases into his system by using a term that he has already applied in a completely different sense. Thus, *sangyō* is to be understood on the one hand as the exercises referring to the *sangen*, on the other hand as the five phases referring to the *sangen*. It is not apparent whether this double encoding was owing to historical reasons (such as earlier texts which Kanetomo built upon), or to Kanetomo's own fondness for multifarious meanings. When he composed the *Myōbō yōshū*, Kanetomo made extensive use of his previous writings; perhaps this explains the two different usages of *sangyō* found in this text. Whatever the reasons may be, in contrast to most other terminological ambiguities, the two meanings of *sangyō* do not only differ in the level of abstractness. *Sangyō* seems to refer to two totally different conceptions so that it may be translated as 'three exercises' in one case and 'the phases of the three' in the other.

Body, speech, and mind

In the concluding passages of the 'triadic section' (which, according to *Myōbō yōshū* interpretation, also form the end of the 'esoteric,' doctrinal part of the *Myōbō yōshū*) Kanetomo finally explains a triad which has already been alluded to from time to time: the three categories of (ritual) behaviour: body action, language and thought. In esoteric Buddhism these are commonly referred to as the 'three mysteries' (*sanmitsu*) or the 'three deeds' (*sangō*) of body, speech, and mind; Kanetomo prefers the latter term. The amalgamation of these Buddhist ritual categories with the Taoist cosmogonic categories of Heaven, Earth and Man seems to be one of the most important points in the esoteric part of the *Myōbō yōshū*. In Yoshida Shinto, the *sangō* triad structures Yoshida ceremonies by combining prayer formulas (speech), gestures (body) and concentration on the object of religious service (mind) to achieve the longed-for merits, just as in Buddhism. The *sangen* triad, on the other hand, serves to link these ritual acts with Taoist and Shinto cosmology, replacing the original Buddhist conceptions. However, as if it were not enough to add yet another triad, Kanetomo's elucidations concerning the relations of the *sangō* and the *sangen* are interwoven with an explanation of the 'Etiquette of Approach and Retreat' (*shintai sahō* 進退作法), a kind of general outline of ceremonial behaviour.

The 'Etiquette of Approach and Retreat' can be compared to the 'Altar of Nine Parts' and the 'Eighteen Shinto' in the sense that it remains unclear to the uninitiated whether this phrase refers to a particular ritual practice or to an allegorical conception of some general aspects of ritual. Again, it appears that the level of abstraction or specificity is being consciously hidden.

Demura Katsuaki believes that *shintai sahō* is related to a certain ritual called *Nichigetsu sahō* ('Etiquette of the Sun and the Moon'), which was designed to celebrate the deities of Yin and Yang.[53] While I do not discount this theory, I believe that the designation 'Etiquette of Approach and Retreat' is intentionally ambiguous, and in one sense may apply to any Yoshida or even Shinto ceremony. Kanetomo finds *shintai sahō* also in the ceremonial behaviour of court officials when they approach the emperor, and maintains that this behaviour was prescribed by Shōtoku Taishi on the basis of a mythical precedent. Moreover, while knowledge of the Altar of Nine Parts and the Eighteen Shinto was not deemed absolutely necessary to please the kami, there is by contrast no merit to be expected from them without *shintai sahō*.[54] Obviously, Kanetomo intended to base any approach to the kami on his own explanation of the Etiquette of Approach and Retreat. His explanation reads as follows:

> A61: [. . .] Approach and retreat, this is the change of movement and stillness of Yin and Yang. (The *Yijing* says: Yang is approach, Yin is retreat.)
>
> To visualise, to meditate, to contemplate[55] – this is the calm energy of the Yin-soul (*inhaku*); it is the secret method to attain the purity of the deeds of the mind.
>
> To read, to recite, to chant – this is the active power of the Yang-soul (*yōkon*); it is the secret method to attain the purity of the deeds of speech.
>
> To bow, to offer, to form a mudra – these are expressions of the movements of Heaven and Earth; they are the secret methods to attain the purity of the deeds of the body.[56]

These remarks finally claim a definitive correspondence between the three deeds and the three foundations. In A44 we found the 'three deeds' already attributed to the *sanmyō* of Man. In this connection, we learned that the deeds of the body are Man's strongest point, while the deeds of mind and speech constitute minor properties. Now we also find a structural necessity for this

136

attribution: to meditate (to think) equals Yin (which is Earth); to chant (to speak) equals Yang (which is Heaven). However, to act with one's body (to move) is attributed to the realm where Heaven and Earth (Yang and Yin) mingle, the realm of Man. If his mind is therefore Man's 'Earth-part,' and his mouth his 'Heaven-part,' then his body is Man's 'Man-part,' and, quite understandably, his primary property.

In this connection, the concept of approach and retreat may be regarded as a means for introducing Yin and Yang, which, as indicated above, have thus far been by-passed. At this point, it is clear that Kanetomo's understanding of the relation between Yin and Yang and the three foundations is quite in line with the references to Taoism set out at the beginning of this essay. On the other hand, the Etiquette of Approach and Retreat is a term flexible enough to refer to all sorts of ritual behaviour in Shinto, which are thus included in Kanetomo's ritual system. Kanetomo's arguments that allow for this inclusion may be briefly summarised as follows: any approach (or retreat) to (or from) a deity comprises the three deeds of body, speech, and mind, that is, acts of meditation, recitation and ritual gestures leading to 'purity.' If one performs these deeds as explained by Yoshida Shinto, one will achieve purity and receive benefits from the deity. If not, one's 'approach and retreat' is bound to bring about evil.[57]

Concluding remarks

Admittedly, there are many odds and ends left open by this exegetic approach to the *Myōbō yōshū*. We encountered Yoshida neologisms such as *sanmyō* and *sangyō*, which serve to synthesise heterogeneous concepts from various older traditions into a new discourse, but seem to change the meaning of these concepts quite drastically in the process. On the other hand, we found terms such as 'purity' or '*kaji*,' which are clearly adopted from other traditions, but are in the *Myōbō yōshū* given such a broad scope of meaning that they are in danger of becoming altogether meaningless. It remains unclear whether there is any religious practice in Yoshida Shinto that is not *kaji*, or whether there is any ritual that does not have the attainment of 'purity' as its aim.

My intention here was to make plausible *Myōbō yōshū*'s initial claim that the *Myōbō yōshū* is neither composed without structuring principle, nor based on a way of thinking that is completely beyond our grasp. In particular, I have identified a central doctrinal part which can be distinguished from the rest of the text by a coherent (yet 'esoteric') line of argument and a deliberately layered structure. On the surface, all statements appear wrapped in a web of classifications. Starting with *genpon* and *sogen*, we encountered the headers 'inner and outer purity,' which lead to all kinds of subdivisions. Notably, 'inner purity' contains the formula *Mujō reihō shintō kaji*. Formally, all of Kanetomo's subsequent 'esoteric' expositions are no more than an interpretation of the various compounds of this formula. Further, we find a second layer that deals with generative principles and organises the argument accordingly. In the arrangement of a monistic, a dualistic, and a triadic section I have sought to uncover a symbolic reference to the generic superstructure of Taoism, '1, 2, 3, all' (the category of the five phases representing the diversification into all phenomena in this perspective). Finally, we find a layer where the text progresses at a leisurely pace from one ceremonial issue to the next. Starting with the stages of ritual abstinence, it proceeds to ritual space, to prayer, to the most sacred objects of worship, to the altars, to one of the most elementary ceremonies, to *kaji*, and finally to the three forms of ritual action to be combined in one's approach to and retreat from the deity, and thus in the movements of Yin and Yang. In this last layer, we find ourselves led from the traditional, open, religious ritual of the court to the innovative, allegedly original, secret forms of Kanetomo's One-and-Only (Yuiitsu) Shinto. This is also a passage from what Kanetomo calls the 'outer (open, exoteric) space' to the 'inner (secret, esoteric) space.' At this level, the shift from open to secret is a gradual one: while Kanetomo adds esoteric Shinto inventions and interpretations to the rules and definitions of the *Engi shiki*, which govern the open realm, he constantly searches for correspondences that can sustain his secret Yuiitsu conceptions in the *Nihon shoki* and the *Sendai kuji hongi* – the texts he defines as the 'classics of the open teachings.'

In concentrating on what I have called the esoteric expositions in the *Myōbō yōshū*, I have sought to show that this widely neglected part of the text is not only carefully composed, but also contains a clue to an understanding of the way in which Kanetomo constructed his esoteric religious system. Kanetomo obviously commanded an intimate knowledge of Chinese philosophy. On this knowledge he based his cosmogonic superstructure, that included Shinto cosmology but excluded Buddhist notions about the cosmic order. He was equally well-versed in the ritual system of esoteric Buddhism. This he took as a model for his outline of Yuiitsu ritual, but only after having replaced a few crucial terms and explications according to his own Shinto conceptions. He combined these elements theoretically and symbolically by identifying the cosmogonic triad of Taoism with the ritual triadic conception of Buddhism. Further, he used the Buddhist notion of a double reality, secret and open, to explain (among other things) the coexistence of traditional and new elements in his teachings, and, on a more general level, the compatibility of Yuiitsu Shinto with the common Buddhist world view.[58]

Yet, Kanetomo's sketch of a theological Way of the kami as expounded in the *Myōbō yōshū* only forms one half of his religious system. The other half consists in the actual creation of rituals. In our analysis, we found ample evidence for the importance of ritual in Yoshida Shinto. Unable though we were to extract the concrete forms of these rituals from the text, we did encounter terms such as the 'Altar of Nine Parts' and the 'Etiquette of Approach and Retreat.' At the first sight, these expressions may appear as empty rhetorical ornaments, merely adding confusion to the explanation of the relationships between more general, cosmogonic concepts. However, in my interpretation, these terms actually represent various ritual implements and activities and serve to relate them to Yuiitsu symbolism. Thus, any object consisting of nine parts may symbolise the three foundations and their respective properties (or powers) by way of the Altar of Nine Parts, and every act of kami worship should be seen as making use of the same powers by way of the Etiquette of Approach and Retreat. Reading the *Myōbō yōshū*, we should never forget the primacy of practice in Yoshida Shinto, which is also reflected in the fact that Kanetomo regarded physical action, rather than mental or verbal activity, as Man's 'strongest point.'

Finally, the doctrine of the *Myōbō yōshū* seems perfectly consistent with Yoshida politics. Between the lines, we read that the focus of Kanetomo's political concern was the imperial court, of which the Yoshida were actually part. Using the relics of courtly shrine administration and the symbolic prestige of the emperor, Kanetomo aimed to usurp the world of Shinto in its entirety. Thus, *Myōbō yōshū* interpretation does not contradict the widespread opinion that Kanetomo's primary objective was the elevation of himself and his own lineage, rather than some idealistic quest for a metaphysical goal such as, for example, a specific Japanese identity. However, whether Kanetomo's theological ideas were merely a by-product of on-going power games between shrine lineages, or whether they were inspired by authentic beliefs, the outcome was a religious system that clearly fitted the needs of his time.

It is my hope, therefore, that the foregoing analysis may serve not only as the outline of an individual priest's musings, but as an example of a larger discourse that existed before him and continued to exist after his death. Few of Kanetomo's conceptions were without precedent. Shrine priests, scholars and even Buddhist monks had worked out similar concepts of kami worship. These influenced Kanetomo to an even greater degree than the original teachings of Buddhism, Taoism and Confucianism.

Again, the influence of Yoshida Shinto in subsequent periods, notably on the amalgamation of Shinto and Confucianism (*shinju shūgō*), is still not adequately acknowledged. Kanetomo denied the influence of earlier esoteric Shinto doctrines on Yoshida Shinto. Edo Shintoists, in exactly the same manner, denied the influence of medieval Shinto (and Yoshida Shinto in particular) on their doctrines. Our understanding of the history of Shinto is still shaped by the notion of a big fissure between medieval obscurantism and/or eclectic syncretism on the one hand, and modern rationality and/or a return to authenticy on the other. Several recent studies have indicated that this fissure was in fact not as large as it would at first appear. While many scholars have questioned the 'rationality' of the Edo period, this essay aims at reconsidering the 'obscurantism' of the Middle Ages. This obscurantism seems intimately related to the use of secrecy or esotericism, which I analysed in the context of the *Myōbō yōshū*. In particular, I have tried to show that there is a logical relationship between the form and the contents of this discourse. Similar studies will be needed to arrive at a more comprehensive picture, and it is hoped that they will help to overcome the stigma, suffered by esoteric doctrines, of being the products of an 'unenlightened age.'

Notes

1 For the sake of simplicity here, I regard Kanetomo as being alone responsible for the doctrines of Yoshida Shinto, and postpone the question as to the degree his ideas were actually already developed by his predecessors.

2 Grapard 1992a: 40.

3 Grapard 1992b See Grapard's article for a historical introduction, which space has not permitted me to repeat here. I am also indebted to his translation but, in order to make my interpretations plausible, I have frequently departed from it, sticking closer to the literal meaning.

4 Teeuwen 1996.

5 Kracht 1986.

6 Scholars who have found positive aspects in Kanetomo's synthesis of various religious currents such as Katō Genchi or Kubota Osamu, also praised him for 'never losing sight of the national spirit or guiding principles of the Japanese people' (Katō 1930: 150), and thus made Yoshida Shinto again dubious in the eyes of many Western observers.

7 Grapard 1992a: 56

8 See, for instance, the article 'The Kami in Esoteric Buddhist Thought and Practice' in this book. Thanks to the intensive studies in textual history by scholars such as Nishida Nagao, Kubota Osamu, Demura Katsuaki, and Okada Shōji, we know much about the individual histories, the mutual influences, and the political motivations that influenced the creation of these texts. However, the inner logic of this esoteric Shinto discourse is mostly put aside, as if its reasoning were either non-existent or beyond any explication.

9 In the *Myōbō yōshū*, the term Yuiitsu Shinto issued most often to denote the Yoshida's own teaching. However, it does not appear in Kanetomo's earlier writings and seems to have replaced the earlier *Genpon sōgen* only gradually.

10 *Daode jing* 42; Wilhelm 1996a: 85. This citation is quoted fully in A75 (NST19: 247, Grapard 1992b: 159) and partly in A60 (NST 19: 231; Grapard 1992b: 151). In the first case, the *Myōbō yōshū* quotes from 'Taoism' in general, in the latter case, mistakenly, from the *Yijing*.

11 These references to Taoism a mainly based on the German editions of Isabelle Robinet's *Histoire du taoisme* (Robinet 1995) and Marcel Granet's *La pensée chinoise* (Granet 1989). As indicated in the above quotation, there is a philosophical distinction between the Dao and the One. Also, there is the question whether Qi (substance, matter) was preceded by Li (principle) as argued by Zhu Xi. It is quite plausible that Kanetomo was aware of these questions, but they do not seem to have a significant influence on his usage of the respective terms and are thus ignored in this article.

12 Wilhelm 1996a: 140

13 Robinet 1995: 27

14 Besides the frequent quotations from the *Yijing* and the *Daode jing* in the *Myōbō yōshū*, research by Nishida Nagao (Nishida 1979) and Sugahara Shinkai (Sugahara 1996) has provided evidence for Kanetomo's profound knowledge and extensive use of the Taoist canon.

15 Robinet 1996: 22–4.

16 The characters 元 and 本 refer to an oracle attributed to Amaterasu which is cited in the *Myōbō yōshū*, but goes back to an earlier Shinto text, the *Yamato-hime no mikoto seiki*. The relevant passage is translated by Teeuwen (1993: 228): '[. . .] you must therefore make the origin the origin and rest in the original beginning; you must make the basis the basis, and depend on your basic mind.'

17 To facilitate the reader's orientation within the *Myōbō yōshū*, I refer to each of the 75 questions and answers by the number of their occurrence in the text (Q1, A1, . . .) which is of course not to be found in the original.

18 As Grapard notes, in Japan this phrase from the *Daode jing* 'has come to qualify the use of expedient means (Skt. *upāya*; J. *hōben*) on the part of those buddhas and bodhisattvas that would have manifested themselves in the form of kami.' (Grapard 1992b: 139, n. 3; cf. *Daode jing* 4)

19 As Kanetomo mentions in A71, the term *sōgen* is taken from the *Nihon shoki*. It might be translated as 'founder.' An esoteric interpretation of this term similar to Kanetomo's is already to be found in Inbe Masamichi's *Nihon shoki kuketsu*, and later in the *Nihon shoki sanso* by Ichijō Kaneyoshi (cf. Kubota 1971: 422), who was probably Kanetomo's most influential teacher.

20 I am indebted here to Ōkuwa Hiroshi's article 'Yoshida Kanetomo no ronri to shūkyō' (Ōkuwa 1996: 67–100) which contrasts these two aspects very sharply. This is the only attempt I have come across so far to analyse the structure of the *Myōbō yōshū* systematically.

21 This phrase is taken from the *Yijing* II/1: 'What is not defined by Yin and Yang, that is called *shin* (Ch. *shen*).' (NST 19: 211, note; Wilhelm 1996b: 279), and is also applied in the definition of *genpon* (A6).

22 *Michi wa tsune no michi ni arazu*. This is a quotation from the first sentence of the *Daode jing* (NST 19: 221, n.), which has been interpretated rather differently in Western translations (e.g., Wilhelm 1996a: 41).

23 This seems to allude to the Watarai concept of 'mind-god' (see Teeuwen 1996: 109).

24 NST 19: 221; Grapard 1992b: 144.

25 According to one interpretation, these two aspects, when separated, are to be understood as Yin and Yang (cf. Hertzer 1996: 36–7).

26 Ōkuwa 1989: 80ff.

27 A74, NST 19: 246; Grapard 1992b: 158.

28 See, e.g., Kuroda 1996.

29 Q66: Are the terms 'exoteric' and 'esoteric' of Buddhist origin, or have they always belonged to Shinto?
    A66: Their contents is similar to that proposed by Buddhism, but the terminology derives from the divine scriptures *(shinsho no bun)*. (NST 19: 237; Grapard 1992b: 155) Subsequently, Kanetomo cites the so-called *kuni yuzuri* myth from the Book on the Age of the Gods of *Nihon shoki*, in which the earthly deity Ōnamuchi cedes the visible things to Ninigi who has just descended from heaven, and announces his retirement in order to manage the hidden things. The 'visible things' are written with the same characters as Kanetomo's term 'exoteric' *(kenro)*, but pronounced *arawani(goto)*, the 'hidden things' contain at least one character of Kanetomo's term 'esoteric' *(on'yū)*, pronounced *kakuri(goto)*. Presumably, Kanetomo's terms were coined by his teacher Ichijō Kaneyoshi (Kubota 1971: 395).

30 A8–13.

31 These names refer to the trinity of Heaven, Earth, and Man and to some other doctrinal principles expounded below.

32 Cf. Teeuwen 1996: 109–14. These two stages were already defined in the Shrine Regulations *(jingiryō)* of the Taihō Codex. *Sansai*, the peripheral stage, refers to the time before and after a ceremony, and *chisai*, the central stage, to the time during that ceremony (the actual length varied according to the ceremony's importance). Further, the peripheral stage is connected with a list of avoidances including mourning, the eating of meat, listening to music, death penalties, and finally any contact with things impure; on the other hand, *chisai*, the central stage, is just defined by concentration on nothing but the ceremony.

33 cf. Takatori 1979: 69–70.

34 cf. Okada 1983: 27ff.

35 The only exceptions are the two altars Bansō and Shogen (Yang and Yin), which are reserved exclusively for the secret realm (A20).

36 My interpretation of this point diverts again from Ōkuwa, who proposes precisely such an analogy in his analysis of the *Myōbō yōshū* (Ōkuwa 1989: 77).

37 The term actually mentioned is *jisshin jūjū* 十心十住. This refers to the fifty-two Bodhisattva rankings (BGDJ: 539–40 and 654), and perhaps also to the doctrine of the ten steps to enlightenment developed by Kūkai in his *Jūjūshinron*); cf. Ishibashi & Dumoulin 1943: 199.

38 NST 19: 218; Grapard 1992b: 143.

39 NST 19: 219–220; Grapard 1992b: 143–4.

40 According to Nakamura Hajime's *Bukkyō daijiten*, *enman* and *jōju* indeed contain quite similar meanings such as 'complete,' 'perfect,' 'mature,' etc. (BGDJ: 116, 744–5); *kannō* 感応, however, is a more specific concept which refers to the response 応 of a Buddha or deity to the feeling 感 or the truly felt faith of the devotee. It can further signify the correspondence or union between devotee and deity. As this amounts to the fulfilment of the devotee's wishes, this term is close in meaning to the afore-mentioned.

41 cf. Demura 1974: 29ff.

42 'I. *Taidai* or essence, which refers to the real, eternal thatatā (*shinnyo*).

   II. *Sōdai* or form, which refers to the myriad forms manifested in the phenomenal world and whose underlying aspect is thatat.

   III. *Yūdai* or function, which refers to the active or functional aspect of thatatā. This *yūdai* is what leads men to do good deeds and strive for enlightenment.' (JEBD: 278) See also BGDJ: 482.

   The actual meanings of these terms may have differed within the various schools of Buddhism, though. In Shingon, the concept is said to be connected with the 'three mysteries,' the exercises of mind, speech and body (Ishibashi & Dumoulin 1943: 202). As we will see below, this connotation may indeed be the reason why the *sandai* appeared meaningful to Kanetomo in this context.

43 To the modern reader it may seem against the laws of logic to place a certain entity (*sangen*) at the same logical level as its properties (*sanmyō* and *sangyō*). However, to express a vertical order as a horizontal one might be a trait common to various forms of religious discourse. If we look at the above-mentioned explanation of the Buddhist *sandai* (see above n. 42), they too seem to consist of a vertical order: 'essence' or 'body' (*tai*, equated with *sangen* in the *Myōbō yōshū*), [this body's] 'functions' (*yū*, = *sanmyō*), and [this body's] 'form' (*sō*, = *sangyō*). Moreover, we should remember the Christian trinity, which also seems to imply an originally vertical relationship.

44 This passage is actually quite obscure. Grapard translates: '. . . gas (Qi) emanations from mountains and marshes, tides of the ocean, and energy of matter (Qi) . . .' (p. 145). Ishibashi and Dumoulin interpret Qi as 'air' (p. 204).

45 Cf. illustrations in Grapard 1992a: 49, 51; Demura 1973: 30; 1975: 51; Okada 1992: 27, 32–3, 38–40.

46 Demura Katsuaki has investigated some twenty descriptions of this ceremony in the Yoshida archive of Tenri University. Even if none are by Kanetomo himself, Demura proves convincingly that the details of the ceremony must have been created by him. It consists of a long initial sequence of prayers and rituals, mostly to purify and to protect the body. Eventually the priest summons the kami of the shrine where the ceremony is taking place, offers some rice to it and chants the request, which seems to be the main purpose of the ceremony. Rites to end the state of protection and the *Nakatomi harae* conclude the ceremony (Demura 1975a,b: *passim*).

47 cf. Demura 1973: 41.

48 BDJ: 1463.

49 A53: [. . .] What the Buddhists call *kaji* seems to be the same as the Shinto term. This is one example of the many words which are the same in India, China and Japan. (NST 19: 226; Grapard 1992b: 147–8)

50 NST 19: 226; Grapard 1992b: 148.

51 NST 19: 228; Grapard 1992b: 149.

52 Kanetomo takes numbers 2–5 from the seven Heavenly Deities in *Nihon shoki* and *Sendai kuji hongi* respectively, which have no connection whatsoever with the five phases. However, the third set makes use of several kami given birth to by Izanami and Izanagi, who are also in the original attributed to the elements wood, fire, earth, metal, and water (cf. NST 19: 229, note; SJ: 707).

53 Demura 1973: 37; for the ritual manual see ibid.: 32–7.

54 A62: [. . .] If you don't understand the etiquette of approach and retreat, there will be lots of punishment and hardly a reward. (NST 19: 233; Grapard 1992b: 152).

55 観, 念, 想. It is not easy to translate these terms, as they seem to refer more or less to the same.

56 NST 19: 232; Grapard 1992b: 152.

57 This interpretation should not exclude, however, any more specific reference included in the term *shintai sahō*.

58 These arguments are mainly included in Kanetomo's remarks on Buddhism which we touched upon only in passing.

CHAPTER EIGHT

The death of a shogun: deification in early modern Japan

W. J. Boot

Ask any Japanese, and he is likely to tell you that deifying humans is just one of those Japanese customs. Perhaps he will even add, that foreigners do not understand. In fact, however, the number of clearly identifiable historical figures who have been deified is not all that great. In the ancient and medieval periods, even if we include such doubtful instances as Hachiman (apocryphally identified with Emperor Ōjin) and Sugawara no Michizane (whose shrine, initially, at least, was intended to placate his angry spirit, his *onryō* and not to worship his person), we still only have a handful of cases. It is true that, once we have entered into the Edo Period, numbers increase. In this period, even living people were deified, and in considerable numbers, as is documented in Katō Genchi's study of this subject.[1] Later, in the Meiji Period, building shrines for the dead and worshipping them almost became a fashion. Well-known examples are the Heian Jingū in Kyoto (for emperors Kanmu and Kōmei), or the Meiji Jingū (for emperor Meiji), Nogi Jinja (for general Nogi Maresuke), and Yasukuni Jinja in Tokyo. This, however, was a new development.

Theoretically, the possibility that all or some Japanese Shinto deities had originally been men was acknowledged at the latest by the end of the middle ages; from time to time one comes across such Euhemeristic interpretations of Shinto gods, both in Japanese and in Jesuit sources. As the word Euhemeristic itself already indicates, however, Japan was by no means the only country where such ideas existed. In other words, the phenomenon is not only too recent, but also not specific enough to be considered a national trait. Under these circumstances, the best thing we can do is to agree on a few very basic hypotheses regarding deifications in Japan and put these to the test. The hypotheses that I would propose are that deification practices changed rather drastically around the beginning of the Edo Period; that the Euhemeristic interpretation is of Chinese, that is Confucian origin; and that the practice of deifying humans was the outcome of specific theological developments.

This chapter is structured around the first and the last of these hypotheses, and its subject is the deification of Tokugawa Ieyasu (1542–1616) and its precedents. The second hypothesis, regarding the origin of the Euhemeristic interpretation of deities, will not be treated here. Although much of the research on which this essay is based dates back to the late 1980s, it will, I hope, still hold its own in the company of the recently published research of Sugahara Shinkai and Sonehara Satoshi.[2]

Deifications used to be left to specialists in religious studies. Real historians preferred to deal in real things, and perhaps felt somewhat ill at ease around such manifestly irrational phenomena as men turning into gods.[3] It is greatly to the credit of the Kyoto historian Asao Naohiro that he has made deifications into an acceptable subject for historical research. This he did in a series of articles, published in the first half of the 1970s. In a nutshell, he argued that in the wars fought in the last few decades of the sixteenth century for the hegemony of Japan a totally new concept of 'power,' or rather, of 'authority' arose.[4] The authority that Oda Nobunaga (1534–82), the first of the three warlords who unified Japan after more than one century of endemic civil war, arrogated for himself was according to Asao quintessentially different from the authority that earlier warlords had exerted over their followers. Nobunaga's authority was absolute and – and this is the important point – religious in nature. In this respect, Nobunaga set the example for his successors Toyotomi Hideyoshi (1536–98) and Tokugawa Ieyasu.

Asao's thesis is that Nobunaga had let himself be inspired by the example of the most zealous and difficult of his opponents, the Buddhist Ikkō sect. The religious fanaticism of its followers and the absolute obedience they showed to their leaders were things that Nobunaga found sorely lacking amongst his own samurai. Asao uses two kinds of evidence to argue his thesis. On the one hand, he shows how, beginning with the bloody suppression of the Ikkō sect in the province of Echizen in 1575, more and more often remarks appeared in Nobunaga's letters and directives to this effect: 'Do as I command you, and you will not only do well in this life, but also in the next,' or 'Honour Nobunaga in all things, and do not even think of turning your feet into his direction.'[5]

The other, and more important piece of evidence to which Asao refers, is a passage in the *Historia de Japam*, a contemporary description of Japan, written by the Portuguese Jesuit Luis Fróis (1532–97). Fróis, who had known Nobunaga personally and knew many people in Nobunaga's entourage, relates in his *Historia* how Nobunaga built a temple, the Sōkenji, next to his castle in Azuchi and ordered that he himself be worshipped there as a deity. Fróis accompanies this story with the translation of an edict that, he claims, Nobunaga had promulgated on this occasion.[6]

Asao combined these two sources, i.e. Nobunaga's letters and directives on the one hand, and Fróis' story on the other, and concluded that Nobunaga consciously and deliberately intended to have himself worshipped as a god even during his life. As with every new idea, this thesis of Asao created quite a stir in Japan. In the second half of the 1970s many articles appeared in which the thesis was not only discussed, but also, following Asao's suggestion, applied to Nobunaga's two immediate successors Toyotomi Hideyoshi, who had been deified as Hōkoku Daimyōjin, and Tokugawa Ieyasu, who had been deified as Tōshō Daigongen.[7]

In the west, too, some scholars, e.g. Herman Ooms, were prepared to argue in favour of the reliability of Fróis' account and, by the same token, of the correctness of Asao's ideas. Others, however – George Elison, who dismisses Asao's ideas as 'extreme and unwarranted' is one such – rejected the notion completely.[8] Criticism focused on the point that Fróis' 'deification of Nobunaga' is not attested anywhere in the Japanese sources. Asao should have known. Already seventy years ago, when the well-known Shinto scholar Katō Genchi was confronted with similar remarks about a so-called deification of Nobunaga, apparently also based on Fróis' account, he reacted: 'I am not yet sure from Japanese historical sources, if he really was deified and enshrined during his life-time, and so far I have never referred to him at all for that reason.'[9] Katō's remarks on this topic date from 1928. Neither Asao nor anyone else has since then succeeded in finding these sources. There are other things that detract from the thesis: the circumstances of Nobunaga's burial, the inconsistencies in Fróis' account, the fact that a deification of Nobunaga is not mentioned as a precedent for the deification of his immediate successors, and other possible interpretations of the linguistic evidence.[10] The fact, however, that not one single Japanese document can be produced to corroborate this Japanese exemplum of the deadly sin of Superbia, is fatal.

Even if his thesis does not hold, however, Asao's articles did serve the useful purpose of kindling a discussion about the other deifications, and, more generally, about the relation between state and religion in the Momoyama and early Edo periods. This is a field that undoubtedly deserves further exploration, and one of the obvious tracks that present themselves for such explorations is the two *bona fide* deifications we have in this period, namely those of Toyotomi Hideyoshi and of Tokugawa Ieyasu. Since the deification of Ieyasu is by far the best documented of the two, this is where we will start.

The common opinion is that Ieyasu was deified in accordance with the terms of his will and testament. Now, it was not uncommon in Japan to make oral declarations on one's deathbed providing for the posthumous disposition of one's body and possessions, but in the case of Ieyasu things are a bit more complicated. Between the day on which he fell ill (Genna 2/1/21; 8.3.1616) and the day on which he died (Genna 2/4/17; 1.6.1616) almost three months elapsed. During this period, to ever changing groups of listeners, Ieyasu formulated a great number of provisions, varying from bequests to faithful servants, appointments of trusted vassals in strategic positions, and wise words of counsel to his son and successor Hidetada, to instructions about what should be done with him after his death.

It is of course this last category of declarations that interests us most. They are all concentrated in the first few days of the fourth month (the second half of May 1616), and can be divided into three groups:

First group: On the first day of the fourth month, Ieyasu orally makes a number of testamentary dispositions in the presence of several of his most trusted vassals: Ōkōchi Masatsuna (1576–1648), Honda Masazumi (1565–1637), Akimoto Yasutomo (1580–1642), and Itakura Shigemasa (1588–1638). Their content is that, after his death, a mausoleum (*byō*) should be built on Kunōzan, and that another vassal of his, Sakakibara Teruhisa (1584–1643), should be appointed as its priest (*shinshoku*). (Kunōzan is the name of a mountain in the neighbourhood of Ieyasu's residence Sunpu, present-day Shizuoka.) This occasion is mentioned in several independent sources.[11]

Second group: On the second day of the month, Ieyasu again formulates a number of instructions, this time in the presence of the Buddhist priests Tenkai (fl. 1643) and Sūden (1569–1633). This occasion, too, is reported in several sources, the most explicit and detailed of which is a letter by Sūden to the governor of Kyoto, Itakura Katsushige (1545–1624). This letter is dated on the fourth day of the fourth month.[12] The substance of this 'testament' was, according to Sūden, that Ieyasu wanted to be buried on Kunōzan, that the funeral ceremony (*sōrei*) should be held in Zōjōji (a temple of the Pure Land sect in Edo that was patronised by the Tokugawa), that an *ihai* (ancestral tablet) should be placed in the Daijuji (a temple in the country of origin of the Tokugawa, the Province of Mikawa, where Ieyasu's ancestors lay buried), and that a 'small hall' should be built in Nikkō, where Ieyasu would be 'invited' (*kanjō*) to reside as a godhead after one cycle had gone by, i.e. in the third year after his demise. He would become the tutelary deity (*chinjushin*) of the eight provinces of the Kanto. In many of Sūden's subsequent letters we find references to these provisions, e.g. in a letter of the sixteenth of the same month, addressed to the same Katsushige. Here, Sūden writes that 'in view of the provisions of his will' Ieyasu's body will have to be interred on Kunōzan and that he will have to be worshipped as a deity. Moreover, the mourning rites (*ontomurai gochūin*) will be held in Zōjōji, but a funeral ceremony (*sōrei*) would not be necessary.[13]

A second tradition, separate from Sūden's account of what happened at this occasion (second day of the fourth month), is reflected in a letter of Date Masamune (1567–1636). According to this letter, dated on the third day of the fourth month, Ieyasu had decreed the day before that, after his death, his body should be placed on Kunōzan and that a temple should be built in Nikkō; as soon as this temple would be ready, his body should be brought there; the funeral ceremony (*sōrei*) should be held in Zōjōji.[14] Masamune does not mention the name of his informant, but in view of the content of the letter, I incline towards the supposition that he is reporting what he has heard from Tenkai. The correspondences with claims that Tenkai voiced at a later stage are, in any case, very striking. What is also very striking is that nowhere in Tenkai's own writings or in his many biographies is this occasion on the second of the fourth month referred to, although his presence at Ieyasu's bedside is attested not only in Sūden's letters, but also in other sources.[15]

147

Third group: An event that in some accounts is dated on the first, and in others, on the sixteenth of the fourth month is Ieyasu's 'trial' of the Miike sword. It is a gruesome story, which the sources narrate as follows: In the deep of the night Ieyasu summons his valet (*nandoyaku*), and orders him to bring him one of his swords, which was forged in Miike. Next, he commands the valet to go to the prison, to take one of the prisoners on whom a death sentence has been passed, and to hack him through the rump with this sword. The valet returns and reports that the sword had gone through smoothly: 'You hardly noticed that you cut.' Thereupon Ieyasu makes him put down the bloodied sword next to his pillow, takes it into his own hands, waves it about several times, and then declares: 'This sword must be venerated as a god who [will make] our descendants [endure] for ever and ever' (*kono tō o motte shison chōkyū no kami to aogubeshi*). This sword, so the story concludes, is even now kept in the Tōshōgū on Kunōzan.[16]

These three groups of 'last wills' can be combined as follows. On the first of the fourth month, Ieyasu – he is very ill; he cannot eat any more, is sick, has a fever, and in general may be sure that his end is near[17] – tells his most trusted henchmen that after his death he wants to be worshipped as a god. On this occasion, he tells them that his shrine should be placed in Sunpu and he appoints Sakakibara Teruhisa as its future priest. These two stipulations must stem from Ieyasu himself. Nobody else had such emotional ties with Sunpu, and nobody else would have had any reason to bestow such a distinguished appointment on Teruhisa.

Ieyasu's henchmen report his words to his son and successor, Shogun Hidetada. Since this is a religious matter, on the following day, Hidetada instructs the two most important religious advisors of the bakufu, namely Sūden and Tenkai, to go to his father and discuss the project with him in greater detail. This discussion leads to a conspicuous proliferation of testamentary stipulations. I do not think, as is maintained by some, that it was Ieyasu who, in the interests of pursuing an even-handed religious policy, had decided to give all religious institutions with which he was connected an equal part in the honour.[18] It seems more likely that it was Tenkai and Sūden who were following a list, that they had drawn up, of things to be done and temples to be remembered. For instance, the stipulation that a 'small hall' should be built in Nikkō was, I think, the answer to a protest raised by Tenkai: 'And I? What do I get?' Only a few years before, in Keichō 18 (1613), the temple complex in Nikkō had been given to him by Ieyasu.[19] Sūden then reported the result of this conversation to Hidetada and his most important ministers, amongst whom we find Itakura Katsushige. Tenkai told his version amongst others to Date Masamune, but did not put it down in writing himself.

Ieyasu's exercises with the Miike sword must, again, be his own personal initiative, if there is any truth to the anecdote at all: every shrine needs a *shintai*, and swords are not an unusual type of *shintai*. What makes one doubt the truth of the story is that the *shintai* that, as we shall see, was installed in the shrine on Kunōzan, was not a sword, but a mirror. Another reason for doubting the historicity of the anecdote is that two different dates are given for the event, namely the first and the sixteenth. On the other hand, both nights have in common that Ieyasu had every reason to suppose that this night would be his last; on the sixteenth, correctly so. If the anecdote is true, however, it underlines that it was Ieyasu himself who took the initiative for his deification and that he himself had a clear idea about the way in which it should be done.

On the fourth of the fourth month, Ieyasu recovers somewhat from his crisis, but one week later things have again taken a turn for the worse: from the eleventh onward, the patient no longer eats and a recovery seems no longer probable. In all temples and shrines prayers are said for him, but Hidetada already prepares himself for the inevitable parting, and on the fifteenth he summons Bonshun (1553–1632). Bonshun, a scion of the Yoshida, was one of the best known Shinto scholars of his age, and a good acquaintance of Sūden, who in the events that followed would be his steadfast supporter.[20] When Bonshun has presented himself, Hidetada interrogates him 'about Buddhism and Shinto.'[21] I assume that his questions will have been about the differences between deification according to Buddhist, and deification according to Shinto rites, i.e. deification as (dai)gongen ('[great] avatar'), or as (dai)myōjin ('[great] god'). That, at least, is the subject about which Bonshun was to be questioned again a couple of weeks later. The inference is that Hidetada had been made aware of the fact that both possibilities existed. The sources do not tell when and through whom this had happened.

Possibly as a result of Bonshun's technical advice about the procedure to be followed, Sūden makes a point of replacing, in his letter of the sixteenth, the term funeral ceremony (sōrei) that both he and Masamune had used initially, by the term mourning rites (ontomurai gochūin). This indicates that between the fourth and the sixteenth theological advice had been sought in connection with Ieyasu's last will, and the most probable advisor was Bonshun. However this may be, Bonshun must have pleaded his case well, because the day after his audience Hidetada decides that Ieyasu 'shall be worshipped according to Shinto rites as godhead on Kunōzan in Sunpu.'[22] On the seventeenth, halfway through the morning, Ieyasu dies. The same night the body (not a word is said about a cremation) is brought to Kunōzan, and the next day, early in the morning, the place is determined where the shrine shall be built.[23] Already in the night of the nineteenth, on the Hour of the Boar (i.e. the hour before midnight), the senza ceremony that installs the new godhead in his shrine can be held. Chief officiating priest is Bonshun; the rites are those of the Yoshida school of Shinto.

The ceremony itself is described in Bonshun's diary and in a letter of the twenty-second from Sūden to Katsushige.[24] The most detailed description is the one in Bonshun's diary: a provisory hall, called 'karidono' or 'utsushidono,' was built, and the area in front of the shrine was marked off with a torii (the entrance gate to a shrine) and a fence. Along the route from the torii to the hall

149

two pairs of lanterns (*tōrō*) were positioned. On the Hour of the Boar, moreover, the route from the *karidono* to the main shrine building (*naijin*) was screened off with rolls of silk cloth and the ground was covered with straw mats, that were also in their turn covered with white silk. People armed with bows and arrows, shields and spears stood to the west of the shrine. Also 'to the west, in front of the god' the procession was formed: in front someone who scattered rice, next followed someone holding the mirror, and then came Sakakibara Teruhisa with the *gohei* and Bonshun who, as the chief officiating priest, brandished a bell; after them followed the portable shrine (*mikoshi*) and, at the very end, the escort armed with its bows, shields, spears, and arrows. Every light had been extinguished.[25]

When the main shrine building has been completed (sic!: *naijin shuttai no toki*), Bonshun orders everything to be purified; next he installs the mirror, which apparently serves as the *shintai*, in the innermost sanctum of the main shrine building (*nainaijin*). Food offerings are set out by Teruhisa, acting on Bonshun's instructions, and then, with the execution of the three kinds of kaji and the three kinds of purification, the central part of the ritual, i.e. the invitation of, and unification with the deity, commences.[26] At the end, the following prayer is read:

> Having selected the nineteenth day of the fourth month of Genna 2, the Hour of the Boar, as an auspicious day and time, we now place on the high peak of Kunōzan in the district Udo in the province of Suruga the image of the Lord Minamoto no ason Ieyasu, Prime Minister and appointee to Junior First Rank.[27] The offerings and herbs (*gosai*) we have placed in front of you. Thus, dwell in peace [in this place] and protect in length of years this fundament of peace in the empire and of ever increasing prosperity – thus we ask filled with awe. By way of taking our leave, the following: if unintentionally someone amongst us present here is not of the correct disposition or is unclean, nevertheless protect us in your magnanimity with your blessings. Thus we speak filled with awe.[28]

Then two bows, hand clapping, and Bonshun retires. Teruhisa puts down the *gohei*, bows twice, and retires. All other people present, too, retire after having made one bow.

On the twenty-second, Shogun Hidetada pays a visit to the shrine, together with his brothers, the heads of the three collateral branches of the Tokugawa family, and on the twenty-fourth he returns to Edo.

One would expect this to be the end of the matter, but nothing is further from the truth. For the theologians, Tenkai, Sūden, Bonshun, their finest hour had just arrived. Hardly had Ieyasu been enshrined than Tenkai started to object. It had been Ieyasu's wish, he claimed, to be deified according to the Shinto-Buddhist rites of Sannō Ichijitsu Shinto that he, Tenkai, knew. The name Sannō Ichijitsu Shinto could be interpreted as the belief that the 'King of the Mountain (Sannō) is the single substance (*ichijitsu*),' but no such theological explanation was forthcoming from Tenkai. The name also suggests close links with the Tendai sect to which Tenkai belonged, for Sannō was the tutelary deity of Hieizan, the mountain on which the main temple of the Tendai sect stood. Sannō Ichijitsu Shinto was, however, most closely linked with Tenkai himself, for no one had ever heard of it until Tenkai brought it up at this occasion. The supposition that, unlike Sannō Shinto which had been around for centuries, it was a personal invention of Tenkai himself is an obvious one, and was also voiced by some of Tenkai's contemporaries, including Sūden.[29]

The theological dispute undoubtedly had a mercenary side to it. My reading of the causal connections is that Tenkai could not tolerate that the Yoshida, for the time being represented by Bonshun, should add the worship of Ieyasu to their religious empire. He wanted Ieyasu for himself;[30] more concretely, he wanted the centre of the worship of Ieyasu and, thus, of all Tokugawa patronage, to be located in Nikkō, which was his. If our supposition that Date Masamune's version of Ieyasu's testament of the second goes back to Tenkai is correct, then Tenkai realised immediately where the crux of the matter lay: with the body. 'As soon as the temple in Nikkō is ready, the body (shitai) must be moved there,' Ieyasu had said, according to Masamune. Neither stipulation is to be found in Sūden's rendering of 'the testament,' which had been accepted by the Shogun and his advisors. Here the operative word is 'invitation' (kanjō): the god was to be invited to Nikkō, not his body reburied. The proviso that 'a small hall' should be built in Nikkō was of secondary importance, and the verb forms that Sūden employs indicate clearly that Ieyasu regarded the 'invitation' (kanjō) to Nikkō not as a condition that would have to be fulfilled before he could possibly manifest himself as the tutelary deity of the Kantō. Additional evidence corroborating the fact that, for others, the founding of a 'small hall' in Nikkō had neither the urgency nor the importance given it in Masamune's letter, can be found in Sūden's letter of the sixteenth where he does not repeat the stipulation that this hall was to be built and the godhead to be invited.

Still, Tenkai eventually succeeded in persuading Hidetada to accept his version of the testament. How he did this is unclear. The best sources do not tell, and later sources, all from the Tenkai camp, give conflicting accounts. The oldest accounts we find in two letters of our faithful chronicler Sūden. The first letter is addressed to Itakura Katsushige, and is dated the twelfth of the fifth month:

In accordance with the stipulations of his testament, Ieyasu has been interred on Kunōzan and glorified as a god. Because Bonshun happened to be in Sunpu, he has already executed the [necessary] rituals, substituting for a Yoshida [priest]. It had already been decided, moreover, that for the name-giving of the god, imperial messengers would have to come. Then, suddenly, it turned out that Tenkai had some ideas of his own, and we quarrelled a bit. I said that, since it was a matter of deities, the Yoshida should know, but Tenkai claimed that he, too, had some knowledge of Shinto. [Fortunately this is a matter that] does not concern me in the least.[31] Are they telling stories where you are [i.e. in Kyoto. W.J.B.] that we have quarrelled about this? It is not really all that important, so you need not be concerned. [For that reason] I have not mentioned the incident in my earlier letters.[32] [However,] because I understand from your letter of the third [that you have heard something], I have this time given you the gist of what happened. Ieyasu, too, often proclaimed regulations that in essence stated that the various Ways should be allowed to establish themselves. I have only once given my opinion, as described above. What happens after that is absolutely no concern of mine. The circumstances are known to all councillors. If strange rumours are being bruited about with you [in Kyoto], please pay due attention.[33]

The purport of the letter is clear. Sūden says that he has of course nothing to do with the matter, but he does not mind confessing that in his opinion Shinto affairs should be left to the Yoshida, and he hints to Katsushige, who after all is one of Hidetada's most important councillors, that he would prefer him to be of the same opinion. In this letter to Katsushige, Sūden does not report any of the arguments that, we may assume, Tenkai brought forth at the time of the dispute. He does give some inkling, however, of the nature of the discussion in a subsequent letter, dated the twenty-first of the fifth month and addressed to another of his regular correspondents, the always-curious retired *daimyō* Hosokawa Tadaoki (1563–1645):

Because [Ieyasu] was going to be glorified as a god, I told the Shogun that this should be done by the Yoshida. Fortunately, Bonshun was in Sunpu; he was ordered, therefore, to take the first measures already. The name of the godhead,[34] his rank and so forth would be determined by the imperial court, and thereupon an imperial messenger, the acting head of the Imperial Council (*shōkei*) and all the others would come here. On that occasion, a priest of the Yoshida, too, could come here; all rituals having to do with the definitive installation [of the godhead] in this shrine (*sengū*) could then be performed. That was the way things had been arranged, and then Tenkai professed that he knew of another [possibility], namely Sannō Shinto. He deceived everybody with remarks to the effect that the shrine of the Yoshida would be subordinate to the Sannō Shrine and other such nonsense. For that reason, things have taken longer than they should. Apparently, here and there the rumour is being bruited about that he has quarrelled with me. Surely such a rumour will have reached you? There is nothing more to it than what is written above, so you need not be concerned about me. What follows I would not like to say to others, but I will tell you, if you keep it a secret. It concerns the Yoshida, and I tell you, that you might know. It seems that

152

recently an itemised letter (*kakitate*) arrived from the capital. I heard this just the way I am relating it to you. I never tell anything that is not the case. [The content of the letter is that Tenkai] is obstructing Yoshida Shinto. Could, then, the country of Japan exist with such a thing as Sannō Shinto?[35] I do not think that former generations would ever have heard of anything as preposterous as that. Recently, however, I have heard that the Shogun wants to make his decision according to the precedents (*kōgi no gobunbetsu senki no gotoshi to oboshimesare*), and that confidential consultations are going on. The *naiki* [i.e. Tadaoki's son Hosokawa Tadatoshi (1586–1641) – W.J.B.] will be able to tell you a bit more about this situation, but the main points I have told you here.

Bonshun is still tarrying here [in Edo]. On the twelfth he presented himself at the castle and had an audience with [the Shogun]. I accompanied him. Also after [this interview] it was still being said that Yoshida, the head of the house, would come to Edo through the good offices of Bonshun. I believe that the imperial edict, too, might still come (*sono bun tarubeshi*). You may not divulge this story. This letter you must throw into the fire.'[36]

It emerges clearly from Sūden's letters that the row had followed very closely upon Ieyasu's death, at such an early date, in fact, that is was possible for the rumours to have reached Kyoto by the third of the fifth month. If we allow a week for the rumour to travel from Sunpu to Kyoto, the *terminus ante quem* would have been around the twenty-fourth, the day on which Hidetada departed Sunpu. From Sūden's letters, it is apparent he considered it a foregone conclusion that a deification must be accomplished according to the rites of Yoshida Shinto, and that he was shocked and irritated by Tenkai's unexpected pretension that he, too, had some knowledge of Shinto. As regards the content of the quarrel, however, he only mentions Tenkai's claim that the Yoshida shrine would be subordinate to the Sannō shrine (a claim, by the way, that is not repeated in subsequent sources). This is only natural. On the twelfth he had had an audience with the Shogun accompanied by Bonshun, and he must have come away from this audience with the impression that his, or rather, Bonshun's case was going well. From his letter of the twenty-first, it is evident that he still believed that Tenkai would be defeated. Why, then, describe a storm in a teacup?

In one of Tenkai's later biographies, the *Jigendaishi engi* of 1679, the quarrel is described at length and with a fine eye for dramatic detail:

A certain Sūden had cajoled Honda Masazumi and had come to an arrangement with a bastard of the Yoshida. Tenkai had not been admitted to the ceremony and hence had not been able to prevent Ieyasu being deified according to Shinto rites. The following morning, when Hidetada gave an audience for all those who had nursed Ieyasu during his illness, Tenkai was sitting on his left and Sūden on his right.[37] Sūden, who was a glib talker, reported that everything had been carried out in accordance with Ieyasu's last will and testament. Thereupon Tenkai edged forward and said that apparently all of Ieyasu's testaments were doomed to be short-lived (*yuigon wa itsu shi ka mina kieusete haberu*). Sūden did not accept that he was implicitly being called a liar, and the row assumed such proportions that Honda Masazumi 'angrily left the room, saying: "It is a grave offence to say such things in the presence of the Shogun who, moreover, is still lamenting his loss; Tenkai should be banished without delay to a distant island." For some days, Tenkai was living in anxious anticipation of his banishment,' but then, to his delight, he was ordered to come to Edo and to tell the Shogun his version of the events. 'And when he had recounted the contents of the testament in full detail, the Shogun said that he himself, ignoramus as he was, understood little of Shinto, but that the late Ieyasu had been an adherent of Buddhism and that, if a Way existed in which Shinto and Buddhism were one [Sannō Ichijitsu Shinto – W.J.B.], that Way would have been to his deceased father's liking. Be that as it may, it was a Way of which he knew nothing, and therefore the imperial court should be asked to arbitrate.' With that assignment Tenkai was sent to Kyoto.[38]

At first, the row seems to have escaped Bonshun totally. Although he had left Sunpu together with Sūden on the twenty-sixth of the fourth month, Sūden apparently had told him nothing of his quarrel with Tenkai. At least, neither Bonshun's nor Sūden's diary indicates he did. Bonshun may have had a first intimation that things were not going well when he arrived in Edo (on the third day of the fifth month), and was met by two emissaries of Hidetada, who questioned him about the relative merits of deification as *daimyōjin* according to Shinto and as *daigongen* according to Buddhist rites. Hidetada may already have queried him about this subject on the day before Ieyasu died.

Bonshun answers that *gongen* is the name of the two creator gods Izanagi and Izanami, and is not given to other gods. To the obvious counter-argument that everyone has heard of a Sannō *gongen* and of a Hakone *gongen*, Bonshun answers that the teachings of the Yoshida do not know a Sannō *gongen* and that, if his memory is to be trusted, the Hakone *gongen* is Izanami. Precedents for giving *gongen* as a divine name do not really exist. For the predicate *myōjin* ('Great god'), however, there are many, many precedents, and in the light of these precedents, it seems an obvious step to appoint someone of Ieyasu's rank as *daimyōjin*. Bonshun argues further that, as regards the offering ritual, a *myōjin* is simpler than a *gongen*. To a *myōjin* one can also offer birds, fish, and the five herbs, which one cannot offer to a *gongen*.[39] For these reasons, he can not but advise that Ieyasu be deified as a *daimyōjin*.[40]

A detailed answer that, as Sūden still believed after the audience of the twelfth, had had the desired impact. Bonshun does not seem to have thought otherwise. The shock comes only on the thirtieth, under which date Bonshun notes in his diary that Tenkai will be sent to Kyoto in order to ask the emperor for a divine name for Ieyasu. Neither Bonshun nor Sūden tells us what Hidetada's considerations may have been. On the eleventh of the sixth month, Tenkai leaves for Kyoto.[41]

Tenkai and Sūden even had a second row. At the origin of this row lay institutional rivalry. Tenkai was the abbot of a number of important Tendai monasteries in eastern Japan (in the vicinity, therefore, of Edo and of the residence of the Shogun), while Sūden was the abbot of Nanzenji, an important Zen temple in Kyoto. It had been decided that the mourning rites for Ieyasu would be held from the seventeenth of the fourth till the thirtieth of the fifth month in Zōjōji in Edo.[42] The official argument went as follows: Since Ieyasu was to be 'glorified as a god' (*kami ni iwawaseraru*), there was no reason to declare an official, national period of mourning. Hence, what happened in Zōjōji was a private affair of the Tokugawa family. With help of this line of reasoning, Tenkai first had Sūden forbidden to say masses elsewhere than in Zōjōji, and eventually he even had Sūden forbidden to invite a delegation of monks from the Zen temples in Kyoto to come to Edo. Sūden was understandably put out by all this, and several times in his letters he made cynical references to the remarkably large numbers of monks from Eastern Japan allowed to participate in this so very private ceremony in Zōjōji.[43]

Tenkai had gained a clear victory in both of his disputes with Sūden, and had thus become the most important Buddhist priest at the court of the Shogun. One of the consequences was that Ieyasu was deified as Tōshō Daigongen and that his main shrine came to be located in Nikkō. On the twenty-sixth day of the tenth month, Tenkai inaugurated the construction work on the shrine, and between the fifteenth day of the third and the fourth day of the fourth month of the following year, Ieyasu's mortal coil was carried in a solemn procession from the Kunōzan to Nikkō where, on the seventeenth of the fourth month, exactly one year after his demise, Ieyasu was installed as *daigongen*. This ceremony, too, has been described in much detail in many sources, and I shall not repeat those descriptions here.

It is axiomatic that there were precedents for the deification and for the controversies between Bonshun, Sūden, and Tenkai. It is inherently unlikely, and contrary to all we know of Japanese culture, to suppose that things of this nature should be done without precedents. That precedents existed is also apparent from the practised way in which the matter of Ieyasu's deification was handled. None of Ieyasu's vassals was horrified or asked himself whether Ieyasu was ill, thinks that after his death he would become a god. The only problem was how he should be deified: as *daigongen* or as *daimyōjin*. The imperial court, too, did not object to deification as such. On the contrary, the court seems to have handled such cases earlier, for when the governor of Kyoto, Itakura Katsushige, suggested that a period of national mourning be declared, the court asserted immediately that this would not be necessary: Ieyasu will become a god, and therefore it will not be necessary to cancel the horse races of the Kamogawa Shrine in Kyoto.[44] Clearly, all the ins and outs were known.

The most recent precedent, also mentioned in the sources relevant to Ieyasu's deification, is the deification of Toyotomi Hideyoshi as Hōkoku Daimyōjin. Unfortunately, we are less well informed about this deification than we would like to be. The most important reason is that after the final ruin of the Toyotomi in Genna 1/5 (June 1615), the victorious Tokugawa degraded and eventually dismantled Hideyoshi's shrine. Many materials have thus been lost. The outlines, however, are sufficiently well known.

Hideyoshi died in Keichō 3/8/18 (18-9-1598), but initially his demise was kept secret. It is often suggested that this was done in order to prevent a rout of the Japanese armies deployed in Korea, and it is a fact that even after Hideyoshi's death his important advisors continued to send messages to the army commanders in Korea declaring that Hideyoshi was recovering from his illness and that before long other messengers would come with new instructions. However, Hideyoshi's death was known; Bonshun, for instance, recorded it in his diary on the very day Hideyoshi died.

As was the case with Ieyasu, in the case of Hideyoshi, too, no period of official mourning was declared, and no festivals or ceremonies were cancelled in order to allow people to mourn Hideyoshi's demise in a suitable manner. Here, again, as in the case of Ieyasu, we find no record indicating that Hideyoshi was cremated.

What did happen was this. Only a few weeks after Hideyoshi's death, rumours became current that a shrine would be built for him in the mountains to the east of Kyoto.[45] Allegedly, Maeda Gen'i (1539–1602), Hideyoshi's governor of Kyoto, had already 'measured' the land. Presently, the first spade cut the ground, and after that, building activities proceeded apace.[46] Maeda Gen'i, who was responsible for the construction of the shrine, stayed in regular contact with Bonshun's elder brother, Yoshida Kanemi (1535–1610), while Bonshun himself was once questioned about the building of the shrine by Ieyasu.[47] The implication seems to be that Gen'i asked Kanemi's advice about the design and the furnishings of the shrine, and about the way in which Hideyoshi's deification should be carried out. After the completion of the shrine, Kanemi was asked to become its chief priest. The reason why the Yoshida were continuously asked for their advice was that, at the imperial court, the Yoshida had of old been the recognised experts in Shinto matters. For many generations they had also had their own variety of Shinto theology, the so-called sōgen-ryū, and the head of the family held an exalted court rank. For instance, in Keichō 2/2/24 (10-4-1597) Kanemi had been promoted to Junior Second Rank. Kanemi's brother Bonshun apparently was a bastard, and for that reason he may have had to become a monk. He had no court rank and held no important position, but his family connections allowed him to act as a kind of free-lance advisor in Shinto matters, and as such he was very active.

When the shrine was almost ready, Gen'i made a petition to the imperial court (Keichō 4/3/5, 31-3-1599). At this occasion, he declared that the shrine had been built in pursuance of the last will and testament of the deceased, who had allegedly announced that 'he wanted to be worshipped in a great shrine on

Amidagatake.' The court established that there were precedents, and the emperor gave his consent. Next, the emperor in his turn consulted Yoshida Kanemi and decided on the name for the new godhead.[48] On the thirteenth day of the fourth month, Hideyoshi's remains were brought to his new shrine from his castle in Fushimi, where they had lain encoffined all these months.[49] On the sixteenth, the new god was installed in the temporary shrine building (*kari sengū*); on the seventeenth, the imperial edict was read in which Hideyoshi's promotion to a god and his divine name were proclaimed and on the eighteenth, at the Hour of the Boar, the new god was enshrined in the Main Hall of the shrine (*shōsengū*).[50] The parallels with Ieyasu will be evident. In the light of these events, neither Bonshun's actions in Sunpu, nor Sūden's conviction that deifications were best left to the Yoshida need amaze us. It is clear which precedents they had in mind when they insisted on deification as *daimyōjin*.

The other precedent that is mentioned in connection with Ieyasu's deification is that of Fujiwara no Kamatari (614–69). The relevant entry in the official history of the Tokugawa bakufu, *Tokugawa jikki*, tells us that Kamatari 'was first buried in Ai in the Province of Settsu and, after one year had elapsed, he was buried again on Mt. Danzan in the Province of Yamato.'[51] In a less official history of Kamatari's shrine on Danzan, *Tōnomine engi*, the story is told as follows. Several years before his death Kamatari told his son Jōe (645–86) that Danzan was the place where he wanted to be buried: 'If I am buried on this spot, my descendants will rise to high esteem.'[52] Jōe was a monk and as such he had, of course, to go to China for further training. While he was in China, his father died. Jōe saw a dream in which he found himself on Danzan. Then his father appeared and ordered him to build a shrine there; when the shrine was completed, he would come down and dwell on this mountain as a god, protect his descendants, and further the spread of Buddhism. Jōe returned home, but upon arrival he discovered that his father had already been buried on Mt. Aizan in Settsu. When, however, Jōe told the head of the family, his younger brother Fujiwara no Fuhito (659–720), about his dream and about the promise he had made to their father, it was decided to bury Kamatari anew. Consequently, his remains were brought from Aizan to Danzan.[53]

Not without divine assistance, a shrine was built on Danzan, which included a special hall in which a wooden statue of Kamatari was placed. This wooden statue guarded the further fortunes of the Fujiwara in a remarkably concrete manner. Every time danger threatened the head of the Fujiwara or other important members of the clan, the mountain on which the shrine was built would start to groan and tremble, special light effects would be seen, and the statue would suddenly show cracks and fissures. The priests of the shrine would report this forthwith to the capital and the Fujiwara would send messengers to close the cracks again through prayers and offerings. According to the shrine chronicles, the first time these phenomena occurred was under Emperor Daigo (r. 897–930) and from the end of the tenth century onward, they occurred fairly frequently. The most recent 'cracking,' occurring in Keichō 12 (1607), is documented profusely, not least because the Fujiwara themselves, on this occasion, proved unable to close the fissures and had to call on the Yoshida for help. The family archive of the Yoshida includes a letter from Ieyasu, in which he congratulates them on the successful conclusion of the operation.[54]

This godhead of Danzan, the deified Kamatari, had received the status of *daimyōjin* from ex-Emperor Go-Hanazono (r. 1428–64). He is known by the name of Taishokkan *shōryō* (i.e. the spirit of [Kamatari, who has received the rank of] Taishokkan) or, especially in texts of the Edo period, as the Tōnomine Daimyōjin.[55]

In these three *bona fide* cases of deification (Kamatari, Hideyoshi, and Ieyasu), we see the same pattern repeating itself. The initiative is taken by the person concerned who, before his death, declares that after death he will manifest himself as a godhead. Thus, we have three cases of posthumous deification. The main shrine is located where the mortal coil of the god lies buried. One conclusion we can safely draw from the above is that, even if Nobunaga had let himself be deified during his lifetime, this could not possibly have been a precedent for the deifications of Hideyoshi and Ieyasu. This means, however, that we are again confronted with the problem that Asao thought he had solved, namely, what is the rationale of such deifications? Not, I think, to render absolute one's own authority over one's vassals. If there is one concept that permeates all the sources that are relevant to this question, it is the concept of *shugojin* or 'tutelary deity.' In a more or less chronological sequence we find the following references:

(a) In the Nō play *Toyokuni mōde* ('Visit of the Hōkoku Shrine'), in which Hideyoshi enters as the god in a speaking role, the godhead says in so many words: 'Place your trust in me, place your trust in me. As long as the god Toyokuni is there, he will protect and preserve the emperor in peace, his children in prosperity.'[56]

(b) According to the testament that Sūden noted down, Ieyasu said he would become the tutelary deity of the eight provinces of the Kantō, the power base of the *bakufu*. Strategical considerations determined not only the location of his residence, Sunpu, that blocked the most important approach to the Kantō from west and central Japan, but also the location of his shrine.

(c) According to *Tokugawa jikki*, Ieyasu had said to Sakakibara Teruhisa, 'on whose knees he breathed his last,' that an enemy would probably come from the west. He had ordered him, therefore, to place his statue in the shrine on Kunōzan with its face to the west. The Miike sword, so this passage continues, was also placed in the shrine with its point turned towards the west.[57]

(d) In connection with the Miike sword, Ieyasu used the words *shison chōkyū no kami*, 'a god [who will see to it that] his descendants will endure for ever.' Evidently, it was not only the Kantō, but also his own progeny he wanted to protect.

(e) In the imperial edict (*senmyō*) of Genna 3/2/21, the emperor 'commanded' that Ieyasu should be the 'tutelary deity of the East.'[58]

(f) In one of Tenkai's biographies, we find the story that Ieyasu told Tenkai on his deathbed, namely that he would manifest himself as a god after his death, and that as such, he would protect, first, the military fortune of his descendants, second, 'the seed of the Buddha and the seed of the sun,' and third, the empire.[59]

(g) In the passage of the *Jigendaishi engi* (1679), part of which has been paraphrased above, several of these lines come together. This is one of Tenkai's later biographies, and therefore less reliable. In fact, a detailed comparison with earlier biographies would show how the story had grown in the telling. Precisely for this reason, it gives a good impression of what by the end of the seventeenth century, many years after Tenkai's victory, had become the commonly accepted opinion amongst the Japanese about the Tōshōgū. The *Engi*'s account can be analysed into three separate aspects:

(1) Ieyasu says it is exclusively due to Tenkai's kindness that he has been initiated into Sannō Ichijitsu Shinto and is thus able to guarantee the continued existence of his lineage.

(2) Ieyasu says he has heard that Kamatari's temple is the ancestral temple (*byō*) of the Fujiwara; evidently, the House (*sō*) of the Fujiwara has flourished for a long period. Therefore he, too, must be re-buried after one year has elapsed, just like Kamatari.

(3) According to this biography, Tenkai's most important argument in his dispute with Sūden had been that a *daimyōjin* was not capable of protecting his own descendants. Tenkai had slipped in this point as follows:

Sūden: 'Our deceased Lord wanted to be deified, remembering the recent example of the Hōkoku Daimyōjin. How, then, could it be against his wishes to deify him according to the rites of the Yoshida?'
Tenkai: 'The one thing that our Lord wished for in his heart, day and night, was that his lineage (*sō*) would continue to exist for a long time. Because the lineage of the Hōkoku Daimyōjin has perished before our eyes, he always kept his distance from that god. To quote such ill-omened precedents amounts to calling down ill fortune over this house!'[60]

'To protect' is a task that closely resembles that of the *ujigami* or 'clan god.' *Ujigami* are already mentioned in the seventh century (*Shoku Nihongi*, under Hoki 8/7/16). They are the tutelary deities of a clan, who are worshipped as such by its members. Their relation with a clan is either geographical in nature (an important god in the area where the clan comes from or has its power base), or genealogical (the divine ancestor from which the clan claims to be descended). In the words of a modern reference work: '*Ujigami* refers to: i) a godhead who is worshipped as the ancestor of the clan; ii) a godhead who from

159

the beginning has been connected with the clan; iii) in later times these gods were confused with local gods of the place where one came from (*ubusuna no kami*), and people started to call the tutelary deities of the place where they lived (*chinju no kami*) by this name; iv) nowadays the word *ujigami* is used in reference to deities in whom the original types of clan god (*ujigami*), local tutelary deity (*chinju no kami*) and local godhead (*ubusuna no kami*) have been fused together. The period in which this fusion occurred was the late Middle Ages.'[61] This dating is borne out by, for instance, a remark of Ise Sadatake (1717–84), who in the eighteenth century felt obliged to protest against this modern practice: 'There are people who think that *ujigami* and *ubusunagami* are the same thing, but this is a mistake. *Ubusunagami* are gods who protect the village where you are born. *Ujigami* are the ancestral gods of your clan.'[62]

The supposition that in such deifications as those of Kamatari, Hideyoshi, or Ieyasu the traditional religious practice of worshipping *ujigami* is asserting itself has its attractions. Objections can be made – I will turn to them in a moment – but there is also evidence that favours the hypothesis. A first point in favour is the proliferation pattern of Tōshōgū shrines.[63] Initially, the main shrine stood in Nikkō, and a second shrine stood in Sunpu. Then the godhead was invited (*kanjō*) from Nikkō to other places, e.g. to the palace of the Shogun in Edo (1618) and to the residences of the three collateral branches of the Tokugawa, the *gosanke* (Nagoya: 1619; Mito and Wakayama: 1621). In this context, the Tōshōgū in Hirosaki domain, allegedly founded in 1617, was very early, indeed. Its founder, Tsugaru Nobuhira (1586–1631), was married to an adopted daughter of Ieyasu, had relations with Tenkai, and may have had reason to be grateful to Ieyasu for excusing him from taking part in the siege of Osaka.[64] Then follows a second round: this time it is the turn of Ieyasu's close associates, i.e. the bonzes who had served him and the *daimyō* who had formed part of his immediate entourage. Tenkai was very quick. Already in 1617, he founded a Tōshōgū in the Kita-in (Kawagoe), the headquarters of the Tendai sect in the Kanto. Enryakuji, by way of contrast, had to wait till 1634 and was scooped by Kōyasan (Kongōbuji), which got its Tōshōgū in 1628. Sūden opened a shrine in the Konchi-in (Nanzenji, Kyoto) also in 1628, and of Ieyasu's warriors one could mention Tōdō Takatora (1556–1630), who built a Tōshōgū in his castle town Ueno (Iga) in 1623. In 1636, Akimoto Yasutomo received a statue from Nikkō, which he had often visited in one or other of his various capacities: regularly as the customary attendant of the Shogun, once in the company of the Korean envoys (Kan'ei 13/12/11), and several times as the intendant of the buildings in the temple complex. This statue of the deity he later enshrined in a temple, the Taianji, which he built within the compound of his own residence.[65]

The worship of Tōshō Daigongen receives a new impulse under Iemitsu, who feels a great debt of gratitude towards his grandfather and bears him a deep, personal veneration.[66] He dreams of his grandfather a number of times, and has each of these dreams recorded in a painting.[67] In consultation with Tenkai he decides to rebuild the shrine in Nikkō on a much more grandiose and costly scale, he increases the landholdings of the complex, and eventually he has himself buried in Nikkō – the only Shogun to be buried there apart from Ieyasu. He also elevates the status of the Tōshōgū, in the sense that he has it put into the category of shrines to be visited annually by an emissary of the emperor, instead of only on special occasions, as had been the case till then.

A second argument is that the *bakufu* did not propagate the worship of Tōshō Daigongen. The parallel that obtrudes itself is the shrines in Ise. Until 'Heian court rule' collapsed in the early Kamakura Period, worship at these shrines was 'the prerogative of the emperor alone.'[68] In the same way, the worship of Tōshō Daigongen was not open to all. One had to be a samurai of a certain rank before one could even enter the temple precincts. There are stories of ministers of the bakufu who spent a night in the shrine, but this will not have been a frequent occurrence.[69] In one of the many collections of anecdotes about Ieyasu, *Ochiboshū* (completed in 1728) by Daidōji Yūzan (1639–1730), we find the question discussed whether those who did not belong to the Tokugawa were in fact allowed to pray to Ieyasu. The answer is that there is no reason why, now that he is dead, one should not beseech Tōshō Daigongen for his blessings, just as one has enjoyed Ieyasu's bounty during his lifetime.[70] This discussion does indicate, however, that this was not a foregone conclusion.

As mentioned above, objections can be made. Both the Toyotomi and the Fujiwara were newly founded real clans (*uji*). It is understandable, therefore, that Kamatari, who on his deathbed had been given the new clan name Fujiwara by the emperor, after an interval of several centuries was deified and came to act as the protector of his descendants. The same applies *mutatis mutandis* to Hideyoshi, but unfortunately not to Ieyasu. He may have been the first to use the family name Tokugawa, but the Tokugawa regarded themselves as belonging to the clan of the Minamoto. To a schooled theologian this may not have presented much of a problem; such considerations may explain why the author of the *Jigen daishi engi* introduces, in the passage paraphrased above, the more modern Chinese term of lineage (*sō*) instead of *uji*. It may not have been an insurmountable difficulty, therefore, but it does make my argument less strong in Ieyasu's case than in the cases of Kamatari and Hideyoshi. Another, and as far as I am concerned stronger objection, is that nowhere in the earliest texts is it mentioned *expressis verbis* that the deifications of Kamatari and Hideyoshi were enacted because they stood at the beginning of a new clan. To my knowledge, neither of them was ever called an *ujigami*. On the other hand, it is quite clear that they acted as *shugojin*. The term is used in connection with Kamatari, Hideyoshi, and Ieyasu. As we have seen, by the end of the sixteenth century this term had become more or less synonymous with *ujigami*. Therefore, I do not think that this objection is strong enough for me to have to revise my hypothesis.

Thirdly, nowhere in the sources relevant to Ieyasu's deification is it mentioned explicitly that the deifications of Hideyoshi and Kamatari were precedents for that of Ieyasu. Tenkai's sneers at the Hōkoku Daimyōjin (= Hideyoshi) for his inability to protect even his own descendants may still be interpreted this way, but that does not hold for the references to Kamatari: Tōnomine Daimyōjin is not cited as a godhead who, in exemplary fashion, with a rumbling mountain and a cracking statue, had guarded his descendants' fortunes, but as a precedent for one single detail only, namely, the removal of Ieyasu's mortal remains from Sunpu to Nikkō.[71]

The problems incidental to Ieyasu's deification can be categorised as 'how' and 'why': how theological developments made the deification possible, and why was it done. The sources do not give a satisfactory answer to the first question. We may surmise that in all probability the 'how' was provided by the Yoshida, who early in the sixteenth century started building shrines over the graves of members of their family and giving them divine names (reishingō).[72] It also seems probable that Tenkai, for all his blustering statements, derived his knowledge of Shinto from Yoshida sources; there is some evidence in favour of this thesis, and no evidence that points to any other sources.[73] If, however, Kamatari is to be regarded as an instance of the same practice, we have a problem, for his promotion to daimyōjin took place more than half a century before the Yoshida began to practise their new burial rites. The history of Kamatari's shrine, the Tōnomine engi, too, antedates the new developments in Yoshida theology. It was written in the middle of the fifteenth century by no less a person than Ichijō Kaneyoshi (1402–81). Further research in this area might throw light on theological developments in the fifteenth century, and, more specifically, on the evolution of the older concept of the ujigami as the divine ancestor of the clan, that antedated sixteenth-century developments.

The problem with the 'why' is not so much one of sources, but of our own, modern presuppositions. The sources are clear enough: Ieyasu is going to protect his descendants, as Kamatari had done, and as Hideyoshi had hoped, but failed, to do. It is a religious matter, which should be interpreted in religious terms. All concerned, beginning with Ieyasu, believed in the existence of gods and buddhas, and in the possibility that Ieyasu would become one. As a god, Ieyasu would become a hoard of divine, magical power that was on the side of the Tokugawa and that, as their ancestor, they were not about to share with all and sundry. The choice that was put to Hidetada, between daigongen and daimyōjin, was a theological choice: which of the two offered the better prospects for maximising the divine protection Ieyasu had promised to give. Within this religious context, I think it is fair to say that the driving force behind the worship of Ieyasu was in the first instance a personal relation to Ieyasu, and a deeply felt, personal belief. Of this, Iemitsu is a prime example.

Of course, Hidetada's choice had a relevance outside the direct religious context, most obviously so for the subsequent fortunes of the Yoshida and of the Tendai sect. As regards the bakufu, considered as the government of Japan, separate from the Tokugawa family, the relevance of both the deification and of the choice of daigongen over daimyōjin is less obvious. Before long, Ieyasu's name would be used to sanctify fundamental bakufu policies: such-and-such was instituted by the Divine Lord (shinkun), and therefore cannot be changed.

Fear to offend the deity may well have been behind this argument. What we do not see, however, is that the *bakufu* seeks to legitimate its authority with references to the deified first Shogun. Gratitude for the fact that he had brought peace to the empire was a theme that was used in *bakufu* propaganda, but no attempt was made to make the worship of Ieyasu into a national religious cult, for example.

Notes

Dates are given according to the Japanese calendar, in the order '(name of the era) year/ month/day'. Where necessary, the corresponding date in the European calendar has also been given.

1 Katō Genchi 1931; rpt 1985. See also Okada 1982: 1.
2 An earlier version of this chapter was published in Dutch as W.J. Boot (1989). For Sugahara see Sugahara 1992 and for Sonehara, Sonehara 1996.
3 Examples are Nakamura 1965, and Kuwata 1975. Both are standard biographies, but Kuwata pays no attention, and Nakamura only perfunctory attention, to the deifications of their respective subjects.
4 Asao 1970: 70–8; 1972: 46–59; 1974: 20–36. See also Elison 1981: 55–85.
5 Paraphrase based on the final article of the instructions that Nobunaga drew up in 1575 for his commander in the Province Echizen, Shibata Katsuie. Text from Asao 1974: 21; text also in *Shinchō kōki* (Book 8). See, for a partial translation, Elison 1981: 73–5.
6 Portuguese text in Luis Fróis, *Historia de Japam III* (Wicki, José, ed. & ann., 1982), 332–3; Japanese translation in Matsuda and Kawazaki 1978: 133–4; paraphrase and discussion in Asao 1972: 55–7.
7 E.g. Kitajima Masamoto 1974: 1–13.
8 See Ooms, Herman 1984: 41; Elison 1981: 301.
9 Katō 1985: Appendix I, 8. See also Proceedings 1928: 61–2.
10 See J.P. Lamers (1998), ch. 6., for a discussion of these points.
11 *Kan'ei shoka keizu den* II, 96–7; *Kansei chōshū shoka fu* II, 272. See also *Tōshōgū Gojikki furoku* 16 (*Kokushi taikei: Tokugawa jikki* I, 285).
12 *Honkō kokushi nikki* III: 382.
13 *Honkō kokushi nikki* IV: 1–2.
14 *Dai Nihon shiryō* (DNS) XII.24, 210–1. See also *Dateshi chike kiroku* 26, quoted in DNS XII.25, 24, where it is said that 'Now that [Ieyasu] has died on the seventeenth of this month, on the Hour of the Horse, he will, so it is said, according to the content of his testament be glorified as a god (*myōjin ni iwaimōsubeki*). It is said that his body will for the time being remain in a place in Suruga, called Kunō (*sic*), but afterwards a temple will be built on Nikkōsan and the body shall be brought there.'
15 See an entry in the diary of one Umezu Masakage (1581–1633), for the second of the fourth month: 'The condition of Ieyasu is worsening by the day, thus Tenkai has related. He also told, that yesterday (*sic*) [Ieyasu] had through Tenkai, Sūden and Honda Masazumi [communicated] all sorts of final wishes and decisions to the Shogun, but has also given to Masazumi, in the presence of Tenkai and Sūden, a number of tasks that greatly redound to his credit.' (*Dai Nihon Kokiroku: Umezu Masakage nikki* II, 253; DNS XII.24, 210).
16 The story can be found in two collections of anecdotes, both compiled a considerable time after the event, namely *Meiryō kōhan* (end seventeenth century)

and *Ochiboshū tsuika* (1728); both works are quoted in DNS XII.24, 224–8. See also *Tokugawa jikki* I, 285.

17 See e.g. the description in *Honkō kokushi nikki* III, 382.

18 Regarding Ieyasu's supposed objectivity and tolerance in religious affairs, see my remarks in W.J. Boot 1988: 418–9 and 1990: 55–7. See also Sonehara 1996: 7, 203–5.

19 Date of the donation of Nikkō to Tenkai in *Jigen daishi nenpu* (*Jigen daishi zenshū* [JDZ] I, 537).

20 For Bonshun, see Tanabe 1992: 40–67; Kakei Iori 1931: 101–4.

21 *Shiryō sanshū: Shun kyūki* V, 3.

22 *Shun kyūki* V, 3.

23 *Shun kyūki* V, 4; *Honkō kokushi nikki* IV, 2–4.

24 *Shun kyūki* V, 4–6; *Honkō kokushi nikki* IV, 3–4.

25 A *gohei* is stick to which white strips of paper have been attached, and which is used in purification ritual. The stick is waved and shook above persons, objects or places that have to be purified.

26 Since the text speaks of the three kinds of *kaji*, it seems likely that the term is used in the Shingon sense of the threefold identification with the deity, through speech (mantra), body (mudrā), and mind (visualisation).

27 The expression used for 'image' in the text is *gyōzō* (var. *katagi*) o *hōmuru*, what could be translated literally as 'to bury the image/effigy.' In view of the verb 'to bury' one would like to interpret *gyōzō* as referring to Ieyasu's body, but as far as I have been able to establish, this word cannot be used to designate 'mortal remains.' The word can be used, however, in the pregnant sense of 'object into which a god descends' (*shintai*), in this case the mirror, but in that context the use of *hōmuru* is rather strange.

28 *Shun kyūki* V, 5.

29 See for this point Sugahara 1992: 197–9.

30 For my conclusions regarding Tenkai's character and aims, see Boot 1992: 54–5.

31 See also the parallel passage in a letter of 6/6: *Honkō kokushi nikki* IV, 31.

32 Sūden could be referring to his letters of 4/27 and 5/5.

33 *Honkō kokushi nikki* IV, 17–8.

34 In the light of this remark, it is strange to see that a later historical compilation, *Taihei nenpyō*, claims that on the nineteenth, at the occasion of his burial on the Kunōzan, Ieyasu was given the appellation Yakusan Daigongen (quote in Okada 1982: 22). This must be a later, spurious tradition.

35 Cf. DNS XII.25, 240, quotation from *Tsuchimikado Yasushigekyō ki* (for Genna 2/7/6), where we find the phrase 'how could Japan possibly exist without the Shira[kawa], the [Yoshi]da, and us' (*Haku, den, warera narade wa Nihon arumajiki*). The Tsuchimikado were hereditary Yin-Yang specialists, and also boasted a Shinto school of their own.

36 *Honkō kokushi nikki* IV, 22.

37 In East Asia, the left takes precedence over the right.

38 JDZ I, 380–2; cf. *Meiryō kōhan* 56–58.

39 *Gosai*, i.e. the strongly smelling herbs chive (*nira*), scallion (*rakkyō*), horseradish (*wasabi*), leek (*negi*) and beanleaves (*mame*).

40 *Shun kyūki* V, 8–9; see also DNS XII.25, 13–4.

41 DNS XII.25, 15–167. N.B. Under Genna 2/5/30 Bonshun still writes that Tenkai c.s. will be sent to Kyoto in order to petition for a divine name for the Kunōzan.' (*Shun kyūki* V, 13).

42 This is the so-called *zhongyin* (J. *chūin*), i.e. the period of seven times seven days after death within which, according to Buddhist belief, the one who died will be reincarnated again. The dates are mentioned in the letter from Sūden to Hosokawa Tadaoki d.d. 5/21 (*Honkō kokushi nikki* IV, 22).

43 *Honkō kokushi nikki* IV, 30. See also Somata 1985: 3–6. In this article, Somata treats these events correctly as part of Tenkai's attempts to make the temples in eastern Japan more independent of the older temples in the west, which were dominated by the imperial court.

44 *Honkō kokushi nikki* IV, 17. See also DNS XII.25, 26–7, esp. the comment of Shirakawa Yoshitomo, quoted ibid., 27. The horse races were a yearly event, and took place on the fifth day of the fifth month.

45 An entry in the diary of the priest Gien under Keichō 3/9/7: *Gien jūgō nikki* I, 299. The shrine was to be built on the model of Kitano jinja.

46 The *chinjisai* ('ground breaking' ceremony) took place on Keichō 3/9/15 (15-10-1598). Gien, who was the chief celebrant at this occasion, gives an elaborate description in his diary (*Gien jūgō nikki* I, 303–4).

47 Bonshun mentions visits by Gen'i under Keichō 3/12/19 (15-1-1599) and Keichō 4/intercalary 3/27 (21-5-1599), and his own visit to Ieyasu under Keichō 3/12/24 (20-1-1599); see resp. *Shun kyūki* I, 161, 179, and 161.

48 See *Miyudono no ue no nikki*, Keichō 4/3/5, quoted in *Koji ruien: Jingi* III, 1655. Ooms writes (1984: 49–50), that 'Hideyoshi requested that a shrine dedicated to himself be built next to the Hōkōji . . . His divine title . . . as stated in his will, was also an abbreviation of a name of Japan . . .' In the absence of the necessary references, Ooms' remark cannot be verified. *Hōkō ibun* does not contain a testament of this purport. A testamentary stipulation is mentioned in *Tōdaiki* (ed. *Shiseki zassan* II, 71), but here the divine name Hachiman Daibosatsu is given, that was later changed into Hōkoku Daimyōjin.

49 For this detail, see Schurhammer 1923: 89–90: 'As he [Hideyoshi] had besides a desire to perpetuate his name to all posterity and thereby be venerated as a god, he expressed a wish, in violation of the custom pervailing throughout Japan that his body should not be burned after death. He ordered instead that he should be enclosed in an artistically made coffin and that this should be placed in his castle, in the very place as a matter of fact which had been set apart, for recreation and games. He wished to be included therefore in the future among the Camis, for it is thus that the great men are called who have in past time distinguished themselves by their military exploits and who, as the people fancy are set up among the gods after their death. He wished besides to have the title of Scinfaciman, the "New Hachiman", for just as Mars was, in former days among the Romans, the god of war, so is Hachiman among the Japanese.' (The original source is a letter from Francisco Pasio to Father General, from Nagasaki, Oct. 3, 1598; Schurhammer quotes J. Hayus 1605: 500).

50 Gien reports (*Gien jūgō nikki* II, 42) that Hideyoshi's body was brought from Fushimi to the Hōkōji in the night of Keichō 4/4/13. See also Aoyama 1925: 3–5.

51 *Tōshōgū gojikki furoku* 25 (*Kaitei zōho Kokushi taikei: Tokugawa jikki* Vol. I, 377).

52 The correct pronunciation of the characters with which the name of the mountain is written, is Tanzan. The original name of the mountain, *tamu*, was contracted in two different ways: *tō* as in Tōnomine, and *tan* as in Tanzan. The pronunciation *dan* derives from folk etymology. Since, however, most dictionaries and reference works use this (mistaken) pronunciation, I have followed it here.

53 See *Tōnomine engi* (*Dai Nihon Bukkyō zensho: jisho sōsho* 2, 481–2).

54 See e.g. *Taishokkan gōharetsu mokuroku*, *Danzan jinja monjo* (rpt., 1985), 1–6. More details about the 'cracking' of Keichō 12 in *Go haretsu kiroku*, ibid., 6–30. Ieyasu's congratulations in Tenri University Library: Yoshida Bunko no. 6526; cf. ibid. no. 43–84.

55 Shōryō-in ('Hall for the Soul of the Deceased') is the name of the hall that was erected in 701, in which Kamatari's statue was placed. Strictly speaking, Go-Hanazono's *insen*, to be dated on Ōnin 2?/11/18 (c. 1468), says that the 'Danzan Myōjin' is to be promoted to 'a *myōjin* of senior first rank' (see *Danzan jinja monjo*, 59).

56 The play is collected in *Yōkyoku hyōshaku* Vol. 9: 230–6; quotation ibid., 235. The play is interesting in many respects, e.g. for the reasons why Hideyoshi is praised, for the notion that, as a god, Hideyoshi was an incarnation of Hachiman, and for the fact that the other protagonist is a Chinese general, who has come all the way from China to pray to the godhead. The author is unknown. It must have been written between 1599 and 1615, but it is not possible to date it more precisely.

57 See *Tokugawa jikki: Tōshōgū gojikki furoku* 16, 285 and the sources quoted there.

58 Quoted from Nakamura 1965: 700.

59 *Jigen daishi denki* (JDZ I, 294). This biography dates from 1650.

60 JDZ I, 381–2. Cf. also *Meiryō kōhan*, 56, which quotes the *Engi* almost literally.

61 *Shintō jiten* (1968), 244.

62 Quoted from *Nihon kokugo daijiten* s.v. 'ubusunagami'; the original source is given there as *Teijō zakki* 16.

63 The following are preliminary conclusions and more research is needed on this point. The lists and figures given in *Kokushi daijiten* Vol. 10, 112–3, s.v. Tōshōgū, help, but are ultimately inconclusive.

64 Tenkai is mentioned in the lemma 'Tsugaru Nobuhira' in *Kokushi daijiten*. The story about the siege of Osaka is supplied in his biography in *Kansei chōshū shoka fu* 725 (Vol. XII, 74), where the preferred reading of his name is Nobukazu.

65 *Kansei chōshū shoka fu* XV, 190.

66 For Iemitsu's veneration for Ieyasu, see Fujii 1997: 187–206.

67 One of these is reproduced in DNS XII.24, opp. 376.

68 See Teeuwen 1996: 21–5; esp. 21, 24.

69 See for more details on this and the following point Boot 1990: 331–7. See also Ishige 1971: 64–81, and Akimoto 1975: 1–29.

70 Quoted in DNS XII.24, 227–8.

71 Compare e.g. the first of Tenkai's biographies, *Jigen daishi denki* of Keian 3 (1650), in which nothing of this nature is recorded, and *Jigen daishi engi* of Enpō 7 (1679), in which the relation is clearly spelled out (JDZ I, 380).

72 I am referring to the lecture 'Medieval and Early Modern Shinto as a Means of Self-Deification,' given at the EAJS Conference in Budapest (August 1997) by Dr. Bernhard Scheid of the Austrian Academy of Sciences. Dr. Scheid in his turn refers to such work by Okada Shōji as his afore mentioned 'Kinsei Shintō no jomaku' (1982).

73 What little evidence there is has been painstakingly assembled by Sonehara. See Sonehara 1996: 180–198.

CHAPTER NINE

Changing images of Shinto:
Sanja takusen or the three oracles

Brian Bocking

Introduction

'The Oracles of the Three Shrines' (*sanja takusen*) are three short oracular utterances attributed to the shrine deities of Ise, Hachiman and Kasuga.[1] In practice, *sanja takusen* usually means the three oracle texts as they appear inscribed or printed on a hanging scroll. Versions of the *sanja takusen* scroll have been known in Japan for almost six hundred years. The deity of Ise (Amaterasu, Tenshō Kōtaijingū) usually forms the central focus, flanked by Hachiman lower down to the right and Kasuga to the left.[2] The various examples of the scroll are by no means identical but they bear a sufficiently strong 'family resemblance' to one another for the *sanja takusen* to be regarded as an iconographical unity. All versions of the scroll contain at least one, usually two and occasionally all three of the following elements: the names or titles of the three shrines; one to three oracular texts (*takusen*); one or more images of the personified deities of the shrines.

Two very different versions of the *sanja takusen* (illustrated in Figs. 1 & 2) will be discussed in this chapter. One version dates from before, and one after, the Meiji Restoration of 1868. This year was a watershed for Japanese religion because of the phenomenon of 'dissociation of kami and buddhas' (*shinbutsu bunri*, *shinbutsu hanzen*) which generated radically new and separate forms of Shinto iconography, ritual and doctrines. The history of the *sanja takusen* graphically illustrates the impact of *shinbutsu bunri* on the Japanese religious landscape.

The standard (pre-Meiji) form of the *sanja takusen*

In the booklet *Basic Terms of Shinto* published by Kokugakuin University, the *sanja takusen* is described as follows:

> Oracles of the three deities Amaterasu Ōmikami, Hachiman Daibosatsu and Kasuga Daimyōjin. According to legend, the oracles appeared on the

Figure 1 *sanja takusen*
(Edo period)

Figure 2 *sanja takusen*
(Meiji period)

surface of the pond at Tōdaiji in Nara during the Shōō era (1288–92). The oracles came to form the basis of moral teachings concerning pureness of mind, honesty and benevolence, and also contributed to the formulation and spread of Shinto doctrine.[3]

168

Fig. 1 shows an example of what I refer to as the 'standard' (pre-1868) form of the *sanja takusen*. The scroll shown here dates from the Edo period and was inscribed by the Zen Buddhist monk Kōgan (1748–1821).[4] It is virtually identical in content and layout to innumerable other examples of the scroll produced by priests, artists, calligraphers and publishers from the late fourteenth century onwards. At the head of the scroll are the names and titles of the three shrine-deities[5] (centre: Tenshō Kōtaijingū, right: Hachiman Daibosatsu, left: Kasuga Daimyōjin). Arranged below the shrine-names are the three oracular texts, one for each shrine, which will be discussed in more detail below. There are many minor variations on the standard form of the *sanja takusen*. Sometimes only the names of the deities are inscribed, and one or other of Hachiman and Kasuga may occasionally be described as *daijin* (great kami) rather than *daibosatsu* and *daimyōjin*. The oracle texts, too, are subject to minor variations and in later versions pictures are sometimes added to, or replace, the text of the oracles.

An English translation of the three oracles in the standard form of the *sanja takusen* appeared for the first time in 1985 in *The World of Shinto*, an anthology published by the Bukkyō Dendō Kyōkai.[6] The translation of the three oracles in *The World of Shinto* corresponds broadly to the standard type of *sanja takusen* scroll shown in Fig. 1 and runs as follows:

Hachiman Daibosatsu
Though one might attempt to eat a red-hot ball of iron, one must never eat the food of a person with an impure mind. Though one might sit above a blazing fire hot enough to melt copper, one must never go into the place of a person of polluted mind. This is for the sake of purity.

Tenshō Kōtaijingū
If you plot and connive to deceive men, you may fool them for a while, and profit thereby, but you will without fail be visited by divine punishment. To be utterly honest may have the appearance of inflexibility and self-righteousness, but in the end, such a person will receive the blessings of sun and moon. Follow honesty without fail.

Kasuga Daimyōjin
Even though it be the home of someone who has managed for long to avoid misfortune, the gods will not enter into the place of a person with perverse disposition. On the other hand, even though a man be in mourning for his father and mother, if he be a man of compassion, the gods will enter in there. Compassion is all-important.

This, with minor variations,[7] represents the text of the oracles found in most examples of the *sanja takusen* scroll and in the commentarial works relating to it from the late fourteenth century up to the Meiji restoration of 1868.[8] The *sanja takusen* scroll was extremely popular in the Tokugawa period (1600–1868) and its ideas, if not its traditional form, retained their influence into the twentieth century. According to one of my elderly informants in central Japan, the moral teachings embodied in the scroll represented *'ippanteki'* (widespread, popular) notions of religiosity during his own childhood in the 1920s.

The post-Meiji form of the *sanja takusen*

Figure 2 shows a quite different version of the *sanja takusen* scroll: the 'post-Meiji' form. This example features the same three shrines of Ise, Hachiman and Kasuga. Though superficially resembling the pre-Meiji version and readily identifiable as a *sanja takusen*,[9] it is significantly different from the standard form. For one thing this version, which probably dates from the late Meiji period (c. 1900), includes pictures of the three deities in a 'pure Shinto' style almost certainly unknown before 1868 and purposely devoid of the Buddhist iconographical features present in illustrated versions of the standard *sanja takusen* scroll. Most significantly, the text of the oracles is different in every respect from the 'standard' wording given above. The text in the post-Meiji version is drawn from the *Nihon shoki*, the eighth century 'Chronicle of Japan.' Three new passages replace the oracle texts on purity, honesty and compassion with the following narrative texts, known in modern Shinto as the *sanchoku* or 'three imperial commands'.

> Amaterasu Sumeōmikami commanded her August Grandchild, saying: 'This Reed-plain-1500-autumns-fair-rice-ear Land is the region which my descendants shall be lords of. Do thou, my August Grandchild, proceed thither and govern it. Go! and may prosperity attend thy dynasty, and may it, like Heaven and Earth, endure for ever.'

> Amaterasu Sumeōmikami took in her hand the precious mirror, and, giving it to Ame no Oshihomimi no Mikoto, uttered a prayer, saying: 'My child, when thou lookest upon this mirror, let it be as if thou wert looking on me. Let it be with thee on thy couch and in thy hall, and let it be to thee a holy mirror.'

> Takami-musubi no Kami accordingly gave command, saying: 'I will set up a Heavenly divine fence and a Heavenly rock-boundary wherein to practise religious abstinence on behalf of my descendants. Do ye, Ame no Koyane no Mikoto and Futodama no Mikoto, take with you the Heavenly divine fence, and go down to the Central Land of Reed-Plains. Moreover, ye will there practise abstinence on behalf of my descendants.[10]

The three shrines (*sanja*)

In *sanja takusen* scrolls the deity of Ise is flanked by Kasuga and the warlike Hachiman. The three deities and their oracles constitute a triad; an iconographic arrangement found often in both Buddhist and non-Buddhist contexts and frequently encountered in Japanese religious art. In his detailed study of the Amida triad at Zenkōji, McCallum observes that:

> The triad format, fundamental in East Asian Buddhist art, is based, of course, on the idea that each of the major Buddhas is accompanied by two attendant Bodhisattvas. The arrangement, with a central Buddha figure flanked on either side by a Bodhisattva, leads to a particularly satisfying symmetrical composition that appears to touch deep psychological roots. . . . Practically all triads belong to one of two basic categories: in one type the central Buddha figure is seated in the lotus position, flanked by standing Bodhisattvas; in the other all three figures are standing. . . . the available evidence suggests that the seated-central-Buddha type was most popular in early Japan, whereas the three-figures-standing type had the greatest popularity in Korea.[11]

The triadic motif of the *sanja takusen* with Amaterasu in the centre is prefigured at the mythopoeic level in the earliest *Kojiki* and *Nihon shoki* accounts by the legend that the sun deity Amaterasu, born from water, is associated with two male siblings.

It is widely known that water is the source of life and growth, and that water, moon and women form the popular symbolical orbit of fertility. We recall that the two brothers of Amaterasu are Tsukiyomi (moon-counting) and Susanoo (impetuous-man): the former is to reign over the world of darkness or night, while the latter the ocean or Netherland. Accordingly, it seems that Amaterasu, Tsukiyomi, and Susanoo form a triad that is closely associated with agricultural life.[12]

As well as the psychological factors, mythological connotations and iconographic traditions which inform the triadic arrangement of the *sanja takusen*, we can note that the specific triad of the three shrines of Ise, Hachiman and Kasuga has a religious, political and symbolic significance which almost certainly predates the linking of these three shrines, the *sanja*, with their associated three oracle texts.

The Iwashimizu shrine of the bodhisattva Hachiman, positioned on a mountain protecting the south-west direction of Kyoto, was established in 859 by the monk Gyōkyō. Hachiman, identified with the legendary Emperor Ōnin, his wife and his mother, was venerated by the imperial court and subsequently by the Minamoto clan. The Kasuga shrine, now called the Kasuga *Taisha* (Kasuga Grand Shrine), is located in Nara. Until 1868 the shrine formed part of what Grapard calls a 'multiplex' – a combined shrine-temple complex whose major integrated elements were the Kasuga shrine and the Kofukuji Buddhist temple.[13] The deity of the entire sacred area, Kasuga Daimyōjin (the Great Deity of Kasuga), was amongst other things the ancestral shrine-deity of the powerful Fujiwara clan who dominated the imperial court from the tenth to the twelfth centuries.

'The Ise shrine' may, according to context, refer to one or both of the Inner and Outer Shrines (Naikū and Gekū respectively) which constitute the imperial household shrine at Ise. The Inner Shrine houses Amaterasu Ōmikami (also read Tenshō Kōtaijin), grandmother of Ninigi, the legendary unifier of Japan, and great-grandmother of the legendary first Japanese Emperor Jinmu. Under the influence of Watarai Shinto, the 'Ise' deity was successfully identified with the Outer Shrine, the pilgrimage destination which was under Watarai control.[14]

Within what the historian Kuroda Toshio has called the medieval *kenmitsu* (exoteric-esoteric) system, the great shrine-temple complexes sanctified and thereby legitimated their own power and that of other elite groups such as the Fujiwara, the imperial court and the bakufu through the rituals and doctrines of esoteric Buddhism. Under the *kenmitsu* system the meaning of each of the three shrines was primarily Buddhist and the shrine-deities were part of the Buddhist pantheon.[15] Hachiman's title of *Daibosatsu* (Great Bodhisattva) is used in most standard versions of the *sanja takusen* and the Iwashimizu Hachiman shrine was first and foremost the shrine of a Great Bodhisattva. The usual title of the shrine-deity of Kasuga in the *sanja takusen* is *Daimyōjin* (great illumined divinity), a term whose meaning is not limited to 'Shinto' or 'Buddhist' contexts. The Kasuga divinity was also known by the Buddhist name of *Jihimangyo bosatsu*, 'Bodhisattva of rounded practice of compassion.'[16]

Ise seems to represent a slightly different case. Buddhist rituals and even Buddhist terminology were officially prohibited in the precincts of the shrine, though pilgrimages to the shrine by Buddhist priests were commonplace. However, the Tendai-Zen monk Mujū Ichien, in his work *Shasekishū*, tells how during his pilgrimage to the Ise shrine in the Kōchō era (1261–4) a shrine official explained to him the reason for the taboos on Buddhism:

In antiquity when this province did not exist, the deity of the Great Shrine [Amaterasu], guided by a seal of the Great Sun Buddha [Dainichi Nyorai, Mahāvairocana] inscribed on the ocean floor, thrust down her august spear. Brine from the spear coagulated like drops of dew, and this was seen from afar by Māra, the Evil One, in the Sixth Heaven of Desire. 'It appears that these drops are forming into a land where Buddhism will be propagated and people will escape from the round of birth-and-death,' he said, and came down to prevent it. Then the deity of the Great Shrine met with the demon king. 'I promise not to utter the names of the Three Treasures, nor will I permit them near my person. Therefore, quickly return back to the heavens.' When she had thus mollified him, he withdrew. Not wishing to violate that august promise, monks to this day do not approach the sacred shrine, and the sutras are not carried openly in its precincts. Things associated with the Three Treasures are referred to obliquely: Buddha is called 'The Cramp-Legged One' [*tachisukumi*]; the sutras, 'coloured paper' [*somegami*]; monks, 'longhairs' [*kaminaga*]; and temples, 'incense burners' [*koritaki*], etc.

Mujū concludes, in typical *kenmitsu* style:

> Outwardly the deity is estranged from the Dharma, but inwardly she profoundly supports the Three Treasures. Thus, Japanese Buddhism is under the special protection of the deity of the Great Shrine.[17]

Broadly speaking, these 'top three' shrines represented the major centres of spiritual-temporal power in medieval Japan.[18] They were already understood to form a quintessential grouping before the *sanja takusen* oracle scroll emerged. According to Tyler, the thirteenth-century *Gukanshō* and fourteenth-century *Jinnō shōtōki* both reflect a public, generally accepted view that Amaterasu had made an agreement with Kasuga which came to fruition in the close connection of the emperor with the Fujiwara ministers; later Hachiman (the Minamoto clan) joined these two deities and their clans in agreement over rulership of the country.[19] A fourteenth-century painting resembling a *sanja takusen* but without the oracle texts shows the resourceful Emperor Go-Daigo (r. 1318–39) seated as a Buddhist priest. In each hand the emperor holds a *vajra*, a symbol of esoteric Buddhism, while above him like a canopy are the titles of the 'three shrines'; Ise, Hachiman and Kasuga. The image is evidently meant to portray Go-Daigo as an emperor whose sacred authority derives from Buddhism and whose rule is endorsed by the three most significant shrine-deities.[20] It seems that by the time the *sanja takusen* first appeared, probably in the early part of the Ōei era (1394–1428), the character and significance of the 'three shrines' motif was already well established.

The Three Oracles

Oracles are brief, authoritative utterances by deities, issued usually in response to a specific request. Oracles occupy an important role in many religious traditions, including Buddhism, and techniques for obtaining oracles vary widely. Well-known pivotal events in Japanese history provided several significant examples of Buddhist priests using specialised techniques to seek oracular guidance from deities. In 735, Emperor Shōmu (r. 724–49) resolved to set up a great statue of Roshana (Vairocana) in what was to become the Tōdaiji in Nara. In 742, with the project still incomplete, the Buddhist priest Gyōgi (668–749) travelled to Ise to seek oracular reassurance that the erection of the statue would not offend the native divinities.

Carrying a holy Buddhist relic, Gyōgi journeyed as an imperial envoy to the great shrine of the Sun Goddess in Ise, to take her opinion as to the erection and worship of the great Buddha by the emperor . . . who was according to the native creed her descendant and her vice-regent upon earth. Gyōgi, then an aged man, after seven days and seven nights spent in prayer at the threshold of her shrine, received an oracle from her divine lips. Using (if we may believe the records) the astonishing medium of Chinese verse, she proclaimed in a loud voice that the sun of truth illumined the long night of life and death and that the moon of reality dispersed the clouds of sin and ignorance; that the news of the emperor's project was as welcome to her as a boat at a ferry, and the offering of the relic as grateful to her as a torch in the darkness . . . The Oracle was duly interpreted as favourable, and it was confirmed shortly afterwards by a dream in which the Sun Goddess appeared to the emperor as a radiant disc, and proclaimed that the Sun and the Buddha were the same.[21]

When in 749 Emperor Shōmu abdicated to become a novice monk in favour of his daughter Kōken (r. 749–58), a second oracle was reported from a kami called Hachiman enshrined at Usa in Kyushu. Hachiman expressed a desire to travel to the capital. His palanquin, the prototype of the *mikoshi*, was met on the road by a retinue of high officials, received at the capital and installed in a special shrine. A high-born priestess of the Hachiman shrine (who was also a Buddhist nun) then worshipped in the Tōdaiji in a ceremony attended by the whole court, including the retired Shōmu, his daughter the Empress Kōken and five thousand monks. Dances were performed and 'a cap of the first grade was conferred upon the god.' Subsequently extensive lands were granted to the Tōdaiji.

Empress Kōken abdicated in turn in 758, but from 764 to 770 reoccupied the throne under the name of Empress Shōtoku, appointing her Rasputin-like advisor, the monk Dōkyō, to be minister of state. Dōkyō soon rose to the unprecedented rank of Hōō (Dharma-king, 'Pope'), but then went too far. Recalling Hachiman's triumphal entry into Nara two decades earlier, Dōkyō announced that a further oracle had been issued by Hachiman via a medium, this time to the effect that if Dōkyō were made emperor, the country would enjoy perpetual tranquillity. The empress, however, sent her envoy Wake no Kiyomaro to consult Hachiman. The envoy returned to say that Dōkyō, not being of imperial blood, could not succeed to the throne. A furious Dōkyō had Wake no Kiyomaro exiled but when the empress died the following year Dōkyō fell from power.[22] Epic interventions such as these confirmed the bodhisattva-deity Hachiman to be a significant and authoritative source of oracular utterances.

Recent Japanese research on the *sanja takusen* suggests that the three oracles brought together in the standard *sanja takusen* scroll probably began life as separate Buddhist oracles;[23] they were just three of many attributed to Hachiman and referred to in various sources. According to the legend mentioned earlier, the Oracles of the Three Shrines (though in what form is unclear) first appeared miraculously floating on the surface of a pond at the Tōdaiji during the Shōō era, 1288–93.[24] Why the oracles should have appeared in a pond is not explained, though there are many legends in Japan of treasures entering this world from the underwater realm,[25] and buried or otherwise concealed scriptures are a feature of esoteric and Mahayana Buddhism. The earliest description of a *sanja takusen* proper occurs over a century later than its legendary first appearance, in a work called the *Daigo shiyōshō* produced around the end of the Ōei period (1394–1428). Mention of the oracles in the *Daigo shiyōshō* suggests that the *sanja takusen* was connected in some way with

Buddhist priests of the southern capital and specifically with the priestly lineage group of the Daigoji temple.[26]

The southern court and capital was established in Yoshino by Emperor Go-Daigo in 1336 while Ashikaga Takauji set up the competing Emperor Kōmyō in Kyoto, following the end of the Hōjō regency and the destruction of Kamakura in 1333. Daigoji, head temple of the Daigo branch of Shingon Buddhism, is located in Fushimi ward, Kyoto. Daigo (*ghee*) refers to the fifth and most clarified period of the Buddha's teachings (literally, the quintessential teachings). The temple, established in 874–6 was visited by the first Emperor Daigo in 907 and maintained links with the imperial court thereafter. The prevailing view is that the oracles included in the *sanja takusen* were already circulating in the thirteenth or fourteenth century and the *sanja takusen* proper had appeared at the latest by 1409. The oracle now attributed to Hachiman, for example, is quoted (with approval) by the thirteenth-century monk Nichiren (1222–82) as a *takusen* of Kasuga.[27] The *sanja takusen* was therefore produced within the context of 'Ryōbu Shinto', Shinto of the two mandalas, that is to say, within the *kenmitsu* exoteric-esoteric system of thought and practice which interpreted the kami or other locally enshrined deities as traces or manifestations (*suijaku*) of the basic buddhas and bodhisattvas (*honji*). The medieval *sanja takusen* motif affirmed the interdependence of Buddhism, the shrine-deities and the imperial institution within an overall *kenmitsu* world-view.

The *sanja takusen* and the meaning of shrines

Shrines and sacred places of many different kinds are found throughout Japan. There is generally little dispute about what constitutes a shrine or where shrines are located;[28] the important question to be asked is always 'what does a shrine mean?' The meaning of shrines, whether ancient or recently-established, has been constantly redefined and renegotiated throughout Japanese history. An important function of the *sanja takusen* as indicated above was to establish the meaning of the three major shrines – and by extension all shrines – within an overall *kenmitsu* religious world-view. The 'standard' version of the *sanja takusen* shown in Fig. 1 does this by relating each of the three shrines to one of three 'inner' spiritual and behavioural qualities or virtues already prominent in Buddhist canonical thought. Hachiman enjoins purity (*shōjō*), Ise honesty (*shōjiki*) and Kasuga compassion (*jihi*). 'Outer' (ritual or physical) pollution and purity are not so important; what is decisive is the inner state of mind. In the oracle of Kasuga, for example, it is made clear that the 'inner' Buddhist virtue of a compassionate mind far outweighs the effect of any external ritual pollution, even the most severe pollution attaching to the death of one's own parents: '. . . even though a man be in mourning for his father and mother, if he be a man of compassion, the gods will enter in there. Compassion is all-important.'

If the idea that the three great shrines promoted the inner virtues of purity, honesty and compassion had been restricted to the *kenmitsu* Buddhist thought of the Daigoji lineage and the southern court, the 'Oracles of the Three Shrines' as a religious icon might have disappeared from view before long. However, in the late fifteenth century the *sanja takusen* motif was appropriated anew by the entrepreneurial shrine priest Yoshida Kanetomo (1435–1511).[29] Born into the twenty-first generation of the Yoshida or Urabe priestly family, Kanetomo inherited responsibilities for the Yoshida shrine in Kyoto at a time when the court nobility was increasingly unable to support this shrine to the ujigami (tutelary deity) of the Fujiwara clan. Kanetomo accordingly developed what we would now call a 'new religion' called *Genpon Sōgen Shinto* ('Shinto of the Original Source') based at the shrine. Incorporating all the major elements of the *kenmitsu* system and adapting Shingon rituals, Ryōbu Shinto and Chinese five-elements theory Kanetomo asserted that the myriads of kami in Japan, the *yaoyorozu no kami*, formed a unity (the 'original source'), rather than an unconnected pantheon, and that this unity of gods should be worshipped at his own shrine on Mount Yoshida. For this reason Yoshida Shinto is also known as '*Yuiitsu Shinto*' ('unique,' 'peerless' or 'unitarian Shinto').

Kanetomo was studious as well as enterprising. In two major works *Shinto taii* ('The gist of Shinto') and *Yuiitsu Shintō myōbō yōshū* ('An anthology of the doctrines of peerless Shinto'), he sought to establish the Yoshida line as the arbiters of shrine orthodoxy in Japan. In 1489 Kanetomo attracted the vigorous hostility of the Ise priesthood when he had the temerity to announce that the deity of Ise had transferred its residence to the Yoshida shrine. Kanetomo also associated the Yoshida shrine with the imperial household, for example by conducting memorial services for the imperial family using a *sanja takusen* scroll personally inscribed by the emperor.[30] Kanetomo's world-view, heavily influenced by Buddhism and Chinese thought and entirely consistent with the import of the *sanja takusen*, held that the *kami* (deities), *rei* (spirit) and *kokoro* (human heart or mind) comprised a form of absolute existence 'prior to the creation of heaven and earth.' The meaning of the shrines, according to the new Yoshida teaching, was intimately bound up with the inner spiritual state of the worshipper.

'Yoshida Shinto' was extremely successful. As a result of Kanetomo's initiatives and the efforts of his successors, the Yoshida family had by the end of the fifteenth century secured the right to award ranks to all shrines and priests throughout the country, with the exception of a few shrines with close links with the imperial household. This privilege was retained until 1868 when all such shrine licensing privileges passed to central government. Because the *sanja takusen* was used to spread the ideas of Yoshida Shinto, Yoshida Shinto was also extremely influential in the dissemination and popularisation of the *sanja takusen* motif, which consequently became known throughout Japan. From the fifteenth century onwards knowledge of the scroll and its contents spread from the imperial family to the samurai classes and the common people, with the help of comprehensible *waka* verse renditions of the oracles (which are written in classical Chinese) and through simple explanatory books. So completely did the *sanja takusen* become identified with the teachings of Yoshida Shinto that the eighteenth-century scholar Ise Sadatake (1717–84) even came to the conclusion that Kanetomo had forged the *sanja takusen* for his own benefit in order to propagate Yoshida Shinto.[31]

Despite such doubts cast upon the authenticity of the *sanja takusen*, the scroll was widely regarded as having a positive moral influence, and the *sanja takusen* continued to receive endorsement – even as a pious forgery – from most religious quarters throughout the Tokugawa period (1600–1868) because of the encouragement it offered to popular piety and the cultivation of virtue. Dissemination of the scroll in the Edo period was supported by popular Shintoists, by followers of the Shingaku ('heart-learning') movement founded by Ishida Baigan and by others connected with Buddhism who supported the 'unity of the Three Teachings' of Buddhism, Shinto and Confucianism. Zen priests made copies of the *sanja takusen* (including the example shown in Fig. 2), among them Hakuin (1685–1768), whose boldly inscribed calligraphy of the *sanja takusen* shrine titles is now preserved in the Jingū Chōkokan museum at Ise. Up to the Meiji restoration large quantities of commentarial works, scroll pictures and prints related to the *sanja takusen* were mass-produced, devotional rituals and services were organised, and votive lanterns were dedicated to the 'three shrines' in various areas.[32]

The oracle of Amaterasu in the standard version of the *sanja takusen* can be invoked to affirm the value of honest uprightness as opposed to magic and corrupt extravagance; this idea was linked in the popular mind during the Edo period with the simplicity of the Ise shrine architecture. The oracles were also widely used in *okina* plays at village festivals.[33] Nagashima observes that although scholars of Kokugaku ('National Learning') may have disliked the 'reek of Buddhism' (*hotoke-kusai*) attached to the *sanja takusen*, they nevertheless seem to have accepted it, thus conforming to the custom of revering 'Shinto' and 'Buddhist' elements together.[34] Mori goes so far as to refer to 'a *sanja takusen* faith which deeply permeated the whole country and had not declined up to recent times,' though this does beg the question of what the '*sanja takusen* faith' meant in practice at different times for different people.[35] The popularity of the scroll over many centuries and within many different religious contexts is thus testament to the broad and enduring appeal in Japan of *kenmitsu*-type Buddhist ideas which stress the cultivation of inner virtues.

There is evidence to suggest that during the course of the Tokugawa period and possibly much earlier, the *sanja takusen* became closely associated with the pilgrimage to Ise. This practice was fostered by the priests and pilgrim-masters (*oshi*) of the Ise Outer Shrine. Pilgrimage to Ise depended on interpretations of the meaning of the shrines supplied by the Watarai priestly lineage at Ise, interpretations which eventually outstripped in popular appeal those of Yoshida Shinto. The Watarai clan were responsible for the Outer Shrine (Gekū), which until the Meiji restoration eclipsed the Inner Shrine (Naikū) as a focus of religious devotion. According to Watarai teachings, the deities of the Ise shrines – including of course Amaterasu – were the source of 'original enlightenment' or innate purity (the Buddhist notion of *hongaku*). Consequently, a pilgrimage to Ise or participation in rituals associated with Ise organised by the *oshi* became a means of self-purification, progress towards enlightenment and the uncovering of the inborn spiritual virtues of purity, honesty and compassion enjoined by the deities in the *sanja takusen*.[36]

It seems likely that pre-Meiji illustrated examples of the *sanja takusen* (i.e., scrolls which feature personified images of the deities in addition to their titles, and sometimes in place of the text of the oracles) emerged in connection with the flourishing pilgrimage trade in Ise. This in turn may have led to more emphasis on the central figure of Amaterasu and the shrine of Ise in the *sanja takusen* and diminished concern for the contents of the oracle texts and the other two shrines of Hachiman and Kasuga. A number of late Tokugawa examples of the *sanja takusen* show the titles of the shrines and (Buddhist-style) images of the three deities, without the oracle texts. This may be because the ideas expressed in the oracles had become unfashionable or, more prosaically, that the medieval Chinese texts could no longer be understood by pilgrims and others buying the scroll. It might even be argued that the oracles were so well known that they had no need to be spelled out. Whatever the reason, the space previously occupied by the standard oracles was soon to be inscribed with new meanings.

The *sanja takusen* after the Meiji restoration of 1868

The 'post-Meiji' scroll shown in Fig. 2 differs from the standard *sanja takusen* of Fig. 1 in all three aspects (titles, texts and images). It reflects very clearly the 'separation of kami and buddhas' (*shinbutsu hanzen, shinbutsu bunri*) formally promulgated within a few months of the Meiji restoration, and consolidated throughout subsequent decades up to 1945. Firstly, the titles of the shrine-deities are regularised in a non-Buddhist form. Kasuga and Hachiman's titles, formerly Daimyōjin and Daibosatsu become, like that of Amaterasu, Daijin or 'Great Kami' (also read Ōkami). Secondly, as earlier indicated, the three *sanchoku* passages from the *Nihon shoki* take the place of the 'purity, honesty and compassion' oracles of the standard *sanja takusen*. Finally, modern pictures of the deities have been added to the scroll.

The renaming and retitling of deities and shrines was a major preoccupation of the new Shinto administrators of the early Meiji period. Shrine officials throughout the country were requested in 1868 to submit a history of their shrine and its traditional Buddhist associations so that the process of 'dissociating' the kami from Buddhism could then take place. Thousands of shrines with Buddhist names, or which enshrined Buddhist or other 'non-Japanese' deities such as Myōken, were renamed or their deities replaced.[37] The retitling of Kasuga and Hachiman in the post-Meiji version of the *sanja takusen* reflects this process. The title *daijin* for Hachiman or Kasuga is found in some pre-Meiji *sanja takusen*, but after the Meiji Restoration use of 'Great Bodhisattva' (*daibosatsu*) for a kami such as Hachiman was prohibited. Many of the new names were drawn from the ancient chronicles, which had been rediscovered during the Edo period by Kokugaku, in particular the *Kojiki* or Record of Ancient Matters completed in 712. This text was considered by scholars and champions of National Learning to be the most authentic repository of pre-Buddhist Japanese culture.

In the case of the Kasuga-Kofukuji 'multiplex' in Nara, its deity Kasuga Daimyōjin now became the kami of the Kasuga shrine alone, separate from Kōfukuji. Grapard describes the day in 1868 on which kami and buddhas were 'separated' at Kasuga and the monks of the Kōfukuji instantly became Shinto priests.[38] The Bodhisattva Hachiman comprised, in addition to his Buddhist identities, the Emperor Ōjin, his wife Himegami and his mother, the warlike Empress Jingū. Before 1868 Hachiman was often represented as a Buddhist priest. After 1868 he was no longer a 'Great Bodhisattva' – instead, his identity became essentially that of the deified Emperor Ōjin. In the post-Meiji *sanja takusen* in Fig. 2 he is depicted as *yumiya* Hachiman, 'bow and arrow Hachiman,' the god of archery and war.

The texts of the oracles in the post-Meiji *sanja takusen* shown in Fig. 2 perform the same function as the texts in the 'standard' version; they establish the meaning of shrines. However, the meaning of the shrines has now changed. The layout of the three oracle texts in the post-Meiji version of the *sanja takusen* suggests that they are not expressly linked to the three deities, and in fact all the texts are related solely to Ise and its deity Amaterasu (now shorn of all Buddhist associations). The first section of text is implicitly concerned with the recent 'restoration' of the emperor to power. It deals with the legitimacy and authority of the imperial line, which is established here by the divine command of Amaterasu to the first of her descendants.

> Amaterasu Sumeōmikami commanded her August Grandchild, saying: 'This Reed-plain-1500-autumns-fair-rice-ear Land is the region which my descendants shall be lords of. Do thou, my August Grandchild, proceed thither and govern it. Go! and may prosperity attend thy dynasty, and may it, like Heaven and Earth, endure for ever.'

The second section explains the divine significance of the Grand Shrine of Ise, where the sacred mirror, one of the three Imperial Regalia of mirror, sword and jewels, is enshrined. After the Meiji restoration, all Japanese citizens were defined as parishioners (*ujiko*) of local shrines and simultaneously as *ujiko* of the Ise shrine. The text explains how the emperor's association with the Ise shrine, which now stood at the apex of a national hierarchy of shrines,[39] offers him privileged and direct access to the divine ancestress.

> Amaterasu Sumeōmikami took in her hand the precious mirror, and, giving it to Ame no Oshihomimi no Mikoto, uttered a prayer, saying:

'My child, whenthou lookest upon this mirror, let it be as if thou wert looking on me. Let it be with thee on thy couch and in thy hall, and let it be to thee a holy mirror.'

The final section describes the origin and purpose of a shrine (minimally a sacred area defined by a fence or boundary). Early in the Meiji period the ritual calendar of local shrines was revised and newly calibrated with the ritual cycle of the imperial household shrines. This created a link between local shrines, the 'national' Ise shrine and the divinised figure of the emperor. The meaning of local and national shrine ritual is redefined in this new version of the scroll as rites on behalf of the imperial line rather than private communion with the shrine undertaken for the benefit of the individual or his or her local community.[40]

> Takami-musubi no Kami accordingly gave command, saying: 'I will set up a Heavenly divine fence and a Heavenly rock-boundary wherein to practise religious abstinence on behalf of my descendants. Do ye, Ame no Koyane no Mikoto and Futodama no Mikoto, take with you the Heavenly divine fence, and go down to the Central Land of Reed-Plains. Moreover, ye will there practise abstinence on behalf of my descendants.'

Finally, the new-style pictures of the three 'Great Kami' (Ōkami, Daijin) epitomise the 'separation of kami and buddhas' that occurred in the Meiji period. Hachiman, riding a horse, carries no hint of his bodhisattva past; he may even be thought to bear some resemblance to the Emperor Meiji, though perhaps accidentally.[41] Kasuga, mounted on a deer, is similarly devoid of any Buddhist imagery. The association of the deer (actual and symbolic) at Kasuga with the deer park at Benares where the Buddha taught his first sermon was displaced in post-Meiji times by the legend of the kami Takemikatsuchi's arrival on a deer from Kashima. In this example of the sanja takusen Kasuga is remarkably similar in appearance to the Chinese god of longevity Shou Lao (J. Jurōjin), one of the popular 'seven good-luck deities' (shichi fukujin) worshipped throughout Japan as harbingers of prosperity and happiness. The central figure, Amaterasu, is that of a young woman outlined by the rays of the rising sun and bearing the 'three Imperial Regalia' of jewels, mirror and sword.

Pre-Meiji images of Amaterasu (including those in examples of the sanja takusen not illustrated here) show her as a Buddhist figure of male or indeterminate gender, adorned with a kōhai (Buddhist halo) and carrying a hōju or wish-fulfilling gem. This raises important questions about the provenance of the modern, immediately recognisable image of Amaterasu as a standing, long-haired young female figure dressed in simple white flowing robes and bearing the three Imperial Regalia. Recent research has thrown some light on this question, tracing the development of the current image of Amaterasu since the Muromachi period from the Buddhist figure of Uhō Dōji. A dōji (Skt. kumara) is a young boy who enters the priesthood; a bodhisattva. Statues and images of Uhō Dōji (see Fig. 3) typically show a long-haired,

180

Figure 3 Uhō Dōji

standing figure dressed simply in white, carrying a jewelled staff and a wish-fulfilling gem. On his head is a *gorintō* (five-storied tower or stupa), the esoteric Buddhist symbol of the five elements. A form of Uhō Dōji as one of the two attendants of the Bodhisattva Kokūzō (Skt. Ākāśagarbha) was worshipped at the Kongōshōji, a Buddhist mountain temple near the Ise shrines which formed part of the Ise pilgrimage circuit. Encouraged by legends which related the manifestation of Uhō Dōji to the legendary monk and culture-hero Kōbō Daishi (Kūkai), pilgrims to Ise would commonly revere Amaterasu in the form of Uhō Dōji at the Kongōshōji. The statue of Uhō Dōji, which over time and in response to growing awareness of Kokugaku-inspired accounts of Amaterasu had acquired the Imperial Regalia of sword, mirror and a necklace, was removed following the 'dissociation of kami and buddhas' decree of 28 March 1868.[42]

The *sanja takusen* today

The *sanja takusen* scroll is sufficiently important and well-known to be mentioned in most contemporary Japanese encyclopaedias and historical reference works, but my own experience suggests that few people in Japan today are familiar with the *sanja takusen* motif. The standard form of the scroll was extremely popular in Japan before and especially during the Tokugawa period. In its post-Meiji form it was widely distributed up to 1945 and the post-Meiji version of the scroll is still on sale today. At Ise in November 1996

I was able to purchase a version of the scroll almost identical to that shown in Fig. 2, the only differences being that the 1996 version is larger and printed in colour, and Amaterasu's expression is less stern. Few ordinary people today, however, are able to identify such a scroll as 'a *sanja takusen*.' As we might expect from the history of modern Shinto since 1868, most Japanese people will inevitably regard the scroll as a representation of Amaterasu, the well-known female deity of Ise, with a couple of attendants. The *sanja takusen* is indeed displayed in scroll retailers' catalogues alongside scrolls bearing images of Amaterasu alone or at most of Amaterasu and Toyouke, the deities respectively of the Inner and Outer Shrines of Ise. Most scrolls in these catalogues are of Buddhist subjects. I have seen no example of the 'standard' *sanja takusen* in scroll catalogues and I understand it is no longer printed, although hand-inscribed versions are occasionally made to order. Like many features of the new Meiji Shinto which have survived into the post-war period, the post-Meiji version of the *sanja takusen* shown in Fig. 2 both embodies the ersatz ancientness of nineteenth-century Shinto and at the same time conceals from our view the authentic pre-1868 form of the scroll in which 'Buddhist' and 'Shinto' themes were indistinguishable. Neither the post-Meiji nor the standard version of the scroll is currently available at the Kasuga Taisha in Nara or the Iwashimizu Hachimangū in Kyoto, the two shrines featured in the *sanja takusen* along with Ise.

Conclusions

In recent years a good deal has been written about the transformation of Japanese religiosity which took place around the time of the Meiji restoration. Other chapters in this book make a further contribution to our understanding of the reality of 'Shinto' past and present. Studies of individual shrines and temples have revealed radical discontinuities, mostly dating from the time of the 'separation of kami and buddhas' carried out by a series of government decrees issued by the new Meiji regime. This activity was designed to undermine the powerful position previously enjoyed by Buddhist institutions under the Tokugawa shogunate and to strengthen and unify national consciousness on the basis of a claimed native tradition. It took the form of attacks on Buddhist temples, the desecration of traditional Buddhist iconography and the violent destruction of any Buddhist artefacts found in shrines. Before the Meiji period it was normal for Buddhist priests to be qualified to perform rituals at shrines. After 1868 government support for Buddhism was withdrawn and thousands of Buddhist clergy left the priesthood or reverted to the role of shrine priest, in shrines newly 'cleansed' of Buddhist influences.

In the following decades a new state-sponsored form of Shinto developed out of the 'Great Promulgation Campaign' (*taikyō senpu undō*) of 1870–84.[43] The new Shinto, officially 'non-religious' or more accurately 'non-denominational' (*hi-shūkyō*), took as its focus the figure of the divinised Emperor Meiji, extolled Confucian virtues of loyalty and respect for superiors, and in the first half of the twentieth century developed into the official nation-building, imperialist ideological structure known retrospectively as State Shinto. After 1945, government support and sponsorship of Shinto was removed, but the post-Meiji understanding of Shinto as a national religion focusing on the Inner Shrine of Ise where the sun-goddess Amaterasu, the emperor's ancestor is enshrined, largely remains. Shinto today is often portrayed as an ancient pre-Buddhist Japanese tradition. As this brief study of the *sanja takusen* suggests, much that is distinctive of modern Shinto originated in the late nineteenth century. The 'separation of kami and buddhas' in 1868 marked a radical break with a Japanese religious past in which 'Shinto,' insofar as it existed at all, was understood to be part of Buddhism.

The extent of the discontinuity that emerges between pre- and post-Meiji Japanese religion calls into question the categories of 'Buddhism' and 'Shinto' as used by modern writers and scholars. The categories that we use today to debate issues in Japanese religion acquired their modern meanings in the late nineteenth and early twentieth centuries. The 'separation of kami and buddhas' meant that the *kenmitsu*-style Buddhist past of both the people and their shrines had to be forgotten. Today, both Buddhists and Shintoists in Japan find that it serves their own interests to emphasise their institutional independence from each other, despite the fact that Shinto shrines and Buddhist temples are, as ever, attended by the same worshippers. Public and scholarly lack of interest in Shinto in the post-war period and the well-established tendency to idealise and 'orientalise' Buddhism, regarding it as something essential and somehow untouched by its social and religious context, remain prevalent.

In turn, Shinto has to some extent become Buddhism's 'other,' not least among outside observers of Japanese religion. Whatever Buddhism is, it seems, Shinto is not. It has often been suggested in accounts of Japanese religion that Shinto has to do with life while Buddhism deals with death; that Buddhism is rich in iconography while Shinto is aniconic; that Buddhism is doctrinal while Shinto is inherently vague in matters of belief, and so on. Such simplistic oppositions are easily contradicted by observation of the complexities of religious life in Japan. Yet the idea, successfully promulgated by the modernising Meiji regime, that 'Buddhism' and 'Shinto' are – and always have been – separate entities, has become entrenched. Approaching the history of Shinto through the iconography of the *sanja takusen* offers a partial solution to the problem of language. The *sanja takusen*, at least in its standard form, identifies itself as neither 'Buddhist' nor 'Shinto.' It provides us with a window through which to observe Japanese religiosity at different times and in different circumstances. The motif of the three shrines and their oracles has a long and significant history which spans the period before and after the watershed of 1868. The apparent continuity in the appearance of the scroll, which allows us to regard both the pre- and post-Meiji forms as *sanja takusen*, masks radical changes in content. The changes in the scroll in turn reflect the profound transformation that occurred in Japanese religion and society in the Meiji period under the guise of the 'restoration' of a pre-Buddhist nativist past. Amongst other things, those changes have profoundly affected our own modern understanding of the relationship between 'Shinto' and 'Buddhism' in Japanese history.

Notes

During a research visit to Japan in Autumn 1996 funded by The British Academy I was able to collect many different examples of the *sanja takusen*, only two of which are illustrated here. This chapter constitutes the prolegomenon to a book on the topic to be published by Curzon Press in 2000. I am grateful to many people for assistance and advice in connection with the *sanja takusen* and full acknowledgement will be made in the book-length study. For the present chapter I am particularly indebted to John Breen and Mark Teeuwen for encouragement and advice and to Michiko Sugino for help with translation.

1 In some early examples of the *sanja takusen* oracles the Kamo shrine occurs instead of Kasuga, marking a shift in the relative status of the two shrines. In this chapter 'the three shrines' means the shrines now known as Ise Daijingū (Ise), Iwashimizu Hachimangū (Kyoto) and Kasuga Taisha (Nara). There is no connection with the *sanja* in Asakusa in Tokyo.

2 In a very few examples I have seen (e.g. in a Yoshida commentary on the *sanja takusen* and in the 1994 *Shintō jiten*) the name and oracle of Amaterasu are on the right, which is another way of indicating priority. In a Meiji period advertisement (found by Michael Pye), the *sanja takusen* figures are shown in mirror-image, with Hachiman on the left. This may be a printer's error or a visual pun – the advertisement is for *hanko* (engraved wooden stamps used for signatures) which are of course cut in reverse.

3 Kokugakuin University 1985: 49. This definition focuses on the oracles rather than their medium of dissemination (the scroll). Both are referred to as *sanja takusen*.

4 Photographed by courtesy of Mr Maezawa Eiichi of Seikan-do Maezawa Co., Kyoto.

5 It is difficult to make any general statements about the relationship between a 'deity' and a 'shrine' in Japan, since the identity, name and conception of the enshrined deity, or as Ashkenazi (1993) prefers, 'moot entity' and its relationship with the divinised shrine vary from shrine to shrine and in different periods of history.

6 The Bukkyo Dendo Kyokai, founded by Mr Numata Yehan, head of the Mitsutoyo manufacturing company, is best known for its publication *The Teaching of the Buddha*, copies of which are left, like Gideon's Bibles, in hotel rooms throughout East Asia. The following quotation is from Bukkyo Dendo Kyokai 1985: 40, 118.

7 This translation is by Norman Havens, based on modern Japanese translations by Kamata Jun'ichi, prepared for the Japanese version of *The World of Shinto*. I will not attempt here a synoptic study of the variants of the standard *sanja takusen* text. Any modern English version is technically another variant, but the important aspect of the standard text is its focus on the mind's purity, honesty and compassion, in contrast to the post-Meiji version.

8 Some early examples of *sanja takusen* scrolls contain completely different texts. For example, in the late Kamakura period some Pure Land Buddhist sects (Shinshū and

Jishū) incorporated the 'three shrines' motif into their teachings. Details of a number of such versions of the *sanja takusen*, whose study falls outside the scope of this paper, are given in Nishida Nagao 1941.

9 Shinto scholars at Kōgakkan and Kokugakuin universities regarded both pre- and post-Meiji versions of the scroll as *sanja takusen*. A representative of the Iwashimizu Hachimangū in Kyoto however was keen to differentiate between the post-Meiji scroll shown in Fig. 2 and the 'real' *sanja takusen* of Fig.1 (which gives Iwashimizu Hachiman his own oracle).

10 Aston 1972: 77–83.

11 McCallum 1994: 56.

12 Nakamura 1983: 178.

13 See Grapard 1992.

14 See Teeuwen 1996.

15 Kuroda 1996: 233–70.

16 Grapard 1992: 79–80.

17 Morrell 1973: 457.

18 'Three' in Sino-Japanese thought also represents multiplicity in a way that 'two' does not, so the three shrines in effect symbolise 'the many shrines.' I am indebted to Youxuan Wang for this suggestion.

19 Tyler 1992: 81.

20 *Go-Daigo Tennō gazō* (portrait of Emperor Go-Daigo). Nambokuchō period (1337–92). Property of Shōjōkōji, Shinagawa Prefecture.

21 Sansom 1973: 133.

22 Sansom 1973: 183–4.

23 Mori 1994 and Nagashima 1991.

24 A 'pond of the three shrines' (*sanja no ike*) has recently been excavated and attractively reconstructed in the precincts of the Tōdaiji.

25 Blacker 1975: 75–8.

26 Mori 1994.

27 Nagashima 1991: 51.

28 A major exception might of course be 'the Ise shrine' where the question of which shrine location – Naikū or Gekū – should be the focus of pilgrimage gripped the two shrines in dynamic tension up to 1868 (Teeuwen 1995, 1996).

29 On Yoshida Kanetomo, see also Bernhard Scheid's essay in this volume.

30 See Mori 1994.

31 Ibid.

32 Ibid.

33 Teeuwen 1996: 200.

34 Nagashima 1991: 52.

35 Mori 1994.

36 See Teeuwen 1996.

37 Myōken ('wondrous seeing,' Skt. Sudriṣṭi), originally an Indian deity, is the divinised form of the Pole Star or Great Bear constellation, believed to protect the country, avert disaster, lengthen the life span and (because of the name) avert eye diseases. In most cases Myōken was replaced by the officially-favoured *zōka no kami* or 'kami of creation,' three deities from the Age of the Gods referred to in the *Kojiki*. On the Meiji reforms, see the chapter by Breen in this volume.

38 Grapard 1992: 249ff.

39 Hardacre 1989: 83ff.

40 Hardacre 1989: chapter 5.

41 I am grateful to Carmen Blacker for this intriguing suggestion.

42 See Toba 1997a.

43 See Hardacre 1989: chapter 2.

CHAPTER TEN

Mapping the Sacred Body:
Shinto versus popular beliefs at
Mt. Iwaki in Tsugaru

Nicola Liscutin

Introduction

In his compelling article on 'Shinto in the history of Japanese religion', the historian Kuroda Toshio challenges the common view that Shinto is 'the indigenous religion of Japan, continuing in an unbroken line from prehistoric times down to the present'. Instead, he proposes that

> The notion of Shinto as Japan's indigenous religion finally emerged complete both in name and in fact with the rise of modern nationalism, which evolved from the National Learning school of Motoori Norinaga and the Restoration Shinto movement of the Edo period down to the establishment of State Shinto in the Meiji period. The Meiji separation of Shinto and Buddhism (*shinbutsu bunri*) and its concomitant suppression of Buddhism (*haibutsu kishaku*) were coercive and destructive 'correctives' pressed forward by the hand of government. With them Shinto achieved for the first time the status of an independent religion, distorted though it was.[1]

Kuroda argues that even the medieval Ise or Watarai Shinto whose doctrines are often regarded as proof of Shinto being an independent religious system accepted Buddhism as 'the overarching principle that embraced and unified both,' and defined itself only relative to Buddhist teachings.[2] While Ise Shinto can be called a sectarian movement, it was actually 'one component of a unique system of Buddhism that emerged in Japan'.[3] A first attempt to delineate Shinto as a system with independent doctrines can be seen in the activities of the 'Shinto-only' school (Yuiitsu or Yoshida Shinto) in the late fifteenth century. But only since the Meiji period can one speak of Shinto as an organised, independent religion that created demarcated sites, distinct theories, practices and representatives.

Another school of thought assigns to Shinto a decisive role in the development of the 'great mix' of religions and rituals assimilated by the Japanese people. According to this interpretation, Shinto has functioned as a kind of adhesive, or even as the agent which transforms imported religious or

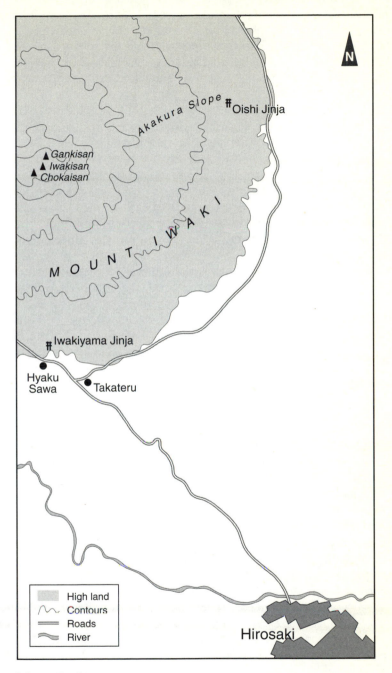

Mount Iwaki

cultural elements into something that is Japanese in character. Yanagida Kunio's work on Japanese folklore or Hori Ichirō's definition of Shinto as 'the underlying will of Japanese culture', are representative of this position.[4] The central idea underlying their view is that Shinto is that which has been 'always, already' there. Shinto thus becomes an all-embracing and harmonising system of which folk beliefs (*minkan shinkō*) are significant expressions and 'true' (i.e. original) practices.

Yet this position appears untenable in historical perspective. Taking Mt. Iwaki in Tsugaru and the cults that evolved around it as an example, I show how Shinto's development into an independent religion involved not only the exclusion of Buddhism, but also of popular cults. In this process, *minkan shinkō* is discernable as a separate system which amalgamated elements of 'the veneration of kami,' Buddhism, Taoism and local cults or customs. Moreover, it created its own sites and representatives such as the shamanic mediums, *itako* and *gomiso*, who constitute a central concern of this study.

Mt. Iwaki and the cults related to it merit close attention for three main reasons.

First of all, the Iwaki-san cults have been limited, geographically as well as historically, to a relative small area, namely Tsugaru, thus providing us with a definite field for analysis. Tsugaru covers the north-western tip of Honshu. Its name appeared first in early Heian-period documents, and in the Kamakura period it became a 'county'. From the late sixteenth to the late nineteenth century, Tsugaru referred to the domain (*han*) as well as its rulers (*daimyō*) who took the name of the area as their family name. When the feudal domains were dissolved and replaced by a system of prefectures in the Meiji Restoration, Tsugaru became a district of Aomori Prefecture.

Secondly, *minkan shinkō* is very much alive in this area. In the Tsugaru district alone, there are approximately 120 shamanic mediums (*fusha*) active; in the whole of Aomori Prefecture there are somewhere in the region of 300 to 350. At the same time, Aomori Prefecture has the lowest proportion of Buddhist temples per 10,000 inhabitants among the six prefectures of Tōhoku. While, for example, the rate in Yamagata is 11.8 temples per 10.000 persons, it is only 3.2 in Aomori prefecture. According to surveys in the mid-eighties, many people to this day prefer to consult shamanic mediums, rather than to seek help at a shrine or temple, or to visit a doctor in case of physical problems.[5]

Finally, Iwaki-san suggests itself as a topic of research because, from the inception of 'state Shinto' and the separation of Shinto and Buddhism (*shinbutsu bunri*) in the Meiji period up until the present day, the divide between Shinto and popular cults and their respective centres manifested itself clearly in a spatial, geographical partition across the mountain. That is to say, Mt. Iwaki, the sacred body of the kami, came to be cut, as it were, into two, the south side with its Shinto shrine representing the obverse (*omote*) of the Iwaki-san cults, and the rougher, wild north side which continues to be the centre of shamanic mediums representing the reverse (*ura*). *Omote*, literally 'front' or 'surface', implies that which is communal, officially sanctioned and often closely related to political authority, whereas *ura* connotes something hidden, individualistic, and often that which is perceived as anti-establishment. In the context of the Iwaki-san cults the concept of *omote* and *ura* was introduced by the ethnologist Kusu Masahiro and further developed by Ikegami Yoshimasa.[6]

The sacred geography of Mt. Iwaki

Mt. Iwaki, a cone-shaped, extinct volcano dominates the landscape of the Tsugaru plain as much as it dominates the perception of its inhabitants. It shields the east and south of Tsugaru from cold north-westerly winds. Thus in winter Hirosaki is, for instance, much less affected by snowfalls than Aomori city. Oku no Fujisan or O-Iwakisama, as the people of Tsugaru call it affectionately, is indeed a beautiful mountain. Dazai Osamu who was born in Tsugaru ardently described its sight:

> . . . It hovered silently in the blue sky, more feminine than Mount Fuji, its lower slopes like a gingko leaf standing on its wavy edge or like an ancient court dress folded open slightly, the symmetry of the folds exactly preserved. The mountain resembles a woman of an almost translucent grace and beauty.[7]

The mountain has three peaks: the central one is called Iwaki-san, the one to its north Ganki-san and the one to its south Chokai-san. The mountain itself is regarded as *shintai*, literally the kami's body. Thus, the word O-Iwakisama refers to the mountain as well as to the set of three deities that are worshipped here. A visitor will in all likelihood arrive first in Hirosaki, the former castle-town and seat of the Tsugaru lords, which lies towards the south-east of Iwaki-san. From there the road to Mt. Iwaki takes one through a pleasant landscape of apple plantations, past the Takateru jinja dedicated to the fourth lord of Tsugaru, Nobumasa, and subsequently to the main site for worshipping which, in the Meiji period, came to be called Iwakiyama jinja. In 'state Shinto', the shrine was designated as the 'northern gate protecting Japan and guaranteeing a peaceful state' (*hokumon chingo*).[8] It is here that the annual ritual on the first of August of *oyamamōde*, the pilgrimage to the top of the mountain, commences. Only the name of the hamlet, Hyakusawa, in which the shrine is located recalls today the impressive temple-shrine-complex of the Edo period, known as Hyakutakuji. All traces of Buddhist presence have been removed. Likewise, only the aforementioned pilgrimage has survived as a sign of the popular cult which, during the Edo period, was integrated within the belief system on this obverse side of the mountain.

The north-side of Mt. Iwaki is much rougher and more difficult to access. It appears that from olden times this reverse side was associated with demon gods (*onigami*). There are countless legends which tell of encounters with the demon god or gods on the mountain, encounters that were not always frightening or

189

harmful, but could indeed be beneficial for humans. It should be noted at this point that, well into the Edo period, the word *oni* had a whole variety of meanings. Beside the meaning 'demon' or 'demon god,' it was used to refer to political enemies, foreigners, and social outsiders, thus in a more general sense denoting the Other or the strange. Many of the Tsugaru legends suggest that these *onigami* who usually appeared in human 'disguise' may, in fact, have been spiritually powerful mountain ascetics (*yamabushi*) or the so-called mountain people (*yamaudo*) who, living and working in the 'other world' of the mountain, were perceived by the farming population as mysterious strangers. Belief in the demon gods is the reason why, when referring to this side of the mountain, Iwaki-san is written with the character for demon (*oni, ki*) instead of the character for tree.[9] There are several shrines dedicated to demon gods, the best-known one of these being the Oishi jinja in which a huge rock is worshipped as the seat or manifestation of the deity. Beyond Oishi jinja lies Akakura no sawa, a steep, rocky slope that leads to the northern peak Ganki-san. It is a rather inhospitable area. At least since the medieval period, the slope of Akakura was one important centre for the practitioners of Shugendo, the mountain ascetics, in the Tsugaru region. It subsequently became the main centre for the ascetic practices of the female shamanic mediums called *kamisama* or *gomiso*.

Itako and *gomiso*

Itako and *gomiso* are, as mentioned earlier, the major representatives of popular cults in Aomori Prefecture. The oldest records mentioning the existence of *itako* in the Tsugaru region date from the early Edo period, but we may assume that *itako* were active earlier in the medieval period.[10] *Itako* are blind, usually unmarried women. Until well into this century, the profession of *itako* was the only way in the relatively poor north of Japan for a blind girl to secure life and livelihood. Thus, parents would give their eleven or twelve year old daughter into apprenticeship with a teacher, an experienced *itako*. There, the girl had to undergo for two to five years severe training involving daily cold water austerities, chanting practices, and the like, until she was 'ready' for the initiation rite in which she was ritually wed to a deity.[11] With the massive social changes in the post-war period, and new child protection laws, the number of under-age *itako* has dwindled. Nowadays, most women enter the apprenticeship well over the age of thirty. Based on the system of discipleship, the *itako* have their own organisation.

Primarily, *itako* exercise *kuchiyose*: they summon the spirits of the dead who communicate with the living using the *itako* as mouthpiece. Traditionally, the *itako* would be called to the house of a deceased, often before the actual funeral, in order to ensure the proper passage of the deceased from this into the other world. Or they would participate in family rituals on the death anniversaries of a relative. On the holiday of Jizō bosatsu (the Buddhist

190

guardian deity of children and the spirits of the dead)[12] in August, groups of *itako* gather at the Kawakura Jizō hall (Kanagi town, north Tsugaru) and at Osore-zan (north-east of Aomori prefecture) to perform for three days *kuchiyose* for a large number of people, mostly women, who come to seek their help. It appears that throughout the history of their profession, *itako* have performed, in particular, memorial rites for the souls of aborted foetuses, *mizuko kuyō*, and these rites also aim at helping mothers to come to terms with their feelings of guilt, their distress, and their anxieties. As Buddhist temples see the performance of *mizuko kuyō* as one of their prerogatives, the popularity of the *itako*'s services has often led to frictions with the established institutions.[13] We shall return to this issue later.

Beside Jizō bosatsu, the *itako* regard themselves as closely related to the Buddhist deity Fudō, and they also revere local divinities as their tutelary deity. In Tsugaru, this is the female deity of Mt. Iwaki. Based on differences in initiation and functions, Japanese scholars distinguish between *itako* and *gomiso*, defining the blind mediums as transmitters of utterances from the other world (i.e. *kuchiyose*), while the *gomiso*, using their inherent power for prophecy (*uranai*), exorcism (*oharai*) and healing, are described as a type of ascetic.[14] The word *gomiso* seems to derive from *go musō*, where *go* is a honorific prefix and *musō*, meaning dream or vision, points to their function as well as to the source of their power. In Tsugaru, *gomiso* are also called *kamisama* (deity), which suggests they are perceived as a kind of manifestation of a deity or of a spiritual, non-human power.[15] *Gomiso* are individual practitioners who do not usually have an apprenticeship; nor are they organised into a group.[16] This may be why nowadays they far outstrip the *itako* in numbers. The majority of *gomiso* are middle-aged women propelled into a religious life by the appearance of a divinity in a dream or in a sudden possession. Frequently, this initiation seems to be preceded by serious illness or temporary mental disorder. After this experience of 'possession', the women often leave their homes for a period of ascetic practice, at the end of which they find themselves furnished with healing and prophetic powers. A common phenomenon among the *gomiso* of the Tsugaru area is that the deity which summons them is the dragon deity of Iwaki-san. Akakurasama, as they call the deity, appears in their dreams and demands that they climb the Akakura slope and undergo ascetic practices. In other words, the guardian deity of the *gomiso* is the most powerful deity of Tsugaru. To the *gomiso* and their religious activities, we shall return later.

The tale of Anjuhime

It was, in fact, the *itako*, also famed for their storytelling and songs, who drew me first to Tsugaru. At the time I was engaged in research on the stories of *sekkyōbushi* and their local roots. *Sekkyōbushi* is a medieval storytelling art which appears to have developed out of Buddhist preaching. However, by the end of the sixteenth century, it had become first and foremost, a kind of

191

entertainment or popular performing art. In the Edo period, it became a thriving form of puppet theatre, and its plays were transcribed and printed. By that time, the stories of *sekkyōbushi* had become far removed from orthodox Buddhist teaching. Although they contain certain Buddhist elements, they reflect to a much greater extent popular beliefs which were current in the late medieval period.

Certainly the best-known tale of *sekkyōbushi* is, due to Mori Ogai's adaptation, 'Sanshōdayū.' It tells the story of Anjuhime and Zushiomaru, the children of the lord of Iwaki, who leave their home in search of their father who has been exiled to Kyushu. They fall into the hands of slave-traders and end up as slaves to the cruel Sanshōdayū in Yura no Minato of Tango province. Anjuhime, the brave elder sister, eventually manages to help her brother escape, but she is then tortured and killed by Sanshōdayū and his men. With her death Anjuhime disappears from the narrative, which then concentrates solely on the plight and career of her younger brother Zushiomaru. Zushiomaru eventually makes his way to the court in Kyoto, gains pardon for his father, and takes revenge upon Sanshōdayū. Finally, he is installed by the emperor as the new lord of Iwaki.

Whether the story of Anjuhime and Zushiomaru originated in the area of Mt. Iwaki or was brought to Tsugaru by Edo-period storytellers, is still a subject of much scholarly debate.[17] There exist, however, several local legends concerning Anjuhime and her brother. The most influential legend among these was – and remains to this day – told by the *itako* of Tsugaru. The *itako*'s version of the legend is entitled *O-Iwakisama ichidaiki*, literally, the life-story of O-Iwakisama. *O-Iwakisama ichidaiki* differs in decisive ways from the *sekkyōbushi* story 'Sanshōdayū'. The protagonist is not the boy Zushio, as in the *sekkyōbushi* tale, but his sister Anjuhime. More importantly, Anjuhime, though born as a human, becomes in the tale narrated by the *itako*, the deity of Mt. Iwaki. Thus, *O-Iwakisama ichidaiki* is, in fact, a narrative of the origins of the Iwaki deity. The *itako* narrate Anjuhime's story in the first person: 'O-Iwakisama, the deity of this province, that is me.'[18] In other words, Anjuhime herself tells her story, while the *itako* function as a kind of mouthpiece.

O-Iwakisama ichidaiki is not only a widely known folk legend in Tsugaru, but for the *itako* it is also an expression of the origin and legitimation of their profession. By transmitting in autobiographical mode the life-story of this important local deity, the close relation between divinity and medium is stressed, and the *itako* appear as descendants to the goddess. As with the *gomiso*, the female deity of Mt. Iwaki is presented as the guardian deity and the source of spiritual power for the *itako*.

The deities of Mt. Iwaki

Thus far we have encountered the female deity of Mt. Iwaki, in one case depicted as a dragon or snake deity called Akakurasama or Iwakisama, in the other case as Anjuhime and closely associated with fertility, growth and water as well. Anjuhime and/or Akakurasama belong to the sphere of popular local beliefs. Let us now look at the 'official' records concerning the origins of the Iwaki-san belief system, and its development particularly in the Edo period.

The *Iwaki-san engi*, an Edo period document explaining the origins of the Iwaki-san cult, merges a variety of narratives including a myth of origin, an allegedly authentic historical record, as well as folk legends.[19] According to the myth, the local dragon goddess Tatsubihime no mikoto, alone on the three peaks of Mt. Iwaki, ruled over the land around it, until Ōkuninushi (here called Utsushikunitama no mikoto) arrived in the area, mated the beauty and civilised the country. Henceforth, they shared the mountain and the rule over the country which, thanks to this combination, thrived and prospered. On their first encounter, the 'shining dragon goddess' emerged from a pool of mud, a symbol of chaos, and offered Ōkuninushi a *tama*, which can either be understood as a jewel or as her spirit, hence a sign of submission to the powerful male god.[20] Thereupon, Ōkuninushi gave her the name Kuniyasu-tamahime no mikoto. The myth follows a common pattern in Japanese mythology, according to which a male deity related to the central Yamato state, as it came to be called, ventures out to expand its territory, to pacify the country, and to bring, at least from the viewpoint of the centre, civilization to these 'uncultured' territories. This invasion is depicted as a peaceful process of civilization represented through the marriage, literally, of local cults and values to the 'superior' values of the centre.

Especially interesting for our present purposes, however, is the name given to the local female deity, Kuniyasutamahime no mikoto. For, when read phonetically in their so-called *on* readings, the central characters of her name, *yasu* and *tama*, become *anju*, as in Anjuhime no mikoto. The identification of Anjuhime with Kuniyasutamahime through the name's rendition in Edo-period texts indicates an attempt to accommodate local beliefs within a complex Iwaki-san cult. This is, indeed, supported by another legend added to the myth of Kuniyasutamahime in *Iwaki-san engi*, which tells the story of how, in the tenth century, the sacred *tama* was stolen by pirates from Yura no minato in Tango province, but then in an act of bravery was retrieved by the son of the governor of Tsugaru. In the same way as in the tales of Anjuhime, whether *O-Iwakisama ichidaiki* or 'Sanshōdayū', the villains in this legend are men from Tango province and are depicted as a threat to the tutelary goddess of Tsugaru.

The so-called historical part of the *Iwaki-san engi* echoes the structure of the myth. According to this record, Sakanoue Tamuramaro came to Tsugaru to fight against rebellious groups, the Ezo (Ainu) people living in the north of Honshū.[21] Thanks to the help of the Iwaki-san deities, he succeeded in defeating these evil forces and, as sign of the pacification of the area and as a token of his gratitude, he built the first shrine, Orii no miya, at the foot of the north-side of Iwaki-san. As mentioned earlier, the north of the mountain continues to be associated with *oni*. This first shrine was transferred in the late eleventh century to Hyakusawa on the south side.

Each of the three peaks of Mt. Iwaki is related to a divinity. The northern peak is associated with the local female deity, Kuniyasutamahime no mikoto (also called Tatsubihime no mikoto, Akakurasama, or Anjuhime). It is worth stressing once more that this peak, Ganki-san, is only visible from the Akakura slope, that is, the north-side of the mountain, which helps to explain why those cults worshipping the local goddess concentrated in this area. Likewise, once the divide between Shinto and popular cults was drawn, Akakurasama and her followers became almost 'naturally' confined to the marginal space of the north.

The southern peak, Chōkai-san, was regarded as the seat of Ōkuninushi, and the central peak, Iwaki-san, became eventually occupied by Kunitokotachi no mikoto.[22] The allocation of peaks appears to reflect a hierarchy among the deities, in which the local, female deity had the lowest position.

Under the influence of Tendai Buddhism and Shugendō in the medieval period, a *gongen* cult was adapted to the Iwaki-san beliefs and the *kami* came to be seen as the manifestations or traces (*suijaku*) of Buddhist deities or of a Buddhist essence (*honji*). Thus, the female deity Kuniyasutamahime became associated with Jūichimen Kannon Bosatsu (the eleven-faced Kannon), Ōkuninushi with Yakushi Nyorai, and finally Kunitokotachi no mikoto was linked to Amida Nyorai. The first Buddhist image, which appears also to have been the main object of worship, was that of Jūichimen Kannon enshrined originally in a little temple hall, again not on the south, but the north side of the mountain.[23] Interestingly, the deity of Ōishi jinja, the main shrine on the north side, was also perceived as a manifestation of Jūichimen Kannon. It seems therefore, that the Iwaki-san *gongen* cult emerged from religious communities, probably mountain ascetics, active at the north side of the mountain, and that the north remained the 'real' centre of the cult throughout the medieval period.

The Iwaki-san cult in the Edo period

Given the significance of Iwaki-san and its cults for all of the area's communities, the Tsugaru family took great care to support and expand the Iwaki-san cult after they had overthrown the former lords of the area in the late sixteenth century. Furthermore, they skilfully utilised the belief system in order to strengthen their rule and to invest their political power with sacred authority. Numerous entries in *Tsugaru ittōshi*, the official record of the Edo-period unification of Tsugaru, or in the governmental diary, *Kuni nikki*, enable us to trace the process in which the Tsugaru lords systematically shaped the Iwaki-san cult.[24] The main aim of their enterprise was to transform the formerly local cult into a cult that would represent in religious terms the unity, independence and power of the new domain of Tsugaru. In other words, the divinities of Iwaki-san were henceforth to function as the guardian deities of the province and its people and, moreover, as the tutelary deities of the Tsugaru family and protector of their rule over the area. Partly, this aim was

194

achieved by a far-reaching integration of popular traditions and temple-shrine cults. The first measures of the Tsugaru lords focused on the temple-shrine complex of Hyakutakuji at the south-side of Mt. Iwaki.

As mentioned above, the first shrine, Orii no miya, had already been moved to Hyakusawa at the southern foot of Mt. Iwaki during the eleventh century. At its side, a Tendai temple, the Hyakutakuji, was built in the medieval period. Around 1610, immediately after the Tsugaru lords had established their rule in Hirosaki, they removed the Tendai monks, put the temple under the control of the Shingon sect, and provided it with a substantial annual stipend. The elevated status of the Hyakutakuji, and the close link between the Iwaki-san cult and the Tsugaru government was emphasised in rituals, such as *amagoi* (prayers for rain), which the priests conducted at the request of the Tsugaru lords.[25] The Tsugaru lords went on enlarging the shrine-temple complex with the construction of several buildings, some of which still stand today. Among the impressive new structures were the main hall in which the three images of Amida, Yakushi, and Kannon were enshrined, and the main gate (*sanmon*) which was built around 1620 under the second Tsugaru lord, Nobuhira. This gate housed an image of Jūichimen Kannon as well as five hundred *rakan*, sculptures, that is, of the five hundred disciples of Buddha. Two rather unusual images can be found among the hundred twenty *rakan* remaining today, namely those of Anjuhime and Zushiomaru of the 'Sanshōdayū' story.

The reconstruction of the main hall of the shrine, and the stupendous decorative works on the buildings resembling those in Nikkō, were ordered by the fourth daimyō, Nobumasa (1646–1710). Nobumasa was known as one of the 'seven wise lords' of the Genroku era, and praised as a great patron of scholars and artists. He fulfilled, it was said, the classic ideal of *bunbu ryōdō*, being accomplished in both literary and martial arts. It is therefore not surprising that already during his life-time, Nobumasa seems to have become a legendary figure. *Oku no Fuji monogatari*, best described as the biography of Nobumasa, depicts his birth as that of a hero, signalled by a bright light coming forth from Mt. Iwaki and pink and violet coloured clouds moving from the mountain to Hirosaki.[26] Another source interprets these signs as Nobumasa being the 'reincarnation' of Iwakisama.[27] There are several other tales of this kind which linked Nobumasa to the deities of Mt. Iwaki, and provided him with an aura of sacredness. The ultimate expression of this special bond between Iwakisama and the lord became the Takateru jinja erected on the southern side. In his last years, Nobumasa ordered that he should be buried at the foot of Mt. Iwaki, despite the fact that the Chōshōji temple in Hirosaki was the house temple of the Tsugaru family and all of his predecessors were buried there. He then began to plan the construction of the Takateru jinja on the same site, which was actually carried out in the year after Nobumasa's death. Obviously, Nobumasa was not only influenced by the architecture of Nikkō, but sought to follow its model of a *gongen* cult revolving around the deified Tokugawa Ieyasu (the founder of the Tokugawa Shogunate). In due course, Nobumasa was deified as well and worshipped in the Takateru jinja. While the *gongen* of Iwaki-san had so far been presented as the guardian deities of the Tsugaru family, the deification of Nobumasa established, as it were, a blood-relationship between the gods and his family. This in turn endowed their political, secular rule with a divine dimension and supreme legitimation.

In order for this reshaped Iwaki-san belief system to spread and take root among the populace, the Tsugaru lords encouraged their subjects to participate actively in the cult. For instance, they transformed the folk tradition of *ōyama mōde*, the pilgrimage to the top of the mountain,[28] into a structured annual observance (*nenjū gyōji*) sponsored by the government, which was to be performed on one particular day, the first day of the eighth month. The saying coined in the early Edo period that 'a man is not a real man unless he has climbed Iwaki-san' shows that the pilgrimage became a kind of initiation rite for the male subjects of Tsugaru.[29] The intended effect of the lords' introduction of this annual observance was to establish and continuously to enhance a feeling of community in geographical, religious, and sociopolitical terms. *Ōyama mōde* thus became also a celebration of the unity between the people, the rulers, and the deities of Tsugaru domain. Or, to put it a different way, the annual pilgrimage was one important element in the definition and demarcation of the 'realm' of Tsugaru.[30]

Women, however, were not allowed to climb the mountain. Probably under the influence of Tendai as well as Shingon Buddhism, Mt. Iwaki became, like Hieizan and Kōyasan, a *nyonin kekkai*, a sacred realm of taboo for women. As the Edo period scholar Furukawa Koshōken (1726–1807) reports in his travel records of Tsugaru, *Tōyū zakki*, it was said that the goddess of Iwaki-san jealously guarded her space from other women. Furukawa comments:

> Since they worship a woman, Anjuhime, as the goddess of the mountain, how can they forbid women to enter the mountain? How strange indeed! If the mountain path is treacherous, they should forbid women to climb it; but there certainly exist no *kami* or Buddha who hate women.[31]

Even after the ban was lifted in the Meiji period, the local sentiment against women climbing Iwaki-san remained strong, and initially only a few women had the courage to participate in the pilgrimage. One side of the mountain was, however, believed to be open for women to enter. Surprisingly, this was the still more rugged north-side, Akakura, which, it will be recalled, was associated with the very female deity that was allegedly jealous of women.

It appears that the Tsugaru lords were quite anxious to popularise the 'official' Iwaki-san cult, as they adopted several elements of *minkan shinko*. For example, the images of Anjuhime and Zushiomaru among the *rakan* of the temple gate point to an integration of the folk legend of Anjuhime into the Iwaki-san belief system early on in the Edo period. Whether the semi-official *Iwaki-san engi*, entries in travel diaries[32] of visitors from Edo, or the explanation of 'Iwaki-san' in Terashima Ryōan's encyclopedia *Wakan sanzai zue*[33] of 1713, all of these texts demonstrate how widespread this legend was. So much so that it overshadowed official mythology. The service to which this

196

folk tale was put is nevertheless striking. It will be recalled that Anjuhime was sold by slave-traders to the cruel Sanshōdayū of Tango province. Out of this strand of the tale developed a belief in the Edo period that Anjuhime, the goddess of Mt. Iwaki, loathed the people of Tango. If a ship from Tango province entered one of Tsugaru's harbours, the mountain would hide in clouds and horrible storms would threaten the land. Likewise, if the weather was bad for days on end, people suspected somebody from Tango of being in the area. It remains unclear as to whether the Tsugaru government took this belief seriously or simply utilised it as a stratagem in their demarcation of the realm of Tsugaru. Whatever the driving force may have been, the government decreed several times the expulsion of people from Tango, and even requested official missions of the Tokugawa bakufu to inquire about the birthplace of their members before they departed for Tsugaru.[34] The Edo-period scholar Sugae Masumi reports in his travelogue from Tsugaru, *Sotogahama kisho*, under the entry for 1798:

> People said: 'These days it is continuously raining; should that not be because a ship from Tango has arrived?' So the administration ordered the captains and sailors of all the ships to gather at the shrine of Iwakisama. There they had to swallow a piece of paper with the magical letters of the shrine [i.e. representing the sacred power of the deity, NL] and, as the kami of Iwaki detests people from Tango province, in particular persons from Yura no Minato, each of them had to swear: 'I am not from Tango province.'[35]

This was, indeed, a most frightening oath, for falsehood would inevitably bring divine punishment onto the liar.

At least in one instance, the government's aim in appropriating this folk belief becomes apparent. In 1784, enormous rainfall had destroyed crops and caused severe famine, and thus in the ninth month of the year the government issued an order to search the whole province for 'intruders' from Tango.[36] The devastating rainfall was thereby presented as a divine act that was not, however, provoked by the people of Tsugaru or, more importantly, its rulers. Moreover, the blame for the subsequent horrendous famine could be diverted and laid on strangers, that is, 'people from Tango.' Put to official use, the folk tale of Anjuhime provided a specific Other which functioned as a scapegoat, but which was also crucial for defining Tsugaru's identity as an autonomous political and religious entity. Likewise, as the decrees of the government apparently supported the belief of the people in the goddess' resentment, so the feeling of belonging to this 'unique' community was strengthened.

Yet, the government's orders also reflect the awe-inspiring nature of the Iwaki-san goddess in particular. The shrine-temple complex at the south side of the mountain, the various rituals performed there, the pilgrimage, the prayers written by the Tsugaru lords,[37] as well as the compilation of tales of origin (*engi*) can be understood as a means of pacifying the deity, but there was still a side to Iwakisama that could not be controlled. The Tsugaru lords repeatedly attempted to integrate the north side of the mountain into the Iwaki-san belief system. For instance, a famous legend recorded in *Tsugaru ittōshi*[38] attributed Tamenobu's enormous success over the previous rulers of Tsugaru in the 1580s to the *onigami* of Akakura. These *onigami* were said to have appeared in a dream vision to Tamenobu, revealing themselves as the messengers of the Iwaki-san deity and offering him their support.[39] Furthermore, the miraculous light shining on the birthplace of Nobumasa emanated allegedly from the Akakura side of the mountain. Nevertheless, Akakura, the *shintai* of the female deity, continued to be perceived as a symbol of the wild side of the goddess and as the space in which her real power, that is, uncontrollable power, manifested itself. Those who dared to live in this area or to climb the mountain from this side were believed to become imbued with this spiritual energy of the goddess.

The attitude of the Tsugaru authorities towards individual religious practitioners such as *itako* and *gomiso* seems to have been somewhat ambivalent. Although the general tendency was to incorporate these people in the Iwaki-san belief system, there were several occasions when *itako* and *gomiso* became the target of government scrutiny and oppression. A major concern of Tsugaru's rulers was the low birthrate caused by the wide-spread practice of abortion and infanticide among the poverty-stricken peasants. The government thus sought to call a halt to these practices by issuing strict prohibition laws and persecuting *itako* who engaged, as mentioned earlier, in memorial rites for the souls of aborted foetuses or deceased infants (*mizuko kuyō*).

In the turmoil of the late Tokugawa years, orders against *gomiso* were issued frequently, accusing them of scare-mongering. It appears that in the mid-nineteenth century, the government started to perceive of the *gomiso* as a kind of agitator who could stir up the population, and thereby challenge the supreme authority of the Tsugaru lords.[40]

The Iwaki-san belief system during the Meiji period

During the Edo period, the Iwaki-san belief system reached its widest integration of Buddhist, Shinto-like, Shugendō and popular cult elements. This changed dramatically with the inception of state Shinto in the Meiji period and the measure of separating Shinto and Buddhism, known as *shinbutsu bunri*. It has been claimed that this separation or rather the removal of Buddhist elements from shrine-temple complexes was not as severe or violent a process in Tsugaru as in some other areas of Japan, such as Toyama or Mino, but it may be that more research needs to be done in this field.[41]

The Buddhist halls in the Iwaki-san shrine-temple complex in Hyakusawa were either changed into Shinto structures, or they were dismantled and moved along with all Buddhist sculptures to Chōshōji in the temple area of Hirosaki. Kodate Chūzō, a scholar from Hirosaki, relates reports of witnesses describing how some of the Buddhist images were just thrown out of the buildings in Hyakusawa, and how the monks came in the dark of the night to rescue them and carry them to Hirosaki. The main image, that of Jūichimen Kannon, however, disappeared and has never been recovered since. The former shrine-temple complex called Hyakutakuji was transformed into what it is still today the Iwakiyama jinja. It received a new state Shinto administration and was designated a state shrine of minor grade (kokuhei shōsha). Interestingly, most of the new line of head priests of the Iwakiyama jinja were not born in Tsugaru (or Aomori prefecture), which suggests an attempt to remove the shrine cult from its previously local context and incorporate it into a cult focusing on the state.[42] Of course, all folk legends as well were omitted from new official records and pamphlets. In other areas of Tsugaru, the separation of Shinto and Buddhism, kami and hotoke, was gradually reversed in the post-war period, but today in the Iwakiyama jinja not a single trace of its Buddhist or minkan shinkō past is to be found.[43]

The separation of Shinto and Buddhism affected not only the shrine-temple complex, but also the practitioners of popular cults, namely the itako and gomiso. Successive Meiji period edicts issued by the central and the Aomori governments prohibited the activities of itako and gomiso, and promised severe punishment for contravention of the laws. For instance, a decree of the prefectural government in June 5, 1874 states as follows:

> Since the Meiji restoration, shamanic mediums and other persons of this kind who spread rumours and tell lies which lead people astray or who deceive others, have been banned. Therefore, such persons should no longer be practising. In Aomori, however, because of manners and customs from olden times, people such as itako, ohira[44] and gomiso are still active. These people go round from village to village, telling completely unfounded and dubious stories, voicing improper opinions and deceiving foolish folk. This is an intolerable state of affairs. It is hereby decreed that when such persons are discovered, they will immediately be arrested and punished. Furthermore, in the event that people do not obey this decree, the official of the village in which such people are found will also be punished for disobeying the law. . . .[45]

Although the government sought to suppress the popular cult of Iwaki-san and, indeed, arrested several itako and gomiso, it is clear from life-histories that many gomiso, and probably itako as well, continued their activities. By the Taishō period a few gomiso had settled at the Akakura slope on the northern side of Mt. Iwaki, which seems to have become something of a safe-haven. Two of them, Kōdō Mura and Yamauchi Saki, became particularly famous for their enormous healing powers and prophetic skills, and drew large numbers of people seeking their help. Especially during the second world war the people of Tsugaru turned increasingly to gomiso and itako for comfort and cure, which they appeared unable to find in other religious or social institutions. Immediately after the war, there seemed to be an even greater need, for the *gomiso* centre at Akakura grew rapidly, until the local government put a stop to the construction of *dōjō*, the small worshipping halls.[46] The increase in numbers and popularity of *itako* and *gomiso* apparently made them competitors in the eyes of Shinto and Buddhist institutions, and engendered a relationship between representatives of popular beliefs and the established religious institution that is far from harmonious.

Afterword

In 1992, I visited the Iwakiyama jinja. Its head priest Sudō Hiroshi provided me with much information about the history of the shrine and the Iwaki-san cult. Unaware, at the time, of the shrine's uneasy relation with popular cults, I asked him if *itako* and *gomiso* would come to the shrine to worship or to participate in its festivals. After a moment of stunned silence, Sudō answered that 'it was not expected' (i.e. not desirable) that *itako* and *gomiso* would come to the shrine. Thus, the spatial distribution of cult sites at Iwaki-san has come to represent the segregation of *minkan shinkō* from Shinto. Ian Reader reports a similar attitude towards individual practitioners by the Buddhist temple at Osore-zan, where a notice 'informs the people that the *itako* have been allowed to use the temple grounds during the festival because of tradition and historical circumstances, and that they really have nothing to do with the temple and its practices'.[47] It appears that the supposed 'direct link' of *itako* and *gomiso* to spirits and deities are perceived as a threat to the established institutions' authority and mission.

There are various approaches to explaining the continuous popularity of *gomiso* and *itako* in Tsugaru. For the larger context of the role of individual practitioners in Japanese religious history, Reader provides a succinct interpretation:

> In a very real sense, individual religious activists and charismatic practitioners are 'standing out' on behalf of and for the benefit of all those who cannot do so for themselves, acting as medium through which others may realise their aspirations and needs, or indeed through which they may project those needs and aspirations. [. . .] Among the abilities widely considered to be possessed in some degree by powerful religious figures in Japan are the powers of divination and of identifying sources of spiritual hindrances that are preventing individuals from attaining their wishes or are causing them illness and misfortune, the capacity to exorcise or eradicate those sources of hindrance, and the ability to communicate with the spirits of the dead and transmit their needs to their living kin. On perhaps a less dramatic level, but equally useful, is the ability to give wise counsel and spiritual advice and comfort to others, for ultimately all these powers focus on dealing with other peoples' unease and problems and the ways of counteracting them.[48]

200

From a historical and social perspective it can be said that it has been, first and foremost, the accessibility of *itako* and *gomiso* which guaranteed for them a steady stream of clients. In contrast to the established religious institutions run by male priests, *itako* and *gomiso* were in touch with the community and its problems; they came from a similar, if not the same background as their customers, and they took particularly care of the needs of the female population, all too often the target of exclusion from the established sects. Furthermore, the services of *itako* and *gomiso* were, and still are today, easily affordable, sometimes even free, whereas an individual ritual at a shrine or temple poses a major strain on a family's budget. Thus, these mediums and their activities also cut across social boundaries: they provide the same individual treatment to anyone who seeks their help.

The range of possible explanations has certainly not been exhausted, but I should like to conclude at this point with an anecdote which nicely demonstrates that ascetic traditions have not been displaced by modern life; that, to the contrary, they appear to have been stimulated by it. A well-known *gomiso* in Hirosaki told me this story when I interviewed her in 1992. In the late eighties, a small circus came to the town of Mutsu in Aomori Prefecture. Among their exotic showpieces was a boa constrictor which escaped. The people of the circus, the police and the fire brigade rushed out to catch the snake, yet without success. When, after a week of intense searching and media coverage, the snake still had not been found, people in Mutsu started to panic. Rumours emerged of dogs and even a baby having disappeared. Fortunately, somebody had the clever idea to consult a blind medium. Calling the deities Oshirasama and Akakurasama for help, or so the story goes, she revealed that the snake could be found under such-and-such bridge. And sure enough, the snake was there. One of the effects of this event was that NHK, Japan's state sponsored television company, became interested in the *itako* and *gomiso* of Aomori, and produced a series of documentaries. Ever since, the mediums of Aomori are said to have increased their custom many times over.

Notes

1 Kuroda 1993:26. For a critique of Kuroda, see Chapter 1 of this volume.
2 Kuroda 1993:25.
3 Kuroda 1993:9.
4 Kuroda 1993:7.
5 Ikegami 1992:34.
6 Ikegami 1984:581–3. The concept of *omote ura* referring to the spatial division of the belief systems which share a common object of worship – Mt. Iwaki – but differ significantly in their ideas, aims, and practices was first proposed by Kusu Masahiro and adapted by Ikegami. According to Kusu's definition, *omote* refers to the spatial representation of the communal cult (*shūdanteki shinkō*) in the Iwakiyama jinja on the south-side of the mountain. This 'communal cult' took shape under the patronage and influence of political rulers and focused on a deity (or a set of deities) that was presented as tutelary and ultimately ancestral deity of the rulers. Thus, a

pyramid of authority and protection was generated, at the top of which stood the Iwaki-san deities guarding the political power, and through and with them ruling and protecting the people of Tsugaru. In contrast, *ura* refers here to a location, the north-side of Mt. Iwaki, characterised by the religious practices of charismatic individuals such as ascetics or mediums who 'stand out' as well as standing outside of established traditions. These individual religious practitioners (e.g. *itako* and *gomiso*) act on behalf of and for the benefit of all who come to seek their help; their practices are mainly aimed at this-worldly benefits (*genze riyaku*). Following Kusu's suggestions, the *omote-ura* division was already in place during the Edo period. However, I hope to show in this study that there was still a strong tendency towards integration in the Edo period, which found an abrupt end and even reversal in the Meiji period.

7 Dazai 1985: 121f. Dazai's travel book of Tsugaru provides a wealth of information and anecdotes of the province's history.

8 Shirai 1979:48.

9 The different ways of writing 'Iwaki-san' are somewhat confusing. The characters used for the northern peak can be read both Ganki-san and Iwaki-san.

10 Bunkachō Bunkazai Hogobu 1986:45f.

11 Very much the best Western study of the whole topic of individual religious practice and shamanism in Japan remains to the present day Carmen Blacker's book *The Catalpa Bow*. She provides an excellent account of the training and practices of *itako* in northern Japan. (1986 [2nd edition]: 140–163).

12 The Bodhisattva Jizō, in Buddhist folklore, is a kind of saviour figure closely related to belief in (Buddhist) hell. He is depicted as guiding the spirits of the dead through hell and saves, in particular, the spirits of dead children and also aborted foetuses. The holiday of Jizō which is according to the lunar calendar on the 24th day of the sixth month coincides with *obon*, the festival of the dead.

13 In the Edo period, the *itako*'s performance of *mizuko kuyō* was also attacked by the authorities which sought to stop the widespread practice of abortion and infanticide. However, repeated famines and the utter poverty of the farmers, particularly in the northern provinces, left many women with no alternative but to ignore the government's regulations. (Kodate 1980:103–107).

14 Eda 1989:128–136

15 The title *kamisama* for these ascetics seem to have become common in the Meiji period. It is unclear how or why it emerged. (Ikegami 1992:130–132).

16 Some of the *gomiso* are, however, affiliated to one of the new religious sects, or established a kind of new religious sect themselves.

17 Sako Nobuyuki provides an outline of the different arguments. (Sako 1992:109–114).

18 A transcription of an *itako*'s narration of *O-Iwakisama ichidaiki* is reprinted in Sako 1992:48–55.

19 Edited and reprinted in Kodate 1975:193–200.

20 In his exploration of the myth and the meaning of *tama*, Kodate refers to the Buddhist legend of the dragon princess, mentioned in the Lotus Sutra, and concludes that in the Buddhist context the jewel symbolises enlightenment, more generally, it symbolises the life force of a being. Thus, when Tatsubihime offers *tama* to Ōkuninushi she presents symbolically the most precious 'possession' of her family (1975:8–11).

21 In another version it actually says that Sakanoue Tamuramaro fought against 'demons' (*oni*) who submitted eventually to his military force and promised to serve henceforth the Yamato state.

22 Although I simplify here to a certain extent the association between peaks and deities, it seems to have been the general picture during the Edo period. After the separation of Buddhism and Shinto in the Meiji period, five divinities came

to be worshipped in the Iwakiyama jinja, of which only Ōkuninushi (Utsushikunitamanokami) and Tatsubihimenokami remained the same as before. The other three deities are Uganomenokami, Ōyamazuminokami, and Sakanoue no Karitamaronomikoto.

23 In the early Edo period, it was enshrined in a hall on the top of the mountain, where it was later replaced by an image of Shō Kannon.

24 Ikegami provides an excellent analysis of this process in his article (1984a).

25 Ikegami 1984a:588.

26 Reprinted by Shinpen Aomoriken sōsho kankōkai (ed.) 1973:195ff.

27 *Tsugaru Zokusetsusen* reprinted by Shinpen Aomoriken sōsho kankōkai (ed.) 1973.

28 Miyata (1970) suggests that the pilgrimage may have developed out of a popular spring festival in which the mountain deity as guardian of water and fertility was invited and brought down to the fields. After the harvest, the deity was send off again to its residence on the mountain.

29 Miyata 1970:281.

30 Interestingly, samurai were forbidden to participate in the pilgrimage. According to an entry in *Oku no Fuji monogatari*, this ban was the result of an incident during the rule of Nobumasa, in which two samurai went missing during the pilgrimage. One of them returned after several days, but some experience on the mountain had left him deranged, for on the next day he returned to the mountain only to disappear again. (Ikegami 1992:157)

31 Furukawa Koshōken, *Tōyū zakki*, p. 99.

32 Beside the aformentioned diary of Furukawa Koshōken, *Tōyūki* (Records of a Journey to the East) of 1784 by Tachibana Nankei (1753–1805) is an important source of information about Edo period Tsugaru, Furthermore there is Sugae Masumi's collection of travel records (e.g. *Sotogahama kisho*) mentioned later in this article.

33 *Wakan sanzai zue*, vol. 9, pp. 295–298 reprinted in the Tōyō Bunko series.

34 For an example see Furukawa's *Tōyū zakki*, p. 99.

35 Quoted in Kodate 1975:14f.

36 *Tsugaru han nikki*, entry of Tenmei 4, 9th month, 12th day. Quoted in Kodate 1975:14.

37 An example of a *ganmon* (written prayer) issued by Nobumasa is given in Kodate 1975:154–157.

38 This legend entitled 'Iwaki-san goshigen ni tsuki, manji shakujō no koto' appears in the second chapter of the official history of the Tsugaru lords, *Tsugaru ittōshi*. Quoted in Sako 1992:87f.

39 Sako (1992:87–95) suggests that the background of this legend may be the military support given to Tamenobu by the followers of Shugendō living to the north of Iwaki-san, many of whom seem to have been (sword) smiths and founders (*imonoshi*). In particular the latter, who worked in the mountains and whose profession was shrouded in secrecy and mystery, became the objects of numerous tales associating them with *onigami*. It should be noted, however, that the Tamenobu legend clearly follows the pattern of the legends concerning Sakanoue Tamuramaro's victory over evil forces, as depicted for instance in *Iwaki-san engi*.

40 Tanaka 1990:36–39.

41 Kodate who makes this claim devotes only three pages to the problem of *shinbutsu bunri* in Tsugaru, in which the Iwakiyama jinja is only briefly referred to (1975: 164–167). Tanaka Hidekazu's study (1990) 'Bakumatsu ishinki ni okeru zaichi shinshoku no dōkō to *shinbutsu bunri*' is an important step in analysing the process of the separation of Buddhism and Shinto in Tsugaru.

42 Kodate 1975:202.

43 Kodate 1980:193–198.

44 It is not clear to what kind of cult and/or profession the title *ohira* refers. Tanaka suggests that these were shamanic mediums engaged in a cult centring on a deity of agriculture (1990:37f). Since the sources mention some kind of 'stick' or simple puppet, it is also possible that it was a version of the *oshirasama* belief. *Oshirasama* puppets are also used by the *itako* (and some *gomiso*) when invoking deities. Core of the belief is a tale about the miraculous bond between a horse and a young maiden, out of which silkworms, hence silk production were born.

45 Quoted in Bunkachō bunkazai hogobu (ed.) 1986: 53.

46 Ikegami 1992: 140–152

47 Reader 1991:131.

48 Reader 1991:110.

CHAPTER ELEVEN

Nativism as a social movement: Katagiri Harukazu and the *Hongaku reisha*

Anne Walthall

On the auspicious first day of 1865 Katagiri Harukazu (1818–66) proposed to a circle of like-minded men that they build a shrine to the four great teachers of the native Japanese way. These included the man they called their teacher, Hirata Atsutane (1776–1843), the eighteenth-century philologist and thinker Motoori Norinaga (1730–1801), the poet Kamo Mabuchi (1697–1769) and the Shinto priest Kada no Azumamaro (1669–1736).[1] The site was to be on the flank of a mountain overlooking the lower Ina valley, a site Harukazu's father and grandfather had many years earlier praised in poetry as one of the eight most beautiful in their locality. Although Katagiri died before the shrine could be built, his associates completed his task and held an inaugural ceremony in the third month of 1867. Called the *Hongaku reisha* ('Spirit hall for the fundamental teaching'), the shrine marked the most concrete realisation of the religious and political fervour that swept the Ina valley in the 1860s.

The nativist movement spread through the Ina valley at a time of intense foreign pressure and increasing domestic conflict. Following a half century or more of intermittent encounters with Russian, British and American ships, the arrival of Commodore Perry in 1853 signalled the start of a new and unpleasant era in foreign relations. The debate over how to deal with it fissured the military ruling class, especially after the disagreement between shogun and emperor over how to respond to Townsend Harris's demand for a commercial treaty in 1858. Taking advantage of this lack of unanimity to promote their own proposals and themselves, low-ranking warriors (*bushi*) rallied around the slogan 'revere the emperor, expel the barbarians' (*sonnō jōi*). The opening of Yokohama to foreign trade in 1859 de-stabilised the currency and brought quick profits to entrepreneurs in the silk trade. These national trends had repercussions at the local level, especially among the men accustomed to wielding power in their communities.

Confronted by the threat of barbarian invasion and domestic turmoil, some members of the village political and economic elite, the *gōnō* or rural entrepreneurs, turned to the Hirata school of nativism for intellectual and spiritual sustenance. They already participated in the yearly round of Shinto agricultural ceremonies designed to placate the tutelary deities, and they remembered their ancestors in Buddhist memorial services. Now they learned that their ancestors were to be worshipped as kami. In addition they were to turn their attention to the emperor who as a living deity mediated between the world of the gods and the Way of man. As Atsutane had written, 'The Way of the gods (Shinto) is the great Way of our country. As the Way governed by the emperor, it is clearly to be revered above Confucianism or Buddhism.' This teaching had a political dimension because 'the emperor rules this sacred country in accordance with the will of the gods and he is the lord of all other rulers.'[2] This is the way it was at the beginning of time in the Age of the Gods. By studying and clarifying the oldest Japanese texts, performing one's duties in accordance with the will of the gods and giving the emperor absolute respect, a disciple could return, at least in spirit, to that ancient past. This was the goal for the Hirata disciples in the Ina valley.

The social movement launched by the Ina valley nativists has received scant attention by scholars in Japan and remains ignored in the West. This neglect is surprising given that with 386 adherents they ended up constituting the single largest group of Hirata disciples. Unlike Atsutane's more famous disciples, men such as Miyaoi Yasuo (1797–1858), however, they came to his teachings late, and none had joined before his death in 1843. Katsurajima Nobuhiro has pointed out that through the 1840s the Hirata disciples maintained a strongly religious orientation in their speculations regarding the afterlife and the supernatural world of the spirits. By the time people from the Ina valley had discovered the school and its centre of gravity had begun a geographical shift westward, its main concerns had become more political and this-worldly under the stress of opening the treaty ports to trade in 1859.[3] While Katagiri wrote his own prayers and proposals for national rejuvenation, his intellectual legacy has never been published in the compendia that would make it easily accessible to intellectual historians.

Why the Ina valley? Writing in the 1920s when agrarianism had become clearly defensive against the attractions of city life, the local historian Ichimura Minato fabricated an unbroken tradition of imperial loyalism in the valley stretching back to support for Emperor Go-Daigo (1288–1339) and his descendants. In the 1850s and 1860s this spirit manifested itself in adherence to the Hirata school's teachings summed up in the slogan *sonnō jōi*. After World War II, the Tokyo-based historian Haga Noboru examined economic and social trends to argue that the village elite joined the Hirata school hoping to transform its dynamic into an enterprising spirit that would increase their region's productivity. Given the Hirata school's emphasis on ancestor worship, its teachings could also be used to shore up the efforts of locally powerful families to dominate lineage groups and hereditary servants (*hikan*). Takagi Shunsuke has taken this now-standard interpretation one step further by stating that the old village elite's aim was really to rebuild a feudal system being eroded by new economic forces through a renewed commitment to worship of the gods who had originally created the status hierarchy.[4] There are also political and geographical reasons why the Hirata brand of nativism proliferated in this particular place. The region was politically fragmented, making it easy for proselytisers and agitators to come and go. In many ways it was less isolated than it is today, for it maintained a major transportation network through which flowed goods and information.[5] One cultural offshoot to the development of communications had been the spread of interest in writing classical poetry (*waka*). It was no coincidence that many of the valley's leading poets joined the Hirata school or that poetry writing circles became nativist cells. Favourable conditions would have meant nothing, however, had certain locally prominent individuals not committed themselves to spreading the word.

The purpose of this paper is to trace the routes by which the Hirata school entered the Ina valley and explore the cultural and intellectual milieu that culminated in the inauguration of the *Hongaku reisha*. The focus is on individuals and their deeds, from the first disciple whose concern for military preparedness led him to the Hirata school, to the proselytiser who brought the Hirata message to the valley by infiltrating already existing poetry writing circles, to the study groups that read Atsutane's texts, to the subscription drive that launched their publication. To deal with the foreign threat and domestic crisis, these nativists took a fundamentalist approach that called for a return to the relations between gods and man mediated by the emperor found in remote antiquity. Their goal was the 'reconstruction of tradition' in the interests of national solidarity.[6] Their efforts may be seen as constituting an alternative or supplemental narrative for the Meiji Restoration that draws on local sources and obscure traditions.

Building the Hirata school

During his lifetime, Hirata Atsutane tried unsuccessfully to interest the daimyo and their chief advisors in his message. Even though they shared a common concern for Japan's ancient history, the nationalistic Confucianists in the Mito school, particularly Fujita Tōko (1806–55), had nothing but disdain for Atsutane's teachings, and other administrators were equally unimpressed.[7] This animosity was not reciprocated; a number of Atsutane's posthumous disciples, Tsunoda Tadayuki (1834–1914) and Katagiri, for example, studied both.[8] Atsutane's chief disciples came from Edo and villages in nearby provinces during the early years of his career and then from the Tōhoku hinterland after the bakufu ordered him back to Akita. Had it not been for the organisational abilities of his adopted son Kanetane (1799–1880), it is unlikely that the Hirata school would have ever attracted over four thousand disciples.

It is well known that the Hirata school attracted more adherents among the villages than the cities of Japan. Itō Tasaburo claims that this is because the urban residents of Osaka and Kyoto found the nativism of the earlier teachers attractive only insofar as it served to enrich their literary and cultural pursuit of taste. Atsutane castigated them for being narrow-minded, petty and corrupt with a refinement that went only skin deep. In his eyes, their scholarship resembled nothing so much as a crested ibis mincing through manure – in contrast to an eagle (himself) soaring across the sky. In the less sophisticated countryside, however, the simple folk were more willing to open their ears and listen.[9]

Kanetane encouraged proselytisers to carry Atsutane's message across Japan, introduce students to the school, and raise funds for the publication of Atsutane's major texts. Disciples had to pay a fee and sign a pledge promising to study the Way of the Gods and follow it faithfully, to obey government regulations, to support the school and to abstain from heretical thoughts. Kanetane urged the men who already took a leadership role in their communities to found study groups where they might read and meditate on Atsutane's ideas.[10] He lent books written by Atsutane and his disciples to eager followers across the country. He maintained a voluminous correspondence that both debated the fine points of Atsutane's teachings and exchanged news.[11] Men who visited him in Edo were given leave to copy the membership lists and share information among themselves. Kanetane thus transformed Atsutane's teachings into a sect. If Atsutane may be seen as akin to the founder of a new religion such as Deguchi Nao (1836–1918) or Helena Blavatsky, then Kanetane played the role of Deguchi Onisaburō (1871–1948) or Annie Besant.

Atsutane wrote voluminously on subjects from philology and history to agronomy, foreign relations and spiritual matters. The common thread was always to ascertain the workings of the gods in the affairs of men. A number of texts consisted of prayers to be recited each day and cautionary statements on how to avoid offending the deities, much like the *Book of Common Prayer*. By studying his texts and putting them into practice, a faithful follower would learn to lead a god-centred life. As he grew older and especially following the death of his beloved wife, Atsutane became increasingly concerned with where spirits go after they leave the flesh. During the devastating crop failures, famines and social upheavals of the 1830s, he and his chief disciples sought men who had passed back and forth between the visible and invisible worlds in order to disseminate accounts of their adventures as widely as possible,[12] much like people today spread stories of alien abduction. A charismatic teacher, he possessed an extremely fertile imagination that coupled with wide-ranging interests and vast erudition produced an enormous body of work that redefined the Way of the Gods.

Kanetane's strength lay in his organisational skills. He set up a clear distinction between the disciples and outsiders, he tried various methods to make the school more cohesive, and although he would have denied it, he redirected Atsutane's message away from a fascination with the occult to more mundane and practical concerns. When one disciple from the Ina valley asked to borrow a volume on travel to the invisible world (*Yūkai monogatari*) for example, Kanetane refused. Instead of wasting time on such foolishness, the disciple should continue his critical study of *Koshiden*, Atsutane's history of the Age of the Gods.[13] Scholars have castigated Hirata nativism for being both incomplete as a religion and lacking clear definition as a political philosophy.[14] As far as the Ina valley disciples were concerned, it offered both.

Military training and cultural enlightenment

Katagiri Harukazu was the first person in the Ina valley to join the Hirata school. Born in 1818, he came from a family that was both warrior and peasant. The Katagiri were one of twenty-six hereditary retainers of the Zakōji *hatamoto* with the qualifications to serve as *karō* (chief advisor) and a stipend of seventeen *koku*.[15] Harukazu began his career at age ten as a page, then became apprentice personal servant (*kinjū*). His family owned and cultivated agricultural land in Yamabuki village north of Iida in addition to forest plots in the nearby mountains. They might well assess corvée labour on their villagers plus yearly supplies of firewood, charcoal and vegetables. Despite their warrior pretensions, however, most of their social interactions, particularly their marriage partners, came through the families of nearby rural entrepreneurs and village headmen.[16] Harukazu thus had a ready-made position that he could use to assert his influence in local affairs.

Harukazu came early to an interest in national politics. On a visit to Edo in 1851, he joined a military science school. Following Commodore Perry's visit to Japan in 1853, he collected the bronze bells from three temples which he hoped to melt down for cannon.[17] In 1854 he organised a troop of thirty gunners from among the Zakōji retainers, eventually achieving licensed proficiency in the use of artillery. (As he later discovered, however, the techniques he had learned were exceedingly old-fashioned when compared to those used in the west.) He supplemented the gunners with a unit of foot soldiers composed of peasant men and drilled them in the use of guns, one of the earliest examples of mobilising peasants in armed units outside of Mito and probably the result of his familiarity with Mito teachings. A total of 227 men participated in the training exercises organised in 1856. These yearly events continued through the 1860s in addition to monthly practice sessions for the most enthusiastic. They were paid for by retrenchment in other areas of domain finances and by donations of money and material from the peasants themselves.[18] In 1857 Harukazu went to Edo again to study the martial arts and military strategy. There he met Kanetane and joined the Hirata school, although a list of books in the Katagiri family library from 1856 provides evidence that he had already begun reading and collecting Atsutane's works along with those of the Mito school.[19] He himself eventually sponsored fifteen people as Hirata disciples, the first in 1862.[20] He exposed many more to nativist teachings through the study group he organised called *Mameo no tsudoi* ('Circle of sincere men'), founded in 1865. Eventually a total of fifty-four domain residents joined the school, seventeen of them warriors, the largest single concentration outside of Iida. In the case of Zakōji domain, military preparedness and the study of Hirata nativism went hand in hand.

The *Mameo no tsudoi* was founded on the principle that in order to understand the ancient Way of the Gods, it was first necessary to communicate with Atsutane's divine spirit.[21] Thus each meeting began with the recitation of a long prayer (*norito*) written by Harukazu before a hanging scroll bearing Atsutane's portrait. Filled with incantations written in an archaic melody, the prayer described the expanse of Atsutane's scholarly achievements, how he had clarified the ancient Way by going beyond the teachings of his predecessors, including Motoori Norinaga, how his vast erudition included knowledge of China, India and the west as well as Japan's ancient literature, and how after his death his influence had attracted so many people to join the ranks of his disciples that it was impossible to count them all. It then stated the study group's intentions:

> Humble but courageous men such as ourselves have received the blessings bestowed by the spirit of our divine teacher to carry out the true practice of the godly Way passed down in our great imperial country from the beginning of heaven and earth, and if we can become enlightened regarding even one branch of the sacred tree, we will delight in the godsend we have received from your [Atsutane's] spirit. . . . If in the course of our debates we should unconsciously stray into error, we ask that you correct us and guide us back to the path of righteousness and truth. [May this prayer express the pious hope that] all those born and living in the imperial country, whether high born or base born might follow the correct course laid down by the gods, that the scoundrels who spread pollution and calamity in confusing substance and form by mistakenly asserting empty Chinese teachings, and the degenerates who mislead the people to follow the path of the Buddha, plus all other disgraceful people who mistake heresy for the true Way, might have their polluted, wicked, perverted and shameless hearts purified and restored to the brave spirit of Yamato.[22]

It ended with a proposal to distribute Atsutane's writings to all foreign countries in order to teach them to respect Japan because it was the peerless ancestor of them all.

Harukazu's prayer exemplified the aspirations of many nativist disciples who strove to connect this world and the world of the gods that had presumably characterised ancient days in order to deal with a contemporary crisis. James Ketelaar has pointed out that the writing of *norito* enjoyed a resurgence during the middle decades of the nineteenth century, although he emphasises their role in new style Shinto funerals created by the governing elite to control death processes and hence life.[23] Harukazu was by no means on the same level as the daimyo of Tsuwano who legislated Shinto practices for his domain in the 1840s. He had only enough prestige in local affairs to cajole men to join with him in a prayer pieced together out of nativist texts; a prayer that in laying claim to the past fitted entirely within the concerns of his own day.

210

A Buddhist priest who later returned to secular life drew up regulations for the 'Circle of sincere men.'[24] These specified where the meeting was to be held, what kind of offerings to place before Atsutane's portrait, and how much food and drink to serve the guests. The monthly meetings were long, from noon to 9 p.m. The fifteen founding members were the Zakōji retainers (seven), headmen from nearby villages, and other officials. Anxious to be as inclusive as possible in spreading enlightenment, Harukazu also allowed ordinary peasants to attend and tried to limit the host's costs to within their means. The 'Circle of sincere men' was just one of several study groups that met regularly to study Atsutane's writings, representing what Itō Tasaburō called the 'true spirit of the nativist movement.'[25]

Harukazu also instituted a *Fumi totonoe no tsudoi* ('Circle for book-buying') in 1865. Its charter pointed out that 'in this area books are few, and it is a matter for deep regret that people interested in literature and scholarship have difficulty finding anything to read. For this reason, people of similar interests are getting together to buy books and lend them to each other as well as to people outside the Circle.' Harukazu had a noble ambition, to lay the groundwork for producing a 'local person of great sagacity' who would rival the sages of the cities. As with the revolving credit associations, the Circle was originally set up to last for ten years, though this was later shortened to six. In 1865 it collected 5 *ryō* 2 *bu* to buy *Rikkokushi*, the six National Histories of ancient Japan commissioned by the imperial court. The next year the purchase was Motoori Norinaga's classic study, *Kojikiden*.[26] Careful records were kept of who owned the book, who had contributed to its acquisition, and who had borrowed it. The Circle's activities attest both to the thirst for knowledge on the part of the local elite and the expense of quenching it.

Before launching his book-buying group, Harukazu had frequently lent his own books to his acquaintances. Between 1857 when he joined the Hirata school and his death in 1866, the number of borrowers increased substantially. They included warriors, shrine priests, peasants and merchants. Fourteen people borrowed *Tamadasuki* ('The precious sleeve cord'), Atsutane's compendium of prayers for living a god-centred life. Twelve other texts by Atsutane such as *Koshiden* ('Lectures on ancient history'), a history of the Tenmangū shrine, tales relating to the supernatural, explanations of ancient rites, chronologies and an attack on Buddhism (*Godōben*) in addition to essays on military strategy, Japan's first poetry anthology (*Man'yōshū*), and a book summarising the basic teachings of the Mito school (*Kōdōkanki*) also found readers.[27] This record both summarises Harukazu's own intellectual interests and points to the scope of his efforts at proselytising. Knowledge was to be shared, not hoarded.

The son, grandson and great-grandson of *waka* poets, Harukazu wrote many poems that expressed his understanding of the relationship between gods and people. One example of his approach is the following:[28]

hoshi yoru wa	The starry night
momita uchikaeshi	above the fields of ripe rice.
mi-tamira ga	I am moved by the sacred people
yoru hiru wakanu	who labour ceaselessly
itatsuki aware	without distinguishing between morning and night.

As a man of some importance in his village, Harukazu reified agricultural work, seeing in it a dignity and beauty that was not necessarily apparent to the people actually slaving in the fields.

Based on the books he had read, his experiences trying to organise a local militia, his efforts to spread education and cultural enlightenment, and his orientation to the Hirata school, Harukazu in 1865 wrote a text stating his proposals for governmental reform, titled *Tenka mukyū taihei kiroku* ('Basic text for the eternal peace of the realm'). The text takes the form of a dialogue that Harukazu claimed to have heard in a dream. The emperor announces through his subordinates that something should be done and the shogun replies, 'It shall be done,' for a total of twenty-five items. This is followed by a list of eleven crimes committed by the shogun and his ancestors for which the shogun apologises, and then a series of orders issued to courtiers, shrine priests, doctors, astrologers, and *daimyō*. In his dream, the reforms result in the practice of governance being restored to the Way of the Gods, peace and harmony descending upon the land, and the people dancing in worship by the light of pine torches to the beat of drums that reverberate to the heavens.[29]

In many ways Harukazu's proposals mirrored those found in Atsutane's texts, modified to fit the greater urgency of the foreign threat and his own position as the chief retainer of a bakufu bannerman. He urged military preparedness, including the study of western military science when appropriate. Both military and literary arts being essential in governing the country, the shogun and *daimyō* should promote military training lest they end up despised by the barbarians. At court as well, a training hall should be erected where the courtiers might learn to fight. Both Atsutane and the Mito school had called for rulers trained in the literary and martial arts. While Harukazu did not suggest that ruling class circles be expanded to include men lower in the status hierarchy, he still took it upon himself to instruct his betters in appropriate behaviour.

Harukazu wanted to reform customary practices, in particular the use of era names to mark the years. They should be abolished and replaced with a numbering of the years beginning with Jinmu's founding of the nation. All foreign ways should be abolished. Court ranks should be labelled in Japanese, not Chinese. The shogun and *daimyō* should show their respect for the gods by performing all rites and ceremonies in accordance with ancient rituals. The names of the gods should reflect their original import before the introduction of Buddhism. All shrine priests of rank five and above should report to the Shirakawa family; those below to the Yoshida family, and the Shirakawa family should take the lead in investigating the way ceremonies were performed in the distant past so as to purify rituals performed in the present. The scripts for prayers, coming of age ceremonies, weddings and funerals, even diplomatic communications, should all be written in the characters used in the Age of the Gods. Chinese medicine, astronomical practices and fortune-telling should be replaced with those native to Japan, although the study of barbarian medicine ought not be neglected. In fact, heathen (*itan*) learning should be pursued insofar as it benefited the state and could be assimilated to the study of the ancient Way. Even the names of plants, animals, mountains and rivers should be revised to conform to ancient practices. People should stop using pen names or sobriquets, which Harukazu called vulgar, and instead call themselves only by their real name (for example, Harukazu) or a name that denoted their service to the emperor (for example, Sukebei or Shōzaemon). Finally they should stop shaving their heads and allow their hair to grow naturally as their remote ancestors had done.

The study of Atsutane's texts was not a passive exercise involving the reading of a few books, but an active attempt to contribute to nativism's development and through that to a defence of Japan. Each disciple had to stake out his own position and develop his own approach to the study of Japan's past. Motoori Norinaga had urged his followers to read his writings with a critical eye so as to correct his mistakes. It was more important to come to a better understanding of the Way than to slavishly accept his ideas.[30] Atsutane had justified his recasting of Norinaga's thought by asserting that as a matter of course a student would go beyond his teacher. Harukazu proposed a much more thorough clarification of the congruence of name and function (the emperor as the supreme ruler should actually rule, the shogun as his delegate should obey him rather than make policy on his own) than Atsutane ever had.

Harukazu criticised the shogun much more severely than had Atsutane. His list of the shogun's crimes included some of recent origin; the others were endemic in a system of rule that had endured for 'three hundred years.' The current shogun had been too young to assume the office of 'barbarian subduing generalissimo' contrary to what a retainer ought to do. Not understanding his responsibilities, he had allowed new regulations to be drafted in dealing with the barbarians. His lack of virtue and discernment gave rise to external afflictions and domestic disorder. The more basic problem was the way the shoguns had been treating the court for centuries. This included not having visited the emperor to inquire after his health, not having thanked the emperor in person for his grants of high office, not having gone to Kyoto to congratulate the emperor on his ascension to the throne, not having ordered the appropriate observances at the emperor's death, not having seen off the emperor's envoy and having insulted him in other ways, not having promulgated imperial decrees, magnifying Nikkō's splendour at the expense of imperial mausoleums, having forced the emperor to send envoys to Nikkō, having had imperial princes serve as masters of ceremony at Nikkō, and so forth.[31] The shogun's most serious mistake was having confused the role and function of ruler and subject by usurping imperial authority. It was not Harukazu's intention to get rid of the shogun, however, but simply to put him in his proper place.

For the sake of the country, Harukazu advocated that the shogun allow the restoration of the emperor to direct rule while still taking responsibility for national defence. He proposed the following reforms by putting these words in the emperor's mouth:

> The laws regarding the court and Shinto affairs are to be revised in accordance with the old rituals and the new laws in effect for the last three hundred years are to be abolished. It also seems to us that the shogun and the daimyo ought to offer us tribute for our sustenance . . . We think the laws issued by the court ought to be followed to the letter . . . The emperor is to be consulted on all matters of importance to the nation and they are to be resolved in accordance with his decree.[32]

Hereafter the shogun was to come to Kyoto once every three years for consultation with the emperor. The *daimyō* too were to appear on a regular basis bringing the products of their domains as tribute before they went on to the shogun's capital of Edo, where they were to stay for not more than thirty days as a demonstration of respect and to promote harmonious relations. They were to be allowed to keep their wives with them in their own castles. No matter what proposals the *daimyō* or warriors might craft for the sake of the country or the emperor, they were to present them to the shogun through the proper channels. Property confiscated from Buddhist temples was to be used to augment the stipends of courtiers and imperial princes. Anyone who disobeyed an imperial decree was to be put to death. Retainers who disobeyed the shogun were to be treated as enemies of the court and punished accordingly. If the shogun made a mistake, he was to accept the emperor's admonition gratefully. He, the *daimyō*, and the warriors were to demonstrate their loyal spirit without favour or partiality by encouraging the commoners to act virtuously. If only the country was internally united and harmonious, then come what might, it would be possible to subjugate the barbarians.

Harukazu's vision of appropriate foreign relations called for the barbarians to be taught that, Japan being the ancestral country of them all with the emperor the ruler over all lands, their proper role was one of subservience and subordination in accordance with the decree of the gods issued in the Age of the Gods. The despicable treaties concluded by the bakufu when the shogun was too young to know any better were to be abrogated. (In Harukazu's dream, the shogun had already abjectly apologised for having requested an imperial approval of the treaties that ran counter to the emperor's wishes.) The agreements reached in their place would close all ports except for Nagasaki and Hakodate, and have the western powers send tribute to the emperor and presents to the chief courtiers and shogun befitting their position as subordinate nations, another example of the congruence between name and function. In return the barbarians were to receive food and drink as well as presents for their rulers, whereupon they should depart immediately. It was all very well for the shogun to receive foreign envoys in Edo, but they were not to set foot in Kyoto. Any military threat against Japan was to be repulsed at once.

Finally, Harukazu launched a violent attack on Buddhism. Naturally he wanted a revival of 'ancient studies' and a revival of Shinto. A university along these lines should be established in Kyoto with branches in Edo, Osaka and the castle towns. To clear the physical and metaphysical ground for this endeavour Harukazu urged the abolition and destruction of Buddhist temples, the monks to be returned to lay life, the wood to be used to build bridges and other useful structures. The precious metals that had adorned their altars should be melted down for use in weapons, wooden statues should be burned, and stone statues should be used to make fences. The worship of foreign gods was to be strictly forbidden, and 'anyone who disobeys should be put to death.'[33] This cultural revolutionary rhetoric had concrete consequences when his neighbours trashed Buddhist temples, beheaded statues of Jizō and threw mortuary tablets in the river, years before the anti-Buddhism movement of the early 1870s.[34] Atsutane had hated Buddhism, but he urged restraint toward its icons because they had been beloved by the ancestors and represented their spirits. Harukazu's family found a way around this weight of tradition. When he died in 1866, they held the first Shinto funeral performed in the Ina valley and enshrined his spirit in a *rei-i*, a Shinto-style mortuary tablet.[35]

Harukazu's 'Basic text' mirrors his position in local society as well as his training as a Hirata disciple. In emphasising the political implications of his thought, Kishino Toshihiko argues that Harukazu was primarily concerned with his family's future. For that reason he wanted the minimal reforms consonant with restoring peace and harmony and he opposed the deeds of grass-roots activists who left their domains to appeal directly to the emperor. Not for him were radical ideas regarding a representative assembly of *daimyō* and samurai such as proposed by Sakamoto Ryōma (1835–67), or worse yet, actions aimed at the overthrow of the bakufu which would have ended the Zakōji family's control over Yamabuki. Given his respect for hierarchy and his dislike of change, the only initiative he could take was to prepare himself and his men should the occasion ever arise when they would be summoned to defend Japan by the Zakōji bannerman acting on the shogun's orders.[36] As he wrote to a friend, 'should the idiots from America come here and commit outrageous deeds, even though I am less than one hair on the cow, I intend to do my best to drive them away.'[37]

While much of the 'Basic Plan' can be subsumed under Harukazu's concern for social stability, it also reflects his grasp of current events. The rumours of the emperor's poverty must have reached his ears. He was obviously aware that political infighting among bakufu leaders had resulted in the appointment of a young malleable man to be shogun, rather than Hitotsubashi Yoshinobu (1837–1913), a mature man of proven competence. He supported proposals for a unity of court and bakufu that would strengthen the nation from incursion by foreigners. He knew enough about the terms of the treaties signed in the 1850s to realise that they put foreign countries on an equal footing with Japan, and he

215

had heard that the foreign envoys were demanding the right to visit Kyoto and have an audience with the emperor. Recognising that intercourse with foreigners was inevitable, he yet wanted to restrict it as much as possible and place it within a hierarchical framework.

Harukazu's study of Atsutane's texts structured the way he perceived Japan's place in the world, the relations between emperor and shogun, and the role of the gods in human affairs. Whereas Atsutane had primarily disparaged China in praising Japan's unique indigenous customs, and only as an afterthought did he show his disdain for the west, for Harukazu, the chief opponent was the latter. Atsutane approved of the first Tokugawa shogun Ieyasu (1542–1616) who in his eyes had reversed a long term decline in the court's fortunes and showed respect for the gods. While being much more critical of the way the shogun treated the court, Harukazu no more than Atsutane was able to imagine a world without him. What the shogun had to do was show his reverence for the gods by reforming customs to mirror the ancient world when they had first issued their decrees. Given the mutually beneficial relations between the Shirakawa family and the Hirata school, it is not surprising that Harukazu supported it in its fight with the Yoshida family over which should be considered senior in the management of Shinto affairs.

Harukazu was able to use the advantages of status and prestige accruing to his hereditary position to enforce his vision of Japan's past and future on his colleagues and neighbours. His activities ranged from concrete if minuscule measures to secure Japan's national defence to a variety of attempts at spiritual rejuvenation in accordance with his understanding of the ancient way. Like other Ina valley men who developed proposals for national defence, he was completed ignored by officials in positions of power and responsibility.

Harukazu left a number of projects unfinished at his death. The first was the publication of the last chapter of *Tamadasuki*, to be paid for by people from his own domain. The second was a major compilation of nativist poetry for which he hoped to solicit contributions from Hirata disciples across Japan based on the membership lists kept by Kanetane. He wanted not love or nature poetry, but poems that reflected the lofty teachings of the true road to the past, strengthened the spiritual pillars of the state, and praised the pure heart of the Yamato spirit.[38] The third was the *Hongaku reisha*. Before examining it, however, let us consider other central figures in the Ina valley's nativist movement.

The proselytiser and the convert

Kanetane travelled only once to the Ina valley in 1869, and with the exception of Harukazu, few of its inhabitants associated with the nativist movement ever visited him in Edo. South of Yamabuki, the crucial intermediary was Iwasaki Nagayo (1807–79), an obscure figure known chiefly for his highly successful career in recruiting for the Hirata school and his prowess at writing long poems *chōka*.[39] At one time he was employed by the daimyo of Awa, but finding the burden of service too onerous, he gave it up. He studied the teachings of Motoori Norinaga before becoming a Hirata disciple at the end of 1839, just a little over a year before Atsutane was forced to return to Akita. Nagayo then spent some years in Kōfu teaching both nativism and the arts of *nō* drama. He also travelled to Wakayama to play the flute at a command performance for the daimyo there. In 1844 the bakufu senior councillor Mizuno Tadakuni (1794–1851) is said to have sent him on a secret mission to Ise to investigate the possibility of reviving the practice of having an imperial princess reside there as the emperor's delegate. Tadakuni's resignation the following year left this plot uncompleted and Nagayo at loose ends. He finally arrived in the Ina valley in 1852, some say at the suggestion of a peddler and fellow Hirata disciple from Suwa.[40]

Nagayo spent seven years in the Ina valley before he recruited his first disciple in 1859. He probably made his living teaching *nō* and poetry, these being skills that the castle town merchants and rural entrepreneurs were eager to hone. They had avidly pursued the study of *waka* ever since the late eighteenth century, but good teachers were few and far between. An Iida pharmacist had taught the superiority of the *Shinkokinshū* to poetry circles centred on the Kitahara house in Zakōji, until his death in 1848 left his pupils without an instructor, a niche Nagayo was delighted to fill. Rather than the elegant craftsmanship of *Shinkokinshū* poems, however, he preferred the more masculine *Man'yōshū* which also happened to be the more direct and accessible. Drawing on its vocabulary and style, he wrote paeans to the creator gods and taught his pupils to do the same.

Nagayo had a decisive impact on the flow of intellectual currents in the Ina valley in the 1860s. He developed connections with the local notables who had the clout to interest other men and women in study groups that focused on Hirata Atsutane's texts. He also began the recruitment of disciples across the mountains in Nakatsugawa.[41] Through his sources in Edo, he brought them news of the wider world. According to local historians, he and his associates learned of the 1860 assassination of Ii Naosuke (1815–60) before the warriors at Iida castle had the slightest inkling that anything extraordinary had occurred.[42] At his suggestion, the disciples published Atsutane's magnum opus, *Koshiden*, that until then had remained in manuscript. Without his presence, it is doubtful that the valley would have ended up with the largest concentration of Hirata disciples in all of Japan. He left for Kyoto in 1863 where he became an assistant scholar in the Shirakawa house. Following the Meiji Restoration of 1868, he served as a priest at various shrines until his death in Osaka.

Of all the people of peasant status who joined the Hirata school in the Ina valley, the most conspicuous was Kitahara Inao (1825–81) from Zakōji village. His father Yorinobu (1790–1862) had achieved a stellar reputation as village headman for his work as an educator, his erudition in western science plus Japanese poetry and his concrete achievements in digging wells and building levees. Iida domain gave his family permission to display swords and use a surname for two generations owing to his work in opening new rice fields along the Tenryū river. Inao had succeeded his father as village headman and school master when he was just 27, and he eventually taught 187 pupils in the years between 1849 and 1869.[43] Zakōji fell well within Iida's orbit, giving Inao easy access to whatever cultural events were taking place and providing him with numerous sources of information. He met Nagayo at the home of mutual acquaintances as early as 1853 although he did not accept the invitation to join the Hirata school until 1859, making him Nagayo's first convert.[44] Joining the Hirata school extended his wide circle of acquaintances beyond his valley to the major metropolitan centres. Even though he was out-ranked by Harukazu, his own accomplishments and the prestige inherited from his father made him a formidable figure in local affairs.

Inao's activities as a Hirata disciple overlapped those of Harukazu in a number of areas. Just as Harukazu had done, he organised a study group for 'like-minded' people in his own and neighbouring villages, a study group that to a certain extent replicated and continued the poetry writing circles he and his father had led for decades. He wrote *norito*; his portrait now hanging in the Kitahara house shows him wearing the headdress of a Shinto priest under one of his compositions. He also solicited converts; twenty-five people ultimately joined the Hirata school through his sponsorship, including Atsutane's first posthumous woman disciple, Matsuo Taseko (1811–94).[45] His brothers too recruited disciples, in fact the Kitahara clan was directly responsible for a total of thirty-seven people joining the school and indirectly through the Matsuo connection for an additional thirty-one.[46] Rather than organise a book-buying group, however, Inao simply lent his own and his father's books to relatives and neighbours.

Inao started keeping a record of the books people had borrowed from him in 1849. At first he lent maps, including one of the world and books on agronomy, astronomy, and poetry, including such famous texts as *Tales of Ise*, *Ehon Chūshingura* (Illustrated Chūshingura) and *Tosa nikki*. Mixed with them were military tales such as *Taiheiki*, said to be the most popular of all the books read by commoners,[47] *Genroku bukan* (a list of *daimyō* houses and their chief retainers) and a curious text called *Namiaiki* about the death in battle of a purported grandson of Go-Daigo in a village south of Iida. By 1851 he had acquired and was lending the *Man'yōshū*, a collection of Kamo Mabuchi's poetry, and a book by Norinaga on transferring a god-body to a new shrine (*Sengū monogatari*). Starting in 1855 he started lending books with a more overtly ideological or political slant, including a list of the Japanese emperors, an introduction to the ancient Way (*Kodō daii*) written by Atsutane, and a grammar for archaic Japanese (*Jindai shōgo*) written by Norinaga. In 1858 he lent a number of Atsutane's texts, including *Seiseki gairon* ('An outline of western countries') first to his cousin Matsuo Taseko who lived just across the Tenryū River and then to a man in Takatō in the northern part of the valley. At the end of that year he started lending out portions of Norinaga's monumental

Kojikiden (and recall that Harukazu's group paid over 5 *ryō* for it). 1859 saw more Norinaga texts, including *Tamakatsuma*, *Tamakushige* and *Tamaboko hyakushukai*. In 1860 he lent Atsutane's *Kishin shinron* (an essay on gods and demons) and *Miyabi no kami godenki* (a biography of the goddess Miyabi whose lewd dance lured the sun goddess from her cave) as well as books and pamphlets on foreign affairs and local conditions. By 1861 he had acquired Atsutane's *Koshiseibun* (a preliminary history of the age of the gods) and *Tamadasuki*.[48] A letter to him from Kanetane makes it clear that he also borrowed books himself, on topics ranging from genealogy to rituals to drive away evil spirits to medicine and agronomy.[49] This record thus attests to the Kitahara family's economic resources, Inao's shifting tastes in reading material, and his determination to share what he knew with other people.

Katsurajima has pointed out that Atsutane claimed to aim his teachings at middle-brow types and people of no education who had neither the time nor the money to read books. In *Tamadasuki* Atsutane even asserted that scholarship was not just a matter of book-learning. He made a number of lecture trips around the Kanto region to raise funds and spread his teachings; in fact some texts attributed to him were compiled by his followers from his talks that 'caused the listeners to laugh and cry by turns.' Despite his castigation of students who kept their noses buried in books, however, most of his disciples found him through his writings and thereafter studied his books as their chief religious activity.[50]

Inao put his family's considerable financial resources to work in publishing Atsutane's manuscripts within a few short months after becoming a disciple. On Nagayo's advice and with Kanetane's approval, he began by paying for the printing of a short chronology, *Kōninreki unkikō*, completed in 1836 but as with so many of Atsutane's writings left unpublished at his death.[51] In this work Atsutane traced the imperial lineage back through the sun goddess to Izanagi and Izanami, then asserted that 1833 marked 4,894 years since the heavenly grandson Ninigi had descended from the great Plain of Heaven to pacify and rule over Japan. His mortal heir was Jinmu, the ancestor to whom all emperors since traced their lineage.[52] Nagayo wrote an epilogue for the text in which he explained that he had settled in the Ina valley because there the people were willing to work hard to learn the Way of the Gods, a commitment manifested in their publication of this book. Its purpose was to demonstrate that Japan is the foundation for all countries and precedes them in all matters. People who read it and listen to it being read will realise the intrinsic value of the incomparable imperial court. 'If stubborn men who prattle on in Chinese and fools who chant the sutras read it, they will understand the essence of the country (*kokutai*) and be transformed into people who are pure in heart.' Although the book was published in Edo in the first month of 1860, Kanetane had no end of difficulties finding a messenger service to send it to Inao. It finally arrived in Ina on the twenty-eighth day of the seventh month.[53] Inao recorded the event in his diary and listed the men to whom he had sent it. To thank him for his efforts, Kanetane sent him a portion of a manuscript in

Atsutane's own hand.[54] In an appeal to the Shirakawa family in charge of Shinto affairs in Kyoto two years later, Inao gave credit to his father for the publication and asked that he be granted a Shinto rather than a Buddhist posthumous name. The name he had in mind was 'the spirit that accumulates meritorious deeds forever' (*banrai reikō sekirei*).[55]

Publishing *Kōninreki unkikō* was but a prelude to the Ina valley's most famous contribution to the Hirata school: the publication of *Koshiden* ('Lectures on ancient history'), Atsutane's twenty volume magnum opus that records everything he was able to glean from Japan's oldest texts regarding the Age of the Gods. This enterprise required such a vast outlay of funds that no single individual had the resources to cover it. While Iwasaki Nagayo signed his name to the prospectus designed to attract potential subscribers, it was backed by Inao, Harukazu, and three other men of wealth and influence.[56] It described how as Norinaga's last disciple, Atsutane had received his teachings, then spent fifty years interrogating Confucianism and researching the texts of a hundred schools to sweep away the last bit of Buddhist-laden dust and clarify the true visage of the divine land. In order to repay one ten-thousandth of their obligation owed the country for having been blessed with peace for three hundred years, his disciples had decided to encourage 'like-minded' people to assist in covering the costs of publishing this text. The organisers promised that 'contributing to this publication will transmit glory to your name throughout the ages and make your good intentions known throughout the land, thus establishing the Way of filiality to your parents and ancestors and also setting a good example for your descendants.'[57]

Sixty-six people, including four women, ultimately contributed to *Koshiden*'s publication. Some were already enrolled as disciples, some became disciples thereafter, some remained merely sympathisers.[58] At the end of each chapter is a paragraph giving the names of the solicitors for the contribution, followed by the names of those who actually put up the money. Inao's relatives and friends paid for the first set of four chapters, then men from Kai Province paid for the second. Nakatsugawa, home to Inao's younger brother, paid for the third section, Ina paid for the fourth, Mino for the fifth and Mikawa for the sixth. People from Shinano, Settsu, Sanuki on Shikoku, Izu, Mino, Mikawa, Shimotsuke, and Buzen on Kyushu paid for the seventh. The entire project was completed by 1864.[59] (In its final form, *Koshiden* runs to over thirty chapters. The last twelve, written by Atsutane's disciples Yano Harumichi (1823–87) and Morooka Masatane (1829–99), were not published until the 1880s.) In a letter to Inao, Kanetane complained that the publication costs had increased to the point that each section cost 1,200 *ryō*. He hoped that they might decline to 800 or 900 *ryō*, still a substantial sum.[60]

As Haga Noboru has argued, one reason why the Ina valley became such a hot bed of support for the Hirata school is because the publication of *Koshiden* gave it a concrete goal around which to rally.[61] It was a large-scale project, one that involved many more people than simply those enrolled as disciples. Just as Inao had done with the text he had published, the subscribers might lend their copies to neighbours and relatives or hold study groups to discuss its contents. Simply knowing a person who had contributed to this project was likely to increase interest in it and aid in bringing in yet more disciples.[62] By organising the publication of one of central texts for understanding Atsutane's thought, the Ina valley disciples attracted welcome attention at both the regional and national level.

During and after the drive to publish *Koshiden*, the Ina valley nativists played host to a number of imperial loyalists on the run.[63] Some came as individuals seeking food and shelter while they plotted their next move. The largest troop consisted of Mito warriors, who forced out of their domain during the 1864 civil war had then fortified Mt. Tsukuba. Defeated there, they decided to appeal to the emperor to reform the government and expel the hated barbarians. They took the mountain road, the Nakasendō, to Kyoto during the depths of the winter. When they reached Lake Suwa, they turned south down the Ina road rather than continuing through the narrow Kiso gorge with its fortified entrance at Kiso-Fukushima. One reason for this decision was their knowledge that the Ina valley harboured many Hirata disciples who had previously helped men dedicated to the imperial cause. An indication of the time that had elapsed since the animosity between Atsutane and the leading exponents of the Mito school was the presence of several Hirata disciples in the Mito troop. What united them and appealed to the Ina valley nativists was their fervent desire to have the emperor play a more active public role, especially in the realm of foreign affairs.

News that the Mito warriors were on the march sent the Iida domain retainers into a panic. They urged the villagers to barricade the road and prepare to fight; the villagers in turn rushed their valuables and women into hiding. Inao proposed that the warriors take a back road around Iida, thus allowing both sides to avoid a confrontation. Having received Iida's silent acquiescence to this plan, he then sent his younger brother Imamura Masara (1830–1906) to negotiate with Mito. Suspicious of strangers, the Mito men feared they might be led into a trap. Only Masara's detailed knowledge regarding the publication status of *Koshiden*, which he had helped fund, plus the promise of 3,000 *ryō* to help defray their travel expenses relaxed their guard enough for them to accept his suggestion.[64] Having got safely past Iida, they then continued their doomed march toward Kyoto.[65] The day after they left the valley, Harukazu showed on horseback to defend Iida, dressed in full armour and leading a contingent of 130 men. Then came bakufu troops in distant pursuit. Their tight-sleeved uniforms in western style prompted Inao to write the following poem:

Mukutsukesa	What is going on
emishi no mane wa	that men from
nani goto zo	the sacred land of the gods
kami no mikuni no	should take on the appearance
sono hito ni shite	of the ugly barbarians?[66]

Inao's last chance to display his commitment to the Hirata school came at the end of 1867. In response to a letter from Kanetane expressing his fear that Edo might become a battlefield, Inao suggested that Atsutane's manuscripts be shipped to the Ina valley for safekeeping. He dispatched Masara and two other men to sort and pack the manuscripts in chests. They sealed them with the Shirakawa family seal because that noble family with its authority over Shinto shrines had long acted as Atsutane's patron and neither bakufu nor imperial troops was likely to question it. (The Shirakawa had given Atsutane permission to lecture to its priests and allowed its retainers to become Hirata disciples. In the 1860s it enrolled a number of Hirata disciples as new retainers and employed a few of them in its offices.[67]) The manuscripts remained in Zakōji until Kanetane was able to settle into a new abode in 1872. While they were there, they became a magnet for the Hirata disciples who met not only to read the words written by their teacher but to touch them with their own hands. Upon their return, Kanetane wrote Inao a long letter thanking him for looking after them so well that not a single new worm hole had appeared.[68]

Unlike his cousin Matsuo Taseko, who went to Kyoto in 1862 to demonstrate her loyalty to the emperor, or his son Nobutsuna (1849–1901), who joined the imperial armies fighting to pacify the north-east in 1868, Inao never let his commitment to the Hirata school take him away from the Ina valley. As the son and grandson of a village headman, it might be assumed that he devoted himself to local administration, but in fact he had quarrelled so violently with one faction of villagers in Zakōji that they were unwilling to submit to his authority. Haga Noboru has argued that the Hirata school was attractive to village officials and landlords because it provided a rationale for asserting an appearance of harmony at a time when their own enterprises were threatening to destabilise social relations.[69] By reminding the peasants of their intrinsic worth as participants in the great agricultural enterprise under the guidance of the gods, nativism served to paper over divisions within the village and buttress the position of the traditional village leadership. Haga thus assumes that the spread of commerce polarised the peasants into the very rich and the very poor. Lest the poor be inclined to revolt against their economic betters, the latter drew on Atsutane's teachings to inculcate a mythical village unity mediated by the gods. On the other hand, a poem that Inao's associate Hara Mayomi (1822–84) wrote might equally apply to Inao:[70]

Toriyari no	Watching the violent
hageshiki ikusa	exchanges in the wars
yoso ni mite	from afar,
kotatsu yagura ni	I've entrenched myself
tachikomori keri	behind the ramparts of my *kotatsu*.

Apotheosizing teachers

The religious culmination to the nativist movement in the Ina valley can be seen in the construction of the *Hongaku reisha*. Harukazu first organised a group of twelve men composed of his family and neighbours, then met with Inao who encouraged the project and promised to help with funding. Kanetane was enthusiastic; similar shrines had been proposed in Satsuma and Akita, but none had ever been built. Gratified at being asked to select an appropriate name, he chose one that emphasised the fundamental character of the nativist teachings.[71] On the first day of 1866 Harukazu sent a manifesto to disciples all over Japan that incorporated Kanetane's proposals for national reform. These included a clarification of the functions of ruler and retainer in order to restore imperial rule, the abolition of the hated unequal treaties, a revival of Shinto worship, the suppression of Buddhism, the revival of the ancient Way of the Age of the Gods, the employment of western military science to strengthen the army and the increase of the nation's wealth and power.[72] From the very beginning it is clear that building the shrine had several purposes besides the worship of the four nativist teachers. These included gaining publicity for the Hirata school, uniting people in the Ina valley behind the Hirata message, heightening awareness of the foreign threat, and shoring up the authority of the local elite.

Selecting a site turned out to be less difficult and time-consuming that acquiring the appropriate god bodies from the teachers' descendants. From Kanetane was requested a stone lingam.[73] He refused at first because he assumed that the other families would send more conventional objects such as mirrors and jewels. Besides, it might have an adverse affect on local customs. The Ina valley side proposed that it be housed in a separate building where the common people would not be exposed to it. Atsutane had been a believer in phallus worship as a manifestation of the creator deities (*musubi no kami*). A number of important Ina valley families had placed similar stones in their gardens to stand for their ancestral deities. As a symbol of the primordial sexual union between Izanami and Izanagi that unleashed the universe's productive forces, it had a direct connection with local efforts to improve agricultural practices.[74]

At first the Ina valley nativists hoped that Kanetane would supply suitable objects for all the god bodies. He sent a necklace of quartz circling a sunstone to stand for and receive Atsutane's spirit. He refused to part with a memento from the Motoori family, however, because it had been given to Atsutane and was not his to give away. Besides, all that was really needed were wooden plaques inscribed with the posthumous spirit names of each teacher. Wanting a closer and more 'real' connection to the departed spirits, Harukazu and his supporters wrote the Motoori, Kamo and Kada families on their own to request objects sanctified through association with each. Once approval had been granted, they then had to send escorts to bring the sacred objects back to the valley with all due ceremony. The Kamo family relinquished a sword that had belonged to Mabuchi, the Motoori house gave a bell and plaque made from a cherry tree beloved by Norinaga, and the Kada family sent a bronze mirror and a plaque. Each object arrived with documentation attesting to its authenticity.[75]

Even before the sacred objects had arrived, the disciples had started construction of the shrine in the first month of 1867. Four bamboo screens were purchased from the Gojō family of court nobles in Kyoto to adorn the shrine, and a disciple from Yokkaichi on the Pacific coast sent a brass bell to be hung in front of it. Kanetane donated two horse loads of printing blocks as an endowment to pay for the shrine's upkeep. Even though Harukazu's brother donated the land and most of the construction materials, the total cost for building and furnishing the shrine still came to just over 282 ryō. Contributions arrived from all over the Ina valley and as far away as Nakatsugawa.[76] Almost two years after Harukazu had first talked to Inao and his associates, the shrine was finally completed at the end of the third month of 1867.

The inauguration of the shrine was performed in accordance with what passed for ancient rites (perhaps based on the Norinaga text that Inao had acquired in 1851) and with all the dignity and solemnity that the disciples could muster. It began with a midnight parade, that being the hour for the easiest communication with the numinous. Lit by pine torches, 118 people wended their way up the mountain along a path lined with spectators. In the vanguard came one man scattering rice to drive away evil spirits followed by another purifying the path with salt. The next to appear were sweepers to clear the way, then men carrying the catalpa bow to summon the spirits. The central part of the procession began with a banner that announced the Kada no Azumamaro god, a staff decorated with zig-zag paper streamers followed by a branch of the sacred sakaki tree, a plaque bearing Azumamaro's spirit name, and finally the god body itself, each bearer accompanied by two attendants. A similar set of objects for Kamo Mabuchi was followed by one for Motoori Norinaga. In addition to those that replicated the objects representing the other teachers, the section dedicated to Hirata Atsutane included a shield and pledge written in Atsutane's own hand. The offerings to be placed before the god bodies came just before the troop that brought up the end of the procession that included three women wearing short swords stuck in their obi. It was said that they cut a most conspicuous figure.[77]

The text used for the opening ceremonies has been lost, but we can assume that it contained prayers similar to those Harukazu had written for his study group. The offerings presented to the god bodies at the crack of dawn included red beans and rice, water, fish, clothing, sake, fans, vegetables, dried persimmons, sesame seeds, indigo and other products of the land and water. Young men then performed a sword dance to pacify the spirits followed by the ancient stately dance called gagaku. A banquet followed at which the participants celebrated the return to ancient days in poetry and song.[78] As Harukazu's son Shigehisa (1846–71) wrote:

Oshi tachi no	Everyone can now
oshie michibiku	follow without error
masamichi wo	the correct path
fumi tagaezute	laid out for us in the teachings
tadore minabito	of our teachers.[79]

At first the shrine enjoyed considerable popularity. One participant took himself to Edo to report the details of the opening ceremony to Kanetane. Kanetane professed himself delighted at the success of this endeavour. To express his gratitude he sent a number of offerings, including a roll of silk, a piece of brocade, some dried candy and sake. The valley's leading disciples could see the shrine during their morning and evening prayers. Even those who lived farther away could feel a connection through the lingams in their gardens.[80] A number of disciples from other areas in Shinano made pilgrimages to worship there, and in 1870 a group from the Saku district presented it with a flag. Local activists petitioned the newly revived *Jingikan* (Shinto Council) for permission to build the (already built) shrine as soon as the Meiji Restoration was announced; acceptance of the petition constituted formal recognition of its existence.[81] It received an official shrine number in 1892. By 1897 however, all of the founders had died, and the Zakōji retainers who had been its chief supporters had scattered. The vast majority of local people never took any interest in the shrine, no one came to perform the twice-yearly ceremonies, the path reverted to fields, and the building collapsed. The Katagiri family removed the god bodies to its own house for safekeeping. A movement to repair and refurbish the shrine collapsed for want of funds in 1917. In 1928 during the commemoration of the sixtieth anniversary of the Meiji Restoration, descendants of the original founders managed to take advantage of a renewed concern for the indigenous Japanese spirit to rebuild the shrine and put in place a retaining wall and stone steps.[82] Thereafter members of the Katagiri family organised twice-yearly ceremonies up to the darkest days of the war in 1943. The shrine was rebuilt again for the hundredth commemoration of the Meiji Restoration in 1968.[83] It still stands today, a ramshackle wooden building with an iron roof. As with so many shrines, it has become a site for children to pray for success in the school entrance examinations.

Conclusion

In his magisterial work on the intellectual history of nineteenth century nativism, H.D. Harootunian focused on a discourse that offered active resistance to the Tokugawa regime and new ways of conceptualising the relationship between commoners and the emperor. He argued that nativism provided the rural elite a means by which to reorder their priorities away from support for the ruling class to a village-centred world ratified by the gods.[84]

James White recently castigated this same rural elite for using nativism as a tool with which to suppress the aspirations of 'the people' who opposed economic and political activities that threatened their livelihood.[85] It seems to me that both men have missed the point of a nativist movement whose populist orientation discovered by Haga Noboru has been vastly overrated.[86] The Ina valley nativists aimed at a god-centred world. While they were indeed concerned with issues of agricultural productivity and village morality, they sought a solution in a renewed commitment to following the Way of the Gods. Furthermore, as Katsurajima Nobuhiro has pointed out, nativist doctrine trapped the rural elite far more than it ever did ordinary peasants and tenant farmers. Their 'illusion of community' was so tightly predicated on the central role played by the emperor that they ended up unable to imagine a polity without him.[87] In the Ina valley, the nativists stayed so tightly wedded to the shogun that they supported him until he was forced to resign in 1867.

Despite the number of people who joined the Hirata school in the Ina valley, it never became a mass movement, there or elsewhere. The cost of joining the school made it prohibitive for most peasants, but even within the village headman class it had to contend with a variety of other teachings, including the nationalistic Confucianism of the Mito school, the eclectic teachings of Ohara Yugaku (1797–1858) and the moralistic message of Ninomiya Sontoku (1787–1856). It never even attracted as many followers as the more popularly-oriented and often suppressed *Fujikō* (predicated on the power of the mountain deity).[88] The disciples worked hard at proselytising among their neighbours and relatives. They formed study groups, bought books and exchanged them with each other. They published one of Atsutane's most important texts and they built a shrine to his spirit. They wrote prayers. They created their own proposals for governmental reform and foreign affairs. None of these had any impact at all. Despite their desperate desire to matter, their vision of a polity governed in accordance with the Way of the Gods constitutes nothing more than an appendix to the master narrative of the Meiji Restoration. Without it, however, that narrative ends up lacking the intrinsic interest of dead ends and thwarted expectations.

Notes

My thanks to Kate Wildman Nakai for her comments on an earlier version of this paper and to Kitajima Eiko for her help in gathering materials.

1 Ōkuni Takamasa (1792–1871) is usually credited with formalizing the nativist teachings in terms of these four men. His followers saw him as the fifth, a view not shared by the Hirata disciples. (Fujii 1975: 127).
2 Quoted in Gotō 1967: 45.
3 Katsurajima 1992:55–60.
4 For this historiographic summary, see Kamijo 1995b: 49; 1995c: 3–9.
5 Wigen 1995.

6 Rothermund 1997: 13–28.
7 Haga 1963: 118.
8 Tsunoda 1989: 10–12.
9 Itō 1982: 292–93.
10 Masaki Keiji emphasizes the importance of a 'point person' in building and spreading the nativist cells. (Masaki 1974a: 6).
11 See, for example, the letter to Kirahara Inao in which Kanetane agrees to send a number of books but refuses to send others, either because he does not have them in his possession or because they are not in good condition. The letter also acknowledges a correction Inao made to *Koshiden*. (Kishino 1978a: 6–7).
12 See an account of this search in Kobayashi 1974: 12–14.
13 Kishino 1978a: 6.
14 See, for example, Gotō 1967: 45.
15 In 1631 Tokugawa Iemitsu had granted Zakōji Tameshige a fief of 1,413 *koku* centred on Yamabuki village. (Shimoina-gun 1980: 513–514). Despite their multi-generational history of close lord-retainer ties, the Zakōji and Katagiri families had a falling out after the Meiji Restoration chiefly because, while the former declined, the latter prospered. (Yamada 1982e: 4)
16 Itō 1982: 213–14.
17 It is not clear whether Harukazu did this on his own or whether he was responding to an imperial directive issued by the Ministry of State (*Dajōkan*) in 1854. See Ketelaar 1990: 3.
18 Tosa began recruitment of peasant soldiers in 1854, Matsue and Chōshū began in the early 1860s. The bakufu ordered *hatamoto* such as the Zakōji to recruit peasant soldiers starting in 1862. For details on Harukazu's military efforts, see Matsushita 1980b: 10–18.
19 Ichimura 1929: 182–83; Matsushita 1980a: 16–17.
20 Masaki 1987a: 106.
21 Miyashita 1975: 280.
22 Itō 1982: 219–220.
23 Ketelaar 1990: 44–46.
24 Miyashita 1962:4.
25 Itō 1982: 221, 223.
26 Itō 1982: 223–24.
27 Matsushita 1980a:10.
28 Itō 1982: 217.
29 The full text may be found in Kishino 1979b: 19–24.
30 This spirit of critical inquiry ended with Ōkuni Takamasa who explicitly ordered his disciples not to contradict his teachings. (Fujii 1975: 124–27, 129)
31 Kishino 1979a: 9: 1979b: 20–21.
32 Kishino 1979b: 19–20.
33 Kishino 1979b: 20.
34 Ichimura 1933: 110.
35 To hold a Shinto funeral, the family was supposed to get permission from the authorities in Kyoto and their local Buddhist temple. It is not clear whether the Katagiri bothered with these formalities. (Murasawa 1936: 214–6)
36 Kishino 1979c: 22–23.
37 Matsushita 1980b: 18.
38 Itō 1982: 216; Matsushita 1980a: 17; Murasawa 1936:96.
39 Haga Noboru claims that Nagayo recruited more disciples than any other proselytiser. (Haga 1975a: 208)
40 Murasawa 1944: 1–9; 1985: 16–20.
41 Gotō 1967: 4–8.

42 Shimoinagun 1977:57; Ichimura 1980a: 444.
43 Haga 1961:26.
44 Murasawa 1944:8.
45 Walthall 1998.
46 Masaki 1978a: 105.
47 Nagatomi 1977: 101.
48 Naganoken 1980: 427–34.
49 Kishino 1978b: 9.
50 Katsurajima 1996: 85–91.
51 Atsutane had to find his own subventions to support the publication of his works. Most were financed by his disciples. When he was exiled from Edo in 1841, he had outstanding debts with publishers of 1,500 *ryō*, and many of his teachings remained in manuscript. (Haga 1976: 105–106; Katsurajima 1996: 83–84)
52 Haga 1963: 138.
53 Kishino 1978b: 6.
54 Murasawa 1944: 9.
55 Haga 1970: 188.
56 These were Inao's uncle Maijima Masayuki (?–?) from Okawara, Hara Mayomi (1822–1884), a poetry-writing friend from Seinaiji, and Majima Toshinari (1811–1868), a doctor from Nakatsugawa.
57 Ichimura 1929: 209–10.
58 Masaki 1974b: 23–4.
59 Haga 1977: 11–12. The text for *Koshiden* constitutes the first two volumes of Atsutane's complete works. See Hirata 1977.
60 Ichimura 1980b: 521.
61 Haga 1975a: 212.
62 Haga 1980: 426. Furuhashi Terunori (1813–92) from Mikawa, for example, contributed to the publication of this opus, then became a Hirata disciple. (Haga 1968: 26)
63 Kobayashi 1943: 107–9.
64 In 1891 Masara compiled his own account of the Mito troop's passage, then in 1901 he raised the funds to build a monument commemorating their 'martyrdom' (*junan*). A few months before he died, his concern for the plight of the poor led him to join the Japan Socialist Party. (Kamijo 1995a: 5) Documents concerning Masara, especially his later career, may be found in Masaki 1978b, 1979a–f.
65 The Mito warriors had hoped to appeal to the emperor through Hitotsubashi Yoshinobu (1837–1913), the shogun's chief advisor and son of the former Mito lord. When Yoshinobu instead announced that he would raise an army against them, they surrendered. 352 were executed, over 100 exiled, and 135 were returned to Mito where they and the relatives of the other men were castigated for having crippled Mito militarily and politically. See Yamakawa 1992: 119–120.
66 Kobayashi 1943: 134, 170.
67 Yano Harumichi, for example, was taken on as an instructor by the Shirakawa in 1863. (Haga 1968: 25; 1975b: 267; Miyachi 1994: 278–279)
68 Ichimura 1929: 227; 1980b: 521–22.
69 Haga: 1980: 497–500.
70 Ichimura 1980b: 602.
71 John Breen has pointed out that *hongaku* or *mototsu no oshie* was a term used by Ōkuni Takamasa (personal communication). None of my sources indicate whether Kanetane was aware of this. The tortured relations between the two men and their followers is a fascinating subject, one beyond the scope of this paper. See Breen 1990: 579–602.
72 Haga 1963: 143–44.

73 The lingam is two feet long, eighteen inches in circumference and weighs about 43.5 pounds. Named Shiokama jinja, the shrine for it was not completed till 1870. See the photograph in Yamada 1982h: 3 and also Yamada 1982a: 7.
74 Haga 1963: 144–45; Ichimura 1929: 243.
75 Ichimura 1929: 245–49; Miyashita 1962: 4.
76 Miyashita 1975: 293.
77 Ichimura 1929: 259–65; Itō 1982: 227–29.
78 Ichimura 1929: 262–63.
79 Itō 1982: 229.
80 Haga 1975a: 216.
81 Ichimura 1929: 276.
82 Ichimura 1929: 280–91.
83 Yamada 1982a: 9; 1982c: 11; 1982g: 29–35.
84 Harootunian 1988: 17, 23, 37.
85 White 1995: 114–15.
86 See, for example, Haga 1976: 236; 1980: 500–503 and the other books by him listed in the bibliography.
87 Katsurajima 1992: 32.
88 Masaki points out that *Fujikō* attracted 309 adherents in the lower Ina valley compared to 272 for the Hirata school. (Masaki 1978a: 110)

CHAPTER TWELVE

Ideologues, bureaucrats and priests: on 'Shinto' and 'Buddhism' in early Meiji Japan

John Breen

Introduction

Over the past few years a series of valuable studies in Western languages has heightened our awareness of the implications for religion of the Meiji Restoration. Four are noteworthy. The first of these was Allan Grapard's pioneering essay on Tōnomine, a 'shrine-temple multiplex', to use his suggestive term, situated in Sakurai, outside Nara, and dedicated to Fujiwara Kamatari (614–69).[1] The focus of early Meiji religious policy fell, in Grapard's words, on 'the disruption of the Shinto-Buddhist discourse and [as such it was] a denial of cultural history.'[2] Cultic centres like Tōnomine constituted 'a fundamental aspect of Japanese religions and culture', and Grapard invites us to see the early Meiji dissociation of Shinto and Buddhist divinities at Tōnomine and elsewhere as 'a major cultural revolution'.[3] If Grapard's interest was in 'shrine-temple multiplexes', Collcutt takes Buddhism, its temples and priests as a distinct entity. Collcutt usefully reminds us that anti-Buddhism was not new with Meiji; that it was a feature rather of the majority of intellectual discourses in the preceding Tokugawa era as well.[4] Collcutt warns us against too simplistic an explanation for the government's assault on Buddhism, but identifies the promotion of 'Shinto' as an important key to understanding. He surveys incidents from different domains and provides valuable statistical evidence, too, on the extent of Buddhist devastation. Out of an estimated total of 460,000 temples in Tokugawa Japan, some 18,000 were destroyed between 1872 and 1874 (and possibly as many again in the period from 1868–72). Some 56,000 monks were returned to lay life. Buddhism, in Collcutt's view, faced the real threat of eradication.[5]

Helen Hardacre has also explored early Meiji religious policy in her book length study of Shinto and the state in modern Japan. What we know as 'state Shinto' began, Hardacre says, 'with the Restoration,' and it was in seeking to raise the status of Shinto that Buddhism suffered mightily. She writes: 'The pent-up resentment of the Shinto priesthood was unleashed in ferocious, vindictive destruction. Buddhist priests were defrocked, lands confiscated, statuary and ritual implements melted down for cannon.'[6] Curiously Hardacre provides little evidence of the involvement of Shinto clergy in these activities, but she offers a much needed and valuable analysis both of institutional change affecting shrines and of ideological change: she discusses the Great Promulgation Campaign, its rise and demise and, most importantly, the implications it had for new religions such as Kurozumikyō and Konkōkyō.[7] Finally, there is James Edward Ketelaar's study of Meiji Buddhism. *Of heretics and martyrs* has certainly done its bit to highlight the dynamics of religion and politics in the new Japan of Meiji. His specific purpose is to chart the modern transformation of Buddhism under the impact of Meiji modernisation. If the Meiji period ended with Buddhists demonstrating the age-old compatibility between their creed and Japanese social and political culture, with Buddhism emerging as a 'national cultural paradigm', it began much more inauspiciously with Buddhism defined, so Ketelaar proposes, as 'heresy', as 'foul and polluted'.[8] Herein lies, of course, the explanation for the devastation that Buddhism suffered in early Meiji. Tokugawa ideologues may have provided the 'source books' for this approach, as it were, but it was inherited and implemented by Meiji bureaucrats. Buddhism's devastation in Meiji was quite simply a consequence of its definition as 'decadent and inherently evil.'[9]

Each of these studies, while drawing inevitably on Japanese scholarship, has made an important and original contribution to our understanding of the religious policies of early Meiji. If they have a shared shortcoming, however, it is that their interest is not sufficiently people-focused. We need to know more about the people involved than we do. Who precisely were the ideologues who formulated religious policy, who the bureaucrats who supported it and what did they seek to accomplish? Only when we know more about the people involved can we refine our understanding of motive. When in the afore-mentioned studies, the focus falls on people, misunderstandings abound. This in turn is a consequence, it would appear, of the shared framework deployed in these studies of Meiji religion: it is one that casts Buddhist as victim and Shintoist – and bureaucrat ally – uniquely as perpetrator.

In this chapter I seek to problematise the framework firstly by identifying the ideologues who formulated early Meiji religious policy and exploring their motives. Secondly, I consider the Meiji bureaucrats and seek to uncover their views on the religious question. In the third section, my concern is to question the idea of 'Shintoist as perpetrator' by examining the bewildering experiences of a provincial Shinto priest.

Ideologues

By March 27 1868, Kamei Koremi (1824–85), *daimyō* of Tsuwano domain, and Fukuba Bisei (1831–1907), a senior vassal and, for some years, the most active ideologue in Tsuwano, had taken effective control of the Restoration government's office for religious affairs. The arrival of Kamei and Fukuba in the office was apparently owing to the sponsorship of the Chōshū leader, Kido

Kōin (1833–77). Chōshū's dominant role in the overthrow of the Tokugawa and the restoration of the emperor, in the military campaigns presently being waged against the Tokugawa and their allies, and Chōshū's dominance in the Kyoto-based government, gave Chōshū men like Kido an influence second to none.

Chōshū sponsorship of Kamei and Fukuba is explained partly by geographical, historical and personal circumstances: Chōshū and Tsuwano shared borders; cordial relations between their *daimyō* throughout the 1860s were based on a commitment to the loyalist cause.[10] Fukuba Bisei had, moreover, moved in the same radical loyalists circles in and around Kyoto as Kido and other Chōshū activists. Kido clearly saw in Fukuba a man of ideas who could be trusted with the ideological dimension of government policy. Fukuba in turn drew much from Ōkuni Takamasa (1792–1871). Ōkuni, one of the great ideologues of the late Edo period, also hailed from Tsuwano and, indeed, only a week after Kamei and Fukuba arrived in the office of religious affairs, Ōkuni Takamasa joined them, at the grand age of 76.

These men, Ōkuni Takamasa, Kamei Koremi and Fukuba Bisei, are the ideologues who formulated state policy on religion and ideology. They were by no means the only ideologues in government, however. Fukuba, for example, was engaged in constant battle with men like Yoshida Ryōgi and Shirakawa Sukenori, who headed the Yoshida and Shirakawa Shinto families responsible for the ritual of the pre-modern imperial court. Fukuba fought bitterly with others, too, like Tokoyo Nagatane, a disciple of Hirata Atsutane, who represented the most vigorous opposition to his policies. Subsequently, Fukuba acquired ideological allies in men like Kadowaki Shigeaya from Tottori and Urata Chōmin from Ise. But it was Fukuba, Kamei and Ōkuni Takamasa who exerted the decisive influence on shrine and temple policy, on all developments in state ritual, and so on the redefinition of the imperial institution.

Kamei and Fukuba were the authors of the infamous edicts known now as the *shinbutsu bunri rei* or 'shrine-temple separation edicts.' They were drawn up, submitted to government and finally published between April and May 1868. But what were they designed to achieve? To what extent were their authors' intentions reflected in the effects they had? Intentions and motives are notoriously difficult to pin down, of course, but in this case there are clues. Firstly, the 'separation edicts' as published were but fragments of a bolder and more comprehensive blueprint for religious reform which has survived in the Kamei family archives. We need to grasp this blueprint in its entirety. We also need to note the edicts' more public context. This was provided by a Council of State declaration of April 6th, four days ahead of the first of the 'separation' edicts. The declaration too was almost certainly the work of Fukuba and Kamei, although no draft is to be found in the Kamei archives. The point is that Meiji religious policy began on April 6th with this declaration, and our own exploration of the early Meiji ideologues, their intentions and motives, can usefully start here too.

The April 6th declaration, published in the government gazette (*Dajōkan Nisshi*), proclaimed the revival of the hallowed principle of *saisei itchi*: namely that emperors as high priests performed state ritual (*sai*) even while, as political sovereigns, they oversaw government (*sei*). The imperial office, in short, was to be defined by the unity (*itchi*) of these two public functions. The declaration reminded its readers that the principle was far from new; that it had defined the imperial office since its foundation by Emperor Jinmu at the dawn of history.[11] It proclaimed the revival of the *Jingikan*, the office that had constituted the ritual centre of the ancient *ritsuryō* government;[12] the *Jingikan* and its rituals were to be reinstated, but so too were ancient rites at shrines throughout the land. Provincial shrines and their priests were hereby declared subject to *Jingikan* jurisdiction, thus severing their erstwhile bonds with the 'private' Shinto families, the Yoshida and Shirakawa.

The focus of the '*saisei itchi* declaration' falls, then, on the imperial institution at the centre, on shrines, their priests in the periphery, and on the inseparable ritual linkage between them. It is, of course, one thing to issue such a declaration; quite another to translate it into policy. But this is what began to happen over ensuing weeks, months and years. The declaration was never rescinded or disowned.

It was four days later that the first of the 'separation' edicts penned by Fukuba and Kamei saw the light of day. The gist: that the many temple priests (*shasō* or *bettō*) serving at shrines located in temple precincts or elsewhere on temple land should desist from so doing forthwith. Many of these men referred to were priests of the Tendai or Shingon sects; others were *shugenja* or mountain ascetics. If they wished to continue serving at shrines, they should now become 'dedicated' shrine priests. A second edict, issued a fortnight later, outlawed the centuries-old practice of applying Buddhist terminology to shrine deities. Hachiman, the 'native' god of war, was no longer a deity in the Buddhist pantheon (as a *bosatsu* or *bodhisattva*), but the indigenous *kami* Hachiman Daijin. Terms like *gongen*, as in *Sannō Gongen*, were likewise banned. *Gongen* defined a deity as a native manifestation of a Buddhist divinity commissioned to guide Japanese to Buddhist salvation. The application of Buddhist terminology to 'native' kami in this way obscured their true Japanese origins and constituted a distortion of religious truth. A third edict, published two weeks on, stipulated inevitably enough that Buddhist symbolism – the bells, pictures, scrolls and statues, that had for centuries bedecked shrines the length and breadth of Japan – be immediately cleared away.[13]

Set in the context of the April 6th declaration, it is clear enough that the prime target was shrines. To isolate shrines in this way from their temples, their clergy and symbols, which alone had given to shrines their social and theological meaning in pre-modern Japan, was, of course, an act of violence. It has to be recalled that not all Buddhist sects embraced shrines; the mighty True Pure Land sects (the Nishi and Higashi Honganji branches of Shinshū Buddhism) remained untouched by these edicts; again, it might be suggested that provincial shrines in the latter half of the Edo period were becoming increasingly aware of their distinctness from Buddhist structures as they came under the sway of the Yoshida and Shirakawa families.[14] Nonetheless, these Kamei and Fukuba penned edicts constituted a first denial and so the start of the destruction of the complex pattern of pre-modern Japanese religious culture.

The Kamei family archives enable us to flesh out further the ideologues' proposals for shrines, and they suggest something too, of the fate in store for Buddhism in the new Japan. Proposals in the Kamei-Fukuba blueprint not (at least immediately) published included the following: that all people of the realm 'venerate shrines'; that census-gathering and anti-Christian checks be transferred from Buddhist temple control to shrines; that the government religious office should be the repository for all such statistical information; that a thorough reform of funeral practice be implemented, allowing for the nationwide introduction of 'Shinto' style funerals (shinsō) alongside Buddhist funerals; and that imperial mausolea and the rites performed there be removed from Buddhist control and transferred to the government office for religious affairs in order that 'classic precedent' might be adhered to. The ideologues' boldest proposal of all was that fukko Shintō ('restoration Shinto') be declared the religion of the imperial realm; this too was ignored by the bureaucrats.[15]

It is curious that Kamei and Fukuba nowhere deploy the now standard term for these regulations, bunri or 'separation'.[16] Bunri suggests the separating out of two distinct, complete entities: Shinto and Buddhism; shrines and temples; kami and buddhas. But what Kamei and Fukuba were engaged in was a much more creative enterprise. They dismissed out of hand the Yoshida, Shirakawa, Norinaga, Hirata and all other schools of Tokugawa Japan as woefully inadequate for the new Japan. 'Separation' was not called for; they demanded rather the forging of an entirely new Shinto.[17] Thus it is that the Kamei-Fukuba blueprint, like the April 6th declaration and the edicts that followed, is concerned primarily with shrines and the definition of their ideal relationship to state and to society. Explicit references to Buddhism in the blueprint are few, but the 'disestablishment' of Buddhism from its position of privilege is everywhere implicit. Just how destructive this creative process could be was already evident in the religious reforms that Kamei and Fukuba had begun to implement in Tsuwano in the summer of 1867. For the insights they offer into the thinking of the ideologues, these reforms merit our brief consideration.

A notice from the Tsuwano office for religious affairs in June 1867 reminded shrine priests impatiently of their calling: to perform rituals night and day to sustain the martial vigour and longevity of the domain lord and the happiness of all his people.[18] The notice admonished priests since the reality was so different from the ideal. Shrine priests were 'incapable of [under-standing] their duties toward the deities'; they were 'immoral', and preached all manner of 'bizarre theories', which left the minds of the people seriously befuddled. In this, they excelled even the Buddhists.[19] Common people in the domain, who should have known better, appeared to regard the building of any new shrine as an auspicious event. At the first sign of the outbreak of some disease or other, they would knock up a new shrine and have summoned to it all manner of deities. In short, shrines in Tsuwano were being treated as the playthings of priests and their parishioners. One consequence of the fad for new shrines was the neglect of older shrines; several now had their sacred treasures exposed to the elements. 'If things continued as they are, respect for the deities will be quite lost.'[20]

'Shinto' in Tsuwano in summer 1867 was in disarray. The solution? The destruction of all shrines founded after 1617, when the Kamei family arrived in Tsuwano and the transfer of their sacred objects to the nearest shrine of long standing.[21] Only in this way would older shrines survive, and their priests be able to engage in the business of morning and night prayers for the benefit of the domain lord. Priests should regard these regulations with gratitude and devote themselves hereafter exclusively to Shinto, amend their bad ways, cut back on costs and, in all things, devote themselves to ancient practice.[22]

The point is that, to Fukuba and Kamei, there were shrines and there were shrines. Shrines' significance for them did not consist in their religious value to the common man or woman – nor yet to the priests – but in their ideological value to the domain authorities, and subsequently, of course, to the Meiji state. Shrines' value to the state was as anchors of state ideology; for this they had, of course, to be 'primed' and in the priming sacrifices had to be made.

If we return to the national scene in the wake of the 'Restoration', it is hardly surprising that shrine priests across Japan were bewildered. As we shall see many came rapidly to find these regulations profoundly disturbing; yet, the edicts seemed at the same time to promise the advent of a new age of privilege. The first flush of enthusiasm in some cases translated into Shinto priests' violence on Buddhist property. It is by no means clear how widespread such violence was, but the government anyway responded swiftly with an admonition to shrine priests who claimed to 'act on behalf of government' when in reality they were 'venting private frustrations'.[23] The authorship of this admonition is unclear, but it was quite possibly Kamei or Fukuba. At any rate, Kamei was echoing these very sentiments a couple of weeks later in a private letter.[24] Fukuba, too, separately penned a warning missive to shrine priests.[25] If Fukuba and Kamei seemed anxious to disabuse shrine priests of the fact that their time had truly come, it was because, in reality and with not many exceptions, it had not.

Over subsequent weeks, months and years, other dimensions of the original Kamei-Fukuba blueprint were gradually published and implemented nation-wide.[26] In May 1868, for example, shrine priests were ordered to perform 'Shinto style' funerals (shinsō), traditionally regarded as defiling. These became an option for the rest of the populace in July 1870. In stages between 1869 and 1871, rites for the spirits of deceased emperors, those at mausolea and those performed within the palace, were reclaimed from the control of Tendai and Shingon Buddhists and entrusted to the ideologues in the government office for religious affairs, the Jingikan. The establishment of 'restoration Shinto' appeared to proceed apace – though a formal declaration of its establishment was never forthcoming.

In a sense, the Kamei-Fukuba proposals reached their culmination in June 1871 in a historic edict penned by Fukuba and issued by the Council of State. It defined shrines as 'sites for the performance of state ritual'.[27] Shrines were no longer private property and they and their clergy were no more to serve primarily the religious needs of the local community. As Fukuba's edict also banned the principle of heredity, the majority of shrine priests now faced summary dismissal with local government bureaucrats assuming responsibility for re-appointment. Other changes followed in rapid succession: income for shrine priests, stipends for shrine upkeep and contributions to offerings used in shrine rites were guaranteed by government edict in spring 1872, appearing to confirm a new privileged status, but they were abolished again – for the vast majority of shrines – a year later. Shrine rituals, too, were now subordinated to the ideological demands of the modern state, as set out in a late 1871 document called the *Shiji saiten* (Seasonal rituals).[28] Fukuba's 1871 reforms meant profound religious reorganisation at the village level, too. Designed to correspond with the reform of the national census registration, they identified one shrine per village as official 'village shrine' (*gōsha*) and placed all others in a hierarchy subordinate to it, ultimately, no doubt, with an eye to the sorts of mergers that had happened earlier in Tsuwano.[29]

Studies of early Meiji religion have tended to focus on the fate of Buddhism, and to cast it as victim to 'Shinto', its shrines and priests. The reality was evidently more complex. Local shrines and their priests quickly came to believe that they were the victims of the modern state, and it is not difficult to see why. What, though, was the fate of Buddhism in the plans of Kamei Koremi and Fukuba Bisei? What were the implications for Buddhism of their 'restoration Shinto' blueprint? James Ketelaar's recent and provocative study of Meiji Buddhism provides us with a suitable entree into this important subject.

Ketelaar's general thesis is that Meiji ideologues and bureaucrats defined Buddhism as 'heresy', as 'decadent and inherently evil', and that this definition is a key to analysing Buddhism's misfortunes in the wake of the Restoration.[30] Ketelaar identifies Kamei Koremi as a central figure here, noting that '[Kamei] consistently refers to Buddhism as the heretical law (*jahō*)'.[31] Ketelaar also draws our attention back to Tsuwano domain on the eve of the Restoration, where in 1867, he tells us, Kamei proscribed all Buddhist funerals, decreeing that henceforth all funeral rites 'would be Shinto', and issuing a 'total ban on priests within the domain' and an 'order to close down all temples'.[32]

In fact, Buddhism in Kamei's vision of the modern age turns out to be a good measure more interesting than Ketelaar allows. In the first document cited by Ketelaar, Kamei makes in fact only one reference to *jahō*, and this one reference quite obviously addresses not Buddhism at all but Christianity. Kamei is referring to the need to ensure shrine priests are rigorous in preventing possible outbreaks of the 'pernicious creed' amongst their parishioners. A careful perusal of the Tsuwano source next cited by Ketelaar reveals another serious misreading. The source begins: 'I, Kamei Koremi,

236

request that dilapidated temples within [my] domain be closed down, that priests be allowed to adopt the lay life and that, with regard to funeral practice, Buddhist and Shinto funerals be carried out side by side.'

There then follow five specific requests: that temples struggling for lack of income and absence of parishioners be merged with the head temple; that temples without resident priests have their buildings destroyed and removed from the land; that priests wishing to adopt the lay life be allowed so to do; that priests who have returned to the lay life be employed in the domain office, if possessed of talent; and that, with regard to funeral practice, the people of Tsuwano, even commoners, if they so wish, be allowed to depart from Buddhist practice and adhere to Shinto, based on the classic texts.[33]

In brief, Kamei issued no orders for Shinto funerals to be made compulsory; no orders to close down all Buddhist temples, and no ban on all Buddhist priests. Nor is there any record anywhere of him framing Buddhism as heresy. The preceding is meant as a corrective to a misreading of Kamei's intentions; not to trivialise the impact of the Kamei-Fukuba proposals for Buddhism either in Tsuwano or subsequently across the length and breadth of Japan. In Tsuwano the impact of their proposals was, as a domain official later reminisced, 'a mighty one'; but, the same official protested, Tsuwano 'did not set out to annihilate the Buddha'.[34] What, then, did Kamei and Fukuba set out to do, locally and nationally, if it was not to eradicate Buddhism as heresy?

In the unpublished blueprint of Kamei and Fukuba, referred to earlier, numerous references are made to Buddhism.[35] The 'disestablishment' of Buddhism, that is the severance of all state ties, an end to all state privileges and the transfer of social functions to 'Shinto' institutions, was clearly a first and most pressing objective. At the same time, these clear cut proposals carried two riders. The first, in announcing the introduction of Shinto funerals, added that people may, as they wished, be exempt;[36] the second, declaring *fukko Shintō* to be the religion of the imperial realm, added that adherents of Buddhism were at liberty to practise privately.[37] In other words, Kamei and Fukuba clearly envisaged *some* place for Buddhism in the new Japan, a Buddhism now distinct, of course, from 'Shinto' and its symbols; and it was clearly to be a restricted, private place. In Tsuwano, Buddhist temples had been subject to the same sort of reduction as shrines, reduction, that is, to pre-1617 levels. Statistics do not reveal the 'progress' made there in Buddhist reduction before the Restoration, but Kamei clearly had every intention of pursuing the matter after the Restoration.[38]

There is a striking continuum in the Tsuwano approach toward Buddhism. It stretches back to the pre-Restoration writings of Ōkuni Takamasa and forward to statements made by Fukuba Bisei after Kamei Koremi left the government in 1869. In his 1862 *Shintō kyōhōben*, for example, Ōkuni dismissed the criticism made by many of his contemporaries that Buddhism's evil derived from its foreignness. Buddhism has its headquarters overseas, it is true, he writes, but 'it is as if it did not'. '(Japanese) Buddhists are, for all practical purposes, based in Kyoto. Provided that they do not shift their loyalties to foreign nations, there can be no harm in them'.[39] He made a point of including here the Shinshū sect whose national strength struck fear into the hearts of many anti-Buddhist Edo ideologues, especially those of the Mito school. Ōkuni rather confessed admiration for their skill at drawing people in to the fold by attaching their hearts to Amida: '[Shinshū] teachings are easy to learn; people remain loyal since priests preach eloquently of Amida's original vow.'[40] Ōkuni's conclusion was this: 'If Buddhists – and Confucianists – help encourage people to be loyal, filial, chaste and industrious; if, too, they contribute to the peace of the realm and the comfort of the general populace; if, finally, they exert themselves in protecting the imperial line, then, they are, without further change, to be regarded as citizens of this sacred realm'.[41]

In short, Buddhism in the approach of Ōkuni Takamasa was, after disestablishment, to be accommodated, valued and deployed for its benefits to the state. This was precisely the line that we find the Meiji government eventually pursuing under the Ministry of Religions (*Kyōbushō*) from 1872. *Kyōbushō* policy granted to Buddhists – especially to Shinshū Buddhists – a major role in countering Christianity and in stirring patriotism. The continuity here is to be explained by the fact that Fukuba played a major role in creating the *Kyōbushō* and in formulating its early policies. He did so along with Kido Kōin, and the Shinshū priest Shimaji Mokurai (1838–1911).[42] Neither Ōkuni nor Fukuba, in other words, saw any contradiction in disestablishing Buddhism only to deploy it again. Fukuba was, in fact, with Etō Shinpei (1834–74) one of two senior ministers in the *Kyōbushō*. Etō was an infamously anti-Buddhist bureaucrat from Saga, and it appears that Fukuba's removal from the Ministry after just two months was actually related to his pro-Buddhist stance. Buddhism, Fukuba insisted, should maintain a distinct identity and not be subject to attempts by government bureaucrats to 'convert all Buddhists to Shinto'.[43] It comes as no *great* surprise in this context to find Fukuba, in 1872, praising the Buddhist saints Saichō and Kūkai for having 'taught the Japanese to lead good lives.'[44]

Bureaucrats

The policies formulated by Kamei and Fukuba in the spring of 1868, by Fukuba subsequently from 1869 through to 1871 and then by Fukuba and Etō under the Ministry of Religions from 1872 saw the light of day because of a meeting of minds between ideologues and government bureaucrats. Neither the *saisei itchi* declaration of April 1868, nor the religious edicts of April and May that followed – all penned by Kamei and Fukuba – were ever rescinded by government: *saisei itchi* defined the nature of the Japanese imperial institution until 1945, and the religious edicts between them redefined Japanese religious culture for the modern era.

Ideologues did not have a monopoly on policy affecting religion and religious institutions, however, and bureaucrats' contributions we need now to consider. Rare is the occasion we are privy to the thoughts of bureaucrats on religious matters, but the opinions that have survived in historical records merit our consideration. The earliest instance I have encountered of direct bureaucratic involvement concerns a submission by Matsukata Masayoshi (1835–1924) to the Tokyo Conference in the summer of 1869. Matsukata was a young Satsuma samurai, presently governor of Hita Prefecture in Kyushu, and is best known for his later role in the commutation of samurai stipends, land tax reform and a range of other policies he implemented as Finance Minister. Matsukata was in the new capital of Tokyo in 1869 for the Conference which appears, not without reason, to have been an emotional affair. The Conference was designed as a celebration of the emperor's new authority, political and religious. The *daimyō* had just surrendered to the emperor their domain registers, symbolising the fact that all land and all people were the emperor's. The Conference also prompted much thought on the emperor's sacred qualities. He had, after all, just arrived in Tokyo via an historic and much trumpeted pilgrimage to the Ise shrines; Conference participants debated 'reviving of the Way of emperors'; and, the Conference's high point was a state ritual celebrated by the emperor in the new Tokyo *Jingikan*.

Such was the atmosphere that prevailed when Matsukata made his submission to Iwakura Tomomi (1825–83), as the senior courtier in government. Matsukata's concern was to strengthen the 'sacred realm'. He discussed taxation, local administration and census, before turning to shrines, temples and their clergy.[45] He lamented the inability of Shinto to better Buddhism in 'this would-be sacred nation of ours', and attributed it to shrine priests' stupidity and negligence. Shrine priests were the 'dregs', while Buddhists were all able, talented and skilled in preaching. The *Jingikan* might make a positive start by appointing men of talent to assume charge of the nation's most famous shrines.[46] Buddhist talents did not suggest to Matsukata, as they had to Ōkuni, Kamei and Fukuba, that Buddhism might have a role to play in the new Japan; far from it. He appeared to favour the annihilation of Buddhism (*metsubutsu*) but was afraid it would provoke widespread unrest. He proposed a nonetheless drastic approach to the Buddhist problem. Where several temples existed, he argued, they should be merged into a single larger one, so that there were nowhere more than two or three temples for every 10,000 *koku* of land; all temple priests should be accommodated together in the surviving temple, and all who objected should be defrocked. Buddhist clergy of ability might then be employed in local government. Buddhist connections with national census should now be severed.[47]

This is an intriguingly emotional statement from a man whose expertise was the economy. Matsukata makes no reference, for example, to temple – or shrine – land-holdings or to their autonomous and often tax-exempt status. That his concerns here are uniquely ideological says much about the atmosphere at the Tokyo Conference. His plan for temple reduction was more drastic than anything Kamei or Fukuba proposed, since its target was

239

indiscriminate: it was not merely the abandoned, the dilapidated or the un-parished. His proposals, designed uniquely to enable Shinto to thrive, found favour with Iwakura Tomomi. Iwakura circulated Matsukata's document with the comment: 'Much of what he says makes good sense; please read carefully'.[48] How wide a circulation it received is unknown, but word of its content did leak out. Buddhists in Tokyo like Matsumoto Hakka heard of it and believed that bans on Buddhist preaching and Buddhist funerals were imminent. Hakka also wrote in his diary that the total eradication of Buddhism was bound to follow.[49] It may well be that eradication was discussed in Tokyo in the summer of 1869, prompted perhaps by Matsukata's submission. But a year passed and no edict to that effect materialised. What began from the summer of 1870 to be discussed in bureaucratic circles, rather, was the question that Matsukata had so conspicuously overlooked a year before: the economic status of religious institutions, Buddhist and 'Shinto'.

Home Ministry (*Minbushō*) bureaucrats, Ōkuma Shigenobu, Ōki Takato and Itō Hirobumi, drafted a succession of proposals in summer 1870 to address the economic autonomy of religious institutions. Their cogitations proceeded in stages from the summer of 1870 through to year's end. First they discussed raising revenue on tax-exempt land; then they looked at the transfer to local government of shrine and temple land scattered, as it often was, at distances from the shrine or temple concerned; and, finally, around the time Matsukata Masayoshi joined the Home Ministry in late autumn of 1870, they proposed the confiscation of all land belonging to all religious institutions.[50]

By year's end, these recommendations had been worked into a draft Council of State document declaring all shrine and temple land hereby confiscated. The purpose was 'to end the anomaly of shrines and temples alone being in possession of private land and people, when *daimyō* had the previous year surrendered both [to the emperor].[51] In February 1871, the notice became law and all land formerly belonging to religious institutions was transferred, nominally at least, to the control of local governments.[52] No distinction was made between shrines and temples, either in terms of land to be confiscated or of stipends to be disbursed by local authorities to disempowered clergy. The only apparent concession to the new age was that bureaucrats now spoke uniformly of *shaji* ('shrines and temples') and no longer of *jisha* ('temples and shrines'), as had been Tokugawa practice. These policies were indiscriminate and so were not strictly-speaking, and in the narrowest sense, ideological; they certainly do not fit into the pro-Shinto, anti-Buddhist framework we habitually apply to early Meiji religious policy. But policies that were of this order, that did seek to complete the disestablishment of Buddhism first proposed by Kamei and Fukuba precisely in order to enhance the status of 'Shinto,' were just now becoming the focus of discussion elsewhere in government.

The Institutions Unit (*Seidobunkyoku*) was accommodated within the Institutions Bureau (*Seidokyoku*); both were located within the Council of State and both were run by the afore-mentioned Etō Shinpei. Fukuba Bisei was seconded to the Unit, and it came to acquire special responsibility for religious reform.[53] It was here that Fukuba's sweeping shrine reforms of 1871 were formulated, for example, before being passed to the Seidokyoku for discussion by Etō and others like Kanda Takahira (1830–98), Katō Hiroyuki (1836–1916) and Soejima Taneomi (1828–1905). Here too, in spring and summer of 1871, the disestablishment of Buddhism was finalised. It was a process that involved, on the one hand, wiping away the last vestiges of Buddhist influence from the imperial court and, on the other, the breaking of Buddhist sect autonomy.[54]

The first of these was a matter of clarifying the manner in which rites for imperial ancestors were to be conducted in the new Japan; and it was not so much Tokyo as Kyoto where Buddhist influence lingered. In Tokyo, the new *Jingikan* had been fitted out with a Shinto shrine to the imperial ancestors (*kōreisha*), and the emperor had been venerating there regularly in a cycle of rituals implemented in autumn 1869. In Kyoto, however, the Buddhist memorial tablets of the emperor's ancestors remained in the *Onkurōdo* chamber of the palace. Even after the transfer of emperor and capital to the east, Shingon and Tendai monks had continued to perform daily ancestral rites in the *Onkurōdo*. In early summer 1871, the sacred tablets were removed to the Mizuyakushiji temple before they were given permanent residence in the Sennyūji.[55] Other edicts drafted by the bureaucrats in the *Seidobunkyoku* ended other Shingon and Tendai rituals that had continued unchanged till now in the Kyoto palace.

Buddhist sect autonomy, as exemplified in the relations between main temples (*honji*) and branch temples (*matsuji*), had already been fractured: by government interference with shrines that Buddhists had long regarded as their own property, and by the confiscation of Buddhist land holdings. Already in autumn 1870, local government bureaucrats were under orders to take an interest in the appointment of chief temple priests (*jūshoku*) in their regions. And then, in early summer 1871, Tokyo bureaucrats pushed through a shock of new policies that stopped once and for all Buddhism's privileged social position: all branch temples were removed from the control of the head temple, and placed under local government jurisdiction; candidates for the priesthood were to be approved now by local government; and the appointment of chief priests was to be subject now to local government veto, too.[56] Any sense of partnership between state and Buddhism had long since evaporated, and it was only a matter of time, autumn 1871 in fact, before the severance of temple involvement in population registration, threatened by Matsukata some two years before, was made law.

We are all too infrequently privy to the thoughts of *Seidobunkyoku* bureaucrats as they set about dismantling state Buddhism. Etō Shinpei had a reputation for anti-Buddhism in excess even of Matsukata. In a communique to Iwakura in the summer of 1870, for example, he had confessed he looked forward to the day when Buddhism, Confucianism and local cults too, were eradicated from Japan and all people venerated 'Shinto'.[57] Iwakura, with whom

Matsukata's earlier communique had found favour, may well have concurred. Yet the policies Etō oversaw and which Iwakura approved were not obviously calculated to eliminate Buddhism; disestablishment and debilitation were their more modest aim. This may partly be explained by bureaucrats' growing concern at rumours of popular unrest in regions like Toyama, where an especially brutal anti-Buddhist programme had been deployed from autumn 1870.[58] Buddhists in Toyama bombarded the government with petitions, protests and claims, too, that Shinshū sectarians were now out of control. So concerned was the Council of State that it took the unprecedented step of ordering the Toyama authorities in June 1871 to 'adopt a more moderate way to proceed . . . given the rumours [reaching us] of widespread distress and anger'.[59]

It is clear, though, that Etō's ideal of a Buddhist-free Japan was shared by some very senior bureaucrats indeed. There is extant a highly suggestive statement on this matter, penned by Ōkubo Toshimichi (1830–78) and Inoue Kaoru (1835–1915) shortly after the abolition of the domains in early autumn 1871.[60] Ōkubo, a Satsuma bureaucrat, was in charge of the Finance Ministry and, with Kido and Iwakura, was one the most powerful men in government; Inoue, a Chōshū man, was his second-in-command. They begin their statement by insisting that the people are the great foundation of national wealth and prosperity. If there is one man who does not work, then by what logic should others provide for him? How much more is this the case when we are talking of not one but tens of thousands of such people? It is far beyond the capacity of government to provide for such people. Provision can only be made by people themselves through their work. The idle are a burden on the state. Education is vital to the cause of government today but nowhere is it more needed than in the Buddhist question. People of all classes are becoming Buddhist priests and nuns only to idle their lives away, sitting there cross-legged, intoning Sanskrit sutras, begging for clothing and food. We have as many as 500,000 idle clerics in this land of ours. We know of no other nation anywhere that has so many. We must plan ahead for the nation's future and deal more strictly still with applications to the priestly life.[61]

The considered view of Ōkubo and Inoue was that 'given the [sheer numbers] of temples and worship halls and stupas dotted here, there and everywhere, a great Buddhist proscription is not feasible'.[62] Clearly there is an element of regret here: neither man is ready to acknowledge Buddhism has any contribution to make to the new Japan. Absent though are concrete proposals for temple reduction – perhaps the Toyama experience has some explanatory value. Equally striking is the absence of any reference to Shinto; there is no intimation that they were as idle and useless as Buddhists, but none either that, as Matsukata had earlier protested, they needed to be given a chance. The authors concluded with a proposal for restricting access to the Buddhist priesthood to 'those capable of mastering sect doctrine'. This was promptly translated into a Council of State edict which became law in November 1871.[63]

A priest's tale

There were many priests of many persuasions who responded in various different ways to the challenges posed them by the ideologues and bureaucrats of the new Japan. There can have been very few who rejoiced for long. There were Buddhist priests like Shimaji Mokurai, for example, who led the assault on government over the destruction in Toyama. Using his links with Chōshū bureaucrats like Kido, Shimaji came to exert great influence over government religious policy. Shimaji with Kido, Fukuba and Etō put together, as we have seen, a set of proposals that led to the creation of the *Kyōbushō* and the (short-lived) promise of a better future for Buddhists. Shimaji Mokurai, as an adherent of the Nishi Honganji sect of Shinshū Buddhism, had impeccable loyalist credentials; his sect, moreover, had no linkage with shrines and so was untouched by the so-called 'separation edicts' and, since Shinshū typically had little landed wealth, his sect was unscathed by the land confiscation edicts. Shimaji accepted the need for Buddhism to reform drastically, however, which explains why neither he nor any of his fellow Shinshū priests voiced any objection when, in autumn 1872, the *Kyōbushō* announced the destruction of all unoccupied and un-parished temples throughout the land.[64]

Again, there were Shinshū Buddhists of the Higashi Honganji sect like Ishikawa Shuntai (1842–1931). We need to know more about them since their ties to the Tokugawa were deep, and their loyalism always suspect. How did this influence their fate in Meiji? There were other priests like Ugai Tetsujō (1814–1891) of the Jōdo sect, also intimate with the Tokugawa. He had played a leading role in setting up the *Shoshū dōtoku kaimei* (Buddhist Ethical League) in 1869. Its purpose was to unite frequently bickering Buddhists in the face of anticipated government attack, to convince government of Buddhist loyalty, to carry out internal reforms, and to fight off the threat of Christianity.[65] But just a few years later Ugai was to be heard preaching that: 'When it comes to teachings there is only Shinto. The imperial nation is special precisely because it has only one creed.' We need to know how typical a Buddhist Ugai was. Again there are the much under-studied *shugenja*, the mountain ascetics who typified in their practice the religious admix that the 'separation edicts' targeted. The future of the *shugenja* was in doubt long before the ban on Shugendō was issued in 1873. Many *shugenja* functioned as *bettō* or 'Buddhist' priests serving at 'Shinto' shrines and so had already been forced to make impossible choices. We need to study the case of men like Seikōin, a *shugenja* from Yonezawa who campaigned bitterly, but vainly, for the survival of Shugendō practice in his domain, as well as men like Gyokusen'in, another Yonezawa *shugenja* who, with no obvious qualms, abandoned Shugendō practice long before 1873, and as a shrine priest exhibited all the enthusiasm of the convert.[66]

Here, however, my focus falls not on Buddhists or *shugenja* in the wake of the Restoration but on the experiences of a provincial shrine priest. The priest's name is Ono Masafusa – his dates are unknown – and he was the chief priest of the Hachiman shrine in Hirosaki, modern Aomori Prefecture.

Ono is known to have registered as a posthumous disciple of Hirata Atsutane, though we know nothing of how his Hirata attachment might have affected his theological ideas or his ritual practices.[67] We also know that Ono was attached to the immensely influential Yoshida school of Shinto. Ono was 'attached' in the sense that so many shrine priests in late Edo Japan were: he received a license, ritual formulae and clerical garments from the Yoshida family in Kyoto, in return for a fee. Indeed, Ono had personally travelled to the Yoshida shrine in Kyoto some time before the Restoration to purchase these symbols of legitimacy for himself and his shrine.

The Hachiman shrine shared in common with other Edo period shrines the fact that it was located within the compound of a Buddhist temple, and Ono Masafusa was in domain terms of subordinate rank to the clergy of the Tendai temple of Saishōin. As was common practice in Edo Japan, Saishōin priests functioned as celebrants in certain Hachiman rites. Ono's position in Hirosaki was not defined uniquely in terms of subordination, however. For he was one of two *shake gashira* in the domain. *Shake gashira* were elite shrine families responsible for ensuring other shrine priests performed their ritual duties correctly, for organising study meetings and for communicating an array of instructions, many from the Saishōin, to some 90% of the shrine priests in Hirosaki.[68]

Thus it was that in summer of 1869 Ono Masafusa received a set of orders from the domain which he duly passed on to the shrines in his charge. The prolongation of the civil war in north Japan no doubt helps explain why the Restoration government's 'separation edicts' took almost a year to reach Hirosaki. Even so no attempt was made to implement them until the summer of 1869, when Ono was notified that he and the shrine priests in his charge were now freed from the control of the Saishōin and its priests. At the same time, he found himself worshipping Hachiman Daijin and no longer Hachiman Daibosatsu. Henceforth, Ono was to take orders directly from the Hirosaki domain office for shrines and temples; the office re-confirmed his status as *shake gashira* and, by the same token, his personal control over a majority of shrine priests in Hirosaki. In summer 1869, Ono began to tour shrines under his jurisdiction to ensure there were 'no obvious signs of mixing [Shinto and Buddhism]'.[69] His approach was hardly that of the fanatic. In adopting a rather perfunctory stance, it appears Ono was not only in tune with the domain office for ritual and religious affairs, but also with the Tokyo *Jingikan*, presently run by Fukuba Bisei. Some time in summer 1869, Hirosaki received a communication from the *Jingikan* which made it clear that 'regardless of our instructions, what is important is to ensure that, as far as you can manage it, the *appearance* of mixing [Shinto and Buddhism] is avoided' (emphasis added).[70]

Sources do not permit us to follow Ono's activities closely through the remainder of 1869 and 1870. It is clear, though, that he encountered significant problems with shrine rites. Since Buddhist priests were no longer allowed to perform rites before 'Shinto' shrines, of course, and since the prestige of the Yoshida family, whose rules had determined all aspects of shrine protocol, had been obliterated in the first few months of the new era, the question of ritual was pressing. Ono Masafusa assumed that the new era meant the supremacy of the ideas and rituals of Hirata Atsutane, whose disciple we have already noted he was. And so it was in a spirit of anticipation that, in July 1870, he dispatched a colleague to Tokyo to meet Hirata Kanetane, Atsutane's adopted son, in order to learn first hand what the new regulations for shrine rites were to be. In Tokyo Ono's colleague must have discovered that the *Jingikan* was in a state of utter turmoil, rent asunder by the bitterest disputes between Hirata disciples like Kanetane and Fukuba over precisely the question of shrine rites. But Ono's colleague did not apparently give any hint of these troubles to Ono on his return to Hirosaki. He simply reported back that the *Jingikan* had yet to come to a conclusion on rituals for provincial shrines.[71] Ono in frustration decided, as stop-gap measure, to promote Kikke Shinto rites, manuals for which were kept in the Yamana family of priests who served at Hirosaki's Ōkuninushi shrine.[72] It was from about this time, early autumn 1870, that the frustrated Ono Masafusa became seriously anxious about his future.

In summer of the previous year, the central government had persuaded domain lords throughout Japan to make the symbolic gesture of returning their lands to the emperor. The gesture symbolised the idea that all land and all people belonged to the emperor; and that domain lords were no longer autonomous but rather his subjects, especially noble subjects.[73] In early autumn 1870, a series of edicts known as the domain reforms (*hansei*) built upon this centralising premise. Two of their features bear mentioning here: the appointment of new domain bureaucrats, selected for their loyalty to the central government, was one; and radical economic reforms seeking to channel income from domains to central government was another. Both had implications for Ono Masafusa and the shrine priests under his control.

Early autumn 1870 began for Ono with his dismissal from the post of *shake gashira* at the hands of these new and nameless bureaucrats dispatched from Tokyo. His failure to bring any sort of rigour to the implementing of the 'separation' regulations, his concern with 'appearance', was apparently to blame. The domain now declared its intention, in the interests of 'reform', to select new and more vigorous shrine priest leaders on the basis of their 'learning and character'. Ono found himself swiftly reinstated, however, since no replacement of similar learning, wisdom or diligence could be found. His reinstatement coincided, however, with the issue of new, tougher regulations on clarification by the new domain bureaucrats. Their target was not Buddhist temples but shrines.

> *Item*: Where a village has two shrines, and the shrine bedecked with Buddhist symbols functions as the tutelary shrine (*chinju*), then its Buddhist symbols must be removed to the Saishōin temple, and the shrine's 'original' deity reinstated. Alternatively, if the second shrine was always free of Buddhist paraphernalia, it may now be elevated instead to tutelary shrine status. In either case, all domain shrines not now defined as 'tutelary' are to be destroyed.

Item: All shrines that are not tutelary, regardless of whether they have Buddhist or Shinto symbols, are to be destroyed, provided that they are of no great historical consequence. In the event of destruction, the Shinto symbols are to be removed to the closest tutelary shrine.[74]

Ono Masafusa, first freed from the financial and ideological control of the Saishōin temple, then given new 'independence' as *shake gashira*, answering to the domain's office for religious affairs, found himself exposed now to the full force of the government bureaucracy. Clarification in appearance – acceptable before the domain reforms – was no longer an option. Research on this subject needs to be carried out over a wider area, but the probability is that shrine mergers of the sort conducted in Hirosaki were the norm rather than the exception. Anyway, of Hirosaki's 252 non-tutelary shrines 246 were destroyed in 1870. These 1870 reforms were also targeted at Hirosaki's *shugenja* population and the temples and shrines they controlled as *mochimiya*. Where these were shrines, they had to be ceded to the nearest shrine priest but if, as a consequence, a *shugenja* were to suffer financial hardship, he could apply for permission to 'convert' to the Shinto priesthood. Where the shrine was known by a Buddhist name, it could not escape destruction once its treasures had been transferred to a safe place.[75]

How Ono Masafusa responded to this new state of affairs is unfortunately nowhere recorded. He appears to have accepted, rather than resisted. His response to another dimension of central interference in shrine affairs is, however, extant.

At the end of 1870, Ono and some six other shrine priests protested to the *Shajisho* (a new title for the office for religious affairs) at the drastic cut in shrine stipends they faced as a consequence of the economic dimension to the domain reforms. *Saisei itchi*, they reminded the bureaucrats, had been resurrected with the restoration of power to the emperor; the Way of the Gods had been revived, and with it ancient shrine rites. Ono and other Hirosaki priests had complied with central government edicts and put an end to the admixture of Shinto and Buddhism. And yet, Ono now lamented, the effect of the recent domain reforms had been tantamount to the abandonment of *saisei itchi* and the Way of the Gods in both name and fact. 'The new [domain] policy not only flies in the face of ancient principles of government; we are most anxious at how the deities themselves might react to the reforms.'[76] Ono ended his petition to the *Shajisho* with a plea that he be allowed to devote himself, without further interference, to the veneration of Amaterasu and other deities and to prayers for the well-being of all people in the realm. This was impossible without a full restoration of stipends.

The precise nature and extent of the stipend cut imposed on Hirosaki shrine priests is unclear. Tanaka Hidekazu points to a shift from shrines deriving income from their own land-holdings to a system of income disbursement from the domain treasury, but suggests, too, that the blow might have been largely psychological: shrine priests, believing their time had come, found in fact that their financial autonomy was being seriously compromised.[77] Ono appears to have been little comforted by the *Shajisho*'s response. He was not reassured to learn that the economic measures were driven by domain reforms, and that 'no diminishing of respect for the shrines of the domain' was implied.[78] Indeed, three days later Ono protested again, this time to the domain registry office (*Kirokusho*). He and seventeen other petitioners declared their sorrow to be 'insufferable', and renewed their plea to the domain authorities not to relinquish their responsibilities for shrines. 'How can shrine priests be expected to survive? We entreat you to relent [and pay us our stipends in full] if only for this present month!'[79] There was no relenting, however; no special case was made for shrine clergy.

Ono Masafusa re-appears but twice in the historical records of the Restoration in Hirosaki. On both occasions, nearly a year later, his purpose was protest. Much had happened in the interim to affect his position as *shake gashira*. In early 1871 Ono had seen confiscated all the land, tax-exempt and otherwise, that had once belonged to the Hirosaki Hachiman shrine. Six months on, Fukuba's shrine reforms had become law: Hirosaki Hachiman was now a 'site for the performance of state ritual', but if this seemed to guarantee special privileges for the shrine and its priests, the promise was undermined by the ban on heredity at shrines.[80] Ono's very future at the Hachiman shrine now hung precariously in the balance. He had already played the decisive role in determining which of Hirosaki's three hundred or so surviving shrines should be selected for definition as *gōsha* for the newly created administrative units (*kosekiku*) of Hirosaki.[81] This selection of one shrine per unit, which included up to four or five villages, was the premise for the Fukuba-drafted shrine registration (*ujiko shirabe*) which was scheduled to begin immediately.[82]

In November 1871, Ono pleaded with the prefectural authorities – after the abolition of the domains, Hirosaki had become Hirosaki Prefecture – for financial help for priests facing expulsion from their shrines. The prefecture responded meekly to Ono's petition by promising to gather statistics on the plight of shrine priests.[83] This was little comfort since in Hirosaki, as elsewhere, the prefectural government had already begun to select new shrine priests, on the basis of 'talent', from a pool of samurai and established priests, just as Fukuba and indeed Matsukata Masayoshi before him, had advocated. Where priests were fortunate enough to be reappointed, they invariably found themselves displaced from their own localities, and transferred to shrines elsewhere.[84]

A month later the always loyal and diligent, but now bewildered and anxious Ono Masafusa learned his own fate. He was to be dismissed and not relocated elsewhere. He responded the very same day with a lengthy and impassioned memorial to the prefectural authorities.

Thirteen generations have now passed since the time of my ancestor Masatoshi. Throughout that time, . . . my family has served at this shrine and served as the head of all the shrine priest families [here in

247

Hirosaki]. I have served without a moment's neglect in my responsibilities. Now under the present edicts, I find myself for the first time relieved of my responsibility. You talk of reforms; for me, [reforms] mean only profound sorrow.

Ono ends his protest with a moving lament:

In the midst of the reforms [that followed the Restoration] I have been overwhelmed with work. Without a secretary, I have worked late into the night every night; I have arisen before the cock crew at dawn. I have made my way to the prefectural office during the day. Day in and day out I have . . . sought the views of shrine priests, working from dawn till dusk. I can not recall having laboured so hard or suffered so much in all my life.[85]

Regrettably, we get no reaction from Ono Masafusa to the introduction of salaries for shrine priests in early 1872, which gave substance to the new idea that shrines were sites for the performance of state ritual; nor, disappointingly, do we hear voices of dismay when these salaries were abolished exactly a year later. We hear no voices, either of protest or acquiescence, when in 1874 Aomori Prefecture – Hirosaki was so restyled at the end of 1872 – successfully petitioned the central government for permission to carry out a further bout of shrine mergers and priest sackings.

Conclusion

Ideology drove change in Meiji religious institutions, whether it was the Shinto ideology of the emperor's divine descent from the Sun Goddess, that 'explained' Japan's supremacy over other monarchies, nations and cultures, or indeed the secular ideology encapsulated in slogans like 'wealthy nation and powerful army' (*fukoku kyōhei*) or 'parity with all nations' (*bankoku taiji*), that demanded economic restructuring. Both merit more consideration than has been possible in this chapter. I have not discussed, for example, the *senkyōshi*, the early Meiji propagandists and the bitter theological debates that paralysed their activities. The *Kyōbushō* ministry and its ideological policies have perforce remained peripheral to my discussion; likewise the substance of successive waves of ritual reform at centre and provincial periphery, and the ideological and theological implications they entailed.[86] Nonetheless, we have seen enough to conclude that the substance of change was much more complex and problematic than has been credited in Western and Japanese studies to date.

How might we summarise the nature of the dynamic change that affected Japanese religious institutions in early Meiji? Well, the ideologues, men like Fukuba Bisei, and bureaucrats like Ōkubo Toshimichi brought about between them nothing less than the birth on the one hand of 'Shinto,' and the birth on the other of a new entity called Buddhism. By legislating an end to the shrine-temple multiplexes that defined pre-modern Japan, the Meiji government was sanctioning a new Buddhism. It was a Buddhism reduced in size, confined in space – to the private sphere – and cleansed of the shrine cults that had been integral to its social meaning before the Restoration in 1868. Not all Buddhism was of this 'syncretic' sort; the mighty institution of Shinshu Buddhism had never accommodated shrines and deities, and they fared better perhaps in Meiji. Nonetheless, the Meiji era gave birth to a new Buddhism, a Buddhism with its soul removed.

What of Shinto? Meiji Shinto, which Fukuba, Kamei and Ōkuni liked to call 'restoration Shinto,' was built on the ruins of the many and diverse Shinto schools of pre-modern Japan: Yoshida, Shirakawa, Hirata and Kikke Shinto, not to mention multiple shrine cults that existed in various states of tension with these throughout provincial Japan. Ōkuni Takamasa dismissed these schools as quite unsuited to the new age;[87] his restoration Shinto alone was fit to steer Japan through the new menace of the international environment.[88] This Meiji Shinto was a new construct: it was a state-ordered, state-penetrated network of shrines, run by state-appointed clergy who celebrated state-approved rituals that conformed, more or less, to state-sanctioned ideology. Where there had been multiple cults at multiple shrines attached to multiple schools – or to none – with multiple rituals reflecting multiple theologies, there was now just Shinto. This, anyway, was the theory. The turbulent fortunes of this new construct are taken up in subsequent chapters of this book.

Notes

1 Grapard 1984.
2 Grapard 1984: 245.
3 Grapard 1984: 265.
4 Collcutt 1986:144–50.
5 Collcutt 1986: 160–1.
6 Hardacre 1989: 28.
7 Hardacre 1989: 51–9.
8 Ketelaar 1990: 62, 68.
9 Ketelaar 1990: 10. On Ketelaar's approach, see above, pp. 236–7.
10 Takeda (1987: 88–90) provides details of the rise to prominence of Kamei and Fukuba.
11 The *locus classicus* is to be found in Aston 1972: 134.
12 See the essay of Nelly Naumann in this volume.
13 Miyachi 1988: 425–7.
14 The best article on the late Edo spread of Yoshida and Shirakawa influence is Mase 1985.
15 *Kansaikō hōmu yōsho zanpen*, unpaginated manuscript. I am grateful to Professor Sakamoto Koremaru for facilitating my examination of this important source.
16 Nor was the term used in contemporary discourse. *Hanzen* or 'clarification' – as in *shinbutsu hanzen* – which suggests something more creative, was occasionally used. *Bunri* only appears to have become standard in early Shōwa (1926–89) with the publication of the *Meiji ishin shinbutsu bunri shiryō*.

17 See for example Ōkuni Takamasa, *Zonnensho*, and *Gokui zonnensho*. They are reproduced in Yasumaru and Miyachi 1988: 5–6 and 7–10.
18 *Oboe* in Kabe 1906: 464.
19 Ibid: 464–5.
20 Ibid: 465.
21 A *kana*-written notice, styled *Satoshigaki*, and addressed to the domain populace at around this time, spoke of there being one hundred shrines, one per village, when the Kamei family arrived in Tsuwano; that number had now expanded to over one thousand. Ibid., 463. The *Satoshigaki* advised the populace that no benefits would accrue to them by venerating these new deities; indeed, they would suffer divine punishments – disasters would be likely to occur – if they did not change their ways. Ibid: 463–4.
22 Ibid: 466.
23 Miyachi 1988: 425.
24 *Kansaikō hōmu yōsho zanpen*. See also Sakamoto 1993: 105–7.
25 Tokushige 1934: 438.
26 Breen 1996a: 82–9.
27 Miyachi 1988: 425. See also Sakamoto's essay in this volume.
28 Miyachi 1988: 437–41.
29 Ibid: 439–40.
30 Ketelaar 1990: 6. Ketelaar curiously fails to point to any government document citing Buddhism as 'heresy' or any government bureaucrat referring to Buddhism as such.
31 Ketelaar 1990: 9. On p. 8 Ketelaar has Kamei as a disciple of Hirata and on pp. 44–5 as a disciple of Ōkuni.
32 Ketelaar 1990: 44 and 241 n. 1.
33 Murakami 1926 (*zokuhen, ge*): 840–1.
34 The official was Saeki Rima. See Saeki 1926: 1135–6.
35 See above pp. 000.
36 *Katte shidai menzeraresōrō koto.*
37 *Butsudō kie no tomogara wa watakushi ni torimochiisōrō gi wa kurushikarazu sōrō koto.*
38 There were also restrictions placed on the frequency of religious gatherings such as the Shinshū *hōe*. See *Gotenpō oboe* in Kabe 1906: 467.
39 Ōkuni 1862: 7–8. I have written at some length on Buddhism in the thought of Ōkuni Takamasa in Breen 1997: 138–48.
40 Ōkuni 1862: 5. In this passage, Ōkuni compares the skilful Amidists with the 'useless *oshi*' priests who operated out of the Ise shrines.
41 Ōkuni 1862: 32. In 1868, Ōkuni made a point of repeating his conviction that Shinshū Buddhism was now properly Japanese. See Breen 1996c: 192.
42 Breen 1996a: 89–90. On Shimaji, see also Nitta and Sakamoto in this volume.
43 On Fukuba's departure from the *Kyōbushō*, see Takagi 1984: 53.
44 Muraoka 1958: 582.
45 Matsukata 1979: 200–3.
46 Ibid: 203.
47 Ibid: 204.
48 Matsukata 1979: 204. It is of interest, in the context of Ketelaar's assertions, that Matsukata nowhere refers to Buddhism as 'pernicious' or 'heretical'. Matsukata's submission to Iwakura is also contained in Iwakura's collected papers, published by Nihon shiseki kyōkai as *Iwakura Tomomi kankei monjo*. A willingness in government to experiment with Matsukata's radical proposals is suggested by measures soon attempted in Toyama domain, where some 1,500 temples were closed down over night and all priests ordered to take accommodation in the one temple that survived for each sect; if they refused they were to be defrocked.

49 Matsumoto 1935: 426–7.
50 Mori 1935: 287–8.
51 Ibid.
52 Miyachi 1988: 436.
53 Sakamoto 1987: 11.
54 Sakamoto 1983: 231–45.
55 Ibid: 224–7.
56 Miyachi 1988: 439, and Sakamoto 1987: 12–3.
57 Takagi cites from *Etō Shinpei monjo* in Takagi: 1984: 56.
58 It is interesting to note that the anti-Buddhism in Toyama was not matched by any obvious enthusiasm for 'Shinto'. The perpetrator there was the fanatical moderniser Hayashi Tachū.
59 *Toyama gōji no tenmatsu*, cited in Murakami 1926 *jō*: 793–4.
60 The statement is cited in Sakamoto 1987: 13–4.
61 Sakamoto 1987: 13–4.
62 Ibid: 14.
63 Miyachi 1988: 443.
64 Miyachi 1988: 449.
65 The most exhaustive study of this league and its activities is Tsuji 1949: 83–166.
66 Seikōin and Gyokusen'in are both discussed briefly in Tanaka 1988: 249–50.
67 Tanaka 1988: 319.
68 Tanaka 1988: 317–8.
69 Tanaka 1997: 204.
70 Tanaka 1997: 204.
71 Tanaka 1988: 322
72 For a contemporary, and interestingly biased, account of the Jingikan crisis in 1870 see *Shinkyō soshiki monogatari* by the Hirata disciple, Tokoyo Nagatane, cited in Yasumaru and Miyachi eds. 1988: 370–1.
73 Tanaka 1988: 322. Kikke Shinto was founded by Tachibana Mitsuyoshi (1698–1750). It was related theologically to Yoshida Shinto.
74 Matsuo 1986: 92; Haraguchi 1982: 70–7.
75 Tanaka 1997: 209–10.
76 Tanaka 1988: 326–7.
77 Tanaka 1997: 181–2 and 220–1.
78 Tanaka 1997: 182. It should be pointed out that shrine priests were not singled out for stipend cuts. Cuts affected Buddhist clergy and domain samurai too; they were applied by domains the length and breadth of Japan and not merely in Hirosaki.
79 Tanaka 1988: 182.
80 Tanaka 1997: 179.
81 Miyachi 1988: 437.
82 On the *gōsha* regulations see Sakamoto 1994: 172–4. Shrine numbers in Hirosaki are given in Tanaka 1997: 326.
83 Tanaka 1997: 225.
84 Tanaka 1997: 226.
85 Tanaka 1997: 172.
86 Some of these issues I have discussed in a different context in Breen 1996a and 1996b.
87 Ōkuni Takamasa discusses these schools in his *Zonnensho*, which is cited in Yasumaru and Miyachi eds 1988: 5–6.
88 Breen 1996c.

CHAPTER THIRTEEN

Shinto as a 'non-religion': the origins and development of an idea

Nitta Hitoshi

Introduction

The idea that Shinto shrines are 'non-religious' was a principle integral to religious administration under the Meiji constitution of 1889. It is frequently maintained that this principle was adopted by the Meiji government in order to dissolve the obvious contradiction between the Meiji constitution's provision for religious freedom on the one hand, and the reality, on the other, that the state was in fact according to shrines the privileged status of a state religion and enforcing public worship at them. Miyazawa typifies this approach when he writes:

> Shrines were in receipt of a quite different treatment from the state – that of a state religion no less – when compared to other creeds. If [the government] were to regard shrines as religious, in the way that, say, Buddhism and Christianity were so regarded, then it would be in breach of the Meiji constitution's provision for religious freedom. So, shrines were not dealt with as 'religious'. They existed uniquely for the purposes of rituals for ancestors, not at all what was meant by religion under the Meiji constitution. As a consequence, it became possible to regard the according of special treatment to shrines, the acknowledgement of their public status, and enforcement of nation-wide worship at shrines as [lying] beyond the bounds of the constitution's guarantee of religious freedom. Herein consisted the essence of the [Meiji] principle that shrines are non-religious. [Meiji bureaucrats] believed it possible to argue there was not the slightest contradiction between providing for religious freedom in the constitution on the one hand, and granting state protection to shrines and forcing people to worship at them on the other.[1]

This analysis, it transpires, can not, however, be applied to the earlier period in which the Meiji constitution was being formulated. There is no evidence to suggest that those responsible for drafting the Meiji constitution believed that enforcing worship at shrines was anything other than a breach of the constitution's provision for religious freedom. This is clear enough from the position adopted by Privy Council member Torio Koyata (1847–1905) before the Privy Council in June of 1888. When Koyata was addressing the question of whether or not bureaucrats should be required to attend shrine rites, he made reference to the question of the attendance of the general populace, and insisted: 'It should not be said that a person's refusal to worship at the local shrine on the occasion of court rituals contravenes either the *kokutai* or that person's duties [as a citizen].' The authors of the constitution raised no objections to this statement of Torio's. He and Sasaki Takayuki (1830–1910), another member of the Privy Council, demanded that stipulations be set down enforcing shrine attendance on bureaucrats, but the problem remained without solution. The position of Itō Hirobumi (1841–1909), Chairman of the Privy Council, on the matter was that 'Torio's concerns relate to government strategy on religion for the future. Who of us will be around in a hundred years' time? Decisions on this matter can be left up to the politicians of the time. There is no need for us to clarify our position on this now.'[2]

All this appears to demonstrate that the Meiji government had no intention of enforcing worship at shrines, but the question remains whether or not it used the 'shrines as non-religious' argument to accord to shrines privileged treatment and grant them public status. The answer to this – the Ise shrines and Yasukuni shrine are notable exceptions – is an unequivocal no. Irrefutable evidence is to be found in the detail of the *Kankokuheisha hozonkin seido* (Regulations for Funding State Shrines) issued by the Home Ministry in March, 1887. These regulations guaranteed funding for 'state shrines' of the *kanpei* and *kokuhei* sub-categories, but for a period of fifteen years and no more, after which time these shrines would be cast off and forced to depend for their livelihood on 'the respect and faith of worshippers'.[3] These Shrine Fund regulations not only marked the end to state funding of shrines; they also meant shrines were *not* being excluded from the religious freedom provision of the constitution. Interior Minister Sanjō Sanetomi (1837–91), who opposed the Shrine Fund system, said it was 'only natural' that 'the survival of shrines should depend upon the faith of the people'.[4] By this time, the late 1880s, regional shrines of various different categories, which made up the vast majority of the nation's shrines, were already being treated by the government as 'private', and were no longer in receipt of any special protection.[5]

We have to conclude from the foregoing that although the Meiji government adopted the principle that shrines were 'non-religious' in the run-up to the constitution's promulgation, it did *not* seek to except them from the provision for religious freedom; indeed, it sought to end shrines' proximity to the state. If, then, the government's purpose was neither to enforce veneration at shrines, nor to guarantee their special public status, why was it that the government took on board the principle that shrines were non-religious?

In what follows, I trace the origins of this principle back to the early Meiji period, to the writings of the Buddhist priest Shimaji Mokurai (1838–1911), to be precise. I then track its development through to its point of adoption by the Meiji government.

Ritual and religion in early Meiji Japan: the Buddhist perspective

In March 1872, the Meiji government abolished the short-lived *Jingishō* (Ministry for Shinto Affairs), set up the broader-based *Kyōbushō* (Ministry of Religions) in its place, and, in April, launched a nationwide programme of 'edification', spearheaded by Shinto, Buddhist and Confucian propagandists who were given the official title of *kyōdōshoku*. The *Kyōbushō*, and the nationwide propagation by adherents of all three creeds which it was designed to oversee, emerged in response to the failure of an earlier, short-lived edification programme by Shintoists only; it was designed to accommodate the wishes of the Buddhist community. At about the same time, the government, with an eye to its relations with the foreign powers, removed the anti-Christian notice boards. This was not necessarily an indication that the government would now recognise the practice of Christianity in Japan, but it was nonetheless seized on by enlightened thinkers as an opportunity to promote debate about religious freedom. Such was the situation that awaited Shimaji Mokurai on his return from a study tour of Europe in July 1873.[6]

Immediately after his return, Shimaji became involved in a campaign to disentangle Shinshū Buddhists from the *Taikyōin* (Great Teaching Institute). Now, this *Taikyōin* was a privately funded body, set up with government approval in January 1873 at the suggestion of representatives of the majority of Buddhist sects to coordinate propaganda, and to serve as a forum for cross-sect discussion on a range of issues. *Taikyōin* members held rank in the *Kyōbushō*, but the two bodies, one private, one official, were only intended to be loosely linked. The Institute was decked out with a shrine and so served as the sacred centre for the propaganda movement; it also served a forum for the discussion of policy. However, from late 1872, the *Kyōbushō* came increasingly under the sway of the anti-Buddhist influence of Satsuma bureaucrats. The result was that the *Taikyōin* was effectively hijacked by a pro-Shinto lobby, and rapidly metamorphosed into a closely monitored institute for Shinto-propaganda. In Shimaji's view, this *Taikyōin* was none other than part of a Satsuma plot to 'convert Buddhist temples into Shinto shrines and Buddhist clerics into Shinto priests'.[7] Thus it was that he determined to have Shinshū Buddhists extricate themselves from the Institute's Shinto influence, and engage independently in propaganda activities. The idea that Shinto was not a religion was integral to the arguments Shimaji now deployed to support his case.[8]

A particularly striking example of the position adopted by Shimaji and others is to be found in a petition drawn up under Shimaji's influence, but penned in fact by an intimate of Shimaji's, Ōuchi Seiran (1845–1918). The petition was submitted by Ōuchi to the *Sain* (Department of the Left), in June 1874:

> What we know today as religions, Buddhism, Christianity etc., are all universal. These religions talk of the mysteries of the other world in terms of the two realms or the three realms; they explain the laws of

cause and effect, known as karma; they offer faith in a truth beyond the realm of experience and knowledge; they lead the believer, by stages, towards good and away from evil. These religions exist in order to offer guidance as to what is right in this life and to give solace to souls in the next. As for the deities venerated in these creeds, sometimes they are monotheistic, sometimes polytheistic; but they are always mysterious and reside in the other realm.

Their deities are not human beings that have been worshipped as spirits. It is true that some religions [of the world] do venerate people, animals, wood and stones, for example, but these are all barbaric, unenlightened practices, not worthy of serious consideration. Shinto, however, is certainly not of this barbaric order. It has always venerated the imperial ancestors, the sacred spirits over the ages and men of wisdom. It goes without saying that ancestors of the emperor, as well as Kusunoki Masashige with his recent national shrine, Tokugawa Ieyasu with his regional shrine and Date Masamune, Matsudaira Masayuki with their prefectural shrines are all men, who have contributed to national life and are now, as a result, venerated as deities. The principle at work here is not that of the two realms or the three realms, nor does Shinto teach that misfortune is a consequence of evil deeds performed. All it is is the worship of lord and father and the sprits of men who were exemplars of loyalty and piety. How can such a creed give rise to faith beyond the realms of knowledge and experience; how can it afford solace to the souls of the dead?[9]

Ōuchi next takes up the question of Shinto as a religion from the perspective of religious freedom:

If you insist on calling this Shinto a religion – we should really call it not merely a polytheistic religion, but a rag-bag religion . . . – if we attach the name religion to the veneration and worship of our imperial ancestors, then, with respect, what will happen is that those who believe that the sprits of the imperial ancestors repose eternally in the other realm will believe, but those who do not will make a mockery of it. Shinto rituals are national or public in character, and so the state should itself perform rites at national shrines [kankokuheisha]; central government should ensure that local governments perform local rites and require the participation of local people. If however we are to regard Shinto as a religion, it then becomes a question of the people's freedom whether or not they believe. You can try all you wish to make people have religious faith, but if the people do not have it of their own accord, all your efforts will be in vain.[10]

Ōuchi's conclusion is that the unity of ritual and state (saisei itchi) is a precious relic from ancient times, but that the state must distance itself from religion, as opposed, that is, to ritual. He makes the following practical proposals:

Shrine priests' business is to engage with ritual; they should be placed under the jurisdiction of the *Shikiburyō* (Bureau for Court Ritual) and be required to devote themselves exclusively to rituals and ceremonies . . . As for religion, the court should set limits and provide some sort of legal framework; these should be adhered to under all circumstances. Preaching and propaganda should be a matter for the free choice of adherents, and should come under the supervision of the head temple. If there are breaches in the law, then we must punish the guilty according to that law. Why the need for a special department or office for these matters? If the judgement is that the situation has not yet proceeded [to the point where this is an option], then an office, styled the Bureau [as opposed to Ministry] of Religions, might be placed within the *Dajōkan* (Supreme Council of State), and be given charge of supervising these matters. It should exist alongside the *Shikiburyō* and not be confused with it. If this [separation] is guaranteed, then shrine priests and Buddhist clerics will not be distracted from their true paths, and ritual and religion will be placed equally under imperial jurisdiction.[11]

In other words, Ōuchi was deploying arguments about religious freedom and Shinto as non-religious in order to effect the separation of Buddhist and Shinto administrative controls – which, in practical terms, meant the dissolution of the *Taikyōin* and the *Kyōbushō*; recognition of Buddhists' right to proselytise unhindered; and, finally, the restoration of autonomy to the Buddhist community.[12]

Ritual and religion in early Meiji Japan: the Shinto perspective

Just as the Shinshū Buddhists were launching their campaign to opt out of the Great Teaching Institute, the Shinto community was embarking on a movement of its own to have resurrected the *Jingikan*, a Shinto office that, for a brief period after the Restoration (1869–71), occupied the highest position in the state bureaucracy, symbolising the special intimacy between state and Shinto affairs. (It, in turn, had been replaced by the aforementioned *Jingishō*, Ministry for Shinto Affairs.) A good indication of the Shinto agenda is to be found in a memorial sent by the Chief Priest of the Ise shrines, Tanaka Yoritsune, to the Ministry of Religions minister, Shishido Tamaki (1829–1901) in May of 1874. Tanaka's petition, styled 'On the need to resurrect the *Jingikan*, and establish within it bureaus for propaganda and imperial mausolea,' puts the case for the most intimate of relations between government and religion:

The relationship of religion to state is akin to that between the two wheels of a cart. That you cannot make do with one and not the other goes without saying. Religion defines the Way and aids government;

256

government implements the Way and protects religion. When government and religion are in total harmony, there can be no better way to rule the realm and comfort the people . . . Russia is a case in point: its sovereign controls sectarians; he occupies a similar situation to the Pope in Rome, with the result that state law and church law are indivisible. Government and religion are one and the people, as a result, support and revere the sovereign. This is poles apart from what happens in other countries. It is, indeed, only with the aid of religion that the Russians are able to lord it over the globe and subsume neighbouring territories.[13]

The focus of Tanaka's state-religion argument here is, of course, Shinto. His proposal is for the state to protect Shinto and deploy it as a means of unifying the spirit of the nation. To this end, the state should resurrect the *Jingikan*, and establish within it a *Kyōdoryō* (Bureau for Religions), to supervise the activities of Shinto and Buddhist propagandists, and set up, too, a *Shoryōryō* (Mausoleum Bureau), which would oversee the mausolea and tombs of emperors and other members of the imperial family since the Age of the Gods. However, it is clear that in his discussions of state and religion, Tanaka is not placing Shinto in the same sort of religious bracket as Christianity:

> The unity of Shinto ritual and government (*saisei itchi*) is the prerequisite of respect for the deities and control of the populace; it is the reason why the polity (*kokutai*), symbolised in the unbroken line of emperors, has thrived throughout history. [The unity of ritual and state] is not to be spoken of in the same breath as the Western example, where the ideal is the separation of religion and state.[14]

The argument presented here for distinguishing Shinto from other creeds can be found replicated in the petitions of other Shintoists as well. At this juncture, however, the nub of the problem was the need for proximity between government and Shinto, and so there was little effort made to argue for such proximity on the grounds of Shinto's special characteristics or its non-religious quality.[15]

The government found itself caught between arguments for the separation of state and religion put by Shimaji Mokurai and other Buddhists, and the case for a new proximity between state and religion proposed by Shintoists like Tanaka Yoritsune. Gradually, however, the government inclined toward the Shimaji Mokurai position. The following memorial submitted by the *Sain* to the *Seiin* (Council of State) in March 1875, advocating the abolition of the Ministry of Religions, is the clearest evidence that this was so.[16]

> The *Kyōbushō* and Buddhist and Shinto propagandists (*kyōdōshoku*) should be abolished; the administration of ritual should be placed under the jurisdiction, as before, of the *Shikiburyō*; shrine priests should be

entrusted with ritual at national and regional shrines. Preaching should be left to those who wish to engage in it. People should be free to select which religion, if any, they wish to adhere to; this will not be a matter for the court or for the law. The Two Principles [of respect for the deities and love of country, and devotion to the emperor and respect for the law] should be inserted into the laws of the land, and adhered to by all preachers. We propose the Home Ministry take charge of shrine priests and Buddhist clerics; their status and their control should be entrusted to their local city or prefectural authority.

It should be clear enough from the wording here that this is very close indeed to the arguments of Shimaji Mokurai and other Buddhists. The *Dajōkan*, to whom this proposal was put, made no decision as yet to abolish the *Kyōbushō*, but in May of the same year, 1875, it did dissolve the *Taikyōin* and permit all denominations to preach unhindered, on condition that they adhered to the Three Principles, declared when the *Kyōbushō* launched its edification programme back in spring, 1872 ('respect for the deities and love of country; clarifying the way of nature and man; devotion to the emperor and respect for the law'). Moreover, in November 1875, the so-called *Shinkyō no jiyū hoshō no kudatsu*, a verbal commitment to religious freedom, was issued. In it the government recognised religions' freedom to propagate, and at the same time explained why it reserved to itself the right to appoint the *kyōdōshoku* as before and have government officials oversee *kyōdōshoku* exams. The reason it gave was that it still hoped religionists would not impede politics, but rather actively support the government.[17] In this way, the Shinshū campaign to extricate itself from the *Taikyōin* proved a success; the Shintoists' campaign to resurrect the *Jingikan*, by contrast, floundered. The Shintoists now changed tack, and responded by creating a privately funded office, the *Shintō jimukyoku*, in order to facilitate cooperation amongst all Shintoists in propagation.

The dissolution of the *Taikyōin*: its significance

How might we assess the significance of the *Taikyōin*'s dissolution in terms of the 'Shinto as non-religious' principle?

Firstly, the dissolution of the *Taikyōin* and the government's recognition of Buddhists' freedom to propagate demonstrate that the government was no longer susceptible to naive arguments demanding a new proximity of state and religion. If Shintoists were to be successful in strengthening their links with government, they would have to come up with some strategy for side-stepping the whole state-religion question. Secondly, the success of the Shinshū campaign was proof that the idea of 'Shinto as non-religious' was one of great benefit to the Shinshū Buddhist strategists. In March 1875, Ōtani Kōson, the Chief Abbot of the Nishi Honganji sect of Shinshū Buddhism, dispatched a memorial, penned in fact by Shimaji, to Prime Minister Sanjō Sanetomi; it was the first 'public' declaration by the sect of the 'Shinto as non-religious' principle.[18] Kōson's memorial declared publicly that Shinshū would insist upon its right to unhindered proselytising, but that it would never slight the emperor, the foundress of the imperial line (Amaterasu, the Sun Goddess) or the spirits of the imperial ancestors. It was this declaration that swung the argument in the Buddhists' favour, since it meant that, from the government's point of view, it could permit the unhindered propagation of Buddhism without destroying that hallowed principle of the unity of ritual and government.[19] Hereafter, Shinshū adhered to this principle in the pursuit of its objectives.

Thirdly, it is important to note that the Shinshū espousal of the principle of 'Shinto as non-religious' was not a recognition of Shinto as it actually was. Shinto was, in fact, not simply something which, to quote Ōuchi's earlier cited petition once more, 'venerated the imperial ancestors, the sacred spirits over the ages and men of wisdom.' Many shrine priests were presently active propagating Shinto as formulated by such men as Hirata Atsutane (1776–1843). In other words, Shimaji's principle ignored Shinto as it actually was, and sought to reconstruct it as a quasi-Confucian system of morality. Inevitably, the potential was always present for Shinshū Buddhists to rely on the construct to attack the reality, and so achieve the overhaul of Shinto along lines they themselves desired. However, the Shinshū purpose in doing away with the *Taikyōin* was simply to achieve its right to proselytise unhindered and so, at this juncture, no demands were actually made for the restructuring of Shinto or the reform of its relationship to the state.

The next point is that, after the dissolution of the *Taikyōin*, the government shifted the thrust of its religious policy in a new direction: it left the business of religious dogma and propaganda to the *kanchō* and refrained from direct involvement in these matters.[20] It did, however, retain the right to appoint and dismiss the propagandists, the afore-mentioned *kyōdōshoku*, and it did so in order that it might 'help the various sects to be an aid rather than a hindrance in matters of administration'.[21] In January 1877, this shift in direction was reflected in the abolition of the *Kyōbushō* which had been directly responsible for doctrine and propaganda. Responsibility for Shinto and Buddhism was now transferred to an office, the *Shajikyoku* or Bureau for Shrines and Temples, within the Home Ministry (*Naimushō*).[22] The Buddhist campaign to opt out of the *Taikyōin* and the Shinto campaign to resurrect the *Jingikan* coincided not only with the potentially disastrous Korean episode, when the government was brought to the brink of collapse in a dispute over whether and when to dispatch an embassy to Korea which would risk provoking war, but also with a wave of samurai rebellions, which seriously tested the government's nerve. Far from supporting the government, religion at this time, owing to the divisions it was itself causing, simply added to the government's woes. It would hardly be surprising if the government began now to doubt the value of religion and to seek to distance itself from it.

In later years, Itō Hirobumi, Chairman of the Privy Council, who at this time was a government councillor (*sangi*), addressed a gathering of the Privy Council with these words:

In the West, constitutional policies have been practised for more than a millennium. The people are thoroughly acquainted with this system and, what is more, they have a religion which serves as its axis [the point about which the whole system turns, as it were]. The same religion has deeply permeated the hearts of the people; all people are unified by it. But in our country, the strength of religion is insignificant. There is no creed that might serve as the axis for the nation. Buddhism once, at the height of its powers, drew together the hearts of the people high and low, but it is now on the decline. Shinto, for its part, is run according to the teachings of its imperial founders, but it quite lacks the ability to unite the minds of the people as a religion. In Japan, it is the imperial institution alone that can serve as the axis [about which the nation might revolve].[23]

Again, in July of 1884, the Home Ministry, *a propos* of some proposals for the reform of the *kanchō* system, had occasion to reflect that, 'There have been many instances of damage done by the government's direct involvement with religion, and no sign yet of any benefit accrued.'[24] It was this sort of understanding that prepared the ground for the government's espousal of the principle of Shinto as non-religious.

The fifth significance of the dissolution of the *Taikyōin* in terms of the 'Shinto as non-religious' principle is that Shinshū's declaration of its intention to accept, as integral to the polity (*kokutai*), 'veneration for the emperor and reverence (which arises from that) for Amaterasu the Sun Goddess as the imperial ancestress,' appears to have provided the government with a guiding principle for coping with the fraught state-religion problem. Thus, the aforementioned memorial of Ōtani Kōson must assume real importance in any consideration of modern Japan's state-religion problem.

The sixth and final point concerns the government's retention of the right to appoint and dismiss *kyōdōshoku*. Under regulations issued in April and July 1874, all temple abbots and anyone wishing to preach had to undergo training, pass tests and be ranked as *kyōdōshoku*, and so the implication of the government's retention of this right to appoint them was that it had won the *de facto* right to appoint and dismiss all Buddhist priests. It would be technically possible, under these April and July 1874 regulations, for the government to deny the right of a given head temple, say, to dictate to temples ostensibly under its control. In fact, this potential for interference had caused major problems in the process of dissolving the *Taikyōin*.[25] As a result, Shinshū, having freed itself from the *Taikyōin*, began to seek the reform of the *kyōdōshoku* system itself, in order to claw back its autonomy.[26]

Shrine priests and the idea of Shinto as a 'non-religion'

Shrine priests who till now had been in competition with Buddhists prelates and indeed played second fiddle to them set up a private office called the *Shinto Jimukyoku* in March of 1875, and took the first step in launching a Shinto propaganda campaign. However, no sooner was this *Jimukyoku* established than arguments began over which deities should be enshrined in the *Jimukyoku* shrine. Should the deity Ōkuninushi be enshrined alongside the three creator deities of Ame no Minakanushi, Takami-musubi and Kami-musubi and Amaterasu? Personnel problems within the office exacerbated the arguments, and a tear began to appear in the fabric of the Shinto world (the so-called *saijin ronsō* or 'Pantheon Dispute'). This dispute reached its peak in 1880, and in January of the following year a national Shinto Conference was convened to debate the pantheon problem. It proved nigh on impossible, however, to bring about a reconciliation between the two opposing sides in the dispute, and in the end delegates agreed to find a solution by inviting along government bureaucrats whose proposals the emperor would then approve.[27]

During the course of the Pantheon Dispute, Shinto priests came to argue the need for the establishment of a *Taikyōkan* (Great Propaganda Office). Motoori Toyokai was one such. He protested that the reason for the theological confrontation in the Pantheon Dispute was that Shinto propaganda had been entrusted 'uniquely to devotees and the intelligentsia,' and that the only way to prevent disputation was for the emperor himself to assume charge.[28] 'He should establish a Great Propaganda Office in the government, and so assert his supreme rights over theology and politics.'[29] The concrete details of this *Taikyōkan* were set out in a joint proposal penned by the Chief Priests of the Ise and Izumo shrines, Tanaka Yoritsune and Senge Takatomi, in February of 1881. Tanaka and Senge envisaged the appointment of a propaganda supremo, to be styled *hakuō*, who would run the Office, assist the emperor in the religious dimension to his duties and occupy a rank senior to that of the Prime Minister. This officer would, in practical terms, exercise supreme control over religious matters. Additionally, as the emperor's representative, he would assume responsibility for court ritual and for the veneration of the deities of heaven and earth and the spirits of the imperial ancestors. He would also have overall charge of shrine priests and propagandists, their various propaganda activities and their appointments. 'As the heart is to the arm and the arm to the finger,' so should this office assume control of all other teachings and set out rules and regulations for the conduct of religious practice; it should draw up rules of etiquette for the various rites in the life cycle; it should distribute a calendar to advise citizens of the main calendrical events, and it should sing the praises of citizens who proved themselves the paragons of such virtues as loyalty, piety and chastity.[30]

It was the idea of Shinto as a non-religion that provided the theoretical basis for the position now adopted by Tanaka and Senge:

We humbly submit that the fundamental teachings of Japan constitute the unparalleled Great Way founded by the imperial ancestors; they are the great rules and rites which Ninigi no Mikoto has to perform in place of the imperial ancestress, Amaterasu Ōmikami. The fact that the words for both 'ritual' and 'government' are read *matsurigoto* in Japanese constitutes a great teaching, a constant reminder of origins. This teaching is the source of all the teachings of the world. This teaching has been inherited by emperors over the ages and there was never a change to its substance. Consequently, there is no distinction between deity and emperor: the Way of the kami (*shintō*) and the Way of the emperor (*kōdō*) are one and the same. Here lies the essence of Japanese teachings; all ethics springs from here; the foundation of the *kokutai* lies here. These teachings we also know as *kannagara no michi*, the Way that sprang from the deities and is coeval with the deities. It should be clear as day that this *kannagara no michi* is not to be spoken of in the same breath as those religions that were founded by the wisdom of men.[31]

Motoori Toyokai argued in the same vein:

The Shinto of Japan is vastly different to other religions; Shinto is the Way of the emperors; the Way of the emperors is none other than the *kannagara no michi* . . . Shinto is not like other creeds; it is the Great Way that came into being with the abundant reed plains that are this earth and constitute the ancient name of Japan. From the ancient period, Buddhism arrived in Japan; in the early modern period, Christianity infiltrated, too. If one were to cling to the ancient way of doings things in such circumstances, there was a distinct possibility that it would fail to respond adequately to the new age. So it was to defend against Christianity and to assert the national dignity that Shinto had no choice but to theorise about the other realm. But in origin Shinto made a clear distinction between this realm and the next. This is clear from our scriptures. It is not something we have now invented. After the Restoration, there was a move to establish Shinto-style funerals. Funeral rites already existed. We had therefore to theorise about the souls in the other realm, as well. This appears not to be that much different from other religions of the world. There were some Shinto funerals in ancient times; these were embellished to reach the state they are in today.[32]

To quote the words of Sasaki, what the petitioners were here insisting was that 'Shinto was synonymous with the Imperial Way; and so it was not possible to view it as one with other religions. Shinto was above those other religions and so was non-religious.'[33] This argument was different to that promoted by Shimaji Mokurai and others when they spoke of Shinto as non-religious in the 1870s. What Tanaka, Senge and Motoori were doing was to take Shinto as it was, 'relabel' it, as it were, as non-religious, and so seek its fusion with the state. Their understanding was that Shinto priests should continue to engage in proselytising and funerals.

The Shinto community found itself having to push to the fore the principle of Shinto as non-religious – albeit in a version modified from that of the Buddhists – because the whole issue of the separation of state and religion had become so firmly established. Motoori, in his earlier cited petition, left little doubt about the pervasiveness of this issue when he said, 'There are three shrines in the imperial palace; it is to conform to the ideal of unity of ritual and government (*saisei itchi*) that the Bureau for State Ritual takes charge of imperial ritual [performed there]. If Shinto were just another religion, then these rituals would not be able to take place.'[34] Again, his view expressed at the national Shinto Conference was that 'If Shinto is taken simply as a religion, then as journalists have already pointed out, this Shinto conference would not have involved the government.'[35]

Buddhist development of the Shinto as non-religious argument

The confusion in the ranks of Shintoists following the Pantheon Dispute provided an ideal opportunity for Shinshū prelates to achieve their erstwhile goals and to contain the Shinto community. So it was that they embarked now upon a vigorous campaign of petitions and memorials to the central government. Representative is the document sent by two Higashi Honganji prelates, Atsumi Keien and Suzuki Ejun to the Home Ministry chief, Matsukata Masayoshi, in March of 1881.[36] They began by confirming the essentially non-religious quality of Shinto. 'It goes without saying,' they insisted, 'that the Way of Shinto is none other than the great Way of rule and ritual founded when the imperial ancestors of heaven determined the position of the emperor and determined, too, that it should be entrusted to the descendants of the Sun Goddess, Amaterasu.' They then drew the Minister's attention to developments in the aftermath of the restoration. The *Jingikan* had been resurrected; an office of Shinto propagandists (*Senkyōshi*) had been set up; then, when the *Kyōbushō* (Ministry of Religions) had taken over, all shrine priests and Buddhist clerics had been appointed as *kyōdōshoku*, state propagandists. Then what happened was that Shinto 'churches' were created and allowed to perform Shinto funerals; they preached not only about the virtues of the kami deities of ancient times and about this realm, but about the other realm and karma, as well; they came to pontificate on all manner of abstract ideas. Their preaching extended beyond the proper boundaries of ritual and politics, and they came to assume the guise of a religion, with the result that 'even under the registration law, Shinto was granted the status of a religion.'[37] The petitioners, having noted the process whereby Shinto became a religion, offered the following somewhat menacing appraisal:

If Shinto is defined as a religion, it would be impossible to take any action against people who did not believe in it since [in civilised nations of the world] government has no right to interfere in the beliefs of its people. It is perfectly possible that people as a result will end up slighting the polity (*kokutai*) . . . Before our very eyes the influence of Christianity is growing in strength day by day. Their followers believe in one deity alone. The deities venerated in other creeds are all dismissed by them as pernicious. As a consequence if Shinto is regarded as a religion, it is my humble view that they will end up slighting the imperial ancestors of heaven.[38]

The petitioners go on to take issue with the arguments of the Shintoists themselves. Shinto has the appearance of a religion; in legal terms it is a religion; two Shinto sects, Kurozumi-ha and Shūsei-ha, are supervised by their own *kanchō*, and they are religions in anybody's terms.[39] Who, then, can believe the Shintoists when they declare – as they do – that Shinto is non-religious? From the petitioners' perspective, the Shintoists' declarations ignored the reality. At the end of the petition, Atsumi and Suzuki set out their demands. The entire system of *kyōdōshoku* should be abolished; anything that made Shinto appear as religious should be prohibited; there should be a distinction in government between the officers responsible for (Shinto) rites (to be known as *daiseisai*) and for Buddhism (to be known as *sōkan*). Under the supervision of these officers, Shinto priests should devote themselves uniquely to the celebration of ritual; Buddhist priests should be allowed to preach their own teachings.

In this way, a clear demarcation should be enforced between the realms of state ritual and religion. Only in this way will it be possible to end the [twin] evils of the desecration of the state, and slights to the imperial foundress.[40]

What the petitioners were demanding, then, was the abolition of the *kyōdōshoku* system, according to which shrine priests became Shinto proselytisers, the proscription of Shinto funerals – the expulsion of Shinto, in other words, from the arena of religious practice – and the distinction, in administrative terms, of Shinto and Buddhism.[41] Only thus could Shinto and religion flourish side by side and serve to support the state. 'In this way, with Shinto severing its ties with religion, and Shinto being restored to pure ritual, adherents of all religions will be able to venerate and worship [at shrines]; for all ages to come, Shinto will be inseparable from the roots of the imperial regime. It will then be the task of religions to discuss abstract [theological] ideas, to stop sin before it is committed; to prevent evil before it occurs; to do what it does best and so aid the progress of the Imperial Way throughout the realm.' In other words, at this juncture, the Shinshū Buddhists employed the idea that Shinto was not a religion to effect a change in the substance of Shinto as it was.

The government response

The government thus found itself in a dilemma, caught between two opposing views of the 'Shinto is non-religious' argument, but gradually it leaned toward the Shinshū position. In July 1881, the Home Minister, Matsukata Masayoshi, proposed to Prime Minister Sanjō Sanetomi that 'unless there were a clear separation of religious teachings from education on the one hand and ritual on the other, there would be real confusion in the relationship between religion and state and all manner of administrative problems.'[42] The Home Ministry, at around this time, began to reconsider the whole question of religious administration. The second volume of the collected papers of Yamada Akiyoshi, (1844–92) held in the Imperial Household Archive, give a clear idea of what sorts of issues were being addressed by the Home Minister in its reappraisal:

1 Ritual before the deities (*kamimatsuri*) should be the responsibility of the state; religion (*kyōhō*) should be left to the beliefs of private individuals.
2 Official ritualists must be appointed and placed under the supervision of the *Shikiburyō* (Bureau for State Ritual).
3 Official ritualists are not to serve additionally as *kyōdōshoku*.
4 *Kyōdōshoku*, both Shinto and Buddhist, are to be under the joint supervision of the Home Ministry.
5 A centre for the study of ritual practice will be established.
6 The government will no longer be involved in the appointment of *kyōdōshoku*; the respective *kanchō* will assume responsibility.
7 The *Shintō Jimukyoku* will be abolished.
8 The Home Ministry will make an administrative distinction between shrine and temple affairs within its Bureau for Shrines and Temples (*Shajikyoku*). In the future, all matters relating to shrine administration will shift to the *Shikiburyō*.[43]

The Yamada papers include the following revealing statement about its reasons for addressing these particular issues:

It is argued that Shinto is non-religious, but after the Restoration the *senkyōshi* office of Shinto proselytising was established; its officials guided Buddhist believers and won not a few converts from Buddhists ranks. It was formerly the practice to deal with deaths in the imperial family with Buddhist rites; these, however, were changed [with the Restoration] and funerals were conducted according to Shinto rites. For such reasons, it is not easy to say, simply, that Shinto is not a religion. As a result, the state should assume unique responsibility for rituals, since they do not belong to Shinto's religious dimension, and require government officials to celebrate them. Shinto, in its religious dimension, should be supervised as a religion together with other religious matters in government without any formal distinction between Shinto and

Buddhism. If we proceed in this fashion, then ritual and religion will be clearly distinct, and there will be no breach in established practice.[44]

It is clear enough then that the position being followed here is essentially that of the Shinshū Buddhists. In December 1881, Yamada Akiyoshi himself, shortly after taking over as Home Minister from Matsukata, proposed to Sanjō Sanetomi that shrine priests should devote themselves exclusively to shrine ritual and have no business at all with anything remotely 'religious'.[45] He cites four main reasons for this position. Firstly, even though all shrine priests had been appointed *kyōdōshoku* in 1872, there was a fundamental difference between their religious role as *kyōdōshoku* and their ritual role as shrine priests; second, such a position was untenable in this day and age when it was essential that all religions be treated on an equal footing; third, there is every possibility that if ritual and religion remain intertwined, then other religious disputes, like the earlier Pantheon Dispute, could recur; lastly, *kyōdōshoku* are exempted from military service, which means that, at present, the priests serving at the 170,000 state shrines are all exempt; this can not be wise policy.

Reforms were evidently called for. Yamada suggested they should be of this order: no shrine priests should hold *kyōdōshoku* positions; an office for the supervision of shrine priests should be set up and the Home Ministry should supervise the now distinct *kyōdōshoku*. As a first concrete measure, Yamada attached to his missive to Sanjo a draft notice ordering all shrine priests to refrain from propaganda activities and from the performance of funerals. In subsequent discussions about this draft notice, it was decided that, for the time being, priests at prefectural shrines, municipal shrines and those of all lower ranks should be allowed to continue performing funerals as *kyōdōshoku*; the ban on both funerals and propaganda should be placed only on priests at state shrines of the *kanpei* and *kokuhei* categories. This was a major set back for Yamada. It appears that opposition came from Kuroda Kiyotsuna (1830–1917) and Mishima Michitsune (1835–88), two high ranking bureaucrats from Satsuma, who pointed out that all the *kyōdōshoku* in Satsuma were shrine priests – there were no Buddhists in Satsuma at all – and that if the ban on shrine priests' performance of funerals were extended throughout the shrine priest community, there would be no one left there to perform funerals.[46]

Scaled down though it was, Home Ministry communication no. 7 of January 1882 on the separation of *kyōdōshoku* and shrine priests was not insignificant. Its significance was, in a nutshell, that the government was adopting publicly the Shinshū version of the 'Shinto as non-religious' argument. For the government, Shinto was now ritual and ritual alone; proselytising and funerals lay in the separate realm of religion. The government did not take the extreme version of the Shinshū position, which held that all religious aspects of Shinto should be cut away; rather, it divided Shinto into two components, shrines and sectarian Shinto; it sought thereby to achieve a happy compromise between its proclamation of May 1871 that shrines were the sites of state ritual on the one hand, and the separation of state and religion on the other. So it was that in

May of the same year, 1882, six Shinto sects were allowed the same freedom of practice as that granted Buddhists.[47] The net effect was that the government was adopting a policy not so much of 'Shinto as non-religious' but of 'shrines as non-religious.'[48]

Shrine priests themselves were up in arms at this latest government policy, but their protests achieved nothing.[49] In August of 1884, the government announced the abolition of the entire *kyōdōshoku* system and advised religionists that henceforth 'the appointment of temple abbots and the promotion of prelates were the responsibility of the *kanchō*.' The next thing government did was to take action against the state shrines of *kanpei* and *kokuhei* status and put an end to government commitment to finance their upkeep for good. In 1887, it implemented the *hozonkin* system (see above p. 251) which promised financial support for these shrines for a limited fifteen year period, after which they would be required to depend for their survival on the faith of the people. This left shrine priests in a dilemma, and some responded by accepting shrines as non-religious so as to make a come-back; they pinned their hopes on a movement which, from 1889, they launched to secure once more the resurrection of the *Jingikan*. This campaign was promoted above all by priests from shrines of prefectural and municipal status, and they made use of the legal loophole they espied in the fact that they had no clear status in law. In legal terms, the abolition of the *kyōdōshoku* meant only the disappearance of public proselytisers who, till then, had been appointed by the state. The point is that shrine priests at prefectural and municipal shrines could interpret Communication no. 7 as sanctioning their involvement in proselytising and funerals in a private capacity.

For the Shinshū priests, of course, this constituted a breach of the 'shrines as non-religious' position; as for the government, it too no doubt wished to stop such practice not least in order to prevent trouble between priests at prefectural and municipal shrines and Buddhists, but it could not ignore the facts, namely that these shrine priests were making a living out of preaching and performing funeral rites. That they were doing so was at least in part because, under regulations of 1872, the state had confiscated shrine land which, till then, had provided priests with a means of existence. If the government were now to forbid these religious activities totally, it would have to provide some sort of financial support for the priests concerned. Yet, there were 170,000 or so shrines that would require such support and the government could simply not cope. The question of what to do with these shrines was a major headache for the government. It was against this background that shrine priests now determined, of their own accord, to stop their proselytising and funeral involvement and to carry through the idea of 'shrines as not religious' to its logical conclusion, and so strengthen their ties with the state.[50] This they would do by campaigning for a resurrection of the *Jingikan*.

It is clear from the foregoing that the arguments defining Shinto as non-religious were the creation of Shinshū Buddhists and in no way confirmed the situation in which Shinto actually found itself. Rather the Buddhists sought to query the relationship between state and Shinto and, indeed, the very existence of Shinto; they sought to pose a problem. The idea that *shrines* were not religious sought to give meaning to the new situation and to confirm it. The Shinshū Buddhist objectives of self-protection, of the securing and expansion of their freedoms, constituted a leitmotiv throughout.

Conclusion

I should like to make two final points by way of conclusion. It should be apparent from the foregoing that the Shinshū sect of Buddhism played a key role in determining the course of Meiji religious policy. The activities of the Shinshū sect have been already noted in numerous studies of the period, but the tendency has been to define the Shinshū role in terms of resistance to government religious policy, and not as a key player in policy formulation. Why might that be? It may have something to do with the fact that the linkage between Shinshū Buddhists and Chōshū domain from before the Meiji Restoration has been overlooked. A more important reason still is the spell cast by that phrase 'State Shinto.' State Shinto has become a keyword in discussions of Meiji religious policy by scholars of religious history and the constitution. It is the unspoken premise of discussions of 'State Shinto' that either the state or Shinto must constitute the focus of religious policy. As long as the analysis centres on State Shinto, it is perhaps inevitable that any facts which do not seem to fit with the idea are either consciously or unconsciously distorted.

The origins of the phrase 'State Shinto,' its popularisation and its application to the study of the whole of prewar religious history are to be found in the so-called *Shintō shirei* ('Shinto directive') issued by the American army of Occupation, in which the phrase is used and defined. In other words, the expansion of the meaning of State Shinto and its application are not a natural consequence of scholarly endeavour so much as a result of the occupation policies. To borrow the words of Yasumaru Yoshio, State Shinto has towered above students of religious history and of the constitution as the supreme principle before which they all must genuflect, and concerning which they all must compete to demonstrate how effective they can be in its service.[51] State Shinto is, indeed, a case of 'in the beginning was the word; all creation came from the word; nothing came into being that was not of the word.'

My second concluding point concerns a suggestion of Miyazawa's. Miyazawa begins by saying that 'It is of interest that the principle of shrines as non-religious, later and to a limited extent, had the good fortune to play its part in guaranteeing a bare minimum of religious freedom.' He then goes on: 'Towards the end of the period during which the Meiji constitution was operational, the linkage between shrines and the state was strengthened and, at the same time, it was argued mainly by scholars, intellectuals and the military who came under their influence that shrines were religious; they constituted the [foundation of the] emperor's religion, and so all Japanese had to revere shrines.' At this point, says Miyazawa, the government began to lend an ear to Buddhists and other religionists who attacked these arguments; they sought to suppress the arguments and once more championed the idea of shrines as non-religious:

> It could be said that this [later usage of the 'shrines as non-religious' argument] was different from the role originally anticipated of it, and from its actual function under the Meiji constitution, and that it was at least to some degree well disposed to the idea of religious freedom. Or rather, if that is going too far, that the [later usage of the shrines as non-religious argument] was not as antagonistic toward religious freedom as it had previously been.[52]

I am not an expert on religious policy under the last years of the constitution, and can make no informed comment about the facts Miyazawa refers to here. But, if Miyazawa is correct in what he says, then it was surely not a case of being different from 'the role originally expected of [the shrines as non-religious position],' but a case, rather, of that being precisely the role anticipated of it.

Notes

1 Miyazawa 1971: 348–9.
2 Shimizu 1973: 244–6.
3 Kankokuheisha were shrines defined under regulations issued in 1871. They were so called because of the funding they were entitled to from central and provincial government. See also, Nitta 1997: 16.
4 Nitta 1997: 169.
5 This had ended in 1873. See Nitta 1997: 106.
6 On Shimaji's experiences in the West, see Fukushima 1977.
7 'Jōmon: Kyōbushō no futeisai ni tsuki' in Futaba 1973, vol. 1: 33.
8 See on this Nitta 1997: 47–66.
9 Cited in Sakamoto 1981: 24.
10 Ibid., 25.
11 Ibid., 27.
12 The Department of the Left passed this petition on to the State Council (Seiin) in June with a note to this effect: 'In the future it is difficult to imagine there will be any other way for us to deal with religion than what is here proposed by the petitioner.' It also passed the petition to the Ministry of Religions for its views. The Ministry responded in December saying: 'It appears the petition is inspired by the confusion between ritual before Shinto deities and Shinto propagation. There are several misunderstandings, so it is not at all possible for us to adopt [the petitioner's views]' (Sakamoto 1981: 28). It is worth pointing out that other Buddhist sects adopted a different position to that of Shinshū; they supported the Great Teaching Institute and were content to share propaganda duties with Shintoists.
13 Cited in Sakamoto 1994: 229–30.
14 Ibid., 230.

15 In May of 1874, the Ministry of Religions passed this petition on to the Department of the Left. The Department of the Left attached to it its views and passed it on to the Council of State. Those views were: 'The most urgent issues facing Japan at present are the establishment of a constitution and the establishment of a state religion. . . Civilised nations of the West acknowledge religious freedom, and only take action against those creeds that are in breach of the law. This approach is correct, but we can not implement it immediately here in Japan. Moreover, Western nations have religions which the sovereign is bound to adhere to; the reasons for this we must carefully investigate. In the present circumstances, we cannot ban Christianity. All we can do is to set down the religion which the emperor must adhere to, and thus show the direction which the people must follow.' (Sakamoto 1994: 232.) A comparison of the Department of the Left's position with that made earlier to Ōuchi Seiran's petition makes it clear that the Department was unable to decide on the respective merits of the Buddhist and Shinto proposals. It appears, though, that there was no conflict in the mind of Department of the Left bureaucrats between establishing a state religion on the one hand, and guaranteeing religious freedom on the other. (Sakamoto 1994: 236.)

16 Sakamoto 1994: 238.

17 Miyachi comp. 1988: 468.

18 Ashizu 1987: 52.

19 Ibid.

20 The kancho were propagandist chiefs; the government had established the position in 1872 in order to facilitate control over the propagandists. The senior clerics from Shinto and Buddhist sects occupied the position of kancho. The position was abolished in 1884.

21 Shinkyō jiyū hoshō no kudatsu.

22 Nakajima 1977: 172–3.

23 Sūmitsuin kaigi gijiroku: 157.

24 'Kyōdōshoku haishi narabi ni shinbutsu kaku shuha kanchō mibun toriatsukai nado no ken', for which see Nitta 1997: 139.

25 Shimaji Mokurai, 'Kengi: bunri kyōka sokushin ni tsuki (2)', in Futaba 1973 (vol 1).

26 Shimaji Mokurai wasted no time in calling for reform of the kyodoshoku system. In May 1875, immediately after Shinshū won permission for their departure from the Great Teaching Institute, he petitioned the Senate (Genrōin) that the right to appoint and dismiss kyōdōshoku be returned from the hands of government to the various sects. See his 'Kengen: seikyō oyobi kyōshoku kan'in ni tsuki (kyōsei kengi)', in Futaba (vol. 1) 1973.

27 On the Pantheon Dispute, see in Japanese, Fujii Sadafumi 1977b, and in English, Hardacre 1989: 48–51.

28 Motoori et al., 'Shintō no gi ni tsuki kengi', in Meiji kenpakusho shūsei vol. 6: 311–2.

29 For an in-depth look at the Great Propaganda Office, see Fujii Sadafumi 1971.

30 Tanaka Yoritsune and Senge Takatomi, 'Daikyōkan setchi kengensho', cited in Sakamoto 1973: 300–3.

31 Ibid.

32 Motoori Toyokai's statement at the national Shinto Conference is cited in Fujii Sadafumi 1977b: 676.

33 Sasaki 1985: 96–7.

34 Motoori, 'Shintō no gi ni tsuki'.

35 See above n. 33.

36 Cited in Fujii Sadafumi 1977a: 477–8.

37 Ibid.

38 Ibid.

39 After the Restoration the government lumped shrines and Shinto-type new religions together under the category and dealt with all as Shinto. In 1874, however, two of these new religions won from the government their independence and the right to propagate as they wished. Kurozumikyō (or, as it was then called, Kurozumi-ha) was one of these. It was founded in 1814 by Kurozumi Munetada (1780–1850) and was centred on belief in Amaterasu. Shintō Shūsei-ha, the other, was founded by Nitta Kuniteru (1829–1902) in 1873.

40 Ibid.

41 Buddhist prelates insistence on the ban on Shinto funerals was 'a reaction to the fact that [Shinto funerals] had begun to threaten prelates' economic base'. (Sasaki 1985: 102–3.)

42 Sakamoto 1973: 88.

43 Nihon Daigaku, ed. 1991: 219–20.

44 Yamada Akiyoshi papers, Imperial Household Archive.

45 'Shinkan kyōdōshoku kubun no ken', *Kōbunroku*, 2A – 10 – kō 3231, Tokyo: Kokuritsu Komonjokan.

46 Tokoyo Nagatane, *Shinkyō soshiki monogatari*, cited in Yasumaru and Miyachi, eds. 1988: 404.

47 These six sects were Shintō Jingū-ha, Shintō Taisha-ha, Shintō Fusō-ha, Shintō Jikkō-ha, Shintō Taisei-ha and Shintō Shinshū-ha.

48 Sasaki 1985: 118–20.

49 Fujii 1977a: 482 and passim.

50 On the Jingikan revival movement, see Hanawa 1941; Sasaki 1987 and Yamaguchi 1993.

51 Yasumaru 1979: 209.

52 Miyazawa 1971: 350–1.

CHAPTER FOURTEEN

The structure of state Shinto: its creation, development and demise

Sakamoto Koremaru

Introduction

The Meiji government's approach to shrine administration in the 1870s and 1880s was based on the principle that Shinto was 'not a religion', but this did not, of itself, lead to the creation of what we have come to know as 'state Shinto'. State Shinto had its roots in the principle, established in 1871, that shrines were 'sites for the performance of state ritual' (*jinja no gi wa kokka no sōshi nite*), but plans for a special office to administer what might be called *Jingi kanga* or 'deity affairs' continued to be rejected, and government persisted in its policy of cutting shrines adrift from the state.[1] As long as this state of affairs prevailed, state Shinto remained a practicable impossibility. The government's approach is typified by the State Shrine Preservation Fund scheme (*kankokuheisha hozonkin seido*).[2] The purpose of the scheme, introduced in March 1887, was to wind down the state's commitment to the financial upkeep of state shrines. For the next fifteen years, the state would continue its support; thereafter state shrines would, like the vast majority of other shrines, have to fend for themselves. The state was clearly not overly concerned with the fate of shrines other than those at Ise and those within the imperial palace itself. And yet, the government never rescinded that 1871 definition. It became a question of how shrine priests and their sympathisers in the Diet, who insisted that the state distinguish shrines from other religious institutions and grant them special status, might bring about a new direction in government shrine administration. The establishment in 1900 of the *Jinjakyoku* or Shrine Bureau was a major turning point.[3]

The Shrine Bureau and the formation of the state Shinto structure

The *Jinjakyoku* was set up in the Home Ministry in April 1900, and it meant a departure from the administrative pattern established in 1877, typified by the joint administration of shrines and Buddhist temples by the *Shajikyoku* or Bureau for Shrines and Temples. This *Shajikyoku* was now replaced by the

Shūkyōkyoku or Bureau for Religions (by which was meant Buddhist and all other religious sects) and the *Jinjakyoku*, the dedicated office for shrine affairs. The expression 'state Shinto' came into general usage in response to the distinction now made between administration of shrines entrusted to a dedicated bureau and the administration of 'religions' under a separate bureau. The following statement by a certain Oda Kan'ichi (1856–1909) to a Diet committee, convened to deliberate government handouts to shrine priests, is indicative of contemporary understanding:

> In 1882, the distinction between 'religious Shinto' (*shūkyō no Shintō*) and 'state Shinto' (*kokka Shintō*) was already clear enough to behold . . . The Shinto that we advocate is state Shinto [as a pyramid structure] with the Ise shrines at its peak and village shrines forming its base . . . Finally, in the year 1900, the government understood. It split the earlier *Shajikyoku* into a *Jinjakyoku* and a *Shūkyōkyoku*. The former now takes responsibility for what we mean by state Shinto; the latter is charged with Christianity, Buddhism and the various sects of Shinto – what we might call religious Shinto . . .[4]

As Oda's statement implies, the distinction between a religious and a state Shinto had its roots in the 1882 ban on shrine priests' involvement in the state propaganda campaign (the *Taikyō senpu undō* or 'Great Promulgation Campaign') and the state's simultaneous recognition of numerous Shinto-based new religions.[5] Petitions calling for a dedicated office for shrine administration that would serve to distinguish shrines from other religious bodies had been frequently submitted by the House of Representatives to government. The government was unable to ignore the offensive, and the Home Minister, Saigō Tsugumichi (1843–1902), responded in July 1899 by submitting a paper calling for the creation of a bureau for shrines and then seeking the cabinet's views.[6] The paper is revealing. It shows firstly that the Home Ministry now believed it wisest to distinguish between shrines and religions institutionally by the creation of a dedicated shrine bureau; secondly, that there was an awareness of a growth of quite separate problems relating to different religious sects, to the point that a dedicated office for their disposal was now essential. Thirdly, the paper reveals that the Home Ministry's priorities were not shrines at all; rather, they were the problems of religious administration as a whole. These were now such that they could not be dealt with under a joint bureau. In a word, in 1899, 1900 or thereabouts, when the Home Ministry began to support the creation of a shrine bureau, it did not do so out of a desire that the significance of shrines to the modern Japanese state be finally acknowledged.

Nonetheless, it is significant that the Home Ministry did take steps to ensure the creation of a new dedicated bureau for shrines, and include in its budget proposal for spring 1900 the costings for such a bureau, as well as those for an expanded religions' bureau. On March 5, 1900, Saigō Tsugumichi formally proposed to the cabinet the creation of these two bureaux; on April 27

Imperial Order 136 announced their creation. The *Jinjakyoku* was a bureau in anything but fact, however. There was only one high level official, the bureau chief; the ten other members of bureau staff were all of low rank. Although the *Jinjakyoku* now took its place at the pinnacle, so to speak, of the administrative structure of government, it was in reality 'a third class bureau'.[7] The government was clearly not *that* enthusiastic. It was, rather, a case of its being unable to ignore the increasingly vociferous movement from the Diet and from the public for the revival of the *Jingikan*, and of its anxiety to appease.[8] It remains, though, that the creation of the bureau added a spur to the chorus of voices calling for reverence for the deities and respect for the ancestors (*keishin sūso*); and it provided a nation-wide boost, too, to those demanding an improvement in the treatment dealt to shrines which, though officially designated 'sites for the performance of state ritual', had been treated with cool indifference since the late 1880s.[9]

The current of opinion demanding the government grant real substance to the ideal of shrine veneration gained impetus steadily with the Russo-Japanese war of 1904–5. That current sprang from the Diet, and it was of such vigour that in 1906 the Shrine Fund scheme was abolished, and replaced by a new scheme guaranteeing continuous funding for shrines from state coffers.[10] With the setting aside of funds for shrine offerings from local government budgets, shrines began now gradually to assert their position as sites for the performance of state ritual.[11] Of course, from the shrines' point of view, all of this was just as it should be. Shrine priests had had to struggle to survive, what with the confiscation of their lands and the shrivelling of shrine compounds earlier in the Meiji period.[12] It was the Meiji state, after all, that had created the present situation: the desperate shortage of priests and no possibility at all of their carrying out traditional shrine rites. The 200,000 *yen* per annum allocated from state funds and a minuscule contribution toward shrine offerings – even then, these new conditions were applicable only to a very limited number of shrines – enabled shrines to cling to their image as 'sites for the performance of state ritual'. Shrine priests could at least begin to inculcate the ideals of reverence for the deities and respect for the ancestors. This was the limited extent of the good fortune now enjoyed by shrines. The fact remains that the vast majority of shrines and their priests were confined as they ever were to impoverished obscurity.[13]

The government had no genuine regard for the plight of shrines, but it continued to demand that priests ensure shrine dignity was maintained and that they impart to parishioners and believers the ideals of reverence for the deities and respect for the ancestors. With the possible exception of priests at 'state shrines' (the so-called *kankokuheisha*), the prospects for the priesthood at shrines of prefectural and lower rank – who made up the vast majority of the 15,000 or so priestly population – were grim indeed. People had venerated at shrines and ensured their survival because they believed; priests were there to strengthen and deepen that belief. But the policy of the Meiji government was to declare shrines 'non-religious', and to suppress wherever possible their religious dimension. The result was that the sphere of clerical activity was greatly restricted. Priests were compelled to adopt a low profile, and that inevitably led to problems in sustaining shrines and to genuine financial difficulties for their priests. It is hardly surprising that priests all over Japan began now to agitate for improved status for shrines and for the betterment of their own conditions.

The *Zenkoku Shinshokukai* (ZSK) or National Association for Shrine Priests, which was formed in 1898, spearheaded a nation-wide campaign for the creation of a special office for deity affairs. Their goal was always a standardised administration for promoting the Way of the Gods and shrine rituals.[14] The ZSK worked on members of the upper and lower houses of the Diet and pressurised the government to improve conditions and elevate the status of both shrines and their priests. The movement was not without success: from the end of the Meiji era (1868–1912) through to the Taishō era (1912–26), the shrine system was rapidly given substance. April 1913 saw an epochal development in the shape of the promulgation of Home Ministry instructions on shrine priests' duties. Article 1 spelt out that the function of shrine priests was to 'attend to state ceremonial and perform state rites'. This was epochal because it was official confirmation that all shrines – from the state shrines to those of prefectural and lower status – were indeed recognised by the state as 'sites for the performance of state ritual' as set out in that 1871 edict. By the same token, it meant that the state's position on the non-religious quality of shrines was more firmly fixed than ever before. Shrines and their priests were left with little choice but to see how best they could attract believers, even as they resigned themselves to abandoning, or at least seriously diluting, shrine religiosity.

There then followed in the first decade and a half of the twentieth century a series of government promulgations on shrines, priests and practice at Ise and elsewhere. Etiquette of ritual practice at shrines (1907), aspects of shrine finance (1908), administration of the Ise shrines (1912), ritual garb at Ise (1912), Ise rites (1914), and rites at all other shrines (1914) were all covered. The promulgation of these regulations effectively erected the state Shinto structure. Nonetheless, there remained an abundance of intractable problems for both government and shrine priests to tackle. The more the state insisted on the principle of shrines as 'sites for the performance of state ritual' and on the non-religious quality of shrines, and the more that insistence was translated into institutional reorganisation, the more striking was the genuine religiosity of shrines in the provincial periphery: for economic and other reasons, peripheral shrines still clung to such 'religious' practices as preaching, funerals, prayers and the selling of charms. The situation was one in which friction and conflict with other religious groups were difficult to avoid.

There were only two possible remedies. The first was for the state to provide shines with financial support so that they could survive without engaging in religious activities; the second was for shrines to work hand in hand with the state and create a system, or a set of social circumstances, that would drive people willy nilly toward shrines, thus obviating the need for direct state support. The first of these was always, of course, out of the question. Leaving aside the question of the capacity of shrine priests and their supporters, the second was a possibility, if the right external factors manifested themselves. The Russo-Japanese war had already provided a precedent here. So it was that the ZSK, with government and Diet members sympathetic to their cause, and aided too by influential members of the public, set about achieving the realisation of this second option. Their campaign endured throughout the Taishō and early Shōwa periods.

Petitioning the imperial diet

The death of the Meiji emperor and the enthronement rites for his son, the Taishō emperor, added great impetus both to demands for the creation in government of a dedicated bureau to deal with Shinto affairs and to the dissemination of the ideal of reverence for enshrined deities. Laments for the death of the 'great Meiji emperor' issued from all classes of society, and they gelled in the form of a campaign for the creation of a shrine dedicated to Meiji's departed spirit. The performance of the Taishō emperor's enthronement rites, too, contributed to the growing sense of reverence for enshrined deities. At the Diet in March 1913, Seki Naohiko (1857–1934) proposed the construction of a Meiji shrine to 'facilitate the worship of the spirit of the Meiji emperor'. His proposal was passed unanimously by the lower house on March 26. By year's end, a feasibility study was being launched by the Home Ministry. In January of the following year, it was agreed that 3,420,000 yen would be put aside for construction and additional expenses, that construction would begin in 1915 and that the shrine would be concluded within five years. The shrine was to be called *Meiji jingū* or Meiji shrine; it was to be dedicated to the spirits of both the Meiji emperor and his wife, and it was to be ranked as a *kanpei taisha* (greater state shrine). The construction of the shrine helped promote reverence for the deities quite simply because the participation of ordinary citizens was called for: the design of the Treasure Hall (*Hōbutsuden*) was put out to tender, and donations of trees for the shrine grounds were invited. A national association was set up to coordinate public help.[15]

Alongside the construction of the Meiji jingū, the state ceremonial of the Taishō emperor's enthronement rites (the *sokui* and *daijōsai*) also merits note. On December 7, 1914, the Home Ministry gave instructions for local shrines to prepare themselves for the great event, and insisted that it would be of much less use to erect a commemorative stone at the shrine than it would be, by way of commemorative gesture, to repair shrine buildings and bring order to shrine compounds. It is clear that the government sought to use the enthronement as an occasion to deepen the attachment of the public to their local shrines. Home Minister Ōura Kanetake (1850–1918) was explicit on the ideological use to which the enthronement was to be put. At a gathering of shrine officials in

April 1915, he demanded that they use the forthcoming occasion to 'spread [understanding of] the origins of the national polity (*kokutai*) and of the [symbolism] of the rites themselves,' and stated that 'the most profound linkage between shrines and the imperial court and the state must be impressed upon people far and wide.'[16] As the year drew to a close, Ōura repeated his warnings about the need for ritual solemnity at local shrines. The construction of the Meiji shrine and the Taishō enthronement together provided an opportunity for government to proclaim the critical importance to the polity of deity veneration, and the centrality of shrines to that enterprise.

Not to be overlooked in this early Taishō context is Japan's participation in World War I, dating from August 1914. It is well known that Japan was motivated by its ambition to oust German military might and authority from Asiatic waters and to establish itself as Germany's successor. Again, after the spiritual crisis occasioned by the death of the Meiji emperor, the empress then died, and Japan was gripped by a sense of imminent collapse. Instability across the globe grew perceptively too. The situation demanded efforts at national unification. Deity veneration at shrines, it was hoped by government, would be the magic wand that would achieve the spiritual unification of the populace. In August 1914, Prime Minister Ōkuma Shigenobu (1838–1922) told a committee of senior local government bureaucrats that it was his 'most fervent wish that the people might be made to shore up their sense of reverence for the deities, and that the military spirit of the nation might be stirred into action'. He made a special point of addressing himself to shrine priests and asking their help in raising 'the morale of this martial nation'.[17]

Three weeks later on August 23, the emperor issued his rescript declaring war on Germany. A week later, imperial emissaries were being dispatched to the mausoleum of the first (mythical) Emperor Jinmu, to the mausolea of the four emperors prior to Taishō, and to the shrines at Ise and the Yasukuni shrine. At each site, a rite of notification (*hōkokusai*) was performed, in which the spirits of the deities and the deceased were notified that war had been declared. At all of the state shrines, too, local officials attended as imperial representatives and rites were performed. Instructions were issued by the Home Ministry for all provincial and local shrines to ensure they put on suitable notification rites. Priests were to help 'fulfil the emperor's sacred wishes', and 'work together to ensure the most solemn performance of rites before the deities'; and, 'with regard to their task of helping raise martial spirit', they were to 'exert themselves to fulfil their separate roles and so contribute to the critical times [in which we live]'. Naturally enough, shrines and the ZSK responded to the call and played a leading role.

The construction of the Meiji shrine, the enthronement rites and WW I all contributed to an enhancing of shrines' significance in early Taishō. The fact remains, however, that the principle of shrines as 'sites for the performance of state ritual' had yet to gain a firm foothold either amongst the people or within goverment. The vast majority of shrines and their priests were in a pitiful state. Priests and their allies in the Diet attributed this state of affairs to government negligence and indifference in matters of shrine policy and administration. Their belief was that if government was, indeed, convinced of the need to disseminate reverence for the deities throughout the populace, then it should work much harder to enhance the status and improve the treatment of shrines and their priests. Naturally views such as these had been circulating amongst Diet members from the latter half of the Meiji period.[18] Now was the time, Diet members believed, to abandon the makeshift, haphazard approach to shrine administration of the past and to adopt an integrated system based on the principle that shrines were, in both name and fact, sites for the performance of state ritual. Their aim, which they sought to impress upon government on the occasion of these great state events, was to plant the seeds not of some ephemeral reverence for the deities but a reverence that would have daily significance.

However, shrines had too many difficulties to overcome before such hopes could be realised. Naturally, the majority of those difficulties were ones that the state's opportunistic approach to shrine affairs had itself created. Not only had the state greatly restricted shrines' religious scope; it had also offered precious little financial help. The Prime Minister and cabinet members seemed to think it was merely a question of them extolling reverence for the deities as a sort of mantra, for people to venerate and revere shrines and so for shrines to thrive. Many priests and Diet members appear to have been of that position. But how much genuine reverence for the deities can there have been in this government, which, after all, had so openly promoted the infamous policy of shrine mergers in which some 80,000 shrines were destroyed?[19] The only forum where people were able to discharge their extreme anger and frustration upon this government was the Diet.[20] And, frequently, that anger was vented in the Diet. In March 1918, Iwasaki Isao (1878–1927) put a petition to the government demanding a specialist office for 'deity affairs'.[21] The unity of ritual and government (*saisei itchi*) is the splendour of our national polity (*kokutai*) and reverence for the deities is the wellspring of our edification, he insisted. Thus it is that we call upon the government to bring some unity to its shrine administration. It should do so with regard to the shrines presently under the supervision of the Home, Army and Navy ministries, and of those under the jurisdiction of the Governor Generals of Korea and Taiwan and the Karafuto (Sakhalin) Office. It should set up a special 'deity office' (*jingi ni kansuru tokubetsu kanga*) to tackle the following issues: rites; shrines; shrine repairs; appointments of shrine priest; the education of shrine priests; shrine surveys; *gagaku* ritual music; public ceremonial and all other deity-related matters.

Iwasaki proceeded to give four reasons for his submission. The first of these was that the hallowed principle of 'unifying politics and ritual' (*saisei itchi*) involved the most basic rituals of the land, and the ideal of reverence for the deities, that went hand in hand with it, was the defining feature of the Japanese nation. The second was that the *Jinjakyoku*, set up in 1900 after the Sino-Japanese war, was charged principally with supervising shrine finances and the appointment of shrine priests, but it was incapable of fulfilling the immense responsibility of ritual and ceremonial that constituted the font of Japan's unique customs. The third reason Iwasaki gave was that Japan was now faced with a major crisis in the form of a world war, and it had therefore to achieve more than a measure of national solidarity, and yet, there was no unity to shrine administration, which was supposed to be at the core of that solidarity. Under the present circumstances, there could be no 'sustaining of national character' in any of Japan's overseas territories: Korea, Taiwan or Karafuto. And, fourthly, Iwasaki insisted that no adequate programme existed for the nurturing of shrine priests. He demanded that the government, as a first measure toward the mobilisation of the people, establish a dedicated office for deity affairs.

Iwasaki's petition was debated at a special deliberative council convened for the purpose on March 11, 1918, and it was discussed on four further occasions before March 19. In the process, the petition was accepted without substantive change. The government voiced no objections to the petition itself, and made it clear that unifying shrine administration was not out of the question. On the 20th, the proposal was passed unanimously in the House of Representatives. This of course added a spur to discussion in the Diet of all manner of deity-related problems.

Three years on, in 1921, another very similar proposal was passed. In 1923, again, this time in the House of Peers, a motion was passed to petition the government to establish a body to implement research into shrines and shrine rituals.[22]

So both upper and lower houses of the Diet gave their overwhelming support for an examination into and the thoroughgoing revamping of the shrine system; they thrust their demands on government. But the government was of the belief that the best option, in view of budget and other problems, would be to expand the existing *Jinjakyoku*. Moreover, with the dismissal of the Diet and the reshuffling of the cabinet in 1923, not only the establishment of the deity office but also the establishment of a body to carry out shrine surveys came under threat. (In July 1923 an imperial order had announced the creation of a body to engage in shrine survey, called the *Jinja chōsakai*, but in November of the following year it was abandoned.[23]) At the same time, there was a need to unify opinion within the Shinto world, torn over the ideal character of the proposed deity office. Should that office house a shrine to the Eight Deities (*Hasshinden*) or should it not?[24]

The political climate in the aftermath of WW I remained volatile globally, and its effects were felt in Japan too. Politics, the economy and society were all being buffeted furiously. There was the social upheaval that accompanied the Russian revolution and the spread of socialist thought; the onslaught of recession following the war; the founding of the Japanese Communist Party; the massive economic and social body-blows dealt by the Kanto earthquake; the eruption of the Toranomon incident, in which an attempt was made on the life of Crown Prince Hirohito; the growing movement to protect the constitution (*goken undō*); the failure of party politics; the establishment and publication of the Peace Preservation Law (*chian iji hō*) to coincide with the granting of suffrage.

It was only natural, perhaps, that Diet members, alert to prevailing social conditions, should press the government for progress in deity matters in order to nurture some sense of solidarity amongst the people. The Taishō period, short but replete with unprecedented turmoil and a strange sense of liberation, came to a close. The funeral for the Taishō emperor and the enthronement of the new Shōwa emperor were major state events which played their part in disseminating reverence for the deities and respect for the ancestors. And, whatever the realities, Japan had, to all appearances, now joined the world community as a great nation. The rites for the emperor, as sovereign of this great nation, had to be performed on a suitable scale and with appropriate solemnity. The funeral rites and the *daijōsai*, the last and most mysterious of the stages of enthronement, were the supreme manifestation of the ideals of reverence for the deities and respect for the ancestors. Then, in 1929, the periodic rebuilding and re-siting of the Ise shrines took place. The funeral rites, the enthronement rites and then the Ise rebuilding, all of them state events – state ceremonial – appeared before the populace as evidence of the inseparable linkage between the state and deity veneration. It was now incumbent on the state to demonstrate clearly its firm commitment to shrines, and to close down perennial arguments over whether shrines were or were not religious. Buddhists and Christians ensured that the argument ran and ran.[25]

The *Jinja seido chōsakai* and the problem of shrine religiosity

The ZSK, which had put its weight behind the movement to establish a dedicated deity office, became a juridical foundation in October 1926. At its first council meeting in November, it adopted a resolution proposing pressure for the creation of such an office be applied relentlessly. The meeting also addressed the question of the religious nature, or otherwise, of shrines, and declared that there was nothing more pressing than to establish clarity on this matter.

The ZSK appointed Egi Kazutoshi, a member of the House of Peers and a leading petitioner, as its head, and set about invigorating its activities. It set up a body to investigate the condition of shrines and shrine rites; it began to expand and revamp its publishing activities (the monthly *Kōkoku* gave way to the thrice-monthly *Kōkoku jihō*); and construction was begun on new premises for the ZSK. In response to these moves, the government itself began to give serious consideration to the setting up of a body of some sort to work on shrine administration.[26] In 1929, Home Minister Adachi Kenzō (1864–1948) wrote to Prime Minister Hamaguchi Osachi (1870–1931) demanding immediate action, 'bearing in mind the state of the world in which we live'.

. . . The shrine system is of the utmost importance, having as it does the most intimate of ties with the national polity. Moreover, shrines have the most wide reaching and complex connection with age-old practices and local customs. In order to establish a policy for maintaining the system . . . the most careful deliberation is called for. Not only must we create an investigative committee; we must employ staff in increased numbers to engage in preliminary investigations, and do all we can to promote and perfect the maintenance of the shrine system . . .

This was, in fact, a revision of one part of an imperial order issued back in September 1920. On August 14, 1929, the content of this proposal was approved by the cabinet in its essentials; it was published on August 22 and deemed operational from that day. Also on August 14, the cabinet approved the creation of a *Jinja seido chōsakai* (Commission for Shrine Research). Its remit was to investigate the legal status of shrines; their economic character; their resources; payments for government offerings to state shrines; shrine rankings; local shrines and local organisations; shrine parishioners, their rites and duties; and shrine charms. On December 10, the Commission itself became a juridical foundation. It was headed by Yamakawa Kenjirō (1854–1931) of the Privy Council (*Sūmitsuin*), under whose supervision were placed some thirty members from both houses. The Home Ministry, the Finance Ministry and the Education Ministry were represented, as was the Imperial Household Bureau, the Justice Bureau and, of course, the world of shrines and shrine priests.

The inaugural general meeting of this Shrine Commission was held on December 17 1929, and Home Minister Adachi addressed the gathering with these words:

Deliberations have taken place over recent years on the question of drafting a religious law, and the government has come under pressure to set up a law to clarify the true nature of shrines, and so to draw a clear distinction between shrines and religious [institutions]. The government responded by acknowledging the need for a means of sustaining the shrine system, but its position was that the most careful consideration was required before deciding whether it was appropriate to determine all matters relating to all shines with a single comprehensive law. As you all know, the shrine system is a vital issue intimately connected to the polity. It is out of the question that we set up a law on shrine maintenance without the most serious deliberations. Thus it is that we have established the Commission.[27]

Adachi made it clear that the key purpose in maintaining and controlling the shrine system was to clarify the real nature of shrines and underscore the distinction between shrines and 'religious' institutions. Ever since 1882 when shrine priests were banned from functioning as *kyōdōshoku* (state evangelists), the government had adhered to the principle of shrines as non-religious institutions, and that principle had been given legal and institutional underpinning with the creation of the *Jinjakyoku* in 1900. But this had been an institutional development only. With the exception of the Ise shrines and state shrines, the remainder, all shrines of prefectural and lower local status, were quite incapable of surviving without engaging in practices that would be regarded as religious. However much government might decide to refer to those participating in shrine rites as 'those who revere' (*sūkeisha*) rather than 'those who believe' (*shinto*), that was not the same as ridding shrines of their religious nature.[28] The government itself was well aware of this, and that is precisely why it was driven into a position from which the creation of the Shrine Commission became inevitable.

The question of the religious quality of shrines had been of the greatest importance ever since the Nishi Honganji priest Shimaji Mokurai (1838–1911) raised it in the early Meiji period.[29] The issue was in appearance, perhaps, settled by the ban on shrine priests acting as religious evangelists in 1882 and the subsequent creation in 1900 of the *Jinjakyoku*. But the religiosity of shrines could not be eliminated with the passing of a clutch of laws and a little institutional adjustment. It remained an unresolved problem throughout Japan's modern period. Indeed, from the end of the Taishō period, the Education Ministry's own *Shūkyō seido chōsakai* (Commission for Religious Reform) had been deliberating a revised draft for a religious law, and the bitterest of disputes broke out at the Commission over precisely this question. Hanada Ryūun (1873–1952), a Nishi Honganji prelate, and the scholar Anesaki Masaharu (1873–1949) argued in no uncertain terms that activities at shrines were unmistakably religious, and pointed up the hypocrisy in the government's position about the non-religious quality of shrines.[30] Nishi Honganji and other sects of Shinshū Buddhism had demanded of the government the total eradication of religious colouring from shrines, and they inspired local movements of opposition to shrines' religious activities. Their aim was to see through to its logical conclusion the non-religious nature of shrines. The campaign reached its zenith with a petition from ten Shinshū sects submitted shortly after the launch of the Shrine Commission on October 30, 1930. The petition made four points: 1) we, the Shinshū sect, will revere orthodox deities; we will not revere pernicious deities; 2) we will revere 'in a spirit of national ethics'; we will not revere in a spirit of religion; 3) we will not pray at shrines for ill omens or good fortune; 4) we will not accept shrine charms that make claims for bringing good or ill fortune.[31]

The Tokyo Shrine Priest Association (*Tōkyōfu shinshokukai*) responded to this with a statement of its own to the Shrine Commission. 'Shrines,' they insisted, 'are the root of the polity of this nation; they are also the source of national ethics *and* they are the ideal object of the people's faith. It is mistaken to insist that shrines are simply a political institution. It is also mistaken to regard shrines as the object of *purely* ethical reverence. How much more a mistake it must be to treat shrines as no different to any other object of religious veneration.'[32] Shrines are the source of politics *and* ethics *and* religion, was their bold claim. Nonetheless, it remains an indisputable historical fact that shrines had survived throughout Japanese history as places of religious veneration. This was a fact of which the government was painfully aware.

The government made no attempt to examine seriously the problem of shrines and religion even in the Shrine Commission. It ended up being taken to task for this in the press: 'The government leaves aside the vital issue of shrine religiosity, and has the Commission debate such issues as the upkeep of state shrines. Yet, in fact this should only be discussed . . . after the character of those state shrines and, indeed, of all shrines has been solved satisfactorily once and for all.'[33] The government and the Home Ministry, not withstanding Minister Adachi's earlier statements, were anxious to sort out the external, institutional aspects of the shrine problem, but there could no longer be any debating the shrine situation without taking full account of the real issues at stake.

At the second meeting of the Shrine Commission, held on February 28 1930, immediately after the exchange on the substance of shrines between the Shinshū group and the shrines, the Home Minister's proposal for ensuring financial support for shrines was deliberated, but Commission members Mizuno Rentarō (1868–1949) and Kanzaki Issaku (1867–1938) demanded debate on the nature of the relationship between shrines and religion.[34] The Home Ministry persisted, however, in its public display of defining shrines as non-religious, whilst intoning the mantra of reverence for the deities and respect for the ancestors. So, for example, in June 1930 at the annual meeting convened by the Home Ministry for prefectural officers with responsibility for cultural and educational matters (*Gakumu buchō kaigi*), the Home Minister insisted that 'revering the deities and treasuring rites was the great Way of the nation and had been since its foundation,' and offered: 'The anchor of people's lives and the source of their ethics are to be found here. It is essential for those in power to explain as widely as possible, and in the most thorough-going manner, the significance of shrine rites.'[35] As long as the Home Ministry repeated these exhortations, local officials whose task it was to tackle shrine issues had no choice but to administrate on the basis that shrines were non-religious. As long as reverence for the deities remained the state's basic ideal, it was only natural that local officials who sought to be faithful to this ideal would engage in such administration, and take such measures as were appropriate to the disseminating of reverence for the deities and respect for the ancestors. It goes without saying that 'administration' could, at a moment's notice, turn into attempts at compulsion. Shrines are not religious; shrine worship, therefore, falls outside the court of religion; consequently, even if we were to compel shrine attendance, make it a citizen's duty, it would not be in breach of religious freedom. Such a stance, sophistry pure and simple, came in time to assert itself. Indeed, this logic, which had never even occurred to the architects of the Meiji constitution, began now to be deployed.[36]

Indeed, for members of the Shrine Commission, that abode of Shintoists, revering shrines and worship before the family deity shelf (*kamidana*) were not so much a question of compulsion as they were activities which Japanese could anyway be expected to engage in, compelled or not. This is apparent from the following statement of Mizuno Rentarō's before the Commission:

> Take, for example, the issue of compelling primary school children to venerate at shrines. You might make them venerate at shrines, and you would do so in the spirit of having them venerate the deities . . . However, to make people participate in shrine rites, and to force belief upon them, that sort of thing would constitute a religious activity. So, for example, you have a purification carried out; if you then [use it to attempt] to make people have belief in [the deity of] the shrine, well, to go *that* far would mean that religious freedom was, indeed, being compromised.[37]

Mizuno's point was that there would be no problem if people were to go to shrines and simply bow their heads, but that, if there were to be compulsory performance of such religious activities as purification, then religious freedom would be compromised. In other words, reverence for the deities in Mizuno's definition meant lowering one's head before an enshrined deity. The general feeling of Commission members was that this was an act substantially the same as bowing before a great man or a superior. Of course, members like Egi Kazutoshi, Hanai Takuzō (1868–1931) and Kakei Katsuhiko (1872–1961) recognised the genuine religious quality of shrines and sought to have that idea embedded in the laws of the land, but they failed to come up with any concrete proposals.[38]

However, many Buddhists and Christians did not share Mizuno's opinion. Given that religious acts quite evidently did take place at shrines, it was not possible, they insisted, for shrines to be *uniquely* the object of secular respect. Further, they argued that if the government was intent on disseminating reverence for the deities and respect for the ancestors, then it would be obliged to wipe out all religious traces from shrines. If that proved to be impossible, it should treat shrines as any other religious body.

What is noteworthy is that the Buddhist and Christian position did not take hold widely amongst the masses. As discussed above, the string of court rites and ceremonial that accompanied the transition from Taishō to Shōwa and the ritual rebuilding of the Ise shrines made the concrete, visual point to the populace that Japan's national ideals were, indeed, those of reverence for the deities and respect for the ancestors. The majority of the populace began to turn their gaze toward shrines with a mind to giving substance to the ideal of revering deities. Naturally this tendency was not prompted uniquely by these rituals and the Ise shrine construction; rather, it had roots in shrine worship enforced from the Meiji period as one of several primary school events and the group participation at the village community level in shrine rites and other events.[39] (However, shrines' economic plight was hardly relieved by such practices; many priests remained impoverished.) There is, of course, the view which sees shrine visits organised by schools or by the local community in a negative sense, and regards them as a link in the chain of nationalist or militaristic policies of government. It is a fact, however, that the majority of Japanese regarded shrines as something familiar and intimate. That this was so emerges clearly from the campaigns against shrine mergers led by Minakata Kumakusu (1867–1941) and others. It is difficult to believe that at the level of the masses, there was any significant gap between respect for shrines and religious belief in their deities.

The mere fact that the majority of people were of this disposition did not mean that one was at liberty to ignore other positions. Those whose religious faith demanded religious purity could not readily bow their heads before the enshrined spirits, however much the government might insist that shrines were not religious. The idea that it was the duty of all Japanese to lower one's head before a deity caused Buddhists, Christians and others all manner of spiritual and, at times, physical hardship. However, neither in the Shrine Commission nor in the government or Home Ministry was there the breadth of mind needed to take seriously the hardships of such minorities. The same applies to a majority of the people at large. It was not long before it became the shared wish of state and populace that consideration for the hardships of minorities be cast aside, and the ideal of reverence for the deities and respect for the ancestors disseminated from one end of the land to the other.

The *Jingiin* and Japan on a war-footing

The funeral of the Taishō emperor, the enthronement rites of the Shōwa emperor, and the ritual rebuilding of the Ise shrines were all state rites and ceremonies intimately related to the ideal of venerating the deities. They played their part in spreading that ideal throughout Japan. Shrine visits had now become established practice at primary school; there was a growing sense that refusal to visit a shrine disqualified one as a citizen of the imperial nation. This tendency was given added impetus when, with the outbreak of the so-called Manchurian incident in 1931, it became customary practice to pray for victory at shrines. This was precisely why the government was in dread lest shrines seek to enhance their religious qualities, and lest there appear, from among the people, an insistence that shrines were, after all, religious. The Meiji constitution had made no provision for a state religion; it sought rather to adhere to the basic principle that, as long as there was no compromise of a citizen's duties and no threat to social order, a diversity of religious belief was permissible. Akazawa Shirō argues that 'shrines assumed a sudden prominence' on account of the fact that 'in state Shinto universalistic norms transcending the state, capable of passing judgement on the state, did not exist, and this led to the absolute legitimation of war as an act of state';[40] but if this had been the case, it would surely have been possible for the government, in a fascist sort of way, to enforce shrine worship and allow no space for debates over the religious quality or otherwise of shrines. However, even in the midst of the Manchurian incident, 'one of those absolutely legitimised acts of state', the government was still struggling with the issue of the nature, religious or not, of shrines. At a special meeting of the Shrine Commission on December 21, 1931, Egi Kazutoshi made the following speech:

> At our previous meeting, Mizuno spoke about some religious person or other who insisted that religious activity at shrines be stopped. This person argued that if shrines are seen as non-religious, then all religious activity at shrines should be done away with. Such opinions are gaining ground. There was the view expressed that it would be appropriate to consider this matter. This is, indeed, a most reasonable view and, at our earlier meeting, frequent reference was made to it. We have not as yet, it is true, devoted our deliberations exclusively to this problem. The opening of the next session of the Diet is imminent. When the Diet reconvenes, I am sure that questions will be raised. The government must address itself to this problem. The Commission must consider its position carefully, and it would, of course, be splendid if the wishes of the Commission coincided with those of government. In any case, it is surely imperative that this whole question is given the most careful consideration in the Diet.[41]

In other words, for the government, the question of the non-religious quality of shrines still constituted a major problem. Of course, in the background was the perennial, unresolved matter of the standardised administration and control of religions under a religious law, which reached back to the 1890s. For the government of the time, *the* issue was how to mobilise the people for a quasi-war footing. Given that this was so, the state's ability to control the world of religion, with its organisational and mobilising capability vastly superior to that of shrines alone, was an issue upon which, at the risk of some exaggeration, the very survival of the state was seen to depend. The state's greatest challenge, therefore, was to create a structure that would facilitate the mobilisation of *all* religions in support of state policy; one which would, in turn, ensure that the ideal of reverence for the deities was sustained without causing friction with other religions. For that reason, too, the government had no choice but to work feverishly to embrace other religious groups. At this juncture, the state did not have the capacity, the 'fascist capacity' if you will, to force on the entire religious world shrine worship and, through it, reverence for the deities.

All the government and Home Ministry could do was insist that shrines were not religious and that 'compulsory' attendance at shrines was not in breach of religious freedom. It goes without saying that compulsion expressed in these defensive terms was quite lacking in force. On September 22, 1934, the Catholic Archbishop of Tokyo asked the Education Ministry about students' and pupils' shrine veneration. The Ministry responded to the inquiry a week or so later: 'The attendance of students, children and pupils at shrines is required for educational purposes. The respect required of such groups is quite simply a sign of patriotism and loyalty.' It is plain enough from this statement that, for government, shrines were nothing more than the objects of 'respect'. It is all too easy to imagine how such a view of shrines dampened their vitality. It is not at all surprising that provincial Shintoists and others disposed to a genuine reverence for enshrined deities attacked such views;[42] nor that many people rushed to join Shinto-type religious groups or other similar religious bodies. The logic of the Home Ministry was that shrine attendance could be enforced since shrines were not religious, but were simply to be respected for reasons of 'national ethics'. This could never lead to more than a superficial concern for the nation's shrines. This government logic was persuasive only to faithless ritualists and modern rational bureaucrats, for whom shrines were on a par with the flag and the national anthem.

So the government sought the restructuring of the shrine system alone, but even this it did not set about with especial enthusiasm. The Shrine Commission, too, gave up arguing about thorny issues and buried its head in secular institutional concerns. Indecisive arguments endured ad infinitum; and the Commission was capable of not much more than making a show of submitting petitions to government, which the Diet itself had anyway submitted ages before. So, for example, the Commission petitioned the government in November 1936 to give urgent attention to the creation of an office dedicated to deity affairs. The government's organisation of the shrine system proceeded in parallel with a whole train of events that were suggestive of a semi-war footing in Japan. I refer to the Manchurian incident in 1931, the establishment of Manchukuo in March 1932, Japan's departure from the League of Nations in 1933, the expanding *kokutai meichō* or 'clarification of the national polity' movement that originated in opposition to the Emperor Organ theory controversy in 1935,[43] the February 26th incident in 1936 and the Sino-Japanese war of 1937. In these extreme circumstances, the movement to achieve national unity on the basis of ideas rooted in the national polity gathered increasing strength and momentum. Actions, words and thoughts which cut across these ideals were suppressed and controlled by means of a range of laws, such as the Law Against Subversive Actions and the Peace Preservation Law. The attempts to enforce national solidarity by means of various 'security measures' were, in terms of their character, quite some distance removed from religion. The government thought its best bet was to command and control the broad framework of regulated religions and religious groups by setting up an integrated religious law; and to regulate anything that escaped that framework with the Peace Preservation Law. In other words, it sought to lay out a system in which religious law was the carrot and the Peace Preservation Law the stick with which religions might be controlled and mobilised.

The government's desire for the invigoration of security laws and for the creation of a law on religions intensified as Japan sank deeper into the mire of the Sino-Japanese war. The strong pull of government toward the latter was, needless to say, inseparable from any restructuring and filling out of the shrine system. The ZSK for its part worked relentlessly on government and Diet for improvements to shrines and the creation of a dedicated organ of government for deity affairs. New impetus was added to these moves with the formation in January of 1939 of a new government by Hiranuma Ki'ichirō (1867–1952). Hiranuma's cabinet came to power with promises to invigorate the national spirit and revamp education; the cabinet's approach to shrines was also a positive one. On February 25th, Home Minister Kido Kōichi (1889–1977) fielded a question by Senshū Suetaka (1875–1941) at a budgetary sub-committee meeting on the issue of the long sought-after government office for deity affairs. Kido said in reply that he hoped such an office might see fruition not long after the start of the following financial year. Hiranuma himself concurred with this view. The Hiranuma cabinet's positive approach ensured swift moves in the direction of shrine system restructuring, and the Home Ministry's *Jinjakyoku*, which since 1933 had been gradually reformed, witnessed a rapid strengthening and a marked diversification in responsibility. Noteworthy among the reforms now implemented was the creation of two new sections, for 'Instruction' and 'Building', and new ranks and a higher status for incumbents. With the Sino-Japanese war dragging on, the question of maintaining and expanding the network of shrines dedicated to the war dead surfaced as a pressing problem. In March, such shrines were restyled *gokoku jinja* ('nation-protecting shrines'), and the whole network of such shrines, fragile till now, was rapidly reinforced.[44]

Such was the state of affairs in 1940, the 2,600th anniversary of the founding of the imperial line. The entire nation was simmering with a mood of celebration; and there was a grandness about the way in which, say, extension works were carried out to the Kashihara shrine in Nara, dedicated to the (mythical) first Emperor Jinmu, and likewise to the creation of the Ōmi shrine in Ōtsu, where the 7th century Emperor Tenchi is venerated. The cabinet, now under Prime Minister Konoe Fumimaro (1891–1945), decided finally to commit itself to setting up a dedicated office of state for 'deity affairs', and the emperor was asked to approve its being named the *Jingiin* in October. The Privy Council deliberated the cabinet proposal, and formed a special committee to give it the closest inspection at the end of the month. At the committee's first meeting, Home Minister Yasui Eiji (1890–1982) explained the idea behind the proposal and then took questions. What is especially interesting here is the Home Minister's view that the *Jingiin* would not be an organ charged with direct supervision of ritual; it would rather concern itself with perfecting the shrine network. There was a major question here concerning the emperor's supreme authority over ritual matters, of course, and committee member Shimizu Tōru (1868–1947) inquired about the 'unifying of state ritual and court ritual', but the only response forthcoming was from Iinuma Kazumi (1892–1982) who ran the *Jinjakyoku*. He agreed the question merited 'due consideration'. The committee approved unanimously the original proposal, and committee chairman, Arima Ryōkitsu (1861–1944), formally advised the Privy Council to approve the creation of the *Jingiin*. He did so with these words:

> Administration of shrines has until now been entrusted to the care of a bureau within the Home Ministry, the *Jinjakyoku*. In recent times, the *Jinjakyoku* has been overwhelmed with administrative work. As a result, basic work on shrines, their rituals and priests and the dissemination amongst the populace of a sense of respect for the deities have not be able to proceed as we should have liked. The capacity of the *Jinjakyoku* until now has simply not been equal to the task. We have, therefore, determined to create a new office, the *Jingiin*, attached to, but outside the Home Ministry, with greater powers and a new expanded capacity.

The Privy Council responded by giving its approval in November, and submitted its considered views to the emperor in order that he might add his seal to the proposal and make it law. The result was the creation of the *Jingiin* by Imperial Order 736 on November 11, 1940. The first of the regulations governing its organisation carried four stipulations:

Regulation 1: The *Jingiin* is under the jurisdiction of the Home Minister and will concern itself with the following items:

 (i) items relating to the Ise shrines;
 (ii) items relating to all shrines, beginning with those of state rank;
 (iii) items relating to shrine priests and other shrine officials;
 (iv) items relating to the dissemination of a sense of reverence for the deities.

The birth of the *Jingiin* marked the first time that government had ever officially added its weight to the dissemination of a political ideology rooted in the ideal of reverence for the deities. For the first time, that is, ideology had been implanted in what had been 'state Shinto' in purely institutional terms. Only now can we talk about 'state Shinto' in the sense in which it is referred to in the 1945 Shinto Directive. This change, in terms of the study of state Shinto, is one of decisive importance. The Home Ministry knew it would be questioned as to why the *Jingiin* was now to be concerned with the dissemination of reverence for the deities. Internal ministry documents disclose the 'model answer' prepared for the eventuality:

> The substance of 'deity administration' covers much ground. But, naturally, it has to do with nothing so much as invigorating the splendid national custom of revering the deities and venerating the ancestors, and clarifying the ideals that sit at the root of the polity. We are at present endeavouring to achieve perfection in this sphere, but until now, regrettably, we were unable to devote sufficient energy into the direct education and edification of the populace. The problems were those of staffing and costs. With the establishment of the *Jingiin*, we are now enabled to devote ourselves with renewed vigour to this matter. Hence the inclusion of this particular item into the regulations for the administration of the *Jingiin*.

Now, for the first time since the *Jinjakyoku* was created some forty years earlier, a system was in place for 'state Shinto' to address itself directly to the people and to begin to disseminate the principles of reverence for the deities and respect for the ancestors. The system, however, was pathetically weak. The *Jingiin* was run by an officer with the title of Bureau Supremo (*sōsai kanbō*); it housed a General Affairs department (*Sōmukyoku*) and an Edification Department (*Kyōmukyoku*). The former had, within it, a Miscellaneous section, an Inquiry section and a Buildings section; the latter comprised an Instruction section, a Rites section and an Investigation section. In the Instruction section (*Shidōka*), which was to spearhead the edification of the masses, there were two instructors and a handful of assistants – that was all. Their main concern, as it turned out, was the nurturing, instruction and education of shrine priests. When it came to its capacity for disseminating reverence for the deities and political ideology to the masses, there was no comparison between this group and the Education Ministry (especially its Doctrinal Bureau, *Kyōgakuka*) which was publishing volumes like *Kokutai no hongi* ('Cardinal principles of the national polity' 1937) and *Shinmin no michi* ('Way of the imperial subject,' 1941). The only publication the *Jingiin* ever issued for general consumption was a text with the title *Jinja hongi* ('Cardinal principles of shrines and shrine practice'). It came out in June 1944 when defeat was imminent. In other words, 'state Shinto' in the sense of a system based on the *Jinjakyoku* and the *Jingiin* did not disseminate or enlighten the populace on matters of revering the deities; it simply did not have the capacity. It was impossible for *Jingiin* bureaucrats to do anything not stipulated under law, and the interests of the elite bureaucrats of the Home Ministry, for whom precedent was always the safe option, did not extend beyond shrine administration. Priests at state shrines, it goes without saying, remained quite uninvolved in the funeral rites for those who died in the war; the bureaucrats were quite unconcerned to involve priests at other ranks of shrine, too. The real limits to the flexibility of the system are well illustrated by the fact that the *Jingiin* did not even have the authority to demand of shrines that they perform rites for the successful conclusion to the war. Indeed, the institution of state Shinto could only function as an institution. It had no authority in the spheres of thought or ideology.

It is, of course, true that children and pupils at primary and middle schools were 'forced' to attend shrines, and the rest of the populace, too, was exhorted to do so. The government continued to call for reverence for the deities and respect for the ancestors. Members of the *Jinjakyoku* would write in their non-official publications that such veneration and reverence was the duty of all imperial subjects, and that those who failed would be 'dealt with under the constitution'. However, no degree of duty or compulsion could be expected to convince those with no interest in shrines to revere deities and worship the ancestors, since respect and belief are not things which spring from a sense of duty or compulsion. This much is clear from the war time lament of a priest at a certain state shrine. He wrote:

I believe that we [priests] too must avoid confusion between shrines and religions, and establish a hierarchy and so confirm our priorities. This much is so clear as to be hardly worth reiterating. However, we must constantly fight off claims and strategies that enable people to think, or make them think, that shrine rites have become merely formalistic; that there is no [ethical] 'Way'; that there are no teachings either. The arguments of Western academia and religion are evident when shrine attendance is justified on the grounds that shrines are merely the object of respect, of ethical importance; they are also to be found in the claims that faith or otherwise in shrine deities is a matter of individual concern, as stipulated in article 28 of the constitution where religious freedom is provided for.

The bureaucrats and priests of the *Jinjakyoku* and the *Jingiin*, helpless except to ensure the performance of shrine rites and the day-to-day running of shrines: these men are the true face of the institution of state Shinto. The fact that after the war, not a single bureaucrat or priest from the *Jingiin* was ever purged is a sure proof of just how far removed the institution of state Shinto was from the ideologies of 'ultra-nationalism', 'expansionism' and 'militarism'.

Conclusion

Why then was it that the government created the *Jingiin*, and what expectations did it have? An examination of the official explanation exposes the fragility of faithless state Shinto.

Rituals before the deities constitute the foundation of our national polity and are the wellspring of national ethics. For these reasons, since ancient times special attention has been paid to organs of government that are dedicated to deity matters. In this way the principle of veneration for the deities has [over the centuries] been brought into relief. Under the prevailing system, the situation is that administration has been carried out under one office of the Home Ministry. When we reflect on the true principle underlying the foundation of this nation of ours, the office offers a good many reasons for regret. Now, however, in response to the unprecedented crisis our imperial nation confronts, the time has arrived when we must make resplendent the national polity and re-invigorate the imperial spirit. Thus it is that the *Jingiin* is to be established. Rites before the deities constitute the foundations of the polity, and the government has made clear its determination to give special attention to establishing an organ for the administration of those rites. In the present climate, we believe that it may make no small contribution to the stirring of the national spirit. When, again, we consider the state of shrine administration, the situation in which the *Jinjakyoku* found itself made

291

any fulfilment of its original brief impossible. Recent times have seen a sharp increase in its administrative work load, and its staff are now overwhelmed. Investigations into shrines and their rites, supposedly the foundation of shrine administration, and work on structures for shrines and their priests were all rendered impossible. Moreover, the dissemination of reverence for the deities has quite lacked the thoroughness it demands. Thus it is that today, in response to the keenly expressed desires of subjects everywhere, and as a consequence of careful deliberations within government, we have determined to establish the *Jingiin*. Our hope is that it may aid the advance of shrine administration.

Here we have then the government's objectives, its reasons for the creation of the *Jingiin*, state Shinto's holiest of holies. In other words, the creation of the *Jingiin* was designed to demonstrate to the people at large that the state was serious about shrine rites as the root of the national polity. In the final analysis, the *Jingiin* was necessary as a symbol. It showed that the state was not merely demanding reverence for the deities and veneration of the ancestors of the *people*; it was also itself a paragon of reverence and veneration. The real reason, of course, was that the administrative work load of the *Jinjakyoku* had become unbearable.

The negative-sounding phrase 'we believe that [the *Jingiin*] may make no small contribution to the stirring of the national spirit' was certainly not mere modesty. It is but an honest encapsulation of state Shinto as it really was. State Shinto, as an institution, had existed since 1882, and it was created to gloss over the vacant, groundless slogans calling for reverence for the deities and veneration of ancestors. What can it have been that bureaucrats (and I include here the majority of priests, too) were expected to contribute to the development of the people's spirit, their inner life? These bureaucrats themselves had no contact with the mystery of the sacred spirits that alone make sense of 'revering the spirits'; they were in no way connected to funeral rites, which alone were the foundation of veneration of the ancestors. The ideal of veneration of the deities and reverence for ancestors was just about sustained amongst the people at large through the application of such laws as the Peace Preservation Law and the Religious Reform Law (published in 1939). 'State Shinto' was merely an observer on the sidelines to all this. It is hardly surprising that the bureaucrats in the *Jingiin*, who remained observers throughout, and ineffective observers at that, never dreamt that the Allied Powers would abolish the *Jingiin*.

Notes

1 Such a dedicated office, called the *Jingikan*, was created, in fact, in the wake of the Meiji Restoration of 1868, but it was soon thereafter abolished. On the fortunes of the early Meiji *Jingikan*, see for example, Sakamoto (1987), Takeda (1987) and in English Breen (1990).

2 On the Shrine Preservation Fund law, see the essay by Nitta Hitoshi in this volume and, for example, Jinja Shinpō seikyō kenkyūshitsu 1986: 89–99.

3 See the 'Shajikyoku' entry in Kokugakuin daigaku Nihon bunka kenkyūjo ed. (1986).

4 Dainijūyonkai Teikoku gikai shūgiin: shinshoku yōseibu kokkō hojo ni kansuru kengian iinkai giroku (sokki) dainikai. Tokyo Daigaku shuppan kai, 1988.

5 See on this, Sakamoto 1981b and Sakamoto 1990.

6 Jingiin chōsa shiryō MS (author's copy).

7 Jinjakyoku jidai o kataru, Jingiin kyōmukyoku chōsakai 1942.

8 On the late Meiji campaign to revive the Jingikan, see for example Yamaguchi 1993 and Sasaki 1987.

9 For prefectural shrines, of course, and those of still lower status, their designation as 'sites for the performance of state ritual' had had no substance since 1873 and, in 1879, even the pretence was dropped. (Ashizu 1987: 89–90).

10 See Sakamoto 1994: 363–84.

11 Sakurai 1992. On late Meiji shrine administration, much profit is to be had from Morioka 1988.

12 See the essay by John Breen in this volume.

13 See Sakamoto 1994: 363–80 and Sakamoto 1987a.

14 See for example Zenkoku shinshoku kai ed. 1935 and Hanawa 1941.

15 See Meiji Jingu hōsankai (ed) 1937 and Yamaguchi 1993.

16 Jinja kyōkai zasshi 5 (1915): 1.

17 Jinja kyōkai zasshi 9 (1914): 39–44.

18 Representative of politicians in the lower house was Ōtsu Jun'ichirō (1856–1932) and, in the upper house, Takagi Kanehiro (1849–1920).

19 On the issue of shrine mergers, see Fridell 1973.

20 In the lower house, Nakamura Keijirō and, in the upper house, Takagi Kanehiro (1849–1920) and Egi Kazutoshi (1853–1932) were most persistent in their protests at the shrine merger policy. See especially, Egi Kazuyuki keireki zadan (ge), Egi Kazuyuki keireki zadankai kankōkai, 1933: 565–88.

21 Teikoku gikai shūgiin giji sokkiroku 34, 1981: 424–5 and 563–4.

22 Egi Kazuyuki keireki zadan (ge).

23 The Jinja chōsakai was shelved as part of administrative streamlining, but the Home Ministry proposed to the cabinet the creation of a smaller scale shrine survey unit within the ministry itself. This was approved at the cabinet meeting on May 8. Yuasa Kurahei (1874–1940), second in command at the Home Ministry, headed the unit, and among those working under him were Mikami Sanji (1865–1939), a Tokyo University professor of history, and Ueda Kazutoshi (1867–1937), a linguist who was presently head of Jingū Kōgakkan University in Ise.

24 When the ZSK gathered in May 1927, the Eight Deity shrine issue headed the list of issues demanding resolution (Zenkoku shinshokukai enkaku shiyō, 42). The history of the controversy surrounding the Eight Deity Shrine was a long one. The controversy was inseparable from that concerning the early Meiji Jingikan. See above n. 1.

25 See Akazawa 1985: 129 and passim.

26 Zenkoku shinshokukai enkaku shiyō: 65–72.

27 December 17, 1929: Jinja seido chōsa kai gijiroku (Dai ikkai sōkai): 3.

28 In article 8 of the Rules for the employment of priests at local shrines (August 87, 1887), the following appears: 'Parishioners – when there are no parishioners, then believers (shinto) – . . .' Sixteen years later, in new regulations governing employment of shrine priests published in February 18, 1903, reference is made to 'representatives of parishioners or of those who revere at the shrine (sūkeisha) . . .'

29 In 1875, Shimaji began the debate with a missive to Sanjō Sanetomi (dispatched in the name of Ōtani Koson) in which he said 'The Sun Goddess is the foundress of the imperial line and all people, regardless of sect, owe reverence.' See Sakamoto (1987); cf. also Nitta Hitoshi's essay in this volume.

30 Akazawa 1985: 129.

31 *Jinja kyōkai zasshi* 29–3: 37–40.

32 *Jinja kyōkai zasshi* 29–4: 55–60.

33 *Ōsaka Asahi shinbun*, February 12, 1930.

34 *Jinja kyōkai zasshi* 29–4: 71–2.

35 *Jinja kyōkai zasshi* 29–7: 1.

36 Tagawa Okichirō 1938.

37 *Shōwa 5nen, 7gatsu, 21nichi Jinja seido chōsakai gijiroku (Daiikkai tokubetsu iinkai)*: 7.

38 On Kakei's ideas, see Kakei 1936.

39 On school worship at shrines, see Yamamoto Nobuyoshi and Imano Toshihiko eds, 1986.

40 Akazawa 1985: 200–1.

41 *Shōwa 6nen 12gatsu 21nichi jinja seido chōsakai gijiroku (Dai22kai tokubetsu iinkai)*: 2.

42 Ashizu 1987: 161.

43 The 'emperor organ theory', popular with intellectuals in the liberal Taishō period (1912–26), held that sovereign power rested not with the emperor but with the state, of which the emperor functioned only as the highest organ. The 'clarification of national polity' movement stood for a 'Shōwa restoration' of power to the emperor and the establishment of a new political and social order.

44 This whole question had of course been debated by the Shrine Commission.

CHAPTER FIFTEEN

The disfiguring of nativism: Hirata Atsutane and Orikuchi Shinobu

Kamata Tōji

There can surely be no nativists so driven throughout their lives by the pain they suffered for their disfigurement as Hirata Atsutane (1776–1843) and Orikuchi Shinobu (1887–1953). Of course, the face of that distinctive nativist from the Kyoto area, Ueda Akinari (1734–1809), was also disfigured with the small pox he suffered as a child of five. Akinari also wrote jestingly in *Ugetsu monogatari* about another physical oddity: the middle finger on his right hand and the first finger of his left were no bigger than his baby fingers. Akinari could never express his pain directly; he always jested, which may constitute evidence, perhaps, of his self-reliance.[1] Hirata and Orikuchi were, however, tormented in a much more immediate way than Akinari by the pain of their disfigurement. Hirata and Orikuchi both bore facial markings.

At the end of 1842, Hirata wrote to his adopted son in law Hirata Kanetane. It was the winter of his 67th year, the year in fact before he died. Around this time Hirata had been ordered by the military authorities to cease his writing activities and was expelled from the capital. He returned to his birth place of Akita. The letter to Kanetane was written by Atsutane when he was in the depths of despair. The letter brims with the pain he felt at his disfigurement.

> I was farmed out and fostered by a poverty stricken lowly samurai family, where I had to endure a lot, until I was 6. Although I had been sent away, when my wet nurse's husband died, I was sent home again and suffered brutality at the hands of my parents and brothers. The pain I endured was absurd as I have always said. Between the ages of 8 and 11, I was placed in the care of a wealthy acupuncturist of the Sakurai family called Sōkyū. Just as I was thinking how unpleasant it was to be in the family of a doctor, they had a child of their own and I was sent home. There I did everything from cooking to cleaning to weeding, running errands and carting night soil around. I was told I worked harder than any of my brothers, but I was still treated with contempt and frequently beaten. There was no end to the bumps on my head from knocks I received. I was born with a sense of justice, even so, and though I never learned anything of worth from my parents, I taught myself how to read and I

had the knack of smiling at those I met and so others were kind to me. On that account, too, I was loathed at home. Moreover, I was always despised for the birth mark on my face. My parents interpreted it as a sign that I would one day engage in fratricide and snatch for myself my brothers' rightful inheritance. It was freezing in winter where I lived . . . When I was one year old, one of my older brothers bought me a small night gown, but when that wore out and was gone, nobody provided me with night wear. I saved up some money from doing chores and bought something called a *moku* that servants wear when they sleep, and I saw through winter after winter without ever once being invited to sit under the warm *kotatsu* . . . How terribly painful it was to be accused of plotting to kill my brothers . . .[2]

This letter was written but it was never sent. Atsutane tore it to shreds. The fragments were later discovered by Hirata Kanetane and pieced together, but the entire piece remains unclear to this day. The lack of happiness in Atsutane's family was abnormal. He was farmed out as a young boy, given over for adoption, his adoptive father then died and his adoptive family had a son of their own son so he was dispatched home again. He was persecuted by his brothers to a degree that Atsutane himself called 'absurd'. What though was the motive for Atsutane writing thus – and so frankly too – of his formative years to his adoptive son-in-law? In the end, of course, the letter was never sent. Perhaps he could not endure the excess of pain it caused him. This pain had its origins in the disfigurement which led his family to suspect him of plotting fratricide, and of planning to deprive his brothers of their inheritance. It was a disfigurement that he could do nothing about. What can Atsutane himself have thought of this facial marking? It led him after all to be despised quite unreasonably as some sort of devil or monster. For the nativist Atsutane to have been ordered to cease all writing must have plunged him into the depths of despair. He was, moreover, in his last years lonely and frustrated. Perhaps he was unable finally to restrain himself from confessing all to Kanetane, and yet the confession he tore to shreds. One can only imagine what Kanetane's only feelings must have been to discover the fragments. Atsutane was after all his intellectual master; his adopted father, too. My belief is that Atsutane's fascination with the Other Realm, his power to see into the Other Realm, are inseparable from his disfigurement. His knowledge of the origins of his disfigurement was intimately related to his theories of the Other Realm. Atsutane's anguish at his disfigurement lay, I suggest, behind his ferocious insistence that the deity Magatsubi no kami was a fundamentally good deity when his master Motoori Norinaga had defined the same deity as evil.

The myths tell how Izanagi, the progenitor of the Sun Goddess, pursued his beloved wife to the nether world, became defiled and then performed a purification rite during which Magatsubi no kami came into being. Norinaga regarded this deity as the root of all evil, and argued that another deity Naobi no kami emerged later to 'amend' the evil done by Magatsubi.[3] Norinaga in other words proposed a dualistic good-evil approach, according to which Magatsubi represented evil and Naobi represented good. Hirata, however, insisted that Magatsubi was himself a good deity who had rectified evil. In *Koshiden*, he wrote that 'Magatsubi was the deity who pleaded that the defilement incurred by Izanagi in the nether realm be wiped clean . . . And so this deity deplores all unclean things; the deity goes wild at the sight of uncleanliness, and only then does he bring about calamities. That is why he earned himself the sobriquet of "Magatsubi, the calamitous".'[4]

However, comparing Hirata's critique of his master Norinaga, with the master's own interpretation of the classic *Kojiki* text, the decision must surely go to his master. In his *Kojikiden*, Norinaga reads a critical passage in the *Kojiki* classic as a nominal, and comes up with: '[Magatsubi] was a deity who came into being as a result of defilement incurred when Izanagi reached the land of pollution'.[5] Hirata, however, in his *Koshiden* prefers a verbal reading and arrives at this: 'Magatsubi was a deity who acted as he did because he had become defiled'.[6] Norinaga is grammatically speaking far more accurate; his interpretation appropriate.

Why was it, though, that Hirata went to such lengths, so far in fact that he wilfully misread the classics, to protect Magatsubi? My view is that Atsutane felt obliged to identify, amongst the deities who performed evil because of their contact with defilement, deities 'whose faces were disfigured and who looked capable of fratricide', who looked as if they might plot to deprive a sibling of his inheritance'. Atsutane was unable to accept the penetrating gaze of Norinaga who saw evil deities for the evil deities they were. To affirm his master's theory unquestioningly would have been to deny his own roots, his own existence. And such a course offered no possibility of redemption.

Magatsubi no kami was not for Atsutane a deity who came into being as the result of evil; rather he was a deity who rampaged and performed evil when he encountered defilement, such was his loathing for it. By defining Magatsubi thus, he sought to slip beyond good and evil, and so transform his own disfigurement from a sign that he was so evil as to kill his brothers and take over the household into a sign of that he was good: that he loathed evil and would seek to rectify it. Atsutane was surely the first of the nativists to take evil and defilement as his own personal problem and to seek to solve it theologically. Atsutane raises his gaze to evil, to pollution, to the other realm and to its possibilities of redemption, all through the medium of his own facial disfigurement.

Nonetheless, it would be rash to assume that Atsutane's nativism was, therefore, arbitrary and dogmatic. Without his internal refractions, his inner wounds, the question of *tengu* and hermits and the rebirth of the soul – those issues that came to obsess Hirata – would probably never have surfaced as a problem in nativism. Atsutane, who boasted that he was the legitimate heir to Norinaga as the master nativist, became legitimate paradoxically because of the light he shed on nativism's more shadowy realm. Atsutane's exploration of this shadowy realm prompted research into the Other World, into the spirit realm, into strange visitors from other realms. At the same time, there emerged the spirit studies of people like Honda Chikaatsu (1822–1889), Deguchi Onisaburō (1871–1948), Tomokiyo Yoshizane (1888–1952) and Asano Wasaburō (1874–1937). Again, there developed the anthropological studies pioneered by men Yanagita Kunio (1875–1962) and Orikuchi Shinobu. Here then we encounter our second disfigured nativist, Orikuchi Shinobu.

The 'love of strangers' in the folklore of Orikuchi Shinobu and Hirata Atsutane

In new year of 1937, the 50 year old Orikuchi Shinobu wrote a poem he called *Osanaki haru* ('The Spring of my youth'). His purpose was to reflect on his early years and express with utter frankness the disharmony he experienced in the midst of his parents and siblings. The unsettled heart that moves the *Osanaki haru* constituted a wound not easily healed.

In the poem, Orikuchi wrote how he was detested by his father, not loved by his mother either and brought up to be different from his older brother and sister; how children in other impoverished families all had 'good parents', and spent their days cheerfully, enjoying themselves, having fun, while he was always decked out in fine silk garments, with a red belt tied high around his waist just like a girl. No doubt this was why he was spurned by children of his own age. He would gaze, he wrote, enviously at these other children, thumb in mouth; his loneliness and ennui reaching a crescendo. Once when an excess of ennui and loneliness brought him to the brink of tears, he had glanced at the border between his house and his neighbour's, and a man had appeared before him, just at the entrance to his family's plot of land. The man stood there waving a delicate white hand. This graceful man, older than Orikuchi's older sister, but quite different in appearance, had looked at Orikuchi and smiled gently. What a fine looking person he was; but who could he be? Orikuchi concluded his poem by reflecting on the sadness he now felt: the image of the man, so vibrant to him as a child who had just come of age, had now faded with the passage of time.[7]

Who was this fine looking man that Orikuchi had seen by the gate waving his white hand? It would be overly bold to say that this man was a stranger from the Other World, and yet the young Orikuchi believed he had caught a glimpse of the other realm, through the mysterious aroma emitted by this beautiful figure. There can be no doubting the strength and depth of his feelings on that occasion. Perhaps we might say that both Hirata and Orikuchi were of a type: they both had the most tenuous of relationships with their parents and siblings; both were able to develop within themselves, as a result, hallucinatory powers that gave them unique perspectives on the other realm.

Yet the truth of the matter is not so much that they espied the Other World and yearned for its inhabitants; rather that they were themselves the object of the Other World's attention; they were gazed upon by its inhabitants. Their powers of vision and the depth of their interest in the other realm were gifts bestowed on them by that other realm and its inhabitants. That their theology was capable of going beyond the dogmatic and arbitrary to produce the most mysterious and the deepest insights was because they were outsiders to the world of humans. Hirata spoke of *Kakuriyo* (the 'hidden realm') as the 'true world' (*moto no yo*); Orikuchi spoke of *Tokoyo*, the Eternal Realm as the 'mother country' (*haha ga kuni*). What they meant by these various terms was, of course, the home of the soul, a place distinct from this realm. What marked them out as distinct from others in this human realm was none other than their facial disfigurement.

In 1948, Orikuchi won a major literary prize for the collection of poems he called *Kodai kanaishū*. Included therein is the long poem *Kotsugaishō* ('The face of the beggar'). It appears in the collection just before the afore-mentioned *Osanaki haru*.[8] The title *Kotsugaishō* is a reference to Orikuchi's disfigurement. When he talks in the poem of 'the face of the one who emerged in to the world, fated to end up a beggar, at arms' length from his mother', he is talking of his own disfigured face. He writes how he had his elder brother to thank for telling him of his deformity. His obsession with his facial disfigurement is abnormal. His mother 'cuts a fine figure'; his father is 'splendid too, glittering'; his elder brother is 'quite unlike me'; his elder sister is a 'handsome woman'. 'I alone am ugly to behold.' Orikuchi is unable to articulate the fact that his fateful disfigurement was a blue birth mark above his right eyebrow. He laments that his face makes him look like a beggar to the mocking eyes of his elder brother, but he never lets on that the mark was a birth mark above his right eyebrow, one that children of the village would jeeringly call his 'ink blot'.

As Muro Saisei (1889–1962) has commented, Orikuchi's failure to mention his birth mark is an indication of just how deep sunk were the roots of both his obsession and his hurt. If he had been able to own up to it and say 'How wonderful that the sun sets on my birthmark and night breaks on my birthmark: how wonderful life is!', then his life would no doubt have been much easier to endure. Just as Hirata was unable to talk of his own disfigurement that convinced others he was a potential killer and destroyer of the family home, so Orikuchi was never able to talk openly of 'the face of the one who emerged in to the world, fated to end up a beggar, at arms' length from his mother'. It is clear to me that without reference to the awareness of how strikingly different they looked to those around them, one can discuss neither the theology nor the thought of either Hirata Atsutane or Orikuchi Shinobu.

Hirata Atsutane's *Senkyō ibun* is a record of his conversations with the 15 year old youth Torakichi who claimed to be able to cross at will from this world to the other. In that book, Hirata laments his plight as the man scorned by all as the *Ōyama mono* and the 'chief wizard'.

What is this fate of mine? What sort of karma is it that led to my present rebirth? [My parents despaired of me], and I passed through the hands of wet nurses and foster parents. Till the age of 20 I never voiced the depth of pain I suffered. From the moment I arrived in Edo till the present day, there can have been few sorrows that I have not known. Such are the trials of this world. I resigned myself to the fact that suffering in this world was the normality. I channelled my energies into the study of the ancient way. I read about it and wrote about it and sought to teach the correct path. I argued that we should apply our compassion not only to the things of the invisible Other Realm but to all animate things, to birds, to beasts, insects and fish, trees and plants too. We should endeavour in this way to ensure we do not encounter the hatred of all things. If we apply ourselves in this fashion, then all people of this world will be able to fill themselves with secret virtue . . . I know that there are many men who scorn me and despise me. Why do they do this?[9]

Atsutane's expresses himself in this work with frankness and not a trace of embarrassment; it is difficult not to be impressed by him. It is possible perhaps to read into Atsutane's manner of expressing himself an excessive self awareness, a pretentiousness. Many people might read the same into the writings of Orikuchi. Even if for both men, this frankness was the only way, the only natural way they knew of expressing themselves, they were obviously oblivious to the bizarre effect it was likely to have on most normal people. Even if they had some inkling of the effect they were creating, suppression was one thing they could not aspire to. They remained, after all, in a state of permanent torment. As Atsutane himself pointed out, it was a question of fate. It was this fate that drove them both towards a folklore dominated by their love for the stranger.

In his 'Postscript' to volume 3 of the *Kodai kenkyū* (Research on the classic age), Orikuchi wrote:

Akinari was dismissive of those who were educated beyond their station and, of their fate, he said it was a 'crucifixion'. He himself was well aware of the ugliness of [the man educated beyond his station], and he ended his own life . . . as a sort of 'stray'. The fact that he nonetheless found a life for himself was a blessing, even though that life was almost certainly one of insufficiency and ennui. He was fostered only to be returned to his parents; he was given a wife only to despair of his acquired family where human relations were a disaster. Such was the tapestry of his life; with old age he became dependent on his older brother. His hair turned white with his confinement to a single room; he was no doubt insulted by his nephews and nieces as a worthless old man. This was no fantasy. This really happened.

Until a generation ago there were many people who lived such vacant lives. I am conscious more keenly than most of this society which now guarantees a living for those unsettled people for whom literature or learning is all. I am well aware that I am of much less value than Hikojirō. That is why I feel not a trace of pride in the fact that I am a scholar and a tutor at a private university . . . My grandfather and his father endured suffering. When I think how they lived lives of much better quality, more modest lives, I cannot bring myself to 'act the scholar' as my elders and friends do.[10]

These words Orikuchi wrote when he was 45. Hirata wrote his earlier cited piece, *Senkyō ibun*, at about the same age. Orikuchi probably knew still better than Atsutane the fate of 'crucifixion' as Akinari had put it. He was a 'wanderer' who himself became 'a worthless old man'; he felt himself to be of little 'value'. If Atsutane's earlier lament was an overly honest confession; this strangely long postscript of Orikuchi's also merits a similar description. It may be that readers will find in Orikuchi a hard-to-swallow theatricality, a pretentiousness. Unquestionably, Orikuchi and Hirata both 'come on strong', but Orikuchi was surely speaking the truth when he said 'I feel not a trace of pride in the fact that I am a scholar and a private tutor'.

What drove both Hirata Atsutane and Orikuchi Shinobu into scholarship was none other than what Socrates called *daimon*.[11] Both would no doubt have concurred with this statement of the youth Torakichi:

Torakichi says this. All learning can lead to evil, and so learning is not good . . . [T]here is yet no man who has studied his way to ethical excellence. In most cases, people learn about life; they flaunt their knowledge with arrogance; they look down on those who do not know books. They say that deities are a myth; that hermits and goblins are fantasy; that nothing in life is mysterious . . . They are full of themselves, and this is all because those who [only] study life are proud and narrow. There are many things which, though they are written in books, are quite obviously wrong . . . There are many levels, many hundreds of them, of higher, greater excellence [of which scholars are ignorant]. It may be that heaven and earth [as we know them] and all creation are located within the stomach of some deity or other. We know, after all, how various insects exist within the stomach of humans. There is no justification for arrogance until one has the capacity to understand how high the sky reaches. Nothing is as bad as arrogance and boastfulness.[12]

It is difficult to imagine that the 15 year old Torakichi was solely responsible for these words. It is likely that Atsutane's own attitude toward learning is reflected here to a very considerable extent. What Torakichi says is anyway a reproduction of what Atsutane appears to have repeated on a daily basis. Here Torakichi, in other words Atsutane, points out that one of the pitfalls of learning is that which leads to evil. What he means by evil is the arrogance of those who study only life. What he insists on is that those narrow-minded people who boast of the quantity of their knowledge, and impose on others their selfish rationality, their self-centredness, made manifest in their dismissal of deities, hermits, goblins and other mysterious phenomena, are victims of the evil way. It is clear that the true learning that Atsutane aspired to was the very opposite of the arrogance and vanity of those who never learned their way to the true ethical way. The true ethical way as understood by Atsutane was very much at odds with that envisaged by his master Norinaga; it was a disfigured nativism.

If we accept that nativism was perfectly formed with Motoori Norinaga, then Atsutane's ancient studies might be thought of rather as the black sheep of the nativist family. If we can talk of Norinaga's nativism as being built upon on the concept of *mono no aware*, then we might venture that Hirata's nativism was built upon *mononoke* (the veneration of spirits); so unmistakably bizarre was his nativism. His nativism was constructed out of blocks fashioned from his obsession with deities, the soul, hermits and goblins. Perhaps it is only natural that Orikuchi Shinobu, our second disfigured nativist, should have given the most accurate evaluation of Atsutane's own disfigured nativism.

In a lecture probably given at Kokugakuin University during the last war, he developed some remarkable ideas on Atsutane. Firstly, he pointed out Atsutane's manic character: 'He read manically and wrote manically'; second was his acute observation that overturns the commonly held view that Atsutane's learning was uncompromising, narrow and ultranationalistic. Rather, Orikuchi suggests, it was immensely 'broad in conception'; it was a learning brimming with compassion and affection for his disciples. Thirdly, although Atsutane is frequently depicted as loathing Confucianism and Buddhism, Orikuchi explained that he took freely from both and certainly did not attack either with malice.[13] Fourth, Orikuchi sought to overturn the view that Atsutane learning was difficult and dry. It was rather brimming with delights.

Finally, Orikuchi pointed out that Atsutane pioneered the fields of spiritualist studies (*shinreigaku*) and folklore studies (*minzokugaku*). He concluded his lecture with these words:

The folklore studies that we pursue can be thought of as a sort of nativist methodology. We as nativists remained long ignorant of [what Westerners call] the discipline of 'folklore'. My feeling is that we are continuing a discipline begun by Atsutane when he brought out Torakichi and Katsugorō. It has given me a certain pleasure to realise this [connection]. Of course, we can only ever hope to achieve a thousandth, a ten-thousandth of Atsutane's success here. That is the truth. I am not being [falsely] modest or untruthful. Now, however, we are fortunate to have superior or more advanced methods than those available to Atsutane . . .[14]

Orikuchi understood folklore studies, those that began with Yanagita Kunio, to constitute a new nativist methodology. Orikuchi said that nativism

(*Kokugaku*) was a discipline which must be cultivated; Shinto by contrast was Shinto as it stood [without the need for human cultivation]. Nativism could only exist by developing it deliberately as an academic discipline. Unlike the natural phenomenon of Shinto, the human phenomenon of nativism had to be developed over the ages.[15] Orikuchi expanded on the idea of folklore studies as the new nativism in the 'Postscript' to the third volume of his *Kodai kenkyū*.

> We need a new nativism. We need to see the original form of those ancient beliefs that have since been rationalised and modernised. The legacy of [old] learning hangs in the air like a dust cloud I can not disperse. Only now has it struck me that the way to straighten this all out is not philosophy or religion. It occurs to me that the new nativism has to start from the study of human society which itself sprung from ancient beliefs. As the inheritor of Professor Yanagita's legacy, I have worked diligently to reconstruct a new nativism. Over the past fifteen years a new structure has come into being. The three volumes of *Kodai kenkyū* constitute an attempt to define the logic of the new nativism.[16]

As a book *Kodai kenkyū* is, in fact, a mess; its text is filled with noise and discordance. It is a bizarre book in which Orikuchi Shinobu traces, very much in fluid form, his own spiritual wanderings and thoughts. There are pieces in the book that can be called neither articles nor essays; pieces that are nothing more than memoirs, collections of fragmented images. In the fragments there are to be found scattered phrases offering a fascinating glimpse of Orikuchi's poetic vision, but it is bizarre that he should have gathered all these memoirs together in a book. Some of the fragments have the power to inspire the imagination; they are truly fascinating. Two such fragments, known as *Oguri hōgan* and *Hyōchaku ishikami*, are in Orikuchi's categories of the Other (*marebito*) and the 'nobleman in exile'. Hirata Atsutane had pushed open a path to the Other Realm through Torakichi and Katsugorō and reported back on his love of the strangers from that realm. In a similar sort of way, Orikuchi relied on all sorts of fragments from his study of 'human society' to engage in the pursuit of his folklore, similarly motivated by love of strangers from the Other Realm. Their efforts here exhibit the workings of that mysterious fate that led them to decipher and to explore the birth place of their own souls.

Orikuchi knew nothing of the disfigurement on Hirata Atsutane's face since it was only after Orikuchi's death that the fragments of the ripped letter were rediscovered. If Orikuchi had known of Hirata's facial scarring, modern Japanese nativism would undoubtedly have taken a different path. At least, Orikuchi's understanding of Hirata would surely have been different. He would undoubtedly have had a keener understanding of the mysterious depths of fate.

Geography, language, and the Other Realm

For Hirata Atsutane and Orikuchi Shinobu, the Other Realm was not merely an abstract idea. Both made serious and passionate attempts to find out about its structure, its geographical position, and even its inhabitants with remarkable passion but also with a strikingly 'scientific' spirit. In their explorations, both writers concentrated on two planes of investigation, one spacial and the other temporal. The first led to questions about the Other Realm's spacial characteristics, structure, and location, and the second linked up with research into mythological accounts of the origin of the universe, and with theories about antiquity. The first, in other words, took the form of a kind of 'mytho-geography,' and the second of 'mytho-linguistics.' The reason these writers spent so much of their energy delving into the Other Realm, *kotodama*, and the writing of the Age of the Gods (*jindai moji*) was that they regarded the Other Realm and its language as their spiritual ancestral home, which demanded clarification. Their quest for knowledge about these matters automatically led them to an interest in such matters as exorcism (*chinkon*) and spirit possession (*kamigakari*). Thus too did they become fascinated with the Taoist Way of the Immortals, with esoteric Buddhism and shamanism. Perhaps we should suggest rather say that Atsutane's and Orikuchi's studies moved on an esoteric plane from the very beginning, as a 'karmic result' brought on by their disfigurement. Obviously, the esoteric character of their studies was built on the conviction that spirits really existed.

Orikuchi described Atsutane the scholar as 'a man who felt free to adopt anything and everything.'[17] Referring to Atsutane's *Ino mononoke roku*, he wrote: 'Atsutane, being the kind of person he is, he must have arrived at the conclusions he did in an attempt to uncover a "kami character" even in ghosts (*bakemono*).'[18] For Orikuchi himself, who traced the spiritual characteristics and phases of transformation of kami, spirits (*tama*), bogeys (*mono*) and demons (*oni*), the distance between ghosts and kami was not all that great. Orikuchi argued that the kami of Japan were what the ancients called 'spirits', and he argued that these sprits had subdivided into the categories of kami and mono.[19] In his *Reikon no hanashi* ('Spirit stories'), he put it as follows: 'Ancient belief held that *tama* were abstract beings who from time to time appeared in physical form. They then became kami, or, on a lower level, beings that came to be thought of as *mono*. In other words, *tama* came to be conceived of as either good or evil, and those parts that appeared as good to humans became kami, while the evil parts were regarded as *mono*.'[20]

For Atsutane and Orikuchi, the standards used to distinguish good from evil could only be human, not absolute. This explains Atsutane's understanding of the kami Magatsubi no Kami, and also Orikuchi's view of Susanowo. While this latter kami was traditionally regarded as an evil kami, Orikuchi saw him as an archetypical 'sacred visitor' (*marebito*) who 'retained vestiges of the [ancient] ambivalence between good and evil.'[21] Similarly, Atsutane described the 'lands of the Eternal Realm' (*tokoyo*) as 'lands ruled by

Susanowo.'[22] These two writers stand on 'the other shore, beyond good and evil' (as Nietzsche might have put it) and from that position overlook the world we inhabit as a 'land where good and evil [have meaning].' Their gaze goes back to the origins of good and evil, and they view the reality of this world from that perspective.

Atsutane wrote in his *Yūgenben*:

> When one grows old and dies, one's body will return to dust, but one's spirit (*tamashii*) will not disappear. Returning to the Hidden Realm (*kakuriyo*), it will be subject to the reign of Ōkuninushi no Ōkami, accept his commands, and from Heaven it will protect not only its descendants but all those related to it. These are the 'hidden matters' (*kakurigoto*) of man, and this is the Way established by Musubi no Kami and governed by Ōkuninushi no Kami. It is for this reason that the [*Nihon shoki*] states: 'The hidden matters constitute Shinto.' . . .
>
> Why then does the Great Deity [Ōkuninushi] allow such evil kami to act in this way when, by rights, he should prohibit them severely; and what does this reveal about his own august heart? . . .
>
> When [Ōkuninushi] fled to the Nether World (*Yomitsu kuni*) [to escape the tortures inflicted on him by his eighty brothers], [his father] Susanowo on purpose put on a stern face, despite his liking for Ōkuninushi, and put him to the test in various painful ways. [Ōkuninushi] underwent his ordeals without flinching, and when he fled back to the Upper World (*Kamitsu kuni*), Susanowo no Ōkami chased him up to the Pass of the Nether World (*Yomotsu hirasaka*), and ordered him to drive away all his brothers and to become the 'Great Lord of the land' (Ōkuninushi no Kami) and the 'Visible Spirit of the land' (Utsushikunitama no Kami). . . . Ōkuninushi did indeed expel his brothers, but during his stay in the Visible Realm (*utsushiyo*) suffered great pains in completing the magnificent task of 'preparing the land' (*kunitsukuri*). Reflecting on these events, it would seem that although the deeds of evil kami and demons [such as Ōkuninushi's brothers] are loathsome, [Ōkuninushi] tolerates them for a while because they have the beneficial effect of bringing a man to true acts of virtue.
>
> It strikes me that this is rather similar to the policy of letting evil persons whose crimes have become known to the authorities live on for a while, even though they deserve swift execution. This serves the cause of investigating good and evil among the people, or arresting those who are in hiding. Only if they have not mended their ways are they later executed. Reflecting further on this, it seems to me that even the most evil things between heaven and earth serve someone's purpose, because even those kami and demons who work only evil benefit the world and mankind by urging man, through their deeds, to perform true acts of virtue. . . .[23]

Here, Atsutane is not merely arguing that good and evil are relative concepts. His view is that human nature is in principle good, because 'human nature is a spirit of the Musubi no Ōkami imparted in man.'[24] He then asks how it is possible that evil is rife in the human world, when all humans are endowed with Musubi no Ōkami's good spirit. He explains that this evil is caused by deeds of evil kami and demons, which serve the purpose of giving humans the opportunity to perfect their ability to perform 'true acts of virtue.' This, he concludes, is the 'fundamental teaching of the "hidden matters" of [Ōkuninushi,] the Great Kami of the Hidden Realm, who allows a man to attain true happiness by urging him to perform real acts of virtue.'[25] Moreover, he argues forcefully that 'this world is a temporary world (*kari no yo*), where the kami make us live for a short while in order to test our good and evil qualities; the real world of man is the Hidden Realm.'[26]

However, Atsutane did not conceive of the Hidden Realm as a distant world that is strictly separated from the material world we know. On the contrary, the Hidden Realm is a very real world, in constant and very close contact, always engaging with the world we inhabit: 'The hidden matters are the fundamental matters, the matters of the spirit-world; but this spirit-world is not a specific place that exists separately from this Visible Realm. It refers to the divine court that [Ōkuninushi] set up within this Visible Realm, wherever it may be, to rule over hidden matters. Its headquarters are in the great shrine in Izumo (Izumo taisha) . . . But as long as one is a human inhabitant of this world, his government is obscured from view, even on pilgrimage to Izumo. Such is the difference between the visible and the hidden: although the visible can be seen from the hidden, the reverse is not possible.'[27]

According to Atsutane, then, the 'spirit-world' does not exist apart from the 'Visible Realm.' Its headquarters are in the Izumo shrine, but it also set up court in 'branches' across the land. However, even on pilgrimage to Izumo we are unable to see the 'government' of the 'hidden,' because just as one cannot see from the light into the dark, the hidden cannot be seen from the visible.[28] Even though the 'visible' and the 'hidden' are mutually autonomous, they are inter-linked in complicated ways. Moreover, the Hidden Realm is just as 'material' as the Visible Realm. Indeed, 'the Hidden Realm has food, housing and clothing, just like our own world.'[29]

In this perception of the world, the 'Age of the Gods' and the 'present age' do not constitute distinct entities. The Age of the Gods is a world just across the border of the same continent, linked directly and very concretely to our own age. For Atsutane, there are no hard divisions between either the Age of the Gods and the present day, or between kami myth and history.

In this light, the reasons for his pursuit of what we might call Shinto-mysticism or Shinto-esotericism become understandable. Atsutane believed that there existed a hierarchical relationship between the different realms making up the world, and that this hierarchy had its roots in the phases of the cosmogony. From this point of view, the relation between (as Orikuchi put it) 'kami and ghosts' can indeed be a very close one. Here, the points of contact between humans, ghosts and kami are not necessarily very clear – just as the distinction between good and evil is rather unclear. Atsutane's sense of the

Hidden Realm is summed up in his remark that 'it is obvious that in many places the Age of the Gods lives on unchanged even now, although we cannot see this because kami and humans have become separated.'[30] Atsutane sensed the Age of the Gods as a physical presence.

This sense of the Hidden Realm alone accounts for a letter Atsutane addressed to 'the servants of the people of Mt. Sōgaku, the Spirit World (yūkai), Mt. Iwama, Hitachi Province'. He asked Torakichi to deliver the letter to his spirit contacts there. It was in all seriousness that Atsutane tried to start up a correspondence with the inhabitants of the 'border regions of the immortals' (senkyō). His letter read:

Recently, I have made the acquaintance of this servant boy of your august mountain [that is, Torakichi], and heard a short account of your activities. This cleared up the doubts that have troubled me for many years, and I cherish my acquaintance with him as the most important meeting of my life. I hope you will not be offended that I have used this opportunity of Torakichi's return to the mountain to offer you this letter. I would like to extend my sincere congratulations to you for the ever-increasing prosperity and diligent works of your servants. Because the visible and the hidden have been separated from each other since the Age of the Gods, the matters of the Hidden Realm are difficult to gauge from this Visible Realm. You are, however, well-informed about the Visible Realm and I trust you are familiar with it. It is my sincere wish to learn about the Ancient Way of the Gods of Heaven and Earth (tenjin chigi no kodō), and to spread this Way in the world. Unworthy though I am, I have striven hard for many years to follow in the footsteps of my master Motoori [Norinaga] and to study his learning. However, as an ignorant layman in the Visible Realm, it is exceedingly difficult for me to gain insight into the Hidden Realm, and I remain troubled by many unanswered questions. Therefore, I would hereafter be most grateful to receive your august instructions about your Realm and thus clear up my doubts. Might you be so gracious as to enlighten me when, from time to time, I might pray that you answer my questions? If at all possible, I beseech you to send me your answers whenever this servant boy descends from the mountain. If you will grace me with your wisdom, I will for the duration of my life diligently perform ritual worship once a month. Also, allow me to show you the book Tama no mihashira which I have recently published. This book discusses the true state of the world (albeit in unsatisfactory fashion) on the basis of the ancient transmission from the Age of the Gods, and also touches upon the Hidden Realm. It contains the feeble thoughts of an ignorant layman, and I tremble to think of the mistakes that will come to light when you cast your eyes over it. If you could, upon your perusal of it, inform me of its failures, that would be a cause of great joy to this world. It would be a reward for my diligent studies and the fulfilment of my life's greatest wish. Please take this letter to your own august master; I pray single-heartedly for your indulgence. With all the sincerity of an ignorant student of the Ancient Way, I submit to your anger at my crime of offering you this letter without any knowledge of the proper procedures of your august realm. Humbly and sincerely yours,

Hirata Daigaku
Taira no Atsutane

[1820]/10/17[31]

Atsutane is seeking instructions from the Hidden Realm here, snatching at the chance offered him by Torakichi to make his acquaintance with the 'mountain dweller of Sugiyama.' Moreover, he has Torakichi present copies of his main works *Tama no mihashira* and *Jindai moji no kō*, and seeks corrections. To cap it all, he promises to repay any answers by means of monthly 'ritual worship.'

Half a year after the sending of this letter, in the fourth month of 1821, Atsutane set off with Torakichi and two of his students on a research trip to the home of the 'mountain dweller of Sugiyama,' on Mt. Asama in Shinano Province. Moreover, from the fourth month of the following year, 1822, Atsutane performed a monthly 'ritual for Mister Takane,' who was none other than Torakichi's master, the same 'mountain dweller of Sugiyama' himself.[32] In his daily prayers Atsutane paid special reverence to a deity called 'Hibi-tsu-Takane-ō no Mikoto' (that is, the same 'Mister Takane'). Atsutane began with worship of Ame no Minakanushi no Kami, Takami-musubi no Kami and Kamimusubi no Kami, and the myriad deities of heaven and earth before turning his devotion to Mister Takane. The text of the prayer implies Atsutane regarded Takane as a member of the retinue of the deity of Mt. Asama, Iwanaga-hime no Kami.[33]

Here, I would like to draw attention to a portrait in *Senkyō ibun* that in all probability depicts this Hibi-tsu-Takane-ō no Mikoto. This portrait is remarkably similar to Atsutane's own portrait: long, slim eyes, which seem to look far into the distance, a rather big, protruding nose, large ears that seem to be straining to catch even the most hidden sounds – all these defining organs show a striking resemblance to Atsutane's own. One only needs to exaggerate the features of Atsutane somewhat to arrive at this portrait of the 'mountain dweller of Sugiyama.' Moreover, there is an equally striking resemblance with Torakichi. In *Senkyō ibun*, Atsutane describes Torakichi's features as follows:

He is an innocent, normal youth, and although he is fifteen years of age, he looks no more than a thirteen year old. His eyes have a whiteness to them and are larger than average, too; they have a piercing quality . . . and the light they emit gives his whole face a strange aspect.[34]

In fact, this characterisation is equally fitting of Atsutane himself, and it is quite possible that Atsutane saw in this youngster an image of his own youth. As described in *Senkyō ibun*, Torakichi became possessed by spirits many times in order that he might serve as a go-between between Atsutane and the

Hidden Realm.[35] However, it is clear that Torakichi meant more to Atsutane than a mere channel of information. I am convinced that Atsutane not only recognised his youthful self in Torakichi, but also saw him as a grown-up version of his first and second sons Tsunetarō and Hanbei, who both died young.[36] In the year Atsutane met Torakichi, Tsunetarō would have been eighteen years old, and Hanbei twelve. The fifteen year-old Torakichi, with his distinctive features, acted as a spirit mediator between Atsutane and his two dead sons. He played the role of a 'stranger' (ijin) who was irreplaceable to the equally strange-faced nativist scholar. Perhaps Atsutane identified Torakichi with his youthful self. He must have happened upon his particular brand of folklore – motivated by his love for 'strangers' (ijin) – through his meeting with Torakichi, and I am convinced that this meeting had an epoch-making impact on Atsutane's nativist thought.

If Atsutane resembled a 'mountain dweller' or tengu, then Orikuchi was more akin to a water-dwelling kappa. In an essay entitled Kappa no hanashi ('On Kappa'), which he published in Chūō kōron in September 1929, Orikuchi wrote:

> I recently spent two summers on the island of Iki. There I learnt that this island is a true repository of kappa legends from the entire region of northern Kyushu. I soon realised that the islanders of Iki are to this day influenced (albeit faintly) by ancient beliefs in the kami of water. Since I believe that it is vital for a folklorist to rely on his own field notes, which convey his own impressions gained during his visit, rather than on reports of oddities and strange rumours by others who are insufficiently aware of the issues, I planned to write an outline of my research into the folklore of Iki and other nearby islands. My basic thesis . . . is that kappa legends were construed on the basis of an ancient belief that highly-respected water kami visit the island from across the sea, to which elements from stories about local water hermits have been added.[37]

This essay also includes nine pictures of kappa, preserved by a swimming instructor of the former Kumamoto domain. The fourth of these shows a striking resemblance to Orikuchi. Under this picture, Orikuchi explains that the half-feared, half-ridiculed kappa is a 'water fairy' who brings wealth, and that the kappa's image is tied up with the 'ancient image of the stranger who arrives with presents, and returns.'[38] Orikuchi's focus on ancient religious life fell on the 'water maidens' who served under various kami; it is therefore easy to imagine that kappa would have been the object of his special affection and interest. It is of little surprise, then, that he preserved these kappa images with devoted care. He must have seen in the kappa, as the much reduced image of a sacred visitor from afar, an image of his own soul. Just as Atsutane, who hailed from distant Akita, felt at home with mountain dwellers and tengu, the Osaka-born Orikuchi recognised his own spiritual roots in the water-dwelling kappa.

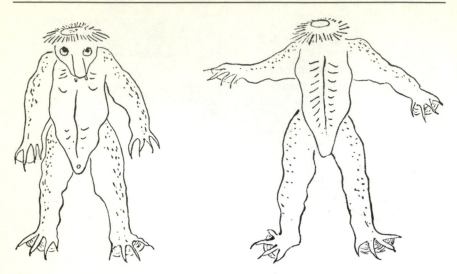

Kappa (Source: Orikuchi hakase kinenkai ed. *Orikuchi Shinobu zenshū*, vol. 3, Chūō Kōronsha, 1973)

In his *Haha ga kuni e, Tokoyo e: Ikyō ishiki no kifuku* ('To the land of my mother, to the Eternal Land: The rise and fall of the awareness of strange lands'), Orikuchi wrote:

If one of the motives behind art is man's yearning for relaxation, both mental and physical, in a world that constrains him on all sides, then the longing for other worlds and other lands is only too similar. While the task of religion and morality may well be to improve the world if only a little, the Pure Land of the common people has to be closer to home than that.

Events from the distant past, when our ancestors arrived in this country, have been handed down in the tales of story-tellers. About their original land (*mototsu kuni*), archaeologists, linguists and historians have offered some additional evidence, but no more than that. Their children and grandchildren may have just heard of the existence of distant lands which their parents had not visited; but even this faint knowledge was soon forgotten, and all that remained was a longing for the 'original land,' infused into them by their fathers. I believe that this force, which inspired our forefathers one, two thousand years ago, is still alive in our hearts today.

Ten years ago, I travelled to Kumano. When I stood on the very tip of cape Daiō, which sticks out far into the ocean, I could not help feeling that my spiritual *homeland* was somewhere far beyond those sun-lit waves. Even today, I cannot dismiss this feeling as a mere affectation of a would-be poet. Is this not an *atavism*, a vestige of the *nostalgia* that once incited the hearts of our ancestors?

Longing for his 'mother's land' distressed Susanowo no Mikoto so much that he turned green mountains into barren mountains; also, it moved Inahi no Mikoto [in the *Kojiki*] to 'walk the wave tops.' Generations of story-tellers have explained that this land carries the name of 'mother's land' (*haha no kuni*) because it is the land to which Susanowo's mother Izanami no Mikoto and Inahi's mother Tamayori-hime no Mikoto retired; but in fact, these are stories which tell of the yearning for the 'original land' that is shared by all human beings.[39]

To Orikuchi, the 'strange land' (*ikyō*) is the 'original land,' the 'homeland of the soul,' and also the 'motherland' and the 'Eternal Land.' It is worthy of note that the channel to Orikuchi's spiritual homeland was water – this in contrast to Atsutane's vision of a 'homeland of the soul' in the mountains. Orikuchi constantly stretched his 'nostalgic' and 'atavistic' imagination to new horizons by manipulating water as a spiritual medium. It was in this way that Orikuchi succeeded in catching a glimpse of his 'spiritual homeland' though 'water maidens' and *kappa*. Here, I shall take a closer look at Orikuchi's fascination with *kappa*, and the process whereby he himself came to resemble one.

Orikuchi wrote about the development of *kappa* beliefs, and about the plate on their head (see illustrations, above p. 310):

> *Kappa* are water deities, or beings from the retinue of such deities. Sometimes, they exhibit great spiritual authority, and at other times they work mischief in the way of naughty hermits. It is also possible that spirits (*bunrei*) of sea kami were thought to reside in wet places on land, and conceived of as flocks of *kappa*. If we approach *kappa* from their modern incarnation, there seems no other way to explain them. However, I propose another view.
>
> Looking at the ideas behind Japanese water kami through a *kappa* lens, we find confusion from an early date. Are they good kami, who have come from across the distant sea, or are they local spirits? The distinction remains unclear. Kami and spirits that oppose them are clearly distinguishable; and yet, deeds of kami are projected onto spirits, and beings that were once spirits come to be treated as kami. *Kappa*, too, were once kami, but ended up as spirits that merely harass the villagers. There are also regions where *kappa* have retained certain characteristics of kami, and have the power to bestow prosperity on those who flatter and serve them.
>
> The plate of the *kappa* seems to be thought of both as a storing place for treasures, and as a hiding place for life-enhancing powers. It is not a plate for holding water; rather, it seems that at places where water beliefs already existed, it came to contain water as a source of the power to control water.[40]

Orikuchi points out that *kappa* have the dual character of 'good kami who have come from across the sea' and of 'local spirits.' His image of the *kappa* is a hybrid one, linked in indistinct ways to kami, human beings and ghosts. With this hybrid image, Orikuchi felt great affinity. His *kappa*, who stand between kami and spirits, are like the *daimōn* in Plato's *The banquet*, who stand between gods and men. This applies, of course, in equal measure to Atsutane's *tengu*. Both the *tengu* and the *kappa* were erotic mediums that provided a channel to the Other Realm.

By using *tengu* and *kappa* as erotic mediums, Atsutane and Orikuchi became conversant with the geography and language of the Other Realm. In order to learn about the geography of this Other Realm, it was necessary first to master its language; and to that end, it was vital to make friends with those of its inhabitants who visit our own world. In other words, by becoming friendly with *tengu* and *kappa*, Atsutane and Orikuchi hoped to be able to learn about their 'spiritual homeland'; and by this somewhat esoteric process, they hoped simultaneously to reach their own 'spiritual homeland,' too.

Orikuchi became aware of the deeper layers of his own perception of 'strange lands' through his piecing together, in his typically precise yet disjointed manner, the process by which *kappa* came to be defined as a cross between water kami from beyond the sea and local water hermits. Atsutane, too, became knowledgeable about the geography and language of the Other Realm thanks to the information he gained with Torakichi's help. Orikuchi wrote about Atsutane's *Ino mononoke roku*:

> Master Atsutane conjures up a never-ending multitude of ghosts over a period of thirty days . . . Part of it must surely be Master Atsutane's creation. There is no way he could have written so much if that were not the case. He writes in great detail what kind of ghosts turned up every night, what they looked like, and what they did. However good one's memory, it would be impossible to remember so many details. Therefore a lot of it must have been invented by Master Atsutane himself. Of every ghost a picture is provided. These pictures show dreadful ghosts. Such ghosts appeared every night, in spite of the fact that they bore no grudge and received no award whatsoever. On the thirtieth day, at long last the boss of the ghosts made his appearance. He was a square, imposing man wearing a *kamishimo*. He praised Inao Heitarō: 'I am Sanmoto Gorōzaemon. I have never met anyone as strange as you. I was hoping to harm you, but I have had no luck. I am off. I can't do it, but there is this fellow I know called Jinno Akugorō. If I bring him along he'll be able to work his mischief on you, but I am no longer capable. Anyway, if ever in your life you need my help, just knock on a pillar.' With that he went home.[41]

Inao Heitarō of Bingo Province, a youth of sixteen years old, was tormented night after night by a succession of ghosts for the whole of a long summer month. Beasts with one eye, women's heads, monstrous crabs, old women: the trembling Heitarō was attacked by them all. However, young Heitarō stood his ground and chased them away one by one, until he finally became friends with their 'boss' (*oyatama*) Sanmoto Gorōzaemon.

312

In Atsutane's text, Sanmoto Gorōzaemon describes himself as follows: 'I am not a human being like you say, nor a *tengu*. I am a demon king (*maō*). I first came to Japan during the Genpei wars. In Japan, there is only Jinno Akugorō of my kind.'[42] Interesting here is that he revealed himself as a 'demon king' who visits Japan from the Other Realm. When an inhabitant of the Other Realm revealed his identity, this meant that he was submitting to the other's power, or recognised his power and wanted to do a deal with him, or again wanted to become friendly with him. It would seem that, strange though this may seem, Sanmoto Gorōzaemon felt some affection for the young Heitarō.

Gorōzaemon's last words to Heitarō were: 'You are a strong-nerved fellow; it is because you are so strong-nerved that you have suffered so much. The time for you to run into trouble came this year. This is something that awaits all human beings in the universe, even if they are only sixteen years old. To scare and frighten people is my duty, and for me it is not a personal matter.'[43] Then he 'took out a hammer' and said:

> Therefore I will give you this hammer, which you must carry with you all your life. If you are set upon by ghosts ever again, turn to the north and say: 'Come quickly, Sanmoto Gorōzaemon,' and strike a pillar with this hammer. Then I will come at once and help you. Thank you for your hospitality.[44]

At this, Gorōzaemon bowed to Heitarō and made his departure. His somewhat humorous and utterly composed manner was very unlike what one would expect of a 'demon king.' Orikuchi hit the nail on the head when he concluded, as we saw above, that Atsutane, as the compiler of this text, 'uncovered a kami character even in ghosts (*bakemono*)'. Gorōzaemon boarded a palanquin (his big feet dangling out) and left in the style of a *daimyō*, with a large escort. 'The palanquin was a normal one, but the escort consisted of strange monsters. They were all wearing formal *kamishimo*, *hakama*, and *haori*, which looked decidedly odd on these monstrous apparitions.'[45] Atsutane described the scene as follows:

> . . . they went up into the sky like the light of a lantern, and their black shadows could be seen for a while in the light of the stars. It appeared as though they would enter a cloud, but then there was a sound like a gust of wind, and they disappeared. Heitarō, unsure whether he was dreaming or awake, just stared at the sky; but after some thought he decided he might well be dreaming, and left the sliding doors open, laying a fan on the lintel as a marker. He went back into his room, hung up his mosquito net, laid out his bed and went straight to sleep, exhausted by his exertions since noon. When he woke up, late the following morning, the fan was still in the same place, and looking out he saw that the garden was covered in marks, as though the ground had been ploughed in all directions. Thinking that perhaps he had not been dreaming after all, he went back in and looked for the corner where he had met Gorōzaemon

the previous night and, indeed, to his shock there was the hammer. This hammer was about six *sun* [18 cm] across, with a handle of one *shaku* [30 cm] long. The handle was too long for it to be a normal hammer . . . In other respects, too, it was a hammer with very strange features.[46]

This was a strange and moving parting between a ghost and a human being. The passage reveals much about Atsutane as a folklorist and his love for strange beings. For Atsutane, it was not enough to love ; he also wanted to be loved in return. Without the experience of this love, this kind of folklore remained meaningless to its practitioners – and this was the same for Atsutane, Orikuchi, and also for Inagaki Ashiho (1900–1974).[47] It was a strange kind of folklore indeed; but it is also folklore's very starting point. Hirata and Orikuchi knew that here was their chance to 'jump and spin' with the gods and the ghosts.

In this respect, even Yanagita Kunio fell short of the ideal – in spite of Orikuchi's following evaluation of Yanagita's scholarship:

If I were to say that the starting point of [Yanagita-] *sensei*'s scholarship is the same as Hirata's, [Yanagita-] *sensei* would not be pleased to hear that, and I am sure you would be surprised as well. But if I now think about Hirata Atsutane, I realise what an extraordinary scholar he was. I think his life before he became a scholar was just too harsh. He was an exceptional reader, a great scholar, and a man who really strove to introduce new knowledge. My strong impression is that he strove too hard. Also on the subject of the Japanese kami, he tried to find out as much as he could, but was too rational in his attitude. Still, there are few *kokugaku* scholars who tackled Shinto in such a methodical manner. His aim was to eliminate 'vulgar Shinto.' Many seem to believe 'vulgar Shinto' refers to the faith of the common people, but that is a gross mistake. He investigated ghosts and believed in immortals (*sennin*). Hirata Atsutane took Torakichi home and brought him up – Torakichi who was 'hidden by the kami' [*kamikakushi* – i.e. suddenly lost to the world]. He then conducted all manner of experiments on him. His attitude to the *kamikakushi* itself was exactly the same. One might expect Atsutane to call this 'vulgar Shinto,' but his view was that unless one took the attitude he took, the kami would always remain out of reach. It was unfortunate that on the one hand he treated [Shinto] as old texts, and on the other hand thought of these real things as something distinct. As a result, the two remained parallel and never came together. If they had come together, he would have benefited the world more, I think . . . However that may be, it is clear that [Yanagita-] *sensei* followed the same route as Hirata Atsutane before him.[48]

Orikuchi defined the aim of Yanagita's work as 'the study of the kami,' and it is indeed true that kami formed the focus of both Yanagita's and Orikuchi's studies.[49] In this respect, Atsutane was similar. He, too, directed his studies at the kami, if anything even more passionately than them. The difference between Yanagita on the one hand, and Atsutane and Orikuchi on the other, consists in the depth and acuteness of their experience of the Other Realm – or, perhaps, the depth and acuteness of their love for that Other Realm. The scholarship of Atsutane and Orikuchi was of too private and personal a character to be accurately described by the term Kokugaku. The prime aim of Yanagita Kunio's folklore studies (*minzokugaku*) was, by contrast, to study and preserve the traditions of the archetypical 'Japanese family' (*Nihon no ie*), but this notion of the 'Japanese family' is clearly missing from Atsutane's and Orikuchi's folklorist studies into the spirit-world. Rather, I would describe Atsutane's and Orikuchi's scholarship as a kind of '*kokugaku* for orphans.' They set out to study the 'kami of Japan,' but their strong personalities pushed them beyond this framework; their body and soul resonated with a longing for a 'homeland of the spirit' that was too strong to allow them to stay within the constraints of the Japanese 'family.' Therefore, their *kokugaku* could only be a 'disfigured' *kokugaku*. Their scholarship was no more and no less than a 'karmic result' brought on by their individual souls.

We saw above that Heitarō had 'just stared at the sky' as Gorōzaemon disappeared with a 'sound like a gust of wind,' feeling 'unsure whether he was dreaming or awake.' Orikuchi explained that this wind was a spirit, and that the 'accompanying noise' (*oto-zure*) was a sure sign of a spirit's 'visit' (*otozure*). Like Heitarō himself, both Atsutane and Orikuchi were tuned in to this mysterious sound.

In his *Ino mononoke roku*, Hirata states that the 'strange hammer' given to Heitarō by Gorōzaemon is preserved in the temple of Kokuzenji in Hiroshima. We are also informed that Heitarō later assumed the name of Take-dayū and took over as family head from his elder brother. One cannot help noticing that the sequence of the bestowal of a spirit-treasure, followed by a change of name and a succession, follows exactly the same pattern as the story told in the *Kojiki* of the initiation of Ōnamuji no Kami, who changed his name to Ōkuninushi after his visit to his father Susanowo in the Nether World. I have made the point frequently that Susanowo was a multifaceted figure, thought of as both an evil kami and a 'sacred visitor.'[50] Like the young Ōnamuji, Heitarō endured great suffering, and thus became the adult 'Take-dayū.' However, Atsutane notes that Heitarō never forgot Sanmoto Gorōzaemon's 'face.'

We can look at the paths of the older Atsutane and Orikuchi towards an ever closer acquaintance with the Other Realm from different angles. Atsutane's research into Taoism, Esoteric Buddhism, Sinology, Indology, and Age of the Gods letters bore the hallmark of his folklore of love for strange beings. The one scholar who realised the importance of this was Orikuchi Shinobu, who like Atsutane was disfigured with a birth mark, and was similarly a practitioner of the 'folklore of love for strange beings.' To understand these figures, we must give due attention to the fact that their 'families' (*ie*) accommodated strange youngsters such as Torakichi, the resurrected Shōgorō, and Fujii Shun'yō, a disciple of Orikuchi's who died an untimely death in the Pacific War, having mysteriously appeared from Keta in Noto. Their families were channels to the Other Realm, too close to that realm to be truly part of the archetypical 'Japanese family'; rather, they were tiny 'non-families' that shared a strange twist of time and space, where a 'meeting with the unknown' was an incident waiting to happen.

However, this Japanese 'non-family' was simply too small to accommodate the disfigured scholars, Atsutane and Orikuchi. Or perhaps we should say that since it formed a channel to the Other Realm, it was too big. Atsutane and Orikuchi were strange relatives, gathered in a mysterious 'non-family' by 'karmic causes' deep within their souls; travellers with looks and a speed of mind that could not be contained by the 'Japanese family.' I think of them as travellers of the soul, who realised they had come to this 'temporary world' from their spiritual homeland, and would soon return to their other, 'original,' Motherland.

Notes

1 Kamata 1986: 223–4.
2 *Hirata Atsutane zenshū* (hereafter *HAz*), 1: 334.
3 The *nao* character in the name of the deity *Naobi* no Kami means 'to amend' or 'to rectify'.
4 *HAz*, 1: 334.
5 *Motoori Norinaga zenshū*, 9: 271.
6 *HAz* 1: 333.
7 *Orikuchi Shinobu zenshū* (herafter *OSz*) 23: 19–22.
8 *OSz* 23: 11–18.
9 *HAz*, 9: 405. On Atsutane's research into the Other Realm, see also Kamata (1988).
10 *OSz* 3: 491–3. The Hikojirō here referred to is Okamoto Hikojirō, son of the family into which Orikuchi's grandfather was adopted.
11 I.e. genius.
12 *HAz* 9: 567–8.
13 *OSz* 20: 331–9.
14 *OSz* 20: 349–50.
15 *OSz* 20: 348.
16 *OSz* 3: 496–7.
17 *OSz* 20: 343.
18 *OSz* 20: 343.
19 *OSz* 3: 261.
20 *OSz* 3: 261.
21 28 *OSz* 1: 327.
22 *HAz* 7: 56.
23 *HAz* (hoi2): 267–270.
24 *HAz* (hoi2): 267.
25 *HAz* (hoi2): 271.
26 *HAz* (hoi2): 274
27 *HAz* (hoi2): 274
28 *HAz* (hoi2): 274.
29 *HAz* (hoi2): 274.
30 *HAz* (hoi2): 275.

31 *HAz* 9: 383–4.
32 See for a detailed discussion, Kamata 1985: 141–6 ('Spirit flying techniques').
33 *HAz* 6: 630.
34 *HAz* 9: 362.
35 For a more detailed discussion, see Kamata (1984–86).
36 On this see Kamata 1996.
37 *OSz* 3: 288.
38 *OSz* 3: 293–4.
39 *OSz* 2: 5–6.
40 *OSz* 3: 310.
41 *OSz* 20: 342.
42 *HAz* 9: 740.
43 *HAz* 9: 741.
44 *HAz* 9: 740.
45 *HAz* 9: 744.
46 *HAz* 9: 744–8.
47 See for a more detailed discussion, Kamata 1985.
48 *OSz* 16: 515–6.
49 *OSz* 16: 512.
50 See, for example, Kamata 1985.

CHAPTER SIXTEEN

Tanaka Yoshitō and the beginnings of *Shintōgaku*

Isomae Jun'ichi

Introduction

Today, there will be few even in Japan who remember Tanaka Yoshitō (1872–1946), and yet he was one of the great names in prewar Shinto studies. While teaching at Kokugakuin and other universities, Tanaka Yoshitō was in charge of the only existing Shinto programme at the time at Tokyo Imperial University, where he was an associate professor (*jokyōju*). Even more importantly, he was the first to advocate the study of Shinto as an independent academic discipline (*Shintōgaku*, perhaps translatable as 'Shintology'), and must therefore be regarded as one of the fathers of modern Shinto studies.

Today, Shintōgaku is regarded as a reactionary discipline tainted by nationalism, and is treated with scant regard. In the prewar period, however, it was a new field that attracted the attention of scholars from many different backgrounds. Its development was bound up with current political issues, such as the non-religious status of shrines and freedom of religion. As we trace Tanaka's career, some aspects of Shintōgaku that are not widely known will become clear. We will find, for example, that Shintōgaku arose from a philosophical movement interested in 'the theory of National Morality' (*Kokumin dōtokuron*), and not, contrary to what some may expect, from National Learning (*Kokugaku*). Also, we will find that its main advocates were not local priests and intellectuals, but academics. In this essay, I shall consider the way in which Shintōgaku originated as an academic discipline, and the ways in which it was entangled with the intellectual and political conditions of the prewar period. In the process, I shall introduce the work of Tanaka Yoshitō and show in concreto what the state of Shintōgaku in his time was.

'National Morality'

Encounter with Inoue Tetsujirō

Tanaka Yoshitō was born in 1872 of a family that had served formerly as *shōya* in Yamaguchi prefecture. After attending primary, junior high and high schools in Tokyo, he enrolled at Tokyo Imperial University, College of Literary Studies, where he graduated from the Faculty of Philosophy in 1903.[1] At the time, one of the professors of this faculty was Inoue Tetsujirō (1855–1944), who actively promoted the notion of 'National Morality', and also gave lectures on Shinto history. As a student, Tanaka conducted a study under Inoue on the topic of 'Merging pedagogy and Shinto.'[2] At Tokyo Imperial University, there was no Pedagogical Faculty at this time; only one course in pedagogy was taught at the College of Literary Studies. In Shinto studies, not even a course existed. These circumstances left Tanaka no choice but to pursue his interests in pedagogy and Shinto at the Faculty of Philosophy.

The roots of the National Morality movement go back to the third decade of the Meiji period (1887–96), when its ideas were first developed in support of the national policy of encouraging emperor worship, and in opposition to what was seen as the world-denying nature of Christianity. As argued, typically, in Inoue's *Chokugo engi* ('Comments on the Imperial Rescripts', 1889) and *Kyōiku to shūkyō no shōtotsu* ('The conflict between education and religion', 1893), this movement regarded 'Western and traditional thought as equal,' and distanced itself from earlier writers on 'Japanese morality' such as Nishimura Shigeki by attempting to systematise ideas on National Morality in a 'theoretical and historical manner.'[3]

After the Russo-Japanese war of 1904–5, an upsurge of capitalism engendered an intensification of socialist labour movements in the Meiji 40sbetween 1907 and 1912. To counter this, and backed by the swell of patriotism of these years, a movement was formed to 'spread National Morality throughout the nation by including in state-enforced school books the moral principles of "unity of loyalty and filial piety" and of our country's unique national polity, as set out by academics such as Inoue Tetsujirō; and by clarifying the essential principles of moral education to teachers of primary, junior high and high schools, as well as teachers' training courses, through lectures organised by the Ministry of Education.'[4] In a strict sense, the term 'National Morality' refers to this movement in the Meiji 40s, when it broadened the scope of its criticism from Christianity to labour movements and Western thought in general. This period in the movement's history is characterised by Inoue's *Kokumin dōtoku gairon* ('Introduction to National Morality', 1912), which 'came close to becoming a state-enforced theory of ethics, and exerted a profound influence on the educational world of Japan.'[5]

During Tanaka's student days at Tokyo Imperial University, that is until 1903, the first signs were emerging of the development of National Morality into a fully-fledged movement. During this period, Inoue published a book on the 'relation between ethics and religion' (*Rinri to shūkyō no kankei*, 1902), criticising those contemporary scholars of ethics who advocated a purely Western style of education. Simultaneously, Inoue wrote extensively on Japanese pre-modern Confucianism, publishing in rapid succession works on the Confucian schools of Wang Yangming (*Nihon Yōmeigakuha no tetsugaku*, 1900), Ancient Learning (*Nihon Kogakuha no tetsugaku*, 1902), and Zhu Xi

(*Nihon Shushigakuha no tetsugaku*, 1906). In these works, he consistently approached his subjects from the standpoint of the 'development of National Morality.'[6]

After completing Tokyo Imperial University's post-graduate course, Tanaka published two works on Kokugaku Shinto thought, both under the influence of Inoue: *Hirata Atsutane no tetsugaku* (1909), and *Motoori Norinaga no tetsugaku* (1912). In 1922 he submitted his doctoral thesis, entitled *Nihon tetsugaku no hatten* ('The development of Japanese philosophy'), based on his earlier books on Kokugaku. This thesis sought to define Kokugaku as a philosophical tradition that was uniquely Japanese, and in it, Tanaka voiced the hope that his findings 'would contribute both to the theory and the practice of our national education.'[7] As such, his works can be described as a 'Kokugaku version' of Inoue's trilogy on Japanese Confucianism. Apart from Kokugaku, Tanaka also turned his attention to Sect Shinto; but what needs to be stressed here is that these were all subjects mentioned by Inoue in his memoirs as topics that had his special interest, and that he felt should be thoroughly investigated.[8] Tanaka's encounter with Inoue was to influence the outlook of his research throughout his life.

Towards a Japanese pedagogical theory

After his graduation in 1903, Tanaka taught 'Practical Morality' and 'National Morality' at Kokugakuin University from November that year, while attending the post-graduate course at Tokyo Imperial University. Soon afterwards, he began to teach pedagogy also at Nihon University and Tōyō University. Both Kokugakuin and Nihon University were well known for teaching Shinto priests and lawyers a syllabus based on ideas about the national polity (*kokutai*). Among Tanaka's colleagues at these universities were Miyaji Naokazu of Kokugakuin (and later the Shinto Research Institute at Tokyo Imperial University), and Hiranuma Ki'ichirō of Nihon University, who was also a politician with a keen interest in Shinto matters. It seems, however, that Tanaka taught these courses as a part-time lecturer, his main occupation being that of teacher (and later head teacher and principal) at his old junior high school.

During this period, Tanaka's research and publications dealt with pedagogy and National Morality. From 1905 onwards, he published a series of articles about what he called his 'New Pedagogy' in a number of specialised journals. His article 'My New Pedagogy' (*Gojin no iwayuru 'Shin-kyōikugaku'*), written in 1905 in the immediate aftermath of Japan's victory over Russia, set the tone:

> This I call Knowledge: that which makes us realise the origins of our nation and the glory of our national polity, and which encourages us to fulfil our given occupation as a member of our national society. This I call Feeling: to love our nation from the heart, and to be loyal to our

nation with true sincerity. This I call Will: the will to exert oneself in one's given occupation without a single thought for one's own benefit or comfort. To perfect these is the true and great aim of our education; this is the fundamental philosophy of what I call my 'New Pedagogy'.[9]

Setting out a nationalistic pedagogy that aimed to instill absolute devotion to the state in the entire populace, Tanaka detailed an educational practice that penetrated into all aspects of people's lives. In his main work in this field, *Saishin kagakuteki kyōikugaku* ('The latest scientific pedagogy', 1909), Tanaka went beyond theoretical questions to address practical teaching methods such as the choice of textbooks, discipline and punishment, and nursing and physical training. In *Katei kyōikugaku* ('Home pedagogy', 1912), he even addressed every-day matters such as prenatal care, clothing, and baby sitting.

The outlook that defined all Tanaka's writings on these subjects was that of *wakon kansai*, 'Japanese spirit, foreign learning': while Western science must be absorbed as formal knowledge, Tanaka argued that this knowledge must be adapted to the unique, historical traditions of the Japanese people. His publications can be divided into works that expound Western principles of pedagogy and ethics, and works that propagate a Japanese adaptation of these principles and advocate a 'uniquely Japanese pedagogy and morality.'

Underlying this was a concept that Inoue Tetsujirō summed up in the phrase 'The phenomenal is the real' (*genshō soku jitsuzai*). This concept defined the particular as identical to the universal, without any intermediary. Tanaka explained it as follows: 'The ultimate goal of education must be absolute and universal. However, its immediate aims and methods must be particular to each state and each historical period, and must be chosen in such a way as to serve the attainment of this ultimate goal in the best possible manner.'[10] In this way, Western pedagogical notions were separated from their social backgrounds, and transformed on the basis of nationalistic principles designed to fit Japanese society. This was the defining principle of the National Morality movement, which stressed the necessity 'to investigate historically and critically our National Morality while referring to ethical theory, and to raise awareness of the guiding role of ethical theory in shaping the policies of the future.'[11]

As the foundation for his pedagogy, Tanaka referred to the Imperial Rescript on Education (1890). As his 'own ideas' inspired by this Rescript, Tanaka stressed loyalty and filial piety in a family-state focusing on an unbroken and eternal Imperial line:

The Imperial line is unbroken over a myriad generations. The innumerable people are loyal (*chū*) and righteous (*gi*), and the relation between ruler and subject is second not even to that between father and son. The Imperial House is the Family Head (*sōke*) of the innumerable people; the people are infants (*sekishi*) of the Imperial House. Ruler and subject are in harmony and, as one body; high and low come together to form one whole. Possessing a national polity unrivalled in the universe, [our nation] maintains eternal independence. This is certainly not coincidental; in truth, these facts form the basis of our education, and constitute the fundamental principle of [my] New Pedagogy.[12]

Japan's 'National Morality,' then, is 'a philosophy unique to our nation, rooted in our history and geography.'[13] Being different from Western ethics, its theories on education must be founded on Japan's historical traditions; and this is the reason why Tanaka studied these traditions as the foundation for his 'Japanese pedagogy.'[14]

Contemporary critics described Tanaka as a scholar 'who has a very distinct message that is rarely heard from others.'[15] He was a well known figure in the world of education, and the reference work *Nihon gendai kyōikugaku taikei* ('Outline of contemporary Japanese pedagogy', Dainihon Gakujutsukai, ed., 1929) dedicated no less than a hundred pages to his works. Some of his books became popular as textbooks for the state examination for teachers, saw many reprints, and sold well even second hand.[16]

However, never until the Meiji 40s did Tanaka refer to his 'uniquely Japanese thought' as 'Shinto'. At the time, Shinto was regarded as different from the Confucian-inspired 'Imperial Way' (*kōdō*), and it was never at the centre of discussions about National Morality. At this stage, Tanaka was still heavily influenced by Inoue and did not venture beyond the well-trodden paths opened up by his teacher. When and why, then, did Tanaka try to place Shinto at the very basis of National Morality, and to systematise it as the 'fundamental philosophy of the Japanese people'? Answering this question will provide us with an important key to understanding the origins of Shintōgaku.

Shinto studies

Towards Shinto studies

Tanaka Yoshitō's first article on Shinto, entitled 'On the differences between the theories of the Masters Motoori and Hirata; including suggestions for future Shinto research,' appeared in 1908.[17] From 1910 onwards, articles on Shinto constituted the bulk of Tanaka's publications. Most of these articles appeared in journals for shrine priests.[18] Other articles, with titles such as 'Shinto and National Morality,' appeared in journals of academic groups related to the National Morality movement, and advocated 'Shinto thought' as the basis of national education.[19] The publication of *Hirata Atsutane no tetsugaku* (1909), *Shintō hongi* ('The essence of Shinto', 1910), and *Motoori Norinaga no tetsugaku* (1912), all in paperback, established Tanaka as an expert on Kokugaku Shinto and Shinto philosophy. Soon, Tanaka became a sought-after speaker on Shinto, rubbing shoulders on many occasions with scholars such as Miyaji Naokazu, Inoue Tetsujirō, Mizuno Rentarō (head of the Shrine

Bureau at the Home Ministry), Kōno Shōzō (of Kokugakuin University), and Saeki Ariyoshi (of Kōten Kōkyūsho, the 'Institute for the Study of the Imperial Classics').

The occasions on which Tanaka spoke on Shinto were seminars for shrine priests, occasionally opened to the general public, and organised by the Home Ministry, local associations of shrine priests, or Kokugakuin University. The scope of his activities in this field is therefore best described as the teaching of Shinto education to shrine priests. Like all contemporary Shinto scholars, Tanaka regarded shrines as places that embodied the principle of 'revering the gods and worshipping the imperial ancestors' (*keishin sūso*), and thus as focal points of Japan's national polity. In this light, the training of priests took on a national importance: 'Priests, who serve at shrines from morning till night, must be of outstanding talent and knowledge, and present a guiding example to society.'[20] Tanaka's move into the study of Shinto, then, did not constitute a break with his earlier interest in National Morality and education. Rather, Tanaka chose a different audience: shrine priests as 'representatives of myself,'[21] rather than the general population. In this context, it is also interesting to find that Tanaka became president of the 'Shinto Youth Association of Kokugakuin University' (Kokugakuin Daigaku Shintō Seinenkai) in 1913, an association whose membership consisted of 'students of Kokugakuin University and Kōten Kōkyūsho.'

In August 1918, Tanaka left Tokyo and his various posts there to become a teacher at a high school in Kumamoto, Kyushu. Rather than as an impediment to his research, Tanaka probably regarded this position as an excellent opportunity to put his pedagogical ideas into practice. Even though the number of his articles and speeches decreased during his time in Kumamoto, Tanaka continued to lecture on Shinto at venues such as a seminar for priests organised by the Home Ministry in Tokyo. He also published some articles in the journal of the Kumamoto Association of Shrine Priests.

Three years later, in April 1921, Tanaka was invited to take up a teaching post as an associate professor at the newly established Shinto programme of the Department of Literature of Tokyo Imperial University. Tanaka was forty-nine at the time. It appears that the institution of this Shinto programme was initiated by Inoue Tetsujirō and Haga Yaichi as part of the University Reforms (*Daigaku Kaisei Rei*), with the aim of 'pursuing the comprehensive study of Shinto, which is deeply related to our nation's morality and mentality.' In contrast to the training courses for shrine priests established earlier at Jingū Kōgakkan (in Ise) and Kōten Kōkyūsho, this programme was to develop into an institute for research and teaching that was open to all, and not just to trainee-priests.

Initially, Inoue was asked to take charge of this Shinto programme, but he resigned, and on his recommendation Katō Genchi, Miyaji Naokazu and Tanaka were selected as its lecturers.[22] Of these, Tanaka's interests were closest to Inoue's own. After teaching Kokugaku for two years, Tanaka established two new courses, one an 'Introduction to Shinto' based on National Morality ideas, and the other 'Reading the Classics', focusing on the *Kojiki*.[23] The Shinto programme (*kōza*) was upgraded to a 'research institute' (*kenkyūshitsu*) in 1923, and Tanaka continued to act as its main lecturer until his retirement in 1938.

The Imperial Way and Shinto

In 1930, Tanaka wrote: 'I know of some who have interpreted the Imperial Rescript on Education as the morality of our nation, but I know of nobody who argues that it is Shinto. Therefore, my impression is that I am the first to interpret this Rescript as Shinto.'[24] If we search Tanaka's writings for this interpretation of the Rescript as a Shinto teaching, we can actually trace it back as far as 1908, and Tanaka's pride of being a pioneer in this respect seems justified.

However, the ideas that Tanaka found in the Rescript on Education were not his own; they had been spelt out decades earlier by his teacher Inoue Tetsujirō. In his interpretation, Tanaka stressed that for the Japanese people, the state forms 'the foundation of our lives,' and he rejected individualism as 'an ideology that antagonises the state and the individual.' He defined the state as an enlarged 'family' (*ie*) with the emperor as the 'family head,' whose tasks are to 'worship the ancestors, honour the family lineage, and ensure the continuity of its rites.' The task of the people, as members of this family-state, was to show 'loyalty and filial piety.'[25] All of these ideas can be traced back directly to Inoue.

The novelty of Tanaka's approach, however, was to place Shinto at the centre of National Morality. While this may seem an obvious argument to make to one who is familiar with later developments in Shinto thought, at the time it was genuinely new. To point up its novelty, it may be useful to consider briefly Inoue's views on Shinto.

In his 'Introduction to National Morality' (1912), Inoue valued Shinto as part of Japan's national polity: 'Being closely connected with Japan's national character (*kokuminsei*), . . . Shinto should certainly not be lightly overlooked . . . The notion of continuity from ancestor to descendant permeates the spirit of Japan, ancient and modern.'[26] Inoue mainly linked Shinto to Amaterasu's oracle promising eternal imperial rule; the oracle that, in its turn, lay at the basis of the Rescript on Education. As mentioned above, Inoue took the initiative to found a Shinto programme at Tokyo Imperial University, and this fact alone indicates his high regard of Shinto. However, in Inoue's opinion, Shinto had some fatal flaws that rendered it unfit as a foundation for government policies.

First of all, there was the fact that Shinto was regarded as a religion, in the same category as Christianity or Buddhism: 'There is no doubt that Shinto is a religion; it has its own share of religious rites.'[27] Since freedom of religion had been guaranteed in Article 28 of the Meiji Constitution (1889), Inoue concluded that 'it is therefore impossible to include Shinto, as a religion, in national education.'[28] Another problem was that when Shinto was considered as a religion, 'it appears to be of a much lower level than Buddhism and Christianity . . . and would not be able to compete with these.'[29] Of many of its kami even the names are unknown, and 'it includes many degraded and heterodox elements,' so that it cannot help being criticised as 'childish' in comparison with founded religions such as Buddhism and Christianity. The concept of 'religion' (*shūkyō*) itself is a Western one, defined with reference to Christianity: it has 'a founder, scriptures, precepts, articles of faith, and missionaries,'[30] and deals with matters of death and the afterlife. Shinto, however, lacks all of these; its lack of interest in the afterlife, especially, makes it unfit for proselytising. Tanaka wrote: 'The general public distinguishes Shinto from the Imperial Way (*kōdō*). The first is regarded as irrational and superstitious, and the latter as rational and orthodox; the former is understood as a religion, and the latter as a moral code.'[31] Indeed, it was the Imperial Way, and not Shinto, that was widely regarded as the spiritual constituent of the Japanese race, and the two were seen as separate. The Imperial Way was identified with the notions of loyalty and filial piety in a family-state, and from the Meiji 30s (1897–1906) onwards it was accepted as the morality of the national polity even by Christians.

Inoue made the same distinction. While placing the Imperial Way at the basis of his National Morality, he merely valued Shinto in a moral sense, in order to include it in the Imperial Way: 'Shinto has modern tendencies in its morality, and is moreover national and racial.'[32] Therefore he argued that, while 'Shinto cannot be separated completely from our national education, . . . it will have to be improved' to an ideal condition in which 'morality has taken the place of religion.'[33]

Tanaka, however, defined Shinto as a comprehensive entity that included politics, religion and ethics: 'Shinto is an extremely wide-ranging Way, that is not easy to grasp in all its aspects. Depending on one's particular viewpoint, one can describe it as political, religious, or moral. Only if one attains a comprehensive overview of Shinto will one discover that it is an awe-inspiring Great Way that includes all these aspects.'[34] Tanaka raised Shinto to a Way that regulates all aspects of Japanese life, and that is 'identical to the Imperial Way.'[35] He regarded Shinto as a supra-historical racial spirit, that not only remained unchangeable even under the influence of imported religions, but in the end even led to their assimilation:

> The premise is that the Japanese people must always follow Shinto. For Shinto is the principle of Japanese life, and without it, the Japanese would be unable to live even for a single day. Before Buddhism and Confucianism arrived, it was the norm and basis for all acts of the Japanese people, and it was through Shinto that they realised their ideals.[36]

This brief passage may suffice to show why Tanaka is regarded as a pioneer in interpreting Shinto as the basis of National Morality.

Shinto and scholarship

On the basis of his interpretation of Shinto, Tanaka laid down the following guidelines for its study:

> The Japanese people all practise the Way of the Japanese people (*sic*) and realise its ideals. Most of us, however, practise this Way without being aware of it. There is a great difference between practising it as a mere custom, and practising it with full knowledge of the reasons why one practises it. That is why it is necessary for us to study and become aware of the spirit, the ideals and the Way of the Japanese people.[37]

Tanaka's Shinto studies aimed at establishing a theology that supported the 'practice of Shinto,' thus allowing the practice of this 'national spirit' to become a conscious effort. Moreover, since this national spirit was a supra-historical entity that absorbed all historical changes without being affected by them, Shinto scholarship served to justify whatever notions scholars chose to read into this spirit. For Tanaka, Shinto scholarship had to serve the same function as his pedagogy: to support the practical activity of preserving Japan's 'national spirit.'

This position naturally throws up the question why this national spirit had to be proven to be supra-historical. The answer is that by superimposing the understanding of the interpreter on the past, his position gained an historical basis, supplying it with an absolute character supported by its roots in the dawn of history.[38] By referring to Amaterasu's guarantee of eternal imperial rule, Tanaka rooted his own nationalistic views in the Age of the Gods:

> The spirit of eternal rule by our unbroken imperial lineage goes back to the dawn of time, and appears in the form of [Amaterasu's] oracle. In her oracle, Amaterasu gave expression to the great source of life that has been cherished by the Japanese people since ancient times. Therefore this oracle and the national life of the Japanese people are inseparable, and it is this that forms the essence of Shinto.[39]

For Tanaka, historical changes were no more than superficial layers that should be explained away by pointing up supra-historical universality. His Shinto scholarship consisted of a theoretical 'Introduction to Shinto' on the one hand, and of historical interpretations of the Shinto classics and other Shinto topics on the other; but it will be clear that the former was much more central to his work than the latter. Indeed, he continued to publish books on this subject throughout his life.[40]

Tanaka founded his interpretation of Shinto on his reading of the Shinto classics and Shinto history. He regarded *Kojiki* and *Nihon shoki*, especially, as 'collections of all that constituted the glory of our race's culture at that time, . . . covering all fields of philosophy, science, history, morality, and religion,'[41] and he valued them as divine classics that embodied the Japanese spirit in its purest form. In his treatment of Shinto history, moreover, Tanaka concentrated on the way 'the Japanese spirit had been clarified by his predecessors.'

326

Because for Tanaka, historical fact was secondary to theory, his historical works on Kokugaku and Sect Shinto are no longer valued academically. His commentaries on the classics, too, are flawed by a lack of philological accuracy, and have been largely forgotten.[42] At the time, however, these works did serve a function in providing Tanaka with an historical foundation for his theoretical framework of Shintōgaku.

From National Morality to Shintōgaku

'Shrines are not a religion'

In Meiji Japan, one could hardly discuss Shinto without being confronted with the problem of religion. Murakami Shigeyoshi summed up the issues surrounding Shinto and religion as follows:

> The religious policy of the early Meiji period set out by attempting to define Shinto as a state religion. After years of trial and error, it finally moved towards the recognition of freedom of religion for all religious groups, provided they acknowledge the religious principles of imperial rule. This development naturally threw up the difficult question of the position of shrines, which contemporary ideology defined as public institutions for the execution of state ritual. In the course of the second decade of Meiji (1877–86), the government solved this problem by distinguishing between ritual and religion. This set the stage for the later development of State Shinto.[43]

Formally, separation of religion and state was established in the Meiji Constitution of 1889, after a long process that passed from the separation of shrine priests and national evangelists (*kyōdōshoku*) in 1882, to the abolition of national evangelists in 1884, and the shrine reforms of 1884–6. The government dissociated shrines as 'ritual institutions' from Shinto, while at the same time stipulating that the Shinto sects were religions.[44] By choosing to argue that shrines were not religious, the government opened up the possibility to place shrines outside the range of the constitutional freedom of religion, and thus to enforce shrine visits on all Japanese nationals.

The government attached importance to shrines as places where loyalty to the state could be instilled in the people. Shrines were no longer associated with the 'degraded and heterodox'; they were places where the ancestors who built the land were worshipped, and where the imperial lineage that founded the state was revered. Because Shinto was widely dismissed as a 'childish' religion, shrines were dissociated from Shinto so as not to give anyone an excuse for refusing to attend shrine rituals or for treating shrines with contempt.

By the time Tanaka entered academic life in the late Meiji 30s, the view that shrines are not religious was established as an undisputed fact. Even so, discussions for and against this view abounded. Various Christians, Buddhists, and scholars of religion questioned the official position by casting doubt on the non-religious status of shrines and their separateness from Shinto.[45] As pointed out by Ashizu Uzuhiko and Sakamoto Koremaru, those who supported the official position and who were in favour of mandatory attendance at shrine rituals, reacted to this criticism in two different ways.[46]

First, there were those who argued that shrines were not religious 'in the sense that shrines must be fundamentally different from religion, and mutually irreconcilable with it.'[47] This standpoint, which was the official one advocated by, among others, the Home Ministry, was also supported by members of the National Morality movement such as Inoue, who wrote: 'As a policy, it will be necessary to separate shrines from Shinto as a religion . . . Shrine worship must be defined as no more than an ancient Japanese ceremony, and be distinguished from religious Shinto. The bad influence of the latter must not be allowed to affect shrines.'[48]

A more aggressive minority opinion, with nevertheless strong support from some quarters, held that shrines were 'not religious' in the sense that shrines, while including religion, were more than religion alone. Advocates of this view argued that shrines and Shinto should not be separated. Tanaka, who belonged to this group, formulated his views as follows:

> The Japanese people, being endowed with a true Japanese spirit, sincerely hold an absolute faith in shrines . . . Therefore I firmly hold that Shinto, as well as shrines, are a religion . . . Buddhism and Christianity are merely religions and nothing more; but Shinto and shrines are politics, as well as morality, as well as a great religion. A combination of these three aspects, that is the Way of the Gods. It is the Great Way of the subjects (*shinmin*) of Japan.[49]

For Tanaka, this position was the logical outcome of his identification of Shinto as the 'national spirit' itself. His opinion was advocated by shrine priests and shrine supporters, as well as a majority in the House of Representatives (Shūgiin). Contemporary coverage of a series of lectures on this subject reported that 'the audiences, consisting of government officials, town headmen, school teachers, parishioners' representatives and shrine priests, ranged between three and five hundred; everywhere, the venues bulged with people. The sincere and devoted lectures of speaker Tanaka, especially, which lasted more than three hours, left a strong impression on audiences and touched them deeply.'[50]

If we consider that during the late Meiji and Taishō (1912–26) periods, there was a 'tendency, not only at Jingū Kōgakkan but also at other specialist schools and programmes related to Shinto, to avoid raising the Shinto banner by subsuming its study under "National History" or "National Literature",'[51] it will be clear that the appearance of a scholar like Tanaka was most welcome to Shinto specialists as a theoretical underpinning of their own position. Tanaka's views on shrines and religion were shared by other academics who, from the late Meiji period onwards, actively sought to raise the prestige of Shinto: Tanaka's colleagues at Tokyo Imperial University's Shinto Research Institute, Katō Genchi and Miyaji Naokazu, as well as Kōno Shōzō and others at Kokugakuin University. Tanaka repeated his views throughout his publications, most representative in this respect being his *Jinja hongi* (1926).

Shinto as a state religion

Tanaka also turned his attention to Sect Shinto, which caught his interest because it 'is active in missionary work, as a pure religion.'[52] Between 1932 and 1937, he completed fourteen articles on the thirteen sects of Sect Shinto, with the addition of the unrecognised sect of Shintō Maruyama-kyō. At the time, Sect Shinto was seen as a group of prototypical 'degraded heterodoxies,' heavily criticised both by the media and by psychiatrists. Tanaka, however, made an effort to describe the teachings of the various sects from a neutral standpoint: neither with the zeal of the believer, nor with the cynicism of the critic. It appears that at this stage of his life, Tanaka became increasingly aware of the limitations of his earlier field of study, Kokugaku, as a medium for the education of the masses:

> The pure Way of the Gods as set out by the Four Great Masters of Kokugaku has been a valuable guiding principle for the intellectual classes, but has also proven to be too out of touch with the masses to be useful for their education. Faced with this fact, our religious genius Kurozumi Munetada appeared in Bizen Province and educated the national mind through his thorough knowledge of the depths of Shinto; improving popular customs, he founded a thriving New Religion.[53]

In the founders of Kurozumi-kyō and other Shinto sects Tanaka discovered 'teachers of the masses' able to compete even with Christians.[54] As such, they had an ability that both Kokugaku and shrines lacked, and that yet was vital if Shinto was to be spread among the people. In his treatment of Shinto, whether it was Kokugaku or Sect Shinto, Tanaka always reduced Shinto's aims to serving the state. As a result, one searches in vain for references to those aspects of Sect Shinto, such as the state suppression of religious groups or certain ideas of their founders, that were incompatible with his own nationalism.

Tanaka regarded Sect Shinto as part of Shinto, in the same way as shrines were. On the reasons for the dichotomy of Shinto in the Meiji period, he wrote

> Our national Great Way, . . . Shinto, . . . contributed to the great mission of restoring imperial government and reviving the founding example of Emperor Jinmu; thus it renewed the whole of the religious world and appeared as a pure state religion. However, in our age of 'civilisation and enlightenment,' society has become increasingly

complicated and it has proved difficult for Shinto to develop as a state religion. It was probably for this reason that the state has emphasised those elements of the Shinto state religion that can be described as the Great Way of politics and the Great Way of morality – or Shinto of the national polity (*kokutai Shintō*) and ethical Shinto (*rinri Shintō*). The development of those elements that pertain to the Great Way of religion, however, has been left to private groups.[55]

The 'Great Ways of politics and morality' mentioned here refer to State Shinto, based at shrines; the 'Great Way of religion' to Sect Shinto. Tanaka regarded both as forming part of Shinto as a 'state religion'. Tanaka's conception of Shinto was identical to Inoue's concept of National Morality in that both aimed to unite the people in an all-embracing nationalism; but while Inoue rejected religious elements and made morality his highest concern, and therefore separated shrines from Shinto and ritual from religion, Tanaka attempted to overcome this dichotomy by advocating the view that Shinto is a supra-religious entity, subsuming religion as no more than one of its aspects. In this way, he tried to restore the unity that Shinto had possessed in the early years of Meiji.

In order to convince his opponents, Tanaka first of all had to recognise that shrines were 'religious' in the same way as the Shinto sects. However, at the same time it was necessary to stress that Shinto was not a religion of the same dimension as Christianity or Buddhism, and therefore 'merely' one among many, as commonly argued in early Meiji. Here, Tanaka took the position that 'there is not a single person who has no religious consciousness.'[56] Every human being had faith, and constitutional freedom of religion gave him the freedom to believe in the sect of his choice. The religious nature of Shinto, however, was of a different dimension altogether; it was a universal presence in the hearts of all Japanese, and constituted 'the essence of our race.'[57]

> Religion [in Japan] must necessarily have its base in the religious consciousness of the Japanese people . . . This religious consciousness can appear as Buddhism, or as Christianity. Only then does it become possible for Christianity or Buddhism not to collide with Shinto. This is the way in which freedom of religion comes about.[58]

Thus, constitutional freedom of religion is only guaranteed on the premise that one agrees to have faith in Shinto. By interpreting Shinto as a supra-religious concept, as the Japanese spirit itself, Tanaka lifted Shinto above all criticism. The questions why Shinto included religion, and why Shinto was to be dissociated from the 'degraded and heterodox,' were not raised; all attention was given to justifying in a theoretical way the *a priori* premise that Shinto is the spiritual prop and stay of the Japanese people. Tanaka duly took his argument to its logical extreme when he wrote that 'if there are believers of particular creeds who cannot abide by this, . . . they will have to emigrate to a foreign country and practise their faith there.'[59]

330

Tanaka's conception of Shinto, then, aimed to re-unify Shinto and resurrect it as a true state religion, and, at the same time, to restrict religious freedom as guaranteed in the constitution. His position represented a departure from Inoue, who regarded Shinto merely as a source of raw material for the Imperial Way. Also, Tanaka's position was clearly different from those of institutions such as Jingū Kōgakkan and Kōten Kōkyūsho in that he did not regard the study of Shinto as the exclusive province of shrine priests.

Such were the characteristics of the Shinto research published by Tanaka, Katō Genchi, Miyaji Naokazu and others from the Meiji 40s onwards. Tanaka was not only the first to argue along these lines, but he was also the scholar who represented these characteristics most fully and typically. It was here that 'Shintōgaku,' in which Shinto became the core of the notions of loyalty and filial piety advocated by the National Morality movement, was first conceived.

Advocating 'Shintōgaku'

The first research organisation to carry the term Shintōgaku in its name was inaugurated in September 1926: the *Shintōgakkai*, based at the Shinto Research Institute at Tokyo Imperial University. In its founding statement this organisation laid down its aims 'to study all aspects of Shinto in a scientific manner, and to complete the systematisation of Shintōgaku' as an academic discipline. Accordingly, the journal this group published, *Shintōgaku zasshi*, described itself as 'the first academic journal specialising in Shinto.'[60] The author of this founding statement was Tanaka, who was in charge of the actual running of the organisation as its secretary. Tanaka was a central figure in this organisation, as well as the main author and editor of its journal; every issue included a foreword and one or two articles by his hand.

The president of the group was Ueda Kazutoshi (professor at the Faculty of Literature of Tokyo Imperial University, as well as director of Jingū Kōgakkan), and its advisory board consisted of an impressive gathering of other senior professors of Tokyo Imperial University, including, among others, Katō Genchi, Miyaji Naokazu, Inoue Tetsujirō, Haga Yaichi, Kakei Katsuhiko, Yamamoto Nobuki, Fukasaku Yasufumi, and Mikami Sanji.

The word Shintōgaku itself was a neologism, first used in c. 1917.[61] It remained unfamiliar even in 1926, and in the first issue of *Shintōgaku zasshi* Tanaka wrote: 'Since the word "Shintōgaku" is hardly used by others than specialists in the field, there may be those who doubt the existence of Shinto as an academic discipline.' It is revealing in this respect that neither the Shinto programme (*Shintō kōza*) established at Tokyo Imperial University in 1920, nor the Shinto Research Institute (*Shintō kenkyūshitsu*) that replaced it in 1923 used the term in their name. Tanaka himself only began to refer to his Shinto research as Shintōgaku in 1924; before this time, he preferred the term 'Shinto philosophy' (*Shintō tetsugaku*).[62] In Tanaka's works, 'philosophy' is defined as 'the academic discipline which studies the fundamental principles of all things, and strives to attain an integrated awareness of this world and of human life.'[63] The *gaku* in Shintōgaku, however, suggests a scientific approach that limits itself to the phenomenal domain – an approach Tanaka deemed inferior to the philosophical study of the true essence of reality.[64]

Shintōgaku was defined as 'the scientific study of facts pertaining to Shinto,' and its methodology was laid out as 'gathering as many experiential facts as possible and organising them statistically by means of experimental, observational, and statistical analysis.'[65] If this definition is taken at face value, it should have meant that the methodology of Shinto studies had changed from a philosophical one to that of the natural sciences. In practice, however, there was little if any difference between Tanaka's Shintōgaku and his earlier Shinto philosophy. Throughout his life, Tanaka's methodology was to set out a theoretical world view, while referring to historical materials and phenomena, and his new scientific definition of Shinto studies as Shintōgaku was no more than lip service to the spirit of the age. If anything, it merely served to camouflage the normative character of his own work.

The problem with Shintōgaku was not so much its attempts to disguise itself as a scientific methodology, as in the ambition of its scholars to unify and systematise Shinto studies as an academic discipline. The members of the Shintōgakkai came from a wide variety of academic backgrounds, and their approaches of Shinto diverged widely: Inoue approached Shinto from the viewpoint of morality, Katō from religious studies, Miyaji from national history, Haga and Ueda from literature and linguistics, and so forth. Research into Shinto, then, was certainly not conducted from within a unified framework as presented by Shintōgaku. Miyaji described this situation as follows:

> Most of the Kokugaku scholars who devoted themselves to studying and teaching after the [Meiji] Restoration had already died, and there were not many of sufficient erudition to take their place. The study of Shinto, both its history and its philosophy, was handed over to a younger generation, and the Restoration school (*fukko gakuha*) that had dominated the realm for so many years had to make way for the new Meiji system. Therefore, while the field has been explored somewhat more widely than before, the number of its specialists has remained small, research has been lacking in subtleness, and it has failed to gain a prominent position in the academic world.[66]

As recalled by Miyaji, the failure of the early Meiji policy to render Shinto the state religion led to the fall of the Kokugaku scholars who had been its advocates. Instead, specialists of philosophy and national history with a background in National Morality began to take up Shinto (Tanaka and Miyaji were two prime examples of this); but they were unable to align the various academic disciplines from which they originated, and therefore failed to close the gap left by the demise of Kokugaku. Moreover, while for some (Tanaka, Katō, Miyaji and others), Shinto was the existential foundation of their scholarship, for many others (such as Inoue and Haga), it was no more than a raw material that had to be reduced to concepts such as the Imperial Way and the national spirit.[67]

Shintōgaku and its organisation, the Shintōgakkai, were founded with the aim of unifying Shinto research, which had up to then been conducted in a disintegrated manner by scholars of philosophy, national history, national literature, and religious studies. However, in order to carry this through, it was necessary to attach sufficient value to Shinto to justify its study as an independent field. This role of 'binding agent' was performed by the theories of Tanaka and others, who defined Shinto as Japan's national spirit. In this light, it was no coincidence that Tanaka played such an important role in the foundation and running of the Shintōgakkai. This organisation transformed the study of Shinto from a disintegrated effort in which scholars from various disciplines used Shinto as a source of raw material for their own research, to an integrated one that absorbed the methods of these various disciplines under the title of Shintōgaku. In the years between the establishment of the Shinto programme in 1920 and the foundation of Shintōgakkai in 1926, Shinto studies grew from a concern of shrine priests alone to a social force in its own right.

The failure of Shintōgaku

The Japanese victory over Russia in 1905 not only took popular patriotism to new heights and thus strengthened Japanese nationalism, but also exacerbated the social contradictions of capitalism. Yamada Kō sketches the social situation of the time as follows: 'During the last years of Meiji, when National Morality was advocated, the end of the Russo–Japanese war was followed by social unrest, and labour and socialist movements became more aggressive. The literary world reflected these developments, and naturalist writing became popular. The Boshin Rescript of 1908 was drawn up to address this situation, and at the 27th Imperial Diet, the promotion of a national moral education was discussed.'[68] The problem of Japanese nationalism versus Western thought was no longer seen only as a problem of Christianity (as, e.g., in Inoue's works from the Meiji 20s), but was broadened in scope to include liberalism, socialism, and communism. It was in this atmosphere that Tanaka first began to study Shinto in earnest. He pointed out the dangers of Western thought in the following manner:

> As a materialist philosophy became the leading principle for action, this led to communism and Marxism in the economic field, and to egoism and utilitarianism in the field of ethics, as well as to any number of other modern Western isms in other fields.[69]

For Tanaka, the essence of Western thought was materialism, with Marxism and individualism as its offshoots. Since a materialist 'has not the least concern for the race to which he belongs, and sees only himself and not his race,' he warned that this way of thinking would lead to the collapse of the Japanese national polity, in which 'the individual self (*koga*) is subsumed in the state-self (*kokuga*)':[70]

> Western philosophy is entering our country at an alarming rate. It is our duty to study our own, unique thought, that was developed by high and low over thousands of years, to Japanise Western philosophy on that basis, and to form a new, great philosophical system. We should certainly not be content to sniff at the drippings [of the West] and to lick up their dregs.[71]

This attitude of Tanaka, as formulated in 1918, remained unchanged throughout his life. His final aim was always to construe a metaphysical system in which Shinto could stand up to Western thought and philosophy. It was beyond doubt this sense of being threatened by Western thought, current among nationalists, that led to the conception of a movement for the study of Shinto even more reactionary than the earlier National Morality movement. The Manchuria Incident of 1931, in particular, plunged Japanese society into a state of semi-war. This inspired Shinto scholars to adopt an even more aggressive tone: 'The sudden occurrence of the Manchuria and Shanghai Incidents will raise the awareness of the people . . . and will lead to a further rise in Shinto.'[72] In practice, 'through Prayer Festivals (*kigansai*), Memorial Festivals (*ireisai*), and the building of memorial shrines (*shōkonsha*) and military shrines (*gunjin jinja*), shrines were pushed to the centre-stage as religious institutions for the protection of the state, and group visits to shrines were encouraged.'[73] In these years, Tanaka used every opportunity to denounce those who held liberal views: Sophia University in 1932, when some of its Christian students refused to pay tribute to the Yasukuni shrine; the Law Faculty of Kyoto University in 1933 after the so-called Takigawa Incident; and Minobe Tatsukichi for his liberal views on the emperor as an organ of the state in 1935.[74] However, as exemplified by Tsuda Sōkichi's criticism of Shinto, even in these years the standpoint of Tanaka and others that Shinto was an all-embracing concept identical to the national spirit failed to convince those who held other positions.[75]

Under the influence of the Kokutai Debate (*kokutai meichō undō*) of 1935, courses in the 'Japanese spirit' were set up at Tokyo Imperial University, Kyoto Imperial University, Tokyo Bunri University, and Hiroshima Bunri University in rapid succession.[76] However, no further Shinto courses were founded at Imperial universities. The Shinto Research Institute at Tokyo Imperial University, moreover, had been denied promotion to a faculty in 1927, and had great trouble in retaining its students. In 1938 it was only with great effort that the institute was able to secure one professorial post and one assistant. The role of Shinto studies in school education, too, was very limited. Tanaka himself said that he had proposed to set up a course of lectures on Shinto philosophy at a private professional school around 1931, but had been rebuffed with the remark that the school 'did not recognise research of that kind.'[77]

The plans of Tanaka and others to establish Shintōgaku soon ran into problems. It appears that within the Shintōgakkai, it proved difficult to arrive at academic unification of the field. Miyaji and other historians stopped publishing in *Shintōgaku zasshi*, and Ueda, who was a specialist in Japanese language and literature (*kokugogaku*), began to offer his academic work to other specialised journals and limited his contributions to *Shintōgaku zasshi* to only very general, normative pieces. Thus the scope of the journal narrowed to only scholars with an interest in Shinto theory based on National Morality: Tanaka, Katō, Fukasaku, and a few others. At the Shinto Research Institute of Tokyo Imperial University, on the other hand, the emphasis changed from philosophy (Inoue, Tanaka, Katō) to national history (Miyaji, Hiraizumi Kiyoshi).

It was some years after the retirement of Tanaka and Katō in 1933 that things began to change at the Shinto Research Institute. Miyaji, who had been a lecturer (*kōshi*) at the Institute, was appointed as a professor (*sennin kyōju*) in 1938; at the same time, Hiraizumi (who was a professor at the Faculty for National History) proposed to expand the Institute with one professor and one assistant. Both Miyaji and Hiraizumi sat on the Committee for Educational Innovation (*kyōgaku sasshin hyōgikai*), based in the Ministry of Education, where they argued for the founding or abolishment of university faculties and programmes with the aim of 'stressing Japanese characteristics in education . . . from the viewpoint of the state.'[78] Hiraizumi himself was in charge of a new programme for 'the history of Japanese thought,' established in the same year, 1938. From this year onwards, then, both the Shinto Research Institute and the programme for 'the history of Japanese thought' – both dealing with the national polity – were led by scholars with a background in National History. Predictably, the new assistant of the Shinto Research Institute (which had no students) was chosen from the graduates of the National History Research Institute, in consultation with Hiraizumi.[79]

Even today, there is a tendency for research into Shinto to be divided into two sections: Shintōgaku in a narrow sense (the theoretical study of Shinto), and *Shintōshi*, the history of Shinto. This division may be explained as an echo of the prewar division of Shinto studies into philosophical and historical research. It goes without saying that both approaches shared the post-Meiji characteristic of regarding Shinto as the core of Japan's national spirit. While remaining true to this conception of Shinto, Miyaji attempted to rationalise the study of Shinto by applying to it the methodology current in National History: Leopold von Ranke's method of textual criticism. To Miyaji, the earlier philosophical approach appeared as 'no more than playing with abstract theories and juggling with mere concepts; . . . mere speculation, stressing only those notions that one finds subjectively attractive, without proper regard for the facts.'[80]

After retiring from Tokyo Imperial University in March 1933, Tanaka became an 'Imperial appointee' (*chokuninkan*) in April. In December of the same year a grand assembly was held in the Great Hall of the offices of the National Association of Shrine Priests (Zenkoku Shinshokukai) in commemoration of

Tanaka's 61st birthday (*kanreki*), featuring speeches by the leaders of this Association and the leader of the Shinto Sect Shintō Taikyō (Kanzaki Issaku), as well as by Tanaka's colleagues Inoue, Ueda, and Katō, and the directors of Kokugakuin and Nihon Universities. Tanaka remained president of the Shinto Youth Federation (Shintō Seinen Renmei Kyōkai), and also became the new director of Shintōgakkai after Ueda's death in 1938. In these positions, he continued to exert considerable influence over the Shinto world.

Tanaka also remained active in education. He continued to teach at Kokugakuin University and at the Imperial Women's College (Teikoku Joshi Senmongakkō), and in 1935 once more took up the post of president of the Shinto Youth Association of Kokugakuin University. In his memoirs, Tanaka recalled his activities during this period as follows: 'While teaching twenty-six hours a week at Kokugakuin and other universities and colleges, I used my free time to give lectures throughout the country. Also, the next issue of *Shintōgaku zasshi* was always waiting to be edited. I was always frightfully busy.'[81] In 1940, he became the director of the Imperial Women's College; the following year, at the ripe age of 69, he personally acted as drill instructor of a 'briefing corps' (*hōkokudan*) made up of students of this College, and in September 1942, he travelled to Peking together with Orikuchi Shinobu to give a lecture at a local branch of Kōten Kōkyūsho there.

However, due to the war situation, Tanaka's beloved *Shintōgaku zasshi* was forced to fold in 1940. In 1945, both the Imperial Women's College and Tanaka's own dwelling at Koishikawa in Tokyo were burnt down in an air raid, and few months later Japan's defeat was a fact. Soon afterwards, Tanaka contracted a stomach ulcer and pneumonia, and he died in March of the following year. Having started his career amidst the excitement of Japan's victory over Russia, Tanaka was forced to end his life as a witness to one of the results of Japan's sacred war: the burnt plain that was once Tokyo. One can only guess at his feelings at this time. He was honoured by the Imperial Women's College with a college funeral, in what was a fitting farewell for an educationalist of unrivalled zeal.

Conclusion

In this chapter, I have traced the development of Shintōgaku through the work of Tanaka Yoshitō. One of the interesting conclusions that emerges, was that Shintōgaku did not grow directly out of pre-modern Kokugaku. Kokugaku scholars failed to recover from the failure in early Meiji of measures to render Shinto a national religion. The gap left by the demise of Kokugaku was filled by the ideology of government intellectuals, who advocated notions of 'National Morality' heavily influenced by German philosophy. After a Japanese version of 'separation of church and state' had been instituted, the advocates of National Morality maintained their nationalist stance by interpreting shrine worship in a moral, non-religious way. Advocates of

Shintōgaku, however, aimed to limit constitutional freedom of religion by defining Shinto itself as the racial spirit of Japan. At this point, Shintōgaku became distinct from its parent, National Morality. Shintōgaku, then, in spite of its supra-historical pretences, was in fact a very recent field of study, first formed only in the course of the 1910s and '20s.

This essay limited itself to the development of the philosophical study of Shinto, in which Tanaka was a major player. To complete the picture of prewar Shinto studies, it will be necessary also to consider the development of the historical study of Shinto, headed by Miyaji Naokazu. A definitive history of modern Shinto studies will only emerge from an analysis of the relation between these two fields.

Today, it is often argued that during the prewar period, shrines had nothing to do with nationalism, and were merely manipulated in various ways by the religious policies of the government. It is indeed reasonable to distinguish shrines from nationalism if one's aim is to identify individual responsibilities. However, it should also be remembered that it was an extremely nationalistic academic group with roots in the National Morality movement that gave Shinto the theoretical identity that saved it from the contempt with which it was formerly treated. As shown by the deep impression Tanaka's speeches left on shrine priests, these priests, too, had a need for the views of an academic like Tanaka to legitimise their position in a theoretical way. It is important not to marginalise the problem of shrines and nationalism as the plot of a small group of individual scholars and Shintoists. Historical phenomena are, of course, influenced by the intentions of individuals, but they appear as trends which exceed the reach of such individuals. These trends are not the result of their intentions; they sweep individuals along, regardless of their intentions, and give them a role within their own dynamics. Both those who construed the theories of Shinto nationalism and those who felt a need for them were determined by historical developments beyond their grasp. It is in order to fathom our own historicity, to throw light on the question how we relate to society and how we fit into its dynamics, that we turn to history in the first place.

Notes

1 For information on Tanaka's career, I have relied on Inoue Nobutaka 1987 and Kishimoto Yoshio ed. 1955.
2 Inoue Tetsujirō 1942 (also 1964: 45); Tanaka Yoshitō 1912: 3 and 1918: 2.
3 Watanabe Kazuyasu 1978: 99; Yamada Kō 1972: 235.
4 Unuma Yūko 1979: 366.
5 Yamada Kō 1972: 235.
6 Inoue Tetsujirō 1905: 6.
7 Tanaka Yoshitō 1942: 2.
8 Inoue Tetsujirō 1942: 46.
9 Tanaka Yoshitō 1905: 30–1.
10 Tanaka Yoshitō 1905: 27.

11 Yamada Kō 1972: 240; see also Inoue Tetsujirō 1912, ch. 2.
12 Tanaka Yoshitō 1905: 28.
13 Tanaka Yoshitō 1905: 27.
14 Tanaka Yoshitō 1905: 31.
15 'Tanaka Yoshitō-shi kyōikugaku', in *Nihon gendai kyōikugaku taikei*, 104–5.
16 *Ibid.*, 105; 'Shohyō', *Kyōiku ronsō* 18–1, 1927, 167.
17 *Zenkoku shinshokukai kaihō* 112.
18 E.g., *Zenkoku shinshokukai kaihō*, published by the National Association of Shrine Priests (Zenkoku Shinshokukai); *Jinja kyōkai zasshi*, published by the Shrine League (Jinja Kyōkai) and initiated by the Shrine Bureau (Jinja Kyoku) in the Home Ministry; *Kokugakuin zasshi*, published by Kokugakuin University and the Institute for the Study of the Imperial Classics (Kōten Kōkyusho); and *Kōten kōkyū zasshi*, published by the Hyōgo branch of the same Institute.
19 E.g., *Tōa no hikari, Tetsugaku zasshi, Teiyū rinri kōenshū*.
20 Tanaka Yoshitō 1925: 34–5.
21 Tanaka Yoshitō 1925: 35.
22 Inoue Tetsujirō 1942: 48–9; *Tōkyō Daigaku hyakunenshi bukyokushi* 1, 1986: 429. On Katō's life and works, see Naomi Hylkema-Vos 1990.
23 Endō Jun 1995; Shimazono Susumu and Isomae Jun'ichi, comp., 1996.
24 Tanaka Yoshitō 1930: 30. See also Suzuki Giichi 1965.
25 Tanaka Yoshitō 1936a: 174, 146, and 151.
26 Inoue Tetsujirō 1912: 131.
27 Inoue Tetsujirō 1912: 146.
28 Inoue Tetsujirō 1912: 147–8.
29 Inoue Tetsujirō 1912: 99–100.
30 Tanaka Yoshitō 1936b: 3.
31 Tanaka Yoshitō 1932b: 1.
32 Inoue Tetsujirō 1912: 141.
33 Inoue Tetsujirō 1912: 72, 73, and 142–3.
34 Tanaka Yoshitō 1936a: 122
35 Tanaka Yoshitō 1932b: 2.
36 Tanaka Yoshitō 1936a: 173–4.
37 Tanaka Yoshitō 1936a: 23–4.
38 See J. Hutchinson 1992.
39 Tanaka Yoshitō 1936a: 174.
40 His main works on this subject are *Shintō hongi* (1910a), *Shintō tetsugaku seigi* (1918), *Kamunagara no Shintō no kenkyū* (1933a), and *Shintō gairon* (1936a).
41 Tanaka Yoshitō 1918: 17.
42 *Shinten Kojiki* (1936c), *Kojiki gaisetsu* (1929), and *Nihon shoki gaisetsu* (1938).
43 Murakami Shigeyoshi 1970: 113.
44 Sakamoto Koremaru 1994; Miyaji Masato 1981; Yasumaru Yoshio 1979; Carol Gluck 1985; H. Hardacre 1989.
45 Akazawa Shirō 1985; Katō Genchi, comp., 1930; Tanaka Yoshitō 1936a: ch. 7.
46 Ashizu Uzuhiko 1987; Sakamoto Koremaru 1994.
47 Ashizu Uzuhiko 1987: 125.
48 Inoue Tetsujirō 1912: 147.
49 Tanaka Yoshitō 1936a: 187. Discussions around these issues abound in *Jinja mondai ronsō, Zenkoku shinshokukai kaihō*, and *Jinja kyōkai zasshi*. On religious policies during this period, see Akazawa Shirō 1985.
50 *Kōten kōkyū zasshi* 109 (1917): 26–7.
51 Miyaji Naokazu 1943: 111. Miyaji also regrets the lack of interest in Shinto in 1939: 181.
52 Tanaka Yoshitō 1939: 181.

53 Tanaka Yoshitō 1932c: 2.
54 Tanaka Yoshitō 1932d: 2.
55 Tanaka Yoshitō 1939: 55.
56 Akazawa Shirō 1985: 54, 94.
57 Tanaka Yoshitō 1932a: 206.
58 Tanaka Yoshitō 1936a: 189–90.
59 Tanaka Yoshitō 1932a: 210.
60 Tanaka Yoshitō 1926.
61 The word appears to have been used for the first time in Endō Ryūkichi 1917.
62 Tanaka first used this term in 1909, in his 'Shintō tetsugaku kōsei no hensen' (*Tetsugaku zasshi* 24–270), and last in 'Shintō tetsugaku no konpon mondai', serialised in *Shintō kōza* 3 between 1929 and 1931.
63 Tanaka Yoshitō 1929–31: 5–6. For an earlier instance of the same definition, see 1910b: 16.
64 Cf. Inoue's distinction between the 'phenomenal' (*genshō*) and the 'real' (*jitsuzai*), referred to above.
65 'Shintōgaku', *Shintōgaku zasshi* 1, 5–6. Tanaka first used the term Shintōgaku in 'Shintōgaku gairon', 1924.
66 Miyaji Naokazu 1941: 239–40.
67 For an overview of contemporary views of Japanese culture, see Minami Hiroshi 1994; Muraoka Tsunetsugu 1962; and Harumi Befu 1993.
68 Yamada Kō 1971: 239.
69 Tanaka Yoshitō 1935a: 25.
70 Tanaka Yoshitō 1935b: 2, 4.
71 Tanaka Yoshitō 1918: 29.
72 Tanaka Yoshitō 1936a: 2–3.
73 Akazawa Shirō 1985: 101.
74 Tanaka Yoshitō 1933b, 1934, 1935a.
75 Cf. Tsuda Sōkichi 1949.
76 *Tōkyō Daigaku hyakunenshi bukyokushi* 1: 429. On the popular interest in theories on the 'Japanese spirit' in the Shōwa 10s (1935–44), see Taira Shigemichi 1965.
77 Tanaka Yoshitō 1929–31: 83.
78 *Kindai Nihon kyōiku seido shiryō* 14: 439–40.
79 Endō Jun 1995; also Isomae Jun'ichi 1993. On Hiraizumi, see Saitō Takashi 1984 and 1985. On Miyaji, see Nishida Nagao 1965, and Isomae 1995. It seems that Miyaji recognised the need for philosophical and theoretical Shinto research, but felt that the field was not yet mature enough to be recognized as an academic discipline (cf. his *Jingishi taikei*, 246).
80 *Shintōshi josetsu* (1938), in *Miyaji Naokazu ronshū* 5: 3–4.
81 Tanaka Yoshitō 1936a: 4–5.

BIBLIOGRAPHY

Abe Yasurō (1980) 'Iruka no seiritsu', Geinōshi kenkyū 69.

Abe Yasurō (1984) 'Jidō setsuwa no keisei, Tendai sokuihō no keisei ni tsuite I & II', Kokugo kokubun 53–8 and 9.

Abe Yasurō (1989) 'Hōju to ōken, chūsei ōken to Mikkyō girei', Iwanami kōza, Tōyō shisō 2, Tokyo: Iwanami.

Agatsuma Matashirō (1982) 'Chūsei Bukkyō Shintō ni okeru Bontennō shisō', Terakoya gogaku-bunka kenkyūjo ronsō 1.

Aida Hanji (1964) Chūkai Yōrō-ryō, Tokyo: Yūshindō.

Akazawa Shirō (1985) Kindai Nihon no shiso doin to shūkyō tosei, Tokyo: Azekura Shobō.

Akimoto Norio (1975) 'Kinsei Nikkō Tōshōgū to minshū no sankei: sono ichikōsatsu', Utsunomiya daigaku kyōyōbu kenkyū hōkoku daiichibu 8.

Antoni, Klaus (1988) Miwa – der heilige Trank. Zur Geschichte und religiösen Bedeutung des alkoholischen Getränkes (sake) in Japan, Münchener Ostasiatische Studien vol. 45, Stuttgart: Franz Steiner.

Arnason, Johann P. (1997) Social theory and Japanese experience: the dual civilisation, London and New York: Kegan Paul International.

Asao Naohiro (1970, 1972, and 1974) 'Shōgun kenryoku no sōshutsu', Rekishi hyōron 241, 266, and 293.

Ashkenazi, Michael (1993) Matsuri, Honolulu: University of Hawai'i Press.

Ashizu Uzuhiko (1987) Kokka Shintō to wa nan datta no ka, Tokyo: Jinja Shinpōsha.

Aston, W.G. (1896, 1956) Nihongi. chronicles of Japan from the earliest times to A.D. 697, London: Kegan Paul, Trench, Trubner & Co.

Aston, W.G. (1972) Nihongi, Rutland/Vermont/Tokyo: Tuttle.

Barrett, T.H. (1994) 'The Taoist canon in Japan', Taoist Resources 5–2.

Barrett, T.H (1996a) Taoism Under the T'ang, London: Wellsweep.

Barrett, T.H. (1996b) 'The fate of Buddhist political thought in China: The Rajah dons a disguise', The Buddhist Forum IV.

Barrett, T.H. (1999) 'Science and religion in medieval China', Journal of the Royal Asiatic Society.

Bataille, Georges (1973) Théorie de la religion, Paris: Gallimard.

Bataille, Georges (1991) The accursed share (tr. Robert Hurley), New York: Zone Books.

Befu, Harumi (1993) 'Nationalism and Nihonjinron', in H. Befu, ed., Cultural nationalism in East Asia: representation and identity, Berkeley: University of California.

Bell, Catherine (1992) Ritual theory, ritual practice, Oxford: Oxford University Press.

Benn, Charles (1987) 'Religious aspects of the Emperor Hsüan-tsung's Taoist ideology', in David W. Chappell, ed., Buddhist and Taoist practice in medieval Chinese society, Honolulu: University of Hawaii Press.

Bian Xiaoxuan (1980) 'Fo-Dao zhi zheng yu Jianzhen dongdu', *Zhongguo shi yanjiu* 1.

Blacker, Carmen (1992) *The catalpa bow: A study of shamanistic practices in Japan.* London: Mandala (Harper Collins).

Bock, Felicia G., tr. (1970) *Engi-Shiki. procedures from the Engi era.* Books I–V, Tokyo: Monumenta Nipponica monograph.

Bock, Felicia G., tr. (1972) *Engi-Shiki. procedures from the Engi era.* Books VI–X, Tokyo: Monumenta Nipponica monograph.

Bock, Felicia G. (1985) *Classical learning and Taoist practices in early Japan*, Center for Asian Studies Occasional Paper, Tucson: University of Arizona Press.

Bocking, Brian (1996) *A popular dictionary of Shinto*, London: Curzon Press.

Bokenkamp, Stephen R. (1994) 'Time after time: Taoist apocalyptic history and the founding of the T'ang dynasty', *Asia Major* (Third series) 7–1.

Bokenkamp, Stephen R. (1997) *Early Daoist scriptures*, Berkeley: University of California Press.

Boot, W.J. (1988) 'Tokugawa Ieyasu no shinkakka o megutte', in Motoyama Yukihiko kyōju taikan kinen ronbunshū henshū iinkai, comp., *Nihon kyōikushi ronsō*, Kyoto: Shibunkaku.

Boot, W.J. (1989) *De Dood van een Shogun: Vergoddelijking in het Vroeg-Moderne Japan*, Oostersch Genootschap in Nederland 16, Leiden: E.J. Brill.

Boot, W.J. (1990) 'The monk and the myth: Jigen-daishi at court', in Erika de Poorter, ed., *As the twig is bent . . . Essays in honour of Frits Vos*, Amsterdam: Gieben.

Boot, W.J. (1991) 'The religious background of the deification of Tokugawa Ieyasu', in Adriana Boscaro, Franco Gatti, and Massimo Raveri, eds. *Rethinking Japan, Vol. II: social sciences, ideology & thought*, Sandgate, Folkestone: Japan Library.

Borgen, Robert (1985) *Sugawara no Michizane*, Cambridge: Harvard University Press.

Breen, John (1990) 'Shintoists in restoration Japan, 1868–1872: Towards a reassessment', *Modern Asian Studies* 24–3.

Breen, John (1996a), 'Beyond the prohibition: Christianity in Restoration Japan', in John Breen and Mark Williams eds, *Japan and Christianity*, London: Macmillans.

Breen, John (1996b), 'The Imperial Oath of April 1868: ritual, politics and power in the Restoration', *Monumenta Nipponica* 51, 4.

Breen, John (1996c), 'Accommodating the alien: Ōkuni Takamasa and the religion of the Lord of Heaven' in Kornicki and McMullen eds., *Religion in Japan: arrows to heaven and earth*, Cambridge: Cambridge University Press.

Breen, John (1997), 'Shinto and Buddhism in late Edo Japan: the case of Ōkuni Takamasa and his school', *Current issues in the social sciences and humanities* 14.

Bukkyo dendo kyokai, comp. (1985) *The world of Shinto*, Bukkyo Dendo Kyokai.

Bunkachō bunkazai hogobu, ed. (1986) *Minzoku shiryō senshū 15: miko no shūzoku II*, Tokyo: Kokudo Chiri Kyōkai.

Chen Yuan, ed. (1988) *Daojiao Jinshi lue*, Beijing: Wenwu chubanshe.

Ching, Julia (1997) *Mysticism and kingship in China: the heart of Chinese wisdom*, Cambridge: Cambridge University Press.

Clastres, Pierre (1989) *Society against the state* (tr. Robert Hurley), New York: Zone Books.

Collcutt, Martin (1986), 'Buddhism: the threat of eradication' in Jansen, Marius and Gilbert Rozman eds., *Japan in transition: from Tokugawa to Meiji*, Princeton: Princeton University Press.

Couvreur, Séraphin (1950) (*Li-chi*) *Mémoires sur les bienséances et les cérémonies*, Leiden: E.J. Brill.

Cranston, Edwin A. (1993) *The glistening cup: a waka anthology*, Stanford: Stanford University Press.

Dainihon bukkyō zensho, Tokyo: Bussho Kankōkai.

Dainihon gakujutsukai, comp. (1929) *Nihon gendai kyōikugaku taikei*, Monasu (reprint Nihon Tosho Sentā, 1989).

Dazai Osamu (1985) *Return to Tsugaru* (tr. James Westerhoven), Tokyo: Kodansha International.

De Visser, M.W. (1935) *Ancient Buddhism in Japan: sūtras and ceremonies in use in the seventh and eighth centuries A.D. and their history in later times*, 2 vols, Leiden: E.J. Brill.

Demura Katsuaki (1972) 'Yuiitsu Shintō myōbō yōshū no seiritsu ni tsuite', *Shintōshi kenkyū* 20–2.

Demura Katsuaki (1973) 'Yoshida Shintō no seiritsu ni tsuite', *Shintōshi kenkyū* 21–5.

Demura Katsuaki (1974) 'Yoshida Shintō ni okeru kenro-kyō no hiden ni tsuite', *Kōgakkan ronsō* 7–4.

Demura Katsuaki (1975a) 'Yoshida Shintō ni okeru on'yū-kyō no hiden – toku ni jūhachi shintō gyōji ni tsuite (1)', *Shintōshi kenkyū* 23–2.

Demura Katsuaki (1975b) 'Yoshida Shintō ni okeru on'yū-kyō no hiden – toku ni jūhachi shintō gyōji ni tsuite (2)', *Shintōshi kenkyū* 23–3.

Derrida, Jacques (1972) *Dissemination*, (English translation by Barbara Johnson), Chicago: The University of Chicago Press, 1981.

Domenig, Gaudenz (1997) 'Sacred groves in modern Japan: Notes on the variety and history of Shinto shrine forests', *Asiatische Studien/Etudes Asiatiques* 51–1.

Du You, ed. (1988) *Tongdian* 185, Beijing: Zhonghua shuju.

Duquenne, Robert (1983) '*Daigensui*' and '*Daiitoku myōō*', *Hōbōgirin* 6, Paris/Tokyo: Ecole Française d'Extrême-Orient.

Eda Yukiko (1989) 'Aomori to Akita no gomiso' and 'Tsugaru no gomiso', in Tanigawa Ken'ichi, ed., *Nihon minzoku bunka shiryō shūsei vol. 6: miko no sekai*, San'ichi Shobō.

Egi Kazuyukio keireki zadankai kankōkai ed., (1933), *Egi Kazuyukio keireki zadan (ge)*, Tokyo: Egi Kazuyukio keireki zadankai kankōkai.

Eichhorn, Werner (1973) *Die Religionen Chinas*, Stuttgart: W. Kohlhammer.

Eichhorn, Werner (1976) *Die alte chinesische Religion und das Staatskultwesen*, Leiden: E.J. Brill.

Eisenstadt, S.N. (1996) *Japanese civilisation: a comparative view*, Chicago: University of Chicago Press.

Elison, George S. (1981) 'The cross and the sword: Patterns of Momoyama history', in G.S. Elison & B.L. Smith, eds., *Warlords, artisans, and commoners: Japan in the sixteenth century*, Honolulu: University of Hawai'i Press.

Ellwood, Robert S. (1971) 'The Spring Prayer (*Toshigoi*) ceremony of the Heian court', *Asian Folklore Studies* 30–1.

Endō Jun (1995) 'Bungakubu Shintō kōza no rekishiteki hensen', *Tōkyō daigakushi kiyō* 13.

Endō Ryūkichi (1917) 'Nihon Shintōgaku no kensetsu', *Zenkoku shinshokukai kaihō* 228–30.

Faure, Bernard (1993) *Chan insights and oversights: An epistemological critique of the Chan tradition*, Princeton: Princeton University Press.

Florenz, Karl (1919) *Die historischen Quellen der Shinto-Religion. Aus dem Altjapanischen und Chinesischen übersetzt und erklärt von Dr. Karl Florenz*, Göttingen: Vandenhoeck & Ruprecht.

Fridell, Wilbur M. (1973) *Japanese shrine mergers 1906–12: State Shinto moves to the grass roots*, Tokyo: Sophia University.

Fróis, Luís (José Wicki, ed. & ann., 1982) *Historia de Japam* III, Lisbon.

Fujii Jōji (1997) *Tokugawa Iemitsu*, Tokyo: Yoshikawa Kōbunkan.

Fujii Sadafumi (1971) 'Taikyōkan, Taireikan no kōsō', *Shintō shūkyō* 62.

Fujii Sadafumi (1975) 'Kokugaku ni okeru hihan no seishin', *Kokugakuin Zasshi* 20.

Fujii Sadafumi (1977a) 'Izumo Taishakyō seiritsu no katei: shinkan, kyōdōshoku bunri o chūshin to shite', in Shintōgakkai ed., *Izumogaku ronkyō*, Izumo Taisha.

Fujii Sadafumi (1977b) *Meiji kokugaku hasseishi no kenkyū*, Tokyo: Yoshikawa Kōbunkan.

Fukui Fumimasa (1995) 'The History of Taoist Studies in Japan and Some Related Issues', *Acta Asiatica* 68.

Fukui Fumimasa (1996) 'L'adoption au Japon du titre d'empereur Tenno', in J.-P. Drège, ed., *De Dunhuang au Japon: Etudes chinoises et bouddhiques offertes à Michel Soymié*, Geneva: Droz.

Fukunaga Mitsuji (1982) *Dōkyō to Nihon bunka*, Kyoto: Jinbun shoin.

Fukunaga Mitsuji et al., eds (1978) *Dōkyō to kodai no tennōsei*, Tokyo: Tokuma.

Fukushima Kanryū (1977) 'Shinto hishūkyōron to Shinshū: Yasukuni jinja mondai wa Shinshū ni totte nan de aru ka', in idem ed., *Jinja mondai to Shinshū*, Kyoto: Dōmeisha.

Fukushima Kanryū (1978) 'Kaigai kyōjō shisatsu: haibutsu jōkyōka no Seiō', *Ryūkoku daigaku ronshū* 413.

Fukuyama Toshio (1977) *Chūsei no jinja kenchiku*, Tokyo: Shibundō.

Furukawa Koshōken (1977) *Tōyū zakki*, Tōyō Bunko 27, Tokyo: Heibonsha.

Futaba Kenkō et al., eds (1973) *Shimaji Mokurai zenshū*, Kyoto: Honganji Shuppan Kyōkai.

Gien-jūgō nikki (1976) Tokyo: Zoku Gunsho Ruijū Kanseikai.

Gluck, Carol (1985) *Japan's modern myths*, Princeton: Princeton University Press.

Godelier, Maurice (1984) *L'idéel et le matériel*, Paris: Fayard.

Goepper, Roger (1993) *Aizen myōō, the esoteric king of lust: an iconological study*, Artibus Asiae supplementum XXXlX, Zürich: Museum Rietberg.

Gotō Tokio (1967) 'Higashi Mino Hirata gakuha no dōkō ni tsuite', *Shinano* 19–1.

Granet, Marcel (1985, 1989) *Das chinesische Denken: Inhalt, Form, Charakter*, Frankfurt am Main: Suhrkamp (tr. Manfred Porkert, from the French *La pensée chinoise*, 1934).

Grapard, Allan G. (1984) 'Japan's ignored Cultural Revolution: the separation of Shinto-Buddhist divinities and a case-study: Tōnomine', *History of Religions* 23–3.

Grapard, Allan G. (1988) 'Institution, ritual, and ideology: The twenty-two shrine-temple multiplexes of Heian Japan', *History of Religions* 27–3.

Grapard, Allan G. (1992a) 'The Shinto of Yoshida Kanetomo', *Monumenta Nipponica* 47–1.

Grapard, Allan G., tr. (1992b) '*Yuiitsu Shintō Myōbō Yōshū* (by Yoshida Kanetomo)', *Monumenta Nipponica* 47–2.

Grapard, Allan G. (1992c) *The protocol of the gods: a study of the Kasuga cult in Japanese history*, Berkeley: University of California Press.

Gunsho ruijū (1903–4) 18 vols, Tokyo: Keizai Zasshisha.

Habito, Ruben (1996) *Originary enlightenment: Tendai hongaku doctrine and Japanese Buddhism*, Tokyo: The International Institute for Buddhist Studies.

Haga Noboru (1961) '*Yoake mae* shūhen: Kitahara Inao o chūshin to shite', *Rekishi kyōiku* 9–12.

Haga Noboru (1963) *Bakumatsu kokugaku no tenkai*, Tokyo: Hanawa Shobō.

Haga Noboru (1968) 'Bakumatsu ishin no henkaku to gōnō no tennō shinkō: toku ni gōnō no Tenmei, Tenpō ishin taiken to kanren sasete', *Rekishigaku kenkyū* 341.

Haga Noboru (1970) *Sōmō no seishin*, Tokyo: Hanawa Shobō.

Haga Noboru (1975a) *Henkaku-ki ni okeru kokugaku*, Tokyo: San'ichi Shobō.

Haga Noboru (1975b) *Kokugaku no hitobito: sono kōdō to shisō*, Tokyo: Hyōronsha.

Haga Noboru (1976) *Ishin o motomete*, Tokyo: Mainichi Shinbunsha.

Haga Noboru (1977) 'Kaisetsu', in *Shinshū Hirata Atsutane zenshū geppō* 6.

Haga Noboru (1980) *Bakumatsu kokugaku no kenkyū*, Tokyo: Kyōiku Shuppan Sentā.

Hagino Kazuhiko (1994) 'Hito ga mori o tsukuru', in Sennen no mori ni tsudou kai, comp., *Sennen no mori pre-symposium hōkokusho*.

Hall, John (1966) *Government and local power in Japan*, Princeton: Princeton University Press.

Hanawa Mizuhiko (1941) *Kokkai kaisetsu zengo ni okeru Jingikan fukko undō*, Kasama Inari jinja shamusho.

Haraguchi Kiyoshi (1982) *Nihon kindai kokka no keisei*, Tokyo: Iwanami.

Hardacre, Helen (1989) *Shinto and the state, 1868–1988*, Princeton: Princeton University Press.

Harootunian, H.D. (1988) *Things seen and unseen: discourse and ideology in Tokugawa nativism*, Chicago: The University of Chicago Press.

Hasegawa Seiichi (1980) *Tsugaru no minkan shinkō*, Tokyo: Kyōikusha.

Hasegawa Seiichi (1984) 'Tsugaru Akakura shinkō oboegaki: gomisokei kamisama no katsudō o chūshin ni', *Bunkyō ronsō* (Hirosaki Daigaku Jinbungakubu) 19–3.

Hasegawa Seiichi (1992) 'Miko to reisan – kamisamatachi no Iwaki-san shinkō', in Akasaka Norio, ed., *Shisō o horu (V): Hyōhaku no mesashi*, Tokyo: Shinyōsha.

Hatta Yukio (1991) *Kamigami to hotoke no sekai*, Tokyo: Hirakawa Shuppansha.

Hayami Tasuku (1975) *Heian kizoku shakai to Bukkyō*, Tokyo: Yoshikawa Kōbunkan.

Hayus, J (1605) *De rebus japonicis . . . epistulae*, Antwerp, dl. I.

Hertzer, Dominique (1996) *Das alte und das neue Yijing. Die Wandlungen des Buches der Wandlungen*, München: Diederichs.

Higuchi Tadanao (1975) *Keikan no kōzō*, Tokyo: Gihōdō.

Higuchi Tadanao (1981) *Nihon no keikan – Furusato no genkei*, Tokyo: Shunjūsha.

Hiraizumi Takafusa (1995) 'Watarai Ieyuki no Shintōron no shūhen', in *Tani Seigo sensei taishoku kinen Shintōgaku ronbunshū*, Tokyo: Kokusho Kankōkai.

Hirata Atsutane Zenshū Kankōkai ed. (1977) *Shinshū Hirata Atsutane zenshū* 1 & 2, Meicho Shuppan.

Hirazawa Takuya (1997) 'Jitsurui to chūsei shinwa', *Meiji seitoku kinen gakkai kiyō* 22.

Hirosaki Daigaku Kokushi Kenkyukai (eds) *Tsugaru-shi jiten*, Tokyo: Meicho Shuppan.

Horii Junji (1974) 'Hōryūji Kondō Yakushi nyorai zō sōmei kō', *Geirin* 25–5.

Hutchinson, J. (1992) 'Moral innovators and the politics of regeneration: the distinctive role of cultural nationalists in nation-building', in A.D. Smith, ed., *Ethnicity and Nationalism*, Leiden/New York/Köln: E.J. Brill.

Hylkema-Vos, Naomi (1990) 'Katō Genchi, a neglected pioneer in comparative religion', *Japanese Journal of Religious Studies* 17–4.

Ichimura Minato (1929) *Ina sonnō shisō shi*, Iida-shi: Shimoina-gun Kokumin Seishinsaku Kyōkai.

Ichimura Minato (1933) *Kyōdo shi danwa*, Iida-shi: Zakōji Jitsugyō Hoshū Gakkō.

Ichimura Minato zenshū kankōkai ed. (1980a) *Ichimura Minato zenshū*, vol. 4, Iida-shi: Shimoina Kyōikukai.

Ichimura Minato zenshu kankōkai ed. (1980b) *Ichimura Minato zenshū*, vol. 5, Iida-shi: Shimoina Kyōikukai.

Ikegami Yoshimasa (1984a) 'Iwaki-san shinkō no kinseiteki engen – shūkyōgakuteki shiten kara no ichikōsatsu', in Hasegawa Seiichi, ed., *Tsugaru-han no kisoteki kenkyū*, Tokyo: Kokusho Kankōkai.

Ikegami Yoshimasa (1992) Miko to reisan – kamisamatachi no Iwaki-san shinkō' in Akasaka Norio (ed) *Shisō o horu 5: Hyōhaku no mesashi*. Tokyo: Shinyōsha.

Imai Jun, comp. (1979) *Nihon shisō ronsōshi*, Tokyo: Perikansha.

Inagaki Hisao (1984, 1988) *A dictionary of Japanese Buddhist terms*, Kyoto: Nagata Bunshōdō.

Inatani Yusen, ed. (1993) *Shingon Shinto shūsei, Tōmitsu jisō kuketsu shūsei 3*, Osaka: Aoyamasha.

Inoue Mitsusada (1956) *Nihon jōdokyō seiritsushi no kenkyū*, Tokyo: Yamakawa Shuppansha.

Inoue Mitsusada (1971) *Nihon kodai no kokka to Bukkyō*, Tokyo: Iwanami.

Inoue Nobutaka (1987) 'Tanaka Yoshitō no kyōha Shintō kenkyū', in Tanaka Yoshitō, *Shintō 13-ha no kenkyū*, Tokyo: Daiichi Shobō.

Inoue Tetsujirō (1905) *Nihon Shushigakuha no tetsugaku*, Tokyo: Fuzanbō.

Inoue Tetsujirō (1912) *Kokumin dōtoku gairon*, Tokyo: Sanseidō.

Inoue Tetsujirō (1942) 'Gakkai kaikoroku', Tokyo: Iwanami.

Inoue Tetsujirō (1964) *Inoue Tetsujirō jiden*, Tokyo: Fuzanbō.

Ishibashi, T. and Heinrich Dumoulin, tr. (1940) 'Yuiitsu-Shintō Myōbō-yōshū: Lehrabriss des Yuiitsu-Shinto', *Monumenta Nipponica* 3.

Ishida Mizumaro (1970) *Kokuyaku issaikyō*, Shiden-bu vol. 18, Tokyo: Daitō Shuppansha (revised edition).

Ishige Tadashi (1971) 'Edo jidai kōki ni okeru ten no shisō (Tōshō-daigongen sūhai shisō no henshitsu)', *Bunka shigaku* 27.

Isomae Jun'ichi (1993) 'Nishiyama Isao-shi intābyū', *Tōkyō Daigaku shūkyōgaku nenpō* 11.

Isomae Jun'ichi (1995) 'Shohyō, Miyaji Naokazu *Kumano sanzan no shiteki kenkyū*', in *Nihon Bukkyō* 3.

Itō Masayoshi (1972) 'Chūsei Nihongi no rinkaku', *Bungaku* 40–10.

Itō Satoshi (1993) 'Ise no Shintōsetsu no tenkai ni okeru Saidaiji-ryū no dōkō ni tsuite', *Shintō shūkyō* 153.

Itō Satoshi (1995) 'Amaterasu Ōmikami – Kūkai dōtaisetsu o megutte, toku ni Sanbōin-ryū o chūshin to shite', *Tōyō no shisō to shūkyō* 12.

Itō Satoshi (1996) 'Chūsei Shintō setsu ni okeru Amaterasu Ōmikami, toku ni Jūichimen Kannon to no dōtaisetsu o megutte', in Saitō Hideyoshi, ed., *Amaterasu shinwa no henshinfu*, Tokyo: Shinwasha.

Itō Satoshi (1997) 'Ise kanjō no sekai', *Bungaku* 8–4.

Itō Satoshi (1998) 'Shinbutsu shūgō no kenkyūshi', *Kokubungaku kaishaku to kanshō*. (March).

Itō Tasaburō (1982) *Sōmō no kokugaku*, Tokyo: Meicho Shuppan.

Iwai Tadakuma and Okada Shōji, comp. (1989) *Tennō daigawari gishiki no rekishiteki tenkai, sokui-gi to daijōsai*, Tokyo: Kashiwa Shobō.

Japanese–English Buddhist Dictionary (1991) Tokyo: Daitō Shuppansha (revised edition).

Jinja Shinpō seikyō kenkyūshitsu, ed. (1986) *Zōho kaitei Kindai jinja Shintō shi*, Tokyo: Jinja Shinposha.

Jōsho, kenpakusho mokuroku, Keiō 4–Meiji 13, Tokyo: Kokuritsu Komonjokan.

Kabe Iwao (1906), *Otoroganaka: Kamei Kansai den* (privately published by Nakayama Kazusuke).

Kadoya Atsushi (1993) 'Ryōbu Shintō shiron, *Bikisho* no seiritsu o megutte', *Tōyō no shisō to shūkyō* 10.

Kadoya Atsushi (1995) 'Ryōbu Shintō', *Kokubungaku kaishaku to kanshō* 60–12.

Kageyama Haruki (1971) *Shintaizan*, Gakuseisha.

Kakei Iori (1931) 'Bonshun no seibotsu no nenji ni tsuite', *Kokugo to kokubungaku* 8–5.

Kakei Iori (1936) *Dainihon teikoku kenpō no konpongi*, Tokyo: Iwanami.

Kamata Jun'ichi, ed. (1978) *Kujiki. Sendai kuji hongi no kenkyū, kōhon no bu*, Tokyo: Yoshikawa Kōbunkan.

Kamata Tōji (1984–86) 'Hirata Atsutane no shinrei kenkyū' (1–10), *Shinrei kenkyū*.

Kamata Tōji (1985) *Shintai no fuiirudo wāku*, Tokyo: Seikyūsha.

Kamata Tōji (1988) *Shinkai no fuōkurōa*, Tokyo: Shinyōsha.

Kamata Tōji (1986) 'Kokugaku no isō to sono tenmatsu' in *Bessatsu bungei 1: gendai shisō no kyoen*, Tokyo: Kawade Shobō.

Kamata Tōji (1996) *Seinarubasho no kioku: Nihon to in karada*, Tokyo: Kōdansha.

Kamijo Atsuyuki (1995a) 'Hirata kokugaku no hattatsu to Inadani no bakumatsu' pt. 1, *Ina* 804.

Kamijo Atsuyuki (1995b) 'Hirata kokugaku no hattatsu to Inadani no bakumatsu' pt. 2, *Ina* 806.

Kamijo Atsuyuki (1995c) 'Hirata kokugaku no hattatsu to Inadani no bakumatsu' pt. 3, *Ina* 807.

Kamikawa Toshio (1989) 'Chūsei no sokui girei to Bukkyō', in Iwai Tadakuma and Okada Shōji, comp., *Tennō daigawari gishiki no rekishiteki tenkai, sokui-gi to daijōsai*, Tokyo: Kashiwa Shobō (this article appeared earlier in *Nihonshi Kenkyū* 300, 1987).

Kamiyo Yūichirō (1977) *Nihon no komyūniti*, Tokyo: Kashima Shuppankai.

Kansaikō hōmu yōsho zanpen MS.

Katō Genchi (1930b) 'The theological system of Yoshida Kanetomo', *The Japan Society Transactions and Proceedings* 28.

Katō Genchi (1931) *Honpō seishi no kenkyū. Seishi no shijitsu to sono shinri bunseki*, Tokyo: Kokusho Kankōkai.

Katō Genchi, comp. (1930a) *Jinja tai shūkyō*, Meiji Seitoku Kinenkai.

Katsumata Shūkyō, ed. (1968) *Kōbō Daishi zenshū*, 3 vols, Tokyo: Sankibō.

Katsumura Tetsuya (1978) 'Shubunden goran ten-bu no fukugen', in Yamada Keiji, ed, *Chūgoku no kagaku to kagakusha*, Kyoto: Kyoto Daigaku Jinbun Kagaku Kenkyūjo.

Katsurajima Nobuhiro (1992) *Bakumatsu minshū shisō no kenkyū*, Kyoto: Bunrikaku.

Katsurajima Nobuhiro (1996) 'Hirata-ha kokugakusha no "dokusho" to sono gensetsu', *Edo no shisō* 5.

Katz, Paul (1995) *Demon hordes and burning boats: The cult of Marshal Wen in late imperial Chekiang*, Albany, NY: SUNY.

Kawakita Yasuyuki (1984) 'Nittō ritsuryō ni okeru kunshu no shōgō', in *Takigawa Masajirō sensei beijū kinen ronbunshū Shintōshi ronsō*, Tokyo: Kokusho Kankōkai.

Kelsey, W. Michael (1981) 'Salvation of the snake, the snake of salvation: Buddhist-Shinto conflict and resolution', *Japanese Journal of Religious Studies* 8–1/2.

Ketelaar, James Edward (1990) *Of Heretics and Martyrs in Meiji Japan: Buddhism and its Persecution*, Princeton: Princeton University Press.

Kimura Bin (1981) *Jiko, aida, jikan*, Tokyo: Kōbundō.

Kindai Nihon kyōiku seido shiryō (1957) Kindai Nihon kyōiku seido shiryō hensankai, comp., Tokyo: Kōdansha.

Kirkland, Russell (1992) 'Person and Cultivation in the Taoist Tradition', *Journal of Chinese Religions* 20.

Kishimoto Yoshio (1955) 'Tanaka Yoshitō hakase shōden', in Kishimoto Yoshio, *Yamato minzoku to josei* (private publication).

Kishino Toshihiko (1978a) 'Ina Hiratagaku kenkyū josetsu' pt. 1, *Ina* 600.

Kishino Toshihiko (1978b) 'Ina Hiratagaku kenkyū josetsu' pt. 2, *Ina* 601.

Kishino Toshihiko (1979a) 'Katagiri Harukazu no "Tenka mukyū taihei kiroku": Ina Hiratagaku no saikentō' pt. 1, *Ina* 612.

Kishino Toshihiko (1979b) 'Katagiri Harukazu no "Tenka mukyū taihei kiroku": Ina Hiratagaku no saikentō' pt. 2, *Ina* 613.

Kishino Toshihiko (1979c) 'Katagiri Harukazu no "Tenka mukyū taihei kiroku": Ina Hiratagaku no saikentō' pt. 3. *Ina* 615.

Kitagawa, Joseph M. (1966) *Religion in Japanese history*, New York: Columbia University Press.

Kitagawa, Joseph M. (1987) *On understanding Japanese religion*, Princeton: Princeton University Press.

Kitajima Masamoto (1974) 'Tokugawa Ieyasu no shinkakka ni tsuite', *Kokushigaku* 94.

Klein, Blakeley Susan (1997) 'Allegories of desire, poetry and eroticism in *Ise monogatari zuinō*', *Monumenta Nipponica* 52–4.

Klein, Blakeley Susan (1998) 'Ise Monogatari Zuinō, an annotated translation', Monumenta Nipponica 53–1.

Kobayashi Kenzo (1974) 'Shimōsa kokugaku to Ina: Chiba-ken Higata-chō Miyaoi-ke o hōmon shite', Ina 559.

Kobayashi Kojin (1943) Mito gigun to Shinanoro, Tokyo: Hōkokusha.

Kobayashi Masayoshi (1990) Rikuchō Dōkyōshi kenkyū, Tokyo: Sōbunsha.

Kōbunroku, Kokuritsu Komonjokan, Tokyo.

Kodaishi hakkutsu '88–'90 (1991) Asahi gurafu, comp., Tokyo: Asahi Shinbunsha.

Kodate Chūzō (1980) Tsugaru no minkan shinkō, Tokyo: Kyōikusha.

Kodate Chūzō (1975) Iwakisan shinkōshi, Hoppō Shinsha.

Kohn, Livia (1995a) 'Taoism in Japan: positions and evaluations', Cahiers d'Extrême-Asie 8.

Kohn, Livia (1995b) Laughing at the Tao: Debates among Buddhists and Taoists in medieval China, Princeton: Princeton University Press.

Kohn, Livia (1997) 'Yin Xi, the master at the beginning of the scripture', Journal of Chinese Religions 24.

Koji ruien (1896–1914) Ise: Jingū Shichō.

Kokugakuin daigaku Nihon bunka kenkyūjo, ed. (1986) Shintō yōgoshū: shūkyōhen, Tokyo: Shintō Bunkakai.

Kokugakuin University, ed. (1985) Basic terms of Shinto, Tokyo: Kokugakuin University, Institute for Japanese Culture and Classics.

Kokuyaku issaikyō (1970) Shiden-bu vol.18, Tokyo: Daitō Shuppansha (revised edition).

Kondō Yoshihiro (1959) 'Ise Jingū mishōtai narabi ni zushi, Eizon no Ise sangū to Mōko jōbuku ni kanren shite', Shintōshi kenkyū 7–1.

Kracht, Klaus (1986) Studien zur Geschichte des Denkens im Japan des 17. bis 19. Jahrhunderts. Chu-Hsi-konfuzianische Geist-Diskurse, Wiesbaden: Harrassowitz.

Kubota Osamu (1959, 1971) Chūsei Shintō no kenkyū, Kyoto: Shintōshi Gakkai.

Kubota Osamu (1973) Shintōshi no kenkyū, Ise: Kōgakkan Daigaku.

Kubota Osamu (1985) 'Tenshō Daijin to Uhō dōji' in Hagiwara Tatsuo ed., Ise shinkō 1: kodai, chūsei, Tokyo: Yūzankaku.

Kumagai Takanori (1984) 'Kinensai hōhei seido no suitai', in Shintōshi ronsō, Tokyo: Kokusho Kankōkai.

Kuroda Toshio (1980) Jisha seiryoku, Tokyo: Iwanami.

Kuroda Toshio (1981) tr. James C. Dobbins and Suzanne Gay, 'Shinto in the History of Japanese Religion', Journal of Japanese Studies 7–1.

Kuroda Toshio (1982) 'Chinkon no keifu', Rekishigaku kenkyū 500.

Kuroda Toshio (1983) Ōbō to buppō, Kyoto: Hōzōkan.

Kuroda Toshio (1989) 'Historical Consciousness and Hon-jaku Philosophy in the Medieval Period on Mt. Hiei', (tr. Allan Grapard) in George Tanabe and Willa Tanabe, eds. The Lotus Sutra in Japanese culture, Honolulu: University of Hawai'i Press.

Kuroda Toshio (1993) 'Shinto in the History of Japanese Religion', in M. Mullins, S. Shimazono, and P. Swanson, eds, Religion and society in modern Japan: selected readings, Berkeley: Asian Humanities Press.

Kuroda Toshio (1996) tr. James C. Dobbins, 'The development of the kenmitsu system as Japan's medieval orthodoxy', Japanese Journal of Religious Studies 23–3/4.

Kushida Ryōkō (1964, 1973) Shingon Mikkyō seiritsu katei no kenkyū, Sankibō Busshorin.

Kushida Ryōkō (1979) Zoku Shingon Mikkyō seiritsu katei no kenkyū, Sankibō Busshorin.

Kuwata Tadachika (1975) Toyotomi Hideyoshi kenkyū, Tokyo: Kadokawa Shoten.

Lagerwey, John (1981) Wu-shang pi-yao, Paris: EFEO.

Lamers, Jeroen P. (1998) Japonicus Tyrannus. A political biography of Oda Nobunaga, Leiden (dissertation).

Lu Zengxiang (1985) *Baqiong shi jinshi buzheng 32*, Beijing: Wenwu chubanshe.

Mabito Genkai, ed. (1979) Wang Xiangrong, *Tō daiwajō tōseiden*, Beijing: Zhonghua shuju.

Maki Fumihiko (1978) 'Nihon no toshi kūkan to *oku*', *Sekai* (December).

Masaki Keiji (1974a) 'Ishin zen'ya no kokugaku shisō: Sakata Tetsutarō no kenkyū' pt. 1, *Ina* 558.

Masaki Keiji (1974b) 'Ishin zen'ya no kokugaku shisō: Sakata Tetsutarō no kenkyū' pt. 2, *Ina* 559.

Masaki Keiji (1975) 'Ishin zen'ya no kokugaku shisō: Sakata Tetsutarō no kenkyū' pt. 3, *Ina* 561.

Masaki Keiji (1978a) *Tokai to Ina: shōhin ryūtsū to seiji, bunka, kōryū*, Nagoya: by the author.

Masaki Keiji (1978b) 'Imamura Masara no shisō henreki' pt. 1, *Ina* 606.

Masaki Keiji (1979a) 'Imamura Masara no shisō henreki' pt. 2, *Ina* 611.

Masaki Keiji (1979b) 'Imamura Masara no shisō henreki' pt. 3, *Ina* 612.

Masaki Keiji (1979c) 'Imamura Masara no shisō henreki' pt. 4, *Ina* 613.

Masaki Keiji (1979d) 'Imamura Masara no shisō henreki' pt. 5, *Ina* 615.

Masaki Keiji (1979e) 'Imamura Masara no shisō henreki' pt. 6, *Ina* 616.

Masaki Keiji (1979f) 'Imamura Masara no shisō henreki' pt. 7, *Ina* 617.

Mase Kumiko (1985), 'Bakuhansei kokka ni okeru jinja sōron to chōbaku kankei: Yoshida Shirakawa sōron o chūshin ni', *Nihonshi kenkyū* 277.

Maspero, Henri (1981), tr. Frank Kierman Jr., *Taoism and Chinese religion*, Amherst: University of Massachusetts Press.

Matsuda Kiichi & Kawazaki Momota, tr. & ann. (1978) *Furoisu Nihonshi* V, Tokyo: Chūōkōronsha.

Matsukata Mineo et al (1979) eds., *Matsukata Masayoshi kankei monjo* (vol.1), Daitō Bunka Daigaku Tōyō Kenkyūjo.

Matsumoto Hakka (1935), 'Rojūkaku sōsho' in Tokushige Asakichi ed., *Meiji Bukkyō zenshū 8: gohōhen*, Kyoto, Shunyūdō.

Matsunaga Zai (1937), 'Maki Izumi no kami no shisō' in Kokugakuin Daigaku dōgikai ed., *Bakumatsu kinnō shisō no kenkyū*, Tokyo: Seinen Kyōiku Fukyūkai.

Matsuo Masato (1986), *Haihan chiken, kindai tōitsu kokka e no kumon*, Chūkō Shinsho.

Matsushita Shin'ichi (1980a) 'Hansei tantōsha no kokugaku juyō: Katagiri Harukazu ni okeru kokugaku no kinō' pt. 1, *Ina* 627.

Matsushita Shin'ichi (1980b) 'Hansei tantōsha no kokugaku juyō: Katagiri Harukazu ni okeru kokugaku no kinō' pt. 2, *Ina* 628.

McCallum, D.F. (1994) *Zenkōji and its icon*, Princeton: Princeton University Press.

McMullen, David (1988) *State and scholars in T'ang China*, Cambridge: Cambridge University Press.

Kyōgi shinbun, in Meiji Bukkyō shisō shiryō shūsei henshū iinkai, ed. (1980) *Meiji Bukkyō shisō shiryō shūsei* vol.8, Kyoto: Dōhōsha.

Meiji Jingū hōsankai, ed. (1937) *Meiji jingū gaienshi*, Tokyo: Meiji Jingū hōsankai.

Meiji kanpaku shūsei, vol.6, (*Tsurumaki Takao comp*). Tokyo: Chikuma Shobō, 1987.

Meiryō kōhan (1912) Tokyo: Kokusho Kankōkai.

Mikkyō daijiten (rev. ed. 1983) Mikkyō daijiten hensankai, comp., Kyoto: Hōzōkan.

Miller, Roy Andrew, and Nelly Naumann (1991) 'Altjapanisch *FaFuri*. Zu Priestertum und Schamanismus im vorbuddhistischen Japan', *Mitteilungen der Gesellschaft für Natur- und Völkerkunde Ostasiens* 116.

Minami Hiroshi (1994) *Nihonjinron, Meiji kara kyō made*, Tokyo: Iwanami.

Misaki Ryōshū (1988) *Taimitsu no kenkyū*, Tokyo: Sōbunsha.

Misaki Ryōshū (1992) *Mikkyō to jingi shisō*, Tokyo: Sōbunsha.

Misaki Ryōshū (1993) *Nihon – Chūgoku Bukkyō shisō to sono tenkai*, Tokyo: Sankibō.

Misaki Ryōshū (1994) *Taimitsu no riron to jissen*, Tokyo: Sōbunsha.

Mitsubashi Takeshi (1984) 'Ōharae kenkyū josetsu', in *Shintōshi ronsō*, Tokyo: Kokusho Kankōkai.

Miyachi Masato (1981) 'Keisei katei kara mita tennōsei ideorogii', in idem *Tennōsei no seijishiteki kenkyū*, Tokyo: Kōsō Shobō.

Miyachi Masato (1994) 'Bakumatsu Hirata kokugaku to seiji jōhō', in Tanaka Akira ed., *Nihon no kinsei 18: Kindai kokka e no shikō*, Tokyo: Chūō Kōronsha.

Miyachi Masato comp. (1988) 'Shūkyō hōrei ichiran' in Yasumaru Yoshio and Miyachi Masato, eds *Nihon kindai shisō taikei 5: shūkyō to kokka*, Tokyo: Iwanami.

Miyai Yoshio (1978) *Fujiwara-shi no ujigami-ujidera shinkō to sobyō saishi*, Tokyo: Seikō Shobō.

Miyai Yoshio (1980) *Jōdai no shinbutsu shūgō to Jōdo-kyō*, Tokyo: Seikō Shobō.

Miyaji Naokazu (1938) *Shintōshi josetsu*, in Miyaji Naokazu sensei isho kankōkai, comp., *Miyaji Naokazu ronshū* vol. 5, Tokyo: Ōfūsha 1984.

Miyaji Naokazu (1939) 'Shintōkai o kaiko shite', *Shintōgaku zasshi* 14.

Miyaji Naokazu (1941) *Jingishi taikei*, Meiji Shoin.

Miyaji Naokazu (1943) 'Shintō no meigi', in *Shintō shichō*, Tokyo: Risōsha.

Miyashita Misao (1962) 'Hongaku jinja ni tsuite: kinsei Ina-gun ni okeru kokugaku shisō to sono tenkai', *Ina* 386.

Miyashita Misao (1975) *Ina kyōdo shigaku ronkō*, Tokyo: Kokusho Kankōkai.

Miyata Noboru (1970) 'Iwaki-san shinkō: sono shinkōen o megutte', in Wakamori Tarō, ed., *Tsugaru no minzoku*, Tokyo: Yoshikawa Kōbunkan.

Miyazawa Toshiyoshi (1971) *Kenpō 2: kihonteki jinken* (new edition), Tokyo: Yūhikaku.

Mori Kazue (1994) 'Sanja takusen', in Inoue Nobutaka et al., eds, *Shintō jiten*, Tokyo: Kōbundō.

Mori Kazuo ed. (1935), *Jiin keizaishi kenkyū*, Tokyo: Sankyō Shoin.

Mori Kimiaki (1983) 'Tennō-gō no seiritsu o megutte', *Nihon Rekishi* 418.

Morioka Kiyomi (1987) *Kindai no shūraku jinja to kokka seido*, Tokyo: Yoshikawa Kōbunkan.

Morita Tei, 'Kuge to jinja', in Shimode Sekiyo and Tamamuro Fumio, eds, *Kōza Shintō*, vol. 2, Tokyo: Ōfūsha.

Morrell, Robert E. (1973) 'Muju Ichien's Buddhist-Shinto syncretism: *Shasekishū*, Book 1', *Monumenta Nipponica* 28–4.

Müller, Claudius C. (1980) *Untersuchungen zum 'Erdaltar' she im China der Chou- und Han-Zeit*, Münchner Ethnologische Abhandlungen 1, München: Minerva Publishing.

Murakami Senshō et al. eds (1926), *Meiji ishin shinbutsu bunri shiryō* (6 vols.), Tokyo: Iwanami.

Murakami Shigeyoshi (1970) *Kokka Shintō*, Tokyo: Iwanami.

Muraoka Tsunetsugu (1958), 'Meiji ishin no kyōka tōsei to Hirata Shintō' in Ishiwara Ken ed., *Hatano Seiichi sensei kentei ronbunshū: tetsugaku oyobi shūkyō to rekishi*, Tokyo: Iwanami.

Muraoka Tsunetsugu (1962) *Kokuminsei no kenkyū*, Tokyo: Sōbunsha.

Murasawa Takeo (1936) *Ina kado shi*, Iida-shi: Yamamura Shoin.

Murasawa Takeo (1944) 'Sonnō no shi Iwasaki Nagayo', *Shinano* 25.

Murasawa Takeo (1985) Iwasaki Nagayo no shinshiryō', *Ina* 686.

Murayama Shūichi (1957) *Shinbutsu shūgō shichō*, Kyoto: Heirakuji.

Murayama Shūichi (1970) *Yamabushi no rekishi*, Tokyo: Hanawa Shobō.

Murayama Shūichi (1974) *Honji suijaku*, Tokyo: Yoshikawa Kōbunkan.

Murayama Shūichi (1976) *Kodai Bukkyō no chūseiteki tenkai*, Kyoto: Hōzōkan.

Murayama Shūichi (1981) *Nihon onmyōdō-shi sōsetsu*, Tokyo: Hanawa Shobō.

Murayama Shūichi (1991) *Onmyōdō sōsho*, 4 vols, Tokyo: Meicho Shuppan.

Murayama Shūichi and Kageyama Haruki, *Hiei-zan no rekishi*.

Nagano-ken, ed. (1980) *Nagano kenshi kinsei shiryō hen 4: Nanshin chihō 3*, Nagano-shi: Nagano Kenshi Kankōkai.

Nagashima Fukutarō (1991) 'Sanja takusen no genryū', *Nihon rekishi* 512.
Nagatomi Chiyoji (1977) 'Edo jidai shomin no dokusho', *Bungaku* 45–9.
Nakajima Michio (1977) '"Meiji kenpō taisei" no kakuritsu to kokka no ideorogi-seisaku: Kokka Shintō taisei no kakuritsu katei', *Nihonshi kenkyū* 176.
Nakamura Hajime, ed. (1981) *Bukkyōgo daijiten*, Tokyo: Tōkyō Shoseki.
Nakamura Kōya (1965) *Tokugawa Ieyasu kō den*, Nikkō: Tōshōgū Shamusho.
Nakamura, K.M. (1983) 'The significance of Amaterasu in Japanese religous history' in C. Olsen, ed., *The book of the goddess*, New York: Crossroad.
Nakano Hatayoshi (1985) *Usa-gū*, Tokyo: Yoshikawa Kōbunkan.
Naumann, Nelly (1970) 'Einige Bemerkungen zum sogenannten Ur-Shinto', *Nachrichten der Gesellschaft für Natur- und Völkerkunde Ostasiens* 107/108.
Naumann, Nelly (1983) 'Die webende Göttin', *Nachrichten der Gesellschaft für Natur- und Völkerkunde Ostasiens* 133.
Naumann, Nelly (1988) *Die einheimische Religion Japans. Teil 1. Bis zum Ende der Heian-Zeit*, Leiden: E.J. Brill.
Naumann, Nelly (1994) *Die einheimische Religion Japans. Teil 2. Synkretistische Lehren und religiöse Entwicklungen von der Kamakura- bis zum Beginn der Edo-Zeit*, Leiden: E.J. Brill.
Naumann, Nelly (1996) 'Taoist thought, political speculation, and the three creational deities of the *Kojiki*', *Nachrichten der Gesellschaft für Natur- und Völkerkunde Ostasiens* 157/158.
Naumann, Nelly (1997) 'Der Tiger in chinesischen Märchen, Sagen und frühen religiösen Vorstellungen', *Fabula* 38.
Nihon Daigaku, ed. (1991) *Yamada Hakushakuke monjo*, vol. 3, Tokyo: Shinjinbutsu Ōraisha.
Nihon Gendai kyōiku taikei, Monasu 1929 (reprint Nihon Tosho Sentā 1989).
Nihon koten bungaku taikei, 100 vols, Tokyo: Iwanami.
Nishida Nagao (1941) 'Sanja takusen no seisaku', *Nihon Shintōshi kenkyū* 4.
Nishida Nagao (1965) 'Miyaji Naokazu', *Shintō shūkyō* 41.
Nishida Nagao (1978–9) *Nihon Shintōshi kenkyū*, 10 vols, Tokyo: Kōdansha.
Nitta Hitoshi (1997) *Kindai seikyō no kisoteki kenkyū*, Tokyo: Taimeidō.
Noguchi Tetsuro, Sakade Yoshinobu, Fukui Fumimasa, Yamada Toshiaki, eds (1994) *Dōkyō jiten*, Tokyo: Hirakawa Shuppansha.
Nosco, Peter, ed. (1984) *Confucianism and Tokugawa culture*, Princeton: Princeton University Press.
Ohase Keikichi (1976) *Nihonkoku genzai sho mokuroku kaisetsu kō*, Tokyo: Komiyama Shuppan (reprint of 1936).
Ōhayashi Tarō (1973) *Inasaku no shinwa*, Tokyo: Kōbundō.
Okada Shōji (1982) 'Kinsei Shintō no jomaku: Yoshida Shintō no sōrei o tsūro to shite', *Shintō shūkyō* 109.
Okada Shōji (1983) 'Yoshida Urabe-shi no seiritsu', *Kokugakuin Zasshi* 84–9.
Okada Shōji (1992) 'Kaidai', in *Shintō taikei ronsetsu-hen*, vol. IX, Tokyo: Shintō taikei hensankai.
Okada Shōji, ed. (1986) *Heian jidai no jinja to saishi*, Tokyo: Kokusho Kankōkai.
Okatani Kōji (1987) *Kami no mori, mori no kami*, Tokyo: Tōkyō Shoseki.
Ōkuni Takamasa (1862), *Shintō kyōhōben*, MS.
Ōkuwa Hitoshi (1989) *Nihon kinsei no shisō to Bukkyō*, Kyoto: Hōzōkan.
Ōmura Seigai (1915) *Shina bijutsushi: Chōsō hen I*, Bussho Kankōkai Zushōbu.
Ooms, Herman (1984) 'Neo-Confucianism and the formation of early Tokugawa ideology: Contours of a problem', in Peter Nosco, ed., *Confucianism and Tokugawa culture*, Princeton: Princeton University Press.
Ōsaka Asahi Shinbun.
Ōsumi Kazuo, ed. (1977) *Nihon shisō taikei 19: chūsei shintōron*, Tokyo: Iwanami.

Otagi Hajime (1993) 'Tōdai Rokan kō', in Yoshikawa Tadao, ed., *Chūgoku Ko-Dōkyō kenkyū*, Kyoto: Dōhōsha.

Ōwada Tateki, comp. (1928) *Yōkyoku hyōshaku*, Tokyo: Hakubunkan (16th printing).

Ōyama Kōjun (1975) *Shinbutsu kōshō-shi*, Kyoto: Rinsen.

Philippi, Donald L., tr. (1959) *Norito, a new translation of the ancient Japanese ritual prayers*, Tokyo: Kokugakuin University; reprint Princeton University Press, 1990.

Philippi, Donald L., tr. (1969) *Kojiki. Translated with an introduction and notes*, Tokyo: University of Tokyo Press.

Piggott, Joan R. (1997) *The Emergence of Japanese kingship*, Stanford: Stanford University Press.

Proceedings of the seventeenth international congress of orientalists, Oxford 1928, London, 1929.

Rambelli, Fabio (1994) 'True words, silence, and the adamantine dance: On Japanese Mikkyō and the formation of Shingon discourse', *Japanese Journal of Religious Studies* 21–4.

Reader, Ian (1991) *Religion in Contemporary Japan*, London: Macmillan Press.

Renondeau, Gaston (1965a) *Les moines guerriers du Japon*, Paris: Imprimerie Nationale.

Renondeau, Gaston (1965b) *Le Shugendō: Histoire, doctrines et rites des anachorètes dits yamabushi*, Paris: Imprimerie Nationale.

Robinet, Isabelle (1995) *Geschichte des Taoismus*, München: Diederichs (tr. Stephan Stein, from the French *Histoire du taoisme*, 1991).

Robinet, Isabelle (1997) *Taoism: Growth of a religion*, Stanford: Stanford University Press.

Rotermund, Hartmut O. (1968) *Die Yamabushi; Aspekte Ihres Glaubens, Lebens und Ihrer Sozialen Funktion im Japanischen Mittelalter*, Hamburg: Kommissionsverlag Cram, De Gruyter & Co.

Rothermund, Dietmar (1997) 'Nationalism and the reconstruction of tradition in Asia', in Sri Kuhnt-Saptodewo, Wolker Grabowsky and Martin Großheim eds., *Nationalism and cultural revival in southeast Asia: perspectives from the centre and region*,Wiesbaden: Harrassowitz.

Saeki Rima (1926), 'Tsuwanohan no jiin shobun' in Murakami Senshō et al. eds *Meiji ishin shinbutsu bunri shiryō* (6 vols.), Tokyo: Iwanami.

Saitō Hideyoshi, ed. (1996) *Amaterasu shinwa no henshinfu*, Tokyo: Shinwasha.

Saitō Takashi (1984) 'Ijō na fūkei: Hiraizumi Kiyoshi', in *Shōwa shigakushi nōto*, Shōgakkan.

Saitō Takashi (1985) 'Hiraizumi Kiyoshi hakase to Shintō' *Shintōshi kenkyū* 33–1.

Saitō Tsutomu (1947) *Ōchō-jidai no onmyōdō*, Tokyo: Sōgensha.

Sakakura Atsuyoshi (1982) 'Gogen – kami no gogen o chūshin ni', in Satō Kiyoharu, ed., *Kōza, Nihongo no goi, 1, Goi genron*, Tokyo: Meiji Shoin.

Sakamoto Ken'ichi (1973) *Meiji Shintōshi no kenkyū*, Tokyo: Kokusho Kankōkai.

Sakamoto Koremaru (1981a) 'Saisei itchi o meguru Sain no 'seikyō' ronsō', *Kokugakuin zasshi* 82–10.

Sakamoto Koremaru (1981b), 'Meiji shūkyō gyōseishi no ichikōsatsu', *Kokugakuin zasshi* 82–6.

Sakamoto Koremaru (1987a) 'Kokka Shintō to wa nan datta no ka' *Seikyō kankei o tadasu kai kenkyū hōkoku*, 3.

Sakamoto Koremaru (1987b), 'Nihongata seikyō kankei no keisei katei' in Inoue Nobutaka and Sakamoto Koremaru eds., *Nihongata seikyō kankei no tanjō*, Tokyo: Daiichi shobo.

Sakamoto Koremaru (1990) 'Kokka Shintō ni tsuite no oboegaki', *Gendai Esupuri*, 280.

Sakamoto Koremaru (1993), *Meiji ishin to kokugakusha*, Tokyo: Taimeidō.

Sakamoto Koremaru (1994) *Kokka Shintō keisei katei no kenkyū*, Tokyo: Iwanami.

Sakamoto Tarō, Ienaga Saburō, Inoue Mitsusada, Ōno Susumu, eds (1965) *Nihon bungaku taikei 68: Nihon shoki I*, Tokyo: Iwanami.

351

Sako Nobuyuki (1992) *Sanshōdayū densetsu no kenkyū*, Tokyo: Meicho Shuppan.

Sakurai Haruo (1992) *Yomigaeru mura no kamigami*, Tokyo: Taimeidō.

Sakurai Yoshirō (1993) *Saigi to chūshaku*, Tokyo: Yoshikawa Kōbunkan.

Sanford, James H. (1991) 'The abominable Tachikawa skull ritual', *Monumenta Nipponica* 46–1.

Sansom, G.B. (1973) *Japan: a short cultural history*, Tokyo: Tuttle.

Sasaki Seishi (1985) 'Shintō hishūkyōron yori jinja hishūkyōron e: shinkan, kyōdōshoku no bunri o megutte', *Nihon daigaku seishin bunka kenkyūjo kyōiku seido kenkyūjo kiyō* 16.

Sasaki Seishi (1987) 'Meiji 23nen Jingikan setchi undō to Yamada Akiyoshi', *Nihon daigaku seishin bunka kenkyūjo kyōiku seido kenkyūjo kiyō* 18.

Saunders, E. Dale (1960, 1985) *Mudrā: A study of symbolic gestures in Japanese Buddhist sculpture*, New York: Pantheon Books.

Scheid, Bernhard (1996) *Im Innersten meines Herzens empfinde ich tiefe Scham. Das Alter im Schrifttum des japanischen Mittelalters*, Vienna: Austrian Academy of Sciences.

Schurhammer, S.J. (1923) *Shin-tō, The Way of the Gods in Japan, according to the printed and unprinted reports of the Japanese Jesuit missionaries in the 16th and 17th centuries*, Bonn/Leipzig: Kurt Schroeder.

Seidel, Anna (1989–90) 'Chronicle of Taoist studies in the West 1950–1990', *Cahiers d'Extrême-Asie* 5.

Seidel, Anna (1993) 'Ōbei no Dōkyō kenkyū hennenshi', *Tōhō shūkyō* 82.

Shimaji Mokurai 'Jobun: Kyōbushō no futeisai ni tsuki', in Futaba Kenkō et al., eds (1973) *Shimaji Mokurai zenshū*, Tokyo: Honganji Shuppan Kyōkai.

Shimaji Mokurai 'Kengon: seikyō oyobi kyōshoku kan'in ni tsuki (kyōsei kengi)', in Futaba Kenkō et al., eds (1973) *Shimaji Mokurai zenshū*, Tokyo: Honganji Shuppan Kyōkai.

Shimaji Mokurai, 'Kengi: bunri kyōka sokushin ni tsuki (kyōsei kengi)', in Futaba Kenkō et al., eds (1973) *Shimaji Mokurai zenshū*, Tokyo: Honganji Shuppan Kyōkai.

Shimazono Susumu and Isomae Jun'ichi, comp. (1996) *Tōkyō teitoku daigaku Shintō kenkyūshitsu kyūzōsho: mokuroku oyobi kaisetsu*, Tokyo: Tōkyōdō Shuppan.

Shimizu Noboru (1973) *Meiji kenpō seiteishi*, vol.2, Tokyo: Hara Shobō.

Shimode Sekiyo (1972) *Nihon kodai no jingi to Dōkyō*, Tokyo: Yoshikawa Kōbunkan.

Shimode Sekiyo (1975) *Dōkyō to Nihonjin*, Tokyo: Kōdansha.

Shimoina-gun gun'yakusho, ed. (1977) *Shimoina gunshi shiryō*, Tokyo: Rekishi Toshosha.

Shimoina-gun kyōikukai, ed. (1980) *Shimoina gunshi*, Nagano-shi: Shimoina Gunshi Hensankai.

Shinchū kōgaku sōsho (1927–31) Mozumi Takami, comp., 12 vols, Tokyo: Kōbunko Kankōkai.

Shinpen Aomori-ken sōsho hankōkai, comp. (1973) 'Tsugaru Zokusetsusen 2', in *Shinpen Aomori-ken sōsho*, vol. 2, Tokyo: Rekishi Toshosha.

Shinpen Aomori-ken sōsho hankōkai, comp. (1974a) 'Tsugaru Zokusetsusen 1', in *Shinpen Aomori-ken sōsho*, vol. 1, Tokyo: Rekishi Toshosha.

Shinpen Aomori-ken sōsho kankōkai, comp. (1974b) 'Tsugaru ittōshi', in *Shinpen Aomori-ken sōsho*, vol. 1, Tokyo: Rekishi Toshosha.

Shintei zōho kojitsu sōsho, Kokushi taikei henshūkai, comp., Tokyo: Yoshikawa Kōbunkan.

Shintō jiten (1968) Anzu Motohiko and Ueda Yoshihiko, comp., Osaka: Hori Shoten (2nd printing).

Shintō jiten (1994) Kokugakuin Daigaku Nihon Bunka Kenkyūjo, ed., Tokyo: Kōbundō.

Shintō taikei, 120 vols, Tokyo: Shintō Taikei Hensankai.

Shirai Eiji and Toki Masanori, eds (1979) *Jinja jiten*, Tokyo: Tōkyōdō Shuppan.

Siklós, B. (1996) *The Vajrabhairava tantras*, Tring: Institute of Buddhist Studies.

Smith, A.D., ed. (1992) *Ethnicity and nationalism*, Leiden/New York/Köln: E.J. Brill.

Smith, Jonathan Z. (1982) *Imagining religion*, Chicago: University of Chicago Press.

Somata Yoshio (1985) 'Bakuhansei-kokka to monzeki: Tendai zasu to Tendai monzeki o chūshin ni', *Nihonshi kenkyū* 277.

Sonehara Satoshi (1996) *Tokugawa Ieyasu shinkakka e no michi: Chūsei Tendai shisō no tenkai*, Tokyo: Yoshikawa Kōbunkan.

Song Minqiu (1959) *Tang da zhaoling ji* 27, Shanghai: Commercial Press.

Song-ben Cefu yuangui (1989), Beijing: Zhonghua shuju.

Sonoda Minoru (1989) 'Matsuri – Kakyō no genzō', in *Iwanami kōza, tōyō no shisō 15: Nihon no shisō I*, Tokyo: Iwanami.

Sonoda Minoru (1990) *Matsuri no genshōgaku*, Tokyo: Kōbundō.

Sonoda Minoru et al. (1985) 'Tōron: Fūdo o dō toraeta ka', in *Nihon no fūdo*, Tokyo: Kōbundō.

Steininger, Helga (1956) 'Der Tennō-Gedanke in einigen Liedern des Manyōshū', in Helga Steininger, Hans Steininger, and Ulrich Unger, eds, *Sino-Japonica: Festschrift André Wedemeyer zum 80. Geburtstag*, Leipzig: Harrassowitz.

Sueki Fumihiko (1993) *Nihon Bukkyō shisōshi ronkō*, Daizō Shuppan.

Sugahara Shinkai (1992) *Sannō Shintō no kenkyū*, Tokyo: Shunjūsha.

Sugahara Shinkai (1996) *Nihon shisō to shinbutsu shūgō*, Tokyo: Shunjūsha.

Sūmitsuin kaigi gijiroku (1985), vol.1, Tokyo: Tōkyō Daigaku Shuppankai.

Suzuki Giichi (1965) 'Tanaka Yoshitō', *Shintō shūkyō* 41.

Tagawa Okichirō (1938) *Kokka to shūkyō*, Tokyo: Kyōbunkan.

Taira Masayuki (1992) *Nihon chūsei no shakai to Bukkyō*, Tokyo: Hanawa Shobō.

Taira Shigemichi (1965) 'Taishō, Shōwa no rinri shisō: "Nihon seishinron" no seiritsu', in Nihon shisōshi kenkyūkai, comp., *Nihon ni okeru rinri shisō no tenkai*, Tokyo: Yoshikawa Kōbunkan.

Taishō shinshū daizōkyō (1924–34), 100 vols., Takakusu Junjirō, Watanabe Kaigyoku, and Ono Genmyō, eds, Tokyo: Taishō Issaikyō Kankōkai.

Taishokkan go-haretsu mokuroku, Danzan Jinja monjo (rpt., 1985), Tokyo: Meicho Shuppan.

Takagi Hiroshi (1984), 'Shintō kokkyōka seisaku hōkai katei no seijishiteki kōsatsu', *Hisutoria*, 104.

Takakusu Junjirō and Mochizuki Shinkō, eds (1942) *Shōtoku Taishi goden sōsho*, Tokyo: Kaneo Bun'endō.

Takatori Masao (1979) *Shintō no seiritsu*, Tokyo: Heibonsha.

Takeda Hideaki (1987), 'Kindai Tennō saishi keisei katei no ichikōsatsu' in Inoue Nobutaka and Sakamoto Koremaru eds., *Nihongata seikyō kankei no tanjō*, Tokyo: Daiichi Shobō.

Tanabe Kenjirō (1992) 'Shinryūin Bonshun kō: Shinbutsu kentai no katsudō to Hōkokusha sōken', *Shintō kenkyū shūroku* 11.

Tanabe, George, and Willa Tanabe, eds (1989) *The Lotus Sutra in Japanese culture*, Honolulu: University of Hawai'i Press.

Tanabe, George, ed. (1999) *Religions of Japan in practice*, Princeton: Princeton University Press.

Tanaka Hidekazu (1988) 'Kindai jinja seido no seiritsukatei: Tsugaru chihō no shinbutsubunri to jinja kaisei' in Hasegawa Seiichi ed., *Hokuō chiikishi no kenkyū*, Tokyo: Meicho Shuppan.

Tanaka Hidekazu (1990) 'Bakumatsu ishinki ni okeru zaichi shinshoku no dōkō to shinbutsu bunri', *Hirosaki daigaku kokushi kenkyū* 90.

Tanaka Hidekazu (1997) *Bakumatsu ishinki ni okeru shūkyō to chiiki shakai*, Osaka: Seibundō.

353

Tanaka Yoshitō (1905) 'Gojin no iwayuru "Shin-kyōikugaku"', *Kyōiku gakujutsukai* 12–1.

Tanaka Yoshitō (1910a) *Shintō hongi*, Nihon Gakujutsu Kenkyūkai.

Tanaka Yoshitō (1910b) 'Shintō tetsugaku kenkyū no hitsuyō', *Jinja kyōkai zasshi* 9–2.

Tanaka Yoshitō (1912) *Motoori Norinaga no tetsugaku*, Nihon Gakujutsu Kenkyūkai.

Tanaka Yoshitō (1918) *Shintō tetsugaku seigi*, Nihon Gakujutsu Kenkyūkai.

Tanaka Yoshitō (1924) *'Shintōgaku gairon'*, Shintō Shōgakkai dai-1-kai kōenkai, kōgi hikki.

Tanaka Yoshitō (1925) 'Shinshoku yōsei ni taisuru iken', *Jinja kyōkai zasshi* 24–4.

Tanaka Yoshitō (1926) 'Shintōgakkai shuisho', *Shintōgaku Zasshi* 1.

Tanaka Yoshitō (1929) *Kojiki gaisetsu*, Nihon Gakujutsu Kenkyūkai.

Tanaka Yoshitō (1929–31) 'Shinto tetsugaku no konpon mondai', *Shinto kōza* 3.

Tanaka Yoshitō (1930) 'Kyōiku chokugo to Shintō no hongi', *Shintōgaku zasshi* 9.

Tanaka Yoshitō (1932a) 'Shinki shūgō', *Shintōgaku zasshi* 13.

Tanaka Yoshitō (1932b) *'Shintō to Kōdō'*, Shintōgaku zasshi 13.

Tanaka Yoshitō (1932c) *Kurozumi-kyō no kenkyū* (Shintō 13-ha no kenkyū, jo).

Tanaka Yoshitō (1932d) *Shintō Shūsei-ha no kenkyū* (Shintō 13-ha no kenkyū, jo).

Tanaka Yoshitō (1933a) *Kamunagara no Shintō no kenkyū*, Tokyo: Nihon Gakujutsu Kenkyūkai.

Tanaka Yoshitō (1933b) 'Kyōdai jiken', *Shintōgaku zasshi* 14.

Tanaka Yoshitō (1934) 'Kokumin kyōiku ni okeru jingi kyōiku', *Kokugakuin zasshi* 40–5.

Tanaka Yoshitō (1935) 'Minzoku to shisō', *Shintōgaku zasshi* 18.

Tanaka Yoshitō (1935a) 'Tennō kikansetsu o haisu', *Kokugakuin zasshi* 41–4.

Tanaka Yoshitō (1935b) 'Minzoku to shisō', *Shintōgaku zasshi* 18.

Tanaka Yoshitō (1936a) *Shintō gairon*, Tokyo: Nihon Gakujutsu Kenkyūkai.

Tanaka Yoshitō (1936b) 'Jinja to shūkyō', *Shintogaku zasshi* 20.

Tanaka Yoshitō (1936c) *Shinten Kojiki*, Tokyo: Ōkura Seishin Bunka Kenkyūjo.

Tanaka Yoshitō (1938) *Nihon shoki gaisetsu*, Tokyo: Nihon Gakujutsu Kenkyūkai.

Tanaka Yoshitō (1939) *Shintō Honkyoku no kenkyū* (Shintō 13-ha no kenkyū, ge).

Tanaka Yoshitō (1942) *Shūseiban Hirata Atsutane no tetsugaku*, Tokyo: Meiji Shoin.

Taussig, Michael (1992) *The nervous system*, New York/London: Routledge.

Teeuwen, Mark (1993) 'Attaining union with the gods: the secret books of Watarai Shinto', *Monumenta Nipponica* 48–2.

Teeuwen, Mark (1995) *The Two Shrines of Ise: an essay of split bamboo*, Wiesbaden: Harrassowitz.

Teeuwen, Mark (1996a) *Watarai Shintō, an intellectual history of the Outer Shrine in Ise*, Leiden: Research School CNWS.

Teeuwen, Mark (1996b) 'Jinja honchō and Shrine Shinto policy', *Japan Forum* 8–2.

Teeuwen, Mark and Hendrik van der Veere (1998) *Nakatomi harae kunge: purification and enlightenment in late Heian Japan*, Buddhist Studies 1, München: iudicium verlag.

Teikoku gikai shūgiin giji sokkiroku 34 (1981), Tokyo: Tokyo University Press.

Terashima Ryōan (1988) *Wakan sansai zue vol.* 9, Shimada Isao et al., eds, Tokyo: Heibonsha.

Toba Shigehiro (1997) 'Amaterasu Ōmikami no imeeji no hensen ni tsuite: nyotaizō, dantaizō kara, Uhō Dōji-zō ni itari zuzōgaku', *Kōgakkan daigaku shintō kenkyūjo kiyō* 13.

Tokoyo Nagatane (1988) *Shinkyō soshiki monogatari*, in Yasumaru Yoshio and Miyachi Masato, eds, *Iwanami kindai shisō taikei 5: Shūkyō to kokka*, Tokyo: Iwanami.

Tokushige Asakichi (1934), *Ishin seishinshi no kenkyū*, Kyoto: Ritsumeikan Shuppanbu.

Tōkyō Daigaku hyakunenshi bukyokushi 1 (1986) Tōkyō Daigaku hyakunenshi hensan iinkai, comp., Tōkyō Daigaku Shuppankai.

Tonami Mamoru (1982) 'Tō chūki no Bukkyō to kokka', in Fukunaga Mitsuji, ed., *Chūgoku chūsei no shūkyō to bunka*, Kyoto: Kyoto Daigaku Jinbun Kagaku Kenkyūjo.

Tonami Mamoru (1993) 'Hōrin shiseki ni miru Tō-sho no Bukkyō, Dōkyō to kokka', in Yoshikawa Tadao, ed., *Chūgoku Ko-Dōkyō kenkyū*, Kyoto: Dōhōsha.

Toyama Ichirō (1998) *Tenno shinwa no keisei to Man'yōshū*, Tokyo: Hanawa Shobō.

Tsuda Sōkichi (1937–9) 'Nihon no Shintō ni okeru Shina shisō no yōso', in idem *Nihon no Shintō*, Tokyo: Iwanami, 1949.

Tsuda Sōkichi (1949) *Nihon no Shintō*, Tokyo: Iwanami.

Tsuji Zennosuke (1949), *Meiji Bukkyōshi no mondai*, Ritsubun Shoin.

Tsunoda Tadayuki okina koden (1989) Nagoya: Atsuta Jingū Gūchō.

Twitchett, Denis (1973) 'The composition of the T'ang ruling class', in Arthur F. Wright and Denis Twitchett, eds, *Perspectives on the T'ang*, New Haven: Yale University Press.

Twitchett, Denis (1992) *The writing of official history under the T'ang*, Cambridge: Cambridge University Press.

Tyler, Susan (1989) *'Honji suijaku faith'*, *Japanese Journal of Religious Studies* 16–2/3.

Ueda Atsushi (1984) *Chinju no mori*, Tokyo: Kashima Shuppankai.

Unuma Yūko (1979) 'Kokumin dōtokuron o meguru ronsō', in Imai Jun, comp., *Nihon shisō ronsōshi*, Tokyo: Perikansha.

Von Verschuer, Charlotte (1985) *Les relations officielles du Japon avec la Chine aux VIIIe et IXe Siècles*, Geneva: Droz.

Wakamori Tarō (1972) *Shugendō-shi kenkyū*, Tokyo: Heibonsha.

Wakamori Tarō et al., eds (1977) *Sangaku shūkyō-shi kenkyū sōsho*, 18 vols, Tokyo: Meicho Shuppan.

Walthall, Anne (1998) *The weak body of a useless woman: Matsuo Taseko and the Meiji Restoration*, Chicago: University of Chicago Press.

Wang Bo, comp. (1991) *Tang Huiyao* 97, Shanghai: Shanghai guji chubanshe.

Wang Zhen-ping (1991) 'Manuscript copies of Chinese books in ancient Japan', *Gest Library Journal* 4–2.

Ware, James (1932) 'Notes on the history of the Wei Shu', *Journal of the American Oriental Society* 52.

Watabe Mayumi (1991) *Shintō to Nihon Bukkyō*, Tokyo: Perikansha.

Watanabe Kazuyasu (1978, 1985) *Meiji shisōshi*, Tokyo: Perikansha.

Watanabe Shōkō and Miyazaka Yūshō, eds (1965) *Sangō-shiiki, Shōryōshū*, Tokyo: Iwanami.

Watson, Burton, tr. (1993) *The Lotus Sutra*, New York: Columbia University Press.

Watsuji Tetsurō (1935) *Fūdo – Ningengakuteki kōsatsu*, Tokyo: Iwanami.

Wechsler, Howard (1985) *Offerings of jade and silk*, New Haven: Yale University Press.

Wei Shou, *Wei Shu* 1, Beijing: Zhonghua shuju.

Wen Daya (1983) *Da-Tang zhuangye qiju zhu* 2, Shanghai: Shanghai guji chubanshe.

Wheatley, Paul, and Thomas See (1978) *From court to capital*, Chicago: University of Chicago Press.

White, James W. (1995) *Ikki: social conflict and political protest in early modern Japan*, Ithaca: Cornell University Press.

Wigen, Kären (1995) *The making of a Japanese periphery, 1750–1920*, Berkeley and Los Angeles: University of California Press.

Wilhelm, Richard (1910, 1996a) *Laotse: Tao te king*, München: Diederichs.

Wilhelm, Richard (1923, 1996b) *I Ging: Das Buch der Wandlungen*, München: Diederichs.

Wright, Arthur (1957) 'The Formation of Sui ideology', in John K. Fairbank, ed., *Chinese thought and institutions*, Chicago: University of Chicago Press.

Yamada Akiyoshi papers, Imperial Household Archive, *Kunaichō shoryōbu*, Tokyo.

Yamada Bōzō (1982a) 'Jōmin no matsuru Hongaku jinja' pt. 1, *Ina* 645.

Yamada Bōzō (1982b) 'Jōmin no matsuru Hongaku jinja' pt. 2, *Ina* 646.
Yamada Bōzō (1982c) 'Jōmin no matsuru Hongaku jinja' pt. 3, *Ina* 647.
Yamada Bōzō (1982d) 'Jōmin no matsuru Hongaku jinja' pt. 4, *Ina* 648.
Yamada Bōzō (1982e) 'Jōmin no matsuru Hongaku jinja' pt. 5, *Ina* 649.
Yamada Bōzō (1982f) 'Jōmin no matsuru Hongaku jinja' pt. 6, *Ina* 650.
Yamada Bōzō (1982g) 'Jōmin no matsuru Hongaku jinja' pt. 7, *Ina* 651.
Yamada Bōzō (1982h) 'Jōmin no matsuru Hongaku jinja' pt. 8, *Ina* 652.
Yamada Kō (1972) *Kindai Nihon dōtoku shisōshi kenkyū*, Tokyo: Miraisha.
Yamagami Izumo (1977) *Nihon geinō no kigen*, Tokyo: Yamato Shobō.
Yamaguchi Teruomi (1993) 'Meiji kenpōka no Jingikan setchi mondai – seikyō kankei ni kansuru ichikōsatsu', *Shigaku zasshi* 102–2.
Yamaguchi Teruomi (1993) 'Meiji jingū no seiritsu o megutte', *Nihon rekishi* 546.
Yamakawa Kikue (1992) *Women of the Mito domain*, tr. Kate Wildman Nakai, Tokyo: University of Tokyo Press.
Yamamoto Hiroko (1990) 'Irui to sōshin, chūsei ōken o meguru sei no metafā', *Gendai tetsugaku no bōken 4: Erosu*, Tokyo: Iwanami.
Yamamoto Hiroko (1997) 'Chūsei ni okeru Aizen Myōō hō, sono poritikusu to erosu', *Nihon no bijutsu* 376.
Yamamoto Nobuyoshi and Imano Toshihiko, eds (1986) *Taishō Shōwa kyōiku no tennōsei ideorogi – (1) gakkō gyōji no ideorogiteki seikaku*, Shinsensha.
Yamasaki, Taiko (1988) *Shingon*, London: Shambhala.
Yasumaru Yoshio (1979) *Kamigami no Meiji ishin*, Tokyo: Iwanami.
Yasumaru Yoshio and Miyachi Masato eds., (1988) *Nihon kindai shisō taikei 5: shūkyō to kokka*, Iwanami.
Yoneyama Toshinao (1989) *Shōbonchi uchū to Nihon bunka*, Tokyo: Iwanami.
Yoshie Akio (1996) *Shinbutsu shūgō*, Tokyo: Iwanami.
Yoshikawa Kōjirō (1968) *Yoshikawa Kōjirō zenshū*, Tokyo: Chikuma Shobō.
Zhou shu 1 and 4 (1971) Beijing: Zhonghua shuju.
Zürcher, Erik (1982) 'Perspectives in the study of Buddhism', *Journal of the Royal Asiatic Society* 2